THE CORRESPONDENCE OF

George, Prince of Wales 1770-1812

VOLUME VIII 1811-1812

George, Prince of Wales

by Sir Thomas Lawrence
Exhibited in 1818

THE CORRESPONDENCE OF

George, Prince of Wales 1770-1812

VOLUME VIII 1811-1812

EDITED BY

A. Aspinall, C.V.O., M.A., D.Litt.

CASSELL · LONDON

CASSELL & COMPANY LTD
35 Red Lion Square · London WC1
Sydney · Auckland
Toronto · Johannesburg

© A. Aspinall 1971

First published 1971

I.S.B.N. 0 304 93712 6

Made and printed in Great Britain by
William Clowes & Sons, Limited
London, Beccles and Colchester
F.371

Editor's Preface

It is again my pleasant duty to express my gratitude to the owners of MSS. from which I have quoted either in the body of the work or in footnotes; to Mr. Mackworth-Young, C.V.O., Her Majesty's Librarian, for the valuable assistance and advice which he has given me; to Miss Jane Langton, M.V.O., Registrar of the Archives, and her staff, who have answered many queries most helpfully; and to Mr. Oliver Millar, F.B.A., C.V.O., F.S.A., Deputy Surveyor of the Queen's Pictures.

This is the final volume in the present Series. It is also the last of the sixteen volumes of Royal correspondence which it has been my privilege to edit. The first Series, under the title *The Letters of King George IV, 1812–1830*, was published in three volumes by the Cambridge University Press in 1938. *The Later Correspondence of George III*, covering the period 1783–1810, was published by the Cambridge University Press, in five volumes, between 1962 and 1970.

In the Preface to Volume I I expressed the hope that the final volume in the present series would contain a comprehensive Index. This is here included. All index entries for the first seven volumes are collated and shown by volume and letter number; and detailed references to Volume VIII are incorporated in the whole.

Contents

Genealogical Tables

Illustrations

Acknowledgement

The publishers wish to express their thanks to the British Academy for their assistance in the publication of this work.

1. The Restricted Regency
June–December 1811

Whether England should be governed by the Whigs or by the Tories was a question which continued to baffle the politicians until the very end of the Restrictions in mid-February 1812. In July 1811 the King again fell so dangerously ill that for a day or two his death was hourly expected, and Arbuthnot was hard at work at the Treasury trying to get rid of all arrears in case he should be suddenly called upon to submit his accounts for audit. The crisis passed but there was no longer any prospect of the King's mental recovery. It was credibly reported that he believed himself to be in Heaven having long conversations with Lady Pembroke, Lord Weymouth and Handel, and for all practical purposes he might just as well have been there. Carlton House was a scene of great suspense, speculation and uncertainty. Not later than February the Regent would have to make up his mind whether or not to change his Ministers: a decision either way would involve him in charges of broken faith or lack of regard for the national interest, and bring upon himself a load of unpopularity. People were wondering whether the impressive amounts of alcohol which he was reported to be consuming would brace his nerves sufficiently to enable him to face the difficulties lying ahead.

Neither the Government nor the Opposition felt confident of the issue. In June Lord Grey thought that if the Caretaker Government lasted until February it would break up as a result of internal stresses, and that the Prince, from necessity if not from choice, would have to make some proposal to the Whigs. They found it hard to believe that the Prince could have forgotten all that had happened at the beginning of the year when he was encouraging them to draw up plans for a Whig Administration, and when he told Perceval that nothing but a regard for his father's health prevented him from changing his Ministers. They considered it would be fatal to his reputation and to his popularity in the country if he deliberately repudiated former pledges and forgot personal obligations. Would it not be wonderfully ironical if he chose as his permanent servants men who had opposed and ill-used him rather than those who had supported him with all the zeal and ability at their command? Grey was one of the least ambitious of politicians, with no strong desire for power, but he felt acute anxiety for the Prince's reputation, fearing that the wrong decision would be taken. 'I look almost with horror to the scenes in which I may be engaged, and would if I could creditably withdraw myself from them.' Though the Whig rank and file were looking forward with eagerness to the end of the Restrictions as the passport to the Promised Land, their leaders, being not too hopeful, made no further efforts to plan an Administration. They must take their ground on public measures, Grey told Grenville. Before talking about arrangements they must find out whether the Regent would support them in their views on the War, on Ireland, on the currency and on economical reform. A change of Government, then, would mean a change of measures.

Had the King died in July a general election would have followed, but whether Perceval or Grenville would have 'chosen' the next House of Commons is a matter for conjecture. Perceval himself then thought that if any reliance was to be placed on what was to be heard from Carlton House, there was no disposition to turn him out. The Prince's general manner, he said, was most gracious. 'He certainly has, to more of his servants than one, distinctly disclaimed any idea of removing us.' But Lord Bathurst told the Duke of Richmond in August, 'I think he will decide on turning us out.' Soon afterwards Moira reported that the Prince was becoming more and more accustomed to his Ministers, that his natural indolence increased his indisposition to change, and that these feelings were encouraged and confirmed by his constant intercourse with Lord Yarmouth and the Duke of Cumberland. Princess Charlotte, who detested 'Prince Wiskerandos' and disliked his 'indecent jokes', called him the Prince's 'right hand'. The Duke's excessive influence, however, was now waning: he had been in the habit of accompanying the Prince almost everywhere—keeping a sort of watch on him, said Brougham, that would have been very laughable had it not been really melancholy. Towards the end of July Lady Holland wrote to Lord Lansdowne: 'The Regent is to live at the Stable Yard, solely to shake off the Duke of Cumberland, the society of whom is becoming excessively irksome to him, but it denotes a lamentable lack of energy that he can only get rid of a troublesome inmate by flying his own home [?]. The other day when he went to Windsor he took Tommy Tyrwhitt in his chaise and bid him keep close to the door when they were to come back in order to escape the Duke of Cumberland's importunities, but he had a more dextrous foe than he calculated upon, for the Duke, after the Prince was seated, got up upon the steps upon the pretence of whispering, and instead of getting down, hollowed out to Mr Tyrwhitt that he had better follow in his chaise. The Prince was either too timid or too much confounded to remonstrate.' Brougham, too, writing to Lord Grey, said that the Prince's going to live at the Stable Yard was simply a manoeuvre to get rid of the Duke.

Before the close of the Parliamentary session (24 July) people were beginning to suspect the Prince of an intention to exclude the Whigs from office when the Restrictions expired, and it was rumoured that though he was disinclined to effect a total change he might favour an all-Party Government. Like the Duke of Northumberland, Moira had always been attached to the Prince rather than to the Whig Party. He told Grey that if the Regent did decide on a patchwork Government and office were offered him (he had the Lord Lieutenancy of Ireland in mind) he would accept it, provided he could approve of the system of policy on which the new Government would act. Grey, however, declared emphatically that if that situation arose *he* would decline office, as he and Lord Grenville had done in September 1809. But Thomas Grenville took a different view. The situation would not be identical with that of 1809: the Whigs would be invited to share in the formation of a new Government, not to join the existing one, and Thomas Grenville could not approve of Grey's refusal to belong to any Ministry that was not formed by him and Lord Grenville 'upon a principle of exclusion.' That the Prince's mind was apparently working in the direction of a coalition Government seemed to the Whigs to afford ample proof of the increasing influence of Manchester Square. Their suspicions were sensibly increased during the recess when Sheridan asked Lord Holland whether he, the Duke of Bedford and any other Foxite would be disposed to accept high office in a new Government 'in the formation of which, Lord Grey and Lord Grenville were not chiefly consulted'. Lord Holland plainly intimated that such projects were quite unacceptable to all 'men of weight' in the Whig party. To send for anyone but the Whig leaders would indicate quite clearly an intention to break up the party. There can be little doubt that Lord Wellesley, who despised his colleagues as much as they feared his ascendancy, was still as anxious as he had been in 1810 to renew his connection with Canning, and rumours of a Wellesley–Canning Ministry which would offer places to the Whigs circulated during the summer. Wellesley was the only Minister for whom the Prince had the slightest regard, and his brother, Wellesley-Pole, the Irish Secretary, thought in the summer that his colleagues had made little progress in gaining the Regent's goodwill. Ryder, the Home Secretary, however, believed that the Prince was satisfied with them.

The nature of the Prince's social engagements shows how carefully he tried to avoid too close a connection with either side. The fact that leading members of the Opposition dined at Carlton House on 1 July in return for a dinner they had given him when, on account of the preparations for the Fete on 19 June, he could not conveniently dine at home, gave rise to rumours that he and the Ministers were at loggerheads and that he was to dismiss them soon after the Prorogation. Ryder was confident that there was no fixed plan in the Regent's mind (and, indeed, the truth of the matter was that his only resolution was to remain irresolute), but Ryder thought that something might depend on the next quarterly report of the Queen's Council on the state of the King's health. 'The reports are so various of what that may be,' he said, 'that I can hardly form a conjecture about it.' The Prince evidently sought to counteract the effect of these rumours by intimating that he would like his Ministers to invite him to dinner: so he dined with Lord Camden on 11 July, with Perceval on the 20th, and with Lord Liverpool on the 24th. These engagements caused consternation at Brooks's Club. Whitbread and his friends did not much like the news of the first dinner, but bore it with tolerable philosophy; but when the dinner at Perceval's was announced, faces lengthened, and the disappointment and astonishment were not to be concealed.

Canning had almost abandoned hope of an early return to office, and his friend Lord Granville Leveson-Gower thought that the best thing that could happen to him would be for him to remain out of office for some years: an opinion with which Canning could hardly have been expected to agree. He said, 'It never has occurred to me that I had any right to think myself aggrieved, much less should I call myself proscribed, because a Government which I quitted (and by quitting nearly overturned) has not solicited me back again on terms that I could accept.' 'I know of no *proscription* of me except Lord Grey,' he said: he was evidently unaware that there were people like Whitbread who had expressed their unwillingness to sit in the same Cabinet with him. It, contrary to his expectation, an offer of some sort was made to Lords Grey and Grenville and the Government fell into their hands, Canning asked Huskisson, in July, not to allow any consideration for him to prevent his accepting the proposal which, earlier in the year, had been in contemplation. Huskisson replied that, in his belief, the Whigs had lost all hope of coming in, but in any case, he would refuse a separate offer.

If, as Lord Bathurst expected, the Prince would eventually decide to change his Ministers, he would seek to represent himself as an ill-used person, and the case of the contest for the vacant Irish Representative Peerage would be one of his grievances. There was an unprecedented clash (Ryder called it a collision) between the two candidates: unprecedented because Lord Leitrim was supported by the Prince, Lord Gosford by the Prince's Ministers. For some years the Prince had been pledged to support the candidature of Lord Leitrim whenever there was a vacancy. Ministers admitted that, however embarrassing the situation, the Regent could not be expected to withdraw his pledged support; on the same principle, they could not retract the pledges which they had given Lord Gosford. Ryder commented: 'I am only surprised that in the strange and anomalous situation in which the Regent and the Government have been placed, such collisions have not hitherto more frequently occurred. All we have to do is to make the best of them when they do, taking care to keep our own faith and honour unsullied.'

After his defeat Lord Leitrim wrote to thank the Regent for his support. Evidently on this occasion, as on the previous one, he had not written to ask for it: in the circumstances it would have been improper to do so. Ryder wrote to the Duke of Richmond with reference to Lord Gosford: 'However usual it might be for a Prince of Wales in that character only to take a part at elections, the case was now different when he was the depositary of the Executive power.... Upon that ground alone such an application would have been improper.... Such an application was never made on any similar occasion to his Majesty.' Ryder told McMahon privately: 'There was a *constitutional* objection to any such assurance of support at an election coming from the Prince while *Regent* which would make it impossible for me as one of his confidential servants to advise such a letter, but that as it was not shown to me in that view I had no opinion to give.'

Another collision seemed likely, for the Prince told Ryder that he had pledged his support to Lord Landaff on a future vacancy. He added, however, that under existing circumstances he should take care to make no more engagements of that kind. The Lord Lieutenant of Ireland heard this news with surprise and dismay, saying, 'The disaffected [in Ireland] are much pleased at General Mathew's getting a Regiment, and anything favourable to his brother will add to their triumph.' The Prince was known to be irritated by the ministerial opposition to Leitrim, and the Opposition naturally encouraged such feelings. Leitrim's friends abused the Prince for insincerity in not having done enough for his own candidate.

The Regent and his Ministers were set on another collision course when, without the knowledge and consent of either the Prime Minister, the Lord Chancellor or the Home Secretary, the Prince offered the office of President of the Scottish Court of Judiciary to his friend William Adam. Perceval declared that if Adam had been foolish enough to accept it, Lord Melville would instantly have resigned from the Cabinet, and the Prince would have been told that the appointment could not be made.

Without reference to Perceval, the Prince promised a Household office to the Duke of Northumberland's son-in-law, Lord James Murray, and the Duke was told that his son Lord Percy was to be called up to the House of Lords 'as one of the first acts' of the Regent's 'emancipation'. The giving away places and the promising of honours was unfair to Perceval, and it was already clear, as Canning said, that the Regent would be 'a most inconvenient master to serve': he himself was to feel the full force of his observation in August–September 1822 when Lord Liverpool secured the Foreign Secretaryship for him only after a severe struggle with his 'master'.

McMahon's appointment as Paymaster of Widows Pensions brought Perceval into conflict not only with the Regent but with the House of Commons. On the death of General Fox, Perceval at once saw the Prince and suggested a suitable arrangement for that office. The Prince told him that he had already promised it to his faithful servant McMahon, and in spite of Perceval's remonstrances he insisted on its being gazetted. He was told that as long ago as 1783 the Tenth Report of the Commissioners for Public Accounts had recommended the abolition of the office as a sinecure, and that this recommendation had been confirmed by the Commissioners of Military Inquiry in their Sixth Report presented to the House of Commons on 25 June 1808. The appointment was sharply criticized in the Whig newspapers (McMahon described himself as 'running a dreadful gauntlet from the daily Press'), and Perceval had the disagreeable task of trying to defend in the Commons an appointment to which he himself had decidedly objected. All he could say was that McMahon had been told that Parliament might well interfere and nullify it, and that this sinecure ought not to be abolished until some alternative provision was made for a meritorious public servant, especially since the Sovereign had no power to grant pensions in lieu of sinecures. Brougham declared that Ministers had flown in the teeth of principles recognised by the House and its Committees. The matter was again raised on 21 February, not by any member of the 'Mountain', but, significantly, by Henry Bankes, an eminent country gentleman, the promoter of the Bill to prohibit the granting of offices in reversion. His Amendment to strike out the salary of the office from the Army Estimates was carried on 24 February by 115 votes to 112. The Duke of Northumberland's members and the Prince's voted with the minority, the 'Saints' with the Reformers.

General Fox's death occasioned another conflict between the Regent and Perceval. Although the Minister knew that the Prince had already promised the military Government of Portsmouth to General Lord Harcourt, the Queen's Master of the Horse, he asked for the appointment of Wellington, but he was defeated. Had Wellington himself known of this affair he might have expressed himself even more emphatically than he actually did, when in May he thought that Ministers ought to resign 'if the McMahon Cabinet should continue to exist'. And Lord Melville told Perceval that 'there must really be some explanation and understanding as to other and irresponsible advisers.' All Governments, irrespective of their party composition, disliked secret advisers.

There is no direct evidence that Perceval supported the pretensions of Lieutenant-General Charles Craufurd to the office of Governor of the Royal Military College at Great Marlow in order to conciliate Craufurd's stepson, the Duke of Newcastle, who returned about seven members to Parliament. If, as seems likely, he did so, he was defeated in this attempt to win parliamentary votes, for the Regent insisted on the appointment of Major-General Alexander Hope, to whom the office had been promised before the vacancy actually occurred. And Craufurd suffered additional mortification when his pretensions to the office of Quarter-Master General were ignored, the Duke of York's friend Colonel Gordon being appointed.

Gordon's promotion caused further trouble for Perceval. The Prince had promised the office of Commissary General to Colonel Drinkwater, but Perceval insisted that it was of essential importance to the public service that J. C. Herries, a very able civil servant who was later to become Secretary of the Treasury and eventually Chancellor of the Exchequer, should be gazetted. Drinkwater had to be content with the post of Comptroller of Army Accounts and a smaller salary than he would otherwise have had. And the Prince failed in his attempt to nominate Lord Hutchinson Commander-in-Chief in Ireland. 'We put a flat negative upon it,' wrote Bathurst.

By insisting on the appointment of the merchant M.P., Robert Thornton, as Marshal of the Admiralty, the Prince took an important piece of patronage out of the hands of Charles Yorke, who would have made a more suitable choice. He told the Prince quite frankly that 'it was not a proper office to be conferred upon a gentleman of Mr Thornton's description.'

The choice of a new Bishop of Oxford following the death of Charles Moss on 16 December caused another clash between the Regent and the Minister. The Prince himself told the story to Wellesley, and Wellesley passed it on to Canning. Perceval called at Carlton House on hearing of the Bishop's passing, and proposed a successor. The Regent replied, 'Mr Perceval, I have always intended to give the first Bishopric that I should have at my disposal in a way to mark my gratitude and affection to my old tutor, Dr Jackson. He declines all such preferment himself, you know, but I think—though upon my honour I have not consulted him, that it would be highly acceptable to him to have my sentiments for him proved by the promotion of his brother. I therefore intend this Bishopric for Dr William Jackson.' Perceval protested that his word was pledged—that he should be placed in a discreditable and awkward situation if he could not keep it, and that the person to whom he had engaged himself had had the King's good wishes. The Prince replied, 'Had I any knowledge of my father's wishes from himself they would have overruled any preference of my own. But I cannot learn them at second-hand. I must hear nothing of what you think he *would have* done. The only question here is between my engagements and *yours*, and it is for you to consider which must give way.' The Prince later remarked to Wellesley, 'Perceval then put on one of his little cynical smiles and observed, "Your Royal Highness perhaps does not know Dr William Jackson's character. He is a notorious *bon vivant*."'

'Oh!, as to that,' the Regent replied, 'I know him very well. I have known him all my life. He has drunk a bottle of port in this house before now, and I hope, when he has got his mitre on, that he will drink another.' The mitre was placed on Dr. Jackson's head a few weeks later.

The Home Secretary was less accommodating than Perceval had been over the Bishop of Oxford when a new Bishop of Dromore had to be nominated in December. Ryder heard from the Irish Government that the Prince meant to propose the Rev. Richard Ponsonby, who was not even a Dean. He therefore informed a person who could be relied on to pass on the information to Carlton House that no such proposition was acceptable; that the Government would resign if it were insisted on; it was out of the question that they could agree to the nephew of the Leader of the Opposition in the House of Commons being placed upon the Bench. The Rev. John Leslie, the Dean of Cork, was appointed, and Ponsonby had to wait nearly seventeen years for a Bishopric. Wellesley-Pole, the Irish Secretary, had advised the Lord Lieutenant to waive his undoubted right of patronage in order to accommodate the Prince who wanted to promote another meritorious clergyman, but neither Wellesley-Pole nor the Duke of Richmond would have accepted the nomination of a discreditable person like Bate Dudley. They knew well enough that the Regent would have liked to make him a Dean if not a Bishop, and soon after the restrictions expired he was in fact given a Baronetcy.

A permanent Regency now being regarded as inevitable, provision had to be made for the Royal Household, the existing one being due to expire with the restrictions. At first, the differences between the Regent's demands and Perceval's more modest proposals created serious difficulties, and Ryder thought that the Prince might change the Government if he could not gain his objects. Anxious to keep on good terms with his family the Prince demanded not only an unnecessarily large establishment for the King but one for the Queen as Dowager, and one for each of the four Princesses, who were delighted at the prospect of partial emancipation. Much more important, however, was the Prince's request

9

that the Cabinet should raise in Parliament the question of his debts which, once more, in spite of solemn promises to live within his income, amounted to the staggering total of £552,000. On 6 December the Cabinet unanimously decided against an application to Parliament, and took the line that the Prince should refrain from imposing fresh burdens on the people and should pay off debt by means of 'his own privations'. Perceval knew well enough that Parliament would never have provided for the payment of such a fantastic sum, and that if the Prince tried to find more complaisant Ministers he would still be unsuccessful. Reliance on the advice of the Carlton House Cabinet instead of on that of his responsible Ministers had caused him to put forward extravagant claims which could not be met and involved him in troubles which ended in humiliating surrender. Moreover, he had to abandon his demand for a sum of £150,000 'for Regency services' and to accept the Cabinet's offer of £100,000. On this point, much to the annoyance of his colleagues, Wellesley had supported the Regent's claims, but in the end he persuaded him to give way.

The Duke of Kent did not see why he should be neglected when something substantial was being done for other members of the family. He too had creditors clamouring for their money, and he thought it would be only an act of justice if their claims were met—at the taxpayers' expense. He remembered that although Pitt had acknowledged the validity of his claims for compensation for losses sustained between 1794 and 1800 by capture and shipwreck, only £4,000 out of £23,000 asked for had been met. Well aware that he could not very well reopen the matter after so many years, he was prepared to forget about it if some other provision were made for him. He complained not only of the non-payment of the promised compensation but also of the partial non-fulfilment of the arrangements which Pitt had made with him and the Duke of Clarence and their three younger brothers: £16,000 a year from Parliament, 'clear of all deductions', an allowance of £5,000 a year from the Civil List 'in lieu of a table', a sum to cover the cost of 'the outfit for our Establishment', and an allowance of fuel, oil and candles from the Board of Green Cloth payable to those residing in the Royal Palace. This last, said the Duke, was a point of some importance because none of his brothers had cellars sufficiently capacious to hold much coal, consequently they had no opportunity of laying in stocks at the cheap season of the year. Moreover, Lord Grenville's Government had decided that they must pay income tax, with the result that their nominal £18,000 a year was reduced to £16,200; and, the Duke complained, 'we have received no allowance for table or sum of money for outfit as promised by Mr Pitt. We have also been deprived of the allowance of fuel, lights, etc.', whilst the Princess of Wales had been supplied by the Board of Works with a complete outfit for her apartments at Kensington Palace,

10

with coal and candles, and with all the produce of the royal gardens at Kensington.

If the differences over patronage and Household arrangements made the Regent reluctant to commit himself to Perceval, Whig blunders contributed to alienate the Prince from his 'old Whig friends'.

At the beginning of the Regency the Prince had been most anxious to restore his brother to the command of the Army, not merely as an act of friendship but as an act of justice. In spite of parliamentary difficulties which threatened, Ministers unanimously favoured the Duke's restoration, but about forty Whigs[1] ignored the advice of their leaders and on 6 June voted against the re-appointment, the rebellion against Ponsonby being led by Lord Milton, the young man who, as a child of three, had been held up in the Prince's arms at Wentworth and ostentatiously displayed to the family and the admiring crowd of bystanders. There was no similar motion in the Lords: Grey in particular would not have supported one.

The Prince had originally been averse to the Spanish expeditions, but under the influence of Lord Wellesley he had come to support the Peninsular War, especially after Wellington's successes had demonstrated its possibilities in contributing powerfully to Napoleon's downfall. The Whigs, however, for the most part questioned the expediency of persevering with an enterprise which seemed ruinously expensive and where success was doubtful. As late as January 1812 Lord Grenville spoke of the 'desperate and hopeless character' of the struggle. The Duke of Northumberland still thought that Wellington had mismanaged everything, otherwise the French would have been expelled from both Spain and Portugal. Even Lord Holland, who had personal knowledge of the situation in Spain, believed that we should never be able to drive the French over the Pyrenees.

The Prince supported Ministers on the question of the Orders-in-Council, but the Whigs demanded their repeal as injurious to British trade and industry, and as bringing the country to the verge of war with the United States, with the consequential risk of the loss of Canada.

The relief of the Catholics had been the object nearest to Fox's heart next to the abolition of the slave trade, and he had left it as such as a legacy to his friends. On the one hand, the Prince would have liked to preserve his consistency on that question, partly out of respect for Fox's memory, partly because he dreaded the abuse and discredit which would be the consequence of abandoning his pledges and professions. Lord Temple suggested that if the Prince began his reign by keeping Perceval

1. The minority of 47 included Tremayne, an independent country gentleman; 'Saints' (Wilberforce, Babington and Henry Thornton); Mildmay, the Canningite; and Radicals (Burdett, Folkestone and Wardle).

11

he would be declaring war against Ireland. On the other hand, under the influence of the Hertfords and his Tory Ministers he was now beginning to pass through the final stage of his tergiversation: neutrality had succeeded support of Catholic relief; a decided hostility to it followed neutrality. No reliance could now be placed on his former engagements to the Catholics, and Lord Hutchinson remarked, 'I had early discovered a close connection between promise and retractation.' When the Prince refused even to discuss the question with Lord Hutchinson, his brother Lord Donoughmore and others, it was clear that the aspect of affairs was unpromising. Moira viewed with apprehension the Government's repressive measures in Ireland and lamented the Regent's acquiescence in them. Ministers succeeded in alarming the Prince with their representations of the dangers to which he might expose himself by offending the Church and the Protestant feelings of the country. The Prince's betrayal of the Irish Catholics would no longer be justified on the ground that the passing of a Relief Bill would be hazardous to the King's life and sanity.

Some members of the Opposition deluded themselves with the idea that the Prince would not be displeased to see the Catholic question again discussed in Parliament before the restrictions expired. But William Adam, for one, believed that in proposing to bring it forward they were behaving very foolishly, showing that they were unequivocally hostile to the Prince, determined to 'take him by storm'. Adam was right, and the Prince was furious when they persisted in their intention. A premature discussion was calculated to produce a substantial anti-Catholic majority and consequently to encourage the Regent to abandon his pledges. Fitzwilliam's Motion in the Lords on 31 January was defeated by 162 votes to 79, and Morpeth's in the Commons was rejected on 4 February by 229 to 135. Canning thought that his young friend had behaved rashly and foolishly.

Whereas the Prince wished to leave the management of the Army precisely as it had been during the King's reign, some Whigs were now taking the line that the Army should no longer be independent of the Civil Government. Grenville said, 'It is a bad principle even under an absolute Monarchy. It is totally incompatible with the principle of a limited Crown.'

Then there was the currency question. In office Grenville would have favoured an early resumption of cash payments, but the Regent supported Ministers who maintained that there had been no currency depreciation but that the restoration of the gold standard should be delayed until peace was restored. Lord King proposed to compel his tenants to pay their rents in gold, thus drawing attention to the fact that banknotes were not legal tender. Lord Stanhope therefore introduced a Bill to remedy this defect. On this question the Whigs were divided.

Tierney had doubts about the wisdom of restoring the gold standard. Some Whigs were afraid to face the unpopularity which opposition to Stanhope's Bill would engender, and only twenty voted against it on 19 July. Nothing could equal the unwillingness of his friends to attend, said Tierney. Some were deterred, too, by the surprising eagerness with which the Prince supported the Bill throughout its progress. Tyrwhitt was summoned from Cornwall to vote for it, and, to the great vexation of the Opposition, Lord Yarmouth, McMahon and Lord Robert Seymour attended daily, whilst Sheridan made a speech in support of Ministers. Tierney believed that the Prince's eagerness for the Bill meant that he had no longer any idea of changing the Government, but some of his friends still thought otherwise.

Lord Holland, and, no doubt, others were of the opinion that the Prince's reluctance to bring in the Whigs arose from his fear of a strong Administration. Now that he was the Sovereign in all but name he had no wish to inherit a weaker Crown than his father's. As a Tory would have phrased it, he had no intention of submitting to being put in trammels.

3057   SPENCER PERCEVAL TO THE PRINCE REGENT

Downing Street, 4.30 a.m., Saturday [*1 June 1811*]

Mr Perceval presents his humble duty to your Royal Highness and acquaints your Royal Highness that Mr Grattan's Motion for referring the Roman Catholic Petition to the Committee of the whole House was negatived after a long debate by 146 to 84.[1] (18088)

1. *Parliamentary Debates*, xx. 369–427, where the minority vote is correctly given as 83. The number is stated as 86 in Colchester, *Diary and Correspondence*, ii. 333. Wellesley-Pole wrote to the Duke of Richmond, the Lord Lieutenant, on 1 June, from the Irish Office in London: 'I sent you an account of our division this morning at half-past four. Perceval's speech was admirable—Grattan worse than I ever heard him—Whitbread blackguard—Montague Mathew very loud but nothing at all like himself last year. Ponsonby made the best speech among the Opposition. You will find the gentlemen spoke out more than they have ever done. The House [was] very thin, the division on the whole good. It is remarkable, and I think very flattering to your Grace's Government, that not one word was said by anybody in the debate that bore the slightest allusion to any part of our proceedings with the Catholic Committee; this I consider as a convincing proof of our complete triumph' (Richmond MSS.).

Ponsonby, Tierney told Lady Holland (1 June), 'made a very good speech . . . and Whitbread a grand splash not quite so much confined to the matter in hand. The Saints got into sad disgrace in the person of their great orator Mr Stephen who was outrageously foul mouthed and was at one time in a fair way to spend the night in the custody of the Sergeant' (Holland House MSS.).

London, 1 June 1811

The Linnæan Society, for the cultivation of Natural History in all its branches, was founded in 1788, & incorporated by Royal Charter in 1802. What particularly led to this establishment was the acquisition of the entire Museum, Library & Manuscripts of the celebrated Linnaeus,[2] purchased from Sweden by Dr. Smith at his own private expense, which was thought so valuable an acquisition to the country that the British Government allowed it to pass without duty or examination.

The Society in question can, by the present Charter, consist of no more than 4 honorary members with an unlimited number of Fellows, foreign members, and associates. The present list embraces nearly all the names of any note in this study throughout Europe. All expenses are borne by the Fellows, who alone sign any obligation or have any share in the government of the Society.

One place of honorary member has been vacant ever since the death of the late Duke of Portland, the Society being under no obligation to fill up such vacancy till they find some 'person of distinguished rank' worthy to be appointed to it.

It is much wished that his Royal Highness the Prince Regent would allow himself either to fill this place under the title of Patron of the Society, or in any other manner most conformable to his exalted station, or that his Royal Highness would, by any alteration of, or addition to, the present Charter, be pleased to declare himself the Patron of the Society. On this subject the President & Council of the Society cannot presume to dictate, only they believe that, as the Charter at present stands, his Royal Highness, by whatever other title distinguished, must come under the denomination of an Honorary Member—which indeed is exactly the place in which his Majesty & all other Royal personages stand in the Royal Society, whose laws they are moreover required to subscribe.[3] (18089–90)

3059 THE EARL OF LIVERPOOL TO THE PRINCE REGENT

Downing Street, 2 June 1811

Lord Liverpool has the honour to transmit to your Royal Highness an abstract of the dispatch of Sir William Beresford on the occasion of the

1. Sir James Edward Smith (1759–1828), founder and President of the Linnæan Society. Knighted, 1814. His memorandum was sent to Tyrwhitt (see No. 3063).

2. Carl Linnæus, the founder of modern botany (1707–78). Professor of Botany at Uppsala, 1742.

3. The Prince Regent later became Patron of the Society.

battle of Albuera,[1] together with a list of the officers killed and wounded.

The dispatches are copying for the Gazette; they will be sent to your Royal Highness as soon as they are copied, and Lord Liverpool will have the honour of waiting upon your Royal Highness any hour this night or tomorrow morning you may be pleased to appoint, with some private letters from Lord Wellington which are very interesting.

As your Royal Highness was absent from town Lord Liverpool has taken the liberty of consulting his Royal Highness the Duke of York on the propriety of firing the guns upon this occasion, and his Royal Highness has expressed his conviction that if your Royal Highness was in town you would decide both in justice to the brave Army engaged, and from the importance of the result of the action itself, that the guns ought to be fired. (18091)

3060 THE IRISH CATHOLICS[2] TO COLONEL MCMAHON
St. James's Hotel, Jermyn Street, 3 June 1811
Having had the honor to present to his Royal Highness the Prince Regent, at the Levée on Tuesday last, a petition from the Catholics of Ireland, to which were annexed the signatures of many thousand respectable individuals, we have to request to be informed if his Royal Highness will graciously condescend to honor us with any expression of his sentiments on the subject of the petition—if not we humbly beg leave to express our hope that his Royal Highness will graciously be pleased to direct that the petition may be inserted in the Gazette in order that it may appear that we have fulfilled the mission with which we have been intrusted.[3] (18101)

1. Fought on 16 May, the French under Soult being defeated, both sides sustaining severe losses. Soult retreated towards Andalusia, and Wellington, joining Beresford's mixed force of British, Portuguese and Spaniards, renewed the siege of Badajoz. The House of Commons voted him its thanks on 7 June.

2. Three not very legible signatures are appended. The first is [?]F. C. [?] Goolden (certainly not Sir F. Goodden); the second is O[?] O'Conor; the third is illegible except for the Christian name 'Geo.'.

3. The sequel is given in the following letters. Wellesley-Pole wrote to the Lord Lieutenant on the 8th: 'I discover'd yesterday that the petition from the Catholics for the removal of your Grace and me from office was to appear in this evening's *Gazette*—and I immediately waited upon Mr. Perceval and Mr. Ryder. They neither of them knew anything of the matter. The petition had been sent from Carlton House to the *Gazette* office with a letter from Genl. Turner conveying H.R.H.s commands that it should be inserted in the *Gazette*. I represented both to Perceval and Ryder that I conceived such an insertion in the *Gazette* might do much mischief in Ireland, and that it would look as if H.R.H. countenanced these ruffians against your Grace and your Administration. They agreed with me and Ryder proposed going to the Regent and endeavouring to stop the proceeding. He accordingly waited upon the Prince,

29 Upper Baker Street, 3 June 1811

I find my conjectures were correct, as the event has proved them to be well founded, and I need not say that the 'reformers' are congregating all their strength to produce what they call 'universal disapprobation of

when I understand H.R.H. told him that the gentlemen who presented the petition were much disappointed at not receiving an answer, and had requested the petition might appear in the *Gazette*, with which request the Regent had complied to stop their clamour—believing that the matter would thus be set at rest. Thus circumstanced both Mr. Perceval and Mr. Ryder say the petition must appear in the *Gazette*, and we have no remedy. It seems a very scurrilous Address from Westminster against Ministers appeared some time ago in the *Gazette* under similar circumstances; and it has been now decided, as I understand, in consequence of what has now happen'd, that in future nothing shall be publish'd that does not go through the Office of the Secretary of State. The best way of acting under the present circumstances seems to me to be to treat the whole affair with sovereign contempt and to consider the insertion as a mere matter of course. I hope it may not produce any bad effect in Ireland, here it cannot at all signify' (Richmond MSS.).

Ryder wrote to the Duke that day: 'You will be surprised to see the Address for your Grace's removal & Pole's in the *Gazette* this evening. Pole informed me yesterday that Rolleston of the Foreign Office had received directions from Carlton House to put it into the *Gazette*. I immediately went there to enquire into the circumstances and I was informed by the Prince that the Petition of the Catholic body & the Address had been presented to H.R.H. the same day, that the former had been sent to be put in as it was put in, on the Sunday last, that the other was withheld, that an application had been made to him by the individuals who presented the Address expressing their concern that the Address was not put in as well as the petition, and requesting that H.R.H. would either return them an answer or direct it to be gazetted, in order that it might appear that they had discharged their duty by presenting it. H.R.H. directed them to be informed that he would return them no answer, but that he did not object to its appearing like other Addresses in the *Gazette*, & had given directions accordingly. Upon my stating to him my apprehensions that the insertion would look like encouragement he said that nothing was further from his thoughts, that he conceived it to be a matter of course, and should be very sorry if it conveyed such an impression; that he had perhaps acted inadvertently, & would for the future send all Addresses, &c., to me who, as I told him, am responsible for what is inserted in the *Gazette*. As, however, he had committed himself, there was nothing more to be said, and in truth the insertion is, I hope, of the less consequence, as Addresses have of late appeared in the *Gazette* full of abuse of our conduct upon the Regency, which, as being contained in complimentary Addresses to the Regent, we thought it best not to stop, but to shew our utter disregard of these libels by inserting them. They went through, or at least many of them, my Office in the regular way; but some, and one in particular presented by Burdett was sent by some carelessness straight to the *Gazette* from Carlton House, which was not only a libel upon us but an atrocious libel upon the Constitution. Similar mistakes are stopped for the future, and have arisen from the people about the Prince being utterly unconversant in habits of business or official routine, and I really believe without the slightest intention to act otherwise than properly. I told the Regent I should think it necessary to explain the circumstances to your Grace, which he desired I would do, and to express his hope that no misconception would arise out of it. I told him the responsibility and the blame would fall upon me' (ibid.).

1. A minor journalist who wrote pamphlets in support of the Government. He was for ever complaining of poverty and writing begging letters. He was eventually given a pension of £200 a year (A. Aspinall, *Politics and the Press*, p. 154).

the measure'. The Examiner[1] of yesterday contained a long article on the subject, & we shall have Common Halls & county meetings in abundance to discuss the measure, therefore I humbly conceive this to be a very proper time to throw a little weight into the other scale & which indeed I have begun under the title of a letter to the Reformers wherein I propose to dwell on the real services done by H.R.H. the Duke of York to the Army, contrast it with the services of other Commanders-in-Chief—expose the views of the faction & by a reference to Ancient Rome shew the people the folly of their proceedings, & where morality stands in the way I propose to extenuate what religion might not justify. I shall touch upon the proposed benefits of reform & dwell upon the good likely to result from the cordiality subsisting between the members of the Royal family at this critical juncture.

I am not ignorant that be the wishes of H.R.H. the Prince Regent what they may on this subject, it would not be proper for them to be given in writing to a person who, however zealous & faithful he may be, is as yet untried, but perhaps a few moments of conversation might obviate all these difficulties. Waiting your commands I have the honor to be [etc.]. (18102)

3062   MRS [?] M. STIRLING TO THE PRINCE REGENT

37 North Audley Street, Grosvenor Square, 4 June 1811

Sir, I have to beg ten thousand pardons for presuming to address your Royal Highness. Nothing cou'd have induc'd me to have taken the liberty but for the full assurance that your Royal Highness possesses a generous & benevolent heart and perhaps may condescend to recollect or listen to the unfortunate circumstances in which I am involv'd from accepting the situation with Miss M. Seymour. I beg leave to represent to your Royal Highness in consequence of becoming an inmate in the family of Mrs. Fitzherbert I gave up the whole of any connection I had previously form'd in the families of noblemen and gentlemen whose children I instructed in music. When Mrs. Fitzherbert propos'd to me to give up my pupils and live with her I pointed out the precariousness of the situation and the chance of its not being permanent which to me wou'd be a most serious disappointment. I therefore declin'd it. Some little time after, Mrs. Fitzherbert again solicited me on the same subject. She said, 'You must not leave me. You are the person of all others I shou'd wish to retain in my family. If you will consent to stay with my darling child you will contribute very much to my happiness, and in

1. Leigh Hunt's weekly paper.

17

return I will grant you any favor in my power.' This was a most painful struggle between interest and inclination, for the very liberal and friendly treatment I receiv'd from Mrs. Fitzherbert during the three months I was staying at Parson's Green to teach Miss Seymour the pianoforte attach'd me very much to them both, but I was oblig'd to start the same objection, when Mrs. Fitzherbert immediately reply'd, 'That shall not prevent you. I have consider'd the matter over and think it but fair as I press you into the service to presume upon the word and honor of a gentlewoman to provide for you for ever—consider you as my friend and treat you as such.' In short, the situation held out not only the comforts of life as long as my existence lasted but promis'd me every happiness my heart cou'd wish, little supposing I shou'd ever have the smallest reason to repent, for nothing cou'd exceed the kindness, friendship and affection of Mrs. Fitzherbert. I am confident I cou'd have sacrific'd my life to serve her. I felt my heart overflow with gratitude, but alas, this mutual satisfaction only lasted a few months before Mrs. Fitzherbert's manner began to change. I was totally at a loss to know the reason, and entreated with the most ardent solicitude to be inform'd how I had been so unfortunate to incur the least displeasure from one I consider'd the best of friends. My mind was soon set at ease by the full assurance that nothing on my part had occasion'd the least coolness, but any external appearance of neglect might have arisen from causes which related to her own affairs. This éclaircissement made me happy as far as concern'd myself but I lamented that one from whom I receiv'd such repeated marks of kindness shou'd from any cause feel a moment's uneasiness. I now hop'd I shou'd go on comfortably in fulfilling the duties incumbent with my little charge. I endeavour'd to acquit myself in the best manner I was capable [of] and devoted my time wholly to Miss Seymour, yet I thought from time to time Mrs. Fitzherbert appear'd dissatisfied without finding any fault with me, which made me again unhappy. At length I was not at a loss to account for the uncertainty of Mrs. Fitzherbert's manner. I found she was influenc'd by a lady who is always about her and who was not kindly dispos'd towards me but from some jealous motive wish'd my removal from the family—therefore devis'd every method to prejudice the mind of Mrs. Fitzherbert against me. She succeeded but too well in her cruel plan as the very unkind treatment I receiv'd affected my health so severely I was compel'd to resign the situation by writing to Mrs. Fitzherbert, being too much oppress'd and agitated to speak on the subject. My letter was receiv'd with no mark of disapprobation—so far from it Mrs. Fitzherbert begg'd I wou'd make myself comfortable while I remain'd and she wou'd do everything in her power to serve me—that I might consider her my friend as my strict principles of honor and rectitude of conduct merited every acknowledgment. Notwithstanding this cruel alternative my drooping spirits began to revive. Mrs. Fitzherbert treated me with her former kindness. I was no longer subject to averted looks but receiv'd every mark of approbation particularly from the lady who had been beaten me [*sic*] so unsuccessfully that if looks cou'd have anihilated me I shou'd not now have been alive to unfold this sad tale. The reflection that I had lost my connection and had no resource left by which I cou'd support myself, together with the returning kindness of Mrs. Fitzherbert, induc'd me to offer to remain in my situation. Mrs. Fitzherbert did not put a negative on my proposal nor give me a decided answer. I was kept in a most anxious state of suspence for nearly three months when my offer was rejected and I was once more driven on the world. It woud surely have been much more humane to have taken my life than to deprive me of the means by which I liv'd. Mine is indeed a bitter fate through the loss of the dearest ties on earth to be left unprotected and unprovided for—to have my bread to seek and when obtain'd with honor and credit to myself to be induc'd to leave my profession for the flattering prospects before me which has ended in my ruin. I have receiv'd no compensation from Mrs. Fitzherbert for the loss I have sustain'd—nothing but cruel disappointment. It is true she begg'd the favor of your Royal Highness to subscribe to my waltzes for which I have and do return a million of thanks, but Mrs. Fitzherbert has procur'd me no other names with the exception of herself and Miss Seymour which has led me into an expence I never shou'd have ventur'd had not Mrs. Fitzherbert promis'd to get me a great many subscribers. I had no other means of paying the publisher who importunes me for the amount of his bill. This last disappointment has added to my distress— in short I have contracted debts I am not able to pay which compel'd me to beg the favor of Mrs. Fitzherbert to lend me a little money but I met with a repulse that forbids another application. I am not without friends but I am much indebted to them. It is now almost a year since I left Miss Seymour. The Hon. Mrs. St. John,[1] whose innate goodness I must ever revere, on whom I had no sort of claim, has indeed been my friend; she has supply'd me with the necessaries of life when I was quite destitute, and lent me money which I am very anxious to repay. She has also recommended me to Lady Charlotte Greville who has been so kind as to procure me a few pupils in families of rank which I fear I cannot decline, attending as I expect very soon from embarrass'd circumstances to be depriv'd of my liberty. I can assure your Royal Highness my heart is almost broken, but how dare I presume to trouble your Royal Highness with my affairs. I am truly sensible I have taken a great liberty. I never shou'd have had courage to do it only that I am certain of the most known fact that your Royal Highness possesses a generous and feeling

1. The Hon. Henry St. John (1738–1818), second son of John, 2nd Viscount St. John, and M.P. for Wootton Bassett, 1761–84, and July–December 1802, married, 31 August 1771, Barbara, daughter of Thomas Bladen, M.P., of Glastonbury.

heart and perhaps will deign to listen to my grievances. I am well convinc'd your Royal Highness will not let the distress'd and the widow plead in vain but with that compassion and humanity inherent in your noble mind will in some measure alleviate my accumulated misfortunes, and Heaven I trust will look upon the charitable deed and send down the reward I merit. (18110–12)

3063 LORD STANLEY[1] TO THOMAS TYRWHITT
Winwick,[2] 5 June 1811

You will not perhaps have entirely forgotten the conversation I had with you in the course of last week at the H. of Commons when I stated to you the commission with which I was charged by our President to endeavour to obtain the distinguished honor of the name of his Royal Highness the Prince Regent as Patron & Honorary Member of the Linnaean Society, or in any other mode that might be considered as most respectful from us, & most consonant to the character & station of H.R. Highness. In pursuance of this object I requested Dr. Smith to furnish me with a written statement of the wishes of the Society in order that H.R. Highness might more clearly understand their nature & extent, & be the better enabled to form a judgement upon the propriety or otherwise of his condescending to gratify them. This paper[3] I last night received, & hasten to transmit to you, who were so good as to say you would endeavour to learn for me whether such an application would be disagreeable to H.R.H. & if not, in what manner it would be most proper that it should be made.

I cannot but confess my earnest hopes that the decision may be favourable, & should feel highly gratified in communicating to Dr. Smith that our Society were to be honoured by so distinguished patronage.

I flatter myself you would have had the goodness to explain to H.R.H. the circumstance of our meeting in London at the very time when he would be informed that I had left town. I trust he would [not] be inclined, from such an apparently positive contradiction, to doubt of my devotion to him or of my readiness at all times to obey any of his commands, but the fact really was that I had left town for ten days or a fortnight with my family, & had only arrived in London that morning,

1. Edward, Lord Stanley (1775–1851) succeeded his father as Earl of Derby on 21 October 1834. Whig M.P. for Preston, 1796–1812; for Lancashire, 1812–32. Created Baron Stanley, 22 December 1832. President of the Linnæan Society, 1828–33. K.G., 1839.

2. Near Warrington.

3. No. 3058.

literally alone & totally unprovided, for the mere purpose of giving my consent in the Committee of the Lords, to set off again that night, or, at farthest, the next.

I will venture to ask when you write that you wd. out of charity communicate any news that may be stirring. You are on the spot & I am 200 miles off. You may therefore conceive how acceptable any intelligence will be in such times as these, & particularly when one knows how much one is kept under deception. Pray direct to Knowsley, whither I go in a day or two. (18113–4)

3064 LETTERS FROM THE QUEEN TO THE PRINCE REGENT

Windsor, 5 June 1811

How unfortunate the day, my dearest son, to be so stormy & rainy as to prevent my young visitor to enjoy a ride of which she talked with so much pleasure yesterday evening. It is the more painfull to me as this place will not afford for the present any great variety of amusements, but you may rest assured that as far as lays in mine & your sisters' power we will use our best endeavours to make Charlotte's visit as little dull as circumstances will admit of.

I saw this morning Drs. Baillie, Willis & Dundas & had a long conversation separately with each. Every one of them are unanimous that the present system will prove beneficial in the end, but that it must take time before we can see essential good arising from it & that it is not in their power to specify any time in particular for this event. The momentary object is obtained (more calmness) by the absence of domestic servants which will in time lead on to further improvement, but of that little can be expected under a fortnight to come. Under these circumstances it struck me to propose to you that as having already put off your intended fête for a week, had you not better add another week to it?[1] My reason for doing this is your amiable & prudent conduct during this, our great calamity, & your wish to do everything most right induces me to suggest this plan to you as by that means you & everybody else may enjoy it more & the world in general may have still more reason to applaud your delicacy.

I beg pardon for intruding myself when your time can be better

1. The Speaker wrote on 31 May: 'The Prince has put off his Fête from June 5th to 12th. Probably it will not take place at all' (Colchester, *Diary and Correspondence*, ii. 334). And on 8 June: 'Regent's Fête put off till the 19th' (ibid., ii. 335). It was thought that Sheridan had tried hard to persuade the Prince to cancel the Fête altogether, and that 'the Lady of Manchester Square' was the real promoter of it, 'being anxious to be displayed thus publicly in an ostentatious state of vanity and influence' (*Dropmore Papers*, x. 150).

employed, but I am sure you will approve my motif, which can only spring from the heart of [etc.]. (36568–9)

Windsor, 6 June 1811
It would not be kind to let your servant go away without an answer to the very affectionate letter I have just received from you. I trust my prudence will not forsake me upon this occasion & that your readiness to take my advice as well as your secret will be kept close by me & that you shall alone enjoy the credit of such a step.

I shall be very happy to see you on Saturday next & to have the pleasure of assuring you by word of mouth how sincerely I am [etc.].[1] (36570)

3065   SPENCER PERCEVAL TO THE PRINCE REGENT
Downing Street, 1.15 a.m., Friday, 8 [7] June [1811]
Mr Perceval presents his humble duty to your Royal Highness, and as the Lord Yarmouth was so obliging to charge himself with acquainting

1. Lady Holland wrote to Lord Lansdowne on 22 July: 'Since the Fête at Carlton House, Mrs. Fitzherbert has inflexibly resisted all his attempts to be admitted within her doors. You probably have seen or heard that she wrote to inquire at which table she was to sit. He replied wherever she chose and begged her to make her own party, but that as rank alone regulated the ceremonial she could not sit at his table. Her answer was spirited. She recalled to his memory her past forbearance, and pressed strongly her *right* to the first place at his table if she were inclined to urge it publicly. This may be relied on; I saw the extract from her letter, but of course it had better not be mentioned' (Bowood MSS.).

Mrs. Fitzherbert's letter to the Prince was written on 7 June, before the announcement of the postponement of the Fête: 'After the conversation your Royal Highness held with me yesterday I am sure you will not be surprised that I have sent my excuses for not obeying your commands for Wednesday next. Much as it has ever been my wish during a period of near thirty years to save you from every embarrassment in my power, yet there are situations when one ought not entirely to forget what is due to oneself. You, Sir, are not aware, in your anxiety to fill your table with persons only of the highest rank, that, by excluding her who now addresses you merely for want of those titles that others possess, you are excluding the person who is not unjustly suspected by the world of possessing in silence unassumed and unsustained a rank given her by yourself above that of any other person present. Having never forfeited my title to your Royal Highness's public as well as private consideration by any act of my life, to what could this etiquette be for the first time imputed? No one, my dear Sir, has proved themselves thro' life less solicitous than myself. But I cannot be indifferent to the fair, honorable appearance of consideration from you which I have hitherto possessed and which I feel I deserve, and for which reason I can never submit to appear in your house in any place or situation but in that where you yourself first placed me many years ago. Yesterday I

your Royal Highness with the earliest information of the result of the debate on Lord Milton's Motion, Mr Perceval cannot deny himself the satisfaction of offering to your Royal Highness his humble congratulations upon the satisfactory manner in which the sense of the House of Commons has been expressed upon the propriety of the reappointment of H.R. Highness the Duke of York to be Commander-in-Chief.[1] (1811b)

3066   GENERAL THOMAS GRAHAM TO MAJOR–GENERAL T. H. TURNER

Cadiz, 8 June 1811

I am sorry to say that I am disappointed of the Seville oranges from Ayamonté & by the report from thence I have some doubt if my commission to Lisbon will be successful.

was too much surprised, when you informed me that from my want of rank I would not be admitted to your table, to be able to express my feelings in due bounds; and today, the impression remaining unabated, I sent my excuse to Colonel Thomas, but on reflection I think it more candid and open to lay my reasons before you, begging you at the same time to believe me [etc.].' (Sir Shane Leslie, *Life and Letters of Mrs. Fitzherbert*, ii. 139.)

1. *Parliamentary Debates*, xx. 470–510. See Nos. 3049, 3055. 'As far as I can at present observe,' Tierney had written on the 1st, 'Lord Milton will not be much supported' (Holland House MSS.). The numbers were 296 v 47. The minority included Whigs, Radicals and 'Saints'. Other Whigs, such as George Ponsonby, William Lamb, William Adam and Piggott, voted with the Government (Colchester, *Diary and Correspondence*, ii. 335). Romilly explained the small size of the minority: 'Several persons, whose votes I should have thought (judging from their past conduct) could not possibly have been influenced by any apprehension of displeasing the Prince, very prudently absented themselves' (*Memoirs*, ii. 391). Lady Spencer suggested to her husband on 31 May: 'Members will be a little shy of going to their constituents for their suffrages after having voted for the Duke's reinstatement, when these constituents rejoiced so sincerely in his dismissal some time ago' (Althorp MSS.). Ryder wrote to the Duke of Richmond on the 8th: '. . . He [the Regent] is delighted with the result of Ld. Milton's Motion, & we have not less reason to be so too. The debate could not go off better than it did, & the division of our opponents upon it has, as of course it was calculated to do, occasioned much uncomfortable feeling. I flatter myself that what passed will give a turn to public opinion. You have probably heard that when the Opposition were to have come in, Ld. Grenville declared he would not consent to it, and Ld. Buckingham canvassed all his friends to vote for Ld. Milton's Motion. The Prince's letter to Perceval desiring him to take the opinion of his colleagues upon the advantages & inconveniences of appointing the Duke of York upon Sir D. Dundas's resignation, and requiring our opinion upon it, was perfectly proper and fair, and I know from undoubted authority that he was much pleased with our unanimous answer recommending the measure' (Richmond MSS.).

The Duke replied on the 12th: 'I rejoice very sincerely at the result of Lord Milton's Motion. I should think it would have been wiser of Lord Fitzwilliam who wants the Ribbon and to be Prime Minister to have prevented his son from taking so mark'd a part. Lord Althorp too will have done his father no good in the eyes of the Prince. The Grenvilles do what they can to disgust his Royal Highness and I hope they will succeed' (ibid.).

23

From Ayamonté they write that the Seville oranges at this season are all so ripe on the trees that there wd. be no chance wth. the most careful packing of their not being spoilt in a few days on board of ship. I shall however give the most particular directions on the subject to the Town Major at Lisbon, formerly an officer of my Regt.—& I am sure, if the thing can be done, that he will send them to you.

Capt. Geddes will write to you if the oranges are sent from Lisbon. (18123)

3067 BENJAMIN WEST TO COLONEL MCMAHON
Newman Street, 10 June 1811

In the month of Augt. last I had the honour to present to his Royal Highness the Prince Regent a letter written by myself on the progress of the Fine Arts and the illustrious patronage given them from the earliest period to our own time: and when his Royal Highness honoured the arts with his preasence [*sic*] at the Royal Academy in Aprill [*sic*] last he was graciously pleased to signify to me his permission for me to have a few copies of that letter printed.[1]

As that letter was written for the purpose of handing down with honour those of high distinction who have patronised the Fine Arts—I wish to avail myself in the printing of that letter, to regester [*sic*] the honour which the arts received in this country by that eloquent Address made by the Prince Regent in the Royal Academy, when his Royal Highness last honoured that body with his preasance. If the Prince Regent should not disapprove of my wish, and would honour me by looking at the inclosed paper to see whether I have caught the heads and meaning of his words—I shall feel a pride in adding them to the glowing honours which the Arts have received in their progress through the world. (18124)

3068 THOMAS MOORE TO COLONEL MCMAHON
27 Bury Street, St. James's, Monday night [?10 or 17 June 1811]

Little as I have had the good luck to see of you I feel quite convinced that it will not be *your fault* if I do not receive a ticket for the approaching fête[2] of the Prince Regent. It was you that first made me known to his

1. On 27 April the Prince Regent went to the Royal Academy Exhibition, and, after dinner, said the Speaker, 'made a long speech in praise of the improvements made of late years in the fine arts, and particularly in the art of painting' (Colchester, ii. 326).

2. On the 19th.

Royal Highness, and to you, I am convinced, I am chiefly indebted for the unvaried attention with which he has honoured me ever since.

I have long been afraid to call upon Mrs. McMahon, from feeling conscious how little I deserve to be received by her. However, pray present my kindest remembrances to her. (18171)

3069 PRINCESS CHARLOTTE TO THE PRINCE REGENT

Windsor, 11 [June] 1811

The Queen has been so good as to invite me to stay here till after your Fête.[1] This being the case I thought it better to write to you myself to obtain your permission. I am very comfortable here & treated with so much kindness that unless you have any objection I shall be very glad to stay. Should you not have time to answer this yourself, will you desire one of your Gentlemen, as it depends entirely upon your answer what I am to do? Before I conclude I must return you my best thanks for your permitting me to go to Montem[2] where I was very much amused. I shall long to see you again. (49667–8)

3070 PRINCESS MARY TO THE PRINCE REGENT

11 June [1811]

I am happy to say the King has passed a particular quiet composed day, been shaved by his own desire, dined well, undressed equally so & has been asleep since 10 o'clock. (Add. Georgian 12/175)

3071 RICHARD RYDER TO THE PRINCE REGENT

Great George Street, 12 June 1811

Mr Ryder has the honor of humbly submitting to your Royal Highness that it would be extremely desirable for the dispatch of public business if your Royal Highness should not find it inconvenient to hold a Council either tomorrow or Friday. Mr Ryder did not, in consequence of some

1. The Regent's consent was given. 'The Queen ... *made me* write to ask him leave,' the Princess wrote on the 13th.

2. She had never been before. Her father was there, and hardly spoke to her at all, & when he did 'his manner was *so cold* that it was very distressing' (*Letters of the Princess Charlotte*, ed. A. Aspinall, p. 2).

mistake, receive this information till this moment or he should have thought it his duty to have made an earlier communication to your Royal Highness upon this subject. (18130)

3072   WILLIAM WALTER[1] TO COLONEL MCMAHON

Audit Office, Adelphi, 13 June 1811

I have had some doubts whether to call on or to write to you on the subject of some animadversions that have appeared in the *Times* on the subject of the Duke of York's re-appointment. The only reason for my offering any explanation to you is—that having on a former occasion solicited your good offices in regard to my father, you had naturally a right, considering your situation with the Prince, to suppose that a battery would not be again opened against the Duke, who, thro' an interference in another quarter, had actually withdrawn the prosecution against my father.[2] All that I have to say on this subject is—that having at the period alluded to drawn up a paper which my father signed, promising that nothing offensive to the Duke should ever again be inserted in the *Times* while he was proprietor, I have used every possible exertion with my father that good faith should be observed on the present occasion. He certainly ought to have exercised a sufficient controul over my brother[3] to prevent any further calumny against the Duke. I have urged everything I can say on the subject, & having asked your assistance formerly on my father's behalf, I am bound to assure you that I have not been wanting in offering remonstrances against a repetition of abuse against his R. Highness. (18135)

3073   THE DUKE OF GRAFTON[4] TO THE PRINCE REGENT

Brook St., 13 June 1811

In obedience to your Royal Highness's commands I communicated to Genl. Fitzroy the grounds upon which your R.H. was pleas'd to recommend that he shd. resign the office which he has long had the honour to

1. The eldest son of John Walter (1739–1812), the founder of *The Times*. In 1795 he had succeeded his father in the conduct of the newspaper, and retired from the management in 1802. He then secured a place in the Audit Office worth £600 a year (the newspaper was then vigorously supporting the Addington Ministry).

2. See Vol. ii, p. 68.

3. John Walter (1776–1847), editor and chief proprietor of *The Times*.

4. Lord Euston had succeeded his father as 4th Duke on 14 March 1811.

hold of Equerry to his Majesty; and I shd. not do justice to the correct view which the General has taken of the peculiarity of his situation, or to his sense of your R.H. condescension, if I did not distinctly inform your R.H. that, when the General learns from such authority what has been H. Majesty's pleasure, distinctly express'd in moments when it has pleas'd God to allow him the exercise of his wonted reason and judgment, he does not hesitate to bow to it (whatever may be his own feelings) and to request of your R.H. to dispose of him as your R.H. may think most conformable to his Majesty's satisfaction. His character, I am persuaded, is safe in your R.H. hands, and will be guarded from the misrepresentation which the resignation suggested, whenever made public, may otherwise naturally occasion.

Without entering at all into the circumstances of Genl. Fitzroy's case, I may be permitted to say that there has been nothing in the General's conduct upon the present occasion which has not been mark'd by a strong feeling of attachment and a grateful sense of duty to his Majesty. It would therefore be peculiarly distressing to Genl. Fitzroy and to his family to have the motives of his ready compliance with any suggestion of your R.H., in any degree misunderstood.

For myself I beg leave to add that (relying on your R.H. justice and kindness) it is most satisfactory to me to be the channel of conveying to your R.H. General Fitzroy's perfect compliance with your Royal Highness's suggestions;[1] and I feel it an honour to have been employ'd by your R.H. in the execution of your commands, or in giving effect to any idea which might seem to your Royal Highness likely to give satisfaction to his Majesty's mind.[2] (18137–8)

3074 SPENCER PERCEVAL TO THE PRINCE REGENT

Downing St., Wednesday morng., 19 June 1811

Mr Perceval presents his humble duty to your Royal Highness and has the honor of inclosing for your Royal Highness's perusal a copy[3] of the

1. General Fitzroy's father, the 1st Baron Southampton, was the younger brother of the 3rd Duke.

2. The letter affords additional proof that the King knew something (after her death) about Fitzroy's attachment to Princess Amelia. See No. 2855.

3. Folio 18148 (*Parliamentary Debates*, xx. 705). A Motion to 'restrain and finally to abolish that cruel, unnecessary and ignominious mode of punishment'. The House rose between 3 a.m. and 4 a.m. The 19th was the day of the Fête at Carlton House: there is a long account in Colchester, *Diary and Correspondence*, ii. 336–9. See also Romilly's *Memoirs*, ii. 403. On the 20th, incidentally, the Prince Regent saw Mrs. Fitzherbert for the last time, before their final separation, at an assembly at Devonshire House (Wilkins, *Mrs. Fitzherbert and George IV*, ii. 124).

Motion of Sir Frances Burdet for an Address to your Royal Highness relative to the punishment of *flogging* in the Army. It was supported by Mr Brougham, Mr Whitbread & Mr William Smith and Mr Hutchinson —and opposed by Mr Manners Sutton, Lord Palmerston, Mr Yorke, Mr Perceval, Sir Henry Montgomery and Mr Adams.[1]

The House divided, Ayes 10, Noes 94. (18147)

3075 VISCOUNT PALMERSTON TO GENERAL T. H. TURNER

War Office, 21 June 1811

Lord Palmerston presents his compliments to General Turner, and will be much obliged by his returning the court martial warrant sent to Carlton House yesterday as soon as it shall have received the Prince Regent's signature; tomorrow being the day appointed for the sitting of the Court. (18153)

3076 CHARLES YORKE TO THE PRINCE REGENT

Admiralty, Friday, 21 June 1811

Mr Yorke most humbly requests your Royal Highness's most gracious permission to be absent from the Council Board *tomorrow*, having made an engagement in the country before he was aware of the Council being to be summoned for Saturday; & understanding that no business of importance is likely to be brought forward at it. (18154)

3077 THE EARL OF MOIRA TO COLONEL MCMAHON

Donington, 23 June [1811]

Let me beg you to have the kindness to send for McCarthy,[2] & learn from him the time of payment of his two notes; also, whether they are made payable at any particular place. I find that I must have left the memorandum of them in town, for I have been toiling in the arrangement of the papers I brought with me and it is not among them. Everything looks beautiful here. Would that you too were enjoying the country! I

1. Charles Adams (*c.* 1753–1821), M.P. for Weymouth and Melcombe Regis, 1801–12. He belonged to the Addington party, and sometimes supported, sometimes opposed, the Perceval Ministry.

2. See Nos. 2707, 2933.

look at myself with astonishment for having anything to do with politics, but I believe it is the lot of man to be always employed in that which is least consonant to his inclination. (18155)

3078 SPENCER PERCEVAL TO THE PRINCE REGENT
Downg. St., 24 June 1811
Mr Perceval presents his humble duty to your Royal Highness and begs to acquaint your Royal Highness that Mr. Pole, who will this day or to-morrow have his writ moved on account of his accepting the office of Chancellor of the Exchequer of Ireland, will be very anxious to leave town for Ireland as soon as he possibly can—and if your Royal Highness should be graciously pleased to honor him with an Audience before he leaves England he would he glad that some hour this morning or to-morrow should be appointed for that purpose.[1] (18157)

3079 WILLIAM RICHARD HAMILTON TO MAJOR–GENERAL T. H. TURNER
Foreign Office, 24 June 1811
I am sorry to trouble you upon the subject of a blue box (one of those marked '*H.R.H. the Prince Regent*') which was sent to Carlton House last Friday night, & which Lord Wellesley, from what he had understood fm. Col. McMahon thought the Prince Regent had seen & had returned to this Office. It has not however yet made its appearance. Lord Wy. would be much obliged if you could send it me, should it be upon one of your tables—as even if H.R.H. should not have seen its contents Ld. Wy. would wish to have it back in order that some other papers upon the same subject should be added to it. (18158)

3080 THE QUEEN TO THE PRINCE REGENT
Windsor, 25 June 1811
Our dear visitor left us yesterday with a very heavy heart & without any compliment we saw her depart with sincere regret on our side, & I return you many thanks for having allowed her to pass some time with us.[2] You

1. Wellesley-Pole was re-elected for the Queen's County on 12 July.

2. Princess Charlotte returned to Warwick House.

have indeed in this child every hope of comfort & delight to come. She is blessed with an uncommon share of good sense; she has talents & facility to learn anything, is easily led to follow good advice when treated with gentleness, desirous to oblige when an opportunity offers, & capable of very strong attachment. She is very sensible of any the smallest attention shewn to her, & also, which is very natural, seems to feel very strongly any apparent neglect. She is already well informed of the history of her own country in particular, & indeed not less so of that of other country's, & seems, notwithstand[ing] her great liveliness & spirit, very desirous of improving herself. She is blessed with a very retentive memory, which is of great assistance to her, & her pursuits when not at her lessons are of that kind to convey information of all kinds necessary to know in her situation.

There are some subjects upon which prudence would not allow us to converse with her, but I am sure that her affection for you is such that by the smallest kindness on your side you may secure her love & attachment for ever. From the bottom of my heart do I wish that she should connect with her filial duty a sincere friendship for you which may be gained by seing a little more of her, & by making her look upon you as the source of every amusement & pleasure granted to her.

In another quarter[1] every possible pains are taken to make her visits the most agreable & every amusement thought of to gain her affection. *In this we cannot blame any attempt*—& I only wish to represent to you that you have the power in your hands to do at least the same, if not to outshine that quarter, & that you have too good an understanding as not to see & to feel the benefit which must arise from attempting to gain not only the love, but even the friendship of so amiable a little being. When I plead my attachment to you I am sure no excuse is necessary for having spoke so openly upon this subject.

As to her manners I will not deny that they are a little brusque, but more society will correct that, which if you please we will talk over when we meet, & now I will release you & only subscribe myself [etc.]. (36571–2)

3081 SPENCER PERCEVAL TO [?] COLONEL MCMAHON, AND AN ENCLOSURE

Downing St., Friday morning [28 June 1811]

As the little incident out of which the enclosed letter to his Royal Highness has arisen has occasioned a good deal of disturbance to Lord Sidmouth in his present affliction—I wish you would put it early under his

1. The Princess of Wales.

R. H's notice, as I am sure his good nature will be anxious to relieve Lord Sidmouth from the anxiety which a state of doubt as to what is to happen to Lady Sidmouth's remains keeps him in.[1] I feel this so strongly that even if his R. Highness should be set off to London this morning before you receive this letter, unless you feel strong objection to it, I could wish you to send my messenger with the box to his Royal Highness at Windsor, that I may be able to give Lord Sidmouth the earliest notice of his R. Highness's permission. (18164)

[Enclosure] SPENCER PERCEVAL TO THE PRINCE REGENT

Downg. St., 28 June 1811

Mr Perceval presents his humble duty to your Royal Highness, and at the request of Lord Sidmouth has the honor of acquainting your Royal Highness that the remains of Viscountess Sidmouth having been removed from London to the White Lodge in Richmond Park[2] previous to their being interred at Mortlake, the Countess D. of Mansfield,[3] as Ranger of the Park, has expressed a doubt whether she should be justified in permitting the funeral & carriages of a very few relations and friends with which it would be accompanied to pass thro' the Park towards the place of interment. It is therefore become necessary to solicit your Royal Highness's permission to that effect in order to remove any difficulty from her Ladyship's mind. Mr Perceval has accordingly undertaken to lay Lord Sidmouth's request with his humble duty before your Royal Highness on this subject. Mr Perceval ventures humbly to submit to your Royal Highness that no objection occurs to him against complying with Lord Sidmouth's wishes, and he is fully persuaded that your Royal Highness's benevolent & humane disposition would incline your Royal Highness to accede to a request so much connected with the feelings of Lord Sidmouth under his present affliction. (18165)

1. Lady Sidmouth (1760–1811) died on 23 June. She was the daughter of Leonard Hammond of Cheam, Surrey, and married Addington on 19 September 1781.

2. Since Addington had had no home nearer London than Woodley, near Reading, the King had assigned to him the occupation of the White Lodge (earlier known as Stone Lodge, built for George II by Lord Burlington) with a garden of five acres, in 1801 (Pellew's *Sidmouth*, i. 408).

3. Louisa, Countess of Mansfield (1758–1843), widow of David, Earl of Mansfield (1727–96). On 19 October 1797 she married her cousin, Robert Fulke Greville (1751–1824), 3rd son of Francis, Earl of Warwick.

3082　THE PRINCE REGENT TO THE DUKE OF YORK

Carlton House, Saturday night, 29 June 1811

I have at this moment only on my return home found your note of recommendation, in consequence of the death of Gl. Scott,[1] & I accord most entirely with you in the intended promotions which you have proposed. (44239–40)

3083　SIR ALEXANDER JOHNSTON[2] TO COLONEL MCMAHON

Madeira, 29 June 1811

I take the present opportunity, which is the very first that has offered since we left England, of saying how much I regretted that I had not the honor of seeing his Royal Highness before my departure, and how much obliged to you I feel for the positive assurances which you gave me that his Royal Highness would confer upon me the dignity of Baronet the first time a creation of Baronets should take place.

The high office which I hold in Ceylon will make that dignity particularly desirable to me & I trust that from what you said the day I took my leave of you that I shall not be long in Ceylon without receiving through your kindness so distinguished an honor from his Royal Highness. The great protection and favor which I have been known to receive from his Royal Highness will I trust fully warrant my hopes on the occasion, & I shall rest perfectly satisfied after what you were so obliging as to tell me that there is not the smallest chance of my being disappointed.

I shall take the liberty of enclosing this letter to my mother & request her to wait upon you with it in order that she may have an opportunity of learning from you whether any thing is likely to be done soon upon the subject & of letting me know. (18167–8)

3084　SIR JOHN MACPHERSON TO COLONEL MCMAHON

Brompton Grove, 29 June 1811

The essay in the Pilot[3] last night was the best that could be written. You have rendered your Prince the best of services. Persevere in that line. It will disarm the worst hostility, & prepare the way for the greatest good.

1. George Scott, Major-General, 1781; Lieutenant-General, 1793; General, 1798.

2. Chief Justice of Ceylon, 1805. Knighted, 1 November 1809. He was never made a Baronet. (1775–1849.)

3. This newspaper had been started in 1807, and the Addington party had thought of securing it for propaganda purposes.

I am confident, from all I saw abroad & have calmly witnessed at home, that our Prince is destined not only to carry his own country safe through the existing storm, but to aid Europe & the world to a restoration of order. He is formed for that noble scene! Yes, the reciprocal progressive distresses of all nations are preparing the way to that great end. India is secure! The system of the actual Chancellor of the Exchequer is favourable to public credit! The command of our armies is fortunately arranged! The support of the rights of nations, espoused in the Peninsula, has drawn the war to its new object. The Sovereigns of Austria, Saxony, Berlin & the North know the Prince's real talents and good dispositions, and that he understood & befriended the wise system of Leopold in 1791. They see in the fortunate union of our Royal family the best basis for the realization of that system; & were our Sovereign's health to return he would, for his own & his country's sake continue the power in the Prince Regent's hands as he had formerly proposed and as Lord Sidmouth remembers well: his Lordship and I had a full confidential discussion on that subject lately—having met at the Duchess of Gordon's—we had but one opinion.

How unfortunate, how awful would the reverse of so grand, so noble a prospect prove if an accident was to happen?—if the enemy in counterplot revenge was to revive the forces of Jacobinism in this country— forces which he formerly aided in extinguishing, and chiefly from his confidence in the honourable system of the Prince. I need say no more to you on this delicate subject. But it is impossible for the true friends of the Prince Regent and of their country to be too active in preventing any impressions to get to France that the Prince's attention to the unfortunate Bourbons goes beyond generous humanity, and that the assassination encouragements of our Press are not *excrated* by his Royal Highness & his particular friends. Vive vale. Keep this note. I know you will do the needful. Vive! Vale! encore. (18172)

3085   THE EARL OF CHARLEMONT[1] TO COLONEL MCMAHON, AND THE REPLY

Brookes, Saturday [29 June 1811]

Upon looking over Ld. Leitrim's[2] letter, written entirely in confidence to me & the production of haste, I do not think I can venture to lay it

1. Francis William, 2nd Earl of Charlemont [I.] (1775–1863) succeeded his father in 1799. M.P. for Co. Armagh, 1797–9; Irish Representative Peer, 1806–63. K.P., 1831; created Baron Charlemont [U.K.], 1837.

2. Nathaniel, 2nd Earl of Leitrim (1768–1854). Styled Viscount Clements from 6 October 1795 when his father was made an Earl, until his father's death, 27 July 1804. Whig M.P. for Carrick, 1790–7, and for Co. Leitrim, 1797–1800 [I.] and 1801–4 [U.K.] Created Baron

before his Royal Highness or dare to ask him to take the trouble of perusing it. But I request you will be so good as to state to his Royal Highness that the Government in Ireland persist in denying that the Prince Regent has any wishes inimical to Ld Gosford[1] *their candidate*, & that *many* have already returned a favorable answer to the Duke of Richmond under this impression. If the Prince could or would consent to your, or some person immediately about Carleton House, writing to each of those Peers who are known to be attached personally to his Royal Highness or *open* to his influence, whether they have promised *Gosford* or *not*, I have no doubt many may still be induced to, at all events, sink their vote, if not to vote for Ld Leitrim. The Duke of Richmond has been, is, & will still remain *actively* occupied in canvassing with all the influence of Government, & to be defeated he must be met with corresponding activity. I would also hint to you that those here who promised to qualify themselves to vote, are very slow indeed in performing their promises; that as yet *Ld Keith alone* has established his right, & that the probable quickly approaching Prorogation of Parliament will render it impossible for others to do it.

Excuse this trouble & believe me [etc.].

I have a *particular* reason for wishing Ld Carleton[2] to be immediately & from *authority* applied to, as I GUESS he may be induced to vote with us altho' under promise to Gosford. But the application must be from somebody authorized by his Royal Highness & *known* to be so. (18169)

COLONEL MCMAHON'S REPLY [copy]

Carlton House, 30 June 1811

I have had the honor to lay your Lordship's letter, with the representations of Lord Leitrim, before the Prince Regent, and am commanded

Clements [U.K.], 20 June 1831. K.P., 1834. The Prince Regent, after deciding to keep his father's Ministers in office, 'kept up for some time his usual habits of private intercourse with members of the Opposition. He dined at Lord Grey's upon his own invitation. He there authorised Lord Hutchinson to insinuate his good wishes, if not actually to use his name, in canvassing the Irish Peerage in favour of Lord Leitrim, the Whig candidate for a representative seat in the House of Lords' (Holland, *Further Memoirs*, p. 94).

1. Archibald, 2nd Earl of Gosford (1776–1849). Styled Lord Acheson from 1 February 1806 (the date of his father's Earldom) to his father's death, 14 January 1807. M.P. for Co. Armagh, 1797–1807. Irish Representative Peer, 1811–49. Captain of the Yeomen of the Guard, July–November 1834, and April–June 1835. Created Baron Worlingham [U.K.], 13 June 1835. Governor of Canada, 1835-8.

2. Hugh, Viscount Carleton [I.] (1739–1826) had sat in the Irish House of Commons from 1772 to 1787. Solicitor-General [I.], 1779–87; Lord Chief Justice of the Common Pleas [I.], 1787–1800. Created Baron Carleton [I.], 17 September 1789, and Viscount, 21 November 1797. Representative Peer, 1801–26.

by his Royal Highness to assure you that he never promised any support whatever to Lord Gosford in his object of attaining the vacant seat in the Representative Peerage of Ireland, nor was his Royal Highness ever even applied to by Lord Gosford for that purpose; but on the contrary, that Lord Leitrim has a very long time since had his Royal Highness's good wishes to succeed to that situation.[1] (18170)

3086   THE PRINCE REGENT TO THE DUKE OF GRAFTON

Carlton House, 30 June 1811

It is with great satisfaction that I express my thanks to your Grace for all the pains you have taken in this (to me) most painful affair, & that acquiescing in the general wish of of [*sic*] my family as well as in what you have intimated to me, I do now receive Lt.-General Fitzroy's resignation of his situation as Equerry in the King's family in the name & behalf of his Majesty.[2] It only remains for me to assure your Grace of my high esteem, & great personal regard with which I am [etc.]. (18177)

1. Ministerial views on the candidatures for the Irish Representative Peerage are given in the Lord Lieutenant's letter of 29 April to the Home Secretary, Ryder: 'Lord Northland cannot live, it will therefore be better to consider to whom the next promise should be given. Besides the two candidates I have mentioned [i.e. Lords Gosford and Mayo] there are a great many. Lord Liverpool was inclined towards Lord Clonmel, but I own I do not think that would be right. He sold a house he had in this country and is trying to sell his house in Dublin. In short, he does not mean to be a resident in Ireland and I do not think we ought to give any honor from Ireland to any but those who usually reside. Lord Thomond is the only Marquis who has not a seat in the Lords. He is anxious to be an English Peer and would not take anything that would interfere with his claim, but if Mr. Percival has decided not to recommend him for a Peerage perhaps he would compromise for a Representative Peerage. His relation Sir Edwd. O'Brien voted against us on the Regency but we must recollect that he was with the Talents when we came into office and that Ld. Thomond brought him over on most questions' (Richmond MSS.).

Ryder replied on 3 May: 'I am afraid that Lord Clonmell has made himself too much an Englishman to be able to bring forward the claims which his fortune and character and uniform support of the Government would otherwise have given him.

Lord Dufferin (if I am not mistaken) mentioned his wishes once to me last year: but it was, I believe, when he was pressing for a dignity in the Church for one brother and a seat at one of the Boards for another; and I told him so plainly that I thought those *two* requests, cotemporaneous as they were, so unreasonable and so impossible to be both gratified consistently with the just expectations of other friends, that I never heard more of the third. He wrote to me some time ago, professing his strong wish to give us support and at the same time his anxiety to remain in Ireland. I have answered him yesterday by saying that however desirable it always was to have a numerous attendance I saw no appearances which warranted me at present to urge him to take so long a journey' (ibid.).

2. See No. 3073.

35

Downg. St., 3 July 1811

Mr Perceval presents his humble duty to your Royal Highness and requests to acquaint your Royal Highness that he apprehends it will be
necessary for Parliament to continue sitting some time longer than
Tuesday next owing to what passed in the House of Lords last night.

Lord King[1] had given notice about a week ago to his tenants that he
would not receive his rent in Banknotes at par, but must either have gold
or more Banknotes to make up what he considers as the difference between the value of the Bank paper and the gold. His tenants are much
alarmed at this proceeding, feeling it to be impossible to procure the
gold. Lord Stanhope on Friday last brought a Bill into the House of
Lords with a view to prevent the mischievous effect, as he conceived it,
of such a proceeding as Lord King's. Lord Liverpool met it by saying
that if he thought it likely the example of Lord King should be followed
it would be very necessary to apply some legislative remedy, but that he
did not think a solitary instance of one individual's so acting created any
such necessity, and he did not think it at all likely that his example
would be followed, or that any number of persons would be found to
countenance it.[2] The Bill was ordered to be read a second time yesterday,
and Lord Liverpool gave notice that, if nothing should happen to alter
his view of the subject, he would move to put the Bill off for six weeks,
that is, to get rid of it altogether.

Yesterday Lord Stanhope, on bringing forward his Motion, mentioned
some few other cases perhaps not sufficiently numerous, to have made it
necessary to have altered the line of conduct intended to have been
pursued: but Lord Grenville, Lord Lauderdale, & Ld. Holland by
their speeches, Lord Grey, Lord Lansdown and others by their presence
& their votes supported Lord King; those who spoke arguing that he had
done nothing but what was perfectly right, and without indeed saying
that they would do the same thing, gave every countenance to the principles on which he was acting, so as unquestionably very much to encourage Lord King to persevere, and others to follow his example.
Under these circumstances it was thought impossible to suffer Parliament to separate without endeavouring to provide some remedy to stop
so serious a mischief, and to protect all the tenantry & bankers of the
country from being liable to be distrained upon, & many of the tenants

1. Peter, 7th Lord King (1775–1833), who knew something about the currency question.

2. The Government, that is, had at first decided to do nothing about it. Perceval had written
to George Rose on 23 June: 'After a great deal of consideration it was determined at last to do
nothing upon Lord King's letter. The hope is very strongly entertained that his Lordship's
example will not be followed, and that no evil will arise from it so great as might result from
the introduction of any measure at present which could be applied to meet it' (National
Library of Scotland, George Rose MSS., 3796).

from being turned out of their farms, for non payment of rent if their landlords under the example of Lord King and the arguments of Lord Grenville were disposed to do so. Lord Liverpool therefore voted for the Second Reading of Lord Stanhope's Bill. The House divided 36 to 12 in favor of it. The Bill cannot come down to the House of Commons before Monday or Tuesday next; and consequently, if it be to pass that House, which Mr Perceval trusts it will, it will occupy that House at least to the end of that week if not some time into the succeeding one.[1] (18184–6)

3088   PRINCESS MARY TO THE PRINCE REGENT

3 July [1811]

I am happy to say the King is quiet; Sophy I hope is not worse. As to myself, I have contrived to get a cold which rather affects my chest, therefore the Queen thinks it better for me not to run the risk of attending her up to town this time for fear of increasing it, as you know this time of year if an *oppression in my* chest *comes on* it ends in a serious long confinement.[2] (Add. Georgian 12/176)

3089   THE DUKE OF YORK TO THE PRINCE REGENT

Horse Guards, 3 July 1811

Secret. Not knowing whether Lord Liverpool may have found you at Carleton House I think it right to acquaint you that in obedience to your orders I have made the following arrangements, the orders for which will go off by tonight's mail.

3 Squadrons of the 4 and 7 Dragoon Guards and of the 3d Dragoons, compleated to 80 rank & file pr. troop to embark for Spain under the command of Major-General Le Marchant[3] as soon as the transports can be got ready for them, as likewise an additional squadron of the 9th Light Dragoons, and a swift sailing cutter is to be dispatched by the

1. *Parliamentary Debates*, xx. 784–832. On 18 July Ryder, writing to the Duke of Richmond referred to Lord Stanhope's Bill as 'our Bill' (Richmond MSS.).

2. The following note from the Princess to the Prince Regent is undated: 'Are we to desire our ladys to come to Carlton House this evening or *not*? Answer yes or no will do by return of the servant.' (Add. Georgian 12/177)

3. John Gaspard Le Marchant (1766–1812). Ensign, 1783; Major, 1795; Lieutenant-Colonel, 1797; Colonel, 1805; Major-General, 1811. Mortally wounded at Salamanca.

Admiralty to Lisbon with orders to Lord Wellington to land the two squadrons of the 9th which sailed about a week ago under Lieutenant-Colonel Chabot.[1]

I am happy to inform you that the Brigade of infantry which was intended to reinforce Lord Wellington from Jersey and Guernsey proceeded directly from these Islands to Lisbon together with a large detachment of recruits for the different regiments in Portugal and are I trust arrived nearly by this time, whereby he will receive a reinforcement of considerably above four thousand men. (44241)

3090 CHARLES MANNERS-SUTTON TO MAJOR-GENERAL T. H. TURNER

Downing Street, Thursday morn., 4 July 1811

I shall be greatly obliged to you to produce for me an Audience of H.R.H. the Prince Regent on Saturday morning. My principal object in soliciting an Audience on that day is that I must request permission to go out of town on Monday next for some days—and the J. A. General[2] ought not to stir out of town without H.R.H.'s consent first obtained.

Do pray therefore if possible procure me this Audience for Saturday next, and I will undertake not to occupy five minutes of H.R.H.'s time. (18190)

3091 SPENCER PERCEVAL TO THE PRINCE REGENT

Downg. St., Tuesday night, 9 July 1811

Mr Perceval presents his humble duty to your Royal Highness and acquaints your Royal Highness that the House of Commons divided on the First Reading of Lord Stanhope's Bill 64 for it & 19 against it. Mr Perceval, Mr Baring,[3] Mr Manning,[4] Sir Meyrick Burrell[5] spoke for

1. William Chabot, Lieutenant-Colonel, 1807.

2. Manners-Sutton was Judge-Advocate-General.

3. Alexander Baring, Baron Ashburton (1774–1848), second son of Sir Francis Baring, 1st Bart. For eighteen years head of Baring Brothers, the merchant bankers. M.P. for Taunton, 1806–26; for Callington, 1826–31; for Thetford, 1831–2; for North Essex, 1832–5. Master of the Mint and President of the Board of Trade, 1834–5. Peerage, 10 April 1835.

4. William Manning (1763–1835), M.P. for Plympton Erle, 1794–6, for Lymington, 1796–1806, 1818–20, 1821–6; for Evesham, 1806–18; for Penryn, 1826–30. Banker and West India merchant, and a supporter of Administration.

5. Sir Charles Merrik Burrell (1774–1862), M.P. for Shoreham, 1806–62. Succeeded his father as 3rd Baronet, 20 January 1796. In 1810 the Whigs considered him a 'hopeful'.

the Bill—& Mr Bankes for the First Reading expressing his doubts whether he would support it in its future stages. Mr Abercombie,[1] Mr Tierney, Mr Whitbread, Sr Francis Burdett and Lord Folkston against it. There were also two other divisions nearly of the same numbers on Mr Tierney's Motion for a Call of the House[2] and for the appointment of a Committee to enquire into the state of the Bank[3]—both which Motions were negatived by nearly the same majority. The House then fixed the 2d Reading of the Bill for Monday next to which day the House adjourned.[4] (18199)

3092   VISCOUNT MELVILLE[5] TO THE PRINCE REGENT

Wimbledon, 10 July 1811

Lord Melville presents his humble duty to your Royal Highness & has the honor to submit to your Royal Highness some letters which have been received from the East Indies by the Barbadoes frigate. There are a great many other voluminous packets on the various details of the several Governments in India, but the letters which Lord Melville has selected contain the substance of the only intelligence of sufficient importance to justify him in obtruding them on your Royal Highness. As reference is made in these dispatches to instructions relative to the enemy's possessions in the East Indies which were sent from England last year, Lord Melville has taken the liberty of submitting those instructions also to your Royal Highness.

He has only further to solicit your Royal Highness's permission to convey to Lord Minto, in reply to his Lordship's letter of the 1st January, your Royal Highness's gracious approbation of the measures he had adopted, in anticipation of orders from hence, for the conquest of the islands of Mauritius & Bourbon.[6] (18201–2)

1. James Abercromby, 1st Baron Dunfermline (1776–1858), 3rd son of Sir Ralph Abercromby. Whig M.P. for Midhurst, 1807–12; for Calne, 1812–30; for Edinburgh, 1832–9. Judge Advocate-General in Canning's and Goderich's Ministries, 1827–8; Chief Baron of the Exchequer [S.], 1830–2; Master of the Mint, July–December 1834; Speaker of the House of Commons, 1835–9. Peerage, 7 June 1839.

2. 63 v 20.

3. 62 v 17.

4. *Parliamentary Debates*, xx. 883–907.

5. Robert Dundas had succeeded his father on 29 May 1811.

6. See Nos. 2863, 2870n. On 10 January 1812 the House of Commons voted its thanks to Lord Minto for these successes (*Parliamentary Debates*, xxi. 129).

See House, Limerick, 11 July 1811

The Primate[2] has sailed for England to pay his duty to the Prince Regent and to entreat the exercise of the Royal Prerogative in the appointment of a Coadjutor to the poor Archbishop of Dublin during his incapacity— an appointment which the interests of the Church, and the discipline of that long neglected Diocese loudly call for. The Archbishop's *insanity* seems to be confirmed, but may live many years.[3]

I wrote to Lord Moira of the Primate's intentions, thinking it essential that the Prince shou'd be apprized as well of the object as of the character of the Primate, which from his retired habits is but little known and very much misunderstood.

Lest Lord M. shou'd not be in town I feel it right to give you a few hints for the Prince's information, if you think them at all useful.

It has been the fashion for the Ministers in both countries to represent the Primate as a most unaccommodating, unmanageable person—which is a very great mistake. He certainly withdrew himself from all communication with the Castle because he disapproved their management of the Irish Church, and did not receive the common attention due to his station—but from my knowledge and the rather intimate acquaintance with which his Grace has honored me for ten years past I can assure you that the Prince will find him a very sensible, clear-headed man of business—with the very purest principles. He is thought to be a *high, proud* man, and probably he has shewn a little of it to the present people in power—but we saw nothing of it in the Duke of Bedford's Administration. Perhaps I ought also to mention that he did *not* go to Court last year when in England and also in Parliament—I believe he had some reason to look to *York* upon the last vacancy,[4] and thought himself not well treated by Ministry.

It is essential to the comfort of the Prince's Government, as it is to the interests of the Church, that a good understanding shou'd be preserved, and I am persuaded his Grace will return to Ireland highly gratified by his reception at Carleton House.

Convinced that my motive in giving you this trouble, renders any apology unnecessary, believe me [etc.].[5] (18203-4)

1. Charles Mongan Warburton. See No. 1077.

2. Dr. William Stuart.

3. Euseby Cleaver (1746–1819), Chaplain to the Lord Lieutenant of Ireland, 1787; Bishop of Cork, March, 1789; of Ferns, June 1789; Archbishop of Dublin, 1809. The Archbishop of Cashel was appointed coadjutor on 27 Aug. 1811.

4. Edward Venables Vernon [Harcourt] became Archbishop of York on 19 January 1808, Dr. Markham having died on 3 November 1807.

5. The Bishop of Limerick had written to ?Lord Moira from Limerick on 20 June 1811: 'I am delighted by a letter from Dublin stating (from the authority of the Chancellor) that the

Regent has offer'd the Scotch seal to your Lordship. The same account adds that you have some scruples of delicacy, not being a native of Scotland! But, my good Lord, be your feelings what they may, the world will feel perfectly satisfied that you are *Scotch* enough by blood & connection to qualify your Lordship for that honorable office—certain it is, that no Scotch Nobleman wou'd think of refusing a high & lucrative office in Ireland—and I hope to see you very soon gazetted.

'By the way, in case of a *demise*, & that our worthy friend of C. Forbes shou'd return to his old office, it wd. be very provoking to see the present deputy (a rich attorney) run away with all the fees arising from the renewal of commissions, which I understand must be the case if the office remains unchanged at the period of demise.

'The better orders of the Catholics in this part of the country are much pleased with your late meeting, and consider the conspicuous part which your Lordship took, as a proof of the Regent's friendly disposition. If the Catholic gentlemen of rank & property will but seize the opportunity, I think they might now rescue the cause from the hands of those low, speculating democrats whose views & conduct have justly called forth the reprobation of every good & loyal subject, and with whom no King or Minister can ever enter into any serious negociation upon the subject: and untill their affairs are committed to better hands, the Regent's Ministers may very fairly, and perhaps wisely, decline entering into the business. In this opinion I am fortified by the respectable Catholics amongst whom I am placed, and who, perhaps with a hope of its being communicated to the Prince, have of late frequently called upon me and expressed themselves extremely solicitous for the royal support of the higher classes of their community, against the dangerous encroachments of low & mischievous speculators.

'I will not apologize for troubling your Lordship with these observations, because I feel it a duty to communicate them; and the same principle impels me to make known a circumstance in which the interests of the Church are concerned (especially in the Diocese of Dublin)— and upon which, I think it probable the Prince Regent must soon receive some application.

'The mental incapacity of the Archbp. of Dublin is now unhappily confirmed—but his bodily health in no sort of danger. That important Diocese is now without any spiritual governor whatever!—for nobody, except the person exercising the functions of the Crown, has the power of nominating a Coadjutor to his Grace—were it a Suffragan Bishop, the Archbp. of the Province wou'd take upon himself the whole duties & patronage of that Bishoprick during the incapacity of its incumbent—but in the case of an Archbishop the Crown only can appoint some Bishop by special commission to take upon him the charge of that Diocese during the incapacity of the Archbishop.

'As Guardian of Lunatics, the Chancellor has, very properly, appointed Commrs. to manage the property of the See, but his Lordship is certainly mistaken in claiming the disposal of the patronage, that not being the private or personal property of the Diocesan, but annexed to the spiritual exercise of his office, and which in the present case, reverts to the Crown. This is not only my view of the case, but that of the Primate & Archbp. of Cashel: a living is now vacant to which the Chancellor has named a gentleman but can proceed no farther, for the A. Bishop being incapable no man has a power to institute in his Diocese. To remedy this inconvenience & to provide for all the other duties of the Diocese, I shou'd think the Primate will entreat the Prince Regent to empower some Bishop by his Royal Commission, as head of the Church.

'The Prince might possibly wish to be apprized of this matter, and therefore I feel it my humble duty to trouble your Lordship with this communication, entreating your Lordship's goodness at the same time to represent my faithful attachment & entire devotion to his Royal Highness's person & government.' (18149–52)

Bury Street, St. James's, 12 July 1811

We have so repeatedly in the course of our long & sincere friendship & mutual confidence talked over many of the circumstances stated in the enclosed Memorial that I should think it scarcely necessary to possess you with documents to support my assertions, were it not that I know you wou'd like to refer to them in the event of either doubt or difficulty; besides, my dear McMahon, it cannot be new to you to hear the more than religious or enthusiastic love & admiration with which I have ever venerated, adored & sworn by our best of masters and England's first & best of Princes. It was an attachment of the heart purely—and frequently was it visited upon me as a sin—but I was proud of the persecution, for I loved the object that gave rise to it—and long, very long, was I made the victim of that vote, in which the Prince was most interested. This you will see by Lord Fitzwilliam's letter[1] to Mr Fox, which I send you.

You & I have been so long in the habit of affectionately thinking of our certainly invaluable and amiable friend the Peer, that we are always anxious that he should have the palm of every boon that attends us; but you well know that my office of Secretary at War in Ireland, in Lord Fitzwilliam's Administration,[2] and the honor of the Baronetage[3] which followed my civil services & retrenchments in the Government of Guernsey, had nothing upon earth to do with that dear good man, the first being Lord Fitzwilliam's own spontaneous act, and the latter the unsolicited & exclusive compliment of Mr Pitt for those services. When I went to Guernsey the inhabitants, if not disaffected, were discontented, and the militia in a state bordering upon mutiny. I restored harmony & good temper—and the militia *are* loyal & efficient. Again, the States of the Island had not for a century contributed anything to its defence; in two years I obtained from them £20,000. Again, the revenue of England lost annually nearly *half a million* by smuggling from Guernsey & Alderney. Pitt had used all the energies of Government for years to put it down, but in vain. I got it suppressed without any commotion. These were the services which Mr. Pitt (whom I had *always opposed*) thought fit to reward with a Baronetage. I should observe that on my return from Egypt, it was suggested to me that as there was no Red Red [*sic*] Ribbon vacant I should be created a Baronet if I wished it. This idea I scouted; the whole object of my life had been to endeavour to earn by *military exertion & enterprize* the only reward worth a soldier's seeking, but I had the mortification to find myself neglected & forgotten untill I *forced*

1. Folio 18217 (25 June 1806. Copy).

2. In 1795.

3. 5 October 1805.

myself upon the attention of Government by the services I had rendered to it in my capacity as a Civil Governor, as you will see by Lord Pelham's & Mr Yorke's letters.[1] By heaven, my dear McMahon, it has almost broke my heart to find that after 40 years hard service in all climates & covered with wounds I should see so many of my juniors in rank & service receive that reward, which I had so often risqued my life to win— and that, merely because I could not be induced to give up my dearest attachments.

My only hope is that our beloved master may have leisure to *read* my Memorial. I have made it as concise as 40 years active service would admit—Will you, my dear friend, find a favorable opportunity to lay it (with my duty & affection) before his Royal Highness? In his gracious & manly mind I have the fullest reliance.

I have heard that he is engaged for the present vacancy, but I trust I may be more fortunate in the next.

God bless you my dear friend. (18208–9)

[Enclosure] SIR JOHN DOYLE'S MEMORIAL

Most dutifully sheweth

That the Lieutenant-General has served his Majesty forty years and in all quarters of the globe.

He served in America the whole War, in Flanders untill disabled by wounds, and in Egypt untill the surrender of the enemy in that country.[2]

In addition to his share in the general actions in those different countries, he was employed as a partizan in several distinct enterprizes, in most of which he commanded, and with success; he was one of those who defended the Stone House in Germantown under Colonel Musgrave, by which Washington's army was kept in check, and the British saved from a surprize.

In the attack upon General Marrion's Corps in South Carolina, he commanded the advanced guard of cavalry with which he charged and defeated the State Regiment of Carolina Dragoons, the killed, wounded, and prisoners of which exceeded the numbers of his detachment.

He repulsed an attack of the French upon his post at Alost in Flanders, where he received two severe wounds, but did not quit the field.

In the deserts of Lybia he captured a valuable convoy of five hundred camels intended to relieve Alexandria, and with it took the escort of 600

1. Folios 18214–5 (31 August 1803). There is a printed copy (folios 18220–2) of *Testimonials of the Services of Lieut.-Gen. Sir John Doyle, Bart.*, and also of *Official Papers* relating to his Memorial (18223–5).

2. In 1801.

of the best troops of France, with their General, cannon, and colours, and this with a force of 250 dragoons only, and which enterprize was planned and executed by himself.

When the Lieutenant-General heard of the intended attack of the enemy's outposts near Alexandria, he was forty miles off in a fever, but got out of his sick bed, rode through the desert under an Egyptian sun in the dog days, and arrived in time to head his Brigade, and succeeded in carrying the objects of attack.

He was fortunate also in facilitating the fall of Cairo, by the intelligence and guides which he exclusively procured.

In consequence of these services Lord Hutchinson recommended Generals Craddock & Doyle 'as officers from whom he derived the *greatest assistance*, and *as highly deserving his Majesty's favours*.' General Craddock was in consequence appointed to the Chief Command at Madrass, and received the Order of the Bath in 1802.

But Lieutenant-General Doyle has remained ever since in the humble hope of obtained this mark of his gracious Sovereign's favor, which outweighs in his estimation all rank and emolument as being the fair object of a soldier's honest pride and ambition.[1]

In the course of these several services the Lieutenant-General has received seven wounds, has been publickly thanked by his Commanders upon nine different occasions, and once by name by both Houses of Parliament.[2] (18210–1)

3095   THE DUKE OF NORTHUMBERLAND TO COLONEL MCMAHON
Alnwick Castle, 13 July 1811
I was extremely sorry to find that your very long silence had been occasioned by illness. It affords me however some satisfaction to learn that you are now tolerably well again, & I hope your excursion to Cheltenham will quite restore your health.

I am obliged to you for the copy of the Quarterly Report of the Queen's Council, which I perceive has been laid before the House of Lords. His Majesty has now been ill for so long a time that I fear his recovery must not be soon expected.

I find a suspicion of a Dissolution of Parliament during the Prorogation is pretty general. I dare say there is not the smallest foundation for it. Certainly whenever such an event is probable it woud be most material to me coud I have any hint of it.

Lord Grey's dinner has had I find a very different effect in the minds

1. He was made a K.B. in 1813.

2. *Parliamentary History*, xxxvi. 191 (12 November 1801).

44

of most people from what according to you it ought to have. It has undoubtedly been taken in general for one of the strongest marks possible of H.R.H.'s predilection for his Lordship, & indeed I was myself taken in by it, altho' after the proceedings which I saw during the interval, before the Prince was declared Regent, I was not a little astonished.

If poor General Fox shoud die, there is no man whose appointment to his place, woud give me greater pleasure than your own; & I beg, by anticipation, to congratulate you most sincerely upon the prospect of getting it.

Mr Raine's silk gown,[1] & what I am extremely anxious about, Captain Haswell's promotion to the rank of Post Captain, will both come in good time. I can hardly conceive Mr Yorke woud be so inattentive to H.R.H.'s wishes as expressed to him as not to promote Captain Haswell soon; at least after all his own friends, whom he is now promoting, are provided for.

As for the state of affairs in the Peninsula, I can only say we had the ball at our foot, & have chosen by ignorance & mismanagement to kick it away. Had things been well conducted not an enemy ought now to be in Spain or Portugal, nor ought the latter to have been desolated & totally ruined as it at present is. I gave my opinion upon the subject freely to our friend Colonel Gordon from the very commencement of the business, & foretold all that woud happen if things were conducted as I perceived they were, but what I said was never attended to, & remembring the old proverb of 'proffered service st—ks' I have held my tongue, but what I foretold has never the less precisely come to pass, exactly as I said it woud happen.

I coud say much upon this subject & America, knowing the Peninsula & that country so well as I do, & being perfectly acquainted with the characters & disposition of their inhabitants, but I am quite tired of war & politicks, & determined never to sport my sentiments again, unsollicited.

Adieu, my dear Colonel—excuse my blots & erasures. (18232–3)

3096 GENERAL THOMAS GRAHAM TO MAJOR-GENERAL T. H. TURNER
Lisbon, 15 July 1811
I have with some difficulty succeeded in obtaining 2000 Seville oranges in the country—they are too ripe—but I trust a considerable number will arrive safe—especially as I have requested Capt. Douglas to have them examined & repack'd, throwing away all that are spoiling.

1. Jonathan Raine was re-elected for Newport (Cornwall) on 19 March 1816 after appointment as a K.C.

I beg you will assure his Royal Highness the Prince Regent that, should I remain in Portugal till the proper season, I shall take care to have more sent for her Majesty's use & that I am very sorry there has been such an unavoidable delay in the execution of his Royal Highness's commands. (18234–5)

3097   LETTERS FROM SPENCER PERCEVAL TO THE PRINCE REGENT
Downing Street, 3 a.m., Tuesday, 15 [16] July 1811
Mr Perceval presents his humble duty to your Royal Highness and takes leave to acquaint your R. Highness that the Second Reading of the Bank Note Bill was carried after a long debate by 133 to 35.[1] (18236)

Downg. St., 16 July 1811
Mr Perceval presents his humble duty to your Royal Highness and has the honor to inform your Royal Highness that Mr Leake, one of the Comptrollers of Army Accounts, has desired to be permitted to resign his employment. He is in the seventy-third year of his age, has been upwards of fifty years in the public service, and has discharged the laborious duties of his situation in the Audit Office & Comptroller of Accounts since the year 1785.

Mr Perceval humbly submits to your Royal Highness that the application is perfectly reasonable, & that Mr Leake deserves to have the largest allowance of superannuation which the length & nature of his services will authorize your Royal Highness to grant under the Acts which passed to regulate superannuation in the last Session of Parliament.[2]

Mr Perceval humbly ventures to recommend Mr Herries[3] to succeed him—Mr Herries has been Private Secretary to Mr Perceval ever since he has had the honor to serve his Majesty as Chancellor of his Exchequer. Mr Perceval can safely assure your Royal Highness that Mr Herries is

1. *Parliamentary Debates*, xx. 914–80. 'All the Prince's friends voted for the Bill,' wrote the Speaker (Colchester, ii. 342).

2. John Martin Leake was succeeded by Lieutenant-Colonel Drinkwater. See No. 3148.

3. John Charles Herries (1778–1855), M.P. for Harwich, 1823–41; for Stamford, 1847–53. Clerk in the Treasury, 1798; private secretary to Vansittart (Secretary of the Treasury), 1801; and to Perceval, 1807. Commissary-in-Chief, 1 October 1811–16; Auditor of the Civil List, 1816; Joint Secretary of the Treasury, 1823; Chancellor of the Exchequer, September 1827; Master of the Mint, February 1828–November 1830; President of the Board of Trade, February–November 1830; Secretary at War, 1834–5; President of the Board of Control, February–December 1852.

one of the best men of business Mr Perceval ever knew; is most intimately acquainted with the duties of the office of Comptroller of Army Accounts and all the other Departments connected with the Treasury, at which he has been a clerk for many years.

Mr Herries has recently gone over to Ireland for a short time to assist Mr Pole in his new situation of Chancellor of the Irish Exchequer, but as he never intended to stay in Ireland except for a few months at the end of the present year his present situation can form no objection to the appointment for which Mr Perceval recommends him, and which he would very much prefer.[1] (18237–8)

3098   PRINCESS ELIZABETH TO THE PRINCE REGENT
16 July 1811
The Queen desires me to say to you that you will understand from your own excellent heart that at this moment she cannot write to her brother, the Duke,[2] but she has given her commission to C. Munster.

We are all in the greatest anxiety as you may easily imagine; my mother is tolerable but in great affliction.[3] (Add. Georgian 11/199)

1. Whilst in Ireland Herries was nominated to succeed Leake, but he never actually took his seat on the Board, as he was soon appointed Commissary-in-Chief. See No. 3148.

Wellesley-Pole had been Irish Secretary since 18 October 1809 and Chancellor of the Exchequer [I.] since June 1811. See No. 3078. He had written to the Duke of Richmond on 17 June: 'In my letter of Saturday I mention'd to you the idea of making Mr. Herries a Lord of the Irish Treasury. Upon farther consideration we find that it would not suit him to take the office, and I have proposed an arrangement which I hope will answer every purpose without being liable to any objection. The office of Secretary to the Irish Chancellor of the Exchequer is in the gift of the Chancellor of the Exchequer, and has usually been given to a personal friend and made a sinecure. This place is worth £500 a year, and I propose giving it to Herries and bringing him to Ireland. He will give up his office of Private Secretary to Perceval, but may retain his other appointments in the Treasury—thus I shall have all the benefit of his assistance, and our Treasury may remain as it is. This plan will give me a full opportunity of settling the business of the Treasury in the manner that may be thought most desirable, and before the meeting of Parliament a general system may be digested. All that will be new at present will merely be my appointment as Chancellor of the Exchequer. If I am to vacate my seat I wish to do it before the Parliament is prorogued, that I may go to my election at once instead of allowing six months for my Papist enemies to work against me. I much fear that the copy of the Patent of the Chancellor of the Exchequer will not come in time, and I am endeavouring to get the Law Officers here to say whether a Patent can be so drawn (as I do not receive any emolument) that I may remain without vacating. I fear the result of the enquiry will be that I must vacate. I shall put it off 'till the last moment' (Richmond MSS.).

2. The Duke of Mecklenburg-Strelitz.

3. 'News that the King was very dangerously ill', wrote the Speaker that day (Colchester, ii. 342).

Princess Charlotte wrote to her friend Mercer Elphinstone that day from Warwick House:

47

3099   THE DUKE OF CUMBERLAND TO THE PRINCE REGENT

Windsor Castle, 7 p.m., 16 July 1811

Halford has this moment left me; he says things are pretty nearly in the same state as they have been for the last 24 hours. The K. has taken 4 jellies, some coco and tea; is totally lost as to mind, conversing with imaginary persons, as he is constantly addressing himself to *Eliza*.[1] His countenance is much flushed and pulse 84. Certainly there is no imediate danger but expects further excitement in the course of the night: 'tis a most melancholy prospect. The Queen certainly better than I expected. Halford is now gone for 24 hours & will call upon you tomorrow morning; he has taken care that one of the medical gentlemen will write this evg. & tomorrow morning. God bless you.[2] (47294)

3100   THE DUKE OF YORK TO THE PRINCE REGENT

Stable Yard, 17 July 1811

I am just returned from Windsor and am truely sorry not to be able to send you a more comfortable account of his Majesty.

He has been quieter the whole of this morning and for two or three minutes when the physicians went into him seemed to know Dr. Baillie and enquired after Dr. Reynolds, but this dawn of reason was soon gone and since then he has remained in nearly the same state as he has been in for the last two days. However, being quiet, all restraint has been removed, but he does not seem to be in the least sensible of it, which Dr. Willis does not like.

I had a long conversation both with Willis and Baillie, who both told me that they do not consider the danger is immediate at the present moment, but Baillie appears to me to have a less bad opinion of the case than Willis.

[*P.S.*] I forgot to add that his Majesty has been shaved, which he bore very patiently.[3] (44242)

'The King has been *cupped* & James powder given him, for he has a *great deal* of fever. I understand from cousin Sophy & from a letter from the Duke of Sussex yesterday that yesterday & *today are very* critical, that is to say that it comes to a sort of *crisis*. The question is whether the King will not be so much enfeebled by the fever as not to be able to bear its effects. Sr. H. Halford, I understand from a letter today, *does not leave* him. He only slept last night for 10 *minutes*, takes no sustenances [*sic*], & is so violent that correction has been necessary & he is confined; both yesterday & the day before, he kept his bed. In short I think him in much danger at present, & there is more to be feard than hoped for' (Bowood MSS.).

1. Lady Pembroke.

2. The King's death was generally expected at this time, and much canvassing for seats was going on throughout the country in the expectation of a general election.

3. Princess Charlotte wrote to her friend Mercer Elphinstone on the 20th: 'As to the accounts

48

3101   SPENCER PERCEVAL TO THE PRINCE REGENT

Downg. St., Thursday morng. 18 July [1811]

Mr Perceval presents his humble duty to your Royal Highness and acquaints your Royal Highness that the House of Commons divided upon the Motion for going into a Committee upon the Banknote Bill, when the numbers for going into the Committee were 74, and against it 11. The Committee went thro the Bill, & it is ordered to be reported tomorrow. The House rose about ¼ p. one this morning.[1] (18241)

3102   VISCOUNT FOLKESTONE TO THOMAS TYRWHITT

Craven Street, 18 July 1811

I have this day received by the post a Petition from one John Collier, an unfortunate man now lying in goal [*sic*] at Lancaster in consequence of the sentence of the Court of Kings Bench on him for a libel. This Petition is addressed to his Royal Highness the Prince Regent. It states the case of the petitioner & prays for his Royal Highness's clemency. And it is intrusted to me, in order that I may convey it to his Royal Highness's hands. Pray inform me in what manner I am to proceed.

Of course it will [be] a subject of much gratification to me if his Royal Highness would allow me to present the Petition to him in person—but I only wish for your instructions in order that I may proceed in the most regular manner & in that most conformable to his Royal Highness's wishes. (18243–4)

3103   VISCOUNT FOLKESTONE TO COLONEL MCMAHON

Craven Street, 20 July 1811

On my return from the House of Commons last night I was honored with your note in reply to a letter which I had addressed to Mr Tyrwhit.

of the King, things are in a very melancholy state, for tho' he is *not at present in immediate danger*, yet he may be shortly so. Till the accounts are such as will justify hopes of his recovery, the family do *not go out into publick*. He is *quite lost* & takes no notice of anything that goes on in his room & knows *no one*. He takes nourishment wh. he did not do before, but gets little or no sleep. Yesterday he passed the day in *much agitation*, dozed a little towards the evg. They gave him an *opeat* [*sic*] last night wh. has produced 4 hours sleep. This mg. I got the following account from Mary: "The opeat has had *no other effect* than making him sleep 4 hours. The head is in *no better a state*. Untill tomorrow nothing can be said; our ONLY hope is in this *opeat*"' (Bowood MSS.).

1. *Parliamentary Debates*, xx. 1013–17.

49

In consequence of the commands of his Royal Highness the Prince Regent, which you signify to me, I enclose herewith the Petition of John Collier—and most humbly beg to recommend his case to his Royal Highness's most gracious consideration. (18247)

3104   THE MARQUESS WELLESLEY TO THOMAS TYRWHITT
Apsley House, Saturday, 20 July 1811
Private & Secret. Although I am thoroughly sensible of the distress under which the Prince Regent's mind must now suffer, & of the indelicacy of intruding upon H.R.H. in the present state of his feelings, it is a duty of personal gratitude & honor for me to endeavour to approach him for a few moments before matters shall come to the last extremity at Windsor. The subject on which I am anxious to address H.R.H., although personal to myself, is deeply connected with the interests of the public service & with H.R.H.'s own view of the present posture of affairs, and if I omitted to make the statement to him before he began to act for himself I might be liable to the reproach of concealment in a case where I wish to satisfy H.R.H. of my entire confidence in his justice & generous temper.

What I have to mention is entirely for H.R.H.'s private information & judgment, nor shall I either communicate with any other person, or act in any manner on the subject matter of these circumstances, otherwise than by H.R.H.'s commands.

I shall be ready to attend the Prince Regent at any time that he may appoint; in the present crisis, I shall not move from town even for an hour. I would have written or waited on the Prince Regent at Carlton House this morning, but I was occupied unavoidably in preparing the Speech for the Lords Commissioners.[1]

1. The Speech of the Lords Commissioners at the close of the Parliamentary Session on the 24th, delivered by the Lord Chancellor (*Parliamentary Debates*, xx. 1118). Why Wellesley should be preparing the Speech is explained in the following letters. Perceval wrote to him on the 16th (the letter is wrongly dated Tuesday the 15th): 'Pray let me have the benefit of your emendatory criticism on this draft of the Commrs. Speech, before I send it in circulation. I should wish to have it back not *later* than tomorrow morning' (Perceval MSS.).

Wellesley replied, later in the day: 'Happening to be out of town until the hour of going to the House of Lords today, I have scarcely had time to read the draft of the Speech with due attention, & you require that it should be returned tomorrow morning.

As you wish for free observation upon it, you will not be offended when I tell you that I object to the whole plan of it, which in my opinion is totally inadequate to the occasion. The great feature of the present Session (with respect to the very existence of this Empire) is the effort which Parliament has made to support the war in the Peninsula; & the principles from which that effort proceeded are in my judgment essentially necessary to be stated in the opening

Pray answer this. I hear very bad accounts from Windsor; this state of things cannot continue many days. (18251–2)

3105   THE DUKE OF NORTHUMBERLAND TO COLONEL MCMAHON

Alnwick Castle, 20 July 1811

I feel infinitely obliged to you for your letter of the 16th, & the communication on a subject so highly interesting to everybody. You may rest most assured that whatever is entrusted to me never will proceed further, and H.R.H. may be satisfied that everything which he does me the honour to communicate confidentially to me will ever continue as great a secret, as far as I am concerned, as if no such communication had been made.

I begin to be impatient for accounts from Portugal. Surely we shall not hear of our army in the Lines of Torres Vedras again. Shoud this really be the case the history of the campaign may be comprised in these few words—much ground traversed backwards & forwards, in pursuits & retreats—some millions of money flung away—some thousands of lives uselessly expended—Portugal laid waste & ruined—two victories—mais pas un pied de gagné. But I cannot bring myself to believe that with the force of which the Allied Army now consists & in a country of such natural strength as Portugal, the present campaign can possibly end in this manner. At any rate, from what I know of that country, I am certain it ought not.

I trust you are now completely recovered from the illness of which you complained, & that Mrs MacMahon is in perfect health.

I must desire you to present my duty to H.R.H. & assure him of my most inviolable attachment. (18253)

of the Speech, quite distinctly from the success of our operations. I have many other objections to the draft both in point of substance & style, but as I really think that the general plan of the Speech is far below the magnitude of the occasion, I state this sentiment to you without delay; I am satisfied that on reconsideration of the draft you will approve very few words which are now on the paper' (ibid.).

Perceval replied (the draft is undated but it was obviously written on the 16th): 'I return you the draft of the Speech. The failure to put the Speaker in the Chair this day, which will render it impossible to prorogue Parliament before Tuesday next has, luckily, in this respect tho I lament it in every other, given us a longer time for the preparation of the Speech. Altho I send you back the draft, yet I conceive from the defects you find in it, it will be infinitely easier for you to compose an entire Speech than to attempt correcting my draft. I hope therefore that you will have the goodness to undertake this trouble. I would most readily undertake it myself if I were at all satisfied that I understand what you mean & hope to execute yr. idea, but I confess I do not know how to set about it. You will only remember that it must be circulated & settled in time to be sent to the Prince by Sunday at latest, as I conceive it must be read to him in Council on the Monday—& we must therefore have our Cabinet upon it on Saturday' (ibid.).

3106   SPENCER PERCEVAL TO THE PRINCE REGENT

Downg. St., 20 July 1811

Mr Perceval presents his humble duty to your Royal Highness and acquaints your Royal Highness that the Gold Coin & Bank Note Bill passed the House of Commons this morning on a division of 95 to 20.[1]
(18255)

3107   SPENCER PERCEVAL TO COLONEL MCMAHON

Downing Street, 22 July 1811

Mr Perceval presents his compliments to Colonel MacMahon and begs to inform him that he has learnt, since he had the pleasure of seeing Colonel McMahon this morning, that the Lord Chancellor will not be able to prepare the Commission for the Prorogation unless the Order-in-Council is made tomorrow instead of on Wednesday. Mr Perceval hopes that this alteration will not be attended with the smallest inconvenience to his Royal Highness, and Mr Perceval, if his Royal Highness will permit him, will wait upon his Royal Highness between one and half past two o'clock tomorrow. (18258)

3108   RICHARD RYDER TO THE PRINCE REGENT

Whitehall, 22 July 1811

Mr Ryder has the honor of humbly submitting to your Royal Highness the dispatch which he received yesterday from his Grace the Lord

---

1. *Parliamentary Debates*, xx. 1038–1106 (19 July). 'Nothing', wrote Tierney on the 20th, 'could equal the unwillingness of our friends to attend, some influenced by disgust at the conduct of Lord King, some really believing the Bill to be necessary, some afraid to face the unpopularity which our opposition to it had to encounter, and not a few perhaps deterred by the eagerness the Prince manifested in support of the Bill through every stage. Tyrwhitt was actually sent for from Cornwall, and last night Sheridan came down to make a speech in favour of Ministers. . . . The Prince is very nervous, as well he may be, at the prospect before him, and frequent in the course of the day in the applications to the liquor chest. I much doubt, however, whether all the alcohol, as they call it, in the world under whatever name administered will be able to brace his nerves up to the mark of facing the difficulties he will soon have to encounter' (Howick MSS.).

Lady Holland wrote to Lord Lansdowne on the 22nd with reference to this debate: 'Romilly made a very short but admirable speech. Perceval sent for the Attorney General to answer him, but he could not, and shrank in a disgraceful manner, though there was a pause in the House, expecting his reply. What do you think of the conflict between Sheridan and Tierney? The latter it is said had the best in the affray' (Bowood MSS.).

Lieutenant together with the three papers to which his Grace has referred. Mr Ryder has already taken the necessary steps to obtain the opinion of the Attorney & Solicitor General[1] upon the legal questions which arise out of the proceedings of the Aggregate Meeting; and as soon as he is in possession of it, which he hopes to be this evening or tomorrow morning, he will have the honor of waiting your Royal Highness's commands at Carlton House.[2] (18261)

3109   SPENCER PERCEVAL TO THE PRINCE REGENT

Downg. St., 24 July 1811

Mr. Perceval presents his humble duty to your Royal Highness and has the honor to enclose for your Royal Highness's perusal & consideration the passage which Mr. Perceval alluded to from the Reports of the Financial Commissioners, as furnishing difficulties in the way of executing your Royal Highness's wishes with regard to Colonel McMahon's appointment to the office of Paymaster of Widows Pensions. Mr. Perceval has only to add to that paper what passed upon the subject of the grants of sinecures towards the close of the present Session in the Ho. of Commons.[3] The conversation arose upon the subject of the late Lord Melville's office in Scotland.[4] Mr. Bankes expressed his hope that the wishes of the House of Commons with regard to sinecure offices, tho' not carried into effect by Act of Parliament as yet, would be recollected by the Government, and that no grant should be made during the recess which might prevent Parliament from regulating any of those offices in the next Session—to which Mr. Perceval replied that any apprehension

1. Sir Thomas Plumer (1753–1824), M.P. for Downton, 1807–13. Second Justice for the Counties of Anglesey, Carnarvon and Merioneth, 1805; Solicitor-General, April 1807; Attorney-General, June 1812; Vice-Chancellor of England (the first), 1813; Master of the Rolls, 1818–24.

2. The Crown lawyers ruled that the Irish Convention Act of 1793 made all sessions of a Catholic Committee illegal, but that the Act could not be extended to suppress meetings called to elect delegates. See Denis Gray's *Perceval*, p. 419, for these opinions dated the 24th and 25th (quoting Westbrook Hay MSS.). The Irish Government was instructed to disperse this convention of Catholic delegates with the minimum of force. The Regent's acquiescence in these repressive measures was taken to imply a step towards the abandonment of Whig principles and a movement in a Tory direction.

3. This was not reported in the *Parliamentary Debates*.

4. His £3,000 a year office of Lord Privy Seal [S.]. The Duke of Richmond wrote to Ryder on 23 June: 'I am very glad Lord Moira is not appointed to Lord Melville's place. He certainly would be improper for the situation as he is inveterately and violently hostile to us in politics. His appointment would also hurt the feelings of the Scotch. They would not be satisfied to be led by an Irishman. I fancy now that Lord Moira is not looked up to as he was for some time. His greatest admirers are the Prince and himself' (Richmond MSS.).

upon that point under present circumstances was quite unfounded and unnecessary; for since, during the Regency, no grant of such an office could be made but during his Majesty's pleasure it would be open to Parliament necessarily in the next Session to consider what should be done upon the subject, and such grant as could be made during the Regency could not impede them, and that it certainly would be right upon any such grant being made during the interval that the grantee should be apprized that the subject was under the consideration of Parliament, and that he must therefore accept it under the impression and with the knowledge that Parliament might not think necessary to continue it.

The above statement with the inclosure is humbly submitted to your Royal Highness in explanation of the difficulty which Mr. Perceval feels in carrying your Royal Highness's pleasure into execution on this occasion.

Mr. Perceval has felt it his duty always when questions have come before the House respecting the abolition of sinecures, to state without any reserve for his objections to such measures—but he feels it next to impossible to resist the abolition of some of them. Those which are paid by a precise vote of Parliament, as is the case *now* with the Paymaster of Widows Pensions, are the most difficult to maintain, and Mr. Perceval would have felt that he greatly neglected his duty to your Royal Highness if he had advised your Royal Highness to give directions for this grant in favor of Mr. Mc.Mahon, which would unquestionably become the subject of Parliamentary consideration in the next Session: and as Mr. Perceval should feel it particularly objectionable to have that considera- tion provoked by an appointmt. in favor of a person so connected with your Royal Highness as Colonel McMahon is known to be, without having distinctly brought these circumstances under the view of your Royal Highness (Alnwick MSS.).

3110 COLONEL MCMAHON TO THE DUKE OF NORTHUMBERLAND

Carlton House, 24 July 1811

Private. I have every grateful acknowledgement to offer for the honor of your Grace's most kind letter of the 20th instant. The state of his Majesty seems to have become such that little satisfactory information is to be derived by a continuation of the confidential bulletins which the physicians send to the Prince Regent, as they appear now to be of opinion his Majesty will 'creep' (their phrase) out this illness without bodily danger, but with no mental improvement.[1]

1. Princess Charlotte wrote to her friend Mercer on the 25th: 'The accounts for a few days

The Prince has commanded me to express to your Grace the very sincere happiness he always feels in your invariable & kind recollection of him, and desires me to make his affectionate remembrances to your Grace & the Duchess, and that your Grace may rely that whenever any material change may happen in either the state of the King or of the country, your Grace shall be the *first* person who shall know it from authority.

Your Grace has probably ere this read of the death of poor General Fox.[1] Lt.-General Maitland has succeeded him in the 10th Foot, & M.-General Leith[2] follows Maitland in the 2d West India Regiment. Lord Harcourt gets the Government of Portsmouth, & his Royal Highness gave his command to Mr. Percival for my appointment to the Paymastership of the Widows Pensions, but owing to some observations that were made by the Finance Committee formerly as to this place, he has stated some difficulty as to Parliament more than the vacating a seat, & I own I fear I may after all the Prince's goodness on the occasion be still thrown on my back, but the Prince kindly says 'You shall not, if it in any way can rest with me,' & this kindness will I trust console my disappointment should I be doom'd to meet one. Brownrigg's commission as Governor & Commr. in Chief at Ceylon, & Gordon to be Qur. Mastr. General in his room, were both sign'd yesterday by the Regent, but they are not to come into operation until the 1st of Octr. next.

There are dispatches from Ld. Wellington from 'Quinta de St. Ivas,[3] dated the 11th inst.' with no particular news nor any very cheering prospects (Alnwick MSS.).

3111   THE MARQUESS WELLESLEY TO THE PRINCE REGENT

Apsley House, 10.30 a.m., 25 July 1811
Secret. Lord Wellesley has the honor to acquaint your Royal Highness that by a secret & confidential letter from Sir James Saumarez which Mr Yorke has received this morning, it appears that a Russian Minister of high rank is on his way to England having been on board the Victory

were better, but nights very *indifferent*. . . . He was very irritable and would not put on his clothes when desired and *refused all* nourishment. However, towards the middle of the day he took a draught of milk and a plate of hasty pudding . . . the *delirium* ran high' (Bowood MSS.).

1. On 18 July.

2. Sir James Leith (1763–1816). Entered the army, 1780; major, 1793; Lieutenant-Colonel 1794; Colonel, 1801; Brigadier-General, 1804; Major-General, 1808; Lieutenant-General, 1813. K.B., 1813. Served in the Peninsular War. Commander of the forces in the West Indies and Governor of the Leeward Islands, 1814. G.C.B. 1815.

3. Quinta de St. Joao, in the *Wellington Dispatches*.

on the 15th instant, & having taken his passage on board the Auckland packet to Harwich. He left Petersburgh on the 24th of June, a few days after the arrival of the Portugese Minister who left London some time since. The Russian Prince stated himself to Sir J. Saumarez as the bearer of important communications to his Majesty's Ministers. Lord Wellesley will have the honor to attend at Carlton House this morning for the purpose of receiving your Royal Highness's commands on this very important occasion. No intelligence has yet reached him of the arrival of the Auckland, although it is probable that she must be arrived.

The Prince declined the offer of a ship of war from Sir J. Saumarez, probably with a view of concealing the object of his Mission.[1] (18269)

3112 COLONEL MCMAHON'S REMARKS ON PERCEVAL'S STATEMENT[2]

[?25 July 1811]

Mr. Perceval grounding his main objections on a paper he encloses containing an 'Extract from the 4to. edition of the Commissrs. of Public Accounts in 1783 (twenty eight years ago) together with an opinion tending to approve what is there recommended given by the Commissrs. of Military Enquiry in their 6th Report in 1808', proceeds to observe, 'In consequence of an expression fallen from Mr. Banks towards the close of last Session on the subject of the late Lord Melville's office in Scotland,' (fully as much an object of Parliamentary regulations at least as that of the P.M. to the Widows' Pensions), that for any grant of such office during the interval of Parliament, that it certainly would be right that the grantee should be apprized 'that the subject was under the consideration of Parliament, and that he must therefore accept it under the impression & with the knowledge that Parliament might not think necessary to continue it'.

To all this, so far, I subscribe and bow.

Mr. Perceval next proceeds to shew that altho' generally disposed to resist the abolition of sinecure offices, yet he feels it 'next to impossible' to resist the abolition of some of them, for instance 'those which are paid by a precise vote of Parliament', in which class he affixes that of the Paymaster to the Widows Pensions by marking 'as is the case now'.

What causes this additional force to be given to the word now I cannot presume to say, for all that I know from the best information is that the

1. Without first consulting the Cabinet Wellesley asked Perceval whether he thought that Saumarez should be authorised to sign preliminaries of peace with Russia (Perceval MSS. To Perceval, 9 August). See No. 3142n.

2. See No. 3115, the Prince having used McMahon's memorandum in writing to Perceval.

late General Fox, in his lifetime, was never paid a salary by the precise vote of Parliament, but was remunerated by a poundage of 1s. in the pound from the Widows Pensions.

Mr. Perceval then concludes his statement of the difficulties attending my appointment to this office by the combination of a sentiment which mankind in all ages have been induced to estimate very differently, namely, that 'of my being a person so connected with the Prince Regent as I am known to be' & making such description to operate as a peculiar exclusion to my succeeding to that employment, leaving thereby a very indefinite (at least) description of that connection, & obviously with-holding the true basis on which it exists, that of the noble & generous nature of H.R.Hs. wishing to increase his bounties to a servant who has faithfully and affectionately served & loved him for *now nearly* sixteen years.

I have but another remark to add, that in the last paragraph of the paper Mr. Perceval enclosed he has interlined in the remark on the Finance Committee wherein it is stated that the Committee has *not adverted* to this office by name, the following line '*Except it may be in their last Report which is not yet printed*' & which upon diligent enquiry I have made I find is not to be in this Report, and therefore I am fairly borne out in those two assertions, namely, that Parliament has not as yet recognised the abolition of this office, and that the deputy has always hitherto been warranted by his principal, and that a warrant to the deputy from the Prince Regent empowering him to assume the functions would to all intents & purposes be at once abolishing the principal. (18266–8 and 42505–6)

3113   THE DUKE OF YORK TO THE PRINCE REGENT
Stable Yard, 25 July 1811
I am this instant returned from Windsor and am truely grieved to inform you that everything continues in the same melancholy way. His Majesty was very irritable in the morning, refused to put on his cloaths when desired to get up and continued to reject all food till two o'clock, when he told Dr. Heberden that if he offered any to him he would take it. In consequence his Majesty tasted some jelly and drank a large draught of milk and then asked for some hasty pudding.

Dr. Willis, who I saw just before I got into my carriage, seems very much cut down and told me that if anything the King was a shade worse today. In short, appearances continue to be as bad as possible. (44243)

3114　THE MARQUESS WELLESLEY TO THE PRINCE REGENT

Apsley House, 7 p.m., 25 July 1811

Lord Wellesley has the honor to acquaint your Royal Highness that having been detained at a Cabinet Council this evening he was not able to see Count Münster. Mr Smith[1] however saw him & brings the following report.

There is a Prince Lubomirsky of a great Polish family, who is married to Czartorinsky's[2] [*sic*] sister. Czartorinsky is not now in office in Russia but he sees the Emperor and is well disposed to England. Lord Liverpool does not recollect Prince Lubomirsky. Care has been taken that his arrival in London shall not be delayed by the Alien Office. (18270)

3115　THE PRINCE REGENT TO SPENCER PERCEVAL, AND A REPLY [copy]

Carlton House, 26 July 1811

The Prince Regent remarks on Mr. Perceval's statement respecting the office of Paymaster to the Widows Pensions, that Mr. Perceval grounds his main objections to the appointmt. of Colonel McMahon to that office on a paper he encloses, containing an 'Extract from the 4to. edition of the Commissioners of Public Accounts in 1783' (TWENTY EIGHT years ago) together with an opinion tending to approve what is there recommended, given 'by the Commissioners of Military Enquiry in their 6th Report in 1808' and in reasoning upon their conclusions proceeds to observe in consequence of an expression fallen from Mr. Bankes towards the close of the last Session on the subject of the late Lord Melville's office in Scotland (fully as much at least, an object of Parliamentary regulation as that of the Paymaster to the Widows Pensions) 'that for any grant of such office during the interval of Parliament, that it certainly would be right that the grantee should be apprized that the subject was under the consideration of Parliament, and that he must therefore accept it under the impression and with the knowledge that Parliament might not think necessary to continue it.'

To those remarks of Mr. Perceval the Prince Regent readily accedes.

Mr. Perceval next proceeds to shew that although generally disposed to resist the abolition of sinecure offices, yet he feels it 'next to impossible' to resist the abolition of some of them, for instance 'those which are paid by a precise vote of Parliament,' in which class he affixes that of the Paymaster to the Widows Pensions.

It appears to the Prince Regent from the Report of the Commissioners

1. The Under-Secretary of State.

2. Prince Adam George Czartoriski (1734–1823), Alexander I's Foreign Minister, 1804–6.

58

of Military Enquiry that by the death of the late Rt. Honble. Chas. Jas. Fox, the patent then became in force only for the life of the late General Fox, and the Prince Regent from information he has received, has reason to apprehend that General Fox in his lifetime was not paid a salary by a precise vote of Parliament but was generally remunerated by a poundage of one shilling in the pound from the Widows Pensions.

The Prince Regent further observes that in the last paragraph of the paper Mr. Perceval enclosed, he has interlined in the remark on the Finance Committee, wherein it is acknowledged that 'the Committee has *not adverted* to *this office* by *name*', the following line—'*except it may be in their last report which is not yet printed*,' and which he believes will not be found in that Report.

The Prince Regent cannot but clearly perceive that Parliament *has not*, as yet, ever recognized the positive abolition of this office; that the Deputy has always hitherto been warranted by his Principal, and that were the Prince Regent to execute a warrant to the Deputy (as now submitted to him by the Secretary at War) empowering the Deputy to assume the functions of that office, it would to all intents and purposes be at once abolishing the office of the Principal, and which he cannot possibly think of consenting to.

The Prince Regent therefore under all those circumstances, and with the fullest consideration of the whole state of the case, together with the willingness of Colonel McMahon to accept such office under the impression and with the 'knowledge that Parliament might not think it necessary to continue it' is induced to direct that Mr. Perceval will be pleased to cause the proper steps to be taken for appointing Colonel McMahon to the situation of Paymaster to the Widows' Pensions, exactly in the same manner and precisely as it was held by the late General Fox (Alnwick MSS.).

FROM SPENCER PERCEVAL

Downg. St., 26 July 1811

Mr Perceval presents his humble duty to your Royal Highness and has the honor to acquaint your Royal Highness that he saw Mr. A. B. Drummond immediately after he left Carleton House yesterday; and applied to Mr Drummond for the advance of so much money as might be necessary to supply the deficiency of the allowance from the Privy Purse for his Majesty's ordinary payments. Mr Drummond said that he should be most desirous of complying with the wishes of your Royal Highness and the Queen upon this subject, but that as Privy Purse he conceived the precise line of his duty was so marked out by the Act of

Parliament, that he could not feel himself authorised in that character to make any other application of his Majesty's Privy Purse money than was by that Act prescribed. Mr Perceval acquainted him that it was not in that character or out of that money that your Royal Highness looked for any such advance, but that the application was made to him in his character of a banker. To that he had no objection, but only desired before he gave an answer which would involve his partners as well as himself that he might have an opportunity of consulting them. The propriety of this could not be doubted, and in the evening Mr Perceval received a note from him saying that 'their respect for your Royal Highness & her Majesty would not allow of any hesitation on their part in acceding to the proposal of advancing as far as four or five thousand pounds.'

Mr Perceval humbly requests your Royal Highness to direct Col. McMahon to send Mr Perceval the precise sum that may be wanted—and Mr Perceval will take care that your Royal Highness shall have the security properly filled up in the course of tomorrow that your Royal Highness may take it down to Windsor to be executed by her Majesty as well as by your Royal Highness, and Mr Brawn may come up from Windsor with that security and a joint draft from your Royal Highness & her Majesty for such part of the sum so to be advanced by Messrs. Drummond as may be wanted for the payments already due for the quarters which are passed. (18271–2)

3116 ROBERT THORNTON TO THE PRINCE REGENT
Grafton Street, 27 July 1811
I venture, with great humility, to lay at the feet of your Royal Highness a request which I can only be encouraged to make from the goodness of your Royal Highness to myself & from the liberality of your Royal Highness's character, to which the world is a witness. Having had my property reduced considerably below one half from the difficulties & hazards of the commercial world in the two last years, & having an income less by £5,000 pr.annm. than belonged to me not long ago, without any immediate hope of encreasing it, I am naturally extremely anxious to maintain something of the situation in society to which I have belonged.

This would be secured to me could your Royal Highness condescend to promote it by obtaining for me an office likely to be immediately vacant; I mean that of Marshall of the Admiralty Court, as Mr. Crickett[1] who fills it is supposed to be at the point of death.

1. John Crickitt. He died in August, in his seventy-seventh year. Thornton was appointed. See Nos. 3168, 3174, 3176.

I did not venture to intrude upon your Royal Highness without having first asked Sir William Scott at the head of the Admiralty Court whether I could be acceptable to him, whose feelings might perhaps be consulted on such an occasion & I know that he would be my well-wisher. The office is within the accustomed patronage of Mr. Yorke as First Lord of the Admiralty & if your Royal Highness could condescend to take up my cause on an occasion of such moment to my interests, it would indeed be serving an individual who at present is grateful to your Royal Highness & who ventures to commit to a mind of so much generosity as that of your Royal Highness what it would not be expedient in every quarter to particularize & to explain. I hope, & indeed I think at any rate that your Royal Highness will forgive this presumption because I know that your Royal Highness will be induced to make great allowances for a person in my own circumstances.

With the greatest possible humility & duty [etc.]. (18277/8)

3117 THE DUKE OF YORK TO THE PRINCE REGENT
Stable Yard, 27 July 1811
I am just returned from Windsor and have little or nothing to add to the melancholy account which you received this morning from Sir Henry Halford except that his Majesty had continued to refuse all nourishment. The Archbishop[1] and the Chancellor went over to his Majesty's apartment in order to judge themselves of his present state without making themselves known to him. I am not able to inform you what opinion they formed concerning him, but I understand from Dr. Baillie that during the time they were in his Majesty's room the King was quieter and less incoherent than he had been during the rest of the morning.

I left the Queen and my sisters very low, but fully aware of and perfectly resigned to what must soon be the probable result. (44244)

3118 COLONEL MCMAHON TO SPENCER PERCEVAL, AND THE REPLY [copy]
Carlton House, 27 July 1811
Private. Col. McMahon presents his respectful compliments to Mr Perceval and is commanded by the Prince Regent to express his Royal Highness's acknowledgements to Mr Perceval for the trouble he has so obligingly taken with Mr Drummond on the subject of the loan wish'd

1. Dr. Manners-Sutton.

for by her Majesty & his Royal Highness on account of his Majesty's Privy Purse; and to acquaint Mr Perceval that the sum proposed to be borrowed of the Messrs Drummond for that purpose is *five thousand pounds* (a few hundred pounds perhaps beyond what may be strictly required at the instant) and at the same time the Prince Regent requests, should Mr Perceval find that such accommodation could in any shape prove the least embarrassing to the opinion of Mr Drummond in making such a loan, he would not think of pressing it, as his Royal Highness can with perfect ease procure, for the convenience of her Majesty, this sum immediately from his own private bankers. (18275)

PERCEVAL'S REPLY

Downg. St., Saturday, 27 July 1811
Mr Perceval presents his compts. to Col. McMahon and begs he would be so good as to acquaint his Royal Highness the Prince Regent that Messrs. Drummonds feel not the least embarrassment in furnishing the accommodation to the amount of £5000 for the payments required to be made on behalf of his Majesty for which a sufficient provision was not made under the Act of Parlt. out of his Majesty's Privy Purse. Mr Perceval begs Col. McMahon would also convey to his Royal Highness Mr Perceval's regret that the Solicitor of the Treasury[1] happening to be out of town, when he was sent for to prepare the Bond, will prevent Mr Perceval from furnishing it for his Royal Highness's and her Majesty's signature till Monday— but Mr Perceval will send it down by a messenger on Monday to her Majesty, together with a form of draft on Messrs Drummond for so much of the money as may be immediately required, which Mr Brawn may bring up to town on Tuesday instead of Monday, and Mr Perceval hopes that this one day's delay will not be attended with any inconvenience, as his Royal Highness will be enabled to satisfy her Majesty tomorrow that the money will be forthcoming on Tuesday. (18280–1)

3119   THE MARQUESS WELLESLEY TO THE PRINCE REGENT

Apsley House, 6 p.m., Saturday, 27 July 1811
Lord Wellesley presents his humble duty to your Royal Highness, & being apprised of your Royal Highness's anxiety respecting the arrival of Prince Lubomirski, has the honor to state that the Prince is not yet

1. Henry Charles Litchfield (1756–1822).

arrived. He would not leave Harwich without his cook & valet de chambre, who have been permitted to accompany him.

Lord Wellesley is now going to dine & sleep out of town, but will return the moment he shall learn the arrival of Prince Lubomirski. (18283)

3120 THE DUKE OF NORTHUMBERLAND TO COLONEL MCMAHON, AND A REPLY
Alnwick Castle, 28 July 1811
I shoud not have troubled you so soon with another letter, but for the message H.R.H. directed you to communicate to me relative to the information I shoud receive in case of any material change. Such marked partiality & kindness fills me with the deepest gratitude, & had I wanted anything to attach me & make me entirely devote myself to H.R.H. such condescension coud not fail to do so. But you know, my dear Colonel, I have long, long ago been totally devoted to H.R.H., and that his interest, his comforts, & his honour & glory are as dear to me as my own. It is his person & not his power to which I am so strongly attached. I am, thank God, placed by nature in a station of life to want little or nothing. It is therefore a dutifull personal attachment & not any selfish or interested views that guide my tongue & heart in anything I ever presume to offer to H.R.H.'s consideration. Woud to God everybody else who has the honour of his confidence may be always guided by the same pure motives.

I hope, my dear Colonel, your apprehensions are groundless, & that you will not at last be disappointed of getting that most comfortable situation which H.R.H.'s goodness intends for you, & I shall feel most particularly & sincerely happy to be informed that you have got your appointment.

I suppose you will soon now be going to Cheltenham, the waters of which I trust will be of great service to you.

I imagine we are not to expect anything of great consequence soon from Portugal. We appear to be very happy & well satisfied if the enemy will only leave us alone, & never seem to think of active tho' defensive operations such I was used to see Duke Ferdinand[1] carry on in Germany during the Seven Years War; & Prince Henry of Prussia's[2] campaign is a most perfect lesson for that kind of defensive operations.

America has at last, thro our encouragement by being too passive, gone somewhat too far. I know the American character perfectly, & hope we shall be cool, firm, & dignified in our language to her, & if we are to act, we shall do it at once with vigour. I trust in God H.R.H. will neither

1. Prince Ferdinand of Brunswick (1721–92), who won the battle of Minden in 1759.
2. Prince Henry (1726–1802), was one of Frederick the Great's brothers.

63

on this occasion nor any other, ever be induced by his Ministers to consent to *half measures*. They are the foundation of all mischief, unworthy of a great & noble character, & never can be conducive to any good end. They are the resource of a low weak mind & fit only for an Old Baily sollicitor. The great mind is always cool, firm & decisive, & if I know anything of H.R.H.'s character, nature has happily endowed him with those necessary qualifications for a Prince.

Adieu, my dear Colonel; assure the Prince of my unabated zeal for his service, & dutifull attachment to his person. (18287–8)

FROM COLONEL MCMAHON
Carlton House, 29 July 1811
The unbounded kindnesses and protection with which your Grace has so long and so generously been graciously pleased to honor me with, will not allow me for a moment to withhold the circumstances which belong to the appointment lately held by General Fox, and which I had informed your Grace, the Prince Regent in his never varying goodness intended for me; besides which, I am strictly commanded by his Royal Highness, with his affectionate regards to your Grace, to send you the copies of Mr. Percival's statement on the subject, and of H.R.Hss.'s answer to that statement, & further to add what pass'd upon the first mention of this business as necessarily requisite to the forming of your Grace's opinion regarding it. Immediately on the death of General Fox (when Mr. Percival suggested the Government of Portsmouth for Lord Wellington, to the embarrassment of H.R.Hss. whom he knew to have previously made another arrangement, giving it to Ld. Harcourt in order to embrace the whole of a plan by which Col. Gordon was to become Qur. Master General) the Prince observ'd to Mr. Percival, 'I hope you have made no arrangement for the office of Paymaster to the Widows Pensions.' 'Yes, Sir,' said Mr. P. 'With great deference we had one to submit' (here he took *no* view of abolition) 'It cannot be,' replied the Prince, 'for being determined to give the first place for life, whether great or small, that should fall to my gift as a mark of my affection & justice to Mc.Mahon, I have promised him this, & will not disappoint him for the world.' 'If such is then the case, Sir, (said Mr. P.) I will be happy to obey your commands, as you could not possibly confer it on a man whom the public voice will more approve than Col. M.' So far very civil, but on a reflection of a few days, instead of carrying H.R.Hss.'s wishes into execution, he transmitted the papers mark'd No. 1 & 2.

The King is quite emaciated, peremptorily & angrily refuses all sustenance, is even with the aid of opium without scarcely any sleep, and totally gone as to reason. It is *now* thought he cannot possibly exist ten days longer without some miraculous change takes place within that time. No news (Alnwick MSS.).

3121 LETTERS FROM THE MARQUESS WELLESLEY TO THE PRINCE REGENT
Apsley House, Monday, 28 [29] July 1811
Lord Wellesley has the honor to submit to your Royal Highness some intelligence of great importance from St. Petersburgh & Vienna. He has also to acquaint your Royal Highness that Prince Lubomirski is not yet arrived. (18284)

Apsley House, 2 p.m., Monday, 29 July
Lord Wellesley presents his humble duty to your Royal Highness & has the honor to inclose a note which he has this moment received; he has sent for Prince Lubomirski & hopes to be able, before the close of the evening, to submit to your Royal Highness whatever communications that person may be charged with. (18300)

Apsley House, Tuesday night, 30 July 1811
Lord Wellesley humbly submits to your Royal Highness that, after full consideration of the circumstances under which Prince Lubomirski arrived in this country, of his conduct since his arrival & of his character it would not be advisable to admit him to the honor of an Audience from your Royal Highness without further inquiry. Lord Wellesley therefore does not propose to present Prince Lubomirski to your Royal Highness tomorrow, but will make further inquiry respecting this person, which will enable your Royal Highness to determine upon the propriety of admitting Prince Lubomirski to your Royal Highness's presence. (18303)

3122 THE ARCHBISHOP OF DUBLIN[1] AND OTHERS TO THE EARL OF MOIRA
Dublin
The Roman Catholic Prelates of Ireland being penetrated with sentiments of loyalty to their gracious Sovereign, and of veneration and

1. John Thomas Troy (1739–1823), Bishop of Ossory, 1777; Archbishop of Dublin, 1786–1823.

65

affection towards his Majesty's representative, the Prince Regent; and being anxious to express these sentiments and to explain their principles and conduct to this august personage at a time when the latter have been misrepresented, humbly solicit your Lordship to be their kind interpreter with his Royal Highness for these purposes.

In endeavouring to prove themselves loyal and peaceable subjects of his Majesty, they trust that they and the Roman Catholic Clergy of Ireland have stronger evidence in their behalf than verbal declarations can be, in their long tried behaviour as individuals, and as pastors of numerous flocks, at different periods of danger, both from the public enemy, and from intestine commotion: this behaviour they offer as the best pledge of their future conduct, should similar danger unfortunately recur; and they presume to express their conviction that the influence of Pastors whose religion exacts of them at all times and under all circumstances these dispositions and this conduct, instead of being detrimental must be beneficial to the State under which they live.

It is true that they claim for their Church and themselves the chief influence and authority in the appointment of their Prelates and pastors, because such is the constitution of their Church, and because they are strictly bound by their religion to provide to the utmost of their power that such persons should be men of the purest orthodoxy, piety and morality, as likewise of adequate theological learning and experience; of all which matters, as well as of the characters and dispositions of their respective clergy, they must be admitted to be more competent judges than persons of other communions can be: but since they hold a steady loyalty and a uniform peaceable conduct to be essential branches of this morality, and since they have twice, of late, solemnly and publicly confirmed 'the rule which they have hitherto followed of recommending such persons only for vacant Bishoprics as are of unimpeachable loyalty and peaceable conduct,'* so far from any detriment accruing to the public welfare from the existing and long tried discipline in this matter, they are convinced that it is for the benefit of their country as well as of their Church that no innovation respecting it should be attempted.

It is also true that they are bound by the fundamental principles of their religion to acknowledge the Pope as the centre of Catholic unity and the depositary of spiritual jurisdiction; but they maintain that no practical mischief to the State can arise from these merely religious tenets; inasmuch as the experience of many past ages in our own and other countries shews that no such mischief has arisen from them; and inasmuch as they, the Prelates, have by their solemn oaths (prescribed to them by Parliament for the express purpose in question) strictly confined these principles to their proper objects. By one of these oaths they swear that 'neither the Pope of Rome, nor any other foreign Prince, Prelate or Potentate hath or ought to have any temporal or civil jurisdiction, power, superiority or preeminence directly or indirectly within this Realm'.† By another they swear that 'No Act, in itself unjust, immoral, or wicked can ever be justified or excused by or under pretence or colour, that it was done, either for the good of the Church, or in obedience to any Ecclesiastical power whatever'.‡ Hence it follows that neither their communication with the Catholic Church, nor their deriving Spiritual jurisdiction from Christ through the Bishop of Rome, can interfere with their civil allegiance or duty to their King & country.

They are bound to add in justice to the persecuted Pontiff and to themselves, that as he has lost his Principality and his personal liberty in defense of the freedom of his spiritual powers and of the choice of his successor, and in defence of the justice which as a temporal Prince he owed to this country;§ so they themselves have solemnly and publicly pledged themselves in a printed circular letter addressed to all the Prelates of their Communion throughout the world, 'Not to acknowledge any successor to the present Pope, who shall not have been lawfully, holily and freely elected.'||

This declaration of their sentiments & principles will, they trust, justify the Roman Catholic Prelates and Clergy of Ireland and their conduct from late misrepresentations, and prove their consistency in what regards their duties both to their religion and to their King and country.

Confiding in your Lordship's well known benevolence and patriotism, they take the liberty of transmitting it to you; humbly requesting your Lordship to make it known to his Royal Highness the Prince Regent and to any other members of the Legislature in such manner as your Lordship's judgment may direct; on the part of the Roman Catholic Prelates and Clergy of Ireland in general.

J. T. Troy R.C. Archb. of Dublin for myself, & on behalf of the Rom. Cath. Prelates and Clergy of Ireland.

On behalf also of the undersigned

Dr. Jn. Milner, Bishop of Castabala, Vicar Apostolic & Agent in England to the R. Cathc. Prelates of Ireland.

London, July 31, 1811 (18304).

* Assembly of Prelates, Dublin Sept. 14, 1808. Ditto, Feb. 26, 1810.

† 13th & 14th.

‡ 23d of his Majesty.

§ Corrispondenza autentica di Sua Santita' cogli Ministri del Governo Francese, Cagliari & Palermo.

|| Actum Dublinii in Conventu generali Episcop. Hib. A. S. MDCCCX.

3123 THE DUKE OF YORK TO THE PRINCE REGENT

Stable Yard, 31 July 1811

I have nothing new to communicate to you since you heard this morning from Windsor except that it being judged essential that his Majesty should take medicine, and the proposal having caused great irritation, it became necessary to put him under restraint when the medicine was taken and he has remained quiet and sullen ever since except when he was asked what he chose for dinner, which produced for a short time a fresh excitement.

Both Dr. Willis and Dr. Baillie stated to me that his Majesty's body has certainly gained strength within the last three days, but his mind remains in the same melancholy state as it has been in since the beginning of this paroxim [*sic*], and Dr. Willis added that though from the body being less under the influence of disease there was less incoherency to be observed in his Majesty's conversation, yet that he had not yet remarked one rational idea and that on the contrary every delusion even of the wildest kind which had appeared in the heighth of the delirium still continued in force.[1] (44245)

3124 THE DUKE OF KENT TO THE PRINCE REGENT, AND AN ENCLOSURE

Castle Hill Lodge, 31 July 1811

If an anxious wish not to intrude on you with my individual concerns, at a time when I deeply felt how cruelly you must be hampered by those degrading restrictions which Mr. Perceval and his colleagues (notwithstanding the united exertions of the whole family and of all the most

1. Princess Augusta wrote to her friend Mrs. Williams on 15 August: 'You will have heard from Sophia how great our distress has been and how much greater *now* from there not being the smallest apparent chance of the mind getting any better. All that nourishment and sleep can do is to strengthen the body, but nothing I fear can have any effect on the mind. It is the greatest example *ever known* of what *wear* and *tear* an *unimpaired* constitution can go through. I have all along had a very bad opinion of my beloved father's case, because *his affections* could never be worked upon. In all his other illnesses he was rejoiced to see us, and vexed beyond measure when we left him, even to such a degree at times as to occasion quite a scene at parting in the forenoon, though he knew we were to see him in the evening; but this time he had just the satisfaction of pouring out his complaints or telling his schemes to us or to anybody else, without caring in the least for the individual to whom he was speaking, and wished us goodbye without the smallest *unconcern*. You who know him and what an excellent and affectionate father he was, can guess what a change this was, for though our reason told us but too evidently that it was complaint, still our feelings were grated to see him so altered. Since the 28th of May I have never seen him but at a distance, and now probably I shall never see him again, for under his melancholy state I would not see him for worlds; as I cannot serve him I could do him no good and he would not know me. He is got so very strong that he may last for a long time though he is grown excessively thin.' (Add. Georgian 10/46)

independant of the hereditary aristocracy of the country) were enabled to impose upon you by *their* Regency Act, has *hitherto* kept me silent relative to myself, I am certain you will *now*, with *that* indulgence I have so often experienced from you, and with that affection which it has ever been the greatest pride of my life to merit, kindly listen to an humble representation of my feelings at a time when a continuation of *that* silence might be construed a want of *that proper* sense of my situation which I trust I never can cease but with my existence to entertain.

Without adverting to events that passed more than eight years since, and which I am sensible must be needless, after receiving such reiterated proofs, as I have done, of the sentiments you *then* so strongly expressed relative to the treatment I experienced, remaining unaltered, or taking up your time with a detail of all I have in consequence suffered, I will only beg leave for a moment to recall to your recollection the single circumstance that, upon my return from Gibraltar in 1803, when you saw how deeply my feelings were wounded by everything I was compelled to submit to, *you* condescended to afford me *the only* comfort I was *then* capable of receiving, in the spontaneous declaration on *your* part, that whenever the power was in *your* hands, *you would see justice done me*; and having said this, I am sure I shall stand acquitted of presumption in *your* mind if I add that, relying implicitly on *that* assurance, the first object of this letter is most humbly yet most earnestly to sollicit that I may be sent out *by you* to the Mediterranean in *that* situation (which alone can prove to the world that however my conduct at Gibraltar in 1802 & 3 was viewed by those in office at *that* time, it was not *then*, nor *ever has been since* considered by *you* as meriting censure) I mean *that* of Commander of all the Forces on *that* Station, which appointment would, of course, as I am Governor of Gibraltar, include *that* fortress, and its dependencies, together with the whole extent, which it has always comprehended prior to the recent nomination of Lord William Bentinck, on which occasion I understand that *Malta* was necessarily excluded from his commission.

Having thus submitted my request I must further sollicit your forgiveness if in *this* place I unequivocally state that the Mediterranean Command is *the only one abroad* which I can reconcile it to *my* feelings to accept of, and *that* upon the ground of its being the only one that *can* again restore me to that place in the opinion of all my old professional friends, to gain which, during the 14 successive years that I passed in the vicissitudes of various climates, ever was, *next* to the happiness of being thought well of by you, the first object of my most zealous exertions.

It may be right for me here to add that nothing is farther from my wishes than to go from England, should it be your kind intention, upon an opening offering to realize the expectation which in 1801 and in 1804 you encouraged me to entertain, of being chosen by you to fill the distinguished office of Master General of the Ordnance, which ever since that time I have naturally been led to look up to as the summit of my military ambition, as, in *that* case, my mere nomination in the *first* instance to the Mediterranean command, without even going out at all to join it, (should such be *your* pleasure) would answer every wish of mine, as my subsequent appointment to the other situation would satisfactorily account to the world for my not proceeding to my destination.

Having thus endeavoured to comprise in as few words as possible my humble representation respecting myself, and having studiously avoided introducing any extraneous subject into it, I shall take my leave of you by saying that it is my intention to call in the morning of tomorrow to see you under the hope that you will then condescend to communicate to me your sentiments upon the subject of this letter, and candidly to tell me how far I may be warranted in looking forward to your deciding favorably upon it.

In the meanwhile I shall only venture to express the confident hope that I may never lose that place in your affection and good opinion which it ever has been as it ever must be the first object of *my* life to preserve, being with the firmest attachment, and the truest devotion [etc.]. (46504–5)

THE DUKE OF KENT'S MEMORANDUM

[*31 July 1811*]

Private. In applying to the Prince Regent for the situation of Comr. of the Forces in the Mediterranean, the Duke of Kent's *first* object is to obtain the high gratification of being placed by the Prince (who so kindly expressed his sense of those professional injuries he had experienced in his recall from Gibraltar in 1803, & the subsequent refusal to give him an opportunity of vindicating his conduct during that twelvemonth he commanded the Garrison) in that situation, of all others, that would most clearly prove to the world the Prince's continuance in the same sentiments and his having avail'd himself of the first moment he had it in his power, to heal the deep wound that had been inflicted on the Duke of Kent at the time alluded to, & that has ever since prey'd on his mind.

His *second.* That, by being nominated to the general superintendence of the forces serving in the Mediterranean it would obviate any interference on his part with the particular arrangements at present judged necessary for the civil Government of either Gibraltar or Malta, or for the particular command of that proportion of the army allotted for the defence of Sicily, which is at present vested in the General Officer recently appointed to be Minister Plenipotentiary to the Court of Sicily.[1]

His *third*, that by fixing Head Quarters at Malta he would be able by the late arrangement of the Packets to receive constant communications from the General Officers commg. at all the different ports and become the channel of transmitting them home, while at the same time he might successively have the different Regiments of the Mediterranean army *there* under his eye.

His *fourth*, that at Malta there would be a very respectable establishment for him as the Palace of the Grand Master in town and his houses at St. Antonio or la Bosquetta in the country afford every accommodation he could wish, while General Oakes[2] as Commandant would occupy the houses which General Villettes[3] had at the time when Sir Alex. Ball as Civil Commissioner had those quarters which it is presumed would be given up to the Duke of Kent.

His *fifth*, that the climate, particularly in winter, is such as the Duke is very partial to, & the confinement would not be so great as that which is experienced at Gibraltar.

In point of emolument, the addition which the Duke of Kent would derive would be simply this, the augmentation of his present Staff pay as General of £6 per day (which by his Majesty's particular order he continues to receive) to £10 (*that* attachd to the commission of Commander of the forces) the bat & forage which is attachd to that rank, amounting to about £900 per annum, and the allowance of his table, which it is presumed could not be under £5000, that being the amount recommended by the Duke of York in 1807, to be given to Sir Hew Dalrymple when appointed Commandant at Gibraltar, & which would then certainly have taken place but for some mismanagement or backwardness on the part of Sir Hew in explaining why the allowance of £3500 was not adequate to keeping his table at Gibraltar when call'd upon to state the same.

If this arrangement were made in the Duke of Kent's behalf, which he considers the most desirable one of any, his idea would be to proceed in May next to Malta & to continue there (presuming his health to continue unimpaird) untill the Prince having the whole power in his own hands, either by the demise of the King or his Majesty's unfortunate

1. Lord William Bentinck.

2. Sir Hildebrand Oakes (1754–1822). Entered the army, 1767; Major, 1790; Lieutenant-Colonel, 1794; Colonel, 1798; Major-General, 1805; Lieutenant-General, 1811. Baronetcy, 1813; G.C.B., 1820; Lieutenant-General of the Ordnance, 1814–22.

3. William Anne Villettes (1754–1808). Major, 1787; Lieutenant-Colonel, 1791; Major-General, 1798; Lieutenant-General, 1805; Governor of Malta, 1801–7; Governor of Jamaica, 1807–8, and died there.

mental disorder being declar'd incurable, should condescend to recall him to fill that situation of confidence *at home* which has long been the heighth of his ambition, his expectation of being nominated thereto having originated in the spontaneous declaration to that effect made by the Prince, *first* in February 1801 & successively in Febry 1804. But if the Prince should see the prospect of being able to appoint the Duke of Kent to the Master-Generalship shortly, then the mere nomination at present to the Mediterranean command and his retaining it for such time as might elapse before the other arrangement could take place, would in such case even without his going out, fully meet his wishes, & satisfy his feelings. (46506–10)

3125   SPENCER PERCEVAL TO THE PRINCE REGENT, AND THE REPLY

Downing Street, 1 Aug. 1811

Mr Perceval presents his humble duty to your Royal Highness and takes the liberty of reminding your Royal Highness that by the death of the Duke of Devonshire[1] the Lord Lieutenancy of Derbyshire is vacant. Mr Perceval humbly conceives that considering the great situation of the D. of Devonshire in that county, and the consideration with which your Royal Highness honoured the late Duke, that it would be your Royal Highness's pleasure that Mr Perceval should offer by your Royal Highness's commands the grant of that office to the present Duke—and if it should be your Royal Highness's pleasure that Mr. Perceval should do so, Mr Perceval will have great pleasure in forwarding to his Grace this intention of your Royal Highness as soon as it may be proper to address him upon such a subject. (18314)

THE PRINCE REGENT'S REPLY

Carlton House, 1 Aug. 1811

The Prince Regent acknowledges the receipt of Mr. Percival's letter which has this moment reach'd him, & for which he returns him many thanks. It was the Prince Regent's intention at his very next interview with Mr Percival to have express'd to Mr. Percival his intention to appoint the present Duke of Devonshire to the Lord Lieutenancy of the county of Derby, which was so long so worthily & so respectably held by the Prince's old & ever to be lamented friend his Grace's father, &

1. The Duke died on 29 July.

therefore the Prince approves that Mr Percival should acquaint the Duke without loss of time of his nomination.

The Prince Regent likewise avails himself of this opportunity of stating to Mr Percival his desire (after having given it every possible consideration) that the appointment should now be made out for his old & faithful servant & friend Lt.-Col. McMahon, subject of course to the wisdom of Parliament should it wish to interfere further respecting that office. (18315-6)

3126 THE PRINCE REGENT TO THE DUKE OF DEVONSHIRE
Carlton House, Thursday night, 1 Aug. 1811
My dear Hartington,

(For I cannot as yet accustom myself to call you by any other name) I cannot help, however, even at the risk of appearing intrusive, and perhaps of breaking through the rules of strict decorum, of trespassing upon you at so early a moment, after the irreparable loss which I with the rest of your family have sustained, still I say, I cannot resist troubling you with these few lines merely to inform you that, in consideration of the very sincere affection I have felt for you from the first moment you drew breath, as well as from the more than common affection, love and veneration I have invariably entertained for so long a series of years for both your dear and ever lamented parents, I have appointed you (if it should be agreeable to you) to succeed my late most inestimable friend your father in the Lord Lieutenantcy, as token and as a proof of that unqualified regard and affection which bound me to him while living, and to his memory, whilst I shall have a particle of life remaining in me. I could wish to say much more to you but this is not the moment; however, I cannot resist the affectionate impulse I feel to tell you that I hear so many things of you at this most trying moment that my heart is quite delighted, and I doubly feel so, for reasons which perhaps you may have some little insight into, but which I shall only be too happy to be quite explicit upon with you at any time hereafter, when you may wish to know them and may give me an opportunity of explaining myself. Now then God bless you, my dearest young friend, and may you ever unite (as I have no doubt that you will) all the unparallelled amiable qualities, merits and virtues, of both your best and most inestimable of parents. Such my dearest Hartington are the sincere prayers of [etc.].

P.S. May I entreat of you to express to my poor dear friend the Duchess how truly I participate at this moment in all her sad sufferings[1] (Chatsworth MSS.).

1. For the reply, see No. 3132.

3127   LORD ELDON TO THE PRINCE REGENT

Thursday, 1 Aug. 1811

The Lord Chancellor thinks it his duty to mention to your Royal High-ness the Prince Regent that the Queen's Council thought it right, upon a meeting at Lord Ellenborough's yesterday evening, to depute a part of their body to Windsor this morning to ask her Majesty's permission that Dr. R. Willis might give Dr. John Willis his representation of & opinion concerning the state of his Majesty's health, the Council, in conformity to what the Chancellor mentioned when he last had the honour of seeing his Royal Highness, conceiving, upon discussion, that it was their bounden duty to omit no means of learning whether anything could be usefully done on his Majesty's behalf in the opinion of any person, though not in actual attendance, & at the same time thinking it due, in respect to her Majesty, to ask her permission in the first instance. The Lord Chancellor will not fail to inform your Royal Highness as to what follows upon this communication with respect to any medical persons who may be talked to, if the permission asked is granted. The Chancellor would unques-tionably have given your Royal Highness this information in the dis-charge of his own duty—but he thinks it right towards Dr John Willis to say that *he* thought it right that this should be expressed to your Royal Highness if, in consequence of any permission, it should be proposed that he should converse with his brother. The Lord Chancellor would have delivered this in person to your Royal Highness if his engagements of this day did not engross his time till late in the evening—probably till nine o'clock. (18312–3)

3128   THE QUEEN TO THE PRINCE REGENT

Windsor, 1 Aug. 1811

I have just seen the A.B. of C., the D. of Montrose & Lord Winchelsea.[1] They came with a proposal of making Dr R. Willis consult with his brother John upon the dear Kg.'s present situation, but not with the idea of seeing him unless it was absolutely necessary. Knowing the Kg.'s dislike to the man & the promise the Kg. extracted from me of never letting him come into his presence or again into the house, I felt a great reluctance upon the subject, but upon their stating that the length of the complaint, & the little progress produced by the different tryals which have been attempted not succeeding they felt it their duty to make this

1. They, together with the Archbishop of York, the Earl of Aylesford, Lord Eldon, Lord Ellenborough and Sir William Grant, formed the Queen's Council, established under the Regency Act, section XV.

proposal, *I immediately answered that I was desirous that not even an interview between the two brothers should take place without the whole family being first apprised of it.* The A.B. will wait upon you accordingly & through yr. means the rest of yr. brothers will be informed of it, as by this candid conduct I feel I must be justifyed in the Kg.'s eyes.

I trust that unless it is absolutely necessary, that J. Willis will not see the King. Pardon this sad scrawl but I thought you could not get this too soon. (36573–4)

3129 LETTERS FROM LORD ELDON TO THE PRINCE REGENT

2 Aug. 1811

The Lord Chancellor, with every sentiment of humble duty, has the honour to acknowledge the receipt of her Majesty's letter, and takes leave to inform your Royal Highness that he will not fail to send her Majesty an answer as soon as possible. Your Royal Highness will be pleased to observe from the other letter, which he was about to send to your Royal Highness when he was honoured with your Royal Highness's note that it was the intention of the Council to collect tomorrow the opinions of the physicians *usually attending*, (both *Dr Baillie* & Dr R. Willis having first seen Dr John W.) and the Chancellor had apprised the Council of what passed between himself and your Royal Highness respecting Drs Simmonds & Monroe, which they will take into consideration after seeing Sir Henry Halford & the other physicians tomorrow. (18317–8)

2 Aug. 1811

The Lord Chancellor, offering his most humble duty to your Royal Highness the Prince Regent, takes leave to mention that her Majesty was pleased to permit Dr Robert Willis to converse *in London* with his brother Dr John, that, that communication having taken place, they met her Majesty's Council last night at Lord Ellenborough's, when it was further arranged that Dr John Willis should wait upon Dr Baillie *in town* today—that Dr Robert Willis and Dr Baillie having thus conversed with Dr John Willis, it was determined that the Council should meet at Windsor early tomorrow morning, the physicians whom they have usually seen there, Lord Ellenborough & the Chancellor meaning to attend that meeting. The Lord Chancellor will do himself the honor of being in attendance at Carleton House on Sunday morning at nine to lay before your Royal Highness all that has passed, and shall pass, if your Royal Highness shall be pleased to see him. (18319–20)

3130 THE DOWAGER DUCHESS OF RUTLAND TO THE PRINCE REGENT

Sackville Street, Friday, 2 Aug. 1811

I scarce know how to venture to address your Royal Highness again, as I fear you will think I presume too much upon your great goodness & the friendship with which you have always condescended to honor me, but it is upon *that* I rest my hope that you will forgive my taking the liberty of troubling you with a second letter, as I am going out of town early on Monday morning & have I fear no chance of seeing your Royal Highness anywhere & cannot help feeling very anxious to know what your Royal Highness in your great goodness has settled about Charles,[1] & I should like much to be able to write him word whether what you so graciously & kindly proposed is likely to be carried into effect, & should be greatly obliged to your Royal Highness (in case you have no objection to it) to allow someone to inform me concerning it, & what I may hope & tell Charles on the subject. Alas, my dear Sir, Bob[2] is at last sailed, & I am sorry to say in a packet from Falmouth, which is a great disappointment & anxiety to me as he had promised me to go in a ship of war, but could not get a passage on board one. Your Royal Highness knows my misery upon the subject of their both being abroad. I will not therefore add to the liberty I am taking by repeating it, only you have always been so kind to me concerning it I could not help thus far mentioning it—& I hope you will forgive me if I still further intrude upon your Royal Highness's time & patience to mention another subject concerning which I am very anxious, & make a request in favor of a very particular friend of mine— General Pigot,[3] whom you have always been so kind to & who would be made most happy if your Royal Highness could in your great kindness bestow a Government upon when any vacancy happens, which may not be unlikely as I believe there are many who are old that hold those situations. General Pigot has (as your Royal Highness knows) all his life been employed in his Majesty's service & I beleive has served with great credit to himself & is an excellent officer & commanded at the seige &

1. Her son, Lord Charles Henry Somerset Manners (1780–1855). See No. 1398.

2. Her son, Major-General Lord Robert William Manners (1781–1835). M.P. for Scarborough, 1802–6; for Leicestershire, 1806–31; for North Leicestershire, 1832–5. Lieutenant-Colonel, 1811; Colonel, 1821; Major-General, 1830.

3. Sir Henry Pigot (1750–1840). Entered the army, 1769; Major, 1781; Lieutenant-Colonel, 1783; Colonel, 1793; Major-General, 1795; Lieutenant-General, 1802; General, 1812. Commanded at the blockade of La Valette, Malta, 1800. G.C.M.G., 1837.

capture of Malta. The General I beleive has applied to the Duke of York who was pleased to say he would lay General Pigot's claim *with others* before your Royal Highness, but I feel so anxious for the General I always meant to take the liberty of mentioning him if I had had the honor of seeing your Royal Highness & hope therefore you will forgive my mentioning him *in writing* to your notice in case a proper opportunity should offer, & that you should be graciously pleased to bestow such a mark of your favor upon him which would give me great satisfaction.

I cannot conclude without lamenting that your Royal Highness should have had in addition to your anxiety to lament the death of one whom you honor'd with your friendship, & feel sure you will have been much concerned for the Duke of Devonshire, for whom I felt a great regard also.

I trust & hope that none of the cares & anxieties you have had have hurt your health & that you are as well as when I had last the honor of seeing you.

I can never express all I feel for your Royal Highness's great goodness to me & mine which is always present to my mind in the midst of all my misery & anxiety concerning my two sons; & must now only hope you will add one more favor to those you have already confer'd & pardon my taking this liberty & allow me to subscribe myself with the highest regard & respect [etc.]. (18321–3)

3131   LETTERS FROM THE MARQUESS WELLESLEY TO THE PRINCE REGENT
Foreign Office, 3 Aug. 1811
Lord Wellesley has the honor to recommend to your Royal Highness's gracious approbation the name of the Revd Robert Marratt Miller,[1] to be Chaplain to the Factory at Lisbon.

Mr Miller has been recommended to Lord Wellesley by Mr Perceval & others, & his character is very respectable. (18326)

Foreign Office, Saturday, 3 Aug. 1811
Having understood from Count Munster, by your Royal Highness's commands, that the state of his Majesty's illness had induced your Royal Highness to leave London this morning, Lord Wellesley has the honor to acquaint your Royal Highness that he did not appoint Prince Lubomirski to attend at Carlton House.

1. He was appointed. He was Vicar of Dedham, Essex, 1819–39 (*c.* 1786–1839).

Whenever your Royal Highness may be pleased to issue orders for that purpose, Lord Wellesley will take care that Prince Lubomirski shall receive proper notice of the honor which your Royal Highness is graciously pleased to confer upon him; & will not fail to attend in order to present the Prince to your Royal Highness. (18327)

3132 THE DUKE OF DEVONSHIRE TO THE PRINCE REGENT

3 Aug. 1811

It would be impossible for me to express the various feelings which agitate me on receiving your kindest of letters. God knows that the pride and object of my life shall be to deserve such kindness, the thought of which almost deprives me of the power of writing. I had notice from Mr Perceval yesterday of the high honor that your R.H. has bestowed on me, and wrote to him, I fear not in the proper forms, but to your R.H. who have so nobly so kindly laid aside form in your valued letter, allow me to give my most ardent thanks for the tribute you have given to my poor father's memory, to thank you as my mother would have done and to tell you that from her, from him, I inherit an affection founded on that knowledge of your heart and character which would make you beloved in any situation. My heart is full, and your R.H. will forgive the manner in which I write. In a very short time I shall have a melancholy duty to perform in returning to your R.H. one of my father's honors, but I shall with happiness embrace the opportunity of receiving your R.H.'s wishes or opinion as to any part of my conduct. In the meantime with every sentiment of esteem gratitude and affection allow me to subscribe myself [etc.].

The poor Dss. has been in a sad state—our hearts bleed for her, and it is the greatest hope of my sisters and myself that we may by our attention in some degree sooth and reconcile her to her cruel change of situation. (19006)

3133 CHARLES ARBUTHNOT TO COLONEL MCMAHON

Treasury Chambers, 5 Aug. 1811

I find upon enquiry at the Home Department that the mode of nominating General Fox was correct. The Sovereign never applies the term of Honble. or Rt. Honble. to any of his subjects. During the life of a person who has the title of Rt. Honble. the Sovereign calls him *His Right Trusty & Well Beloved Counsellor*; but after the person's death, he only calls him *such a one Esqr.* To leave no doubt upon the subject I desired that Mr Perceval's patent might be brought to me. He has *not* the titles of *Hon.* or *Rt. Honble.*, & is merely called Spencer Perceval. Lord Henry Petty is called in the same patent *Henry Petty Esqr.*; & I recollect that in my Commission of Ambassador to the Porte,[1] his Majesty designated me by no other appellation than that of Chs. Arbuthnot Esqr. Indeed it would be below the dignity of the Sovereign to give to his subjects the title of *Hon.* or *Rt. Hon.*; & this it is which has established the etiquette in question. I hope the explanation I have given will be thought satisfactory.

It will be necessary for you to communicate with Mr Pollock, the Head Clerk in Mr Ryder's office, as he will take the charge of passing the patent for you thro' the several offices. (18332–4)

PRIVATE
I had a long conversation yesterday about you with Mr Perceval, & nothing cd. be more satisfactory. He said that he was very anxious to find something for you that would be sure to be permanent & therefore better. (18334)

3134   ROBERT PEEL TO COLONEL MCMAHON
Downing Street, 6 Aug. 1811
Mr. Peel presents his compliments to Colonel McMahon and takes the liberty of acquainting him by Lord Liverpool's desire that it would be material that the accompanying dispatches should be returned to the Office at an early hour if it would not interfere with the convenience of his Royal Highness the Prince Regent. (18335)

3135   THE MARQUESS WELLESLEY TO THE PRINCE REGENT, AND ENCLOSURES
Foreign Office, 6 Aug. 1811
Secret. In submitting the inclosed intercepted letters to your Royal Highness, Lord Wellesley humbly requests to observe that the former letter from Mr Lorentz[2] on the same subject was never communicated to any person excepting your Royal Highness, after it came from the hands of Mr Smith, the Under Secretary of State.

1. He was Ambassador, 1805–7. His full powers were issued on 12 September 1804.
2. See No. 1832.

Considering the general tenor of these letters, Lord Wellesley proposes to use the same precaution unless he should receive your Royal Highness's commands to a different effect. He certainly would not wish to conceal from Mr Perceval the judgment of Mr Lorentz respecting the severe contests in the Cabinet & Lord Wellesley's ambitious projects.

Your Royal Highness will not fail to estimate the degree of credit due to Mr Lorentz when the imposture which he practised on Mr Adam (& through that gentleman on his Royal Highness the Duke of York) shall have been made apparent by Mr Lorentz's curious confession to his own master:[1] a person of Mr Lorentz's zeal, fidelity, integrity, & veracity is well calculated to appreciate the pretensions & views of the public characters of this country: but as his observations on Lord Wellesley are so blended with the general subject of his letter that it is impracticable to separate them, Lord Wellesley cannot think himself justified in any other request to your Royal Highness than that you would be graciously pleased to make any disposition of these papers which may be suitable to your Royal Highness's wishes. (18338)

[Enclosure] R. LORENTZ TO WILLIAM ADAM [copy]
6 July 1811
It is more than three months ago since I wrote several letters to you repeatedly requesting the favor of an interview upon official business. I have also at different times left my card at your door, not finding you at home, but I have never received any answer to the one or any return to the other. Not being used to this kind of cavalier treatment from you I was inclined to attribute the cause to your being perhaps no longer charged with the pecuniary concerns of his Royal Highness the Prince Regent. I therefore wrote to Colonel McMahon on the 4th of May last to obtain from him some information on that head, by whose answer dated Carlton House, 6 May I was however assured that (to use the Colonel's expression) Mr. Adam is the Chancellor to the Prince Regent, and all the important private business belonging to his Royal Highness is transacted by him. Not having met you ever since in the street or at Carlton House at the Fête it was out of my power to come to any explanation with you on the subject, but as my duty to my Sovereign always supercedes with me all minor considerations, and as I should not think myself justified in being wanting in that duty from motives of resentment, I leave your motives for acting thus to your own feelings, and I have only to transmit to you the enclosed No. 1 of which No. 2 here annexed is the sequel,

1. The Elector of Hesse Cassel.

from which you will perceive that the interest due amounts now to £85,375 17s. 7d, and I have to request that you will acquaint me for the information of his Electoral Highness my master, whether the short interruption which (agreeable to your letter to me dated Bloomsbury Square the 29 June 1809) had been caused to the measures in view for proceeding to the liquidation of the debt of his Royal Highness has not yet found its limit, and whether nothing is in contemplation to fulfill the promise which you held out to his Electoral Highness by your before-mentioned letter to me.

I have moreover to acquaint you that the proposals which I wished to communicate to you verbally when I requested the interview above-mentioned cannot now be executed any longer, and I have finally to request that you will cause the sum of £716 13s. 4d. which was due on the 14th ult. to his Electoral Highness from H.R.H. the Duke of York, to be forthwith paid to Messrs. P. & L. van Notten & Co., the Elector having assigned upon the said instalment part of the allowances granted by him to me. (18340–1)

[Enclosure] WILLIAM ADAM TO R. LORENTZ [copy]
Bloomsbury Square, 7 July 1811, recd. 9th
Your letter of the 6th inst. with it's inclosures I shall without delay submit to the perusal of the Prince Regent and I will convey to you whatever commands his Royal Highness may be pleased to honor me with thereon.

The concluding paragraph of your letter I shall lay before his Royal Highness the Duke of York, thinking it right in the meantime to inform you that the payment to van Notten & Co. will be made as soon as the Duke of York receives his Midsummer payments. (18341)

[Enclosure] R. LORENTZ TO THE ELECTOR OF HESSE CASSEL [copy, translation]
London, 9 July 1811
After the departure of my last of the 3d of May, a copy of which I have the honor to enclose, I heard for certain that M. Horn[1] was expected to arrive here: of this I was extremely glad as I felt persuaded that he would bring me a letter from your Electoral Highness. Unfortunately I have been disappointed; for that gentleman arrived but brought me nothing; and he informs me that he offered his services at his departure to your

1. An agent employed by the British Government to collect information on the Continent. See *Letters of George IV*, No. 391.

Highness to be the bearer of dispatches, but was not honored with any for me. Accordingly I still continue as on the 3d of May without the smallest commands from your Highness excepting those of the 25th and 30th August 1810. I need not add that this want of instructions greatly embarrasses me, but I shall refrain from all complaints, especially as I am justified in expecting every day to receive one or more letters from your Highness. In my letter of the 30th August 1810 I shewed what according to my judgment was the best and least expensive way of realizing the expectations (which your Highness had never quite given up) arising from the Convention concluded at C—l by his Royal Highness the Duke of York on the 17th July 1802; and the non-arrival of orders from your Highness is therefore greatly to be regretted.

Since my last there is become due seven instalments of principal and interest, but not a shilling has been paid. The 8th is now also due; consequently some decisive measures should be adopted especially as the Duke of York has been appointed the second time, since the 25th of May, Commander-in-Chief of the whole English Army, and has thus fully regained his former influence.

Mr. Horn likewise informed me that your Highness looked with anxiety for an answer from the Prince Regent to a letter which your Highness had written to him. Upon this head I think it my duty most humbly to observe that it is very prejudicial to your electoral Highness's interests here, and productive of many unpleasant consequences which I dare not describe, if your Highness writes letters to this country without permitting me to present them, or furnishing me with a copy of them, unless they contain matters of a private nature; for it thus is made to appear that your Highness has interests here which do not require my assistance, or of which it is thought proper that I should remain ignorant. My fervent wish to contribute to the utmost of my power to your Highness's welfare obliges me to repeat that your Highness's interests are best protected and watched on the spot—and that no place but London furnishes the means by which the point in view can be attained—and that all steps taken in the business in question without my knowledge must necessarily be productive of evil consequences—for I may thus most innocently take steps or make observations which, ignorant as I am of what statements have previously been made, lead to results the very reverse from what I intend, for according to the mode in which diplomacy is conducted in this country, no documents are communicated which it is presumed one is perfectly acquainted with.

My zeal for your Highness's true interests obliges me moreover to recur to a subject which I mentioned at the end of my humble report of the 24 January 1810. I shall not repeat in this place what I then so fully stated, but to those details I have to add some particulars, unquestionably true, and with which I have only lately become acquainted. The fact is that supposing three of the four persons in whose names the capital is placed, to be dead, and the last, meaning the fourth to be also dying, the disposal of the capital would exclusively devolve to the heirs of this fourth person; thus situated these heirs would have at a great expense to produce proofs of the nature of the trust and having succeeded in this they would have in their own names to take out Letters of Administration in order to transfer the whole capital to other trustees. These circumstances would be unavoidable in case of such decease, and the business would not only cause immense expenses but might even produce a delay of several years, during which period there would be no disposing of the capital, nor would it be possible to receive a shilling of the interest. I therefore humbly submit it to your Highness's consideration whether it would not be advisable to adopt the arrangement I proposed in my said letter of the 24 January 1810. This leads me to the subject of the capital itself, and principally to its value at this time. That part which is in 3 pcts. and which was purchased at the rate of 65 9/10 p. ct. is now worth only $62\frac{1}{2}$ p. ct., consequently there is a loss upon it of $3\frac{2}{5}$ p. ct. But this would be no serious matter, though the price has been continually falling during the last 15 months, if many circumstances had not lately taken place which merit the most profound considerations—and if the want of confidence amongst the public which is rather increasing than diminishing did not make me apprehend a still farther and considerable deterioration of your Highness's funds. I regret that prudence prevents me from explaining myself so fully on this head as I could wish, but I think this will serve as a sufficient hint—and conformably to the 9th §. of my instructions I must hesitate no longer in informing your Highness that after the most mature reflexion I have resolved to advise your Highness to sell all or at least the greatest part of your funds—being persuaded that circumstances will become still more unfavourable. The money thus arising might be lent upon secure landed property at 5 p. ct. till such time at least when the course of exchange, which is now $24\frac{1}{2}$ p. ct. against this country—has recovered. I shall conclude by observing that not even the smallest fraction of your Highness's funds can be sold till the survivors of the four persons in whose names they are placed are furnished with full Powers of Attorney by you. (18342–4)

[Enclosure] R. LORENTZ TO THE ELECTOR OF HESSE CASSEL [translation]
London, 4 Aug. 1811
When I had the honor of sending off my last of the 9th July (a copy of which is enclosed I had not yet received an answer to my letter to Mr Adam of the 6th of that month. I have the honor to enclose a copy of that

letter and have to observe that I pretended to have received your Electoral Highness's order to receive the £716 13s. 4d. being the instalment due the 14th June, as part of my salary, thinking that his Royal Highness the Duke of York would thus have an additional motive for paying that sum; but to this hour no money has been paid—nor have I received any answer from Carlton House except the dry and laconic one from Mr. Adam which is annexed.

During the last fortnight all official business is greatly impeded by reason of the unfortunate state of his Majesty's health, which is such at present that his Majesty's decease may be daily expected, and accordingly the physicians have published bulletins every two hours for the information of the Royal Family and the Ministers. Though the physicians do not explicitly pronounce the King's life in danger, yet I believe they are unanimous in giving up all hopes of perfect recovery.

In this state of things the verbal answer I received from the Under-Secretary of State was not quite unexpected: I had asked that gentleman confidentially, a short time since, whether, all Parliamentary business being now finished, this was not the proper time for writing an official note to the Marquis Wellesley and reminding him in strong terms of your Highness claims, which I have now so long but in vain urged. He replied very candidly and without hesitation that owing to the precarious state of affairs at Windsor he considered the present moment as most unfavourable for such a purpose and that he was convinced that my note, however pressing, upon the subject in question, would not produce the effect I desired. Thus situated I must still longer exercise my patience, though almost exhausted, and inform your Electoral Highness that your affairs in this country are not better now than they were at the date of my letter in May 1810. In the meantime there are rumours amongst the public of changes in the Administration, and it is said that five of the twelve members of the present Cabinet will shortly resign, and make room for some of the Opposition party. The rumours however, are not strong nor are any names mentioned; but it is expressly stated that Mr. Perceval, the Marquis Wellesley and the Earl of Liverpool are not amongst those who will resign; nevertheless it is asserted that there is likely to be a severe contest between Mr Perceval and the Marquis Wellesley who is ambitious to be the Premier, to which Mr Perceval will not consent, particularly as the Prince Regent has bestowed many marks of approbation upon him. By what means such different interests are to be united is not known. If this jealousy actually exists between the present Prime Minister and the Marquis Wellesley, it accounts for the little progress I have made in your Highness's affairs.

I have now the honour to submit for your Highness's consideration another subject: should the crisis at Windsor be decided, or in the month of March next an unlimited Regency be established—it will be necessary that your Highness furnish me with new credentials; indeed many of my friends in this country are of opinion that this should have been done at the commencement of the present year: and I most humbly supplicate your Electoral Highness to reconsider what I stated in my letter of the 4th of August 1807 respecting the title of *Chargé d'Affaires*, for I conceive it to be conducive to your Highness's interest that I resume the character given me in July 1803 of your Electoral Highness's *Resident* at this Court; and I therefore humbly request, if it meet your Highness's approbation, to insert that title in my credentials. (18346–7)

3136 THE DUKE OF CLARENCE TO THE PRINCE REGENT

Bushy House, noon, Friday [*?9 or 16 Aug. 1811*]

My motive for troubling you is in behalf of Colonel Butler who is naturally very anxious to succeed General Le Marchant as Lieutenant-Governor to the Royal Military College.[1] I have been acquainted with him for near six years and can bear the most honourable testimony to his conduct on every occasion during that time. If he had continued in the Royal Artillery he would at present be a Major-General and very near having a battalion: thus situated and being much senior to Sr. Howard Douglas[2] he hopes you will consider him as the fittest person to be the Lieutenant-Governor: more particularly as Sr. Howard Douglas was first brought forward by Colonel Butler and would now only be a Brevet Major if he had continued in the Royal Artillery. Colonel Butler has superintended at the Military College fifteen hundred lads since he has been in his present situation, and trusts that all these circumstances considered you will be gracious enough to let him succeed to the situation of Lieutenant-Governor. I can only add from his great attention to my three sons that I must ever feel very much interested in his welfare. (44980–1)

1. The appointment was gazetted on 20 August 1811. James Butler (*d.* 1836) became a Colonel in 1810, and Lieutenant-General in 1825.

2. Sir Howard Douglas (1776–1861) succeeded his brother as 3rd Baronet on 25 May 1809. Lieutenant, 1794; Lieutenant-Colonel, 1806; Colonel, 1814; Major-General, 1821; Lieutenant-General, 1837; General, 1851. Governor of New Brunswick, 1823–9. C.B., 1814; K.C.B., 1821; G.C.B., 1841. Groom of the Bedchamber to the Duke of Gloucester. M.P. for Liverpool, 1842–7. Commandant of the Senior Department of the Royal Military College, 1804.

See House, Limerick, 10 Aug. 1811

I have to acknowledge the honor of your very kind note communicating the promotion of my son[1] to the rank of Lt.-Colonel, by the appointment of an Inspecting Field Officer in Canada, and I entreat your goodness to lay before the Prince Regent the deep sense of gratitude I feel for this mark of royal protection to my son, whose correct principles & attachment to his profession afford the surest pledge of his not discrediting the royal favor now conferr'd upon him. The only regret he can feel is that of not being able to serve the ensuing campaign upon the Peninsula, for which he had just got his Regt. in order to embark, & quite recover'd from their heavy losses at Corunna, & the Welcheren [*sic*] fever.

The Prince Regent's condescension & goodness in approving my being the Coadjutor to the Archbishop of Dublin, quite overwhelms me, & must ever be remember'd with feelings of pride & gratitude—but I must explain to you that when I had the honor of communicating the Primate's intention on that subject, I had no view to the office myself; on the contrary, I early declined it for various reasons, but principally from a sense of duty to my own Diocese, which must have been neglected had I taken charge of Dublin at so great a distance—for at this moment I have nineteen new Churches built & building in the counties of Limerick & Kerry—where the Protestant religion has hitherto been known only by name, and where I am anxious to establish Churches & resident clergy before it may please Providence to remove me. The Primate had some difficulties about the person to be Coadjutor. It was claimed as a right by the Bishop of Kildare,[2] as senior Bishop of that Province & living in Dublin;—then, I understand, Mr. Pole named the Bishop of Killalla as his friend:—to get rid of the struggle, I suggested the propriety of the Archbishop of Cashel[3] taking upon himself the charge of Dublin during the incapacity of its own Diocesan—to which his Grace has assented, & thereby all difficulties got over.

I take the liberty of troubling you with this little detail of our Church affairs, feeling it right that the Prince Regent shou'd be acquainted with every circumstance in which the interests of the Established Church are concern'd in this part of the United Kingdom. (18379–80)

1. Augustus Warburton.

2. Charles Dalrymple Lindsay (*d.* 1846). Bishop of Killaloe, 1803; of Kildare, 1804–46.

3. Charles Brodrick (*d.* 1822). Bishop of Clonfert, 1795; of Kilmore, 1796; Archbishop of Cashel, 1801–22.

Carlton House, 13 Aug. 1811

I am, my ever dearest Lady B., only this very moment return'd here,[1] & the post is just going out, but I can neither forego the promise I made you nor the pleasure of writing to you again today, although it be ever so few lines. The account Sir Henry Halford brought me just before I left Windsor is, according to his own words, the most unfavourable he has ever had to detail, not so much as to the immediate danger of the moment but as to the mischief he sees again brewing & (according to his perception & view of the state of things) just approaching, together with a more complete disorganization of all power of intellect than he has ever as yet witness'd at any period of this particular attack & malady, or indeed in the case of any other patient; & he also tells me that Rt. Willis views it exactly in the same light as he does, & never was so entirely confirm'd as by the state of today, that it is a completely gone case. All this, my best & ever dearest friend, coupled with the melancholy manner in which we passed yesterday, has, to tell you the truth, worried me very much, as I do not see the prospect clearing in the least, nor the least probability at present of its doing so, & I am sorry to add that it has made me very unwell, & therefore I am glad to be return'd to town, for if I am not better tomorrow morning, I shall send for my old friend Sir Walter Farquhar, & see what he can do to patch me up again, for I really am but in a sorry way just at present, exactly what my cousin Fanny[2] calls *rather poorly.* However, it is nothing of any consequence, but you shall be fairly told the truth, you may depend upon it, in my letter of tomorrow. Pray tell Lord Hertford that it grieves me not to be able to send him even the smallest scrap of news, but I have not found on my return either a letter or box, nor do I beleive that there is a single Minister at this moment in the metropolis, so pray tell him, with my best & kindest remembrances, that he must accept in the present instance out of sheer necessity the will for the deed.

It is a shame to tresspass upon you, my ever dearest Lady B- any longer with so very dull a scrawl as this is, & in the very stupid tone in which my mind is just now. I therefore shall hasten to conclude, by assuring you, that whether absent or present, I am ever [etc.].

P.S. Pray tell me something of dear Ragley, (& which I hope soon to see again) in your next epistle (Egerton MSS. 3262, ff. 77-9).

1. His birthday was celebrated at Windsor in a private manner because of the King's illness.
2. See Nos. 1425 and 1427.

Carlton House, 13 Aug. 1811

About an hour yesterday before the Prince Regent set off from hence to Windsor to pass his birthday in private with the Queen, I had the honor & happiness to receive your Grace's most kind letter of the 9th instant, and the pleasing satisfaction of shewing it to his Royal Highness.

The Prince has commanded me to make his love, affectionate remembrances and grateful acknowledgements to your Grace for the very many distinguish'd proofs you have given him of friendship and disinterested attachment, and to assure you that H.R.Hss. was too long and well acquainted with the innumerable and noble acts of generosity & magnificence which have characterised your Grace's life to feel any new cause for admiration & applause at the princely manner (& so worthy of yourself) in which, by the splendid endowment of so great a seminary at Alnwick, you have exhibited the grandest display of the finest humanity this country had ever yet to boast, and placed his Royal Highness's name on an immortal record of national attachment and esteem. Indeed he commanded me to say that his feelings are quite overpower'd by this peculiar and unrivall'd mark of goodness, & at the same time to assure your Grace that the Life Guards or any other Guards shall never have priority in his favor & estimation to the Royal Regt. of Horse Guards Blue, in augmentation, or anything while he lives, & especially while 'his friend Hugh Duke of Northumberland is their Colonel.'

As to myself, what can I presume humbly to say to your Grace, for your matchless & unbounded generosity to me? Never surely had man the good fortune to possess so munificent a patron & protector as your Grace has been to me. I can only add that my gratitude & devotion to you is interwoven with my life, & can only cease with my existence. The Prince is highly delighted with the Prince Regent of Portugal's attention to what H.R.Hss. conceived to be your Grace's wishes respecting General Silviera, & it has struck him with a little remorse in not having yet sent him his portrait, but he says he will speedily surprise your Grace with it and prevail on you to make his *amende honorable* to the Prince Regent of Portugal. I am just setting off for Cheltenham, from whence I shall have the pleasure to occasionally obtrude a line on your Grace; and I shall return for good at farthest by the 20th of September (Alnwick MSS.).

Bushy House, Tuesday morning [13 Aug. 1811]

I am sure you will do me the justice that I am never troublesome, and believe me if it was not at the request of a lady I would not at this moment apply. You will not be surprized that I could not refuse this lady when I inform you that I write at the desire of Mrs. Jordan and relative to her daughter Mrs. Alsop.[1] Alsop, her husband, is a clever fellow and a very useful servant of the public, having put everything relative to the making and arranging the small arms for the country in the best possible state, but he has outlived his means and is under difficulties. Thus situated he is anxious to go abroad, and the situation of Collector of the Customs being now vacant in the Island of Dominica he would be too happy to go out to that office, and I write these few lines to request you would have the goodness to appoint him to the Collector-ship. (44989)

3141   SAMUEL PEPYS COCKERELL[2] TO MAJOR-GENERAL T. H. TURNER, AND AN ENCLOSURE

Saville Row, 13 Aug. 1811

I beg leave to enclose an extract of a letter which I have just received from my son[3] at Athens containing the accot. of an important discovery in the ancient Temple of Jupiter Panhellinius in the Island of Ægina, which is highly interesting to the Arts, and respectfully to request that you will do me the honour to communicate the substance of it to his Royal Highness the Prince Regent whose commands will be attend[ed] to [*sic*] with all respectful duty.

Knowing the interest you take in everything worthy of notice in antiquity and relating to the Fine Arts, I have by the recommendation of my friend Mr. Wm. Hamilton, to whom the subject is familiar,

1. Frances (or Fanny) Daly (1782–1821), Mrs. Jordan's eldest daughter by the Dublin theatre manager, Richard Daly (*d.* 1813). In circumstances still unknown she changed her name to Bettesworth, and in 1808 she married Thomas Alsop (*d.* 1826), a clerk in the Ordnance Office. 'Alsop', wrote Mrs. Jordan, probably on 14 April 1811, 'has ruined himself and consequently poor *Fanny* by his unpardonable extravagance and I fear it must end in the King's Bench' (*Mrs. Jordan and her Family*, ed. A. Aspinall, p. 192). In November 1812, or thereabouts, he had to resign his situation (ibid., p. 240). In April 1813 Lord Moira took him out to India, but Mrs. Alsop remained in England, the marriage having more or less broken down.

2. The architect (1754–1827).

3. Charles Robert Cockerell (1788–1863), the distinguished architect. He had been travelling in the eastern Mediterranean since May 1810. Hamilton, the Under-Secretary of State, entrusted to him despatches for Constantinople.

taken the liberty of making this communication thro' yourself, as the most direct channel to his Royal Highnesses notice. (18391)

[Enclosure] CHARLES ROBERT COCKERELL TO HIS FATHER [extract]
Athens, 13 May 1811
We passed the channel in the night & reached the Temple after crossing the Island the day after; as it was our intention to examine thoroughly this curious Temple, we pitched the tent you remember under a rock & took possession of a cave which, close by, made a famous dwelling for our troop, servants & janissary.

The better to put our object into execution we set three men to dig & turn over stones that were interesting to our measurements. The second morning we found in the interior of the portico two heads in helmets in high preservation, the noses &c entire, of Parian marble; after these a beautiful leg & foot appeared & not to tire you with the detail of our progress, we found in the two fronts east & west of the Temple 16 figures & 13 heads, legs, arms &c in proportion, in the highest possible preservation. They were not three feet under the surface of the ground; they appear evidently to have fallen from the pediments by an earthquake; in the fall they are broken, but the pieces are found, & now that we have put each in its proper place make almost as many entire figures; you may easily imagine in the progress of this extraordinary discovery we were not a little astonished at our good fortune, and that of the many travellers of all nations who have visited this famous Temple for the last 1000 years we should have been the first with curiosity enough to dig three feet deep.

In the middle of our progress the Primates of the Island, who farm the rights of the Captn. Pasha, came in a body reading a statement made by the islanders in general, begging that we would desist from our operations, for that Heaven knew what harm we might do to the Island, & more particularly to the land immediately surrounding; with so miserable an excuse as this, we soon found that their object was to induce us to give a sum of money. We sent our dragoman with the Primates to the village to agree about the sum which we found it necessary to give. Suspecting some impediment, we had ordered a boat to be ready to convey what we had already found to Athens. The Primates were hardly out of sight when the boat arrived at a port near the Temple & we embarked the marbles, Forster[1] & one of our German friends attending to convey them to Athens, which they prudently did from the Pireus to the town

1. John Foster, the Liverpool architect (?1787–1846), who designed, *inter alia*, Lime Street Station.

90

by night, lest it should make too much noise among the Turks, which we feared exceedingly.

Haller[1] & I remained to carry on the digging which we did vigorously, finding legs & arms each moment. On the return of our friends we compleated the bargain with the Primates for 800 piastres (equal to about £40) for the antiquities we had found & leave to continue the digging.

We did not finish our great work until the 16th day after our arrival, when with our sixteen statues &c we compleated our researches, drawings &c of the Temple of which we have made some important discoveries in the architecture, & a restoration of the hypethral & other circumstances, a sketch of which I shall send to Abany [sic].

So interesting a time I never spent, every hour produced some discovery; it was a continued scene of surprise; we slept in the tent far from the town; purchased our meat of the shepherds, & by a large fire which we made at night roasted it on a wooden spit.

You will say 16 days were enough to be employed there, but it was necessary to make oneself a workman, to rest, & to overlook them lest anything interesting should escape. All heads &c we were obliged to take out of the ground ourselves, lest the workmen should ruin them. Upon the whole, however, we have been very fortunate, & few are broken by carelessness. I write to you now on the 3d day after our arrival, & till now we have been occupied in joining the broken pieces, for which purpose we have taken a large house. We have restored a great portion of them & I assure you the effect of them is magnificent. We have not yet discovered the subject of the groups, the figures are about 5 to 5.6 high in very powerful action, evidently in combat, the costumes are of the most antique kind I have ever seen, the helmets are made to cover the nose & face, as those you have seen in Mr. Hope's book,[2] greaves to protect the skin & large bucklers; there are two in high preservation which draw a bow, the hands pulling the string & arrow are wonderfully beautiful, some are clad in a leathern coat & a costume something resembling the Roman; in general, however, they are without drapery of any kind & the anatomy & contour I assure you are equal to anything I have yet seen. Our council of artists here consider them as not inferior to the remains of the Parthenon, & certainly in the second rank after the Torso, Laocoon & other famous statues; we conduct all our affairs in respect to them with the utmost secresy, for we greatly fear the Turks may either reclaim them or put some difficulties in our way. The few friends we have here & consult, such as they are, are dying with jealousy, literally. One who intended to have farmed Ægina of the Captn. Pacha is almost ill on the occasion.

1. Baron Haller von Hallerstein, architect to the King of Bavaria.

2. Possibly *Costume of the Ancients* (2 vols. London, 1809) by Thomas Hope (?1770–1831), author and virtuoso. He collected marbles and sculptures.

Fauval, the French Consul, hardly recovers the shock, altho an excellent man, he does not suffer his envy to prevail against us; on the contrary he is on all occasions most obliging & has given excellent advice to us. You may easily imagine the finding such a treasure has tried everyone's character most powerfully. He saw that might be the case, and lest it might operate to the prejudice of our beautiful collection, he proposed our signing a contract of honour, that no one should take any measure as to the sale or division of it without the consent of the other three; this we put into execution. We all agree that it is not to be divided, as of itself it forms a large portion for a Museum & is a collection which either a King or a Nobleman should make a point of having for the sake of the Arts of his country.

Our Germans have accordingly written to their Ministers; I have done the same to Mr. Canning,[1] & Fauval who has a general order for the purpose from his Minister will make an offer to us. I had hoped that Lord Sligo[2] would have offered for it, but our Germans, who calculate by the price of marbles at Rome, have named such a monstrous price that it has frightened him. They have talked of from 6 to £8000, altho' I have promised to give my portion for half price, in the desire of their going to England. I have made the same offer to Mr. Canning so much do I feel interested for the British Museum. (18392–5)

3142 THE MARQUESS WELLESLEY TO THE PRINCE REGENT
Foreign Office, 15 Aug. 1811
Lord Wellesley has the honor to acquaint your Royal Highness that in examining the private correspondence between his Majesty & the present Emperor of Russia, he has found that the last letter was written in English, & answered by the Emperor Alexander in the same language, in which it appears that his Imperial Majesty takes particular pleasure.

The letters are inclosed for your Royal Highness's perusal together with a note of reference. Lord Wellesley humbly submits for your Royal

1. Stratford Canning, Lord Stratford de Redcliffe (1786–1880), George Canning's cousin. Précis writer in the Foreign Office, 1807; Second Secretary of the Mission to Copenhagen, October–November 1807, and of the Constantinople Embassy, 1808–9; Secretary of Embassy at Constantinople, 1809–12 and Minister there, 1810–12. Envoy to Switzerland, 1814–19, and to Washington, 1820–3; Special Mission to Petersburg, 1824–5; Ambassador to Turkey, 1826–7. Tory M.P. for Old Sarum, 1828–30; for Stockbridge, 1831–2; for King's Lynn, 1835–42. G.C.B., 1829. Ambassador to Turkey, 1842–58. Peerage, 1852. K.G. 1869.

2. Howe Peter, 2nd Marquess of Sligo (1788–1845) succeeded his father on 2 January 1809. Styled Viscount Westport until 29 December 1800 (when his father became a Marquess) and as Earl of Altamont subsequently until his father's death. Governor of Jamaica, 1833–6.

Highness's gracious approbation the draft of a letter in English to the Emperor of Russia. If your Royal Highness should be pleased to approve this draft, Mr Smith, the Under-Secretary of State, who takes charge of this box, can copy it immediately for signature; & Mr Céa can be dispatched tomorrow night. If your Royal Highness should think it more proper to employ the French language on this occasion, Lord Wellesley will be prepared immediately to obey any commands with which he may be honored for that purpose. Lord Wellesley has put into this box the note which your Royal Highness has already been pleased to approve, in order that reference may be made to it if necessary.

Lord Wellesley wishes M. Céa to leave England previously to the departure of any other agent.

The latest advices from Russia are contained in this box for your Royal Highness's information.[1] (18398)

1. Wellesley had been wondering whether power should be given to Sir James Saumarez or to anyone else to sign preliminaries of peace with Russia, and Perceval had replied to his inquiry, on 9 August: 'I have read your paper intended for Russia, and I have very little to observe upon it, as it meets with my ideas entirely. I enclose, however, on a separate paper as a suggestion for your consideration another mode of turning the passage which introduces the mention of the restrictions on trade—I think it will equally convey your meaning and I prefer it as being less capable of being construed into an implied conditional promise of direct aid to Russia.

'I should see no objection to your giving power to Sir James Saumarez to put an end to the war directly with Russia by signing preliminary Articles of Peace, except that I doubt whether it might not, by betraying too great an eagerness and forwardness on our part, rather tend to defeat our object. But for the purpose of enabling Great Britain to maintain her exertions in that quarter to the extent in which the interests of the Peninsula may require them it would be of essential advantage if the Emperor of Russia would lead the way in emancipating not only his own dominions, but by his example other nations of the Continent from the severe pressure of that system of prohibition & exclusion of British commerce from the ports of the Continent of Europe, which France has imposed with such relentless rigour in defiance of the established principles of the law of nations and to the general distress of trade throughout the world. For altho' Great Britain has made exertions (notwithstanding the effect of these restrictions upon commerce) greater than she ever made in any former contest, yet unquestionably the continuance of these exertions would be rendered more easy, in proportion as that system was relaxed, and at least the extension of them in any other direction as the necessities or occurences of the war might open the opportunity, in the direct aid either of Russia or of any other Power of Europe must fully be considered as impracticable while the effect of that system continues to be felt.

'But upon this point particularly I lament that we have not had a Cabinet, for I think our colleagues would be a little surprised to find such a measure taken without any previous communication with them. And indeed I think you will feel that if it would occasion too much delay now to have a Cabinet upon this paper, yet before it is dispatched (& we could not hope to have one assembled before Monday next) it will be very desirable that the paper should be circulated as soon as possible—for tho' I do not conceive that there is any point in it on which any of our colleagues can differ from us, yet it is not impossible, especially with those who are every week in town, that they might feel hurt at not having so much as the appearance of being consulted upon such important subjects. This last observation applies to the dispatch

SIR JOHN MACPHERSON TO COLONEL MCMAHON

Farm near Tunbridge Wells, 16 Aug. 1811

I have now the pleasure to enclose to you the India document which I mentioned to you in my last note. How creditable is it to your Royal friend & master to have received such a reply from the successor of our first Asiatic ally? Were your friend the Earl of Moira to proceed directly to the Government-General of India he might peruse the enclosed with advantage & I leave it at your disposal. Fifteen years ago our Prince Regent was was [*sic*] master of this subject. If the accounts stated in our newspapers of Lord Minto's determination to return to this country after the reduction of Batavia be true, it is equally true that a day should not be lost about not only the nomination but departure of his successor. Incalculable might be the confusions that would follow in India on Sir George Barlow's consequent succession to the Government General. The expedition to Batavia may lead to Walcheren maladies. The Malays are a most sanguinary people. Should an accident happen to Sir Samuel Achmooty[1] on that expedition & that Lord Minto left India—the successor in regular rotation to Sir George at Madras would prove most offensive to the army.

The Earl of Moira by manners & obliging sincerity as well as dignity of conduct conciliated all the convulsions of Scotland, when he commanded there. Never was conciliation more seasonable! Very few of our best informed statesmen of that period knew the extremeties to which Jacobinical intrigues were approaching at that moment. The key to this real knowledge was obtained from the enemy in September 1801. It came to the cottage at which I now reside, and from Mr. Otto. I went to town, saw him & Mr. Addington—their hands were united, & the Prince Regent then at Brighton had the first intimation of that event, as he well remembers. The preliminaries were immediately signed. That act saved London from convulsion. It took place without special previous approbation from either our own Sovereign or the ruler of France. 'Je regarde ma responsabilité *morale* infinement au dessus ma responsabilité *politique*' were the words of Mr Otto's letter on the occasion. It was his Audience from the Prince in the subsequent month of March that closed the *Peace of Amiens*. Indeed it was the countenance of his Royal Highness that

respecting the mediation with the S. Amn. colonies of Spain & the answer to Mr. Smith. I think we should be able to have a pretty full Cabinet on Wednesday next about 2 o'clock—if you would summon it for that day, & you might then read to us your instructions to Mr. Wellesley on the first point, and also your letter to Mr. Smith' (Perceval MSS.).

1. Sir Samuel Auchmuty (1756–1822). Joined the Army, 1775; Lieutenant, 1778; Captain, 1788; Lieutenant-Colonel, 1795; Colonel, 1800; Knighted, 4 May 1803; K.B., 22 February 1812; G.C.B., January 1815. Major-General, 1808; Lieutenant-General, 1813. Commander-in-Chief at Madras, 1810–13.

effected the whole. It is upon a corresponding system that it is, I trust, reserved to him to settle in time the general peace of Europe. He has not been christened *Augustus* as well as George, in vain. But my reason for touching upon this subject *now*, is that I am apprehensive *unless his Royal Highness has received* SECRET & VERY PARTICULAR CONCILIATORY PROPOSITIONS *from Napoleon*, our enemy has taken up the old directorial system, and the state of Ireland with the possession of Flushing &c &c &c will confirm him in it. *Pensez y* —!

I am hopeful America will be managed and I wish I could hear that the Earl of Fingal,[1] of whom I have the best accounts, instead of having difficulties with his Lord Lieutenant were to have a private invitation to Carlton House. The easterly storms of *September* have been always in the contemplation of the French Government.

Pardon these observations from a retired farmer. (18404–5)

3144   THE EARL OF LIVERPOOL TO [?] MAJOR–GENERAL T. H. TURNER[2]
Fife House, 17 Aug. 1811
Will you have the goodness to inform his Royal Highness the Prince Regent that the Algerine Ambassador will attend at Carlton House[3] on Monday to have his Audience on taking leave, either before or after the Council, as may be most convenient to his Royal Highness, and that Lt.-Genl. Maitland will likewise attend on the same day upon his return from the Government of Ceylon. (18410)

3145   LETTERS FROM WILLIAM RICHARD HAMILTON TO MAJOR–GENERAL T. H. TURNER
Foreign Office, 17 Aug. 1811
I had the pleasure of receiving your private letter of yesterday's date respecting the marbles at Ægina, and have this morning seen Mr Cockerell on the subject. In the course of a day or two, that is by Monday at farthest, I shall be able to communicate to you what appears upon

1. Arthur James, 8th Earl of Fingall [I.] (1759–1836). Styled Lord Killeen until he succeeded his father on 21 August 1793. One of the Leaders of the Irish Catholics in their agitation for relief from political disabilities. K.P., 1821. Created Baron Fingall [U.K.], 20 June 1831.

2. The letter cannot have been sent to McMahon, who was then in Cheltenham.

3. According to *The Times* (17 August) the Prince Regent, on his arrival in town from Windsor, took possession of York House, St. James's, where he was to reside whilst extensive repairs to Carlton House were being carried out.

consideration to be the most eligible way of executing the commands of his Royal Highness the Prince Regent. (18411)

Foreign Office, 17 Aug. 1811
Since I acknowledged your letter this morning, I have received the enclosed from Mr. Cockerell, whose proposition I have made known to Lord Wellesley, and have received his orders to communicate with the Admiralty for a ship of war to be sent to Athens as soon as is compatible with the Service. This will be acted on immediately if it meets with his Royal Highness' approbation.

P.S. I will thank you to return me Mr. Cockerell's letter. (18412)

[Enclosure] SAMUEL PEPYS COCKERELL TO W. R. HAMILTON [extract]
17 Aug. 1811
On the presumption that no specific terms have been mentioned, I beg to suggest the following to your consideration as giving every advantage to the British Government, without any actual expence, & which I have no doubt but my son & those concerned with him will readily acceed to, namely, that with the prompt aid of this Government & the assistance of any armed ship at present in the Mediterranean, of sufficient force to repel the attack of a privateer, the marble may be transported to England on acct. of Government & that when here they be taken on the public acct. at the lowest estimated value stated in my son's letter viz. six thousand pounds, & that if upon their arrival & inspection here the Govt. should be disinclined to take them at that sum, they be delivered over to the present proprietors, freight & duty free, with liberty to export them. (18413)

3146   THE EARL OF LEITRIM TO COLONEL MCMAHON
Killadoon,[1] *19 Aug. [1811]*
As I think it my duty to repeat what I have already communicated through Lord Charlemont, the gratitude I feel to the Prince Regent for the very gracious manner in which his Royal Highness has interested himself in the success of my election, I have the honor to request that

1. His seat in Co. Kildare.

you will express to his Royal Highness how sensible I am of this most flattering instance of his condescension. Yesterday was the last day for receiving writs, when the contest terminated in favor of Lord Gosford by a majority of twelve votes. Gratified however, as I am by the distinguished proof which I have received of the Prince Regent's good opinion, I have none of the feelings which might be supposed to arise from disappointment. His Royal Highness by his support has conferred an honor upon me of which no Minister can deprive me, & I hope his Royal Highness will do me the justice to believe that I shall ever remember it with pride & gratitude.

I trust it is unnecessary for me to add any assurance of the most devoted attachment to his Royal Highness.[1]

1. See No. 3085. Lord Holland had written to Grey, earlier in the month: 'The Prince's understanding with Perceval about Lord L. seems to be in an odd state. Lord Gosford is ten ahead. Not above five or six more Peers will vote for Lord L. unless pressed by the Prince, who says no more upon it, and the result of all this is that Goodwin is in despair and often quotes his parting words to you that he would be damned if he did not turn out a rogue at last' (Howick MSS.).

Leitrim's situation with regard to a Representative Peerage is referred to in the Lord Lieutenant's letter to Ryder, 12 June 1811: 'As to the future Representative Peer after Lord Gosford it is a most difficult case. I enclose a list of these who at different times have been candidates and ask'd for the support of Govt. Lord Leitrim and Lord Barrymore are candidates but do not ask for our support. Lord Dunally certainly is in opposition though he states himself as unconnected with any party. I have made observations on each candidate in the list I enclose.

It seems to me that the contest lays between the Earls of Farnham, Mayo & Clonmell and Lord Bantry. Lord Farnham claims the Duke of Portland's promise. He is a good sort of man but certainly would not add much lustre to the House. He has at times been confined and and at other times is certainly a very weak man: Lord Mayo says he is the only Peer who supported the Union not a Representative.

If this be the case it gives him a claim certainly. Lord Clonmell supports us so steadily that we must wish to do him a kindness, but he certainly has sold two houses he had in Ireland. It is true he has bought land in Tipperary but he seems to have done that on speculation and evidently does not mean to reside, for I cannot call it residence to be a few days every year at an hotel in Dublin and a few weeks at an agent's house.

Lord Bantry has a very considerable property in the south and has succeeded to a large share of Lord Longueville's estate. He is a great friend of Lord Shannon's who is anxious for his becoming a Representative Peer' (Richmond MSS.).

The Duke enclosed the following list of candidates:

Earl of Aldborough, Not respectable

Lord Ashtown, Respectable but no interest

Viscount Bantry, Respectable, great property and encreased by the death of Lord Longueville

Lord Blaney, Old family and considerable influence in Monaghan

Earl of Clonmell, Very respectable good property, strenuous supporter but not resident

Lord Dufferin, Not to be satisfyd; do what you please for him

Lord Dunally, Respectable, led by the Ponsonbys

Lord Dunsany, Old family, not respectable

I enclose a list of the Peers who voted both for Lord Gosford & myself, which perhaps his Royal Highness may like to look over. (18425–6)

3147   THE EARL OF MOIRA TO THE PRINCE REGENT
Donington, 19 Aug. 1811

Irregular as the enclosed Address is, there is no reason (as it is not to be presented formally) why I should withhold from your Royal Highness the profession of attachment & gratitude from any portion of the community, however humble.

Those anxious feelings for the prosperity and honor of your Royal Highness which will never cease while I have life, impel me to solicit earnestly that you will condescend to read the remarks on the late steps against the Catholics, contained in the newspaper I presume to send. There is no merit in the stile; and the publication is ill-judged if not mischievously intended. But it is an accurate exposition of what is thought by an infinite majority of the people of Ireland as far as I can gather from my letters: and the point is much too serious not to claim your Royal Highness's consideration. If the discontent of Ireland be unavoidable, it is to be met firmly, like any other calamity which foresight cannot parry. If it be capable of prevention, it never can be for the interest of your Royal Highness to let an evil pregnant with such formidable consequences be gratuitously entailed.

I refer myself, Sir, to your own observation whether I have not, in the confidential intercourse to which you have deigned to admit me, most strictly abstained from any unfavorable remarks upon the measures of your Ministers. I have thought such censure secretly offered to your ear would be not only unconstitutional but unworthy. When I can bring myself to address your Royal Highness upon a public topic, in deviation from a principle so strongly defined, my judgment may be in error, but my heart must be conscious of an imperious duty.

Without exactly analyzing the policy, for I am sure they would then reject it, Ministers may indistinctly perceive a benefit for themselves in involving your Royal Highness in what they think only a petty contest with the great body of the Irish people. The opposition of sentiment between your Royal Highness and the Ministers respecting the mode in which Ireland should be treated formed the great obstacle to your

Earl of Farnham, Good property & interest, well meaning but very weak
Lord Frankfort, Rich in interest
Earl of Mayo, Respectable, no interest
Lord Muskerry, Not respectable
Lord Tara, Respectable, no interest.

98

Edward, Duke of Kent
by Sir William Beechey, 1818

Arthur Wellesley, 1st Duke of
Wellington

by Goya, 1812

Part of a letter dated 23 November 1811
from the Prince Regent to the Marchioness of Hertford

retaining them, when you should have to act professedly according to your own wish, in your counsels. This obstacle they might imagine they should remove if they could implicate you in differences with the Catholics on any collateral ground. Unfortunately, an incorrect procedure is never sure to stop where those who hazard it may wish. The zeal, or the intemperance or the designs of associates will always be likely to improve upon the measure and give it a quality it was not intended to possess. The petulant insults in which the dependants of Administration indulge themselves towards the Catholics can do no good, and not only may but must do excessive harm. Those sneers do not apply to a few insignificant individuals but to a vast connected body conscious of numerical strength and equally sensible of the advantage which the difficulties of the Empire give to them at this juncture. It is easy for clever men with profligate views to sharpen and direct the indignation of a multitude so wantonly provoked. One must be mentally blind if one is not aware that separatists, neither few in number or of inferior class, are actively at work in propagating their doctrine; and no expatiation is requisite to show what would be the amount of the inconvenience were the mass of the Catholics to embrace that disposition thro' disgust and resentment. I do firmly believe that the greatest bar which the separatists have experienced in inculcating notions very seducing for the common people has been the confidence entertained throughout Ireland that under your Government there could not be a continuance of oppression. This opinion is too inestimable to be risked lightly. A rebellion, unconnected with any other circumstances, must be regarded as one of the greatest calamities to the Empire. But we know it could not be unconnected; we know that Bonaparte would not let slip the moment of our embarrassment; and, with all our just reliance on ourselves, there is no measuring the degree of wound which his sagacity and enterprize might in such a case inflict. He is watching for this juncture, which I doubt not he has secretly been endeavouring to create. (18419–22)

3148　LETTERS FROM SPENCER PERCEVAL TO THE PRINCE REGENT

Downg. St., 20 Aug. 1811

Mr Perceval presents his humble duty to your Royal Highness and acquaints your Royal Highness that Lord Grosvenor[1] has applied to be permitted to turn the King's Road which leads from the bottom of Grosvenor Place to Westbourn Bridge at Chelsea. The line in which he

1. Robert, 2nd Earl Grosvenor (1767–1845) succeeded his father, 5 August 1802. See No. 197.

proposes to turn it is represented by Mr Wyatt to whom the application has been made as more convenient to the public, as well as advantageous to his Lordship, and if your Royal Highness sees no objection to it, Mr Perceval would humbly venture to recommend to your Royal Highness that the application may be complied with. (18428)

Downg. St., 20 Aug. 1811

Mr Perceval presents his humble duty to your Royal Highness and acquaints you Royal Highness that he has seen Col. Drinkwater[1] upon the subject of the arrangement which Mr Perceval submitted to your Royal Highness respecting the office of Commissary in Chief and Comptroller of Army accounts—and Mr Perceval stated to Col. Drinkwater the arrangement which he had submitted to your Royal Highness yesterday, namely, that instead of appointing Col. Drinkwater to the office of Commissary in Chief, Mr Herries, one of the present Comptrollers of Army Accounts, should be appointed to succeed Col. Gordon, and that Col. Drinkwater, whose late employment as a Commissioner of Military Enquiry seemed very particularly to qualify him for the situation of a Comptroller of Army accounts, should succeed Mr Herries as Comptroller. Col. Drinkwater, as might naturally be expected, did not withold from Mr Perceval the expression of his disappointment as he had for the last two months been looking with expectation to the appointment of Commissary in Chief, which is an office of more value, and which from understanding from your Royal Highness that you would recommend him to Mr Perceval in the most favorable manner for that situation, he had entertained a confident belief would have been granted to him. Mr. Perceval fully stated to Col. Drinkwater that your Royal Highness had been pleased in the most gracious manner to mention Col. Drinkwater to him for that situation, but that Mr Perceval had stated to your Royal Highness how peculiarly that situation was connected with the Treasury, and how particularly he felt it of importance to the public service that he should if he could present to it a person from the experience of whose former services Mr Perceval could entertain the most confident opinion of his complete fitness for the situation, and in whom also Mr Perceval had such perfect confidence—that at the same time Mr Perceval was very far from having any disrespect for Col. Drinkwater, which indeed he conceived himself to prove by recommending him to a very important situation as Comptroller of Army Accounts. Col. Drinkwater admitted that the office of Comptroller was a very highly honorable and important office, expressed himself thankful for being considered fit to fill it, and

1. Lieutenant-Colonel John Drinkwater. Major, 1794; Lieutenant-Colonel, 1795.

altho he could not forbear feeling & expressing the disappointment which Mr Perceval has mentioned before, yet he certainly could not but feel that his late employment as a Commissioner had brought him acquainted and familiar with much of the business connected with the Comptroller's Office, that he could not desire to resist Mr Perceval's wishes in this arrangement, and that he would be ready to acquiesce in it if your Royal Highness should approve of that arrangement.

Col. Drinkwater expressed his intention of waiting upon your Royal Highness himself. Mr Perceval humbly hopes your Royal Highness will permit him to acquaint Mr Herries that he is to have this appointment, as it will be extremely desireable that he should have the earliest notice of it, as his coming over from Ireland to make himself acquainted with the detail of the office as carried on under Col. Gordon, before Col. Gordon quits it, will be very useful to him.[1] (18430–2)

3149 LETTERS FROM HENRY FRANCIS GREVILLE TO GENERAL T. H. TURNER, AND AN ENCLOSURE

No. 2, Little Argyle Street, Friday [*? 23 Aug. 1811*]

By the inclosure you will see a mistake has occurred of a most distressing nature to me. I am of course in the dark as to the proceeding adopted by Col. MacMahon—there can however be no indiscretion in communicating to you confidentially the circumstances that induced my direct application to the P.R.

1. Drinkwater's appointment as Comptroller of Army Accounts was gazetted on 21 October. Herries' appointment as Commissary in Chief, *vice* Col. J. W. Gordon, was gazetted on 1 October. Had Richard Wharton shown the least willingness to move to another office, Herries would probably have succeeded him as Secretary of the Treasury, the office, Arbuthnot told him, for which above all others he was 'exactly suited'. Arbuthnot wrote to Herries on 6 August: 'I am delighted however, to be able to tell you that Perceval thinks of you in the manner which you would like best, & it was but the other day that he gave me a proof of his desire not to leave you in your present situation. It has been settled that Gordon should go to the Horse Guards the 1st day of October, & Col. Drinkwater, having obtained knowledge of his [destination], wrote to me to propose himself for the Commissariat. When Perceval saw Col. D.'s letter, he said to me, "I think Herries would do admirably at the Commissariat, & perhaps Col. Drinkwater might be made a Comptroller of Army Accounts." Nothing has since passed upon this subject, but when Perceval spoke to me upon it, his only doubt seemed to be whether you could get from Ireland in time to be initiated into the business before Col. Gordon had quite left the Office. I said what I think, that you would require very little initiation, versed as you long have been in business of all descriptions.

'Pray let me know what you think of the Commissariat, & what your wishes are, as my language shall be guided accordingly; but don't let what I have written to you transpire' (Herries MSS.).

101

Some time ago I transmitted to my old & most respected friend Col. M. a distinct narrative of my peculiar case & I solicited him to use his influence for my appointment to some situation whereby I could maintain myself & family since, as it has been judged necessary to withdraw altogether a Crown Licence, I remained completely & entirely ruined.

The Col. replied in a most feeling & friendly manner & *advised me as from myself* to address a few lines to his R. H. stating the nature of my grievances & the mode of amelioration, with an assurance that whatever means he had of furthering my suit he would afford me. I in consequence transmitted the letter to the Prince under a flying seal, begging him to make any alterations he might think proper. As Col. MacMahon is at Bath[1] it is useless to trouble him. I therefore trespass upon you with the above explanation & will thank you for a line in answer. (18442–3)

[Enclosure] H. F. GREVILLE'S MEMORIAL TO THE PRINCE REGENT

15 Clifford Street, 22 Aug. 1811

Sheweth

That your memorialist, having seen in the public prints that Mr. Taylor, Proprietor of the King's Theatre, had received an intimation from Col. McMahon that your Royal Highness had recognised your guarantee of protection to the King's Theatre and would accordingly protect it, most humbly craves permission to know if this intimation means that your Royal Highness disapproves of your memorialist's making use of a Licence, granted to him for Italian Burlettas, to be followed by Ballets, and to be fixed at the Pantheon; because if so it becomes as much his duty as it has ever been his endeavour to take no steps not perfectly in conformity with your Royal Highness's wishes.

AND your memorialist is certain that if a thought could be entertained by either the committee or the subscribers that to establish a Theatre in the Pantheon was contrary to your Royal Highness's pleasure, they would in no manner countenance such a measure, and it is a justice due to them all that he should so state it: but he most humbly hopes he may be honored with your Royal Highness's sentiments without delay, on account of the vast expence he has incurred and is incurring.

And your memorialist shall ever pray. (18439)

1. On 13 August he said he was setting off for Cheltenham (No. 3139).

FROM H. F. GREVILLE

[*Undated*]

A statement having this day appeared in the papers *by authority* announcing an Italian Opera at the Pantheon under the management of noblemen, I think it right to mention *to you* that not only do I know nothing of such arrangement but that I have not even applied for *any licence* & I have reason to believe the statement is put in without any sanction of the noblemen who did patronize that Theatre & who are trustees for the creditors.

Should therefore any remark to the predjudice of my interests be made *in any quarter* where you may happen to be present I take the liberty of entreating you to state my ignorance of the intelligence thus apparently *officially* announced. (18444–5)

FROM H. F. GREVILLE

2, L. Argyle Street [*undated*]

I return you many thanks for your very obliging communication—but I am so dreadfully ill from excess of spasm & cramp that I am unable to come to you without great difficulty, tho I could do it if you would wish to see me.

I never for a moment believed but that Col. McMahon would do all he could to serve me—never did human being stand more in need of a patron than I do at this moment & indeed my conduct *if known* renders me deserving one.

If to Col. McMahon's kind offices you will unite yours you will confer a lasting obligation on [etc.]. (18446)

3150   THE MARQUESS WELLESLEY TO THE PRINCE REGENT

Ramsgate, 23 Aug. 1811

Lord Wellesley has the honor to submit to your Royal Highness a dispatch just now received from Mr Henry Wellesley at Cadiz containing a pretended letter from Ferdinand the 7th to his Majesty. An extract of a private letter from Mr Vaughan[1] is added which tends to confirm Mr Wellesley's suspicions of the letter from the King of Spain.

1. Sir Charles Richard Vaughan (1774–1849), brother of Sir Henry Halford (formerly Vaughan). Private Secretary to the Foreign Secretary, Lord Bathurst, 1809; Secretary of Legation (later of Embassy) in Spain, 1810–20, and Minister there *ad int.*, 1815–16. Secretary of Embassy in Paris, 1820; Minister to Switzerland, 1823–5. Minister to U.S.A., 1825–35. Knighted, 4 February 1833; G.C.H., 1833.

103

The Duke of Infantado is arrived at Portsmouth on board the Comus frigate. Lord Wellesley left in town the necessary orders for his Excellency's reception at Portsmouth, & also directed Mr Richard Wellesley, who is intimately acquainted with the Duke, to proceed to meet his Excellency at Portsmouth, & to attend his disembarkation & his journey to London.

As soon as Lord Wellesley shall know that the Duke has left Portsmouth he proposes to return to town in order to see his Excellency, who will probably be able immediately to ascertain the authenticity or forgery of the supposed letter from the Catholic King.

Lord Wellesley submits for your Royal Highness's notice a memorandum of dispatches received from Mr Wellesley at Cadiz by this conveyance. The dispatches are at the Office if your Royal Highness should be pleased to direct the Under-Secretaries of State to send them to your Royal Highness.

Lord Wellesley humbly requests that your Royal Highness will be pleased to honor him with the necessary commands respecting the time, place and manner of receiving the Duke of Infantado for the presentation of his Excellency's Credentials.

Lord Wellesley takes the liberty of acquainting your Royal Highness that he has dispatched by express a private letter to the Duke of Infantado. (18449–50)

3151   LIEUTENANT-COLONEL BLOOMFIELD TO THE MARQUESS WELLESLEY

Oatlands,[1] *24 Aug. 1811*

Lt. Colonel Bloomfield, in immediate attendance in the absence of Colonel McMahon & M. Genl. Turner, who is ordered to be in waiting in London, is commanded by the Prince Regent to acknowledge the receipt of Lord Wellesley's dispatch of the 23rd inst. & to request that his Lordship will do everything that is right & proper in respect & attention to the Duke of Infantado. Lt. Colonel Bloomfield is further commanded by the Prince Regent to acquaint Lord Wellesley that it will not be in his Royal Highness's power to receive the Duke of Infantado for the presentation of his Excellency's credentials sooner than Tuesday or Wednesday in the first week of September. (18454)

1. The Prince Regent had just arrived at Oatlands from Bognor.

3152   MRS. MARGARET SCOTT TO THE PRINCE REGENT

67 Upper Berkeley Street, 25 Aug. [1811]

Most gracious Prince, your nurse most humbly prays that your Royal Highness will condescend to peruse this paper.

One morning soon after I weaned your Royal Highness, when I carried my Prince down to the Queen's appartment, her Majesty being alone, said to me, 'Mrs Scott, what do you mean to do now the Prince of Wales is weaned?' I answered 'What your Majesty pleases.' The Queen then said 'the King and myself wish you to continue with the Prince.' I said, 'it is a great happiness to me to know the Royal pleasure but I am a little distress'd with regard to my family. I find they do not go on so well as I could wish at the great distance they are from me; it would be a comfort to bring them nearer to me, but it is difficult to accomplish my wish with the expence attending it.' At that moment the King came into the room. Her Majesty most graciously told the King what I had been saying. His Majesty said it was just and proper, and going out of the room returned immediatly and gave me a fifty pound note, saying, that was the first quarter, and that he hoped I would place my family to my satisfaction. This donation from the King of two hundred pounds a year was first paid me by Madam Schulenberg, afterwards by Mr. Mathias,[1] and lately by Mr. Rowland.[2] Since his Majesty the King's present illness I have ceased to receive it; there were two quarters due at Midsummer last.

I hope your Royal Highness will pardon the liberty I take in presenting this but the encreased dearness of the times has reduced my income very much in value.

I continue to offer my constant prayers for your Royal Highness's health and happiness. (18456-7)

3153   ROBERT STERNE TIGHE TO COLONEL MCMAHON, AND AN ENCLOSURE

Cheltenham, Monday the 26 [Aug. 1811][3]

I have the honour of enclosing a paper of observations on some points connected with the present unsatisfactory state of Ireland—in presuming to submit them to the consideration of his Royal Highness the Prince Regent—I shall rely on your goodness to secure me from any suspicion of being influenced by any motive that could in the slightest degree be

1. Thomas James Mathias (?1754-1835), satirist and Italian scholar. Clerk to the Queen's Treasurer, the Earl of Ailesbury. Later, he was Vice-Treasurer.

2. Hugh Rowland, Clerk to the Earl of Effingham, the Queen's Secretary and Comptroller.

3. The letter is endorsed, evidently wrongly, 26 September 1811.

offensive to his Royal Highness, or inconsistent with that high respect so justly his due. In other respects I have only to add that as my opinions are totally uninfluenced by any bias of party or personal hostility or partiality I can have no desire to withhold any fact or opinion which I may have stated from those who may appear to be affected by them if it should be thought desirable to ascertain the correctness of the facts or of the inferences I have drawn from them. (1860I)

[Enclosure]
Cheltenham, 24 Aug.
The present state of Ireland appears to me to be such as to excite the apprehension of all who are interested in its welfare and to call for the united efforts of every loyal subject to guard against the danger. The first necessary step is a correct knowledge of the sources of that danger, that knowledge must be founded on information of the state of the country and of all circumstances likely to operate upon its inhabitants. With every sentiment of respectful duty towards his Royal Highness the Prince Regent I presume to offer such observations as have occurred to me, well aware that his Royal Highness's judgment will assign to them their proper value & trusting to the interest his Royal Highness is known to take in the prosperity of Ireland as well as to his Royal Highness's acknowledged condescension & goodness to pardon whatever may appear to proceed from an honest zeal for the interests of my Sovereign & my country.

His Royal Highness is too conversant with the history & state of Ireland to render it necessary to dwell upon the assertion that the internal prosperity & comfort of its inhabitants, its advantages as a member of the British Empire and its security against a foreign enemy are all most intimately connected with the religious divisions of its inhabitants and liable to be materially affected by the policy & conduct of its Government as applicable to those divisions, but I feel it my duty as a Protestant & faithful subject of that Empire over which his Royal Highness is one day to reign and which to the satisfaction of a people in that point unanimous, is now entrusted to his care in the name & on the behalf of his Royal father—humbly to state my conviction that there can be no safety for Ireland in the system which has been lately pursued in that country—a reverse of that system can alone secure its peace & happiness. It would be presumption in me to intrude upon his Royal Highness those arguments in favour of the wishes of my Roman Catholic countrymen which have been so often & so ably stated and of the force or weakness of which his Royal Highness is so competent a judge to the decisions of the Legislature it is my duty to bow with submission even whilst I feel that everything dear to me & to my children as Protestant inhabitants of Ireland may be affected by those decisions, but whilst I feel that it must be the anxious desire of his Royal Highness to render his Government a source of comfort & consolation to those who have failed in their applications to Parliament for an object so just & so honorable as a full participation of all the rights & privileges of the Constitution they live under, I feel it my duty to state explicitly & with feelings of deep regret that the conduct & principles of his Royal Highness's servants in Ireland have produced an effect the very opposite of his Royal Highness's benignant wishes. To all who know Ireland & the temper of its people it is manifest that the manners which grow out of the laws affecting the Catholics have been more grievous, more productive of irritation & of mischief than the laws themselves or than any refusal to repeal them. His Royal Highness's present servants in Ireland have not by their Administration tended to soften those refusals to those who have experienced them or to correct those manners which must ever result more or less from the triumphs of party where party principles are allowed to prevail. It is said & with some truth that the mass of the Catholics of Ireland feel little interested in their applications to Parliament, but they are deeply & feelingly interested in the conduct & principles of their local Government as applied to local objects, & they are too easily made to believe that the opposition to the great objects of their Petition is intended to & made to influence their pursuits in a more confined sphere. They can too easily be made to believe that they are objects of mistrust & suspicion to a Government uniformly hostile to their Petitions, & they are as likely to suspect that such a Government will be adverse to many of their pursuits as individuals. A wise, a strong & a humane Government would feel that all this was natural & would endeavour to counteract this natural effect by marks of favour & of a prudent confidence. I am sorry to say that the present Government of Ireland has not acted upon this principle, & the result has been encreased & encreasing irritation of the publick mind, alienation on the part of the Catholic & an universal & gloomy apprehension among all thinking & disinterested men of renewed animosity between Catholic & Protestant. I will venture to state, not reports of which numbers have reached me & on good authority but a few facts within my own knowledge which will I think shew that the present Administration in Ireland has uniformly acted under the influence of suspicions & of prejudices which would in their progress very naturally lead to the present lamentable crisis of affairs in that country.

And here I must beg to be allowed to disclaim every feeling or opinion disrespectful to the Lord Lieutenant or to the Lord Chancellor. I revere & I love their characters whilst I lament that they have not been able to guard themselves against the influence of those prejudices & suspicions which it has been the object & the interest of others to instil into them or to secure themselves from the ill effects of information founded upon or derived from those prejudices or from private interests & passions rendering those prejudices subservient to their purposes. The defective system of County Government in Ireland necessarily exposes the Ld. Lt. & the Lord Chancellor to many serious inconveniencies. In England the Lords Lts. of counties form a proper & a safe channell of communication between the seat of Government & the counties. In Ireland the old spirit of jobbing deprived Government of that advantage. Every man of fortune in a county wished to be a Governor, and the office, to oblige them, was split into so many parts as totally to do away any responsibility—so that in point of fact there was no responsible authority in the different counties from which could proceed the recommendations of persons to fill the office of magistrate. The consequence has been that sometimes one representative or one Governor recommended men who were afterwards displaced at the solicitation of the other member or of another Governor—sometimes a number of R. Catholics have been placed on the Commission; at others they have been removed. The mischievous effects of such a system upon the magistracy of Ireland have been manifest & therefore I am convinced Lord Manners has felt & wished to remedy it. His Lordship has been at times deceived or given way in cases bearing most unhappily upon the feelings excited by the Catholic question. The following instance is within my knowledge. Two magistrates, one a Protestant, the other a R. Catholic quarelled; the former publickly asserted that he would have the latter removed & accordingly he was removed without any charge being assigned & with circumstances which attached to his case the appearance of having been sacrificed on account of his religion so far as to call forth a remonstrance from some of the first Roman Catholics & some Protestants of the neighbourhood with a Petition to the Ld. Chancellor that he would be pleased to restore his Commission or assign the grounds on which he had been removed. The Ld Chancellor thought proper to refuse this request & in a short time & in the progress of the quarrell between the two gentlemen the Protestant magistrate was prosecuted for illegality—for gross & malicious oppression in the execution of his office. I was one of the Special Jury consisting of some of the principal gentlemen of the county that tried the cause—in which the Protestant magistrate was found guilty & sentenced to pay £200 damages to the gentleman, the son of the Catholic magistrate who had been imprisoned by him. On the trial some of the witnesses deposed upon oath that it was beleived & publickly talked of in the country that the Catholic magistrate had been removed from the Commission of the Peace at the solicitation of a gentleman, a brother officer & personal friend of the Duke of Richmond made at the request of the Protestant magistrate to whom I have alluded. I am fully convinced that the Ld. Chancellor was utterly incapable of being influenced by any motives such as were supposed to have operated, but the effect of the step into which he was led could not fail to be a beleif of a prejudice in favour of a party, and this could not fail to be greatly aggravated when it appeared that the Protestant magistrate, notwithstanding his conviction, was allowed to remain in commission & the Roman Catholic still unrestored, though that conviction of his opponent might naturally have excited some doubts of the correctness of the charge against him on which he had been removed—& I cannot place in a stronger or juster point of view the lamentable system upon which the magistracy of Ireland has been governed or is supposed to be governed than by the statement of what followed in this case. It became a matter of open & notorious negotiation between the two parties when the friends of the convicted Protestant magistrate undertook to have the other restored upon condition that the latter should stop a further prosecution which had been commenced on account of another instance of misconduct—& the Roman Catholic magistrate felt so certain of the influence of his opponent to obtain his restoration to the commission that he acceded to the terms & put an end to the prosecution—but I beleive was not restored. His Royal Highness will feel the disgrace that must attach to Government by such transactions—let the source of them be what they may—& it must be evident that in a country where they are considered as likely to occur, strict impartiality and a total abstinence from party principles in the Government becomes doubly essential. In fact, if a party spirit be allowed to prevail or to appear in the conduct of Government no independent gentleman who can have no motive but a sense of duty for taking upon him the office of a Justice of the Peace will risk his reputation upon any chance or prospect of his being removed from the office by the influence or private information of those who may be adverse to him.

I shall now state another instance in which it appears to me that the present Government of Ireland evinced a very unfortunate proneness to suspicion & in which it was misled by that vicious policy of the Old Irish school which endeavoured to draw everything & everybody within the vortex of the Castle & which has always had the effect of bringing the magistrates of the country into a constant reference to the Castle in all cases connected with their duty—thereby throwing upon the Govt. that responsibility which the magistrates ought to take upon themselves & too often exposing it to the odium of acting wrong upon the most groundless information. Upon such information about three years ago the Lord Lieutenant was led to beleive that a depot of arms was concealed in the house of a R. Catholic inhabitant of the town of Athboy. Trusting to this information, with a precipitation which strongly marked a predisposition to suspicion, a detachment of troops was ordered from Kells & another from Navan—and a Staff Officer sent from Dublin to conduct the expedition. The town was surrounded to the great consternation of its inhabitants—but the most vigilant search could discover no arms, & upon a too late communication with those gentlemen of the neighbourhood who could have given a correct opinion, it appeared that the person suspected was in fact the person of all others whose former conduct had least deserved suspicion.

On a more recent occasion in which I was in part concerned I humbly conceive the Irish Government to have displayed & acted upon the same feelings of mistrust & adverse disposition, & the same imprudent & precipitate reliance on private information, received with an eagerness which may very fairly be attributed to that mistrust & adverse disposition towards a large portion of those who are under their Government. When the Union between the two countries appeared to be compleated and the Government in Ireland encreasing in popularity I had presumed to take the liberty in some communications with Ld. Hardwicke to give it as my opinion that that popularity would be still further augmented—the disposition of the people still further improved & additional means of security as well against the foreign enemy as against internal disturbance, acquired—if gentlemen of fortune throughout the country were encouraged to mark a prudent confidence in their Roman Catholic neighbours by the formation of supplementary corps of yeomanry selected from a knowledge of the general characters of the individuals and without distinction of religion. Lord Hardwicke fully concurred in these sentiments, & in their spirit I formed and clothed at my own expence a small corps consisting of infantry & cavalry composed with one or two exceptions entirely of Roman Catholics. The permanent sergeant & all the non-commissioned officers were of this persuasion & I can only say that I should have had no hesitation of entrusting the safety of everything dear to me to their good conduct, or to have pledged myself with their assistance to have maintained the peace of the district under any circumstance of mere internal disturbance. In the month of November last, being detained in England by my state of health, I was informed by a letter from the Irish War Office that the Lord Lieutenant had received information from respectable authority that the arms of the corps were not safe & that his Grace had therefore thought proper to direct that they should be immediately called in. I instantly expressed my submission to his Grace's pleasure but expressed also my regret that there should appear to be any necessity for a measure which could not fail to be construed into some mistrust of men who had always borne good characters or of a neighbourhood which had been uniformly peaceful & submissive to the laws & which from every observation or information I could collect still continued to be so, & I expressed my hopes that his Grace would direct a further investigation into the grounds of the information he had received, stating at the same time that I had directed my agent, a gentleman of the first respectability, to attend at any appointed time to deliver up the arms & ammunition of the corps—a circumstance the more necessary for me as the ammunition was deposited in a part of my house which could not be properly opened except in the presence of my agent. I afterwards was informed that the persons whose duty it was to carry the Lord Lt.'s orders into effect, without waiting for the day on which my agent had been appointed to attend, had sent a conveyance escorted by a party of men & carried off the arms that were in my house & order'd the men who had theirs to surrender them, and when my steward remonstrated & urged that surely in a country so peaceable & quiet as that had been they might wait till the day appointed—which would have been the next—the brigade major said he could not wait an hour. I had afterwards an opportunity of proving that the information on which the Ld. Lt. had been induced to act was not only groundless in every respect but that it in point of fact originated in a motive so excessively absurd & childish as to have excited a smile of contempt or of pity —if the haste with which it had been receiv'd & acted upon had not produced the mischievous effect of marking mistrust & ill will where none had been deserved and of exciting in the people afresh that dread of being the victims of private information & the well founded apprehension of not being able to guard against it by the most peaceable & orderly conduct, though the mischief was manifest & the information evidently false in point of fact & absurd in its origin. A spirit of party or some other spirit interposed to prevent the removal of the mischievous effects of the measure by any declaration which could have been satisfactory to the wounded feelings of those who had thus been held forth as objects of suspicion. I could obtain none such from the justice or policy of the Castle—I therefore felt it my duty to resign my commission as captain of the corps—that I might have an opportunity in a farewell address of stating those assurances in which the Lord Lt. had been pleased to express his reliance upon the peaceable & loyal disposition of the inhabitants of that district in general & of the individuals who had composed the corps. The inference which I humbly conceive must be drawn from the instances I have mentioned—is that the present Irish Government has been under the influence of a strong mistrust of or of an adverse disposition towards the great mass of the people they were sent to govern, a circumstance which would naturally lead to the present unhappy state of irritation that prevails in that country—& which it was most peculiarly the duty of a Government so circumstanced as the present Irish Government was to endeavour to guard against—without presuming to give an opinion upon any of the measures that led to the removal of the late & the appointment of the present Irish Govt. I must be allowed to say that a wise Government composed of men kindly disposed towards the people

111

would have made allowances for the degree of irritation which might be naturally expected from the lamentable cry of No Popery which preceded & accompanied their entrance into power. I do think that a wise Govt. even whilst it steadily adhered to that rejection of the prayer of the Catholic Petitions should have even gone out of its course to have marked in every other respect a conciliatory disposition & by language & by acts of kindness to have proved to that portion of his Majesty's subjects that they were not a suspected or unfavoured party in the State—that such conduct would have been right Mr Pole has proved by his own assertion—though unfortunately he has not acted up to that assertion in his justification before Parliament of his circular letter.[1] He thus states the principles of his Government—He states it to have said to the Catholics—'you are to expect no new privileges from us—but you shall have the law equally administer'd that justice shall be dealt out to you, nor shall anybody in the country, either Protestants or Dissenters, insult or degrade you.' I totally acquit the Duke of Richmond & the Lord Chancellor from all participation in the terms & tenor of this boast—it bears the true genuine stamp & character of the Old Irish school of policy with which Mr Pole seems very fully imbued. At what period since the accession of the illustrious House of Hanover has it ever occurred in England that the people stood in need of the assurance of a Secretary that they should have the benefits of the law 'that justice should be dealt out to them & that they should be protected from insults & degradation'? But if Mr Pole in his memorable boast displays the principles of the Old Irish school he also evinces a knowledge of that system of Government under which alone such principles could operate or exist—& the fact is that the conduct & principles of the Irish Government bear more closely & strongly upon the pursuits, the occupations & the enjoyments of the people than can be well conceived by those who view Ireland through an English medium. A spirit of party produces mischiefs more immediately felt by every individual there than can be the case here—& that mischief is dreadfully aggravated in reality & still more in imagination whenever the Govt. appears as the leader or supporter of party. The enlarged powers of our Grand Juries, the importance which from those powers is attached to the appointment of Sheriffs—the defective system under which this high office is administer'd from the permanence in office of the Sub-Sheriffs contrary to law—their practising as attornies in the counties in which they are Sub-Sheriffs—the influence they acquire over all the embarassed inhabitants of their districts, the manner in which they often apply this influence & are still oftener suspected of applying it to pack juries to serve the purposes of those who employ them as attornies or who have influence to procure

1. See No. 2888. The date: 12 February 1811.

112

grants from the Grand Juries. All these & other circumstances in our internal policy—well worthy of deep consideration—will explain to those who are acquainted with them the manner in which the Castle may be made habitually the instrument of much that is grievous & much that is irritating without any evident or gross violation of law or of justice. The Irish Government is in fact more constantly in contact with the people than can be well understood here & for that very reason should be more conciliatory, more strictly impartial, more divested in reality & in appearance of everything like a party spirit. If it be not so it will inevitably be the cause or be duped into being the instrument in the hands of others to cause much of that 'oppression of that infringement of rights of that degradation & insult' from which Mr Pole so kindly promises to protect the Catholics & from which in England the law alone would suffice to protect them. Though I have the satisfaction of being able to state that many of those evils & defects of our internal policy have diminished yet they would still revive with a spirit of party or their final removal would at least be retarded. The evils of party in Ireland are deplorable even to the extent of shaking all confidence in the laws in the minds of those who conceive that they are classed under those that appear to form the weakest, and it cannot be otherwise, for I take upon myself to assert that I have known Juries packed for particular purposes. I have known large sums disposed of contrary to law to gratify Sub-Sheriffs & other publick officers with the due administration of whose offices the security, the properties & the comfortable existence of the people through every gradation are very closely connected & which are very liable to be ill administered to serve the purposes of those from whose influence these officers have derived such gratifications. These abuses are too often the result of private party but they have always been felt with aggravated weight where party has appeared to rest upon some publick principle; & the difficulty of applying a remedy to such abuses when they do prevail & are supported by a strong party spirit may be conceived when I state as a matter within my own knowledge that Judges have been reluctant & have declined to prevent a positive infraction of the law even when pointed out to them. I have referred to these points as tending to shew how essential it is that the Irish Government should evince the most decided impartiality in words, in manners & in conduct. It is difficult to attain this character but it is necessary and it was of tenfold necessity under the circumstances that attended the formation of the present Irish Government—circumstances which I will also admit rendered it more difficult to guard against being misled by those who at all times wish to see the Castle at the head of a party. Upon an impartial view of the subject I feel myself warranted in the opinion that the present Irish Government has from its commencement been considered as the head of a party & that its conduct in many instances have afforded the most plausible grounds for that opinion. And I much fear that recent events render it utterly hopeless that it should ever acquire the character of impartiality or of being favourably disposed in any respect towards that very important portion of our population which more than any other in the Empire calls for the exertion of every just source & means of a beneficial influence over their minds. That such an influence might have been attained & still may be attained even under the circumstance of persevering delays to the prayers of their Petition I have no doubt, & I think an impartial review of the conduct of the Roman Catholics & of the Irish Government even down to the present moment would tend to confirm this opinion. What has been the conduct of the Roman Catholics in 1799? They met the demands of Mr Pitt in terms as cordial & as acquiescent as the English language could furnish—more than was asked they were ready to agree to—what the Prelates signed was known to all the efficient men of the Catholic body & was tacitly acquiesced in—it remained in that state & might have been acted upon at any period during the succeeding 7 years—not a symptom of retraction appeared; they experienced unexpected delays but they relied upon the support of their friends. They saw those friends driven from their offices by a cry of No Popery which it might be right to raise & which might be justified, but which candour must allow to have been irritating & as it was disclaimed by Ministers it called for everything that could be soothing—called for everything that could prevent ill intentioned, violent or ambitious members of the body from taking advantage of such irritation to enable themselves to act a prominent part in the pursuit of Catholic Emancipation. Nothing was done to sooth—& it would be easy to point out much that might have been done acceptable to the Catholics & most beneficial to Ireland. Much was done that at least afforded a handle for misrepresentation & for aggravating feelings already ulcerated. Under these circumstances the friends of the Catholics most unfortunately brought forward those concessions which had been made in 1799—& had for 7 years been unproductive of advantage to those who made them. It is to be lamented but unfortunately it is not unnatural that passion should blind people to their own interests. The R. Catholics thus called upon to concede to those whom they considered as their enemies that which under more happy auspices they had acceded to their declared friends and at the same time told that the concession would be of no avail to procure for them their objects—appear to have given way to irritation or to the arts of those who were at all times watchful to take advantage of that irritation & have committed themselves against those measures to which they had before consented. Here again was a case in which allowance ought to have been made & which called for a conciliatory conduct on the part of Government. Nothing like it marked the conduct of the Irish Government towards the Roman Catholics—irritation encreased

114

with encreasing alienation on both sides. That Committee of Catholics met which has led to the present state of things. There is no justifying the violence & intemperate language of many of the members of that Committee; it was mischievous in the extreme not only to the general peace of the country but to the interests of the Roman Catholic body, but it was the natural & almost inevitable result of preceding causes. Those causes ought never to have occurred, or having occurred, their force should have been weakened by prudence & even kindness blended with firmness. Mr Pole should have interfered at a more early period & if his interference had borne the character of a friendly disposition towards those who were the objects of his interference as well as of a firm determination to prevent the mischief of such intemperate conduct there can be little doubt that it would have been successful. If it had not produced an effect upon the violent members of the Committee it would have so strengthened the moderate as to have ensured a change of language in the Committee. By the course adopted the Irish Government was made to wear the appearance of looking on with sullen silence or with a feeling of satisfaction at the mischief which the Catholic cause was likely to suffer from the intemperance of the Committee: everything that was irritating—everything that was likely to revive the old animosities was allowed to be sent forth to the world without an attempt on the part of Government to stop it—and when the Committee was evidently falling to pieces from its own violence, which had drawn upon its members as much contempt as odium—when several members who had for a long time absented themselves again attended & had actually shamed or reasoned their colleagues out of some objectionable measures & prevailed upon the Committee to rescind others & to adjourn for a fortnight when it was evident that the Committee could never again have been assembled in the same spirit of violence—Mr Pole seized that moment to send forth his circular letter as if eager to deprive the Catholics of the credit of a return to moderation & anxious before it was too late to bring forward an act of Government to encrease & perpetuate the odium upon the Catholics—which the transactions of the last day of the Committees meeting gave reason to hope would be removed in the most desirable manner, by the subsequent more temperate conduct of its members. The effect of that circular letter was such as might be expected, an effect which would have been useful to the country—though it might be unpleasant to a party. It reunited all the Catholics & in reuniting them it ensured moderation & decorum in their proceedings— & it was evident that their measures to petition Parliament & their language would be in the spirit of the Constitution & in terms decorous & respectful. Lord Fingal & all the rank & character of the Catholic body were again in their places—they had firmly resisted every attempt to obtain their sanction to the Address for the removal of the Ld. Lt.—

& the Catholics in general had approved of their conduct. I will venture to assert that so long as the proceedings of the Catholic body wore this appearance no Protestant in Ireland would have felt alarm. It becomes Government at all times to be watchful—but there was no danger or appearance of danger when the late Proclamation was issued. That Proclamation has evidently grown out of the Circular letter & not out of any danger to be apprehended from the Catholic Committee. It was meant to bolster up the credit of the letter & to prove the propriety of the latter by a presumed necessity for the former. The Proclamation must produce one or other of these effects: 1st, the magistrates of Ireland, called upon to act, & called upon when it was evident that there was a doubt as to the law, will by acting revive the old feuds between Protestant & Catholic—as formerly occurred upon that memorable occasion when in the Administration of Ld Westmorland[1] the Protestant Gd. Juries were arrayed against the Catholic Petitions & then abandoned by the Government which had urged them on: or 2dly, as is most probable, the magistrates will either openly refuse or secretly evade acting in support of the Proclamation & thus exhibit the Irish Government abandoned by those whose duty it ought to be to support it—& if there be really any-thing mischievous in the designs of the Roman Catholics it must derive encouragement from the exhibition of a magistracy affraid or unwilling to act even when solemnly called upon: 3dly, by the Proclamation a dis-cussion will be opened & kept alive upon a law which, however it might have been required by the circumstances of the times in which it was passed, is evidently in contradiction to the spirit of the Constitution & ought not to have been brought forward except in a case of urgent necessity. It is clear that the Catholic Committee was framed for the purpose of petitioning; any other object must be mere matter of sus-picion. A Jury will very reluctantly apply such a law to such an avowed & evident object—& if it does appear to be the law according to the sense of the Proclamation the consequence will be aggregate meetings of the Catholics in all the counties to frame those Petitions which they are prevented from doing by delegates. These meetings will be held under the influence of the irritation occasioned by the failure of their first attempts, & were the Protestant country gentlemen of Ireland consulted I believe it would be found that they would have prefer'd the meeting of a Committee to the tumultuous meetings of all the Catholics around them. If these meetings are to be prevented other laws of a harsh nature must be passed, & what then becomes of all the boasted good effects of the Union, which, as Dr Duigenan alledged, 'would render it un-necessary to curb the Romanists by any restrictive law'? I hope his Royal Highness will beleive that I should never have presumed to have presented to his Royal Highness any opinion upon the state of Ireland

1. 1790-5.

116

tinged in the slightest degree with party views or principles. Totally un-connected with all party I have no interest in any measure except that which results from the stake I possess in the country likely to be affected by the measures of its Government. I therefore venture with humble confidence to state my opinion that his Royal Highness's present servants in Ireland never can govern that country with that spirit of conciliation so essential to its safety & to the interests of the Sovereign & of his Royal Highness. What has been done cannot be undone by those who were the authors and advisers except by such concessions as would degrade them & through them the Government. The good nature of the Duke of Richmond can no longer produce its usual good effects—& the talents & activity of Mr Pole, however useful they may be elsewhere, can in Ireland only produce mischief. I humbly presume to assert that a speedy change of persons in the Irish Government is at all events essential to the final preservation of peace in that country. Without touching upon the great subject of Catholic Emancipation—which must be left to time & to superior wisdom—I may presume to say that much might have been done & may still be done well calculated to sooth the regrets of rejection or delay—much that would gratify the Catholics & benefit Ireland. The mass of our people are less connected with the Government by an in-fluence founded on benefits such as are likely to be felt by the people than is the case in most parts of Europe. An improved system of educa-tion might at once have been made a source of beneficial influence & of eminent service to the State. The appointment of the Board of Education by the Duke of Bedford gave room to expect something. The importance & the necessity of attending to that subject in Ireland are manifest in the documents laid before the Board. Those documents deserve attention. They have been very inadequately conveyed to the public in the Reports of the Board to the Ld. Lt. as laid before Parliament. It is a matter in which the middling & lower classes take a considerable interest—among them the education of their children is a matter of more anxiety than is generally beleived. The poor hoped to be assisted & the middling class look for better description of school than is now to be found in the country parts of Ireland. Four years have elapsed & nothing has been done. Still much that is defective, wasteful & irritating remains to be removed, & no benefit has been extended to the lower classes—& much I fear that nothing can be done in the present state of the dispositions of the Irish Govt. & of the Catholics towards each other—& though the Board is at this moment apparently occupied with plans to fulfill that most important branch of its duty—namely 'to extend the benefits of education to the lower classes of his Majesty's subjects in Ireland' the attempt will I fear prove abortive if it be not even productive of the mischief of throwing difficulties in the way of future attempts. In the present state of things the Catholics look with apprehension upon every

117

plan. It would have been prudent & it would have been kind, & in Ireland kindness towards the people is wisdom, to have consulted the Catholic Clergy & respectable laity upon the best & most acceptable manner of assisting the Catholic poor in the education of their children. It has not been done & I have before me letters from several Catholics expressive of apprehension & mistrust, & much I fear that these are more likely to encrease than to diminish, & if so it would be better not to agitate the subject till a more favourable opportunity. It may only serve as in the case of the 'Veto' to commit many against a measure which under more favourable auspices they may be enduced to support. Much time has been lost & opportunities allowed to pass by when an application to respectable Catholics for their cooperation would have been conciliatory & wise. Tithes afforded to the Irish Government another means of gratifying the Catholics & of serving the country. Promises on that head had been held out at the Union—nothing has been done or attempted. It has even been most mischievously stated in Parliament by men in office that the oppressions of the landlords & not tithes were the great grievance of the people in Ireland. The fact is that tithes are a great & an irritating grievance, not from any spirit of avarice or exaction in the Clergy who are in general most moderate in their demands—but from various causes peculiar to Ireland. Tithes are unequal in their operation & vexatious in their collection. The former is in great measure the effect of that vicious & barefaced spirit of party which governed the old Irish school of politics & to which the interests of the Crown, of the Church, the State & the People have in their turns been sacrificed. The tithe of agistment was wrested from the Clergy first by a vote of the House of Commons & lastly by a law passed to remove an obstacle to the success of the Bill for a Legislative Union. The consequence has been that in the richest tracts of Ireland thousands & tens of thousands of acres have been exonerated from tithe & the Clergy have been obliged to lay additional burthens on the small holdings of the poor—so that in one parish or district potatoes & the milk of the poor are heavily taxed whilst the rich grazier under whom they live is entirely exonnerated—& in an adjoining parish perhaps from a different system of occupation of the land no tithe is levied on the potatoe garden or on the milk of the labouring poor. All this appears susceptible of some better arrangement & many other modes of lessening or removing objections to tithes might be devised if it were ever possible for an Irish Government to bestow serious attention to the interests of the people they are sent to govern. Many other means presented themselves by which the present Govt. in Ireland might have marked a friendly disposition towards those whose Petitions they conceived it to be their duty to reject. By recommendations from the Castle those offices which are open to the middling & lower classes of Catholics might have been more generally cordially bestowed upon them & the

118

effect would have been more extensively beneficial to the country & more widely conciliatory than any system of courting a few leaders of the body. So far as has come under my observation, & it has not been very limited, a Roman Catholic is hardly ever to be found among the excisemen, the Collectors of publick or of county taxes, the Constables which form a numerous body on good annual salaries, or in any other situation of similar description. I am very far from supposing that any English Govt. in Ireland would endeavour to prevent the Rom. Catholics from participating in these offices, but the fact is that they do not participate & that even now the great mass of the middling & common Irish think their religion a ground of exclusion. I know this to be the case, & it would be wise in Govt. actively to interpose its influence to remove the impression & to enduce Roman Catholics, whose characters & situation are proper, to put themselves with confidence forward with their Protestant neighbours as candidates for the numerous small offices that are to be disposed of in their respective counties. It is hardly to be conceived what an effect may be produced in a small circle of a parish by the appointment of a Roman Catholic to the situation of a police officer. It at once conciliates the Roman Catholics by raising them in their own estimation & checks that air of superiority which is more prevalent among Protestants of the lower than of the higher orders. This effect was most evident in my immediate neighbourhood when Lord Hardwicke's Govt. gave the arms to my corps of Catholics—& most assuredly an attention to such points would have been most peculiarly desirable in a Government circumstanced as was that of the Duke of Richmond on its arrival in Ireland.

I feel that I have been led by a deep interest in the subject to a length which I fear must be troublesome, & yet the subject is very far from being exhausted. I have now only to add the expression of my humble reliance on the goodness of his Royal Highness to construe favourably what I have written candidly but hastily, & my most sincere prayer for the prosperity & honour & comfort of his Royal Highness's Government at all times & under all circumstances. (18602–19)

3154   RICHARD RYDER TO THE PRINCE REGENT

Whitehall, 28 Aug. 1811

Mr Ryder has the honor of humbly submitting to your Royal Highness that in consequence of the facts disclosed in the petition which your Royal Highness commanded to be transmitted to him in favor of John Francis and of the communication which he has since had with the Lord Chancellor upon the subject, he has directed the execution which was to have taken place tomorrow to be respited till the Judges have had an opportunity of conferring upon the case.

Mr Ryder is concerned to state that there are no circumstances alleged by Mr de Souza on behalf of Antonio the Portugueze which can justify him in recommending the prisoner to your Royal Highness's favorable consideration. (18460)

3155 THE DUKE OF CLARENCE TO THE PRINCE REGENT, AND ENCLOSURES
St. James's, noon, Monday [*26 Aug. 1811*]
Knowing how your time is occupied and the goodness of your heart I only enclose the two letters and subscribe myself [etc.].[1] (44993)

[Enclosure]
MAJOR JAMES MCDERMOTT TO THE DUKE OF CLARENCE
Royal Military College, Great Marlow, 25 Aug. 1811
The situation of Commandant to the Junior Department of the Royal Military College having become vacant by the promotion of Colonel Butler; relying upon your Royal Highness's goodness I take the liberty to entreat you to solicit the Prince in my favor. Tho' I can obtain testimonials from every officer in existence under whom I have had the honor to serve during a space of 36 years and upwards, yet as you are so well acquainted with the merits of every officer of the Institution I shall request you to give me the character I deserve, and I enclose a letter to his Royal Highness the Prince Regent which I request you to read, and

---

1. The Prince had been to see his daughter at Bognor. She wrote to Mercer Elphinstone on the 26th: 'To begin then first by telling you how the visit went off. I may say that I believe *all parties* were *mutually* satisfied; *all* in *good humor* & spirits, the Prince looking *veritably well*. He was *very kind* & seemed pleased *with all* our proceedings. He arrived at 7 in the eg. with the D. of Cumberland & Mr Tyrrwit. Colonel B[loomfield] was with us according to command in attendance. We retired to bed about 11 o'clock. The Prince slept in Lady de C[lifford's] rooms, his valet in a chair bed in my dressing room. Ly de C. went up to Mrs Udney's room; she got a lodging close by where the D. of Cum[berland], Mr. Tyrrwit & the servants slept. The next mg. I drove the Prince out by his *own desire* in the phaeton. We went to see Dr. Jackson's house ... Ernest was in high spirits & for a *wonder* in *perfect* humor; in short, the whole was *couleur de rose*. The next mg. at half past 10 they left this for Oatlands. The Prince gave me a melancholy account of the D. of Sussex who has been *dying*. Thank God for the *present* he is *better*, & if he does not have a relapse he will do' (Bowood MSS.). Dr. Jackson, the Dean of Christ Church, lived in retirement at the Manor House at Felpham, near Bognor.

if you approve of the contents to have it put under an envelope and forwarded, but if not to return it with such remarks as you may be pleased to make. I humbly beg pardon for trespassing on your time and hope to be favored with an answer particularly as delay in the application may be a cause of its failure.

Henry[1] tells me he means to write by this post. I need therefore say nothing more about him but that he is in perfect health and improves both in appearance and progress. (44994–5)

[Enclosure] MAJOR JAMES MCDERMOTT TO THE PRINCE REGENT

Great Marlow, 25 Aug. 1811

Having already experienced many favors from your Royal Highness I feel a degree of dread in presuming to ask another, but aware of your benign disposition I venture once more to lay myself at your feet humbly to solicit the vacant appointment of Commandant to the Junior Department of the Royal Military College. I found my hopes of success on your partiality to an old officer, to a faithful service of my King for thirty-six years and upwards, eleven and a half of the time in America and above eight at the Royal Military College from which it may be presumed I am acquainted with the arrangement and detail of the Institution. A zealous attachment to your Royal Highness and to the Royal Family, the expectation of favor after having served many years under your immediate command, add to all this that by giving me the appointment you will derive the pleasure of having conferred upon a father of eight children, five of whom are intended for your service, the means of amply providing for and educating them.

May God Almighty protect your Royal Highness and give you a long and happy life; may you be your country's glory and the protector of your faithful servants is the sincere wish of, Sir [etc.]. (44996–7)

1. The Duke's second son (1795–1817). In 1808 he had been serving as a midshipman on the *Superb* under his father's old friend Sir Richard Keats, and the squadron had then been in the Baltic. In 1809 he sailed as a volunteer with the expedition to Walcheren, and in the summer of 1810 he sailed for the Mediterranean to join Captain Blackwood's ship. He disliked the navy so much that in May 1811 he was sent to the Royal Military College, and he soon received a commission in the Fusiliers. He joined the German Legion on the Continent in 1812, and served in the Peninsula in 1813. He and his brother George got into trouble with Colonel Quentin, their commanding officer, in 1814, and both were practically coerced into going to India where Lord Moira, the Governor-General, could be relied upon to look after them. Henry FitzClarence died of fever in India in 1817.

15 Clifford Street, Monday [26 Aug. 1811]

Private. In the absence of Col. MacMahon who I am sure would be so kind as to mention to the P.R. what I am going to state & what I did not think correct to put into my official paper, may I ask of you the favour to name it previous to his Royal Highnesses imparting to me his answer, namely that hearing as I conceive from *undoubted authority* that H.R.H. did not wish to be at all troubled on the business of any Theatre, & having only removed a licence I long had possessed & against which no objection had been made, I scrupled not to comply with the wishes of the Committee by engaging the Pantheon & having now taken the building to peices it will cost me thousands to put back in [the] same state, & utter irretrievable ruin must be my fate if his R.H. forbids a Theatre there.[1] (18440)

No. 2 Little Argyle Street, Tuesday, [?27 Aug. 1811]

Private. H.R.H. being come to town I take the liberty of saying to you that my only hope lies in his being made acquainted with the irretrievable ruin that will attend his declaration of hostility to the exercise of my licence—should he deign either to ask a question on the subject or to listen to an information which your kindness may prompt you to give, I think the following facts will strike him. By the licence & the Argyle establishment I actually lose £8000, & by the preparations for changing the Pantheon into a Theatre an expence of some thousands has already been incurred. An answer from H.R.H. signicative [*sic*] that he does not interfere with licences given by authority will at least save me from what has been done at the Pantheon—otherwise I & all my boys & *who are all* in the service of H. Majesty will be quite ruined. (18441)

3157 LETTERS FROM SPENCER PERCEVAL TO THE PRINCE REGENT

Downg. Street, 26 Aug. 1811

Mr Perceval presents his humble duty to your Royal Highness and has the honor to inclose for your Royal Highness's perusal, a letter which he has received from his Grace the Archbishop of Canterbury upon the subject of Dr. Bell's[2] & Mr Lancaster's system of education, together

1. See No. 3149.

2. Andrew Bell (1753–1832), an Anglican clergyman who served as an army chaplain in India where he founded the Madras system of education, the boys being alternately masters and

with an extract from a newspaper which accompanied his Grace's letter. Mr Perceval has thought it right to trouble your Royal Highness with these inclosures in order that he may be enabled, if your Royal Highness shall be graciously pleased to authorise him, to assure the Archbishop that your Royal Highness will at all times be ready to pay all due attention to any communication which his Grace may be desirous of making upon any subject which he may feel to be so interesting to the cause of the Establishment and of religion, as his Grace appears to conceive that to be which is the subject of his letter: or that, in all events, your Royal Highness may be apprized of the subject on which it is likely that his Grace will be desirous of humbly requesting to be permitted to have an Audience of your Royal Highness.

Mr Perceval ought to add that he has the opportunity of knowing, from a communication which he has recently received from the Bishop of Durham,[1] that it is not only amongst the Clergy of London that the apprehension which the Archbishop expresses upon the subject of the Lancastrian system of education prevails. It is indeed to be lamented that Dr. Bell's system, which contains all the same mechanical advantages as Mr Lancaster's, with the additional recommendation of being applied to the education of children in the principles of the Church of England, had not been brought forward to notice with as much industry as Mr Lancaster's. In that case it cannot be doubted that many persons who have given their countenance to the Lancastrian system, principally if not entirely from the great mechanical advantages which belong to it, would, at least as gladly, have patronised that of Dr Bell. If however the Clergy of the Church of England feel it to be their duty at present to exert themselves in favour of the latter, it appears, as Mr Perceval humbly submits, a favorable opportunity for introducing it with every advantage to the public notice.

Mr Perceval at the same time conceives it to be due to his Grace the Archbishop not to omit pointing out to your Royal Highness the proper & laudable anxiety felt by his Grace lest any measure in which his Grace should be engaged should be misunderstood or misconstrued as intended disrespectfully towards those branches of the Royal Family who, from

scholars. The monitorial system was introduced in England in 1798, and was further popularized by the Quaker Joseph Lancaster (1778–1838) after 1803. Bell's adherents formed the 'National Society for Promoting the Education of the Poor in the Principles of the Established Church throughout England and Wales'; and Lancaster's Royal Lancasterian Society (1808), favoured by Nonconformists and Quakers, provided religious instruction on a nonsectarian basis. William Lamb wrote, in later life, 'I was taught to read, as usual, with considerable difficulty, having had the misfortune . . . to have come into the world long before the new system of instruction (Dr. Bell's or Mr Lancaster's) had made almost an amusement of that which was before a work of heavy labour and most grievous suffering' (Melbourne MSS.).

1. Shute Barrington (1734–1826).

not having their attention sufficiently called to the important considerations which weigh so strongly with his Grace & his brethren, have lent their names, as sanction to the plan of Mr Lancaster. (18458–9)

Downg. St., 27 Aug. 1811
Mr Perceval presents his humble duty to your Royal Highness and humbly represents to your Royal Highness that he has just heard that a Canonry of Windsor is vacant by the death of Dr Hallam.[1] Mr Perceval does not presume to know how far your Royal Highness might, from the local situation of this Canonry, be disposed to suspend for the present making any appointment to it. But subject to that doubt, Mr Perceval ventures humbly to recommend the Revd. Mr. Stopford,[2] the brother of the Earl of Courtown,[3] to your Royal Highness for this vacancy. Mr Perceval believes him to be a very respectable and worthy Clergyman as far as he is acquainted with his character, highly deserving the favor of your Royal Highness. Mr Perceval is more particularly led to name him upon this occasion because he has reason to believe that the late Duke of Portland had promised to apply to his Majesty for the next Stall at Windsor for Mr Stopford, and that the Duke had mentioned his intention to his Majesty, who had received the mention of it with the expression of his perfect approbation. Under these circumstances, tho' Mr Perceval does not conceive himself absolutely bound by the Duke of Portland's promises, yet he can never fail to refer to them with great respect, and considering the respectability of Mr Stopford himself, he thinks he would not be acting properly if he submitted to your Royal Highness's approbation any other person who from other considerations he might conceive to have stronger claims upon Mr Perceval individually than Mr Stopford. Mr Perceval submits the above accordingly for your Royal Highness's approbation & commands. (18463–4)

1. John Hallam (1728–1811). Canon of Windsor, 1775–1811; Dean of Bristol, 1781–1800.

2. Richard Bruce Stopford (*c*. 1774–1844). Rector of Barton Seagrave, Northamptonshire, 1798; Vicar of Nuneaton, Warwick, 1803; Chaplain to the Queen; Prebendary of Hereford, 1810; Canon of Windsor, 1812–44.

3. James George, 3rd Earl of Courtown (1765–1835) succeeded his father, 30 March 1810. Tory M.P. for Great Bedwyn, 1790–6 and 1806–7; for the Linlithgow Burghs, 1796–1802; for the Dumfries Burghs, 1803–6; for Marlborough, 1807–10. Treasurer of the Household, 1793–1806 and 1807–12; Captain of the Band of Gentlemen Pensioners, 1812–27. K.P. 1821; Captain of the Yeomen of the Guard, January–April 1835.

Ramsgate, Wednesday, 28 Aug. 1811

Lord Wellesley has the honor to acquaint your Royal Highness that in obedience to your Royal Highness's commands the Duke of Infantado has been received with every possible mark of respect & attention. At Portsmouth his Excellency was received with the most distinguished honors by all the naval, military & other public officers, was admitted to see the Dockyard, publicly entertained at dinner, & repeatedly greeted with marks of satisfaction & applause from the people.

Mr Richard Wellesley met his Excellency at Portsmouth (having been intimate with him in Spain) & attended him to London, where the Duke arrived at a late hour on Saturday night.

Lord Wellesley visited his Excellency at the Clarendon Hotel on Sunday afternoon, & on Monday received him, & had a long conference with him at Apsley House; & on the same day had the honor of entertaining the Duke at dinner together with the Portugese Ambassador, Admiral Apodaca & several of the Duke's personal acquaintances.

The Duke's manners & conduct are in the highest degree interesting & satisfactory, & truly worthy of his illustrious rank & of the noble cause which he represents. Your Royal Highness will accordingly appretiate the reverence and affection with which he conducts himself towards his aged & respectable mother the Duchess Dowager of Infantado; they would not be separated during this Mission; & accordingly the Duchess accompanied the Ambassador on board the Comus frigate.

At the Duke's request, in consequence of the extreme age of the Duchess, the Comus was ordered round with the Duchess on board to the Nore, where she arrived yesterday, when one of his Majesty's yachts attended for the purpose of conveying the Duchess to Greenwich, whence she is to proceed in the Admiralty barge to Whitehall. Lord Wellesley is convinced that your Royal Highness will graciously approve these marks of respect & attention on such an occasion. The Duchess of Infantado is a daughter of the House of Solm; she is a most accomplished, excellent & sensible woman, of the highest manners & the most agreable & lively conversation. She speaks French with the greatest ease & propriety.

Lord Wellesley takes the liberty of humbly suggesting that any mark of personal condescension from your Royal Highness to the Duchess of Infantado would produce the most favorable effect.

In obedience to your Royal Highness's commands Lord Wellesley has appointed Wednesday the fourth of September for the presentation of the Duke of Infantado's credentials; & on the same day, with your Highness's permission, Admiral Apodaca will present his recredentials & take leave.

If your Royal Highness should be pleased to postpone these ceremonies to any more distant day Lord Wellesley humbly requests early notice of your Royal Highness's pleasure.

It has been the accustomed etiquette for an Ambassador not to appear in public, or to visit in London previously to the reception of his credentials by the King; the Duke of Infantado, however, having stated that he had the honor of the personal regard of his Royal Highness the Duke of Sussex (to whom he also acknowledged considerable obligations) and having expressed an earnest desire to visit the Duke of Sussex in the present condition of his Royal Highness's health, Lord Wellesley did not hesitate to assure the Ambassador that your Royal Highness would be satisfied to wave all considerations of form in such circumstances. The Duke of Infantado, however, most particularly requested that Lord Wellesley would submit his Excellency's motives for such a departure from the established rule to your Royal Highness's gracious indulgence.

In the conference with the Duke of Infantado the points of importance which were stated were these:

The urgent wants of the Spanish Government with respect to pecuniary means, & the necessity of coming to some distinct arrangement with regard to supplies & plans of combined operation.

Doubts whether the proposed mediation with the Colonies will be successful in Spanish America, although it may tend to remove jealousies in Spain.

An intimation that the Princess of Brasils[1] had many friends in Cadiz, & that the general disposition towards her was favorable.

Lord Wellesley communicated to the Duke of Infantado the pretended letters from Ferdinand the 7th, lately received through Mr. Wellesley, when the Duke, having examined those papers in Lord Wellesley's presence, without hesitation pronounced them to be forged. (18469–72)

THE PRINCE REGENT'S REPLY [copy]

31 Aug. 1811

The Prince Regent returns his thanks to the Marquis of Wellesley for the letter which has just reach'd him. The Prince most highly approves of every mark of attention that has been manifested on the part of this Court towards the Duke of Infantado & the Duchess his mother since their arrival in this country, & the Prince will not fail, after his return to London & as soon as he shall have receiv'd the credentials from his Excellency the Duke of Infantado, to call in person upon the Duchess: it will, however, not be in the Prince's power to reach London earlier

1. The Prince Regent of Portugal, afterwards John VI (1767–1826) married (1790) Charlotte (1775–1830), daughter of Charles IV of Spain.

than Friday next the 6th inst. as he must necessarily make some stay at Windsor previous to his return to town. In the meantime the Prince Regent desires the Marquis of Wellesley to assure the Duke of Infantado of his highest respect & best regards & that the Prince will have the pleasure to receive his Excellency on that day at three o'clock. (18476–7)

3159 COLONEL MCMAHON TO THE DUKE OF NORTHUMBERLAND

Cheltenham, 2 Sept. 1811

As any news or interesting information (of which there is none at present) could only from hence reach your Grace at least third handed, I should not but for your kind permission have thus obtruded my scroll upon you, but under that indulgence I cannot resist the pleasure of acquainting your Grace that I have again received my usual benefit of many past years from the use of this to me, efficacious water with its attendant change of air and consequent repose from business, and that unless call'd up, (which from what I hear from Windsor I do not now expect to be) I shall continue to sojourn here until the 15th instant, when I shall return to my duty in town & settle myself for the winter campaign, which I fear may be far from a mild one, although I apprehend that, should the King continue in even his present state, there will be no meeting of Parliament until after Christmas, towards the end of January.

The Duke of Norfolk pass'd through here a few days ago in his way to Home Lacey[1] in Herefordshire, and told me that [he] had heard in town from very good authority that a violent difference had taken place in the Cabinet between Mr. Perceval & Lord Wellesley, the latter proposing & the former resisting the measure of taking the whole Spanish army into our pay. The Irish Chancellor (Lord Manners) has likewise been here, and states that the business of the Catholics in that country is by no means in that enflamed state which the public prints describe it to be, and that the question now at issue regarding the Convention Act will be brought, without any intemperate proceedings, to a legal decision, & in the meanwhile the several Catholic meetings throughout the country are confining themselves solely to the right of petitioning, and which right had never been denied them; at the same time he professes his complete belief that the meeting in Dublin was assuming a legislative shape for ulterior & very different purposes, had not the Government promptly check'd & stop'd their proceedings. I have not heard from the Prince, but I have heard (thanks to God) that he is extremely well, & this day going to Windsor where everything is as wretched as wretched can be (Alnwick MSS.).

1. Holme Lacey, near Hereford.

3160 RICHARD RYDER TO MAJOR–GENERAL T. H. TURNER

Great George Street, 4 Sept. 1811

I called upon you this morning in consequence of having just heard from Lord Bathurst that it would be necessary to hold a Council for Affairs of Trade in a few days, and that after tomorrow it may be very difficult to collect six members together (the number requisite for that purpose) for some time to come: and I meant to have requested you to take the earliest opportunity of laying these circumstances before his Royal Highness the Prince Regent after his return to town in order to know whether it might not be his Royal Highness's pleasure to hold a Council either at York House or at the Treasury in the course of the day.

I understand from Lord Bathurst that the business would not take up many minutes.

If it should be his Royal Highness's pleasure that a Council should be summoned for tomorrow, I will trouble you to acquaint me with his Royal Highness's commands both upon that point and the time and place of its meeting, in order that I may give the necessary directions without delay. (18484–5)

3161 LEWIS GOLDSMITH[1] TO MAJOR–GENERAL T. H. TURNER

76 Charlotte Street, Fitzroy Square, 4 Sept. [1811]

Mr Goldsmith presents his compts to General Turner begs he will have the goodness to transmit to his Royal Highness the Prince Regent a book which accompanies this letter, entitled Recueil des Manifestes, Discours &c Par Bonaparte. Comme General, comme Consul, et comme Empereur, in 3 parts bound in one volume, all extracted from the Moniteur.

Mr. G. has sent to his Royal Highness the Prince Regent, his several works when they were first published, namely 1. 3 & 6th edition of his 'Secret History of the Cabinet of Bonaparte', & a translation of that work into French, as also a pamplet [sic] on the 'Conduct of France towards America', but he does not know that his Royal Highness has ever received them. General Turner will very much oblige Mr Goldsmith if he can ascertain that those publications were put into the hands of his

1. Political writer and journalist (?1763–1846). He conducted *The Anti-Gallican*, afterwards *The British Monitor*, an anti-French weekly paper started in January 1811. In 1810 he had published a highly scandalous 'Secret History of the Cabinet of Bonaparte, including his private life, character'. In 1801, under the title, 'The Crimes of Cabinets: or, a Review of their Plans and Aggressions for the Annihilation of the Liberties of France and the Dismemberment of her Territories', he had made a virulent attack upon his own Government, and in 1809 he had narrowly escaped a charge of high treason. His new venture earned him a secret service subsidy of £1200 a year (Aspinall, *Politics and the Press, passim.*).

Royal Highness, whose approbation will always be an encouragement for Mr Goldsmith to continue his exertions in the exposure of the greatest enemy human nature ever had to encounter. (18487)

3162 DAVID ALLAN TO COLONEL MCMAHON

Heligoland, 5 Sept. 1811

Lieut.-Governor Hamilton, ever anxious to promote my welfare, has by this packet recommended me through Mr. Harrison[1] to the Lords of the Treasury to the appointment of Agent for the lighthouse of this Island. Your kind support and influence would add much to his recommendation. I have taken the liberty of inclosing a copy of his letter on the subject (inclosure A. No. 1).

Whilst I had the charge of the old coal light the heavy expenditure attending the same struck me forcibly and in 1809 I submitted for the consideration of Government at different times the great advantage that would be derived from the substituting of an oil in lieu of a coal light, which substitution was subsequently made, and is now the cause of a saving of upwards of £2,000 per ann:. In obtaining the Governor's support with a view to have the change carried into effect, I had to encounter much opposition arising from the strong prejudices of the natives and other individuals on the Island. By persevering however I was ultimately successful and have now the gratification of seeing the new lighthouse an ornament to the Island and perhaps the first in the world, and I am still more gratified at having been the means of so great a saving to the public. I also at different times pointed out to Government the propriety of tolls being collected here for the light, and which last year amounted to upwards of £500—(inclosure B Nos 2 & 5).

For what I have done I never expected or should have asked for any remuneration, conceiving it no more than my duty, had it not been that others and whose duties are comparatively triffling [*sic*] to those which I executed under the old light, and which I will now be called upon to perform should the appointment of agent take place, the one Mr Fredericks, keeper of the light being paid a salary of £200 per annum, and the other Mr. Brown, the harbour master, being allowed 20 per cent. for collecting the tolls, which in some months has yielded him £40 per month what is remarkable, these two gentlemen were perhaps the most hostile to the change, yet they have reaped all the advantages and left me all the trouble. I trust therefore that the liberality of the Treasury

1. Sir George Harrison (*d.* 1841), Assistant Secretary of the Treasury, August 1805. Knighted, 1831.

129

will grant me an equitable allowance in the event of my being named agent, as I humbly concieve my claims are at least equally great as theirs.

By the inclosed abstracts which form but a small part of my correspondence you will be able to form some opinion of the great trouble I have had and the pains I have taken respecting the Lighthouse, besides which I have to mention that I have constantly the comptrolling and receiving of the tolls, and that with a view to bring the negotiation with Hamburgh to a close, I have been twice on the Continent for that purpose and have had a discussion with Commodore Brunswick at Cuxhaven on the part of the Senate, during which I was made prisoner by a party of French dragoons who unexpectedly entered the town, was marched into the country, and procured my release only by a considerable ransom which never was charged to Government (B. Nos 2 & 5).

I trust that in taking all these circumstances into consideration you will be of opinion that my claims in this instance are well founded, and my expectations neither presumptuous nor unreasonable, and I have most respectfully to entreat you to use your interest with their Lordships in procuring me the situation with an adequate salary attached thereto.

I know not how to apoligies [*sic*] for the length of this letter but I have found it impossible to compress it into a smaller space. But throughing myself entirely on your goodness and liberality I do assure you with the greatest truth that I ever remain [etc.]. (18489–90)

3163   LEWIS GOLDSMITH TO MAJOR-GENERAL T. H. TURNER

76 Charlotte Street, Fitzroy Square, 6 Sept. 1811

Mr Lewis Goldsmith presents his respectful compts. to General Turner & is very much obliged to him for the note which he received yesterday, but as H.R.H. is just arrived[1] Mr. G. will feel himself particularly obliged to General Turner to ascertain from H.R.H. if his different publications *have* been received.

If General Turner has not yet read Mr G.'s Secret History of the Cabinet of Bonaparte, he will be happy to send him a copy of the sixth edition. (18504)

1. At York House.

Donington, 11 Sept. 1811

Ld Manners was right enough in saying that there was no such spirit of
turbulence in the distant parts of Ireland as might be inferred from what
one sees in the Dublin papers. It is not turbulence that one has to
apprehend. What we have to dread is that silent disgust which can wait
in patience for an hour of advantage when its effect will be more
formidable from not having been precipitate. Nobody will question the
general discontent of Ireland at the time of the Rebellion tho' peculiar
circumstances prevented the whole mischief from exploding. Let us ask
ourselves what has been done since to remedy the causes of dissatisfaction & win over the people to us? No one thing. You would thence
rationally suppose the multitude to continue in the same unfavorable
disposition if you heard no particulars. But do not all informations concur
to apprize you of a smouldering fire which may at any moment burst into
flame? I enclose to you the copy of a letter from Ireland transmitted to
me the other day by one of the first merchants in London who has great
commercial dealings with Ireland. He was a supporter of Pitt's Administration & is leagued with the present Ministers, yet he thought it
expedient to warn me of an evil which he fears may grow to dreadful
magnitude. As to Ld. Manners's assertion that the Catholic Committee
had objects dangerous to the State in their meeting, I dare say he believes
it as firmly as we do the contrary. When assumptions are so at variance
the only way of judging between them is by appeal to facts. Now, we
know that the Aristocracy & Prelacy of the Catholics, alarmed at seeing
the management of the concern in the hands of factious barristers, had
made a great exertion & had succeeded in gaining to themselves a decided
preponderance over the demagogues. Was this an indication of mischievous purposes? Ought not the Government to have rejoiced at this;
unless, indeed, it had made up its mind at once to do that into which as a
necessity it will find itself soon plunged, I mean the repressing by
arbitrary violence alone the assembly of subjects for framing a Petition?
This is the question which will in a month be agitated; a question not
attaching upon Catholics alone, but in which you will see the feelings of a
vast body, in this country as well as in Ireland, of Protestants called into
play. And this we hazard with Bonaparte at our gates. (18527–9)

[Enclosure: copy, unsigned]

Cork, 21 Aug. 1811

The statement I gave you some days ago of the export of live cattle
proves the encreasing value of this country to England. In the space of

three years the export of horned cattle considerably more than trebled—pigs quintupled & sheep nearly trebled.

Neither the people nor the Government of England know or they don't wish to know either the value or moral or physical force of this country; history shews that there is no other cause of action gives such a momentum to the physical force of a country when put in motion as religion or anything therewith connected. The abstract cause of civil liberty does not propel a people to violent exertion so much as religious liberty, but when both these causes are permitted to exist & operate what obstacle will not they struggle with & perhaps overcome? The host of religious liberty is a hydra in itself—every head that is cut off leaves a stock that produces two at once. And so we see that the strength of Catholic Emancipation has encreased with every effort that has been made to put it down.

If the torch of discord & disunion be once lighted fairly in this country 'twill be very hard to put it out; and the Government that has produced the present unnatural state of Ireland has a great deal to answer for. The fact is, tho' the ferment is great, it only extends to the higher & midling class of the Catholics of Ireland. No immediate fear of disturbance should be apprehended. The lower orders know nothing of the foolish conflict between the other classes & the Governmt.

But the sad effect of such a misgovernment will be the estrangement & alienation of the bulk of the nation that will be produced by these unwise & imbecile acts of Mr. Pole.

Depend upon it, no interruption will take place to commerce, but the sooner Mr Pole is dismissed & a different line of Government adopted, the better for Great Britain—for the cause of the state of Ireland is infinitely of more interest to Great Britain than to us.

I am far from approving the conduct of the people of Dublin: but when I see them backed & encouraged by a large portion of the wealth, the magistracy & even aristocracy of Ireland, I think it high time to go to the source of the misfortune & to apply the cure. (18530–1)

3165 MICHAEL ANGELO TAYLOR TO COLONEL MCMAHON

Raith, Kirkcaldy, 13 Sept. 1811

Most private. By two letters which Sir Wm. Manners[1] has confidentially written to me respecting the future seats at Ilchester (which letters were

1. The son of John Manners, of The Grange, Grantham (a natural son of Lord William Manners, M.P. for Leicestershire), and of Louisa, Countess of Dysart (1745–1840). He was M.P. for Ilchester, 1803–4 and 1806–7, and was created a Baronet in 1793 (1766–1833). See *Letters of George IV, passim.* He had asked Pitt for an Irish peerage in 1793, and in 1812 vainly offered his three seats to the Government in return for a U.K. peerage. This was evidently

immediately returned by his express desire) I am placed in a situation of extreme delicacy. Sir William informs me that he is inclined to continue the present representatives[1] on reasonable terms if I will undertake to lay before his Royal Highness *certain conditions* which he will then communicate. I dare not of myself presume to do anything. Pray collect what answer I should return. Sir William presses for a reply. I cannot understand why he did not write to you on the subject.

I beg you will offer to our illustrious friend & master my most humble respects & duty. (18537)

3166　SIR JOHN CRADOCK TO COLONEL MCMAHON

Government House, Cape of Good Hope, 14 Sept. 1811

To so kind a friend I will give myself the pleasure to state our safe arrival on the 5th inst after an excellent passage of eleven weeks. This may appear somewhat tedious, but we had only one day of anything like bad weather. I cannot as yet form correct judgements, but everything here has a favorable prospect, & were it not for home & all its charms & peculiar gratifications—this ought to be the best & happiest of stations. By the next opportunity I will write again a little more fully upon all circumstances. It may be too much to expect at times a line from so occupied a person as you must be—but I feel, you know, how deeply interested I am in every event that passes under your roof. My thought will be incessantly there, & it will ever be the highest gratification I can experience to be ascertained of the happiness & prosperity of 'that Person', to whom I owe so much.

I shall say no more—than that I shall ever be ready to return to England to throw myself at the feet of that personage, & that no consideration can ever counterbalance that paramount feeling. In your friendly hands, I commit the expression of my unbounded devotion.

I have done everything in my power to shew the highest respect &c to General Grey upon my taking the command, & I know he is sensible of it to the utmost; besides a personal regard, I thought it would be acceptable where I am most anxious to please.

I have often, my dear McMahon while in London attempted to say to

what he wanted in 1811. Farington wrote, 16 November 1807: 'Lord Dysart . . . has more than £30,000 a year, and, being a widower without children, will leave £30,000 a year to Sir William Manners, son of the late Jack Manners, the usurer, who has already £30,000 a year, he being Lord Dysart's nephew' (*Diary*, iv. 216).

Sir William bought the Ilchester seats in 1802.

1. Taylor and Sheridan. John William Ward and George Philips were returned at the general election in 1812.

you how much I felt all your kindness—& I find it here equally inadequate—therefore I can only declare that I shall ever be [etc.].

Best regards to Lord Hutchinson—when you see him. (18539–40)

3167 LETTERS FROM THE MARQUESS WELLESLEY TO THE PRINCE REGENT

Dorking, 16 Sept. 1811

Lord Wellesley presents his humble duty to your Royal Highness & has the honor to state that he remained in London from Monday the 2d of September untill yesterday evening the 15th. He did not request an Audience of your Royal Highness on your return to town,[1] having carried all your Royal Highness's commands into execution, & not being desirous of giving unnecessary trouble.

He was compelled to leave his house in London on account of the necessity of painting it, which circumstance will oblige him to reside here for some days, but he will be at the Office from time to time, & can always attend your Royal Highness's commands in three hours from the time that he may have the honor to receive them. (18541)

Dorking, 16 Sept. 1811

Secret. Lord Wellesley has the honor to acquaint your Royal Highness that M. Zéa, General Nugent,[2] & Colonel Dornberg arrived safely on board Sir James Saumarez's Flagship in Wingo Sound on the 30th & 31st of August, & that every facility has been given to them by the Admiral for the prosecution of their respective Missions.

All the further orders respecting Prussia have been issued in obedience to your Royal Highness's commands; a person is appointed to proceed forthwith to Sweden, and has received instructions from Lord Wellesley. The arms & ammunition for Colberg are embarked, & the requisite instructions have been sent to the Admiralty for Sir James Saumarez with respect to the prospect of war between Prussia, Russia, & France.[3] (18543)

1. The Prince Regent had been visiting Lord Yarmouth at Sunbury Hall, near Woodbridge, for a few days' shooting.

2. Count Nugent, afterwards Field Marshal in the Austrian army.

3. See No. 3232*n.*

Admy., 17 Sept. 1811

Mr Yorke most humbly begs your Royal Highness's pardon for pre-suming to trouble Y.R.H. again upon a subject so inconsiderable as that of the Marshal of the Admiralty, but as Y.R.H. has been pleased to express some interest about the disposal of it, Mr Yorke is extremely anxious before any final arrangement is made to ascertain Y.R.H.'s present intentions with regard to it.

When Mr Yorke had last the honor of paying his personal duty to your Royal Highness he took the opportunity of stating such circumstances respecting this office as appeared necessary for Y.R.H.'s information; & Mr Yorke then presumed to lay before Y.R.H. some of the reasons which induced him to think that it was not a proper office to be conferred upon a gentleman of Mr Robert Thornton's description, & that it might be more properly given to Mr Price whose pretensions to some considera-tion from Government were already known to, & in some degree sanc-tioned, by your Royal Highness.

Mr Yorke has now the honor of informing Y.R.H. that he has since conversed with Mr R. Thornton on the occasion & explained to him the circumstances belonging to the office in question; acquainting him at the same time with the doubts which Mr Yorke entertained as to the propriety of his (Mr Thornton's) appointment to it. Mr R. Thornton certainly appeared not to enter into these considerations as far as he was personally concerned, & expressed on the contrary his readiness to accept of the employment, such as it was, if offered to him.

Mr Yorke submits most humbly to your Royal Highness that after mature reflection he cannot divest himself of the doubts which he originally entertained as to the propriety of conferring the Marshalship of the Admiralty on a person of Mr R. Thornton's description (a gentle-man of rank, a merchant of eminence & a Member of Parliament) nor of his impression that Mr Price would be on the whole a more proper selection.

But Mr Yorke is at the same time sollicitous to conform in this matter wholly to Y.R.H.'s pleasure as to what may be most fitting to be done, & he has now only most humbly to request the communication of Y.R.H.'s gracious commands respecting the disposal of this office, which will be implicitly and immediately obeyed.[1] (18554-5)

1. See No. 3116.

York House, 17 Sept. 1811

The first anxiety of my heart is to know how your Grace does, for on my return from Cheltenham on Sunday I had unfeigned grief to hear that your Grace was confined to your bed by illness, and I have the joy to know that the same sympathy of feeling in the breast of the Prince Regent has almost this very instant induced his Royal Highness to earnestly command me to make your Grace his best love & most affectionate regards, & to repeat the question how your Grace does.

I find from the Prince that his Royal Highness, in my absence, had caused Colonel Gordon to inform your Grace of the earnest recommendation which the Ministers had made for the recall of Lord Strangford as a point not to be relinquish'd on any consideration, and at the same time submitting the name of Lord Louvaine[1] to his pleasure, as the successor to the Embassy. The Prince commands me to say the extreme pain he felt at finding the former proposition to be indispensable, from the reflection most particularly that his Lordship had been honor'd with your Grace's friendship & protection; and that with regard to the succession, it had been placed before H.R.Hss. as a measure the Ministers thought must prove agreable to him as being entirely offer'd by them with a view of a personal compliment from the *Prince Regent* to *your Grace*, and the Prince commands me again, *and in confidence*, to assure your Grace that he will not allow such appointment to be carried into effect unless with your fullest & most perfect approbation. H.R.Hss. desires to add that he will have shortly an occasion to communicate with your Grace on some most *interesting* & *important* points respecting Portugal, for his own individual benefit & advantage, for without your advice he was resolv'd not to determine upon them.

I am return'd much better for Cheltenham, but am running a dreadful gauntlet from the dayly Press, for my Royal master's last act of bounty & graciousness[2] (Alnwick MSS.).

1. George, Lord Lovaine (1778–1867), M.P. for Bere Alston, 1799–1830. He was the son of Lord Algernon Percy (1750–1830), who was the second son of Hugh, Duke of Northumberland, and who became Lord Lovaine on the death of the Duke, 6 June 1786, and who was created Earl of Beverley on 2 November 1790. George succeeded his father as 2nd Earl of Beverley on 21 October 1830, and succeeded his cousin as 5th Duke of Northumberland on 12 February 1865. A Lord of the Treasury, 1804–6; a Commissioner of the Board of Control, 1807–12; a Lord of the Bedchamber, 1821–30; Captain of the Yeomen of the Guard, 1841–6.

Lord Strangford remained Minister to the Prince Regent of Portugal (in Brazil) until 1815, being recalled on 31 December 1814. See No. 3189.

2. Colonel Gordon wrote to the Duke from the Horse Guards on the 14th: 'Having this day returned from Ipswich, where I had been in my official capacity attending the Prince, I was on the point of writing to inquire after your Grace's health, when I received a message from the Prince desiring my attendance, from which I am this moment returned. H.R.H. made a confidential communication to me, which he commanded me, (i[n] the temporary absence of

3169A MAJOR-GENERAL F. DECKEN TO [   ]

2. James's Str. Terrace, Buckingham Gate, 17 Sept. 1811

Secret. I have received the following intelligence from Berlin written the latter part of last month. Bonaparte is stated to have demanded the fortresses Colberg and Graudenz. The King of Prussia has positively refused to comply with this demand but has promised to prevent all possible intercourse with the country and has given verry [*sic*] severe orders to that effect. This demand of Bonaparte has caused much negociation between Berlin and Paris, the result of which was not yet known. Meanwhile the King of Prussia has begun warlike preparations, and has assembled an army at Colberg of about 371,000 men. The Cabinet of Berlin is stated to be divided in two parts, one for and the other against the French. The nobles for the greater part are for the French, being much displeased with Count Hardenberg's[1] arrangements, by which they lose a great part of their incomes and privileges. The King is very indecisive. The nation at large is stated to be verry violent against the French. The French are stated to have a large force on the Prussian frontiers. (18556)

3170 LORD ELDON TO THE PRINCE REGENT

Encombe, 18 Sept. 1811

The Lord Chancellor humbly takes leave to state to your Royal Highness the Prince Regent that he waited upon Mr Perceval for some hours on Sunday last. They had much conversation upon the subjects which your

MacMahon) to communicate direct to your Grace, and which I will endeavour to do in his own words, lamenting only the impossibility of doing justice to his kind expressions of regard & friendship for your Grace.

'The Prince said that Lord Wellesley had been with him to propose that Lor dLovaine should be sent to the Brazils to relieve Lord Strangford who was to be recalled. To this the Prince gave no other answer than that he would consider of it. "Now," says H.R.H., "before I give my decision upon this point I must know whether this arrangement would comport with the Duke's wishes with regard to his family, for he may rely upon it that I will do nothing contrary to his inclinations, and I am never more happy than when I think I am meeting them." "The fact, unfortunately is," the Prince continued, "that Lord Strangford, with every zealous & good wish, has materially erred, & he must necessarily be recalled, though he deserves and shall receive every favorable consideration. With respect to myself I cannot have any objection to Lord Lovaine, nor any other predilection for him than as he may stand well with my friend the Duke, and therefore it is that I am anxious you should ascertain for me his Grace's wishes upon this point, assuring him that I will not act contrary to them."

'All this was done i[n] the most gracious manner, which I can only thus inadequately express' (Alnwick MSS.).

1. See No. 40. He had succeeded Stein as Frederick William III's Chancellor in June 1810.

Royal Highness had the goodness to mention on Saturday. Their extreme importance precludes the possibility of coming to any resolution upon them in a first conversation, if their nature did not necessarily render them matters for Cabinet consideration, upon which, therefore, Mr Percival & the Chancellor could only converse generally as individuals. The Chancellor left Mr Percival, understanding that he meant humbly to propose to your Royal Highness to allow a Council to be held on Tuesday the first of October with reference to the Prorogation of Parliament, at which, if it should be your Royal Highness's pleasure to hold the Council, the Chancellor will not fail to attend, and he agreed with Mr Percival that he would remain in town till the end of the week, in the hope that the Cabinet, in general, would also be in town in order to discuss the subjects to which the Chancellor alludes.

The Lord Chancellor begs permission to express his dutiful & grateful thanks for the condescension and kindness with which your Royal Highness was graciously pleased to honor him at Windsor. (18557–8)

3171 LIEUTENANT-COLONEL CHARLES PALMER TO COLONEL MCMAHON

Brighton Barracks, 18 Sept. [1811]

At the desire of Col Quentin[1] I reply to the enclosed letter by assuring you that the fact therein stated is untrue, & at the same time cannot help expressing my surprise & regret that the writer should on such slight grounds take upon himself to decide against the Regiment in a case which he conceives to be so discreditable to its character, but which if true, would in my humble opinion be rendered much more so by adopting the mode of compromise he recommends. The fact is this, the man Wilson whom he alludes to, was certainly sentenced to, & did receive 200 lashes, but *only* 200, of which the Adjutant of the Regiment who (as usual) took down the number on paper & whose authority from that circumstance, & thro' being in the habit of it, is most to be relied on, & who could have no motive but his duty to actuate him, will make oath— fortunately too, the surgeon of the Regiment, Mr Morrison, from the attention he paid at the time, is enabled to make oath of the same, nor am I aware of anyone who can contradict it, altho I know that a report to that effect was circulated at the time, & which originated entirely with the farriers of the Regt. who flog by turns but who on this occasion by

1. Sir George Augustus Quentin (1760–1851), Cornet in 10th Hussars, 1793; Colonel of the 10th (Prince of Wales's) Light Dragoons. Lieutenant-Colonel, 1808; Colonel, 1814; Major-General, 1825; Lieutenant-General, 1838. K.C.B., 1815; K.C.H., 1821. He came from an old-established German family, in Göttingen.

accident or design (& I strongly suspect the latter) shifted their places in their rank, & thereby occasioned the doubts of those who calculated the punishment by the number of farriers & the turns which came to each.

With respect to the writer's apprehensions of an enquiry in the House of Commons, I can only say for the sake of the service that I should not have the least objection to it, as I am sure nothing could be easier to prove than the absurdity & danger of the system of a total abolition of corporal punishment—for instance in our own Regiment, previous to the punishment of this Wilson, none had taken place since the discussion alluded to in the House of Commons, & had it not again been resorted to, I believe a mutiny must have been the consequence, but from that period the general conduct of the men has been as orderly & creditable as ever & fully justified the propriety of the step taken—at the same time there are not wanting those who as in all other Regiments, are anxious to create discontent, of which we had another instance yesterday which Col. Quentin will explain to his Royal Highness or yourself. I trust you will forgive me if I have expressed myself more warmly than the occasion justifies & believe me [etc.]. (18563)

[Enclosure] FROM REAR-ADMIRAL HENRY WARRE[1]
Grenada Cottage, East Barnet, 11 Sept. 1811
A circumstance has this day accidently come to my knowledge by the means of a man of the name of Wilson, a taylor at Finchley. I employ him and I saw him this morning. He has a brother it seems in the 10th Dragoons, his Royal Highness the Prince Regent's Regt. N. Wilson was order'd to recieve two hundred lashes by the sentence of a court martial *lately* at Brighton; by some great inattention (as I cannot impute it to any other cause) the man recieved two hundred & twenty lashes. I know the brother has been at Brighton about the business and has evidence of the fact. A Lieut.-Col. Palmer, it appears, superintended the punishment.

I have no other motive by this communication to you than to prevent if possible unpleasant circumstances being brought before the public; and the more especially so, from what *lately* passed on the subject of corporal punishment before the House of Commons.[2]

In my own opinion I think the friends of the man may be inclined to drop the subject by the man's discharge and some compensation from the party whose duty it was to see the prisoner recieved no more punishment than the court martial awarded. The case, as far as my humble

1. Lieutenant, 1781; Captain, 1790; Superannuated as Rear-Admiral, August 1810.

2. For the discussions on flogging in the army, see *Parliamentary Debates*, xx. 320 (25 May); 698 (18 June); 759 (26 June), and 776 (1 July).

judgement goes, must in being agitated operate to ye prejudice of the Service. I am persuaded my friend will at least give me credit for good intentions in acquainting him with this circumstance, and will entirely act as his much better opinion guides him. (18565)

3172 THE EARL OF MOIRA TO COLONEL MCMAHON

Donington, 18 Sept. 1811

It was curious that an illustration of the species of mischief which I supposed to be generating by the conduct of Government in Ireland should immediately occur after I had stated to you the probability of it. I have perused a letter from an officer in a regt. of English militia to his brother, giving an account of what passed the first night he & others went to the theatre in Dublin. A voice in the gallery called for a groan for the English militia, upon which a yell echoed from every side. Then a groan was demanded for John Bull. It was given with every show of inveteracy. Afterwards, God Save the King was struck up in the orchestra. The tune was opposed with loud clamour by the galleries, & Patrick's Day in the Morning was insisted upon in its stead. The officer says, 'to us uninformed folks this looks as like a prelude to violence as anything that could be imagined.' And we forget that Bonaparte is watching the game! Be assured the dissatisfaction is running to formidable consequences, & those not distant.

I enclose to you a strange letter from Capn. Byng. My answer was that, as he professed himself to be too deeply embarked to recede, any opinion on the subject was out of the question; that the Prince never could sanction an opposition to his Ministers; & that I thence regarded his letter as only a polite intimation meant for his Royal Highness to preclude the suspicion of any cooperation with persons hostile to the Prince individually.

Can a Barrack-mastership be obtained for Frederick Forbes?[1] He is a Yahoo: but by Sir John Doyle's account he certainly had hard measure on his court martial. Were he to starve alone it would not signify, but he has a wife. It would be hard to have Ld Granard saddled with him, when Ld G. has had such cause of estrangement to him as not to have had communication with him for years. A West India station is what would best suit him, & there is not much competition for the opportunity of forming acquaintance with the land crabs.

I further submit a letter of Lady Myers's; leaving you to judge whether

1. Lord Granard's brother (1776–1817). In 1796 he married Mary, daughter of William Butler, from whom he was divorced.

140

or not it should be laid before the Prince. Let me amuse you with another point of parish business. There is a Madame de Willford who came to this country with the first swarm of émigrés from France. She was so circumstanced as to receive remittances from her relations who staid behind; and she thence thought it would be unhandsome to apply for an allowance here. Till now she has subsisted without aid from Government, but recently her sources of supply from France have been annihilated. She is a real object, & it would be a pity that her delicacy should be a bar (as it is a point of form) to her receiving assistance. The prayer is that she may be recommended to the Committee, which, without such an authorisation, could not take her case into consideration as it would be deemed a new one. The Prince de Condé would make the solicitation earnestly if that be necessary.

[P.S.] It is surmised that Ld. Gosford's election may be made void thro' his having neglected some form in qualifying himself as candidate; but this is not explained to me. (18559–62)

3173   THE EARL OF MOIRA TO THE PRINCE REGENT

Donington, 19 Sept. 1811

When I entered upon my functions as Constable of the Tower, it was explained to me to be my duty that in all arrangements relative to the fortress I should take the pleasure of the King directly & not thro the channel of any Minister. A proposition is now made to me by the Treasury to which I conceive there can be no objection, but which I yet consider as coming so much within the sense of the line pointed out to me as to require my having your Royal Highness's sanction. It is only that I should appoint a person on my part to determine with one delegated from the Ordnance & one from the Keeper of the Public Records as to the distribution of the buildings which belonged to the officers of the Mint. As far as relates to the convenience of the garrison such a reference is likely to be superficial, but it is still a preliminary to a degree of alteration on which the signification of your Royal Highness's pleasure appears to me previously requisite. If no objection shall occur I will humbly solicit that your Royal Highness may deign to direct M. General Turner to notify your approbation for my proceeding in the way proposed. (18571–2)

3174 ROBERT THORNTON TO THE PRINCE REGENT

Grafton Street, 19 Sept. 1811

Mr. Yorke has this day offered to me the place of Marshal to the Admiralty Court, which I have determined to accept.

This, Sir, brings me to the moment when I have to perform the duty of thanking your Royal Highness not only for the most substantial benefit but for the most condescending marks of favor & partiality in obtaining that benefit for me. The impressions I now have can never be changed & I am bound to your Royal Highness for my life in humblest duty, in strongest gratitude & in most unqualified respect & veneration. The mind that is properly grateful in common cases finds some relief, but at my humble distance to have received such marked condescensions & liberality is almost a weight too oppressive, yet that oppression is even [*sic*] relieved when my illustrious benefactor condescends to confer so great a benefit as your Royal Highness has done. It is but justice to Mr. Yorke, altho' he offered some observations which are known to your Royal Highness, that I should state the very handsome manner in which he executed your Royal Highness's commands on this day.[1] (18569–70)

3175 HENRY GOULBURN TO COLONEL MCMAHON

Whitehall, 19 Sept. 1811

Mr Goulburn presents his compliments to Coll. MacMahon & takes the liberty of requesting that he would take the earliest opportunity of submitting to his Royal Highness the Prince Regent for his Royal Highnesses signature the enclosed order for sending Jean Bart out of the country, as some circumstances have occurred to render it necessary to put it immediately in force against him. (18573)

3176 CHARLES YORKE TO THE PRINCE REGENT

Admy., 20 Sept. 1811

Mr Yorke has the honor most humbly to acquaint your Royal Highness that having in obedience to Y.R.H.'s commands (communicated thro'

---

1. Wilberforce mistakenly thought that Thornton owed his appointment to the influence of the Duke of Cumberland. Referring to his party of 'Saints', he wrote (1 October), 'This is one of the instances in which the whole connection will be discredited by the misconduct of one man' (Wilberforce MSS.). Thornton wrote to Lord Melville from the south of France on 14 February 1815 resigning his office on account of 'extreme ill health and some family afflictions which have greatly increased my present illness' (Thornton MSS.).

Colonel McMahon) again seen Mr R. Thornton, & after restating to him a full description of the office of Marshal of the Admiralty, offered it to him finally for his acceptance or rejection, Mr R. Thornton has this day thought proper to decide on the former alternative, & the usual warrant has been directed to be made out for his appointment accordingly.

Mr Yorke humbly presumes to entertain a hope that the pretensions of Mr Price to favorable consideration on this occasion, may entitle him to the gracious recollection of your Royal Highness at some future opportunity.[1] (18584)

3177   COUNT MÜNSTER TO THE PRINCE REGENT
Clarges Street, 20 Sept. 1811
Count Munster most humbly communicates to your Royal Highness an abstract of a letter from Colonel Gneisenau[2] which he received yesterday. He intends, with your Royal Highness permission, to send it to the Marquis Wellesley.

Count Münster has also received a most minute and satisfactory account of the present state of the Russian army.

A messenger from Hannover is arrived at Harwich and is likely to reach London tomorrow. (18585)

3178   THE EARL OF YARMOUTH TO THE PRINCE REGENT
Seymour Place, 20 Sept. 1811
Enclosed are some further words &c. suggested in addition by Count Nugent. I will add them properly to your Royal Highness's dictionary whenever it may be under your Royal Highness hand. I would have deferred this but it is possible he may soon write.[3] (42518)

1. Later, William Price, who had been Equerry to the King (1782–7), Groom of the Bedchamber (1795) and Vice-Chamberlain to the Queen (1792–1801) was Secretary and Comptroller of the Queen's Household (1814–16).

2. August Wilhelm Anton von Gneisenau (1760–1831). Fought in the Imperial army in the War of the Bavarian Succession, 1778; entered the Prussian service, 1785; defended fortress of Colberg, 1807; later, Blücher's Chief of Staff with rank of Lieutenant-General; rose to rank of Field Marshal.

3. The enclosure is missing.

3179 WILLIAM ADAM TO COLONEL MCMAHON

Richmond Park, 20 Sept. 1811

The sensations excited in my mind respecting the proposal made by the Chief Baron of Scotland,[1] communicated to me by the Prince with such marked kindness & gracious regard to my interests, so completely absorbed my thoughts & excited my astonishment that it prevented me, in the short conversation which I had with you as we walked to Carlton House, from telling you that I had had a very different account of the Ch. Bar.'s objects, and of his brother Mr Wm. Dundas's—and that it had been publicly stated on the authority of the Justice Clerk & propogated [*sic*] throughout Scotland that the whole was settled and that Wm. Dundas was to be made the Exqr. Baron in the room of Norton,[2] and I was to be Chief Baron. And so much was this current that George Drummond[3] was canvassing Kincardineshire & securing my friends to support him on the strength of it. I little thought while this was the view of their friends in Scotland that the C. B. & his br. were ushering in a proposal so totally inconsistent with his former professions and grounds of refusal—and so entirely out of all bounds in point of propriety and fitness to be submitted to the consideration of his Royal Highness.

I never can have effaced from my mind the Prince's conduct to me throughout the whole of this procrastined bss. It makes an impression which no words are equal to expressing.

The manner in which his Rl. Hss. pressed on me the situation of Presidt,[4] as the only practicable thing now—can only encrease the security & strength of those feelings—& the desire that I shd. take time to consider it adds to all.

I will attend his Royal Hss. tomorrow to submit the imperative reasons against my acceding to this wish & I am sure they will convince.

How the Ch. B. & Wm. Dundas—for Lord Melville is entirely free from any connection with this outrageous proposal—can think of reconciling it to the consistency which they ought to preserve as regards themselves or their professed respectfull desire to accede to the Prince's wishes—only obstructed by that state of health which a title is to cure, I cannot conceive.[5]

The appointment I made with you yesterday will stand good. (18588–9)

1. Robert Dundas (1758–1819), Chief Baron since 1801. Mentioned as Lord Advocate (1793–1801) in No. 746.

2. Fletcher Norton (1744–1820), second son of Fletcher Norton, 1st Lord Grantley, and father of the 3rd Baron. M.P. for Appleby, 1773–4; for Carlisle, 1774–5. Baron of the Exchequer[s], 1776–1820.

3. George Harley Drummond (1783–1853), M.P. for Kincardineshire, 1812–20.

4. President of the Court of Session in Scotland. Charles Hope succeeded Robert Blair (1741–1811), the appointment being gazetted on 22 October.

5. Had the Prince Regent's offer of the office of President of the Court of Session been

144

[*21 Sept. 1811*][1]

Ld. Melville met the Chief Baron at Boroughbridge; persisted in not altering his decision as to the non-acceptance of the Presidentship.

accepted by Adam, Lord Melville's resignation from the Cabinet would have followed. Melville wrote to Perceval on 4 October: 'I wrote some days ago to Mr. Ryder on the subject of the Chief Baron's declining the situation of president of the Court of Session, & I regret the necessity which compels me to trouble you with the inclosed correspondence which has recently taken place on that subject. If you have seen my letters to Ryder, you will have observed that though I think the Chief Baron perfectly entitled now or at any time to look to a Peerage, I did not concur in the propriety of bringing forward those pretensions at the present moment, because it was liable to misinterpretation, & I think it would have been more *graceful*, if he chose to accept the office at all, to state his wishes after that acceptance rather than before. On the other hand I cannot possibly admit the justice of Mr. Adam's charge that there was anything derogatory to the honor of the Prince Regent in the proposition, from the state of the Chief Baron's health. It would have been at least as derogatory to have pressed the Chief Baron to accept a situation to which he repeatedly stated his health was unequal, from no other motive than creating a vacancy for Mr. Adam. It must also be re-collected that the Chief Baron had no idea or intention that the matter should be mentioned at all to H.R.H. unless you had previously concurred in the propriety of the request, & it was probably from his allusion (in his letter to you) to his brother's correspondence with you, that the mentioning it to H.R.H. became unavoidable. The Prince Regent's Government have been hitherto placed in embarrassing circumstances; but when it assumes a more settled form if we are to continue in his service, there must really be some explanation & understanding as to other and irresponsible advisers. I presume that the offer of the President's situation to Mr. Adam was without the knowledge & concurrence of either yourself, or the Lord Chancellor or Mr. Ryder. If I am right in that supposition, I should be glad to know if there can be anything more injurious to the Prince's character or more derogatory to his honor than the promulgating in writing that such an offer had been made under those circumstances. It is fortunate that Mr. Adam declined it, & he acted wisely. If he had accepted, & H.R.H. had insisted on the appointment, it would not have required one moment's hesitation or doubt to have induced me to request his permission to retire from his service, because I could not possibly have concurred in a measure that would have been so repugnant to the feelings of this part of the kingdom, or so disrespectful & injurious to the character of the Bench & the Bar. I was most anxious that the proper & reasonable wishes of H.R.H. in favor of Mr. Adam should have been gratified, but not at the expense of everything that is due to the public & of the respectability of our Courts of Justice. He was perfectly qualified to be Chief Baron, & he is totally unfit to be President' (Perceval MSS.).

1. Endorsed by William Adam: 'This is in the handwriting of the Prince Regent and was written by H.R.H. in my presence on my reading to him the statement and observations I had made respecting Mr. Wm. Dundas's proposal to make the C.B. a promise of peerage—to induce him to accept of the Presidentship—and on H.R.H. pressing me to accept the office of President.—21st Sepr. 1811.'

Perceval had written to Eldon on 2 September: 'I have had a *queerish* letter from William Dundas. The Chief Baron's health it seems is improved *so far* that, provided that *strengthener of the nerves, a British peerage*, could be promised, the danger which otherwise his constitution might apprehend from the change of situation would be no longer alarming!!! It might have been all very fair if it had been said and felt, at first, that the present situation was what he much preferred and what he would not leave, but under the inducement of the advantage of a peerage to himself and family, but to have been resisting it on the score of ill health for two

After that, met his brother, Wm. Dundas, at Harrowgate, when in consequence of that meeting, Wm. Dundas wrote to Mr. Percival, stating his brother's continued objection to the change of situation, but at the same time plainly stated that if an English peerage was offer'd or admitted, it would be a douceur which his brother would not refuse, and would be the inducement to him to accept of the desir'd exchange. Percival almost immediately answers, either through Wm. Dundas or directly to the Chief Baron himself, in the most amicable but at the same time, in the most decided terms, that this was a proposal that could in no way be listen'd to or recommended by him to the P.Rt. This then drew almost an immediate answer from the Chief Baron, thanking Mr. Percival for the very friendly manner in which he had treated his brother's, Mr. Wm. Dundas's, letter and proposal, but stating that he totally disagreed or differ'd with Mr. Perceval's train of argument and reasoning, and further stating that in consequence his determination was finally fix'd, and that therefore he was induc'd not to come to London, as it had been propos'd to him to do, and as he had originally assented to do, because in all probability he would have then been honor'd by a

months and then to be disposed to accept it with the peerage annexed did, I must confess, not a little surprise me.' He concluded, 'You know how embarrassing anything which increases the number of competitors for the peerage is to the Government at present, and yet with the Prince's anxiety for the ulterior arrangement I should not wonder if he approved very much of the proposition, to be executed in due time' (Eldon MSS.).

The following is probably a complete list of applicants for peerages whilst Perceval was Prime Minister: First, *Irish Peerages*.

Vice-Admiral Sir William Sidney Smith recommended himself. Lord Westmorland recommended Viscount Longueville and Lord Caher for Earldoms (the former died, 23 May 1811 and Caher was given an Irish Earldom, 22 January 1816); also, unsuccessfully, John Bagwell, M.P. Colonel Strutt asked that Lord Lecale's peerage might be entailed to his nephew, the Colonel's son. The Irish Attorney General told the Duke of Richmond that it would be illegal (presumably by the provisions of the Act of Union).

Second, *U.K. Peerages*.

Viscount Curzon was recommended, unsuccessfully, for an Earldom by his daughter-in-law, Sophia, Baroness Howe (her son, who succeeded his grandfather as Viscount Curzon, was created Earl Howe in 1821). Lord Harewood asked for an Earldom, and was given one on 7 September 1812. Sir Cecil Bishopp, 8th Baronet (1753–1828), asked for a peerage—without success until 11 August 1815 when the abeyance of the Barony of Zouche was terminated in his favour. Colonel Beaumont, M.P., vainly sought a peerage, Mrs. Beaumont recommending him for one. R. E. Drax-Grosvenor's personal application was also unsuccessful, as was Sir William Langham's, he alleging that his father had been promised a peerage by the Duke of Portland. The Earl of Elgin [S.] wanted a U.K. peerage, but was given 'no encouragement'. A similar reply was given to Ralph Sheldon, who was brought into Parliament by Lord Pembroke. 'Sorry, but unfavourable,' was the gist of the reply given to General Craufurd, who had married the widowed Duchess of Newcastle. The Duke of Atholl asked for a peerage for his second son, Lord James Murray (the Duke of Northumberland's son-in-law), but it was not given until 1821 (title, Lord Glenlyon). The Duke of Marlborough's application for a peerage for his second son was similarly deferred—until 1815. The applications of Sir William Manners and Lethbridge have already been noticed.

personal interview with the P.Rt., and when he must have declin'd the furtherance of his R.Hss.'s views and wishes respecting his change of situation on the Bench of Scotland (Blair Adam MSS.).

3181 THE DUKE OF NORTHUMBERLAND TO COLONEL MCMAHON

22 Sept. 1811

Most Confidential. Altho again confined to my bed & hardly able to hold my pen I can no longer delay begging you to lay me at the Prince's feet & to assure H.R.H. how sensible I am of his kindness & partiality. I am sorry that Ld. Strangford's conduct shoud make his removal necessary, but I shoud feel more miserable than it is possible for me to express, was Lord Lovaine to be appointed Lord Strangford's immediate successor. The appearance this appointment must have to H.R.H. the Prince of Brazil, Lord Strangford & his friends I need not mention, as well as how injurious as well as false the conclusions must be on the occasion. I trust therefore H.R.H. the Prince will permit me to supplicate him in the most earnest manner that Ld. Lovaine may not be the *immediate* successor to Ld. Strangford.

Of Lord Lovaine's abilities for filling such a situation I know nothing, nor woud I wish to be supposed to interest myself in any way about his future appointment. I find from a part of your last letter that it is necessary I should explain in confidence the situation of Lord Beverley's family with respect to mine. Soon after my father's death, my brother waited upon me to say that he shoud look upon himself & family in politicks, as having no connection with, & perfectly independent of me, and in conformity to this he immediately join'd Mr Pitt & procured his own advance in the Peerage, & different other advantages without even my knowledge till the circumstances were effected; nor has any political intercourse of any kind ever subsisted since between Lord Beverley's family or mine. Ld. Lovaine's appointment therefore to the situation mentioned must be as perfectly indifferent to me as if any other person was appointed. But unfortunately, not just so in the present instance, from the injurious appearance that the appointment of *my nephew* as the *immediate* successor to Ld Strangford must carry with it.

Desiring you, my dear Colonel, to lay all these things before H.R.H. for his most serious consideration I beg you will assure him that I shall ever feel the gratitude I owe H.R.H. for his confidential communication, whatever may be his decision upon this point.

I wish you may be able to make out this letter, but I will no longer delay writing adieu. (18590)

147

H. Guards, 23 Sept. 1810 [1811]

Private. I have been some days in possession of your letter of the 17th instant & its enclosures—and I assure you I fully appreciate the confidence you have reposed in me by favoring me with the perusal of your brother's[1] letter. It would be uncandid not to confess that his case is hard, but I should make an ill return for the confidence which marks your communication if I did not state with equal candour that in my opinion a junior off[ice]r has no right to complain of supercession in the course of the Service. It is what we are all liable to—and I have often experienced the mortification of giving up a flattering command to a senior offr. and of relinquishing to him the credit which I had had the ambition to look to, as the reward of much labour & exertion. However I may have felt upon such occasions I considered it my duty to submit with a good grace—and I am confident that when the irritation arising from the disappointment of an honorable ambition shall have subsided in the mind of your brother, he will likewise see the necessity of yielding to the unavoidable circumstances of the case respecting which he complains: it is quite impossible that any discredit should attach to an offr. who is superceded by the arrival of a senior; every person must look upon it as the common course of the Service—particularly as Col. Spry[2] is a *full Colonel* in our service—and I am confident you will agree with me in thinking that a young Lt Col. whose legitimate station is the Command of a Regt. has no right to complain because he is not continued to act as a General. Besides it appears by Col. D'Urban's[3] letter that Col. McMahon was led to expect this supercession. While I argue in this way I must repeat that I think your brother's case very hard. But I am equally of opinion that he should submit to it. I shall conclude with the expression of a hope that you will do me the justice to receive in good part the frankness with which I have communicated my sentiments upon this subject. I return the letter and remain [etc.].

N.B. I know not what to say respecting yr brother's removal from Portugal—But if any plan should occur by which it might be effected I

1. Sir Thomas McMahon (1779–1860) succeeded his brother, Colonel McMahon, as 2nd Baronet on 12 September 1817. Lieutenant-Colonel, 1809; Colonel, 1814; Lieutenant-General, 1838. Adjutant-General in India for thirteen years, Commander of South-west District in England for five years, and Commander-in-Chief, Bombay, 1840–7.

2. William Frederick Spry (*d.* 1814). Lieutenant-Colonel, 1800; Colonel, 1808; Major-General, 1813.

3. Sir Benjamin D'Urban (1777–1849). Entered the army, 1793; Captain, 1794; Major, 1799; Lieutenant-Colonel, 1805; Colonel, 1813. K.C.B., 1815; K.C.H., 1818; Major-General, 1819; Governor of Antigua, 1820; of Demerara and Essquibo, 1824; of the Cape of Good Hope, 1833–7. Lieutenant-General, 1837. G.C.B., 1840.

shall be very happy to consult with you. I think however you should persuade him to remain where he is for the present at least. (18593–5)

3183 COLONEL MCMAHON TO THE DUKE OF NORTHUMBERLAND

Carlton House, 25 Sept. 1811

MOST SECRET. Believe me that the sight of your Grace's handwriting was received by the Prince Regent with inexpressible delight and by me with heartfelt joy & happiness, for nothing could exceed the uneasiness & anxiety which your recent illness had occasion'd. The Prince with all affection to your Grace commands me to assure you of his best love & regard, and to entreat that you will most confidently rely *that no consideration upon earth* shall ever induce his Royal Highness to allow of Lord Louvaine being appointed to the Embassy to the Prince Regent of Portugal; and that [neither] Lord Louvaine nor any person living shall ever know of his reason for this determination. That H.R.Hss. is now overjoy'd at the sagacity & happy foresight which led him so quickly to apprehend there might possibly be doubts in your Grace's mind on the subject of this appointment, and that he had the good fortune to have thus early apprized you of it. The Prince, coinciding with your Grace in all the feelings you have express'd on the occasion, & agreeing entirely in the force and propriety of your reasoning upon it, is most anxious to devise some mode for dispensing with the measure regarding Lord Strangford which the Ministers represent to be so very indispensable, by averting either his removal or causing it to be done (if unavoidable) in a manner the most complimentary to his feelings & character, from the weighty & primary consideration that his Lordship has been so honor'd & distinguish'd by your Grace's favor & protection, with [*sic*] still retaining an earnest desire to serve Ld. Strangford individually. I hope so long a scroll may not disturb your Grace's repose, and with every kind wish for the health & felicity of all at Alnwick Castle that love & gratitude can send, I have the honor [etc.][1] (Alnwick MSS.).

1. Colonel Gordon wrote to the Duke on 1 October, from the Horse Guards: 'The enclosed will shew you the result of the Prince's decision which you will see accords exactly with your wishes. I was aware that the younger branch of your Grace's family differed with you in politics, but I did not quite so intimately know the causes: indeed my connection with that part of Julia's relations has never been very much cultivated. Your Grace at the outset of my marriage was pleased to address me in what I then considered very handsome & condescending terms, & your whole conduct to me has been such as I ever have upon all occasions, and ever shall, very gratefully acknowledge, and the only return I could make was to look up to you as the head of the family into which I had the honor to connect myself, and as far as was necessary to frame my opinions by yours. This I have done without deviation upon all

Apsley House, 4 p.m., Friday, 27 Sept. 1811

Lord Wellesley has the honor to acquaint your Royal Highness that Lord William Bentinck is arrived in London from Sicily. Lord William Bentinck had a conditional permission to come to England if your Royal Highness's service should appear to require such a step.

Lord Wellesley expects to see Lord William immediately, & will instantly submit the result of the conference to your Royal Highness.[1]

Lord Wellesley humbly proposes with your Royal Highness's gracious approbation to attend at York House[2] to morrow (Saturday) at two o'clock. (18621)

Apsley House, 5.15 p.m., Friday, 27 Sept. 1811

Lord Wellesley has the honor to submit to your Royal Highness the dispatches received by Lord William Bentinck whom Lord Wellesley has seen since the date of his former note of this day. Lord Wellesley deems it an act of duty to submit to your Royal Highness his humble opinion that Lord William Bentinck has acted with great judgment, temper & resolution, and that his Lordship has pursued the true spirit of your Royal Highness's commands, with honor to the national character & to your Royal Highness, & with a prospect of advantage to the public service, in bringing the affairs of Sicily to a short & plain issue.[3] (18622)

publick affairs, and this perhaps has tended to disincline me from any intimacy with the most respectable persons of the younger branch, so that I cannot in truth boast of much acquaintance or influence there' (Alnwick MSS.).

1. Lord William Bentinck had arrived at Palermo on 24 July, and suddenly left for England on 28 August. His departure alarmed the Sicilian Court, which became much more amenable after his return (7 December) to the reforms he proposed to introduce. The real ruler was not the incapable Ferdinand IV but Queen Caroline, who hated the English and was intriguing with the French.

2. The Prince Regent was still living at York House, and it was not until the middle of December that he moved to Carlton House, following the completion of alterations. Princess Charlotte remained, in a very comfortless state, at Warwick House, which was 'full of work people'.

3. Friction had been growing between the British authorities in Sicily (by the Treaty of Palermo, March 1808, Great Britain had undertaken to defend Sicily against the French with a force of at least 10,000 men, and to subsidize the Court to the amount of £300,000 a year) and the intriguing Queen.

Horse Guards, 7 p.m., 28 Sept. 1811

I am this instant returned from Windsor and have to acquaint you that the account of his Majesty continues exactly the same without the least shade whatsoever of better though he is today in rather a milder mood than yesterday.

Sir Henry Halford shewed me the answers which have been given by the three consulting phisicians which he will bring to you tomorrow morning. The most explicit is certainly Dr. Monroe's, but except overturning everything that Dr. Heberden had wished to propose they seem to me to contain little or no information whatsoever, and though Dr. Simmonds says that he has known some patients of the age of his Majesty who have recovered, yet to the question when that is put directly to him he says that he is not able to give an answer. Dr. J. Willis I understand from his brother is very sorry for the answer which he has given to the last question.

Sir Henry asked me if I had seen his letter to you to which I answered in the affirmative, upon which he asked me if I liked it, when I told him that I was sorry that he had written it, as I thought, though I had no doubt with the best intention, that he had stept out of his sphere. I had not time to say more to him as I was then called to attend the Queen. I found her Majesty rather low. She began immediately by asking me what I thought of the answers of the consulting phisicians, when I told her that they seemed to me to contain nothing at all except a complete contrary opinion to Dr. Heberden's remarks upon the treatment of his Majesty; that, however, I thought it my duty to put her upon her guard as to the possibility of the Council taking advantage of that paragraph in Dr. Simmond's answer in which he seems to hold out his Majesty's recovery as less improbable than any of the other phisicians, to press her again to admit of his personally attending the King, and in case of her continuing to refuse it, of their tendering their resignations, to which to my great surprize she said that she should not be astonished at it, as the Duke of Montrose had some time ago dropt something to that purpose. I then endeavoured to lead her on to talk upon what probably [will] be the course of proceeding at the meeting of Parliament, but she would not enter into it but changed immediately the subject, only saying that she was perfectly aware that there must be an examination of phisicians.
(44246–7)

3186   GEORGE COLMAN[1] TO [?] COLONEL MCMAHON

28 Sept. 1811

I have drawn up a memorial to the Prince Regent, and it is of much importance to the interests of the Haymarket Theatre that it should be submitted to his Royal Highness's consideration as speedily as possible.

My inability of attending at present with this memorial, and of paying my personal duty at Carlton House is among the first of many mortifications which my restricted situation has render'd unavoidable.

Allow me to introduce to you by this letter my friend Mr Winston; he is my partner and theatrical Aide-de-camp; and let me further intrude upon your goodness by requesting you to point out to him when and in what manner he may have the honour (if not contrary to etiquette) of presenting the paper in question to the Prince Regent. (18627)

3187   THE EARL OF MOIRA TO MAJOR-GENERAL T. H. TURNER

Donington, 29 Sept. 1811

So many solicitations have been received by me respecting the living of Little Halingbury, vacated by the death of Doctor Raine[2] & in the gift of the Governors of the Charter House, that I suppose it must be a very good thing. In that case there may be some individual whose aims at it the Prince may be desirous to support. The Duke of Kent wrote to me immediately on the vacancy, requesting my vote for a Doctor Maule. My answer was that I should be happy to obey his Royal Highness's wishes, under the reservation of the Prince's having no person to protect on the occasion; for that I must always feel my suffrage bound to anyone whom the Prince might countenance. Pray learn for me the Prince's wishes in this point, as likewise on the Mastership about which I have many letters. (18628–9)

3188   THOMAS TYRWHITT TO COLONEL MCMAHON

Plymouth, 29 Sept. 1811

Upon any subject the Prince's wishes are to me commands.

I am apprehensive there will be some difficulty in softening our friend B.'s enthusiasm to represent this Borough. This can be only be done [*sic*]

1. The dramatist (1762–1836), Manager of the Haymarket Theatre, 1789–1813. See No. 3191.

2. Matthew Raine (1760–1811) was Headmaster of Charterhouse, 1791–1811. He was presented to the Living of Little Hallingbury (Essex) in July 1810. Jonathan Raine, one of the Duke of Northumberland's Members, was his brother.

152

by its being stated to him I am not permitted to abandon the footing I have here.

In spite of all cabal I shall be quite sure of my return & without expense—but I protest my ambition to be again in the House is very small—it will be politic to request B. for a short time to say nothing upon the subject.[1]

I think Sr. C. Pole has been very steady to H.R.H. throughout all the discussions of last Spring, and having answered the whip whenever I requested him to come up, I do not see how I can abandon him as my future colleague—but of this more when we meet.[2]

No man can be more rejoiced than I am to hear you are returned much improved in looks. Old England, with whom I dine today, is as thin as a whipping post, & must have drank oceans from Mrs Fonty's hands.[3]

With my most humble duty upstairs, I remain [etc.]. (18630–1)

3189 COLONEL MCMAHON TO THE DUKE OF NORTHUMBERLAND

Carlton House, 30 Sept. 1811

Private. I this morning had the honor to receive your Grace's favor of the 27th instant, and was inexpressibly delighted at the sight of the hand-writing which appear'd to indicate considerable progress in your Grace's recovery. I lost no time in laying it before the Prince Regent who earnestly participated in this feeling & opinion, and, commanding me to make your Grace his affectionate regards, to express H.R.Hss.'s delight at your amendment, and to assure your Grace that without disclosing any cause or reason, nor even leaving the possibility of its ever being known to Lord Louvaine himself that such a measure was ever in con-templation, the idea of sending his Lordship to the Prince Regent of Portugal is completely & entirely abandon'd for ever: and further, H.R.Hss. has settled & arrang'd that Lord Strangford shall not be recall'd, but on the contrary, that should he be able to atchieve certain

1. Sir Charles Morice Pole (1757–1830) and Tyrwhitt were elected for Plymouth at the general election in 1807. Bloomfield was elected, *vice* Tyrwhitt, on 22 June 1812, shortly before the Dissolution, the by-election being caused by Tyrwhitt's appointment as Gentleman Usher Daily Waiter to the King.

2. Pole was M.P. for Newark, 1802–6, and for Plymouth, 1806–18. See No. 264. He had been reckoned an Addingtonian in 1804 and 1805. In 1806 he was appointed a Lord of the Ad-miralty (re-elected for Newark, 17 February 1806). Like Sheridan and William Adam (but unlike Tyrwhitt and McMahon, who were only 'hopefuls'), Pole was reckoned by the Whigs as a 'thick and thin' Opposition man in 1810. He was therefore no longer a member of Sidmouth's dwindling connexion.

3. The allusion is obscure.

points confided to his charge he shall be advanced to the rank & station of full Ambassador to that Court, with all its attendant privileges & advantages[1] (Alnwick MSS.).

3190 THE MARQUESS WELLESLEY TO THE PRINCE REGENT
Foreign Office, 30 Sept. 1811
Lord Wellesley has the honor to acquaint your Royal Highness that in consequence of your Royal Highness's gracious approbation, the following appointments will be notified in the Gazette tomorrow.

Mr Henry Wellesley, Ambassador,[2]
Mr Charles Vaughan, Secretary of Embassy, in Spain.[3]
Mr Stuart,[4] Captain George Cockburn,[5] and Mr J. P. Morrier, Commissioners to Spanish America.
Mr Hoppner,[6] Secretary to the Commission in Spanish America.[7]
Mr Thomas Sydenham to reside at Lisbon[7] during the absence of Mr Stuart. (18632)

3191 GEORGE COLMAN TO [   ]
3 Oct. 1811
The Memorial, a copy of which I have already had the honour of conveying to your Royal Highness's hands, will be sent to Colonel MacMahon this evening, who has kindly promised to present it, immediately,

1. Lord Strangford attained Ambassadorial status only in 1821 when he was sent to Constantinople.

2. Hitherto he had been only Envoy Extraordinary and Minister Plenipotentiary (to Spain).

3. Charles Richard Vaughan's promotion from Secretary of Legation to Secretary of Embassy naturally followed Wellesley's advancement.

4. Charles Stuart, Minister to the Portuguese Regency.

5. Admiral Sir George Cockburn (1772–1853). Lieutenant, 1793; Captain, 1794; Rear-Admiral, August 1812; Vice-Admiral, 1819; Admiral, 1837; Lord of the Admiralty, 1818–27, 1828–30, 1834–5, 1841–6. K.C.B., 1815; G.C.B., 1818. M.P. for Portsmouth, 1818–20; for Weobley, 1820–8; for Plymouth, 1828–32; for Ripon, 1841–7. Succeeded his brother as 10th Baronet, 26 February 1852.

6. Richard Belgrave Hoppner. In 1814 he was Consul-General *ad interim* at The Hague, and was Acting Consul-General in charge of affairs at Lisbon, 1831–3.

7. The Commissioners were to attempt to mediate between Spain and her rebellious South American colonies. They accomplished nothing, and the colonies soon established *de facto* independence.

8. As Minister Plenipotentiary.

to the Prince Regent; and I wait the issue with the utmost anxiety, for my future 'daily bread' will depend upon it.

I had flattered myself that I had, some time ago, arrived at the most frozen latitudes in distress, but I find there is still an '*ultima Thule*'; a ruin beyond St. George's Fields;—and that without relief I shall touch the very North Pole of embarrassment. Should my case appear peculiarly hard (which I presume to be evident upon the fact of it) allow me, Sir, most respectfully to solicit your Royal Highness to assist me so far as to communicate some points to the Prince Regent, which I know not how to insert in a Memorial, unavoidably too long already. The points are as follows:—

I do not mean to be *querulous* against the Winter Managers; but to obviate if possible the ruin in which their protracted seasons threaten to involve me. In respect to the Lyceum, I am confident, from experience, that no two *Summer* Theatres can go on in London for several years and each of them prosper. They must either divide the comparatively scanty number of play-goers, in the dog days, so equally, that it would scarcely pay them for their labour, or one must ruin the other. How Mr Arnold[1] has, now, the pull, is explain'd in the memorial; and how Mr. Sheridan gave him that advantage, against his own interests and in forgetfulness of me, is a little surprising. The two Winter Theatres pledged themselves, with me, that we should all *three*, as regulars, join our forces to repel any invasion that might happen to any *one* of us. Soon after the Lyceum started up (which was an invasion upon *all* of us) Mr. Sheridan not only deserted me but mingled his interests with those of the invader. Possibly he might not have been able to help this, *at the moment*; and, therefore, I do not *complain* & cry *murder*; but if he is killing me by a kind of *chance-medley*, it is time to call out for assistance. From the best information I can gather, 'tis likely a City Theatre Bill may pass through Parliament. Mr. Sheridan has done me the honour to state, in the House of Commons, that, if a third Theatre were allow'd, I have the strongest claim to an interest in it. This is a handsome & generous declaration; & '*laudari à laudato viro*' is very flattering: but if an extension of license were given to me it would supersede one grand argument of the City speculators, namely, a want of competition, and would probably be the means of putting their project at rest; which project, if carried into execution, upon the extensive scale intended, would produce a much more formidable rivalship to Drury Lane than any plans I could ever enter into in the Haymarket.

At present, should my license be extended into the winter, the Haymarket and the Lyceum will not give more accommodation to the town than the late Old Drury, when it was open against Covent Garden.

---

1. Co-proprietor, with Tom Sheridan, of the Lyceum.

I respectfully entreat pardon for this intrusion; to which I have been impell'd by the hope that, through your Royal Highness's great goodness, the above explanations may meet the Prince Regent's consideration much about the same time as the presentation of the memorial—the effecting of which (so that a favourable impression upon *all* points might be obtain'd at *once*) is a most material object. (18643–4)

3192   GEORGE COLMAN TO COLONEL MCMAHON, AND AN ENCLOSURE

3 Oct. 1811

Accept my cordial thanks for your attentions to Mr Winston & for the very kind and friendly readiness you express'd to him in respect to presenting my memorial to the Prince Regent—which memorial I now enclose to you open, that you may be convinced there is no gunpowder put into it with a view to blow up any of my regular allies. I am merely acting upon the principle of preserving myself. Much innovation has already taken place in play-houses; & the clouds of revolution are gathering over the heads of the old theatrical constituted authorities. I think in such times my old colleagues, King Sheridan and King Harris, should (for their own interests) support me (& not suffer my small state to be annihilated in a grand impending convulsion. The Little Theatre is a little Poland: I would, if possible, still preserve my dominions. In regard to Mr. Sheridan's interests I know not how to express my sentiments better than by enclosing you an extract from a letter which I have just written on the subject of my memorial.

I think it will be much against Mr Sheridan's solid & ultimate interests to oppose me. I think it will tend much to his solid & ultimate interests (for reasons which you will perceive in the enclosed *extract*) to forward my plans. If Mr. Sheridan, under the present difficulties of the late Drury Lane Theatre, must coalesce with anybody, I should imagine that his policy—I should hope that his sentiment—would make him lean towards me—his old ally in particular—his admirer in common with all those who are capable of feeling the force of his talents. If your friendly propensities towards me should induce you to explain all this, *at the time the memorial is presented*, you must be aware of the infinite obligations under which you would place yours, my dear Sir [etc.].

P.S. Excuse, my dear Sir, the very rough scrawl I have sent you of my extract of a letter. I am fagg'd, by theatrical business, almost to death. (18645–6)

[Enclosure]

28 Sept. 1811

TO HIS ROYAL HIGHNESS THE PRINCE REGENT

The Memorial of George Colman, principal Proprietor of the Theatre Royal in the Haymarket,

Humbly sheweth,

That your memoiralist [*sic*], with the utmost duty and respect, implores your Royal Highness's consideration, in relief of the above Theatre, which is labouring under extreme difficulties—the causes of which difficulties have been, of late years, rapidly increasing; particularly through the protracted seasons of the Winter Theatres, and through the recent license obtain'd for the performance of new English Operas and Ballets during the Summer, at the Lyceum—and also through the many places of nominally limited exhibitions which have started up, in addition to the Surrey Theatre, Sadlers Wells, and Astley's. In all such last mention'd numerous places of subordinate entertainments, the Act of Parliament is evaded. Pieces, though constructed in verse, are not *sung*, as the Statute directs, but *spoken*, so as to appear like prose; while a harpsichord, only just audible, is touch'd, occasionally;—and thus dialogue and complete dramas are nightly given under the pretence of slight burlettas and recitative accompanied by musick. Even old plays, operas, and farces, appropriate to the regular Theatres, are, by similar artifice, frequently perverted to their purposes, and instances of subterfuge are so multiplied that all the above places have virtually become Play Houses—to the great injury of *all* Theatres, but especially of that in the Haymarket, which must contend with them in the midst of the summer, when their attractions are most strong and the town most empty.

Your memoiralist further humbly sheweth that in consequence of the Winter Theatres having so far extended their seasons, the season of the Haymarket Theatre, now licenced for *five months*, is reduced to about *seven weeks*, unless it exercise the whole of its grant to its own destruction.

For your memoiralist most humbly prays your Royal Highness to consider that he has *twice* attempted to collect an almost entire new company of performers from the country, and that in these experimental struggles to maintain his independence of the Winter Houses, in the fair exercise of his license, while their Theatres have been open, he has fail'd and suffer'd loss—and experience has now convinced your memoiralist that histrionick talents are too scarce to enable a London manager to present to the publick of this metropolis nearly a full company of new provincial performers all at once, which would give satisfaction.—A company might be establish'd in the course of two or three seasons by adding to a few performers, who have newly succeeded with the town, others who may from time to time arise; but, without a further extension of license, this

157

cannot be effected in the Haymarket Theatre—for when new performers become favorites there they are engaged by the Winter proprietors; and the talents which have struck root are transplanted, and lost to the soil that reard them.

And your memoiralist further sheweth that the monopoly of performers which the Winter proprietors possess over him is occasiond by their unlimited power of employing the actors for the greatest part, or the whole, of the year, while your memoiralist can only hold out to them less extended and less solid emoluments. Even after their Theatres are closed the actors are only allow'd to perform with *him* by courtesy from the Winter managers, according to their agreements with *them*—so that, although the Haymarket Theatre has for so long a series of years boasted the sanction and protection of his Majesty, the Winter managers can keep its doors shut *ad libitum*, or otherwise they must be open'd to a heavy loss, from the reasons and causes above stated.

And your memoiralist further sheweth that no longer ago than in the year eighteen hundred and nine, his Majesty's then Lord Chamberlain (the late Earl of Dartmouth) granted a summer license to Mr. Arnold to open the Lyceum for the performance of new English Operas and Ballets; on which grant your memoiralist respectfully remonstrated; and the Lord Chamberlain was pleased to inform him in writing that 'Mr Arnold being in *possession* of his license, it could not be revoked, because he had expended money *upon the faith of it*', but adding that 'When he granted it he *did not imagine that it would materially interfere with the interests of the Haymarket Theatre.*'

But your memoiralist most humbly states that if Mr Arnold's expenditure of money in a *new* scheme *on the faith of his* RECENT *license* be an abstracted argument in his favour, it is plain, *à fortiori*, that the proprietors of the Haymarket Theatre have infinitely more serious claims upon consideration—that Theatre having been *in possession of the Lord Chamberlain's annual License since the year* SEVENTEEN HUNDRED AND SEVENTY EIGHT, and having proceeded *upon the faith of his Majesty's most gracious protection*—upon which faith the proprietors have (as Mr Arnold has NOT) RISK'D THEIR WHOLE FORTUNES. The avowal, also, that the license was given to Mr Arnold 'with no conception that it would materially injure the Haymarket Theatre' (which it materially has) involves it in a candid admission on the part of the late Lord Chamberlain that the above Theatre should be defended from invasion and ruin.

And your memoiralist further sheweth that the license for the new English Opera render'd the Lyceum in the first instance equal to the Haymarket Theatre: it has since proved superior to it. How cramp'd your memoiralist is in the means of procuring and retaining attractive performers has been above shewn; but, by the connection of the holder of the Lyceum with the proprietors of the late Drury Lane Theatre, he is

158

enabled to make his Winter speculations with them profitable to his summers scheme; to blend his double interests, and to modify his summer engagements with nearly whom he chooses of the Winter company, and, thus, both in point of saving and attraction, to command very great advantages. As to the exhibition of *new* Operas, Operas produced years ago, and musical Farces brought out in the winter, have been already acted under this grant; and, by a subterfuge, new Plays of any description, by the insertion of a few airs, may be easily made new Operas. The first season of the English Operas hurt the receipts of the Haymarket Theatre; the second most materially diminish'd them; and the third (in the present year) has involved the proprietors in a loss of *several thousand pounds*.

Your memoiralist, therefore for himself and for his partners, humbly prays your Royal Highness,

First, that he may be relieved from the opposition set up against him by the summer license at the Lyceum, which was not given as a permanent grant, but merely as an experiment to ascertain whether new English Operas might proceed without injury to others whose property has been for years under the protection of the Crown—and

Secondly, in consideration of the protracted seasons of the Winter Theatres, in consideration of all he hath suffer'd and doth suffer, in the apprehension of his property being totally crush'd, and himself reduced to the utmost point of distress, that your Royal Highness will be pleased to grant him such an addition, namely, that of three months, to his present annual license, as will enable him to retain a company of performers exclusively; and as the only means of procuring him that subsistence which it was his Majesty's most gracious intention to afford him, when his Majesty originally allow'd him to enjoy the Lord Chamberlain's license; but which most gracious intention is now frustrated by the causes above mention'd.

And your memoiralist will ever pray &c. &c. (19112–3)

3193 LORD WILLIAM BENTINCK TO COLONEL MCMAHON

Brampton Park, 5 Oct. 1811

I am about to act irregularly, but the shortness of my stay and the goodness of my object must be my apology. I want his Royal Highness's aid in procuring a decision upon the questions relating to Sardinia and the Archduke before my departure. I wish the Prince to ask Lord Wellesley what instructions I am to have upon these subjects, & to add that he hopes it is not intended to send me away without them. I know from

Nugent, & I myself perceived that his Royal Highness understanding foreign politics better perhaps than anyone of his Cabinet, takes a most lively interest in this cause. I have no difficulty in stating my opinion that if this question is taken up in time, if the plan is properly organised and systematically acted upon, if there is established in Sicily under British protection such a model of rational liberty as shall make the happiness of that people & shall become the object of desire to the whole of Italy, I do say that with the Archduke for their leader, we may raise against Bonaparte a power infinitely more formidable than that of Spain. The Prince is entirely of this opinion I beleive. But my good friend, we are losing much valuable time and many valuable officers. Delay is the rock upon which we split. It is the bane of all our political operations. In the multitude of our Counsellors there is much wisdom & integrity, but we want promptitude. Excuse these reflections, to which I shall put an end. I have to entreat very urgently one favor, that this request may not reach the ear of any Minister. I cannot, however conscientiously, omit any means within my power of promoting the success of so great and good a cause. The Prince & the nation may gain infinite honor & advantage from it. But no delay.[1] (18641)

3194   THE DUKE OF YORK TO THE PRINCE REGENT

Windsor, 5.30 p.m., 5 Oct. 1811

I have waited to the last moment in hopes of being able to communicate to you what had passed at the Queen's arrival, but they are still talking and it does not appear probable that they will finish yet for some time.

The only particulars I know are that the Lord Chancellor, the Archbishop of York[2] and Lord Ellenborough saw his Majesty almost immediately upon their arrival. In consequence of the earnest request of the phisicians, who stated the necessity of not delaying to give him some medicine, they were but a short time in the room, as fortunately his Majesty gave them every proof that could be necessary of his disease. They then began by examining Sir Henry Halford and delivered to him at the close of the examination some questions to be answered in writing, the fourth of which is whether he considered his Majesty's malady as amounting to insanity.

Everybody is to be examined, among the rest Colonel Taylor, who I have not yet seen as he has been in waiting all the morning.

When I had got thus far Colonel Taylor came to me, having just been

1. See No. 3198.

2. Dr. Vernon.

examined; nothing can be stronger or fairer than the questions which were put to him. When he came away the box[?] was sent for, and I suppose it will be still some time before the Council concludes their business. (44248)

3195   PRINCESS ELIZABETH TO THE PRINCE REGENT
Saturday, 5 Oct. 1811
The Queen commands me to say that she had intended having Charlotte here tomorrow[1] but the scarlet fever not being over & the Lower Lodge so near the stables, Sir Henry Halford thinks it safer & wiser to put it off. My mother has commanded me to write also to Lady De Clifford. I grieve to say all is very uncomfortable here, no sleep & the talking going on the same. (Add. Georgian 11/200)

3196   RICHARD RYDER TO THE PRINCE REGENT
Great George Street, 6 Oct. 1811
Mr Ryder has the honor of humbly submitting to your Royal Highness that he has just heard from Mr Pole that the Bishop of Dromore[2] is dead.

    Mr Ryder has not received any letter from the Lord Lieutenant yet upon the subject, but he begs leave respectfully to state to your Royal Highness that from the communications which he has had with his Grace on a former occasion, he knows it must be his Grace's intention to recommend the Revd. Dr Hall,[3] the Provost of Trinity College, to your Royal Highness as the individual who, after much enquiry and consideration, appears in point of character, attainments and situation in the

---

1. Princess Charlotte had returned to Warwick House from Bognor about a fortnight earlier. She had written on 24 September: 'The *charming* D. of Cum[berland] came here yesterday & was as disagreable as usual.' Her father was to dine with her that evening. 'The D. of Cum. told me he should dine here, wh. I am sure will spoil it in a great measure, but you know it is *quite impossible* for the Duke to let the Prince dine *even* here *without* him' (Bowood MSS.).

    The Princess was delighted that the week's visit was postponed. It would have been 'dreadfully dul to be shut up for 5 hours in the eg. in the *royal menagerie*'.

2. Thomas Percy (1729–1811), editor of the *Reliques of Ancient English Poetry*. Bishop of Dromore, 1782–1811. He died on 30 September.

3. George Hall (1753–1811). At various times Professor of Greek, Modern History, and Mathematics, and Provost (1806–11) of Trinity College, Dublin, between 1790 and 1811. He was nominated Bishop of Dromore on 10 October, consecrated on 17 November and died six days later.

country to have the strongest claims to succeed to a seat on the Bishop's Bench. (18653)

3197   GEORGE COLMAN TO COLONEL MCMAHON
4 Melina Place, Wester Road, 7 Oct. 1811
I know not how to express my thanks to you for the very kind & friendly readiness you have shewn (as Mr. Winston has explain'd to me) on the subject of the memorial. If I could possibly have an interview with you *previously* to my having any intercourse with the Winter managers, according to the suggestion of the Prince Regent, it would relieve me from much difficulty & tend much to the clearness of any propositions which I might submit to them, for at present I am somewhat at a loss to know what those propositions should specifically be till I have *minutely* gather'd from you all that his Royal Highness has said. You have given me so much encouragement to come begging to you that you have drawn upon yourself one more request—namely, that you would have the charity to favor me with a call, as I am unable to wait upon you. It would much expedite anything that may be done for my interests and save a world of time in making arrangements. On *any* morning after two o'clock [*sic*] I shall be happy to see you.

I am sure you will excuse the liberty which I have taken. Again & again, accept my best thanks. (18656)

3198   COLONEL MCMAHON TO THE DUKE OF NORTHUMBERLAND
Carlton House, 7 Oct. 1811
Private. Indulging the fond hope of your Grace's perfect recovery, & fearful of interrupting it, I have abstained for several days past from obtruding myself on your quiet & privacy, nor have I now any object beyond repeating my anxious enquiries on that head to trouble your Grace with, for there is a dearth of public news, & little of any sort which could either interest or amuse you. The Prince again yesterday on going to Windsor renew'd with encreased affection his interrogatories respecting your Grace's health, & commanded me to send you and her Grace his best love & unalterable regards. Although the King has scarcely had one single lucid interval for those [*sic*] five months past, and notwithstanding that the violence of his incessant irritations cannot but have made a considerable inroad upon his bodily state, yet by the Machievalian [*sic*]

Above left

William Cavendish, 6th Earl of Devonshire

by Sir Thomas Lawrence, 1811 (detail)

Above right

Richard, Marquess Wellesley

by Sir Thomas Lawrence
Exhibited in 1813

Robert Jenkinson, 2nd Earl of Liverpool

by Sir Thomas Lawrence, 1820

Samuel Whitbread
by Thomas Gainsborough, 1788

Charles Manners-Sutton,
Archbishop of Canterbury

by an unknown painter, *c*. 1805

propensities of the physicians & Ministers for confusion & fallacy, they have cook'd up another quarterly report on Saturday last, which still holds out his Majesty to be in a condition which does not demand an immediate assemblage of Parliament, which consequently will not I believe now meet before the first week in January.[1]

Lord Wm. Bentinck (whose conduct in quitting an army of which he was Commr.-in-Chief, is condemn'd by some & defended by others on the urgency & nicety of the case) goes back to Sicily next week, carrying with him a considerable reinforcement & powers sufficient to cramp the genius & passion of that intriguing jade the Queen of Naples. Bonaparté is drawing all his force towards Magdeburgh; & everything respecting Lord Strangford has subsided into satisfactory measures, which are not now likely to be further disturb'd (Alnwick MSS.).

3199   SPENCER PERCEVAL TO THE PRINCE REGENT
Downing Street, 8 Oct. 1811

Mr Perceval presents his humble duty to your Royal Highness, and begs leave to acquaint your Royal Highness that he has been given to understand that Doctor Reynolds, whose illness has prevented him from continuing his attendance on his Majesty, feels great inconvenience from not having received any payment on account of that attendance, and that his anxiety on that account is considered by his friends as really aggravating the effects of his disorder. Mr. Perceval has therefore ventured to direct a warrant to be prepared for granting Dr Reynolds £1500 on account of his remuneration for such attendance. It will be afterwards time enough to come to some distinct arrangement respecting the amount of payment to be made.

1. Ryder, the Home Secretary, had written to the Duke of Richmond on Thursday the 3rd: 'The result of our meeting in Cabinet on Tuesday last, which was summoned for the purpose of considering whether Parliament should be assembled before Xmas, has been, that, as Perceval is of opinion, that as far as money questions are concerned, it is not necessary that it should meet before the *first week in January*, and as the Prince appears to have no wish upon the subject one way or the other, it is upon the whole desirable to defer the meeting till that period. It is possible however that the quarterly report of the physicians upon the state of the King's health which will be made on Saty. next may be so desperate as to hopes of recovery as to alter that determination, and therefore till that report has been taken into consideration we can only hold our present view of the question as conditional, and depending in some degree upon the colour of that report, as it may strike the Prince or his servants. But my present impression is, that though the report must be far more discouraging than any other has been, it is not probable that it will be so hopeless as to make any change in our sentiments upon this question. At the same time we cannot circulate the knowledge of our decision amongst our friends generally as long as this chance remains that it may be altered' (Richmond MSS.).

Mr Perceval regrets that it would be attended with an inconvenience almost amounting to an impossibility to find funds at the present moment applicable to the payment of the other physicians, who must as he apprehends be obliged to wait till the pecuniary arrangements necessary upon the expiration of the restrictions on the Regency will open some fund for that purpose. (18662)

3200 THE EARL OF LIVERPOOL TO THE PRINCE REGENT, AND AN ENCLOSURE
Fife House, 8 Oct. 1811
Lord Liverpool presents his humble duty to your Royal Highness, and having been desired by your Royal Highness confidential servants to make the necessary enquiries respecting the security of the British Army in Sicily in the event of a French force being landed in that island, he has the honour of submitting to your Royal Highness a memorandum containing the result of those enquiries. (18663)

[Enclosure]
The Island of Sicily may be subject to attack in two different ways—the first—by collecting a considerable force on the opposite coast of Calabria, and taking advantage of the favorable circumstances of wind & weather, to pass this force in small craft through the Streight of Messina. This appears to have been the plan intended to have been adopted in the last year (1810) under the superintendence of Murat, but the only attempt to carry it into execution proved entirely abortive.

The other plan necessarily depends upon a large armament to be prepared at Toulon or in some distant part of France or Italy, from whence a considerable body of troops must be carried to the neighbourhood of Palermo or to some part of Sicily remote from Messina.

This armament would constitute the main part of the operation whilst a force was collected in Calabria to threaten an attack on Messina by the Streights, & thereby to keep the British Army in that quarter in check.

The British Army at present in Sicily, including a proportion of foreign regiments, consists of almost 15,000 effective rank & file. This force is assembled in the neighbourhood of Messina, with the exception of one battalion at Agosta and one at Syracuse, and may be said to occupy a triangle of the island of Sicily, the base of which would be a line drawn from Taormina to Cape de Calava.

There can be little doubt that the British force thus collected, aided by a flotilla, is sufficient according to the probable chances of war to defend the island of Sicily against any attack made by the enemy from the opposite coast of Calabria. But if a French force could be brought from Toulon or elsewhere & landed near Palermo or in any other remote part of the island, and a force could at the same time be collected in Calabria as a diversion, the British Army would not in such case be sufficient for the two purposes of defending the part of the country which it now occupies against an attack from Calabria, and at the same time of detaching a force into the interior to operate against the main body of the enemy.

The success, however, of such an expedition on the part of the enemy must depend upon their escaping the British Fleet in the Mediterranean, an event certainly improbable but not altogether impossible.

The question then arises whether, if such an event should occur, either with or without treachery on the part of the Court of Palermo, the British Army in its present position could be considered as in a state of security, and would be enabled ultimately, if circumstances should render it necessary, to effect its embarkation from Sicily.

Upon this material part of the subject it appears upon enquiry that no doubt need reasonably be entertained. The country between Palermo and Messina is so mountainous and strong—the roads so few—the soil so deep—that it would be scarcely possible for an enemy to bring the heavy artillery by land at all, and certainly not under many months, which would be necessary to enable them to attack Messina and Melazzo, under the protection of which places the British Army could always embark in safety. Melazzo indeed from its position might easily be rendered nearly impregnable, and the Bay which it commands is the finest possible position for the embarkation or disembarkation of troops. The transports & small craft which could easily be collected would be sufficient to remove the British Army to Malta, to the Ionian Islands or to any other safe station. But even if it were judged expedient to require the protection & assistance of a part of the British Fleet, there could be no doubt that the British Army could maintain itself in the principal positions which it now occupies 'till such time as a sufficient part of the Fleet could be detached for its relief. (18664-9)

3201   THE QUEEN TO THE PRINCE REGENT, AND AN ENCLOSURE

Windsor, 9 Oct. 1811

The inclosed is the paper which I received at six a clock this evening from the Council, which was followed by the arrival of the three consulting physicians about a quarter of an hour afterwards, very unexpectedly. They were not allowed to see the King untill the attending physicians could all be present, which was just at the time when the King went to bed, & after that visit they went to the inn where they are to lodge. I believe no conversation took place this evening between the two parties.

If I had known that you had not been informed of the decision of the Council I should have sent it by the return of the messenger; it was Sr. Henry Halford who told me you was ignorant of what had passed.

I beg pardon for sending such a bad piece of writing but it is late & I am afraid not to be in time for the Duke of Cambridge who is the bearer of this. I wish you a very good night's rest, or if you please, *a bon repos*, & though half asleep most sincerely [etc.]. (36575)

[Enclosure] THE QUEEN'S COUNCIL TO THE QUEEN, AND THE QUEEN'S REPLY [copy]

Lambeth Palace, 9 Oct. 1811

Her Majesty having been graciously pleased to propose that Dr. Monro, Dr. Simmons & Dr. Willis should conjointly have access at stated periods to the King's apartment in order that they may be enabled by their personal observation of his Majesty's habits, demeanour & constitution, both of body & mind, to form an accurate judgement of the extent & nature of the disorder, to make their reports to the Council & to advise whether any & what alteration of treatment is likely to produce any beneficial change in his Majesty's state, her Majesty nevertheless objecting to their interference during their access, in the management of the King, & insisting upon Dr. R. Willis's still retaining that management, & objecting to their making themselves known to the King, & requiring that they should be considered as consulting physicians & that they should not sign the bulletins, the members of her Majesty's Council now assembled do therefore request Dr. Monro, Dr. Simmons & Dr. Willis to repair to Windsor as immediately as may be to the intent of conjointly having access to his Majesty for the purposes before mentioned, at such stated periods as may be agreed upon between them & the physicians already in attendance upon his Majesty, having regard to what her Majesty, as is before mentioned hath objected to & insisted upon. (Signed) C. Cantuar, Montrose, Winchilsea, Aylesford (36576)

THE QUEEN'S REPLY [copy]

Windsor Castle, 9 Oct. 1811

The Queen has this moment received the communication from her Council inclosing for her information a copy of the instructions given by them to the consulting physicians, & her Majesty has observed with satisfaction that they have so explicitly stated to them and also made known to the physicians actually in attendance the conditions upon which alone the Queen could consent to the former having access to the King's apartment. (36577)

3202   COUNT MÜNSTER TO THE PRINCE REGENT, AND AN ENCLOSURE

Clarges Street, 10 Oct. 1811

Count Munster in obedience to your Royal Highness commands most humbly communicates herewith Colonel Ompteda's[1] Memoire on the plan of defence adopted by Prussia. (18674)

[Enclosure]

London, 8 Oct. 1811

My interview with Colonel de Gneisenau took place on the 12th of September at night. The apprehension of all the persons in office at Berlin of being detected by French emissaries in any the least of their intercourse with individuals suspected to be attached to England, caused a variety of mysterious precautions to be adopted previous to my intro-duction, though I did not arrive at Berlin till long after it was dark and immediately before my visit to the Colonel. I never saw him before. But having been previously informed of my destination, he entered into the subject at once, almost instantly after my being introduced to him by my brother.

He prefaced the explanations which he was about to communicate over a large map of the Prussian dominions, by expressing the lively joy imparted to him but one of those last days past, from the statement of a gentleman—Colonel de Perponcher—recently arrived at Berlin from this country, of the magnanimous dispositions of his Royal Highness the Prince Regent, for the assistance of all those powers, oppressed under the yoke imposed by France, who should attempt to liberate themselves

1. Christian Ompteda, of the King's German Legion. Lieutenant-Colonel, 1805; Colonel, 1813.

167

from their bondage. That he had particularly heard with an animating hope that the affairs of Germany and the present crisis of Prussia attracted his Royal Highness's peculiar interest. That from this circumstance he hoped that the illustrious House of Brunsvic would finally restore the liberty of that country, in which their ancient & glorious family had stood foremost for ages. That, encouraged by this idea, he supposed that by enabling me, by communications from a military man to a military man, to convey to England the main features of a plan for the defence of the Prussian dominions in the case of a probable attack from France (which he had submitted to the King of Prussia and which had been adopted) the determination of his Majesty's Government with respect to the assistance wanted & requested at the hands of Great Britain, might be facilitated.

He next alluded to the momentous crisis in which Prussia evidently must be placed by the renewal of the war, from her political, geographical and military situation. With Magdeburg in front, Stettin in their right flank, Danzic & the Poles in their rear, Custrin & Glogau occupied by the French in their very centre, and a formidable body of Saxons quartered for several months past on the open frontier of their left flank— 17,000 men at Stettin, a numerous French corps d'armée on the Mecklenburg frontier, within less than a day's march from the Priegnitz, and, upon the whole, an army of 154,000 men (computing native French and Poles & the Allies of the Confederacy of the Rhine) between this latter river and the Vistula—and in this position Prussia left to her own resources, with a view of 'la bombe sur le point d'éclater'—all this they knew, but there was no choice, and whatever seemingly insurmountable difficulties there might be, must either still be tried to overcome or not minded. Under this impression, and with the firm resolution rather to fall gloriously than to yield with ignomony [sic] it next behoved to survey the resources actually left to them.

These consisted chiefly in a very numerous army, provided the whole could be properly armed, & in 8 fortresses, which afforded as many most important rallying points; and, as a final resource, the 'Heerbann' or rising of the whole country. From these elements of their defence, the plan proposed by him was exactly the reverse of the measures hitherto adopted by the Continental Powers in their wars with France. To collect all their troops in one grand body and to risk the existence of the Monarchy in the event of a single battle, they had, at their severe expence, learnt to avoid. What then seemed the most advisable was *to establish four distinct main theatres of the war*, corresponding with the very number of provinces left to the King of Prussia by the Peace of Tilsit, and managed so as to serve each other for a mutual support, in order that if they should be defeated in one quarter, all might not be lost, but still the war kept up in the rest.

Thus all their means of resistance were to be collected, 1) in the Margraviate of Brandenburg, 2) in Pomerania, 3) in the Kingdom of Prussia and 4) in Silesia. That, as to the first of these theatres, being the most exposed, though the most important from containing Berlin and most of the Royal residences, the King, from the almost thoroughly open nature of this part of his dominions, had decidedly thought of giving up the country between the Elbe & the Oder, & retreat with the troops and whatever could be saved behind the latter river, that, however he, Colonel Gneisenau, upon seriously examining the country, had found out a position near *Spandau*, at about 10 English miles to the westward from the capital) which seemed to him to afford facilities for one of the strongest intrenched camps. That its main advantage consisted in the peculiarity of the river *Havel's* (which at this point receives the *Spree* from Berlin) branching out in a succession of lakes, below and even above the fortress, establishing a breadth of water over which it was impossible to throw a bridge of pontons [*sic*]. That besides he had taken advantage of 5 small islands, situated at convenient distances above and below Spandau, every one of which was fortified by strong redoubts, so as to strengthen the front of the position. That under these topographical advantages a line right and left from Spandau of four German miles, from *Tegel* (a village near Berlin) down to *Potsdam*, might be esteemed impenetrable to whatever invading force; that under these circumstances, the enemy must advance upon the intrenched camp near Spandau by a long circuitous way, which would afford the troops stationed there the opportunity of sallying through the fortress to assail him in his rear, while he moved to either flanc, or to attack him in detail if the length of the front should induce him to take up an extensive line opposite. That at any rate Colonel G. hoped by this position to gain time; was it but for three weeks, what would be of the utmost importance to them; that, as this advanced point was certainly the most critical and might be considered as of a doubtful propriety of choice, he had entreated the King to give him the command of the intrenched camp, prepared for 15,000 men; that the King had granted his request; that he hoped to check the enemy & should do his best to make him repent if he should too rashly attempt either to attack him in a position rendered formidable by nature and art,[a] or pass by him and leave the force under his command in the

(a) The following circumstance will perhaps not be deemed totally undeserving of notice, as it tends to corroborate the opinion of the importance of Spandau. Nearly a fortnight previous to my interview with Col. de Gneisenau was spent by me at a villa near Potsdam belonging to a gentleman of my acquaintance, where I waited for the result of my brother's negociations with Baron Hardenberg and Colonel de Gneisenau, for which I delayed my journey to England; avoiding by this apparent party of pleasure the notice which my appearance at Berlin might have attracted. This villa being one of the most elegant & pleasant in the vicinity of Potsdam, had during the constant passage of the French Army in 1806 and 1807

rear. That besides he relied on the moral impression of the measure, as hitherto nobody had thought of defending a country apparently so open as that whole tract between the Elbe and Oder, and therefore the novelty and seeming boldness of the idea might inspire confidence.

Colonel G. mentioned the circumstance that Count St. Marsan, the French Minister at Berlin, and the rest of the diplomatic characters of the Allies of France had lately taken their rides towards Spandau, in order to look on at what was doing there. A numerous body of men, consisting of soldjers [sic] who formerly served in the old and totally disbanded army, who purposedly [sic] have hitherto been suffered to stay quietly at home, whilst the young population has been successively embodied in the present regiments, and again dismissed to make room for other recruits, so as to train to arms the greatest number possible—is employed at the fortifications. The same system is pursued at Colberg, Pillau & in Silesia.

Colonel Gneisenau next passed to the second & most important stage of their preparations—the fortress of Colberg, the rallying point of the forces in Pomerania. The successful defence made by this fortress in the Seven Years War & latterly in 1807, when Colonel Gneisenau himself, as Commandant of the place, acquired the honor of a most gallant & fortunate resistance to the French besieging army under Mortier,[1] would alone be sufficient to fix the eyes on this point as one of main importance. But this strong fortress is at present rendered considerably more formidable. A triple position is intrenched in its vicinity. It admits of so many successive retreats. The last position, partly traced on the downs, where the right wing and the centre are covered by the fortress, and the left reclined towards the sea, with strong redoubts for its appui, may be considered as one of the strongest possible. Besides, if the access by sea is kept open, provisions and succours of every description may be thrown in continually, & in this respect the easy intercourse with Pillau is of great importance. Nor has the anchorage been neglected. The river *Persante*, which falls into the sea about within gunshot distance to the westward of the fortress, affords a safe harbour for vessels of ten feet draught. The entrance is protected by two ancient forts. But at present the whole of the left bank of the river, higher up than the anchorage extends, is covering by new works of considerable strength; a precaution,

been generally chosen for the reception of several of the French Generals, amongst others General Nansouti, the family of my friend being thereby in possession of a number of anecdotes relative to these characters, they formed frequently the topic of the conversation, and among these, the gentleman, who is not a military man, once mentioned, before Colonel Gneisenau's project relative to Spandau was known to me, that he had been very much surprized to hear the French Generals observe *that Spandau was a place whose importance had been strangely overlooked, and that it might be rendered extremely strong from its natural advantages.*

1. Marshal of France, 1804; given Duchy of Treviso by Napoleon (1806).

to which the late attack of the French on that side, seems to have been conducive, & which now appears to preclude the apprehension of a similar approach.

A personal inspection of these fortifications, on my passage through Colberg, where the highest activity in building then prevailed, has impressed me with a strong opinion of their importance & efficacy. Nor will the superior construction of these works be questioned, since General Scharnhorst[1] is the officer by whose directions they have been raised.

With respect to the third stage of the operations, the Kingdom of Prussia, Colonel Gneisenau briefly observed that the fortress of *Pillau*, though small, was of similar strength and importance with that of Colberg; that both were to support each other mutually; that Pillau was chosen for the protection of an intrenched camp, intended for the forces in Prussia in case of the necessity of a retreat; but that as *Danzig* lay between the two Prussian fortresses, and that even *Graudenz*, the fourth Prussian fortress in the northern provinces, might through the enemy's junction from *Thorn* in the south and from *Danzic* in the north, be occasionally reduced to its own strength (intended to be augmented by a strong tête de pont on the left bank of the Vistula) and thus the direct communication between the Kingdom of Prussia and the rest of the country by the road of *Marienwerder* be intercepted, it was highly desirable that some naval protection might insure the navigation between Colberg and Pillau on the one hand, and with the Islands of *Usedom* and *Wollin* on the other.

Colonel Gneisenau then took a rapid view of the theatre of the war in *Silesia*, pointed out the resources of that province in population and wealth; the points d'appui afforded by the four valuable fortresses of *Neisse, Glatz, Kosel & Silberberg*; the convenient situation of that country for an eventual junction with a Russian Army; the facility of passing from thence to offensive operations by the invasion of *Saxony* through *Lusatia*, of which *Dresden*, the capital, might be the immediate object; and seemed to suppose, as a matter of course, an intrenched camp in Silesia, similar to those in the other provinces. Probably this may be intended near *Schweidnitz*, though the place itself has been dismantled, by restoring the famous camp of *Bunzelwitz*, or perhaps on the *Bober*, near *Löwenberg*, in the camp of *Schmotseifen*, where King Frederic II and his brother, Prince Henry of Prussia, repeatedly kept the superior forces of the Austrians in awe, & from whence the passage into *Lusatia* is the most easy.

The command of the four main districts seems to be intended, (1) that of *Brandenburg* for Colonel de Gneisenau under the King himself,

1. General Johann David von Scharnhorst (1755–1813). Fought in the Flanders campaigns of 1793–5 and in the 1806–7 campaigns. Reorganized Prussian army and introduced short-term service.

(2) that of *Pomerania* for General *Blücher*, who has been stationed there for these last years past, and who during my stay at Colberg (from September 15th to Sept. 20th) was invested with full powers of an uncommon latitude with respect to the measures which he should think requisite for placing this province in the most respectable posture of defence; (3) that of *Prussia* for General *Scharnhorst*, who even was there, when I passed at Berlin, and (4) that of *Silesia* for one of the Princes of the Royal Family, whose name I did not learn. Colonel Gneisenau just observed, en passant, on this subject, that as the Silesians had a considerable deal of pride, he was sure that this distinction would go a great way in stimulating their spirit.

One circumstance, which Colonel Gneisenau only seemed to mention by the way in the course of a very animated conversation on the topics above reported, was a project, which he stated to enter into his plans of annoyance against the enemy. This was no other than a diversion *between the Elbe & Weser*, where, he said, it would be proper to send round *by sea* a body of four thousand men, or thereabout. Surprized at a scheme rather strange, considering the naval resources of Prussia, I interrupted him by observing that I supposed, he meant to say the coast of Mecklenburg between Stralsund and Lubeck, and that even there a force so inconsiderable appeared to me to be extremely exposed. But Colonel Gneisenau maintained his original statement, and said that in plans of such magnitude possible sacrifices must not be attended to. He then asked me what was my opinion of the probability of the effect which the appearance of the alluded to expedition would produce on the inhabitants of that part of Germany (the Electorate of Hannover.) I told him, 'that of the spirit which prevailed among them, there was no doubt, & that I well knew men there, who desired no better than to be enabled to come forward; but that I very much doubted whether a *Prussian* force would be considered by them as a rallying point of their choice.' The subject was then dropped, and I indeed almost suspected that this idea was started with an intention either to learn whether I might be possessed of some conjectures as to some possible plan of a diversion from this country to that quarter, or even to create a sort of jealousy which might in so far serve the general plan as to determine the British Government on a new attempt in that part of the Continent.

It appears certain that from the totally altered relations of the three Hanseatic towns, Hamburg, Lubeck & Bremen, the operations in the north of Germany afford combinations entirely new and different from former times, and that these three important places, leaving out of sight their commercial consequence, might be considered as a sort of basis for operations embracing the north of Germany and even the Netherlands.

I took hold of a convenient opportunity to enquire of Colonel Gneisenau whether he had any prospect of a cooperation on the part of

Russia, what he thought of their forces collecting on the frontiers of Poland & what was his opinion of their amount? His answer was that, as to a concert between his Court and that of Russia, he knew nothing but that indeed it never entered into his calculations, for that his opinion was that the only safe reliance was on one's own firm determination & activity. That he was perfectly familiarized with the idea of their having to fight it out by themselves. That the Russians, however, were indeed assembling very strongly on their western frontier. He stated their force at 17 divisions, & the establishment of a division at 15,000 men. However, making allowance for contingencies, he supposed each division at 10,000 men, which would give an effective force of 170,000 men, of which however two divisions had been lately detached for the reinforcement of the army of Walachia. However, on my observing that in my private speculations I had always imagined that Silesia might be a favourable quarter, in a military point of view, where the Russians might form a junction with the Prussians, he perfectly coincided with this opinion and in a manner which made me believe that, after all, the probability or possibility of such an event was not entirely kept out of sight.

The strength of the Regular Prussian army was computed by Colonel Gneisenau at from 100,000 to 124,000 or 130,000 men & more, according to their possibility of arming them. The levy en masse was, of course, computed much higher, and any sort of weapons admitted for them. In general, Colonel Gneisenau seemed to incline to measures of the most decided energy, even in an administrative point of view, as the only means of meeting the enemy on his own ground. He certainly seems the man, though apparently cool, to be equally good with his word.

Colonel Gneisenau having probably expressed in his letters his hopes and sentiments with respect to the great reliance he places in the support of England, I shall not dwell on what fell verbally from him on this subject. It is not a subject of surprize that his ideas of this country should be enlightened, having begun his military career in a British army; for he served when very young, in the Anspach troops in America at the time of the American War. (18675–87)

3203   RICHARD BRINSLEY SHERIDAN TO THE PRINCE REGENT

Cavendish Square, Thursday, 10 Oct. [1811][1]

The unvaried & protecting kindness with which you have so long regarded my private situation and circumstances (placing wholly out of the

---

1. Docketed 16 September 1811 (a Monday).

question all political considerations) induces me to address to you these few frank lines. I hate to intrude myself upon you respecting small matters especially when they relate to myself, but the truth is that while I am on the point of parting with my theatrical property on an arrangement which would leave me discharged from a single debt to anyone [on] earth, & give me what remains of my life to the exertions of my own fond & I trust active exertions in your R. Highness's service, I find my hopes thwarted by disputes in the Committee under the Act of Parlt., the main cause of which is a difference of opinion respecting the merits of the candidates for building the new Theatre, a difference and a difficulty which I am confident your Royal Highness's interference would immediately settle but your's alone.

The particulars I cannot presume to trouble your R.H. with in writing, but I will have the honor of attending your commands in the morning. (18727)

3204 THE DUKE OF NORTHUMBERLAND TO COLONEL MCMAHON

Alnwick Castle, 11 Oct. 1811

I have to thank you for your letter of the 7th. I do not think the last quarterly report of his Majesty's health holds out any flattering hopes of his speedy recovery. Why not therefore call Parliament together, state fairly the King's situation, & repeal, most at least, of the restraining clauses in the Regency Act? But this is too strait a line. There are in the Cabinet some, I fear, who admire the crooked path & half measures, by which they have, & by which, if persisted in, they will continue to involve this country daily into greater & greater difficulties.

I confess I was a good deal astonished to learn that Lord Wm. Bentinck was returned to England. To his Lordship was entrusted all power, both diplomatic & military, together probably with such instructions as it was thought necessary to give him for his conduct in this double capacity. How then can his Lordship justify his leaving *himself*, his army, his mission, & the Island at such a crisis; & trusting, to whoever happened to be the second in command, the decision of such steps as may be necessary to be pursued, till his return to Sicily, together with all the awefull responsibility attendant upon such a situation? Viewing it merely in a military light, one might almost be inclined to term it desertion. Allow me to own, that I was not a little surprised also, my dear Colonel, at the Gazette of the first of this month.[1]

I think I can now venture to say that I am recovering from my late

1. The diplomatic appointments were the main feature of interest. See No. 3190.

174

violent attack, altho', as yet, I improve by very slow degrees. I feel as I ought the interest the Regent takes on this subject, & trust my conduct towards H.R.H. will ever be such as will prove I am not unworthy of the partiality his Royal Highness is graciously pleased to honour me with. (18689)

3205 THE DUKE OF YORK TO THE PRINCE REGENT

Windsor, 12 Oct. 1811

After a very short examination of the King's regular phisicians the Queen's Council proceeded to see the consulting phisicians, and after putting a few questions to them, in answer to which I understand that all three fully approved of everything which had hitherto been done, they gave them one question to answer separately in writing, 'Whether they had had sufficient opportunity of judging of the King's state from his demeanour, conversation and habits, or whether they wished to have further access, and lastly, whether they had any advice to offer'. Dr. Simmond's answer is that so far as he could judge from what he had seen of the King and from the very full communication he had had from the regular phisicians, he had recommended some medicines which he hoped would do good, but that he could not as yet form a conclusive judgement.

Dr. Munroe's answer is much less strong in regard to the expectation of any beneficial effect from the medicine but agrees with Dr. Simmonds in the wish to have renewed access.

Dr. John Willis, on the contrary, does not state any hope of improvement from the effect of the medicine, nor does he express any wish to see the King again upon the ground of necessity.

The Archbishop, in delivering a copy of the question and answer to the Queen, asked her Majesty if she had any objection to these gentlemen returning again to Windsor, to which she replied that she had not the least objection to their returning on Friday next to make their report on Saturday, and as Dr. John Willis seemed to have made up his mind and had very particular business in the country she would dispense for the present with his return unless fresh circumstances should produce any proposal of alteration in the treatment, when she would require his attending urgently with the others. Her Majesty's intention is to shew you these papers tomorrow but you will find the above contains their substance.

I have now seen both the Willis's and find that Dr. John fully coincides with his brother in the unfavourable opinion which he has formed of his Majesty's case. (44249-50)

175

3206 VISCOUNT MELBOURNE TO MAJOR-GENERAL T. H. TURNER

Whitehall, Sunday [13 Oct. 1811]

Frederick Lamb leaves town on Tuesday early. I wish you could procure him the honour of seeing H.R.H. the Prince Regent for a moment before his departure to thank him for all his kindness during the long time he was obliged to be absent from his duty.[1] (18697)

3207 THE EARL OF MOIRA TO COLONEL MCMAHON

Donington, 14 Oct. 1811

Excuse my inattention respecting Ld. Hardwicke's letter. People had come in to get letters franked while I was making up the packet to you, & thence I was hurried. As it happened it was of no consequence, for in consequence of your letter I have found that I burned the letter of Ld Hardwicke's which I meant to keep, retaining by mistake another that only alluded to it. The one I meant to send was only a lamentation on the dangers of Ireland, & an expression of his hope that (in an interview which was to take place for the annunciation of his daughter's marriage)[2] he should have the opportunity of detailing his sentiments to the Prince upon it. The Prince shirked that opening dextrously. Be assured with regard to Ireland that Bonaparte is prosecuting his views there most actively. I do not speak from guess. A person who gives me information but would not trust himself for the world to the Ministers, is watching the matter closely.

You tell me that the Prince thinks Dr Scott a very fit candidate for the living. Now that is in answer to a statement of mine of my having promised the D. of Kent my vote for a friend of his in case the Prince did not countenance anyone specially. Do let me know how the Prince wishes my vote to go for this & the other appointments.

Who is to get the 5th Dragoons?[3] I speak with reference to the Atkinsons,[4] who have got but one (the Hertfordshire) of the militia regiments. It is quite heart-breaking to poor Joe. (18698–9)

---

1. Frederick Lamb, Viscount Melbourne's third son, was at this time attached to the Legation in Sicily, and was on leave of absence.

2. Lord Hardwicke's daughter, Lady Catherine Freeman Yorke (1786–1863), married the Earl of Caledon (1777–1839) on 16 October 1811, and she brought with him as her dowry Tittenhanger House, near St. Albans.

3. The Regiment was disbanded.

4. The Army Agents.

Dover Street, 15 Oct. 1811

I communicated to Mr Benjamin Wyatt[1] and to Mr Wilkins[2] the gracious permission of his Royal Highness the Prince Regent that they should send their models and designs to Carlton House for the inspection of his Royal Highness tomorrow, & I have received their grateful acknowledgments of the condescension of his Royal Highness.

It has since occurred to me that as there are plans of other architects of emminence before the committee it might be considered unjust to them if that fact were not submitted to his Royal Highness; & however the committee may have decided upon the superiority of the designs of the two Messrs Wyatt, or Mr Wilkins over the rest, there might possibly be a feeling of dissatisfaction in the minds of the other competitors if upon enquiry they should [discover] that his Royal Highness had not been informed of their labours. Might I then presume to hope that thro' your kind offices his Royal Highness may be induced to allow the designs of the other architects before the committee to be sent to Carlton House? They are drawings only & not models, & if permission is granted I will take care of the conveyance.

I feel great uneasiness on the subject of the two designs by Messrs. Wyatt, & cannot help expressing it to you. If the committee had adopted a mode of advertisement not unusual in cases of the same sort, to have advertised for plans & proposals designated by letters or mottos, we should have avoided all the painful discussion which is now before us on the subject of family differences. We should have selected the design in our opinion the best adapted to our proposal, & treated at once with the successful architect after we had discovered his name. *Now* should either of the Mr Wyatts be successful, we have a family feud to go into before we can begin to build, & by what I have learnt I am fearful our time of building will have elapsed before the preliminary step can be accomplished.

I have no acquaintance whatever with the Wyatt family, & had never seen Mr Benjamin Wyatt when he became a competitor for building the Theatre. But it is only justice to him to say that his first proposals were given in, & his designs & model ready by the 10th of May last, that no whisper was ever uttered to the Committee that his design was not his own till long after that period, & that it cannot be the province of the Committee to decide upon a point so delicate & difficult between two brothers.[3]

1. Benjamin Dean Wyatt, architect (1775–?1850), son of James Wyatt (1746–1813). He designed Drury Lane Theatre (1811), and Crockford's (1827).

2. William Wilkins, architect (1778–1839). He designed portions of Downing College, Cambridge (1804), University College, London (1827–8), St. George's Hospital, London (1827–8), and the National Gallery (1832–8).

3. Benjamin Wyatt was assisted in many of his works by his brother Philip (*d.* 1836).

It would however be a great misfortune if, after having accomplished so much & atchieved a labour so unexpectedly as that of yesterday, we should on the account of an unhappy family dissension be prevented from going on, & executing the intention of the General Assembly who have instructed us to come to a decision upon some design & to have contracted for the execution of the work before tomorrow fortnight. My wish is, with a view to the complete success of the undertaking, to have workmen at the spot on Monday morning next; & if this unhappy obstacle did not arise to the ordinary and obvious mode of proceeding I am sure it could be done whichever plan of the three shall be adopted. *Much depends upon it.*

I am fully sensible of that goodness of heart which has induced his Royal Highness to go so fully into this matter, and I do my full homage to the feeling which so evidently, so nobly fills his breast & actuates his conduct upon the occasion, & I will contribute my efforts, humble as they are, to so good a work.

But I earnestly & anxiously hope that the consideration of this matter may not destroy our undertaking. We have no time to select, combine & produce a plan out of divers plans & then to find a person independent of them all to execute it. We must, as far as I can judge, decide upon the plan the least objectionable, correct its errors and employ one man to do the thing. If one of the Wyatts should be the successful candidate, which ever it may be, it will then be the time to try whether they will both consent to divide the reputation. If they consent they must give us one of them to look to & treat with; if they will not, we must look & treat with the man whose design we have selected. I have taken the great liberty of disburthening my mind to you upon this subject, and am quite sure you will pardon me. In the whole progress of these complicated concerns no difficulty has weighed so heavily upon my mind, none was ever so unlooked for—in truth its occurrence was not within the range of probability.

The three competitors themselves will be at Carlton House to wait the commands of his Royal Highness & to explain their plans. The discernment of the Prince Regent will be most satisfactory & beneficial to the Committee, & if with his gracious assistance & concurrence we shall decide upon the design of either of the Mr Wyatts I earnestly hope his benevolent feelings will be gratified in their reconciliation.

In the whole matter I am completely sensible of the value of the exalted support we received & of his Royal Highness's benignity.

[*P.S.*] I am ashamed to add to this long letter, but a very particular friend of mine at the other end of the town has expressed a great desire to see the interior of the Prince Regent's stables at Brighton.

It would be esteemed a great favour by me if I could obtain that permission for him—perhaps you would be so good as to assist me. (18706–9)

Foreign Office, 1.45 p.m., 15 Oct. 1811

Lord Wellesley presents his humble duty to your Royal Highness & has the honor to submit the intelligence received respecting Mr Burr. (18716)

[Enclosure] WILLIAM RICHARD HAMILTON'S MEMORANDUM

Foreign Office, 15 Oct. 1811

Colonel Burr was in England in 1809, and it was in agitation to order him to quit the country as a notoriously bad character. But he claimed the rights of an English subject, as having been born in America before the separation. The question was referred to the Attorney-Genl. who declined giving a decided opinion *against* his being a British subject, because Lord Kenyon had decided a former question on a similar subject in favor of this claim of persons so circumstanced. The result was, tho' Lord Liverpool was clearly of a contrary opinion, that it was agreed that Burr shoud leave England for France. He went to France, & has been lately taken on his return to America on board an American vessel from the Texel which has been captured under the Orders in Council. Burr was one of 58 or 59 passengers on board the same vessel, and they have been allowed by the Home Dept. to take their passage, as they could, on board other ships. Some are gone—& others are coming to London (among the last is Colonel Burr) on their way to some port in the west— or with a view to get a passage on board some ship in the river—but all under the engagement that they shall remain as short a time as possible in England.

Rather than again stir the question of law, the decision of which in favor of the Americans might be attended with unpleasant consequences, it has been thought adviseable to allow Burr to come to London for a short time, & to watch him strictly—for which the proper measures have been already taken by the Home Department.

Burr is expected in London this evening. Burr *represents* himself to have been very ill treated while in France. (18717–9)

3210 THOMAS TYRWHITT TO COLONEL MCMAHON

Ton Royal, Tavistock, 15 Oct. 1811

From the tenor of your letter I am quite satisfied Plymouth had better remain as intended, viz—that B.[1] should represent it. If the P. was to order otherwise he would I am certain manifest ill humour, which would make our master wish both of us & Plymouth too, at the devil.

Let me know therefore if anything has been announced to B.; if not, all shall stand as intended & I will invite him down to me to explain circumstances he does not seem to understand. As for myself, and I know you will believe me sincere, that I care not a fig whether I am in Parliament or not—but, if matters slide on smoothly, Government will take[2] of me I have little doubt.

Not having said a word of your health, I am sanguine in my hopes your trip to Ramsgate is not on that account—so God bless you says your sincere friend. (18720)

3211 THE DUKE OF NORTHUMBERLAND TO COLONEL MCMAHON

Alnwick Castle, 15 Oct. 1811

I was very happy to find that you had got a fortnight's leave of absence to enjoy the sea breezes & sea bath. From both of which I sincerely hope you will receive great benefit.

I have been waiting in expectation of hearing your account of Lord Wellington's victory confirmed, but as yet in vain.

I want, my dear Colonel, your advice on a subject which I have a good deal at heart. Mr. David Hume,[3] who is nephew to the late Mr. David Hume,[4] married a very near relation of my late father's. He has been many years Professor of Law in the University of Edinburgh, & most of the Judges now sitting on the Scotch Bench were educated under him. He is besides a person held in high esteem by the Scotch Bar. Being now somewhat advanced in years, and the fatigue of his lectures in the University, & his business at the Bar & as Sheriff Depute having affected his health, Mrs Hume, my cousin, has strongly sollicited me to get him seated on the Bench, & she is particularly anxious I shoud make some application now, as Mr. Baron Hepburn[5] of the Exchequer Bench has

1. Bloomfield. See No. 3188.

2. Word (?care) omitted.

3. David Hume (1757–1838). Professor of Scots law at Edinburgh, 1786; Principal Clerk to the Court of Session, Edinburgh, March 1811; Baron of the Exchequer, Scotland, 1822.

4. The philosopher and historian (1711–76).

5. Sir George Buchan Hepburn (1739–1819). Solicitor to the Lords of Session [S.], 1767–90;

been taken very ill & is not likely to recover. I shoud undoubtedly be very happy to see Mr. Hume placed there because I know he is in every way properly qualified for the situation, & I know some years ago he might have had a seat on the Exchequer Bench, but at that time modestly declined it, saying there were others more advanced in the profession whom he did not wish to supersede in their pretensions. Now, my dear Colonel, knowing nothing of the Scotch chart du pais I wish to know to whom I ought to apply upon this occasion, for, however anxious I may be for the success of Mr. Hume, I cannot think of troubling the Regent upon the subject, remembering well my having placed H.R.H. in a situation unpleasant to him about Captain Haswell,[1] & God forbid I shoud ever again commit such an error. Do let me know who has the disposal of these Scotch places, for altho' I am not well enough with any of the present Cabinet or Ministers to hope for success, yet I confess I shoud be inclined, for Mr. Hume's sake, to make the attempt if I only was informed of the person who has the disposal of these Scotch preferments. I trust, my dear Colonel, to your friendship & goodness to excuse me for the trouble I am giving you, but I really shoud feel myself most particularly obliged to you woud you give me your advice how to act, or coud in any way be instrumental in procuring for me the accomplishment of my wishes on this occasion.

I wish you may be able to make out this scrawl but, altho' I am much better, writing is still very painfull to me. (18721–2)

3212   THE EARL OF LIVERPOOL TO THE PRINCE REGENT

Downing Street, 17 Oct. 1811

Lord Liverpool presents his humble duty to your Royal Highness and has the honour of informing you that he has had a conference with Mr Yorke, Adml. Dommett[2] & Sir Joseph Yorke, on the subject of the eartholmes, and on the security which it might be practicable to afford to Colberg, in the event of a war between France and Prussia during the winter.

Lord Liverpool has transmitted the correspondence which has taken place on the subject of the earthworks in the years 1808, 1809 & 1811,

Judge of the Admiralty Court, 1790–1, Baron of the Scottish Exchequer, 1791–1814. Baronetcy, 1815.

1. See Nos. 2928, 2952, 3011, 3095.

2. Sir William Domett (1754–1828). Lieutenant, 1777; Captain, 1782; Rear-Admiral, 1804; Vice-Admiral, 1809; Admiral, 1819. A Lord of the Admiralty, 1808–13; Commander-in-Chief at Plymouth, 1813. K.C.B., 1815; G.C.B., 1820.

and it appears to be the opinion of the professional men that at the late season of the year an attack could not be made upon the eartholmes with any reasonable prospect of success, and that even if it was successful it is very doubtful whether the station would answer the intended purpose.

Lord Liverpool thinks it right to add that as he is informed the Island of Boernholm[1] contains no post whatever capable of affording shelter to ships of war.

Lord Liverpool understands from Mr Yorke that instructions have been already given to Sir James Saumarez upon quitting the Baltic to leave a force of gunbriggs in the neighbourhood of Colberg under the command of Capt Fanshawe,[2] who is particularly well acquainted with the navigation of every part of the Baltic; and at the same time Rear Adml. Geo. Hope[3] is directed to remain in the Baltic with two 84 gun ships as long as he can possibly obtain shelter for them in any quarter.

Lord Liverpool has further settled with Mr. Yorke that the intended force of gun briggs at Colberg shall be considerably augmented, and that in conformity to your Royal Highness intentions they shall have directions to remain there at all events under the command of Capt. Fanshawe during the whole of the winter.

Lord Liverpool thinks that it may be material to add that in the opinion of the professional Lords this description of force will afford the best protection to Colberg during the winter on the side of the sea, as from drawing very little water they will be able to lay in close to the shore, and may seek protection in the river which runs up to Colberg at the time when the French flotilla my be exposed on the open beach.

Lord Liverpool humbly requests your Royal Highness to return the accompanying papers when your Royal Highness has done with them. (18728–9)

3213 THE DUKE OF BRUNSWICK-OELS TO THE PRINCE REGENT
Belmont House, ce 17 d'Oct. 1811
Je viens de réçevoir une letter d'Allemagne, dont l'objèt est de la plus grande importance pour moi; sur le quel cependant je ne me permettrai pas, de me décider avant de connoître les intentions de Votre Altesse Royale, qui seules me guideront, dans mes démarches; ayant constament à coeur d'exécuter très exactement les ordres, qu'elle daignera me faire parvenir.

1. Bornholm, in the Baltic.

2. Robert Fanshawe. Lieutenant, 1799; Commander, June 1801; Captain, November 1801.

3. Sir George Johnstone Hope, K.C.B. (?1767–1818). Lieutenant, 1788; Captain, 1793, Rear-Admiral, August 1811. M.P. for East Grinstead, 1815–18. A Lord of the Admiralty, 1813–18.

On me mande, qu'on désire ma prèsence en Allemagne, au moment que la guerre y récommencera avec la France.

Mes dévoirs envers le Gouvernement Britanique, me sont connûs, et je suis pénétré de réconnoissance, envers lui, des bontés et de la bien-veillance, dont il m'a honoré : cependant j'ai encore d'autres dévoires tout aussi sacrés à remplir, ceux que m'impose l'interèt de ma patrie mal-heureuse et celui de mes pauvres enfants.

Ce sont ces sentiments qui m'excuseront auprès de Votre Altesse Royale, si je la supplie de porter un moment son attention, sur le projèct de mon voyage en Allemagne; que j'ose soumettre à sa décision.

Dans la supposition, que la guerre eût éclaté dans le nord de l'Alle-magne, il sagit de savoir quel seroit le point de mon débarquement? Les côtes de la mer Baltique n'offrent point des moyens, qui répondent à la tâche, qu'on me déstine, et cependant ce ne seroit qu'à Colberg, à Pillau, où dans un des ports de la Russie, que je pourrois mettre pied à terre. Arrivé dans une de ces places, qui séront sans doute investies par les troupes ennemies, on rencontreroit la difficulté d'en rèsortir, pour se rembarquer et chercher à débarquer sûr un autre point, pendant que l'ennemi, qui ne pourra pas ignorer cette entreprise, trouvera tous les moyens de la faire èchouer.

Il ne me sera pas plus facile, de connoître l'emploi que Sa Majesté le Roi de Prusse voudra me donner dans son armée; ni de réussir à engager aucune des autorités constituées, à m'obèir, à moins d'un ordre exprès du Roi.

Si toutes ces considerations sont propre à me faire hésiter, de me rendre à l'invitation très honorable et très flatteuse pour moi, je n'en ai pas moins conservé le désir ardent, de servir la bonne cause, en concevant le projèt, que je vais soumettre très réspectueusement, aux ordres de Votre Altesse Royale : mon idée est de demander à Votre Altesse Royale la grace de m'accorder le commandement de mon corps, pour une expédition en Allemagne.

L'Isle de Helgoland pourroir servir de point de rassemblement, aux troupes, qu s'y rendroient sans donner de l'ombrage à l'ennemi en les faisant partir des différents points, où elle se trouvent à prèsent : sans les faire venir en Angleterre.

On a tout lieu d'éspérer, que cette dèscente sur un point de la côte opposée réussira en l'entreprennant au mois de Décembre ou Janvier, dans un moment où l'ennemi ne s'y attendra pas; on se dirigera, ou dans le paye de Mechlenburg pour saisir les barques canonieres, qui font mine d'attaquer Colberg, quand la flotte Angloise aura quitter la Baltique, ou sûr Spandau, en tâchant de gagner les routes militaîres, qui conduisent de la France en Allemagne et au câs, que la supériorité ce l'ennemie ne permét pas de s'y tènir, il faudra tâcher de gagner les vallées de Silésie et se mettre sous la protêction d'une de ces fortresses, ou de révenir sur mes pas pour gagner l'Isle de Rügen, si les circonstances politique entre le Gouvernement Anglois, et celui de la Suède le permettront, pour n'être pas absollument coupé de la mèr et prèt de rentrer en campayne, quand la saison le permêttra. Il n'y a de doutte, que dans un cas pareille, la prèsence d'une partie de la flotte Angloise dans la Baltique seroit d'une grande importance.

L'exécution de ces idées dépendra des circonstances et principalement, de la bonne volonté des peuples.

C'est avec les sentiments, de la plus profonde soumission et ceux d'une réspécteuse vénération [etc.]. (18730–1)

3214   DRURY LANE THEATRE

Sub-committee appointed to consider of, and determine upon the plan to be adopted for rebuilding the Theatre Royal, Drury Lane, 17 Oct. 1811.

Resolved, that the designs & model exhibited by Mr. Benjamin Wyatt appear to the sub-committee to be, upon the whole, the best adapted to the purpose of the subscribers to the rebuilding of the Theatre.

That Mr. Benjamin Wyatt be informed thereof, and that the sub-committee are prepared to treat with Mr. B. Wyatt & Mr. Rowles for the building of the same according to the specification addressed to the committee by that gentleman for executing the work; & that the chairman do enter into provisional contracts with Mr. Benjamin Wyatt and Mr. Rowles, under securities, for the performance of the same, which contract shall contain such clauses as may be necessary for securing to the committee a discretionary controul over the work in its progress, and the adoption of such alterations as may by the said committee be judged expedient, without a violation of the terms of the contract, such alterations to be the subject of previous and distinct estimate. Also for securing to the committee the advantage of such professional experience in the construction of the stage or other parts of the Theatre or its machinery, as they may judge proper to select.

That the subcommittee have witnessed with the highest satisfaction the display of talent evinced in the competition for rebuilding the said Theatre.

That the plans of Messrs. Foulston Cabanel & Robinson appear to the sub-committee to possess strong claims to approbation, and discover much inginuity [sic] & professional knowledge.

That the models and designs exhibited by Mr. William Wilkins, junior, bear full testimony to the depth of his research amongst the great specimens of antiquity, and the success with which he has cultivated his natural genius, and adapted the great examples which he has personally viewed to produce a design of great erudition, simplicity and magnificence.

That the model and designs produced by Mr. Philip Wyatt appear to the sub-committee to be deserving of high commendation. The finished beauty of the model of Mr. P. Wyatt appears to the committee to surpass in execution anything that has ever been produced of the same nature; and the elegance, richness and architectural knowledge shewn in the whole design, as well as judicious distribution of most parts of the design, to claim the warmest applause.

The committee have found it difficult to make a selection in a contest of so much genius, and in determining upon one they deeply regret the necessity of rejecting either of the other two designs, that of Mr. Wilkins, or that of Mr. Philip Wyatt—but they congratulate the country on the possession of such powers, and they cannot help remarking upon the distinguished rank held in this competition by the two sons of Mr. James Wyatt, himself confessedly preeminent in the profession of architecture.

That the chairman do submit a copy of these resolutions with all humility, in the name of the sub-committee, to his Royal Highness the Prince Regent: and do express the grateful sense entertained by the sub-committee for the condescending favour shewn by his Royal Highness in his patient & enlightened investigation of the different plans and models submitted to the consideration of his Royal Highness at Carlton House.

That these resolutions be reported to the general committee at their meeting tomorrow for their consent and approbation.

Unanimously agreed to

Signed { Samuel Whitbread
P. Moore   (18736–8)
Thomas Hope

3215   THOMAS TYRWHITT TO COLONEL MCMAHON

Ton-Royal, 17 Oct. 1811

From a communication from Yarmouth[1] it is quite clear not a word has been said by anyone to B. respecting Plymouth—nor is it *now* necessary there should be. If I had been commanded I should have obeyed—as it now is, I am certain it is for the *harmony* of all that I should give it up,

1. Lord Yarmouth.

which I do with joy. I shall lend every assistance to B. in my power.[1]
(18739)

3216   THE EARL OF MOIRA TO MAJOR-GENERAL T. H. TURNER
Donington, 18 Oct. 1811
As I believe Colonel McMahon to be absent from town I beg leave to
address [you] respecting Mr Wilkins who is to present a model of a
Theatre for the inspection of the Prince Regent.[2] On the merits of the
model I can have of course no judgement, but I will beg you, if conversation should arise upon it, to lay before his Royal Highness my humble
assurance that Mr Wilkins is in personal character as well as in cultivated
talent, very deserving of any protection which the Prince may deign to
extend to him.

I do not infer from the Gazette that the French will be driven beyond
the Pyrenees this winter. (18741)

3217   THE DUKE OF YORK TO THE PRINCE REGENT
Windsor, 19 Oct. 1811
I have seen only three of her Majesty's Council who came here today:
the Archbishop, the Duke of Montrose and Lord Ailesford. They began
by examining first the two consulting phisicians, who, as far as I can
understand, at first laid a great stress upon one or two more rational
sentences which his Majesty spoke during the phisicians' visit this
morning as a proof of the medicines they had proposed having taken
effect, but upon a further enquiry into what had passed as well as to the
occurrences of the week, the Council found no grounds for a more
favourable view of the case. These two phisicians, however, being again
asked their opinion as to the general state, returned for answer that they
had not yet seen enough of his Majesty to form any judgement. It was
therefor proposed to her Majesty that they should return again on Friday,
to which the Queen consented, and upon the Archbishop stating that it
was possible that Dr. Monro could not come on that day, her Majesty
said that she had no objection to Dr. Simmonds seeing his Majesty in
the presence of Dr. Robert Willis if it was clearly understood that he was
not to be admitted to the King's room without them. Her Majesty has

1. See No. 3188*n*.
2. See Nos. 3208, 3214.

likewise agreed to an alteration being made in the attendance of the phisicians, whereby Sir Henry Halford will come here on the Wesnesday and stay till after the Council has met on the Saturday. Dr. Baillie will come on Friday and stay till the Monday, and Dr. Heberden relieve Dr. Baillie on that day till the Wednesday and return again on the Friday, as the Council has insisted upon all the phisicians being here on Friday and staying till after their examination on the Saturday.[1] (44251)

3218 **THOMAS HARRIS TO COLONEL MCMAHON**

Bellemonte, 20 Oct. 1811

When I wrote to you the other day I little thought that I shou'd so soon have been compell'd to trespass again upon your valuable time—the present subject is as painful to my feelings as the former one was gratifying.

I have recd. information from my son that you have had from Mr. Colman a Petition to present to his Royal Highness the Prince Regent, praying for an extension of the Haymarket license to eight months—that is neither more nor less than to establish a third regular winter Theatre—which must effectually compleat the destruction of all regular theatrical property—his own among the rest.

The pretences on which Mr. Colman founds his application I understand to be these—viz—the late Ld. Chamberlain's license to Mr. Arnold for the English Opera—the innovations practis'd by the numerous public places acting under the Lord Chamberlain's & the magistrates' license in performing regular dramatic pieces—and the protraction of the seasons of the patent Theatres—it is but too true that the unprecedented licenses granted by the late Lord Chamberlain have been a material injury to us all. The late Lord Dartmouth was the first Lord Chambn. who ever exercis'd that power on his own authority which heretofore was always understood to be a branch of the Royal Prerogative, & under that conviction the two patents belonging to Drury Lane & Cov. Gardn. have been from time to time purchas'd, & large sums have been advanced

1. Princess Charlotte wrote on the 16th to her friend Mercer Elphinstone: 'Sir H. Halford called upon me yesterday. I saw him for a few minutes. He told me *fairly* that there was *not the smallest* chance of the K.'s recovering his reason, but that he might live for a considerable time. In a letter yesterday from Mary she says other mad doctors were called in for *the sake of giving* their *opinion*. A *consultation* therefore took place in wh. Dr. John Willis gave his *decided opinion* of things *being irrecoverable*; so did Baillie [and] Halford &c., but Dr. *Monroe & Simmonds*, tho' they *think* the *same*, beg for *another consultation when* they will give their *decided* opinion, as they wish for a few days for *consideration*. The K. *suffers no pain* & is *perfectly happy in himself*' (Bowood MSS.).

upon their validity so consider'd. The license granted by Lord D. to Mr. Astley (who thereupon erected a small building in Wych Street, Drury Lane which he has this year considerably enlarged) has so diminish'd our nightly receipts (our galleries being almost deserted) that we have been compell'd to have recourse to similar exhibitions at an enormous expence, without which the regular drama cou'd not have been supported. The license granted to Mr. Arnold, obtain'd under the shallow pretense of encouraging native musical talent (as if we had not been always eager to encourage it wherever it was to be found)—& also the license which I understand Mr. Greville has obtain'd must be of serious injury—but while we are suffering in common with Mr. Colman, is it reasonable that he shou'd by an extension of his license be enabled to become himself the *chief* of those *innovators* of whom he so justly & heavily complains?

I shall not at present dwell on the irregularities practis'd at the numerous public places acting under magistrates' licenses—for it is to the distress'd state & confusion of the regular Theatres alone that they have so long been suffer'd thus grossly to violate the restricting Act of King Geo. 2nd.

Mr. Colman's last ground of complaint is the aggression of the patent Theatres. I must here revert to the original grant of the Haymarket patent to prove that the aggression has been progressively on his part & not on ours—Sam Foote[1] hunting with the late Dk. of York[2] met with an accident. The Dk. in compassion to his misfortune solicited his Majesty for a patent authorizing Mr. Foote to open the little Theatre in the Haymarket—during his life—particular attention was then paid to the interests of the patent Theatres by restricting the opening of the Haymarket Theatre to the 15th May & the close to the 15th Septemr. It was also understood that Foote wou'd perform merely his own pieces or such others as wou'd not interfere with either the patent Theatres, their actors or their performances. The elder Colman,[3] having purchas'd Foote's life interest, at his decease obtain thro' Lord Hertford[4] an annual license merely (his petition to have the license during his life being refused) which was continued to the pres. Mr. G. Colman at the decease of his father. Heretofore the patent Theatres had frequently perform'd the whole year round, but in order to give an interval of rest to theatrical exhibitions, that the public might return to them with more avidity, they shut up for three & sometimes 4 months. Until the Haymarket Theatre came into the possession of the present proprietors the performances seldom interfered with what is call'd the stock pieces of the patent

1. Samuel Foote (1720–77), actor and dramatist.
2. Edward Augustus, Duke of York (1739–67), George III's brother.
3. George Colman (1732–94), dramatist; father of George Colman (1762–1836).
4. The first Marquess (1718–94). He was Lord Chamberlain, 1766–82.

Theatres, & consequently the end proposed by closing for a time at the patent Theatres was answer'd.

From the intimacy & friendship which has ever subsisted between Mr. Colman & myself I have been induced for a long series of years to allow any part of our Company, stock pieces &c, to be at his service, & have always paid our performers their full salaries even when acting at the same time, in opposition to Covt. Gardn., at the Haymarket Theatre. Mr. Colman forgets to state that about two years since he prevail'd on the late Lord Dartmouth (without any communication, as I have good reason to believe, with his Majesty) to extend the term of his license another month—that is, to the 15th Octobr.—which extension on a former application direct to his Majesty thro' Ld. Salisbury, his Majesty has been pleas'd to refuse. That month certainly more than compensates for the contingent protraction of some of our seasons, occasion'd by unavoidable circumstances. I can feel no hostility to Mr. Colman for this second attack on us by his prest. petition, which indeed I consider more as the act of his partners, especially of Mr Morris, who for some time has done all in his power to injure the interests of Covt. Gardn Theatre merely because I have from time to time giv'n every theatrical assistance to his partner Geo. Colman, with whom he is at bitter variance, & is now, & has long been contending in the Court of Chancery. Perhaps it may not be known that Mr. Colman some years since sold the half of his interest in the Haymarket Theatre for six times the sum that his father gave for the whole—at which time his license was for 4 months only. His other half is now so entangled with law expenses that it may be said to be in the hands of his attorney—& I am credibly inform'd that shou'd the application for the extended license prove successful, that Mr Colman's partners in conjunction with his attorney & some speculating discontented actors, have agreed to erect on a much larger scale an entire new Theatre. Thus, my dear frd. have I as briefly as possible (tho I am afraid very tediously) gone over the grounds of Mr Colman's pretensions.

A clamour has lately gone forth of a want of theatrical competition—but already the competition for histrionic talent is so general in London, Dublin, Edinbro' & the numerous provincial towns, that at any expence whatever, one good company worthy of a great national Theatre can hardly be collected. Three of our performers left us this year rather than accept a salary of £18—19 & £20 pr week each—exclusive of a Benefit by which they generally clear'd from four to five hundred each—& Mr Colman confesses that it is from *our Company* that he must create *his own*.

Drury Lane Theatre will now speedily rise from its ashes supported by all the powerful interest of a charter'd corporation. I know from dear bought experience how difficult it will be to contend with such a rival,

189

for there is no instance on record of Dry. Lane & Cov. Gardn. Theatre's haveing had in one & the same year each of them a fair profitable season.

I have now only to add that shou'd our every gracious & illustrious founder be induced to withdraw his protection to our patent rights which he has hitherto so repeatedly & so kindly supported, I intreat that you will in your friendship give me the earliest notice of such a misfortune. I must then make the best arrangement I can with my numerous creditors who are now pressing very seriously for their heavy debts, & by ridding myself of my precarious & hazardous concern altogether. I shall extricate my family from a property which must have long since led me among so many others to the walls of a prison, had I not for so many, many years experienced the unceasing favour, the protecting power & justice of the Throne. (18743-6)

3219   THOMAS TYRWHITT TO COLONEL MCMAHON, AND ENCLOSURES
Plymouth, 20 Oct. 1811
I enclose another letter, and I trust the last from my Worthing correspondent.

It is now settled B.[1] comes in here—He is sure of his election and without expence—not a word has or will be said to the P. upon the subject. Yarmouth thinks B. would have shewn very ill humour, & is quite happy, the thing is so arranged that harmony will be the order of the day.

Between you & I, B. is acting a silly part. He, as the Duke of C. writes me word, is wishing to go to Ireland to see his ESTATES, the Duke says. The P. will not give him leave. I will bore you no longer but in all cases believe me [etc.]. (18748)

[Enclosure] J. RYAN TO THOMAS TYRWHITT
Worthing, 15 Oct. 1811
In addition to what I had the honor of communicating to you relative to Col. Wardle's movements, I beg leave to observe further, as the result of minute subsequent inquiries, that he had been here about six weeks prior to his late visit, accompanied by a poor miserable looking female, who, from the description and other circumstances, appears to be Mrs Wardle[2] —at Bognor usually called, in derision, 'Mrs Rum & Onions'—'Mrs

1. Bloomfield. See No. 3215n.
2. Wardle married a Miss Parry of Carnarvonshire about 1792.

Tabitha Skinflint'—'The little Jew Old-Cloaths-Woman,' &c., &c. Without giving his name, he introduced himself to a fisherman of the name of Wicks, who also keeps bathing machines, as the particular friend of Sir Francis Burdett, with whom Wicks is well acquainted, having been frequently in the habit of bathing him, and attending him out a-shooting when in his neighbourhood, as well as of sending him to town a present of the first herrings he takes in the season: for the worthy Baronet is as fond of first fruits as the parson himself. Hence it would seem that Sir Francis & Mr. James Wicks, the fisherman, are old cronies, tho' I think the latter by far the better subject of the two.

The illustrious Colonel wishing to pass incog. in a place where he thought himself not personally known, announced himself at the warm bath as a Mr Bonnet—still as the intimate friend of Sir F. Burdett: but, rather unluckily for his view, he was soon recognised, and the noted, the patriotic Col. Wardle, Mr. Browne, and Mr. Bonnet were identified as being one & the same individual personage! Surely this man never could attempt to avail himself of any mistake in regard to his name in an action at law, by pleading a misnomer. He could no more prove it than he could an *alibi* when detected under the feigned name of Browne with his mistress at the Cadogan Arms in Sloan Street.

At the time above-mentioned, he was also negociating with a brother of the said Wicks about the hire or purchase of a large boat: for what purpose he best knows. At his late visit he commissioned Wicks to engage a furnished house for him during the remainder of the season or till Christmas. He was about leaving Worthing immediately, but was to be back in a day or two. He left his lodging near Broadwater[1] early on Saturday morning, the 5th inst. but has not yet returned.

Sir Francis Burdett not having been seen in or about Worthing yet this season, tho' his name had been entered in the books at both the libraries, it is doubtful whether he was actually the person who accompanied Col. Wardle from this neighbourhood.

Could the enterprising Colonel by any means contrive to put the Heiress Apparent of England into Buonaparte's power, he may unquestionably make his own terms. That a man of his description, and in the present desperate state of his character & circumstances, would stick at the commission of no crime, however atrocious, to gratify his hatred to his Majesty's family & Government, on the one hand, and with the certain prospect of ample emolument on the other, hardly admits of the least shadow of doubt; while at the same time he could take the necessary measures for his personal security by removing to another country. In this he has no interest, or next to none. I repeat it, that his motions should be watched with the utmost care.

At Felpham, the Revd. Dr. Jackson (distinguished by the title of

1. One and a half miles north of Worthing.

Mother Jackson) late Dean of Christ Church, Oxford, and the Revd. Mr. Bede, the annihilator of the aspirate,* and, at Bognor, Lady Collins[1] and Sir Thos. Trowbridge[2] & family are the principal if not the only advocates for Wardle and Wardelian politics in that neighbourhood. Mr. Bede is his declared friend, and ready to serve and assist him in any enterprise whatever. Three-fourths of the inhabitants of Chichester are still infected with the like mania. In fact, Chichester may well be considered an hospital for political incurables.

Conceiving the celebrated Mrs Clarke the very properest person I could possibly consult on the choice of a lawyer to prosecute my claim on Wardle, to her I accordingly applied, and obtained the information I wanted. In a few days after, she sent me a slip of paper with these words:
'Col. Wardle is not at Heen[e].'
'Mr. Ryan'
To which I returned the following answer:

'Madam,
'On my return, after a walk on the Steyne yesterday, I observed a printed hand-bill posted up, offering a reward for the discovery of the person or persons who lately committed depredations on some poultry at Heene: I should be glad to know if your assuring me that *Col. Wardle is not at Heen* was meant to obviate any suspicion of his having been concerned in robbing a farmer's hen-roost?'
                              'I am, Madam &c.
                                        J. Ryan'

'Mrs. Clarke.'
I herewith inclose an extract from my letter to Lady Collins last winter, occasioned by a disgraceful transaction in which she & her daughters took an active part with her friend, Mrs Wardle. I have stated or alluded to none but real incontrovertible facts and have the honor to remain most respectfully [etc.]. (18749–50)

---

* This truly bad man & most worthless character commits some very ridiculous mistakes by his determined hostility to the poor (h) . . . 'The Lord poured down '*ail* . . . Madam, shall I ride your '*orse*?' &c. Mr. Bede.

1. Possibly the wife of John Collins, Captain R.N., who was knighted on 4 July 1783.

2. Sir Edward Thomas Troubridge (*c.* 1787–1852) succeeded his father, Rear-Admiral Sir Thomas Troubridge, as second Baronet in February 1807. Entered the Navy, 1797; Lieutenant, 1806; Captain, 1807; Commander-in-Chief at Cork, 1831–2; M.P. for Sandwich, 1831–47; a Lord of the Admiralty, 1835–41; C.B., 1838, Rear-Admiral, 1841.

Felpham, 18 Jan. 1811

When 'tis known that Lady Collins and her daughters are the intimate friends & associates of a family deservedly detested & shunned by every loyal subject in the Kingdom—a vile mixture of Jews & rank Jacobins;—a family where even the children are from their infancy taught to lisp the name of our august & revered Sovereign with contempt, to deride his infirmities, and to cherish disaffection to his Government and hatred to his family: when, I say, this circumstance is known, what will the world think of such a connexion? No one who wishes well to the Royal family and knew the Wardles as I do at present, would have the least intercourse with them.* Had I known that at first as well, I would just as soon have engaged in the family of a Despard[2] or a Margaret Nicholson.[3] Since I began to know their real character I have studiously avoided all freedom or familiarity of communication with them as much as possible. I have faithfully & conscientiously discharged my duty towards their children, tho' I could not help abominating the parents for their detestable principles—principles from which every well-disposed mind must shrink with abhorrence; and this opposition of sentiments & principles was the true & only substantial ground of misunderstanding between us, whatever other they may *now* chuse to allege.—*Taffy* and *Skinflint* are perfectly sensible there was no other in fact. (18751)

* Our acquaintance commenced and the transaction was managed principally by the agency of a third person, employed, as I afterwards found, by Col. Wardle.

3220   LORD ERSKINE TO COLONEL MCMAHON

2 Upper Grosvr. Street, 21 Oct. 1811

I came to town today from our friend Lord Keith's near Portsmouth, but there being a sale of trees at Stockwell I stopped there till after the post was gone out, & only found your letter on coming home. I will make a point of seeing Perry[4] before breakfast tomorrow. *He shall not continue* in the manner you naturally complain of. I think it most wicked & unjust, and *Perry cannot* refuse to abide by my wish and opinion on the subject. I will also see others not less important. There is not any disposition to find fault with you as the object either of the Prince's favor or of the attention due to an honorable man. It goes to *the office*—for the

1. Addressed to Frederick's Place, Bognor.

2. Edward Marcus Despard (1751–1803), the traitor. See No. 1690 (iv. 323).

3. The lunatic who tried to murder the King in 1786 (*c.* 1750–1828). See *The Later Correspondence of George III*, i. 240.

4. James Perry, proprietor of the *Morning Chronicle*. See No. 1338.

abolition of which as you know my opinion there is no foundation whatever. Let Parliament abolish it, if it pleases, and then the Prince knows
what to do, but why should he abolish it? And now, my dear friend, let
me give you a lesson. Are you not sufficiently a man of the world com-
pleatly to despise all the trash which gives you so much pain? I can say
to you in confidence that I believe there are not many persons who enjoy
more than I do the confidence & esteem of the people of this land, & yet
(for the Press is a two-edged sword) I have been abused in newspapers
not now & then but for a pelting of 20 years incessantly *every, every*
day, *& I never cared for it the thousandth thousandth part of half a farthing*;
& let me counsel you WHOLLY to disregard it. Nevertheless as you suffer
uneasiness I shall not relax in my exertion to to [*sic*] do what will remove
pain at a distance from you, being as you know I am [etc.].[1] (18756)

3221   LETTERS FROM THE MARQUESS WELLESLEY TO THE PRINCE REGENT

Dorking, at night, 21 Oct. 1811

Lord Wellesley has the honor to submit to your Royal Highness a very
interesting letter received this day from Count Nugent. The opinion
respecting Sweden will no doubt be satisfactory to your Royal Highness,
your commands having anticipated every suggestion which has arisen at
Berlin on that most important point. A most extraordinary interception
is also contained in this box which Lord Wellesley submits to your Royal
Highness with considerable regret, as it displays the character of his
Majesty's Minister at the Brasils, & of that Court, in the most disgraceful
state of intrigue & corruption.

Your Royal Highness will perceive that his Majesty's Minister at the
Brasils has, under an assumption of your Royal Highness's authority,
forced the Prince Regent of Portugal to confer honors on the Portugese
Minister in London; and this system of force is to be reciprocated upon
your Royal Highness by the Count of Funchal (lately M. de Sousa) who,
in return for Lord Strangford's successful violence at Rio de Janeiro,
intends to force your Royal Highness to gratify whatever expectations
of honor or advancement Lord Strangford may entertain, & to sanction
whatever engagements the Portugese Minister here may have concluded
with his Majesty's Minister at the Brasils, respecting your Royal Highness's favor in the distribution of the patronage of the Crown in the
diplomatic department. (18753)

1. The appointment of McMahon to the sinecure office of Paymaster of Widows' Pensions
was criticised in the *Morning Chronicle* and other newspapers, and in the House of Commons
in 1812 (*Parliamentary Debates*, xxi. 112–24 [9 January]; 900–07 [21 February]; 911–31 [24
February]).

Dorking, at night, Tuesday, 22 Oct. 1811

Lord Wellesley presents his humble duty to your Royal Highness, & requests permission to offer his grateful acknowlegements [*sic*] for your Royal Highness's gracious condescension in forwarding Count Münster's letter by an express messenger: the intelligence which it contains is most interesting, & (unless it can be supposed that Prussia is treacherous to herself) satisfactory, since it is certainly desirable that more time should be given for the preparation of the Northern Powers against France.

Lord Wellesley will not fail to consider with serious attention the expediency of submitting for your Royal Highness's commands a letter to the King of Prussia in the present crisis. He proposes to be in town tomorrow, & to attend at York House on Thursday; before which time he hopes to have access, by Count Munster's kindness, to the communications received from Vienna. (18759)

3222   THE EARL OF MOIRA TO COLONEL MCMAHON

Donington, 22 Oct. 1811

Thank God, my dear friend, you are enjoying a little tranquillity & sea air. You are not, however, out of reach of letter-shot, so I assail you tho' it is more to indulge my own propensity of communing with you than for any business. Some time ago Forster (of Lubbock's Horse) asked me to propose to the Prince to become a President of the Linnaean Society. I said that acting as Sovereign of the country, the Prince ought to be Patron not President. Forster replied that he thought the Charter indicated nothing but a President: to which I rejoined that the Prince could not be enrolled as functionary in any Society & should be Patron or nothing. I hope the distinction was right.

The account of what took place at the Catholic Meeting has not yet reached me. The assembly would be dispersed of course. I do not apprehend riot, but there may be circumstances on such occasion capable of encreasing the dissatisfaction already entertained; therefore I look with anxiety for the narrative. You must have learned from your brother the lamentable persuasion adopted by the Catholics that the Prince has espoused all the hostility of his Cabinet towards them. This conviction is so strong that if it be eradicable by any subsequent procedures our luck will be better than what I reckon upon. See what this goes to. The Catholics compose at least five sixths, & by far the most active part, of the population of Ireland. As Irishmen simply, they were embittered by past grievances against England. The belief that the Prince favored their just pretensions afforded the hope of a more equitable Government & suspended their animosity. That prospect is now dispelled. Nothing

195

checks their misconstruction of England: and the Protestants, with the miserable exception of the Corporation of Dublin, the Castle dependants & the tythe jobbers instigate the ferment of the Catholics, some from seeing no security for their property but in joining so irresistible a mass, others by way of avenging themselves on the Prince for political disappointment. Surely, surely, it requires no sagacity or peculiar foresight to distinguish whither all this is tending. Men in that humor never calculate their solid & ultimate advantage; they look to nothing but the way in which they can wound those with whom they are irritated. It is therefore idle to think that such folks will be deterred from listening to Bonaparte because of his treacheries exhibited elsewhere. They will listen to him, they do listen to him, & the storm will burst upon us as it did on the Prussians who thought him, good loitering fellow, many days march from their camp on the very morning in which he was to subvert their Monarchy. All the preparations opposite to Jersey & Guernsey are referable to Ireland either as destined active instruments or as curbs on your interference with the efforts to be made from other quarters. Unimportant as the matter may appear, the recent appointments in Ireland are not indifferent. There was nothing to object to Hall[1] for the Bishoprick, but the bestowal of the Provostship on Elrington[2] (especially against such a candidate as Magee[3]) has had very injurious effects: for, Elrington had no recommendation but the virulence of his language & his publications respecting the Catholics. The latter necessarily regard his elevation as the reward of his dispositions against them; & there is no explaining away so prominent a fact to the multitude who regard it as the display of the Prince's own sentiments.

Ld Wellington's dispatch is quite sufficient to settle my opinions about him. They were tolerably made up before, but now my judgement has not one floating doubt.

I shall direct this to London lest you may have been suddenly called up, tho' I trust nothing will occur to interrupt your enjoyment of your retreat. (18762–5)

1. See No. 3196.

2. Thomas Elrington (1760–1835), a Professor at Trinity College since 1799. The Lord Lieutenant, the Duke of Richmond, appointed him Provost of Trinity College in November 1811. Bishop of Limerick, 1820; of Ferns, 1822.

3. William Magee (1766–1831), Professor of Mathematics at Trinity College, 1800; Dean of Cork, 1813; Bishop of Raphoe, 1819; Archbishop of Dublin, 1822–31.

Addington, 23 Oct. 1811

I must trouble you to submit my humble request to the Prince Regent that I may be permitted to lay at his Royal Highness's feet ye proceedings & resolutions of a meeting convened for ye purpose of establishing a Society entitled The National Society for promoting ye education of ye Poor in ye principles of ye Established Church throughout England & Wales. I venture to submit this request to his Royal Highness in consequence of ye following resolution of ye meeting: 'That ye ABishop of Canterbury be requested to lay ye proceedings of this meeting before his Royal Highness ye Prince Regent.'

If you will have ye goodness to take his Royal Highness's pleasure as to ye day & hour in which I may be permitted to pay my duty to him, you will much oblige me. It is fit I should state to you that ye publication of our proceedings is suspended untill they shall have been submitted to ye inspection of ye Regent.[1] (18766)

3224 THE DUKE OF YORK TO THE PRINCE REGENT

Windsor, 26 Oct. 1811

Only three of the Queen's Council attended today, the Archbishop, the Duke of Montrose and Lord Winchelsea, and the examinations of the phisicians were very short. I understand that they all agree in opinion that the medicines proposed a fortnight ago have rather done harm than good and they have in consequence determined to give his Majesty occasionally doses of julep, as it is not wished to increase the irritation which has always been the case for a length of time when medicine has been administered; it is intended that the jelup [sic] shall be mixed in his food.

The Council afterwards went to his Majesty's room to see him while he dined; his Majesty quieter than usual but every symptom of his disorder was manifested.

[P.S.] The Council have not noticed the Queen's letter[2] and when her

1. The Society was formed under the patronage of the Established Church as a rival to Joseph Lancaster's Royal Lancasterian Institution, which became in 1814 the British and Foreign School Society.

2. She wrote to the Archbishop on 23 October: 'Altho' your letter of the 21st instant did not appear to require any immediate reply, I have felt that it would be advisable to convey to you previous to the meeting of the Council on Saturday next a few observations which have occurred to me & which I had at first proposed to have stated verbally on that day.

'I am glad to find that the order which the Council left with Dr. Willis was not intended (as I had conceived it) to be considered as dispencing with the condition which I had prescribed, that the consulting physicians should attend here conjointly, but I cannot deny to you that the representation made on Saturday by Dr. Simmons, added to my knowledge of his presumption & to other circumstances which have occurred, confirms my suspicion that he has it still in view if possible to introduce himself into the exclusive management of the King & is therefore proceeding towards the attainment of that object by such means as shall appear to him best suited to his purpose. I am confident that upon reflection it must strike the Council as it does me that no well grounded or even plausible plea of personal convenience can be assigned by Dr. Simmons which should render it a matter of necessity during his & Dr. Munro's occasional conjoint attendance, that either should have access separately to the King's room. The nature of their practice does not render them liable during their short attendance here to any applications from the neighbourhood requiring even a temperary absence from the Castle, & the particular object of their attendance must be more satisfactorily ensured by their joint observations of the King's demeanor. There cannot therefore be any reasonable ground for Dr. Simmon's representation, & while it strengthens the suspicion to which I have before adverted, it adds to my desire that the condition upon which I consented to his having access should be executed in its full extent.

'I am sensible that it may occur to the Council that I am more pointed & more determined in my opposition to Dr. Simmons than to any other person, & that having waved my original scruples the present objections may be termed preposterous, or at least superfluous. I must, however observe to you that the original ground of opposition which applied equally to Dr. Simmons & Dr. Willis was confined to a principle of deference to the King's injunction & was wholly free from any personal objection which I or any of my family entertained towards Dr. J. Willis. This is far from being the case in respect to Dr. Simmons, whose conduct & proceedings (exclusively of the prejudice generally imbibed by the King towards individuals similarly circumstanced in regard to his Majesty) had render'd him justly obnoxious to the King, to myself, to the whole Royal Family & to the individual attendants. I believe I have more than once expressed my sentiments verbally to this effect to you & to others of the Council, & altho' we have unfortunately differed in this point & altho' you have considered it necessary, from motives to the purity of which I do full justice, to urge measures in which I could not concur or to which I could assent only with reluctance, I am persuaded that you are all sincerely disposed to consult as far as you may consider it to be consistent with what is due to public feelings & prejudice, the comfort & the tranquillity of the King's family, & that you will not therefore press upon *me* & *them* any measure which, while it must at best appear to you one of very doubtful utility, to us, one of hopeless benefit, would be calculated greatly to heighten the distress & to encrease the difficulties by which our feelings are already so greatly harrassed. Of such nature would certainly be any proposal for extending to Doctor Simmons facilities of access beyond those already given, still more for sanctioning any interference on his part in the management which, I must repeat, I am confident is the object of his wishes & of his proceedings.

'I am aware that he has laid great stress upon having attended the King in the last illness from which it pleased God that he should recover, but I do not see upon what grounds he presumes to claim *exclusive merit* as it stands on record that the King had recovered from two *previous illnesses* under the management of other physicians. The disappointment of our anxious hopes on the present melancholy occasion has been, I verily believe, attributable under Providence not to any want of skill or attention in those who have attended him, but to circumstances of a general & public nature which had upon no former occasion prevailed to such extent.

'I am not callous to the great responsibility which attaches to the situation of the Council & far be it from my intention to add to the difficulties which they must encounter in the discharge of their painful duties, but conscious as I am that I am maintaining certain sentiments upon just grounds & from the purest motives, confident as I am that no individual subject of the King can feel more tenderly alive to his welfare & interests, more warmly anxious for

198

Majesty mentioned it to the Archbishop he merely bowed an acknowledgment of the receipt without saying anything upon it. The Council has proposed that the consulting phisicians shall return next Friday, and I understand that there is to be a meeting of the Council at the Archbishop's next Wednesday. (44252)

3225   THE DUKE OF NORTHUMBERLAND TO COLONEL MCMAHON

Alnwick Castle, 26 Oct. 1811

It is impossible to say how much I feel myself obliged to you for your letter of 20th & the trouble you are so kind as to take on account of my wishes to serve my relation Mr. Hume.[1] By a letter I received from him this morning I find that Mr. Baron Hepburn,[2] whose death was hourly expected, is relieved for the present, so that the expected vacancy of a Baron of the Exchequer has not taken place. This perhaps is fortunate, as it may enable you thro' your kindness to secure a future vacancy by giving us more time.

I see by the papers that the D. of Cumberland always goes down to Windsor with the Regent, & attends H.R.H. almost constantly. Is this really true, or only a newspaper fabrication? As the Duke is such a staunch friend to the present Administration I find from my letters that people in general, believing the account, look upon it as a strong proof that the present Ministers will continue to hold their places.

My neighbour, Lord Grey, has got quite well again, altho' I understand he will be always liable to returns of his troublesome complaint. If I remember right the late Lord Thurlow was troubled with gall stones for some years.

I hope Lord W—y has by this time had a surfeit of his zenana & will apply heartily & assiduously to the business of his Office. He will have enough to do with Spain and Portugal if all the other Powers on the Continent remain quiet, besides the attention which other parts of the world, such as Sicily—South America—&c. &c. &c., will require. I hope you are receiving great benefit at Margate, & that Mrs Mac Mahon is quite well, to both of whom the Duchess & the rest of my family desire

his recovery, than I do, I am willing to share the utmost responsibility which may be thrown upon the Council, & further, shall not shrink from that of having persisted in my opposition to a measure the adoption of which I should never cease to *deplore*.

'In vindicating Dr. J.W.'s character I beg it may be understood that I do not wish either him or Dr. Munro to be established here.' (36579–81 [copy])

1. See No. 3211.

2. See No. 3211.

to offer their compliments with my own. I am recovering daily, but very slowly. Pray when do you return to London? (18778)

3226   GEORGE COLMAN TO [?] COLONEL MCMAHON
4 Melina Place, Westminister Road, 26 Oct. 1811
The day before yesterday I had the pleasure of an interview with Mr. Henry Harris who informs me that I am to expect (as I did before) a decided opposition to my memorial from the proprietors of Covt. Garden Theatre. He tells me also that his father has written to you on the subject,[1] & as far as I can gather from him the contents of the letter there do not appear to me any formidable arguments against my cause. Trusting that it will be permitted me to rejoin to them I shall throw upon paper such reasonings as occur to me for your inspection on your arrival in London—till when I hope nothing will be laid before the Prince Regent, for I presume you will think it most eligible to collect all that *all* the parties can have to state, & *then* submit the whole to his Royal Highness's consideration. This mode, I conceive, would be less troublesome to the Prince, certainly more for my interests and perfectly fair towards all.

Mr. Sheridan is, I understand, on a visit, for a few days, at Oatlands; & as you are so nearly on your return, may it not be as well to defer my conference with him till your arrival? Have the goodness to favour me with one line as to your sentiments on this.

Mr. H. Harris does not think it necessary that a Covent Garden proprietor should attend a general meeting of parties, his father's sentiments being made up, & fully before you. (18779)

3227   THE QUEEN TO THE PRINCE REGENT, AND AN ENCLOSURE
Windsor, 27 Oct. 1811
Mary having just informed [me] that you are prevented coming here today on account of a cold, I will not let the messenger return without a few lines to say how sorry I am of being prevented seing you, & also to add that I beg you not to think of comming tomorrow unless you are quite free from pain.

Inclosed I send the copy of a letter I have just sent off to the A.B. of C.

1. See No. 3218.

200

concerning Dr. W.[1] nightly attendance, which I trust you will find respect-full to the King & just to the Dr. God bless you. (36578)

[Enclosure] THE QUEEN TO THE ARCHBISHOP OF CANTERBURY [copy]
Windsor, 27 Oct. 1811
Dr. Willis having communicated to me the wish expressed to him by you yesterday that he should take my pleasure in regard to some arrangement which might relieve him in some measure from the most fatiguing part of his attendance, I have after due consideration determined upon that which will, I trust, appear to you and the other members of the Council unobjectionable, as it does to me.

I conceive that the object in view is to secure Dr. W. during the night from that continual interruption of his rest from which his health has already suffered and which it is impossible that any human being can support in the long run, and I am convinced that the Council will feel with me that it would be most unreasonable to suffer the *undimminished zeal* of any individual to operate to his prejudice when the excessive exertion of it is not a matter of absolute necessity. On the other hand the Council cannot feel more anxious than I am that the King should in his present melancholy situation have the benefit of the immediate assistance of the physician in attendance when required. I have therefore directed that Dr. W. shall occupy a room in his Majesty's apartment and on the same floor, where he will be sufficiently removed from the King's bed-room to be able to enjoy his rest and where he will nevertheless be within immediate reach of a summons if the two men who sit up with the King should find it necessary to call for his assistance. You are I conclude aware that one of the pages is in attendance every night in the outer room and that such has been the invariable practice during this and former illnesses, while in no former illness have the physician or physicians in attendance been called upon to occupy the room adjoining the King altho' they have alternately set [*sic*] up during the more critical periods.

Independantly of the arrangement which I have made in consequence of what passed between you and Dr. W. yesterday, I proposed that the other physicians should occasionally relieve Dr. W. from the attendance below stairs during the night, which, altho' it will be henceforth less necessary, must still, as possibly subject to frequent interruption of rest, be considered in my opinion more fatiguing than it would be reasonable or necessary to impose upon him. (36582)

1. Dr. Willis.

201

Wimbledon, 28 Oct. 1811

I understand from your correspondent that 'if the paper which I wish to present to the Prince Regent is of a *public* nature it is the usual custom to transmit it through you when there are no Levies [*sic*]; but if it be of a *private* nature and personal to myself, you are thoroughly sure his Royal Highness will receive me with very great pleasure, and with every attention to its object.'

I am exceedingly flattered by the very handsome expressions in your letter relative personally to me. I am however very sorry for its contents and can only transmit the paper to you open to be considered by yours and others better judgement. (18783)

[Enclosure] SIR FRANCIS BURDETT TO THE PRINCE REGENT

Wimbledon, 28 Oct. 1811

With every sentiment of respect and humility I beg leave to approach your Royal Highness with this intrusion, believing that I shall thereby merit your approbation not your displeasure.

Nathan Wilson,[1] a private in your Royal Highness's own Regiment the Tenth Light Dragoons, a private but a decent man and creditably allied and at this time only twenty three years of age, having been nearly six years in the Regiment and never committed not even the slightest offence against military discipline so as to receive even the smallest rebuke, till the twelfth his Colonel's birthday when he was not in barracks at nine o'clock, for which he was tried by a court martial the following day and sentenced to receive two hundred lashes; which sentence was carried into execution the next day.

It is important that your Royal Highness should know this, and that the court martial consisted of Captain De Gramont, President, twenty three years of age, Smith, twenty one years of age, Cotton, twenty years of age, Hill, twenty one years of age, Fitzgerald, seventeen years of age.

This sentence was confirmed by Lieutenant Colonel George Quintin and given by him to Lieutenant [*sic*] Charles Palmer to be carried into execution. The following persons inflicted

George Ellis	twenty lashes	Benjamin Nott	twenty lashes
John Adams	twenty lashes	William Afflick	twenty lashes
James King	twenty lashes	Thomas Whebbles	twenty lashes
James Thinnes	twenty lashes	George Ellis	twenty lashes
John Hoole	twenty lashes	John Adams	twenty lashes
Christopher Pole	twenty lashes		

1. See No. 3171.

So that it appears Wilson received twenty lashes more than his sentence although he twice during the punishment begged for forgiveness of Lieutenant-Colonel Palmer on the score of character and it was the duty of Adjutant Bromley to have scored punctually the lashes which were given, and yet this man had served in Sir John Moore's army, had had his horse shot under him a[t] Benevento at the taking of General Lefevre;[1] suffered great privations and hardships in that retreat; and during near six years' service was never in the gaurd [*sic*] house nor as a prisoner in any sense of the word. His crime, his only crime, was being absent at nine o'clock on his Colonel's birthday.

This Nathan Wilson is a man of twenty three years of age, of exemplary good conduct and behaviour and seems rather to deserve remuneration for services than redress for such sufferings in consequence of so slight an offence.

On Monday the twenty third, Colonel Palmer called him from the ranks and wished Nathan Wilson to tell him whether he wanted his discharge or money: to which Nathan Wilson replied (and I repeat his Christian name because your Royal Highness may find hereafter that his Christian name is of great consequence) he could not answer. And on Friday morning Colonel Palmer threatened to bring Nathan Wilson to a general court martial for refusing to answer some question in his parlour.

Your Royal Highness's own benevolent heart will best judge what is fit to be done on this occasion. (18784–5)

3229 SAMUEL WHITBREAD TO [?] COLONEL MCMAHON
Southill, 31 Oct. 1811
My exceeding earnestness to complete the business we have now I think so nearly accomplished must be my apology for the liberty I am about to take, but Mr Sheridan has informed me that a list of subscribers is preparing under your friendly direction towards the rebuilding of the Theatre; and I feel so sensibly that such a list under the auspices of his Royal Highness the Prince Regent would at the present crisis be most conducive to Sheridan's interest that I cannot refrain from stating so much to you.

The meeting yesterday went off well beyond expectations, & if followed up by a strong appearance of such support the business will be done. My zeal must be the excuse for my freedom. Sheridan knows nothing of my writing, and I had rather he should not. (18791)

1. Lefebvre. See Nos. 2747, 2990, 3020.

Whitehall, 31 Oct. 1811

Mr Ryder has the honor of humbly submitting to your Royal Highness that he has received from the Lord President of the Court of Session[1] the arrangement which in consequence of the changes that have recently taken place amongst the Scotch Judges, his Lordship recommends as most likely in his opinion to have the effect of putting both Divisions of the Court of Session upon the most respectable footing.

Mr Ryder has reason to believe that your Royal Highness might postpone without public inconvenience, the consideration of the greater part of this arrangement till your Royal Highness's return to London, and on that account he is extremely desirous not to give your Royal Highness any unnecessary trouble.

The only part of the plan which presses for decision, and which obliges Mr Ryder very reluctantly to presume to intrude upon your Royal Highness at this time, is the proposal made by the Lord President that Lord Woodhouselee,[2] who is now a Judge of the First Division, should be transferred to the Second.

At present in consequence of the vacancies occasioned by the resignation of Lord Polkemmet,[3] the death of Lord Newton[4] and the removal of the late Justice Clerk, the Second Division has only a quorum & no more; and consequently unless it receives immediately the addition of another Judge, the administration of justice would be stopped if sickness or any other accident should prevent one of the quorum from attending at the commencement of the term on the 12th of November.

Mr Ryder has consulted with the Lord Chancellor & Mr Perceval upon this subject, and they concur with him in the propriety of acceding to this part of the Lord President's suggestions without delay, and in the necessity of his losing no time in humbly submitting it for your Royal Highness gracious approbation.

Mr. Ryder has received another letter from the Lord President this morning strongly pressing upon him the urgency of taking steps to give immediate effect to it.

Mr. Ryder takes this opportunity of respectfully soliciting your Royal Highness's commands, upon what day in the next week your Royal Highness would be pleased to direct that a Council should be holden for the further prorogation of Parliament.[5]

1. Charles Hope, of Granton succeeded Robert Blair, who died, 20 May 1811. Hope had been Lord Justice Clerk since 1804, and he was succeeded by David Boyle (1772–1853).

2. Alexander Fraser Tytler, Lord Woodhouselee (1747–1813), appointed a Lord of Session, 1802; a Lord of Justiciary, 1811.

3. William Baillie, Lord Polkemmet (*d.* 1816), a Lord of Session, 1793–1811.

4. Charles Hay, Lord Newton (*d.* 1811), a Lord of Session, 1806–11.

5. Ryder had to make this inquiry because the Prince Regent, accompanied by the Duke of Cumberland, Lord Yarmouth and Bloomfield, had left London for Brighton on the 29th.

Mr. Ryder understands from the Lord Chancellor that his Lordship had the honor of humbly submitting to your Royal Highness that the Council could not be deferred later than Friday as the Proclamation must be in the Gazette on Saturday. (18793-4)

3231   THE DUKE OF CLARENCE TO [?] COLONEL MCMAHON

Cobham Hall,[1] *noon, Wednesday* [? *earlyNov. 1811*]

I am to acknowledge yours of Monday which has only this moment reached me: Mrs. Jordan is becoming more moderate: I have a very proper letter from her and my answer I think will bring matters into a proper and favourable train: the next interview you have with Mrs. Jordan I conceive will bring her mind to do everything that is right. I have satisfied Sophia[2] and she is quite reconciled to my marriage. My accounts from Broadstairs are progressive in my favour and I think I shall hear from thence every day: indeed I have a direct message from Miss Long[3] to the Duke of York which you will deliver. She is most anxious to get rid of Colonel Swain,[4] and being informed he is a good officer Miss Long trusts the Duke will employ him and so remove him from Broadstairs. You will of course explain everything to the Prince Regent. Lord Mayo[5] is master of all circumstances till Saturday last,

1. Near Gravesend: the seat of the Earl of Darnley, where he stayed for about a week.

2. The Duke's eldest daughter by Mrs. Jordan (?1797-1837). She married the first Baron De Lisle and Dudley (1800-51) on 13 August 1825.

3. Catherine (1789-1825), the young daughter of Sir James Tylney-Long (*d.* 1794), and an heiress reputed to be worth £40,000 a year. The Duke had decided that he and Mrs. Jordan must part, so that he would be free to form this very desirable connection; and he was confident that he could secure from his brother the Prince Regent that consent to the marriage which the Royal Marriages Act of 1772 required. The Duke had been pursuing 'the bewitching Catherine', 'the lovely little nice angel' at Ramsgate in mid-October, but within a few weeks 'the lovely and fascinating Catherine' had become engaged to William Wellesley-Pole (1788-1857), Wellington's nephew. They were married on 14 March 1812. He squandered her fortune and broke her heart, she dying at the age of thirty-five.

4. Hugh Swayne (*d.* 1836). Lieutenant-Colonel, 1800; Colonel, 1810; Major-General, 1813; Lieutenant-General, 1825.

5. John, 4th Earl of Mayo (1766-1849) succeeded his father, 17 August 1794. M.P. for Naas [I.], 1790-4; styled Lord Naas from 20 April 1792 when his grandfather died, until his father's death. Irish Representative Peer, 1816-49. He was already, in 1811, hoping for an Irish Representative Peerage, as appears from Richard Ryder's letter to the Duke of Richmond, the Lord Lieutenant, on 26 April 1811: 'Ld. Mayo desired an audience of me a few days [ago] upon the subject of his pretensions to the support of Government upon the next vacancy in the Representative Peerage, after Ld. Gosford's had been satisfied. I told him that we had

since which I have not any reason to complain. Direct to me at the Dockyard, Chatham as I shall remain there from tomorrow till Monday, on which day I hope to be in town early. God bless you and ever believe me [etc.].¹ (45001–2)

3232 THE MARQUESS WELLESLEY TO THE PRINCE REGENT
Foreign Office, 1 Nov. 1811
Lord Wellesley has the honor to submit to your Royal Highness the communications received this day from Mr. Thornton.²

determined not to commit ourselves in any degree as to what our conduct might be on an event at such a distance, and more than once in the course of our conversation desired to be understood as giving no encouragement whatever to his Lordship's claims. He said if that was the case it would be of no use for him to see Mr. Perceval, who I had told him, concurred in opinion with your Grace & me, & therefore he should not desire, as he had intended to do, an interview with him. I find, however, that he changed his mind and went to Downing Street but, as I had previously furnished Mr. Perceval with a copy of our correspondence he did not gain a more satisfactory answer from him' (Richmond MSS.). The Duke replied on the 29th: 'He is a very worthy, good man, but he is unreasonable about the Representative Peerage. He held an office in the Irish House of Lords and has the income for life. Any claim he might have had for borough interest must have been settled at the Union. He has now no Parliamentary interest. The Duke of Portland's letters to him were strong as were those to Lord Farnham but it was thought also that his Grace did intend to have decided in favor of Ld. Gosford. Lord Mayo thinks he ought to have the next promise. I have told him that I dont conceive the Duke intended to promise more than for one vacancy as he had desired me to stick to that rule. I also told him I did not conceive Mr. Perceval would think it necessary to fulfil a second promise even if the Duke had given it and that I certainly should not' (ibid.).

1. Lord Auckland, hearing that the Duke of Clarence had offered himself in quick succession to Miss Tylney Long, to Princess Charlotte's friend Mercer Elphinstone, and even to Lady Berkeley, and, in addition, that he had been busy reviewing regiments and inspecting dockyards, suggested that there might be more work pending for the Willises (Colchester, ii. 347). 'There is another history,' wrote Princess Charlotte (23 November) 'which says that the Duke *has* or is *going* to offer himself to the Dowager Lady Downshire' (Bowood MSS.). And W. H. Fremantle wrote on 28 November: 'Before . . . [the Duke of Clarence] went to Ramsgate he wrote to Lady C[harlotte] L[indsay] to propose, who wrote him a very proper letter in answer, declining the honour in the most decided terms . . . He wrote to Lord Keith to propose for Miss Elphinstone, who, in the most decided and peremptory terms, rejected him' (Buckingham, *Memoirs of the Regency*, i. 146).

2. Sir Edward Thornton (1766–1852). Secretary of Legation at Philadelphia, 1796–1804, and Chargé d'Affaires there, 1797–8 and 1800–3; Resident to the Hanse Towns and Minister to the Circle of Lower Saxony, 1805–7; Minister to Sweden, 1808 and 1812–17; Minister to Brazil, 1819–21, and to the Portuguese Court, 1823–4. G.C.B., 1822.

Diplomatic relations with Sweden were suspended from 1810 to 1812, but in 1811 Thornton was sent on a special mission in H.M.S. *Victory* to negotiate treaties of alliance with Sweden and Russia. He arrived at Wingo Sound, 17 October, and negotiated with Netzel, the Swedish plenipotentiary, at Amal, 10–19 November. The negotiation was broken off on the 19th and

It may be necessary to observe that a dispatch from M. de Rehausen,[1] under date the 20th of Septr, (containing a report of his conference of that day with Lord Wellesley, & of which your Royal Highness has seen a copy) had not reached M. d'Engerstrom in consequence of some accidental error in the mode of conveyance. Dispatches from M. de Rehausen of subsequent dates to the 20th Septr. had been received by M. d'Engerstrom, & M. de Rehausen had received the most satisfactory replies with respect to the general disposition of the Swedish Government & to their acceptation of the mission of Mr Thornton.

It appears, however, that no orders had been issued by the Swedish Government to Count Rosen, Governor of Gottenburgh, on this very delicate subject; nor had M. de Rehausen written to Count Rosen, excepting the letter sent by Mr Thornton. No conclusion adverse to the ultimate success of the negotiation can justly be drawn from these circumstances; the caution observed both by M. de Rehausen & by the Swedish Government is not blameable, nor in any degree inconsistent with perfect sincerity in the professed views of Sweden.

Lord Wellesley has sent in this box a communication received this day from M. de Rehausen, & also the papers from M. de Rehausen which your Royal Highness has seen: it is probable that your Royal Highness might be pleased to refer to them in forming your judgment upon the probable intentions of Sweden.

Your Royal Highness will learn from every source of information that the conduct of the Swedish Government in every respect indicates a favorable inclination to the common cause against Bonaparte.

Every facility has been afforded in Sweden to persons passing, under the protection of the British Government, to Russia & Prussia, & the most cordial intercourse has been maintained with Sir James Saumarez.[2] (18801)

3233   HENRY ERRINGTON[3] TO COLONEL MCMAHON

Red Rice,[4] 3 Nov. 1811

A thousand thanks for your letter, which I have rec[e]ived this morning, it has given me spirit & life, is there then any hope of getting rid of these

Thornton returned home. Sweden was not brought into the grand alliance against France until 1812.

1. The Baron de Rehausen was Swedish Minister in London before the suspension of diplomatic relations, and resumed his functions in 1812.

2. See No. 3212.

3. Mrs. Fitzherbert's uncle.

4. Near Andover, Hants.

207

miserable Ministers? Surely he wont wait till they have quite undone us, I was always convinc'd their own acts would sooner or later do their business, but then our destruction would go hand in hand with theirs. I do hope *he* will stop in time, & as the eyes of the publick must be opened by the late events in Spain he may with great propriety make a change at present, & the publick voice will be with him & feel grateful to him for rescuing us from destruction. Perhaps I am too sanguine in my expectations, but I shall observe your caution & keep all this to myself. Mrs F. has run it very near. Does her approach hasten his removal from Brighton or prevent him going to Ld. Egremont's?[1] *Entre nous*, I wish she would commute her residence at Brighton for some other country house. The inhabitants will think she drives him [from] the place. There is no kicking against the pricks.

I am sorry nothing can be done for poor Beaver.[2] I thought the Prince would remember him; he never forgets anyone. Perhaps at a future period something may be done: he is in real distress. Stuart is here, so have the goodness to send his money to me, or to him *Grateley Cottage, Andover*. Between Cheltenham and Ramsgate I hope you have acquired *une santé de fer* to enable you to bear all the fatigues of office, and to keep it as long as your best friends can wish, among the foremost of whom I beg you to believe your very [etc.]. (18805–6)

3234   THE MARQUESS WELLESLEY TO THE PRINCE REGENT
Dorking, 6 p.m., 4 Nov. 1811
Lord Wellesley has the honor to return his most grateful acknowledgments for your Royal Highness's very gracious commands of the 2d instant, which reached him in London yesterday morning. Count Munster being at Windsor a messenger was immediately dispatched to him with Mr. Nicholas's paper, & other documents on the same subject, or connected with it. This day by Lord Wellesley's desire Count Munster was so good as to call at Dorking, when he entered fully into the subject of Mr. Nicholas's paper, & has promised to prepare notes upon the plan, in order that the whole may be laid before the several Departments of Government without delay.

Count Munster has prepared for your Royal Highness's approbation, the draft of a dispatch to M. Ompteda at Berlin, in the propriety of which Lord Wellesley entirely concurs. It is requested that your Royal

1. At Petworth.

2. The Weymouth apothecary who had attended Princess Amelia whilst she was in residence there. See Vol. VI, *passim*.

Highness will be pleased to return this draft (sent by this conveyance) by the messenger who carries this box & who will call at Dorking on his return.

Lord Wellesley will not fail to have the honor of attending your Royal Highness on Friday in London when he hopes to be able to make some more satisfactory communication respecting Sweden.

Dispatches have been received from Mr Stuart & Mr Wellesley containing nothing of sufficient interest to require your Royal Highness's immediate attention. Lord Wellesley humbly requests your Royal Highness to accept his most dutiful thanks for the great condescension which has been manifested towards him by your Royal Highness most gracious commands respecting his proceeding to attend at Brighton if your Royal Highness's service should demand his presence there before Friday next. (18811–2)

3235 JOHN NESBITT TO [?] COLONEL MCMAHON

Bolton Street, 5 Nov. 1811

Private. There's no person's health I am more interested for than yours, both on account of your uniform kindness to me as your being one of my oldest and best friends. Therefore, to guard you against any *complaint in your stomach*, I have sent you four bottles of cognac brandy of the year 1746. I inherited it from my uncle, who died thirty two years ago. As the Regent sometimes invites himself to dine with you, I have sent you some eau de vie de Handaye [*sic*], which is very old and good. I know his Royal Highness prefers it to any other liqueur. When you taste it it will bring to your recollection [etc.]. (18814)

3236 COLONEL MCMAHON TO THE DUKE OF NORTHUMBERLAND

Carlton House, 8 Nov. 1811

Private. After I had the honor to receive your Grace's ever kind letter of the 26th ulto. at Margate, I left that place on the same day, & on returning to London found a command which carried me immediately to Brighton, where the Prince Regent then was, & where I did not fail to lose an instant in obeying your Grace's wishes by expressing all those valuable sentiments of affectionate esteem which your Grace had confided to my delivery, & for which I received H.R.Hss.'s express directions to return with a sincere reciprocity of love & never ceasing regard.

209

During my absence from town, Lord Liverpool had sought me (for as I never can have a secret from your Grace, it was to him I convey'd, *as entirely an idea of my own alone*, what a civil thing it might be to the D. of N. to promote Mr. Hume[1] to the Exchequer Bench of Scotland) to say how thankful both Mr. Perceval & he were for even my *unauthorised* suggestion; that they had both consulted with Lord Melville on the appointment (taking it for granted to be vacant) of Mr. Hume, when Lord Melville had assured them he was pre-eminently qualified & entitled to the situation, & that his high talents & character could not fail to adorn it, but that the Lord Advocate, who could not be embraced in the recent Law promotions of Scotland, had felt so sore on being given an *unavoidable* go by, that he felt so disgusted as to declare his wishes to be placed on the Exchequer Bench on the first vacancy & to resign the Lord Advocateship. That should he persist in this splenetic notion, they could not possibly but indulge him in this object, but (as was most natural) should he not do so, Mr. Hume should then have no other competitor. At the same time (as cannot be a matter of surprize to be expected) a wish was clearly thrown out how gratifying it would most assuredly be to them 'that the *D. of N.* would condescend to convey his wishes for Mr. Hume *more directly* to Mr. Perceval (or to the Ld. Chancellor if he prefer'd it) but that I might be assured the most mark'd respect & attention would meet such a communication.' To this I merely answer'd, 'I have only ventured the liberty of this suggestion entirely from my own idea, & cannot pretend to say how it can be brought about for the *D. of N.* to personally ask it, but to every man who knows the greatness & magnificence of his Grace's mind, it will at once appear the happiest road to his favor, for the high & proud liberality of his nature never suffer'd him to *owe* obligation to any mortal, tho' ever with a greatness & kindness peculiar to himself at all times most willing to acknowledge it.'

A Council was this day held which prorogues Parliament to the 7th of January, meaning then to meet for *the dispatch of business*.

[*P.S.*] There is no public news nor any private interesting. I am now fix'd in London till at least next August, God willing, & overjoy'd shall ever be to be honor'd with your Grace's commands, & the indulgent permission of continuing to address you, being ever with a heart full of affection and gratitude [etc.] (Alnwick MSS.).

1. See Nos. 3211, 3225.

3237 SAMUEL WHITBREAD TO [?] COLONEL MCMAHON

Dover Street, 9 Nov. 1811

The committee appointed under the Act of Parliament for the rebuilding the Theatre Royal Drury Lane have directed a common seal to be prepared for the Joint Stock Company.

Very little consideration appears necessary for them to determine upon the most appropriate device, and the most gratifying to the general feelings of the subscribers: and I am commanded by the committee to request that you will have the goodness humbly to express to his Royal Highness the Prince Regent their anxious wish that he will be graciously pleased to permit the bust of his Royal Highness to form the subject of the common seal of the Company.

Sensible of the very important assistance they have derived from the exalted patronage of his Royal Highness, they are desirous that all their acts should bear record of the distinguished honour conferred upon the proprietors. (18827)

3238 THE QUEEN TO THE PRINCE REGENT, AND AN ENCLOSURE

Windsor, 10 Nov. 1811

I have this morning sent my answer to the Council agreing [*sic*] to Dr. J.W. giving his assistance to his brother, & I hope that you will approve of it when you read it. I allow it to be long, but in the predicament I stand with our dear invalid on account of the promise never to let J.W. re-enter the house to attend him, it was necessary to recapitulate strongly to the Council the hard task I am put to by them & *how cutting it is to my feeling to do that which if the King recovers* may perhaps forever make me forfeit his good opinion. Therefore I wish'd to state in black & white which they will not destroy, & what must shew to the King & the public, that nothing but the perseverance in their request to have the consulting physicians in the first instance & now again the attendance of Dr J. W. could have made me yield in any way. My conscience is clear, for I have kept off the attendance of J.W. above a year & the plague of the consulting physicians very near two month, by a constant opposition, & by now yielding with the greatest reluctance & almost with a broken heart, I have a right to expect that no further cutting proposals will be made by them.

In a day or two I shall write to you again about dear Charlotte, but would not introduce it in this letter.[1] (36583-4)

1. The Queen had written to the Princess on 30 October: 'I have the pleasure to inform you, my beloved Charlotte, that, sanctioned by the Faculty, I may now invite you to Windsor,

[Enclosure] THE QUEEN TO THE COUNCIL, AND THE REPLY

Windsor, 10 Nov. 1811

The Queen has learnt with satisfaction from the communication made in writing by her Council dated the 4th instant & which was delivered to her yesterday by the A.B. of Canterbury, that the arrangement which she had directed on the 27th October, as stated in her letter of that date, with a view to relieve Dr. Willis from the unnecessary disturbance of his night's rest, had met the wishes of her Council.

Her Majesty has given due consideration to the proposal of her Council that they should be permitted to call to the assistance of Dr. R. Willis in the discharge of his important & laborious duties the skill & experience of Dr. John Willis, & she is too well convinced of the anxious zeal & the solicitude for the King's recovery & welfare by which her Council are actuated, not to feel desirous of co-operating with them in whatever measure may in her opinion be conducive to an object so justly dear to herself & not to prove such disposition by her early decision upon one which they so earnestly recommend.

The Council are in full possession of the objections which the Queen had made to similar proposals upon former occasions. They have equally been made aware of the principles upon which her Majesty so long resisted them & they cannot but have perceived the difficulty with which she waved her scruples to the extent even of suffering Drs. J. Willis & Simmons to *have access to his Majesty's apartment* as consulting physicians. They have learnt from subsequent communications that altho' the original ground of opposition applied equally to Doctor Simmons & to

where I hope to embrace you on Sunday next. I cannot promise much amusement nor entertainment, but I will insure you a most hearty wellcome from, my dear Charlotte, your affectionate grandmother & friend' (Bowood MSS.). From Windsor she was to be sent on to Oatlands, 'a much more agreable place than that wh. I shall leave,' she wrote next day, in a letter further illustrative of the instability characteristic of her mother's family: 'You will be surprised to see me seal with black, but accounts were sent me *today* from the Pss. that her brother George has *suddenly died*, so, tho' I do not *mourn much inwardly* I must *outwardly*; from her letter I should judge that she was not *much afflicted either*. It is curious how he came to die so suddenly, as there were letters from abroad about 3 weeks ago giving an account of his having *eloped* with a young lady, the wife of a gentleman who lived with him' (ibid.). Prince George (1769–1811) the imbecile brother of Frederick William, Duke of Brunswick and of the Princess of Wales, died on 16 September.

'When I go to Windsor,' she said in a subsequent letter, 'I feel as if *banished* & in *prison*. I recvd. a letter a short time ago from thence saying that the *scarlet fever* & *sore throat* is in the stables & therefore I take up my aboad [sic] at the *Upper Lodge* instead of the *Lower*, but will you have the goodness still to direct yours to Warwick House as I can then *be sure* of their *coming safe*. I shall give you a *full account* of all the *proceedings* wh., being so *unlike anything* or *anybody*, will perhaps afford you some little amusement' (ibid.). 'The old girls,' she wrote (6 November) were all very happy to see me, & to *do them justice* nothing can have been more *attentive* or endeavoring to be *civil* than they all have in *their different ways*. Yet their life is dreadfully dul' (ibid.).

Dr. John Willis, it was wholly free from any personal objection entertained by herself or any of her family to Doctor J. Willis.

The Queen does not hesitate upon this occasion to repeat this declaration with respect to Dr. J. Willis & to state the high opinion which she entertains of his character & of his professional skill; she is also willing to admit that she considers his regular attendance upon the King to be wholly divested of many of the objections which would have operated strongly against that of any other individual. Nevertheless she feels that she would be wholly unworthy of the confidence which was reposed in her by the country when she was entrusted with so sacred & important a charge, if she could be so regardless of an engagement entered into with the King as not to yield with the utmost reluctance to a proposal which requires an infraction of it, yet more positive than that to which she had already consented in deference to the urgent advice & solicitations of her Council, under the impression made by circumstances of which the melancholy extent could not be foreseen when she contracted the engagement in question & under the pressure of encreasing difficulties & embarassments.

The Queen has more than once declared that she gave her Council full credit for the pure motives, the principles of duty & attachment by which they are guided & she does not deny that this conviction & her earnest wish to admit the advice of men who are influenced by such honorable feelings tend in a great degree towards weakening her scruples upon the present occasion. H.M. has also in a recent communication noticed the obligation under which her Council may consider themselves placed to defer in some measures to public feeling & public prejudice, but she is far from condemning the influence of that obligation, aware as she is that it is fully justified by the earnest interest which the country takes in their proceedings, an interest which arises from the warmest attachment to the best of Sovereigns & from a no less anxious solicitude for his continued comfort & his preservation, to which every act of his meritorious life, public & private, has established a claim which H.M. is persuaded is strengthened rather than weakened in the public consideration of the King's present melancholy state.

With these feelings the Queen yields to the earnest request of her Council that Doctor J. Willis should be admitted to the King's appartment & permitted to cooperate with his brother, & she fervently prays that their skill & united efforts may, under Providence, realize her anxious wishes & those of the family & the country for his Majesty's ultimate recovery.

She trusts, however, that in consideration of the feelings which the Queen has expressed upon former occasions & the reluctance with which they must be sensible that she now acquieses in this proposal her Council will not hesitate in releiving her & her family in some degree from the weight of uneasiness by conveying to her an assurance that the concession which has thus been drawn from her will secure her from future proposals for the introduction to the treatment of the King's disorder of any other individual or for any further change.

The Queen cannot conclude without observing to her Council that three of the individuals in actual attendance, Sir Henry Halford, Doctor Heberden & Mr. Dundas, were bound by the same pledge which she had given & would have been precluded from further attendance by the same scruples which imperious circumstances have led her to abandon, if she had not taken upon herself the responsibility of calling upon them for their services & had not in a manner exonerated them by holding out her own example as justifying, upon the same general principles, their departure from such an engagement.

P.S. The Queen takes it for granted that upon the admission of Doctor John Willis to cooperation with his brother, the further periodical attendance of Doctor Simmons & Doctor Monroe will be considered unnecessary. (36585–6)

THE COUNCIL'S REPLY[1] [copy]

12 Nov. 1811

Your Majesty's Council acknowledge with gratitude your Majesty's gracious condescension in approving the motives by which your Council are actuated; doubtless they are of the same nature with those which have uniformly governed your Majesty, arising from an anxious wish to leave no means untried that may be reasonably expected to contribute to his Majesty's recovery. If in the pursuit of this object they have sometimes suggested measures difficult for your Majesty to approve, your Majesty has been pleased to sacrifice your own feelings to the earnest and urgent representations of your Council.

With every disposition to obey your Majesty's commands and with no present intention whatever to recommend the introduction of any other person than Dr. John Willis to the management of the King's apartment, professing at the same time to be perfectly unconscious of the particular grounds of your Majesty's objections to Dr. Simmons, your Council humbly implore your Majesty not to impose upon them a pledge to exclude from his Majesty's medical assistance the assistance of any man who may hereafter he deemed capable of affording it, a pledge that cannot, as they humbly conceive, be given by your Majesty's Council without incurring a breach of their official duty and of the oath by which they are bound to perform it.

1. Though slightly out of order it seems best to keep this and the previous letter together. It was enclosed in No. 3243.

Presuming on your Majesty's consent to the cooperation of Dr. John Willis with his brother, your Council have desired Dr. John Willis's immediate attendance at Windsor. (Signed) C. Cantuar, Montrose, Aylesford, Eldon, Ellenborough, W. Grant. (36589)

3239   LETTERS FROM CHARLES MANNERS SUTTON TO MAJOR-GENERAL T. H. TURNER
Downing Street, 11 Nov. 1811
Many thanks for your note—but all my endeavours did not enable me to discover that any of the Ministers were to have audiences of H.R.H. yesterday, therefore I did not venture to request one for myself.

Today I conceive also the Recorder's Report will so long occupy H.R.H. that I dare not entertain any expectation of an audience.

Will you then have the goodness to request an audience for me on some early day at any hour which H.R.H. shall be pleased to appoint?

Unless I hear from you that H.R.H. should wish to see me today I shall not attend the Council at the Treasury. (18828)

Downing Street, 11 Nov. 1811
The reason for my suggesting that I should not attend at the Treasury today is that I cannot sit at the Council during the Recorder's Report, not being one of the Cabinet;[1] and conceiving it might from its size last a long time, and knowing the Ministers will want audiences themselves afterwards—and in addition having much to do at home—I did conceive therefore that it would be better, unless H.R.H. should think otherwise, not to expect an audience today—

Your suggestion however makes me the more anxious to learn H.R.H.'s pleasure. (18829)

3240   WILLIAM TAYLOR TO COLONEL MCMAHON
King's Theatre, 11 Nov. 1811
I had the honor duly to receive your letter of the 11th of August communicating to me the most gracious sentiments of his Royal Highness the Prince Regent respecting his royal protection of the interests of this

1. Not the Cabinet Council, but the 'Grand Cabinet'. See No. 2363*n*.

establishment; but in your absence, I did not like to trouble General Turner, who was not, like yourself, acquainted with the business, and besides I wished to ascertain the proceedings at the Pantheon before I took the liberty of troubling again his Royal Highness upon the same subject.

I now inclose you a printed prospectus which has recently been generally circulated and published, announcing a complete Italian Opera Establishment at that place, in the most undisguised opposition to this property, which, as you know, had become responsible for the losses of a similar enterprize at the Pantheon 20 years ago to the amount of nearly £40,000 altogether, in consideration of which the Italian Opera was re-established here permanently and exclusively, and therefore to set up again the same opposition would be such an act of injustice as I am persuaded never can be tolerated. Competition indeed in this respect is certain ruin, as the unfortunate experience of 1791 afforded a dreadful example; and if one foreign establishment has not hitherto, even in times of peace, been supported with benefit to the undertakers of it, what must be the fate of two in the present state of intercourse with the Continent?

At first it was said that the licence in question was merely a renewal of that formerly granted for the Argyle Rooms, which was but for music and dancing in a place where there was neither stage, scenery or anything of a theatrical nature; whereas the licence at the Pantheon appears to be for the permanent establishment of a new and additional theatre; a measure which the Privy Council had so recently refused to sanction, doubtless on account of its injustice to the interests of the three long established Theatres as recognised by the arrangement of 1791; and the opposition too to this undertaking has been so directly hostile, that almost all the performers in their list have been seduced and taken away from this place by encreased terms so great as in several instances to have reached the very double of their former salaries here; a competition so certainly ruinous, that I have contented myself with retaining the principal performers requisite to the support of this establishment, in the confidence that it will be suffered to continue without opposition; otherwise it must cease to exist as a property.

I feel the credit of the undertaking so completely shaken by the opposition so set up that it is impossible to compleat the necessary arrangements for opening it, without incurring dreadful sacrifices both of present interest and in future example. I therefore humbly throw myself and the justice of my case at the feet of his Royal Highness the Prince Regent, and do most earnestly beseech his Royal Highness to be graciously pleased to direct an enquiry to be made into the rights and property of this Theatre under the final arrangement of 1791, sanctioned equally by his Majesty and by the Prince Regent, a final decision upon which being absolutely necessary to the very existence of this place as a public concern.[1] (18831–2)

3241   SAMUEL WHITBREAD TO [?] COLONEL MCMAHON
        Newmarket, 12 Nov. 1811
        I have just received the favour of your note enclosing a list of subscribers to the new Theatre Drury Lane of the gentlemen in the Establishment of his Royal Highness the Prince Regent, which I will not fail to lay before the committee at their first meeting, who will I am sure partake of the grateful feeling I experience at the condescension of his Royal Highness in allowing a list to be formed under his immediate auspices.

        May I take the liberty of asking what number of shares is to be attached to the each name [*sic*], & of requesting the deposits may be made at Messrs Hammersleys & Co. in Pall Mall? Your answer directed to Dover Street will find me.

        I cannot omit any opportunity of expressing our obligation to yourself, personally, for the friendly interest you are so good as to take in this concern. (18833)

3242   THE DUKE OF NORTHUMBERLAND TO COLONEL MCMAHON
        Alnwick Castle, 12 Nov. 1811
        I have to acknowledge the receipt of your letter of the 8th, & return you many thanks for the trouble you have taken in order to procure the appointment of my relation Mr. David Hume to the situation of one of the Barons of the Exchequer in Scotland. I fear however the Lord Advocate will not desist from his desire of obtaining this appointment, & therefore that Mr. Hume has no chance of success. Indeed, as I wrote you word, I understand that Baron Hepburn, who was expected to die hourly, is now so much recovered as not to be likely to make an immediate vacancy. In this situation of circumstances, as the Ld. Advocate is to have the seat, any application of mine immediately & directly to Mr. Perceval coud not possibly be of any service, as it woud only subject me to a refusal, a circumstance which I shoud feel extremely unpleasant, & embarrassing, after, by my application, having shown some readiness of

        1. It was not until 3 April 1813 that William Taylor received from McMahon the sum of £467 which had been owing to him since 1796 and 1797 'for the subscription of two Boxes at the Opera House and some masquerade tickets'. (30031)

217

laying myself under an obligation to the Minister. Indeed, I never coud consent to make any application to the Ministers without having the most positive assurance given me that such my request would be complied with. Totally unconnected at present with any Party, & only devoted to the wishes of the Prince, I wish to continue so; and it was for this reason I presumed to make the imprudent application to H.R.H. in behalf of the late Captain Haswell, as it was to the Regent alone, to whom I have wished to owe *personally* any favours I might receive. Your letter however to me, on the subject of Captain Haswell, cut off all my wishes in this particular; as it informed me that such applications were disagreable & distressing to the Regent. I shall therefore take care not to err again; &, as I do not wish to lay myself under obligations to any Party, go on, as heretofore, by informing my friends that I am not able to procure them anything. God knows it is very little I ask for any of them; for myself nothing.

I see it still reported in the papers that the Regent hardly goes anywhere without being accompanied by the Duke of Cumberland. I confess I am rather surprised, as I did not know the Duke was so confidential a favorite with the Prince. Perhaps however it is only newspaper invention.

I suppose everything now is in a great bustle in the political world. Parliament will meet now pretty soon, & it will not be long before the removal or continuation of the restrictions on the Regent must be finally determined upon. The different Parties I know are in a state of great anxiety: the present Ministers hoping & flattering themselves that H.R.H. will continue them in power, & the opposite Party, the Lords Grey & Grenville, indulging themselves with the expectation that, when the Regent becomes wholly unfettered, he will indulge his inclination towards them & place them at the head of affairs. At any rate they keep up a good countenance in this neighbourhood, & their friends insinuate that this is a settled point.

The times are growing daily more & more critical & require experienced, able & energetic heads to conduct affairs properly. I cannot say I like the appearance of things in Spain and Portugal. Millions of money & thousands of lives seem to have been flung away there to very little purpose. Long, long ago I gave Colonel Gordon my opinion of affairs in the Peninsula, and even then ventured to foretell what the consequences woud be of the measures pursued; & the day before yesterday I received a letter from him in which he does me the justice to say 'Your opinion, upon our campaigns in Portugal, are realizing very fast [*sic*].' I am grieved to think our dispute with America has been protracted so long, & has given this country so much trouble. It ought not to have done so. Decisive measures are more necessary in all transactions with the United States than with any other Power whatever; & I will venture to say that nowhere will half measures be attended with such bad consequences. I have seen a great deal of the Americans, & know them well. Lord Percy will be in town by the meeting of Parliament, desirous of doing whatever is most agreeable to the Regent. Perhaps, however, as he is a young man, it may be as well if H.R.H.'s wishes were conveyed to me, & I coud then direct him & any other friends how to act, as from myself. If the Regent is in town, I beg you will assure him of my most steady & dutifull attachment. All here unite with me in compliments & best wishes to you & Mrs MacMahon. I am now, thank God, getting pretty well again. I have been well enough to write a long account of myself to Dr. Jones, & to ask his advice. (18834–5)

3243   THE QUEEN TO THE PRINCE REGENT
Windsor, 15 Nov. 1811
I received yesterday evening the answer from the Council to the letter I wrote on Sunday, a copy of which I send you & by which you will perceive that tho' they are sensible of the concession I have made to their proposal of Dr. J. Willis comming here to assist his brother, they nevertheless are urging to continue the attendance of Drs. Simmons & Munro, *& specify in particular that 'They are perfectly unconscious of the particular grounds of my objections to Dr. Simmons'*. I do not deny that I feel most extreamly hurt at this very singular expression, as in every letter I had occasion to write upon that subject I have stated my reasons without any hesitation, & I cannot help fearing that they still mean to force this man upon us, & I have therefore thought it proper to prepare an answer directly which I inclose herewith & which, after perusing it, if it meets with your approbation I must beg of you to seal it with my seal, which I also send, & to forward it to the Archbishop immediately, as I wish him to have it before he comes on Saturday to Windsor.

Our conversation on Fryday last in which you & I were quite unanimous upon this subject makes me the more anxious that you should read it before it goes to the Council & makes me flatter myself that you will not less approve of this letter than the last which of course you may easily believe must prove a great satisfaction to [etc.].
[*P.S.*] May I beg to have my seal returned? The copy of my letter to the Archbishop I will send by the evening or give it you on Sunday when I see you. (36587–8)

Windsor, 15 Nov. 1811

The Queen sincerely lament[s] that in acknowledging ye communication from her Council of the 12 instant received yesterday she cannot refrain from noticing particularly that part of it in which, although they state that they have no present intention whatever to recommend the introduction of any other person than Dr. John Willis to the management of the King's apartment, they clearly admit that such intention may be entertained by remonstrating against the exclusion of any man whom they may hereafter deem capable of affording his assistance, which by their previous mention of Dr. Simmons they as clearly point him out to be the man in their contemplation.

When the Queen took the painful resolution of assenting to the proposal of her Council that Dr. J. Willis should be admitted to cooperate with his brother, she had flattered herself with the hope that in consideration of all that she had stated upon that occasion & all she had stated upon previous occasions, in consideration of the sacrifice of her own feelings, which the Council admit to have been made to their earnest & urgent representations, her Majesty might indulge the consoling prospect that her peace of mind & that of her family could not again be harrassed, her scruples of conscience not be again assailed by proposals for the introduction of any other individual & under that sanguine hope she was led to express her confidence that her Council would by an assurance to that effect relieve her & her family in some degree from the weight of uneasyness under which they must labour.

The Queen is sensible that she cannot impose a pledge upon them to which they think proper to object & she never could wish, even if she had the power, to impose one which should be inconsistent with the official duty of any man & with the oath by which they are bound to perform it.

The Queen, impressed as she is with feelings of the truest regard for the individuals forming her Council, cannot view without great apprehension & concern the possibility of any serious difference with them, & she trusts that she has already given ample proofs that such is far from being her disposition & that her opposition to their advice has been wholly uninfluenced by captious motives or trivial prejudices. She has waved her scruples, she has rendered her own duty subservient to that which her advisers stated to be theirs, but there are certain bounds beyond which concession cannot be carried without becoming not less disgraceful than it must appear to her a most reprehensible abandonment of the charge imposed, & there are also certain points upon which the Queen is confident that she shall stand justified in the eyes of her family & of the whole country in exercising her own judgement particularly as her object has invariably been to combine the admission of that which may prove useful to the King in his melancholy state with that which shall not prove distructive of his remaining comfort. Nor can it be said that the Queen is guilty of presumption in opposing her judgement in this instance to the united opinions of her advisers as it is unfortunately too well known that she has had the melancholy experience of three illnesses by which the King had been afflicted previously to the present & as she has possessed in each the same means of information which she now possesses & to as great extent as those upon which her advisers ground their opinions, further, as in the exercise of her judgement, resting upon such melancholy experience & upon such ample means of information, she is borne out by her situation, by the nature of the charge imposed upon her & supported by the concurrent sentiments of her family. (36590–1)

3244 COLONEL JAMES WILLOUGHBY GORDON TO COLONEL MCMAHON

Chelsea, 15 Nov. 1811

As I can offer no sufficient apology for intruding my political disquisitions upon your attention I shall trust wholly to your good nature and kind regard for me, and at once enter upon the subject, promising, however, that the circumstances of the times, the critical situation of the Prince, and the personal obligations I owe to him are the motives that impel me to this communication.

The text of every conversation in every company is the question, what will the Prince do when he has full power? Will he change the Government? Will he abandon his old friends, and will he concede anything to the Catholicks? This I need not tell you is the substance of every conference at every table & in every society at this moment in the metropolis, & probably in the kingdom. Not being any politician myself, at least having no political expectation, but having a very general acquaintance & a business kind of communication with the several leading men of the day, and being known also to be honoured with the Prince's regard, I am perhaps as much in the way of ascertaining the various bias [*sic*] and bearings of opinion, as any man, and I thus endeavour to lay them before you.

You know that the present Ministry, with Mr. Percival at their head, owe their situations and power wholly and solely to the undivided support of the King, arising from his Majesty's conscientious opposition to the Catholick Petition. You know also that this Administration is the remains of the Pitt School, of which School, however, *two* most important members are schismatic—Canning and Castlereagh, each of whom have their supporters & followers and may be considered as possessed of a large share of the confidence and respect of the House of Commons and also of the country.[1] The other party (of this School also) is the Sidmouth party,[2] of which Mr. Bathurst is the usual organ, and they also have their share of power in the House. This, I believe, may be considered as the main body of the Pitt School, orthodox and heterodox, but all sprung from the tree of Pitt.

The opposite party, those hitherto distinguished by the appellation of the Prince's friends, are the remains of the Fox School, the head of which may be considered Earl Grey, uniting the whole Grenville family and followers, and having as their organs in the House of Commons, Messrs. Whitbread, Ponsonby and Tierney.[3] There are many eminent young

1. Canning's friends in the Commons in 1810 were Barrington Pope Blachford, William Sturges Bourne, Colonel George Canning (his cousin, later Lord Garvagh), John Dent, Charles Rose Ellis, George Bellas Greenough, William Huskisson, Hylton Joliffe, Robert Holt Leigh, Lord Granville Leveson-Gower, William Taylor and Edward Bootle Wilbraham. For the list in 1812, before and after the General Election, see 'The Canningite Party', by A. Aspinall, in *Transactions of the Royal Historical Society*, 1934, page 223.

Castlereagh's friends: G. P. Holford, F. J. Robinson, William Sloane, Charles William Stewart (his half-brother), and Thomas Wood.

2. According to the Whig calculators, the Sidmouth party in the Commons in 1810 consisted only of Charles Adams, John Hiley Addington, Alexander Allan, Charles Bragge Bathurst, Henry Bowyer, T. G. Estcourt, Davies Giddy and Benjamin Hobhouse (one would have expected to see Vansittart's name here). This once numerous phalanx had shrunk severely since Addington had ceased to be Prime Minister in 1804. The strength of these 'floating' parties depended appreciably on the ability or inability of the leaders to reward their adherents.

3. The 'thick and thin men, who vote against Ministers on all occasions' were as follows, the list being compiled by the Whig party managers early in 1810: J. Abercromby, R. Adair, W. Adam, E. F. Agar, Lord Althorp, G. Anson, Sir J. Anstruther, Lee Antonie, Sir J. Astley, Sir J. Aubrey, W. Bagenal, J. F. Barham, A. Baring, F. Baring, G. C. Berkeley, Scrope Bernard, C. Bewicke, T. C. Bligh, E. Bouverie, A. C. Bradshaw, T. Brand, Brougham, J. W. Butler, G. Byng, J. Calcraft, N. Calvert, D. Campbell, G. Campbell, Lord J. Campbell, Lord G. Campbell, W. Cavendish, R. Chaloner, E. C. Cocks, J. Cocks, T. W. Coke, E. Coke, N. W. R. Colborne, H. C. Combe, B. Cooke, J. Craig, Creevey, Curwen, J. R. Cuthbert, D. B. Daly, W. Dickinson, C. Dundas, L. Dundas, R. L. Dundas, G. Eden, W. Elliot, Earl of Euston, N. Fellowes, R. C. Fergusson, Lord H. Fitzgerald, M. Fitzgerald, R. Fitzpatrick, Lord C. Fitzroy, Lord W. Fitzroy, C. Fleeming, A. Foley, T. Foley, Sir M. Folkes, Visct. Forbes, W. Frankland, W. H. Fremantle, D. Giles, Earl Gower, G. M. Grant, Grattan, R. Greenhill, P. Grenfell, Lord Geo. Grenville, T. Grosvenor, Sir J. Hall, J. T. Halsey, Lord A. Hamilton, G. Hibbert, Sir J. C. Hippisley, W. Honywood, Horner, H. T. Howard, W. Howard, H. Howarth, W. L. Hughes, W. H. Hume, R. Hurst, W. Hussey, C. H. Hutchinson, J. Jackson, Jekyll, T. Johnes, T. Kemp, T. Knox, M. Laing, W. Lamb, R. J. Lambton, W. G. Langton, D. Latouche, J. Latouche, R. Latouche, J. Leach, C. S. Lefevre, C. Lemon, J. Lemon, Sir W. Lemon, B. L. Lester, Sir E. Lloyd, J. M. Lloyd, G. Longman, E. Loveden Loveden, Sir J. Lubbock, W. H. Lyttelton, J. Macdonald, W. Macdowall, W. A. Madocks, Lord Mahon, J. Markham, H. Martin, R. Martin, M. Mathew, W. Maule, W. Maxwell, J. Meade, Earl of Mexborough, Sir R. Milbanke, Lord Milford, Sir T. Miller, C. Mills, W. Mills, Sir W. Milner, Lord Milton, P. Moore, Lord Morpeth, Sir O. Mosley, Sir T.

men on both sides, but certainly of no leading capacity, and it is therefore unnecessary to mention them in this disquisition.

As the Fox Administration in fact dissolved itself upon the Catholick question, it may be fairly considered as a great political party indisputably pledged and committed to carry it when in power, and if taken into power they would not have an alternative but must effect it or resign their seats as ill-judging & incompetent men.

Upon a due consideration of these points it appears to me that the Prince stands between these two parties as the arbiter upon the Catholick question, that is, if he rejects it he draws upon him at once the united hostility of his former friends and also of the great mass of the people of Ireland, and he unites himself for ever as the head of the Pitt party, subjecting himself also to the violence of decided opposition upon a great publick question, and which if ever carried would be a sort of assault upon the Crown. If on the other hand he forms an Administration of which Catholick concession is the basis, he unites against him the Percival part of the Pitt School (the remaining part of that School will be hollow supporter [sic] for the popularity of the moment) and he risks all the consequences attendant upon a failure which in this Protestant and, I may add, Protestantly bigotted kingdom, I doubt whether any man can safely predict—indeed, if I may trust my own limited observation I should certainly say that as an English question the Catholick Petition is decidedly unpopular, and unless the temper of the people is very much changed, there is nothing which would be more likely to create a popular ferment if handled by designing knaves (of which there is never a scarcity) than on Catholick concession.

In this state of political difficulty let me appeal to your good sense whether it would not be practicable and easy for the Prince to avow himself wholly unfettered by any conscientious feelings upon the Catholick cause, and to be ready to do that which shall appear to be the true sense of the nation upon the case, but that he will not himself personally interfere in the discussion, seeing that his family is a Protestant family and

Mostyn, R. Neville, Sir J. Newport, D. North, W. Northey, Sir G. Nugent, J. O'Callaghan, C. O'Hara, W. Ord, Lord F. G. Osborne, Lord Ossulston, C. Palmer, H. Parnell, H. Peirse, C. A. Pelham, G. A. Pelham, R. Mansell Phillips, Sir A. Piggott, Sir C. Pole, Lord Pollington, Ponsonby, Lord Porchester, R. Power, F. A. Prittie, F. Pym, W. H. Quinn, Sir M. W. Ridley, Romilly, Lord W. Russell, Sir J. St. Aubyn, F. Savage, R. P. Scudamore, R. Sharp, H. Shelley, T. Shelley, Sheridan, W. Shipley, A. Smith, G. Smith, J. Smith, S. Smith, W. Smith, Sir M. Somerville, Lord Stanley, T. Stanley, J. Stewart, Lord W. Stuart, T. P. Symonds, R. W. Talbot, B. Tarleton, Lord Tavistock, C. W. Taylor, M. A. Taylor, Lord Temple, Lord Templetown, T. Thompson, Tierney, W. Tighe, Lord J. Townshend, C. H. Tracey, Vansittart (surprisingly), G. G. V. Vernon, Lord Walpole, G. Walpole, J. W. Ward, Sir G. Warrender, C. C. Western, J. Wharton, Whitbread, F. J. Wilder, O. Williams, Sir R. Williams, W. Williams [sic ?Wilkins], Windham, Sir T. E. Winnington, C. W. W. Wynn, Sir W. W. Wynn. (Total, 211.)

seated upon this throne upon sound Protestant principles, and seeing also that his father was uniformly adverse to it. That he wishes the question to be decided as a great national question, unfettered by party, unbiassed by power, and that his fiat will be given when the decision of the Legislature shall be duly laid before him—in short, that he wishes it to be discussed as was the slave trade where every individual spoke as his mind dictated.

If the Prince should see this matter in a point of view similar to this, he would be at perfect liberty to form an Administration as extended as he pleased, and by including in his Household establishment the heads and heirs of the great families of this country, viz. the Devonshires, Bedfords, Northumberlands, Rutlands, Beauforts, Hertfords, Moira; he might then, aided by his old friends, dictate to any Administration he chose to form, nor could any formidable power be raised against him. No reasonable objection could be made by the King's old friends, as it must be a natural proceeding for every new Monarch to surround himself with those who, from political & personal interests, he may consider most useful to his Government, and most satisfactory to himself.

This is the outline of what I wished to lay before you, and when I assure you that it is most exclusively the result of my observation and reflection, and that no man living is privy to the secret of this letter, I need not entreat of you to keep it perfectly confidential and to yourself. (18839–42)

3245   SIR RUPERT GEORGE[1] TO MAJOR-GENERAL T. H. TURNER

Transport Office, 15 Nov. 1811

I have the honour to acknowledge the receipt of your letter of yesterday's date, conveying to me the pleasure of his Royal Highness the Prince Regent that Mr. Tyrwhitt should be permitted to enlist Germans from among the prisoners of war at Dartmoor for his Royal Highnesses own Regiment, and inform you that in obedience to his Royal Highnesses commands, orders have been sent accordingly to the Board's Agent, Capt. Cotgrave.[2] (18843)

1. Lieutenant, R.N., 1770; Captain, 1781. He was superannuated. He was a Commissioner of Transports in 1800 (*Later Correspondence of George III*, iii. 463) and was created a Baronet in August 1809.

2. Isaac Cotgrave. Lieutenant, R.N., 1780; Commander, 1797; Captain, 1802.

Windsor, 16 Nov. 1811

I am extreamly sorry for the cause which prevents my having the pleasure of seeing you, but trust that by taking care of yourself & the assistance of Mr. Home, you will not only recover soon but be prevented of doing too much before it is proper to do so.[1]

I send inclosed the copy of my letter to the A.B. of C. as also the questions to & answers from the consulting physicians of the 26 Octbr. which are the last the Council gave me. I am glad you approved of my letter. I shall not fail to acquaint you with the result of it as soon as I hear anything. (36592)

Windsor, 17 Nov. 1811

I am sorry to learn by Sr. Henry Halford's letter to Augusta that you are threatened with a very long confinement to your couch. I wish most sincerely that you may have patience to bear up under such a severe calamity, for without doubt it is the only remedy that can recover such an accident, but requires much fortitude. With infinite pleasure do I hear that the violence of the pain is abated, & flatter myself that today's account may bring us the good news of yr. being quite free of all unpleasant feels.

The Duke of York promised to relate what had passed between the Council & me yesterday: it really was so little that it was not worth while troubling you with a letter about it. John Willis is not arrived nor do I think he can reach this place till tomorrow or Tuesday; when he arrives I shall let you know.

Having nothing to entertain you with it is better not to trouble you any longer with my scrawl. (36593)

3247   THE DUKE OF YORK TO COLONEL MCMAHON

Oatlands, 17 Nov. 1811

I send you, by the Prince's commands, the enclosed letter[2] which I received yesterday and which he wishes that you would communicate as

1. Princess Charlotte, writing to her friend Mercer Elphinstone on the 16th, referred to her father's accident whilst at Oatlands. 'You have seen of course by the papers of the Prince's accident. It was not, however, with me, but in trying to recollect the *Highland Fling* with Mr Adam. One of the *small tendons* of the foot *is snapped*' (*Letters of the Princess Charlotte, 1811-1817*, ed. A. Aspinall, p. 14).

2. Missing.

soon as possible to Mr. Conant and take the necessary steps to investigate fully the worth of its contents. Secrecy seems absolutely necessary, and the Prince and I have agreed not to mention the subject to the Duke of Cumberland.

Of the writer of the letter I have some knowledge and have reason to believe her a person of respectability. I have put our friend Adam au fait of all I know about her as well as of some of her connections, and he has desired me to tell you that if you will appoint Mr. Conant to be at your house tomorrow at twelve o'clock he will not fail to meet him there.

I am happy to acquaint you that the Prince is better this morning, though he has had a very uncomfortable restless night. (44253)

3248 THE MARQUESS WELLESLEY TO THE PRINCE REGENT

Foreign Office, 17 Nov. 1811

Lord Wellesley has the honor to present his humble duty to your Royal Highness & to submit that he has seen M. Turri (who passes under the feigned name of Castelli) but Lord Wellesley cannot yet venture to offer to your Royal Highness any decisive opinion with regard to M. Turri's mission.

M. de Rehausen, at his own desire, had an interview with Lord Wellesley yesterday in which he stated with great additional earnestness his confident expectation of the success of your Royal Highness's propositions to Sweden. M. de Rehausen read an extract of a dispatch from M. d'Engerström directing the former to take a house in London for the facility of communicating with your Royal Highness's servants. M. d'Engerström's dispatch contained several expressions from which it would be reasonable to draw a conclusion favorable to the issue of the negotiation. M. de Rehausen mentioned that M. Netzel[1] (appointed to meet Mr. Thornton) is a person of good disposition & principles, but not much known in any official capacity.

M. de Rehausen suggested that if France should betray any inclination to seize the Island of Ze[a]lland or Elsineur, such a project ought to be defeated in its origin by the combined exertions of England & Sweden. He considered Denmark to be utterly unable to resist France, & viewed the remnant of the Danish power as a mere instrument in the hands of France for the execution of her Continental System.

Lord Wellesley has the honor to send in this box some papers for your Royal Highness's notice.

He has sent by Mr Smith a letter from Mr Adair on which he requests

1. See No. 3232n.

your Royal Highness commands. He also hopes to receive through Mr Smith your Royal Highness's orders respecting the letters from the Duke of Orleans to the Duke of Kent. (18845–6)

3249   THE DUCHESS OF DEVONSHIRE TO THE PRINCE REGENT
Portsmouth, Crown Inn, 17 Nov. 1811

I have directed that a copy of the *Characters*[1] should be sent to your Royal Highness in their present state, because the delay has been so great of their being ready for distribution that I have been disappointed in the one which I shall have bound in a particular manner for you, my dear Sir, yet I could not bear that *you* should not be the first person to whom they were sent; this was right from every consideration—never I believe was affection & regret greater or more sincere than yours, Sir— and much do I wish to know if your R.H. approves of & is satisfied with this character of your lov'd friend, my most ador'd husband. Allow me, my dear Sir, to profit of this opportunity just to mention myself, for you have taught me to believe that your R.H. is interested about me. The blow which has fallen on me feels as if it had crush'd me—but I do what I can & what I am told. I am come to Portsmouth where Lord & Lady Bessborough & their two sons[2] are to join me, & where Caroline,[3] my son Frederick[4] & Clifford are with me. The Cephalus is still in the work-men's hands, but he is hurrying them on & is eager for some fresh opportunity of deserving your R.H. kindness to him—& from the bottom of my heart I thank you, my dear Sir, for that timely interference wh. promoted Clifford, & for having now seen this dear young man; your kindness to him has encreased his attachment to your person tenfold. We are here in an hotel to ourselves. I see nobody, but being close to the sea I get to the beach by a little quiet subterraneous passage under the ramparts. As circumstances prevent my returning to Chiswick, I have taken the smallest of Lady Yarmouth's two houses. I am afraid it will be more than I can afford to go on with, or that she will not give a lease of

1. A volume of *Public Characters* was published annually at this time.

2. Viscount Duncannon and Sir Frederick Cavendish Ponsonby (1783–1837). See No. 2961.
    Lord Duncannon (1781–1847) succeeded his father as 4th Earl of Bessborough on 3 February 1844. M.P. for Knaresborough, 1805–6; for Higham Ferrers, 1810–12; for Malton, 1812–26: for Co. Kilkenny, 1826–32; for Nottingham, 1832–4. First Commissioner of Woods and Forests, 1831–4 and 1835–41; Home Secretary, July–November 1834; Lord Privy Seal, 1835–9; Lord Lieutenant of Ireland, 1846–7. Created Baron Duncannon [U.K.], 19 July 1834.

3. Caroline St. Jules (1785–1862). See No. 2560n.

4. Frederick Thomas Hervey Foster (*b.* 1777), her first son by her first husband, John Thomas Foster, who died in 1796. M.P. for Bury St. Edmunds, 1812–18.

it. I sd. have lik'd a house in the Green Park best as less publick, but I was oblig'd to fix on something. Do you think, my dear Sir, that Lord Yarmouth would express to Lady Yarmouth any wish about it, or is that out of the question?

I have just heard from Sr. Walter Farquhar that you have hurt your ankle. My dear Sir, I anxiously hope that it [is] not a hurt of consequence to your health. May God preserve to you that & every other blessing. Desolate as I feel in the world, yet is my heart alive to every sentiment of the warmest & most gratefull affection to your R. Highness, & ever will be.[1] (18848–9)

3250   J. KING TO COLONEL MCMAHON

35 Howland St., Fitzroy Square, 18 Nov. 1811
A friend of mine[2] has been engaged to give a compleat life of Lord Nelson, for which purpose all his Lordship's papers are put into his possession; among them is found a plan to prevent or repell invasion in Lord Nelson's own handwriting; my friend assures me that it is of the utmost importance, and will certainly be adopted when it is known. I wrote to Lord Moira on it, and offerd to confide the papers to his Lordship if he would be so good [as] to hand them to the Prince Regent. His Lordship has answerd that the proper way would be to address you on the subject, and to propose to wait on you with it, whenever you should appoint to receive it.[3] (18851)

3251   SPENCER PERCEVAL TO JOSEPH LANCASTER

Downg. St., 18 Nov. 1811
Private. I think I told you that H.R.H. the Prince Regent authorised me to state to the A.B. of Canterbury that he approved of the new school *for*

1. In August Lord Holland had written: 'The situation of the Duchess is deplorable, for whatever faults the man may have had they are expiated by this calamity, for to the Duke she was always affectionate, good and grateful. And as he was the inducement and cause of her betraying and injuring others, so was he her protector, and now to be deprived of him her only support she becomes an object of very great compassion and pity, and though at no time did she excite any friendly feeling in me, yet from the bottom of my heart do I feel for her present sufferings' (Howick MSS.).

2. James Harrison. See No. 3271.

3. Nelson's memorandum on the subject of coastal defence is in iv. 535 (No. 1845).

National Education and would accept the office of its PATRON. H.R.H. also told me that he would subscribe to it the same sum which he authorised Mr Adam to subscribe to Mr *Lancaster's school*. The A. Bp. was with me this morning and his Grace was desirous of knowing what *sum* that was, as it would be necessary in publishing a list of the subscribers to publish the amount of their subscriptions. Perhaps you can learn for me what that sum was, and if you can I will thank you to let me know. I send this to you instead of Colonel McMahon because the former communications on this subject passed between you & me, when the Col. was out of town. (18852)

3252   WILLIAM WELLESLEY-POLE TO COLONEL MCMAHON
Dublin Castle, 19 Nov. 1811
Private & Confidential. I laid your private & confidential letter of the 12th instant before the Lord Lieutenant, and his Grace has commanded me to acquaint you for the information of his Royal Highness the Prince Regent, that the living held by the late Dean Dawson[1] is in the gift of the Primate.[2] Upon the appointment of Doctor Warburton to the Bishoprick of Limerick[3] his living of course lapsed to the Crown, and the presentation was in the Lord Lieutenant; but the present presentation is in the Primate, the living being in the patronage of the See of Armagh. The Lord Lieutenant laments that under these circumstances he has not the power to obey the commands of his Royal Highness the Prince Regent. His Grace has directed me farther to acquaint you that he has not deem'd it proper to forward your letter to me to the Primate without his Royal Highnesses permission, and that he shall await his Royal Highnesses commands on that subject. (18853-5)

3253   J. KING TO COLONEL MCMAHON
35 Howland St., 21 Nov. 1811
I should never have presumed to address you or Lord Moira respecting the plan in question if I did not consider it of the utmost importance. Lord Nelson gave extraordinary proofs of a naval genius, and he would

1. Thomas Dawson, Dean of Clonmacnoise. The living was wanted for that disreputable clergyman, the Rev. Henry Bate Dudley. See No. 3273.

2. William Stuart, Archbishop of Armagh.

3. In June 1806.

have exerted it to its utmost on a subject that he must have deemd of more consequence than any other. The enclos'd, which is a transcript of a paper which is also in his Lordship's writing, evinces what idea he entertaind of the plan. I was appointed to correct a publication which is intended to be given to the world; among the papers is this plan, which I should have considered it a species of treason to withhold from the Prince Regent. I am pleasd to be instrumental in a matter that serves the country. I could have wishd to have the honor of delivering the papers to the Prince Regent or to you, but you have directed them to be given to Genl. Turner, which shall be done on Monday if I dont hear of any other command from you before then. (18861)

3254   LETTERS FROM PRINCESS AUGUSTA TO THE PRINCE OF WALES

Thursday morning, 21 Nov. [1811]

We are all most anxious to hear how you are today, but were not satisfied with Sir Henry's[1] account of you last night—therefore the Queen sends over to Oatlands in the hope of having a *very particular account* either from Sir Walter[2] or Mr. Home. The Queen orders me to say how vexed she is at your undergoing so much pain, and how sincerely she hopes you will soon be able to get out of bed again.

I am sorry I cannot give you even a tolerable account of the dear King; he is not so much excited as yesterday but still there has been a great deal of very unpleasant laughing very early this morning which I fear may increase in the course of the day into the same sort of instability as we suffered so much from yesterday. God bless you. (Add. Georgian 10/47)

Thursday night, 21 Nov. 1811

Sophia and myself will ride over to visit you tomorrow. We will be at Oatlands between twelve and one o'clock and stay with you so as to be at home again time enough to dress for dinner at four o'clock. I need not say how happy we are at the thoughts of seeing you. Mary and Eliza will come on Monday next. God bless you. I send this by an orderly to-morrow morning.[3] (Add. Georgian 10/48)

1. Halford's.

2. Farquhar.

3. Princess Charlotte wrote on the 23rd: 'Mary and Sophia went yesterday to see him, but what I think extraordinary, considering the *many* and *great sacrifices* he has made her, that *neither* the Queen nor Elizabeth were of the party' (Bowood MSS.). The Queen, however, went to Oatlands on the 25th.

Bloomsbury Square, 21 Nov. 1811

There was a ground of subscription—distinctly for the building Lancaster's School &c and one personal for the relief of his family. I will in the course of this day obtain the amount applicable to each which I subscribed by the Prince's commands & send or take them to you. (18862)

Bloomsbury Sq:, 22 Nov. 1811

The Prince Regent's subscription to Lancaster was as follows:

For the building	£210
For payment of the debts contracted by Mr Lancaster	105

I reckon the first sum the subscription; the other was in the nature of private relief—& was so understood by the subscribers. (18865)

3256 THE MARQUESS WELLESLEY TO THE PRINCE REGENT

Apsley House, 22 Nov. 1811

Lord Wellesley has the honor to submit to your Royal Highness dispatches received by Count Munster & Mr. Smith from Colonel Dornberg. It was intended that Mr Smith should have carried these papers to your Royal Highness this morning, but as he was going to the Office he was overturned in his carriage & so much hurt that he cannot leave his room. There is no reason however to apprehend that he will not be quite well in a day or two. There is no arrival from Russia. Your Royal Highness will no doubt have observed that the want of communication which Colonel Dornberg laments has been equally regretted by Sir James Saumarez on the other side for nearly a month past. As Sir James Saumarez & Colonel Dornberg were to meet, it may be hoped that this scene of confusion will at length be closed by some appearance of order & activity.[1] (18863)

1. Colonel Dornberg wrote to Culling Charles Smith, the Under-Secretary of State, on the 23rd, on board the *Victory*: 'I have the honor to send you herewith a letter for Count Munster, which I beg you will be pleased to forward to him. I came here by the express desire of Sir James Saumarez to concert with him the measures to be taken about the arms etc. send [*sic*] for the support of Prussia. I very much fear we will be obliged to send them back, considering the very advanced season and the uncertainty of the breaking out of the war—though I have not the least doubt but Bonaparte will attack Prussia as soon as he thinks her deprived of every assistance from England. Sir James has given the most positif orders to

3257 THE PRINCE REGENT TO THE MARCHIONESS OF HERTFORD

Oatlands, Saturday, 23 Nov. 1811

I begin, my ever dearest Lady B., now really to hope that there will be little or no interruption to our further correspondence, for, though it was a restless one, still, it was a much less bad night the last I pass'd than the preceeding one, & which indeed surpass'd in every respect everything that you can form to yourself the smallest idea of. When Bloomfield wrote yesterday I was incapable of moving a single joint in my whole frame, & it was therefore quite impossible for me to hold a pen within my fingers. Today I am certainly upon the whole easier but never one instant free from pain. The greatest blessing is that laudanum has not in the least lost its effect, notwithstanding the immense quantities I have taken & must still for a time be under the unavoidable necessity of taking; nothing but the steady perseverance in these frequently repeated dozes [*sic*] can or does afford me the smallest relief. I must now reluctantly bid you adieu, my best & ever dearest friend, & leave everything else to be told you by Bloomfield. Assure Lord Hertford of my best regards & beleive me yourself, my ever dearest Lady B., most unalterably, your ever & most affectionate

P.S. Francis[1] never better, & has been sitting for the last three hours in the best possible health & spirits by my bedside (Egerton MSS. 3262. f. 81).

3258 THE MARQUESS WELLESLEY TO THE PRINCE REGENT

Apsley House, 25 Nov. 1811

Lord Wellesley has the honor to acquaint your Royal Highness that in obedience to your Royal Highness's gracious commands he intimated to Mr Perceval & to the Cabinet that it would be expedient that some of the principal members of the Cabinet should attend your Royal Highness for the purpose of which your Royal Highness is apprised.[2] It was

use the utmost endeavours to get these arms landed, if asked for in time, and I hope to find things advanced far enough on my return to be authorized to try to get them landed.' (18866)

1. Lord Yarmouth. On 10 October Princess Charlotte thought he was looking very ill and old. Lady Holland had written to Lord Grey on 7 October: 'Lord Yarmouth is supreme in favour and confidence *apparently*, but he swaggers and boasts so much that one is tempted to suspect he endeavours to persuade himself and others more of the reality of his favour than he feels is true. However, he has contrived to get Colonel Bloomfield discarded, at least kept at a distance, which, considering the great partiality once entertained for him by the Prince, is remarkable' (Howick MSS.).

2. The Cabinet had a preliminary discussion about the King's Household on the 19th. Wellesley had communicated to Perceval the Prince Regent's views two days earlier.

determined that Mr Perceval should attend your Royal Highness, &
that gentleman will accordingly solicit the honor of an audience from
your Royal Highness at Oatlands.[1] (18869)

3259   RICHARD RYDER TO THE PRINCE REGENT
Great George Street, Monday, 25 Nov. 1811
Mr. Ryder has the honor of humbly submitting to your Royal Highness
that he received an express from Mr Pole late last night to inform him
that the jury had brought in a verdict of acquittal in the case of Dr.
Sheridan. His was the first trial under the late prosecutions.[2] Mr. Pole
was obliged, in order to save the tide, to dispatch his letter the moment
after he was informed of the verdict, and had not been able to learn
correctly any particulars respecting the trial. He understands, however,
that the opinion of the Judges concurred with that which had been
delivered by the Law Officers of the Crown that the jury were out one
hour & ten minutes in considering their verdict, and that they grounded
the acquittal on the defect of evidence. (18870)

3260   SPENCER PERCEVAL TO THE PRINCE REGENT
Downing Street, Monday evening, 25 Nov. 1811
Mr Perceval presents his humble duty to your Royal Highness and
requests to know at what time he may be permitted to have the honor of
waiting upon your Royal Highness at Oatlands for the purpose of learning your Royal Highness's pleasure upon the subject of the arrangement
to be proposed to Parliament respecting his Majesty's Household. Mr
Perceval will hold himself in readiness to wait upon your Royal Highness
at any time on Wednesday or any subsequent day which may be most
suitable to your Royal Highness's convenience. (18872)

1. Wellesley wrote to Perceval on the night of the 26th: 'With the Swedish papers (which I
sent to the Regent this morning) I have received an order to attend at Oatlands tomorrow, for
the purpose of meeting Count Münster & of discussing the affairs of the North, on which
H.R.H. is very anxious. I am afraid that I shall not be able to return in time for Lord Westmorland's dinner' (Perceval MSS.).

2. The Catholic Committee in Ireland had been proposing to elect delegates to what would
be, in effect, a Catholic Parliament in Dublin. Dr. Sheridan and others who took part in the
meeting on 9 July which considered the scheme were arrested and brought to trial.

3261 THE EARL OF MOIRA TO COLONEL MCMAHON

Holkham, 27 Nov. 1811

I write instantly to the Bishop of Limerick,[1] & if no pledge be already given to another, there is no doubt of carrying the point. This appears to me better than writing directly to the Primate, for, as I know him but little, I fear he might make a sudden excuse & then think himself bound to abide by it. Now Warburton has tact enough to comprehend the thing, tho' my name alone shall appear to him; & he will urge it efficiently with the other. (18873)

3262 THE ARCHBISHOP OF CASHEL[2] TO THE BISHOP OF FERNS[3]

18, Glocester Place, 27 Nov. 1811

I had the honor of receiving your Lordship's letter, enclosing Mr Dudley's[4]—which I now return. I can do nothing else than leave this gentleman to make his appeal to the tenderness of Dr Duigenan. He is not the best of the legacies which your Lordship's predecessor has left you.[5] (18874)

3263 PRINCESS CHARLOTTE TO THE PRINCE REGENT [copy]

27 Nov. 1811

I can no longer remain silent or resist the impulse of taking up my pen to tell you, my dear father, how much happiness this day's good account has afforded me, & how very anxious I have been during this severe confinement. Often & often I have been tempted to write, but as often remained silent, fearing I might appear intrusive or worry you when in pain; even now I am not wholly divested of that fear but I trust to your kindness to me. Another wish has been still more predominant &

1. Dr. Warburton.

2. The Hon. Charles Brodrick.

3. The Hon. Percy Jocelyn (1764–1843), third son of Robert, 1st Earl of Roden. Bishop of Ferns, 1809; of Clogher, 1820–2. In October 1822 he was deprived of his Bishopric for scandalous crime.

4. The Rev. Henry Bate Dudley (1745–1824). See Nos. 1333, 2167, etc.

5. Note by the Bishop of Limerick (on the back) of the letter: 'This letter, just recd., will shew you that my opinion as to that person, is not lightly taken up—it is from the Abp. of Cashel to Bp. of Ferns, and sent to me for advice.'

234

ardently wished for—that of seeing you. Till I heard my aunts had been with you I remained silent (tho' not the less anxious) but now may I say how happy, how very happy it would make me could I enjoy the same indulgence (indulgence I call it, as I always feel it so when you permit me to be with you) for ever so short a time, as I should fly down at all hours & days &c that you liked best. I am longing for you to come to town; you must be well soon for your sake [as] for mine. Pray don't forget & believe me [etc.][1] (Bowood MSS.).

3264 EARL BATHURST TO [?] COLONEL MCMAHON

Portman Square, 1 Dec. 1811

I shall be obliged to you if you will have the goodness to let me know where the goods are belonging to his Royal Highness which he is desirous should be imported under licence into this country.

I hope the wine and the packages are at the same port, otherwise by creating a necessity for different licences, it will very much add to the difficulty of getting the whole over.

You have I believe been misinformed as to the supposed prohibition on the part of the French Government to allow wine to be exported except to a given amount. That regulation applies only to cases where the remaining part of the cargo is grain & some other enumerated articles. It is true that if the vessel to which the licence is to be given were to be allow'd to import only the goods of his Royal Highness which you have mentioned in your letter, they would form only a very small cargo. It would be better on many accounts that this licence should be separate, & made to attach upon some vessel which may have a licence to make imports under the existing regulations. If therefore you would give instructions to the person in France who may have these goods of his Royal Highness in custody to deliver them over upon the production of the

1. Princess Charlotte wrote to Miss Elphinstone on 3 December: 'I must now tell you, my dearest Mercer, all that passed yesterday. I arrived quite safe at Oatlands a little before 1, was recvd. by everyone with great kindness, & everybody seemed as if they were glad to see me again, wh. I *was a little* flatter'd at. The Fitzroys are still there & remain till the Prince comes to town. The little Duchess was as kind as possible. Lord Yarmouth is there & I had the *supreme felicity* of seeing him. We had musick, wh. made the time pass very agreably. *At length my friend* Mr Adam made his appearance; he was in *high spirits* & feather. *Marquis Welsley* [sic] I had some conversation with, & *found* him (what I did not except) [expect] *pleasant*. The Prince at length sent for the Duchess, myself & Lady de Clifford; he was *kind* in *his manner* to *us all*. He looks *extremely well* but suffers a great deal of pain still. We were near 2 hours during wh. time he *talked entirely* of the *King* & gave a *most distressing & lamentable account*. He is in hopes of being able to move to town Thursday. He was *more easy* in *his manner* than I *have seen yet*, wh. *is a step I think*' (Bowood MSS.).

235

licence (a copy of which I will in that case enable you to send him), the whole might be managed in a manner much less objectionable & therefore I am sure in a way more conformable to his Royal Highness's wishes. (18878-9)

3265   THE EARL OF MOIRA TO COLONEL MCMAHON

Holkham, 1 Dec. 1811

I ought to have returned Pole's letter. I now enclose it, apologising for the former omission.

I likewise send for your perusal one from Plunket.[1] My intervention could not be necessary to ensure to the representation from the Fellows of Trinity College every degree of urbanity as to the reception, whatsoever may be the ultimate decision upon their memorial: but it is advisable for me to have it to say that I did not neglect Plunket's entreaty.

It was with anguish I viewed the extravagant step of the Irish Government in moving new indictments against the Catholic Delegates. Were the Viceroy and Pole the only persons responsible to public opinion for the irritating perseverance in this desperate controversy, still I should have lamented the measure as pregnant with evils which no future palliations might suffice to remedy. It would, however, be a mischievous concealment to the Prince to suppress the fact that in the eyes of the

1. William Conyngham Plunket, 1st Baron Plunket (1764–1854), M.P. for Charlemont [I.], 1798–1800; for Midhurst, January–April 1807; for Dublin University, 1812–17. Solicitor-General [I.], 1803–5; Attorney-General [I.], 1805–7 and 1822–7; Chief Justice of the Common Pleas [I.], 1827–30. Peerage, May 1827. Lord Chancellor [I.], 1830–4 and 1835–41. A leading advocate of Catholic emancipation. He had declined the offer of a seat in Parliament at the end of 1809 (the Duke of Bedford would then have been happy to bring him in for Camelford *vice* Lord Henry Petty). Plunket's being without a seat from 1807 to 1812 is explained in the Duke of Bedford's letter to Lord Holland, 19 November 1809, and it is interesting to note that although there was a 'total' change of Government in March 1807, Plunket, as the Irish Attorney-General, could have remained in office. Referring to his resignation of the office of Lord Lieutenant of Ireland in 1807, the Duke wrote: 'When I quitted Ireland Mr Plunket behaved in so very handsome a manner to me personally, desiring to attach his fortunes to mine, and positively refusing to retain the Attorney Generalship notwithstanding the pressing solicitations of the present Ministers and of many of his immediate and personal friends. He declined at that time coming into Parliament on account of his circumstances and his large family making it necessary for him to stick closely to his professional pursuits at Dublin. Since that, the death of his brother has made him independent in fortune, and I understand he is not unwilling now to come into Parliament. I am therefore anxious to offer him the seat, and independent of the satisfaction I shall have in giving him this testimony of my regard, I think it cannot be matter of indifference in a party view to have the accession of his weight and abilities in the discussion of the Catholic claims now about to be renewed in Parliament.' (Add.MSS.51661,fo.140)

country he is not (& cannot be) clear of implication in this business. The plea that, as he keeps them, he must let these Ministers follow their own judgement, is not admissible in a case of vital importance to the tranquillity of the United Kingdom. I should not express the point so forcibly did I not know from informations entirely beyond question what the extent & the strength of feeling is upon this matter. The contest is not with a portion of the Catholics or the whole body of the Catholics alone, but with the whole population of Ireland. The adherents of the Castle are too insignificant to be put into any scale. That the Prince, after the spontaneous pledges he had before given, should allow an attempt at opposition of a quality such as was never offered under his father's Government, bewilders the minds of all classes. And I do most solemnly assure you that it dangerously affects the best link that existed for keeping the countries together. Can I put this too strongly when the view of the Irish Government to involve the Prince directly & personally in this frantic warfare is obvious from the procedure of putting off the trials so as that the legal issue shall not be determined before the period at which the Catholic Committee is to meet? The dispersion of that Committee, to which Government is pledged, is an act of outrage that (altho' it will produce no riot) is to draw the line between the parties *for ever*: and the base purpose of those who have been upon bad ground & are ashamed to admit it is to include the Prince in their squad, so as to cover their error with his name, at the trifling expense to him of the loss of confidence from so vast a proportion of his people. The consequent mischief is not either problematical or remote. The exigency is even now upon us: and, if the means which ought to parry it shall on the contrary co-operate in the purpose, it requires no sagacity to foresee the result.

I shall be in town by the middle of the week; but the uncommon anxiety of my mind would not allow me to delay the avowal of these sentiments. (18880–2)

3266   THE EARL OF LIVERPOOL TO THE PRINCE REGENT

Downing Street, 2 Dec. 1811

Lord Liverpool has the honor to send your Royal Highness again the dispatch of Lord Wellington of the 6th of Novr, according to your Royal Highnesses desire, and at the same time the copy of a private letter of Lord Wellington of the same date, with an enclosure address'd to his Lordship by Lt. -Genl. Hill.[1]

1. Rowland Hill, 1st Viscount Hill (1772–1842). Entered the army, 1790; Lieutenant-Colonel, 1794; Colonel, 1800; Major-General, 1805; Lieutenant-General, 1812; General, 1825. K.B.,

Considering the services of Lt.-Genl. Hill in the Peninsula for the last three years, as well as the brilliant & successful termination of the late important military operation, it would be a particular satisfaction to Lord Liverpool if your Royal Highness should be graciously pleased to authorise him to acquaint Lord Wellington and Genl. Hill that your Royal Highness would confer the Red Ribbon upon the latter whenever you might think proper to create any Knights of the Bath.

Lord Liverpool begs leave to add that Genl. Beresford (who is a junior officer in his Majesty's service) is already in possession of the Red Ribbon, and Lord Liverpool is not aware of any Genl. Officer on service not already in possession of this honour who has as strong and peculiar a claim to such a mark of distinction as Lt.-Genl. Hill, with the exception of Lt.-Genl. Graham, to whom your Royal Highness was so good as to promise the same favour after the battle of Barrosa.

Lord Liverpool has great satisfaction in transmitting to your Royal Highness a letter which he has received this day from Lt.-Col. Green[1] which gives a very favourable account of the state of the war in the province of Catalonia.[2] (18883)

3267 THE DUKE OF NORTHUMBERLAND TO COLONEL MCMAHON, AND AN ENCLOSURE
Alnwick Castle, 6 Dec. 1811
I will trouble you to give the enclosed to H.R.H. the Prince Regent. Lord James Murray,[3] my son-in-law, being extremely anxious to have the honour of belonging to the Regent's family, & finding that the number of Aides de Camp (which situation he first thought of) is compleat & full, has strongly urged me to apply to H.R.H. for the appointment of one of his Lords of the Bedchamber whenever H.R.H.'s Household shall be established, thinking this situation highly becoming his rank; and, at the same time, knowing that his amiable manners, natural politeness & sweetness of temper woud please the Regent, I have ventured to sollicit this situation for him, & shall be truly happy & gratefull to H.R.H. shoud he

22 February 1812; G.C.B., 1815. M.P. for Shrewsbury, 1812–14. Created Baron Hill, 17 May 1814. Colonel of the Royal Horse Guards, 1830–42. Viscount, September 1842. See No. 3297.

1. Nuttall Green, Lieutenant-Colonel, 1810.

2. The letter is endorsed: 'The Prince Regent's full concurrence was immediately communicated to Lord Liverpool by Mr Culling Smith under the commands of his Royal Highness, Decr. 2, 1811.'

3. Lord James Murray (1782–1837), second son of John, 4th Duke of Atholl, married the Duke of Northumberland's daughter Emily Frances (1789–1844) on 19 May 1810. Created Baron Glenlyon, 17 July 1821. M.P. for Perthshire, 1807–12; a Lord of the Bedchamber, March 1812–32. A.D.C. to the Prince Regent, 1813–19.

be graciously pleased to listen to my application, & grant me this favour.

I hope to hear that H.R.H. is now perfectly recovered from his disagreable accident. Adieu, my dear Colonel, accept the compliments of us all.

I hope you have settled everything with Wilson[1] about your re-election?[2] Genl. Hill's action is the ablest thing we have done this war. He truly merits a Red Ribband.[3] (18887)

[Enclosure] THE DUKE OF NORTHUMBERLAND TO THE PRINCE REGENT
Alnwick Castle, 6 Dec. 1811
Lord James Murray, who is married to my youngest daughter, being extremely desirous of having the honour of being about your Royal Highness's person, I have ventured to trouble you with this letter in order to sollicit your Royal Highness to honour him with the appointment to be one of your Lords of the Bedchamber whenever your Household shall be established. Of Lord James's character and manners I need say nothing, for as he had the honour of being in your Regiment, with them your Royal Highness is perfectly acquainted; & altho' he is not a Peer, yet as the late Lord Robert Bertie[4] was a Lord of his Majesty's Bedchamber when he was Prince of Wales, and afterwards when his Majesty came to the Throne; and as Lord Charles Spencer is now actually one of his Majesty's Lords of the Bedchambers[5] [*sic*] precedents are not wanting of the second son of a Duke being honoured with such an appointment.

If your Royal Highness shall be graciously pleased to do Lord James Murray the honour of complying with my humble request I shall esteem it, Sir, as a personal favour granted to myself, in addition to the many others with which your Royal Highness has been graciously pleased to honour me.

Permit me, Sir, before I conclude to express my anxious hope that your Royal Highness is perfectly recovered from the accident you lately met with. (18888)

1. Richard Wilson, the Duke's agent.

2. McMahon was re-elected for Aldborough on 15 January 1812 after appointment as Receiver and Paymaster of the Royal Bounty to Officers' Widows.

3. The reference is to Hill's defeat of General Gerard near Merida on 28 October. General Brun, the Prince d'Aremberg and 1,300 men, were taken prisoner.

4. Lord Robert Bertie (1721–82), a son of Thomas, 1st Duke of Ancaster. Major-General, 1758; Lieutenant-General, 1760; General, 1777. M.P. for Whitchurch, 1751–4; for Boston, 1754–82. Lord of the Bedchamber to George III as Prince of Wales and King, 1751–82.

5. His appointment is first noticed in the Red Book in 1808.

Carlton House, 6 Dec. 1811

Confidential. The Prince Regent not having yet return'd to town, although from general health so perfectly enabled to do so, on account however of his foot only, wishes to continue where he is until he can (without the inconvenience of the smell of paint which may prevail in this house for some days longer) move in here at once in preference to again taking up his abode at York House, and this arrangement has carried me so often to & from town to Oatlands that I have scarce had a moment to myself, or I should have had the honor of writing to your Grace earlier in the week and to tell you that Mr. Percival has already submitted to his Royal Highness, preparatory to the meeting of Parliament, the projet of a Civil List, and of a future Establishment for the King, from the admitted improbability of his Majesty ever recovering again. Between this proposition & the Prince's expectations some considerable & many shades of differences are seemingly likely to arise. The Household of the King is to be on a scale of the greatest comfort & of the highest possible dignity that can accord with his Majesty's unhappy situation, in which all the parties are of course entirely agreed. He is to retain the Groom of the Stole, four Lords of the Bed Chamber, four Grooms of ditto, the Master of the Robes, all his Equerries & Pages, &c. &c. &c. with carriages, two setts of horses, servants, horses &c. and his Privy Purse (subject to medical attendants &c.). The Queen wishes a separate Establishment for herself, & also for each of the Princess's, the same as if the King was *actually* demised, and to this the Ministers disagree, as they contend (& which in everything else the Prince consents) that in the case of a possibility that the King should recover, his Majesty is to find his Government, his family, and his everything exactly *eo ipso* as he left them, but from the improbability of such an event H.R.Hss. is induced to favor the wishes of his mother & sisters. The solution of this plan may perhaps be the means of developing much as to what may produce some ministerial arrangements, for it would seem to go to either schism or approbation, and whatever turn it takes, your Grace shall have the earliest information, with all the various points of discussion & of final determination. The Prince excepting his not [having] yet been able to stand on the left foot, is as well as man can be; still politicians & stock jobbers have spread many contemptible reports respecting his health which I *assure* your Grace are, thank God, all false[1] (Alnwick MSS.).

1. Tierney wrote to Grey on the 13th: 'The Prince came to town very unexpectedly . . . He is nervous to the greatest degree, as he necessarily must be if the stories are true about the quantity of laudanum he takes' (Howick MSS.). He returned to London (to York House, Carlton House not being in a fit state to accommodate him) on the 9th.

3269   CABINET MINUTE

6 Dec. 1811

That it was the clear, decided and unanimous opinion of Mr. Perceval and all his colleagues, most reluctantly & unwillingly adopted, that to bring these debts before Parliament for the purpose of discharging them by whatever gradual instalments out of money to be raised on the people for that purpose would be most inconsistent with the true interests of H.R.H. himself.

That it was also their unanimous opinion that the idea of founding or strengthening any claim upon the public for the discharge of these debts by any reference to the former demands on account of the Duchy of Cornwall after the manner in which the determination to abandon the suit for that demand was recorded in Parliament, would not be consistent with what appeared to be the plain meaning of that transaction, and that his Royal Highness could not be properly advised to attempt to distinguish between that abandonment of the suit & an absolute abandonment of the claim.

This paper was shewn & read to the full Cabinet on Friday last, when it was agreed by every one present correctly to represent the decision of the day before.[1]

                    S.P.
                        Monday Dr./9, 1811 (Perceval MSS.)

3270   SAMUEL WHITBREAD TO [?] COLONEL MCMAHON

Southill, 7 Dec. 1811

Many thanks for your letter. I had the highest expectations from the Prince Regent's name & sanction, & I am gratified by the example given of its influence in the case of Mr. Angerstein.[2] I am much obliged by your having been so good as to send his note to me.

I may be allowed to express some disappointment that the gentlemen of his Royal Highness's Establishment have limited their subscriptions to one share each & to hope that this determination on their part may not operate to restrain your liberal intentions towards us.

Your name has been placed in the list for some considerable time to

1. The revived question of the Prince Regent's debts (a question connected with the threatened revival of his claim to the arrears of the Duchy revenues) was calculated to embarrass the Opposition as well as the Government. If they opposed the payment they would mortally offend him; if they supported it they would be likely to lose what little popularity in the country they still possessed.

2. See No. 2449.

five shares; to alter the number by reducing it now would have a very bad effect for us. If continued as it stands it may counteract the influence as to quantum of subscription which the limitation of your colleagues might otherwise produce.

Here is another subject of great delicacy which I hardly know how to mention but I am sure your good nature will supply my deficiencies, & not take what I say amiss. I mean the deposits upon the shares which his Royal Highness has condescended to take himself in the concern. Perhaps you would do me the additional favour of putting this in train.

May I be permitted to express my sincere sorrow for the accident & suffering of his Royal Highness, & my earnest wishes for his speedy & complete recovery from their effects? (18889)

3271 JAMES HARRISON TO THE PRINCE REGENT

Mount Pleasant, Richmond, 7 Dec. 1811

On examining a very large collection of Lord Nelson's original papers intended for publication, I have discovered a plan in his Lordship's own handwriting[1] to prevent any invasion of our country, which being, as I conceive, quite improper to appear from the press unless previously carried into execution, is now most respectfully transmitted to your Royal Highness by favour of General Turner in consequence of an application through Mr. King to Lord Moira and Colonel McMahon.

From the first moment of seeing this important paper, which several circumstances induce me to believe has never been perused by any other person, I determined carefully to conceal what it recommends till I could obtain for it the honour of being delivered immediately into the hands of your Royal Highness, fully satisfied that it would there meet with every merited attention.

I have too intimate an acquaintance with Lord Nelson's private correspondence not to know the very great personal attachment of our chief naval hero to your Royal Highness; the affectionate regard of your Royal Highness for Lord Nelson is well known to all the world.

I should feel highly honoured by your Royal Highness's commands on this or any other occasion within the scope of my humble ability. In making the present communication I am merely performing what I consider as my duty to the memory of Lord Nelson, to your Royal Highness and to my country. (18890)

1. No. 1845 (April 1804).

3272   WILLIAM ADAM TO SPENCER PERCEVAL

Oatlands, 8 Dec. 1811

I came here yesterday to lay the paper which you sent to me on Friday night before the Prince Regent—and H.R.H. has commanded me to inform you that he wishes you to attend him here on Tuesday at 12 o'clock upon the whole of the matter connected with your paper—but that he wishes any opinion of the Cabinet on the whole subject to be deferred until he shall have seen you—in order that the result of the interview may be communicated to the Cabinet before they proceed farther in the consideration of the subject—as any previous opinion might produce such embarassment as it might be difficult if not impossible to overcome: and which the Prince deprecates & would most sincerely regret[1] (Perceval MSS.).

3273   THE BISHOP OF LIMERICK TO THE EARL OF MOIRA

Limerick, 9 Dec. 1811

Very private. I am only just now honor'd with your letter of the 27th Novr., from Holkham expressing a wish of obtaining from the Primate the preferment of Loughgilly (vacated by the death of Dean Dawson) for Dr. B. Dudley, as an event that wou'd be gratifying to the Prince.

I need not take much pains to convince your Lordship of the extreme happiness I shou'd feel in being any ways instrumental to the gratification of H. Royal Highness.

The living in question (Loughgilly formerly held by me) by the death of Dean Dawson fell to the patronage of the Primate, and which I know his Grace disposed of three weeks ago to Dr. Bisset of that Diocese—and here, my dear Lord, I feel myself bound, from every sense of duty and attachment to his Royal Highness, to freely state my opinion to your Lordship upon this point in the *strictest confidence.*

From various circumstances which occur'd in the Duke of Bedford's Administration as well as from late conversations with the Lord Primate, I am persuaded that his Grace never wou'd grant any preferment himself to Dr. D— and that if he took a part at all it wou'd be that of opposition to his receiving (even from the Crown) any sort of dignity in the Irish Church. It is but justice to that honorable & worthy man, the Duke of Bedford, to assure the Prince that I was witness to the extreme anguish he felt in not being able to accomplish the wish of H.R.Highness upon this subject. The strong prejudices of the late Bishop of London[2] were

1. See No. 3275.

2. Beilby Porteus, died 14 May 1809.

conveyed to the heads of the Church in this country, which were so strengthen'd by a similar letter from a high & respectable member of your Cabinet to the Duke, that his Grace was with difficulty able to confer upon him a preferment in Ardagh Diocese, and that through a little management of mine with the A. Bishop of Tuam.[1]

From this statement, my dear Lord, you will perceive there is nothing to hope from the Primate, who, in addition to very good understanding, possesses many oddities; his prejudices not easily removed, and he piques himself upon independence—mixes but little with the world, & therefore apt to form mistaken opinions. He is good natured at bottom & very kindly permits me sometimes to combat these erroneous opinions.

When Bishop George Beresford[2] was to be translated from Clonfert to Kilmore in the province of Armagh the Primate took it into his head to write immediately to the King, against Lord Hardwick's recommendation; and the other day he told me a laughable circumstance of Lord Erskine applying to him for that very living of Loughgilly for his son[3] who wishes to marry the Primate's niece—'His Grace had no objection to the match, but Lord Erskine must provide for his son himself.'

These little anecdotes will give your Lordship some idea of the man's peculiar turn—from which little is to be expected upon the subject of your letter.

I understand Mr. *Pole* has got his relation, Dean Leslie[4] of Cork, recommended for the vacant See of Dromore. Shou'd this promotion take place the Lord Ld. will have the Deany. of Cork (£1300 p.an.) and a living of £900 to dispose of.

Now I do think that the Lord Lt. in common decency ought to consult the Prince Regent's wishes upon this occasion, who has shewn such unexampled forbearance & unusual indulgence to the Irish Minister in the uncontroul'd disposal of so many Bishopricks. The Duke of Richmond himself express'd his surprize when his first recommendation, in favor of Dr. Hall to Dromore, came back accepted; he took for granted the vacancy wou'd not be filled up untill the restrictions expired.

1. The Hon. William Beresford, Baron Decies (1743–1819), Bishop of Dromore, 1780; of Ossory, 1782; Archbishop of Tuam, 1794–1819. Peerage, 1812.

2. George de la Poer Beresford (1765–1841), Bishop of Clonfert, 1801; of Kilmore, 1802–41; son of John Beresford (1738–1805), who was the second son of Marcus, Earl of Tyrone.

3. Henry David Erskine (d. 1859), later Dean of Ripon, married (4 May 1813) Mary Harriet (d. 1827), daughter of John, 1st Earl of Portarlington.

4. John Leslie (d. 1854), Bishop of Dromore, January 1812 (nominated 5 December 1811); of Elphin, 1819; of the united diocese of Kilmore, Elphin and Ardagh, 1841. Ryder wrote to the Lord Lieutenant, 1 January 1812: 'The Prince has not yet recovered the effects of his sprain and confinement, and the consequence has been that Dr. Leslie's appointment and many others have been delayed from wanting his signature, which spasms in the hands prevented him from giving' (Richmond MSS.).

From my personal knowledge of B. Dudley, and particularly from the Prince's anxiety to promote him, I shall feel extremely happy in being at all useful—but from what I have stated your Lordship will see that (unless as preferment from the Crown) it will be difficult to accomplish the object—and even then, some little management will be necessary on our part.

I cannot with safety be more explicit by a post letter, but shall probably after Christmass have an opportunity of personally stating to your Lordship such information as may be necessary for his Royal Highness to be in possession of; especially respecting the situation & management of our ecclesiastical affairs in this country. (18893–6)

3274　CHARLES ARBUTHNOT TO COLONEL MCMAHON

Downing Street, Tuesday, 10 Dec. [1811]

Confidential. In the first place let me mention that Lord Bathurst would be very much obliged to you if you wd. call upon him tomorrow at the Board of Trade between ½ past 12 & 3, as he wishes to speak to you about some French articles which are to come for the Prince. Lord B. will propose a mode of bringing them over which seems unobjectionable.

Don't say it to any one, but Ld. Yarmouth has been with me today, & I think it right to apprise you that talking to me of £200,000 to be voted to the Prince as a sum to cover the expences of this last year, I observed that I feared Perceval wd. not be able to propose so large a sum, upon which he told me that *you* on Sunday had said that it was now the intention of Ministers to give £200,000. He afterwards desired that I wd. say nothing to you about it, so you must not let him have an idea that I have repeated it to you. I have however been desirous that you shd. know how yr. name has been brought forward but I must intreat you to say nothing which could make it appear that you & I have communicated together.

I shd. be very glad if so large a sum of £200,000 could be voted, but what Perceval says makes me fear that such a sum would not be possible, & he has more than once told me that the Prince's own declarations at the beginning of the Regency, of not allowing the Regency to be any burthen to the country, increases the difficulty of proposing any sum.

I don't put my name on the outside, as I wish this letter to get to you without its being known from whom it comes. (18897)

3275

Memorandum of the observations made by the Prince Regent on the paper which was sent by Mr. Percival to Mr. Adam on Friday evening the 6th of December, approved by the Prince Regent as a correct account.

[Perceval's comments in pencil] This is the foundation of the great & leading difficulty—as long as the Prince continues to feel, and is permitted by such persons as he consults out of the Cabinet to be impressed with this idea, there is no hope of inducing him to believe that Parlt. could make any difficulty, or that he could be expected to make any sacrifice.

The fair inference from what passed in Parlt. in 1803 is that there might at that time be pecuniary debts to the amount of between 2 & £300,000, that the Prince had determined upon setting apart immediately a large sinking Fund, say about £50,000 per anm., which would *soon* completely discharge all his debts— whereas the result is that at the end of nearly double the time which could have been expected to be required to pay the whole, there now exists near twice the sum which could reasonably have been inferred as existing then.

This transaction did not take place till full 5 years after the settlement in 1803—therefore for 5 years nothing was attempted to be done towards discharging these *foreign* debts—and it is to be remarked that it certainly was supposed by the Govt. & by the

The Prince observed that he could not consider the claims and arrears which he was bound to discharge as standing in the unfavourable light in which Mr. Percival placed them. On the contrary H.R.H. said that he considered all his creditors entitled to the protection of Parliament—on the soundest principles of equity and fair dealing.

That in 1803 the House of Commons authorized a sufficient portion of his income to be set apart for the payment of debts which had a claim upon his justice and honour, and sanctioned the suspension of his assuming his State till that should be accomplished.

Under this sanction publicly recorded on the Journals of the House of Commons and then made known to his Majesty and the nation, the Prince's servants entrusted with his pecuniary concerns made distributions and payments of demands, which had originated subsequent to the enactment of the Legislature prohibiting the Prince of Wales from contracting debt: and in pursuance of the plan of liquidation thus undertaken with the full knowledge and approbation of Parliament, the creditors have signed

1. 'Read to Mr. Percival at York House.—10 December 1811 previous to his seeing the Prince Regent.'

people that the Prince was to have allowed her £5,000 pr. annm. more than he did.

agreements and under them have regularly accepted of instalments in discharge of their claims. Thus much with respect to the creditors here.

With relation to the loan from the Lan[d]grave of Hesse (to which allusion was made in the discussion in the House of Commons in 1803) it was about to be put in a similar train of liquidation when an unexpected call was made upon the Prince to discharge the debts of the Princess of Wales. The sum[s] intended for the payment of the debts of the Langrave were appropriated by H.R.H. to answer this call, and that circumstance was communicated to the Langrave's Agent with an assurance that the fund should be applied to reduce the debt to his Serene Highness as soon as the creditors of the Princess of Wales were satisfied. So that the Langrave must be considered has having an equitable right under the sanction of the Legislature to that fund.

The Prince farther observed that the funds out of which his Royal Highness had proposed to render those payments as speedy and effectual as his situation and necessary expenditure would admit, were much and very unexpectedly diminished soon after that time, and here his Royal Highness remarked that having a certain fixed income not liable to encrease or decrease it is self evident and undeniable that any decrease must prove a delay or loss to creditors—every reduction having been previously made to the utmost extent that the strictest economy could point out.

The imposition of the property tax not formerly affecting the Prince of Wales—the call to pay the debts of the Princess of Wales—the farther call to encrease the income of her Royal Highness—all since 1803—have unexpectedly created a deficiency of funds for liquidation to the amount of £160,000, whilst the whole sum in arrear up to the 11th of October

247

1811 amounts to £192,000, including a whole year of Regency unprovided with salary or allowance.

On this view of the subject (which must satisfy every fair and candid mind that the arrear has not arisen from want & extravagance or careless management) his Royal Highness considered that being called upon, in consequence of his Majesty's afflicting illness, to discharge the duties of Regent, and to deliberate upon arrangements for the Establishment, and expenditure suited to that station, the income pledged to his creditors, might be encroached upon or suspended. He felt it therefore to be an obligation of justice and honor to take care that the Minister should, in making those arrangements, provide a secure fund for the fulfillment of the obligations which he had thus been authorized to contract, not by a discussion of the debts publicly but by taking care that the interest of the creditors was kept constantly in view. His Royal Highness added that he felt completely convinced if these things were fairly and candidly, earnestly and liberally explained that they would be favorably received by Parliament—as founded upon the immutable principles of justice— which required that an imperative change in his situation, by the great calamity which the nation laboured under in the incapacity of our beloved Sovereign, should not weaken and dissolve the claims which he had become bound, with universal consent as to their justice, to discharge.

The Prince could not forbear to add that he trusted no part of his conduct in the present arduous crisis has produced any impression on the public mind calculated to lower him in public estimation. And that an honest effort to secure the discharge of just claims would not alter any favorable impression or weaken the hold which he was said by Mr. Percival to have in the hearts of the people.

With respect to the claim for the Duchy arrears, he only said that fortified with the opinion of such high legal authority, he could not in common justice to himself and his creditors give up his own opinion in its favour, and recollecting all that passed in 1803, the direction that his Law Officers should withdraw the suit was never to be understood as an abandonment of the claim.

His Royal Highness added that it was not his intention to press the payment of the creditors in any particular form, the means of arranging with them effectually in a manner suitable in time and amount was what H.R.H. required: it therefore appeared to the Prince that Mr. Percival has been under misapprehension as to the means by which the object was to be accomplished. H.R.H. added that he had a plan of general arrangement to communicate and for that purpose should direct Mr. Percival's attendance at Oatlands on Tuesday—the 10th.—
Oatlands, Sunday, 8th Decr. 1811
(Perceval MSS.).

248

There appears to be no solid reason why the sum required for the maintenance of an Establishment suited under the present circumstances to the rank and comfort of the King should necessarily be supplied in total from the Civil List; on the contrary, a distinct vote of a specific annual sum to his Majesty will simplify the statement to be made to Parliament as a single operation, and will avoid the double process of taking from the Civil List that which it is intended immediately to restore to it. The adoption of this mode of providing for the existing difficulty will, independent of its other advantages, possess the material one of placing the encreased charge to its proper head of expenditure, namely, a provision for the King and his family—for the King in reason of his situation—for his family because deprived of his paternal support and assistance. It will further be calculated to meet the anxiety expressed by Mr. Perceval to mix as little as possible the Prince Regent in a question where Mr. Perceval thinks encreased demands on the public may diminish the affection and attachment of the people towards his Royal Highness.

Adverting on the one hand to the necessity of providing a suitable income for the Queen and Princesses, whilst deprived of the supplies afforded them hitherto by his Majesty, as well as to the impossibility of placing the Queen in the situation of appearing to withdraw from the King's comforts whatever she may apply to her own separate expences, and on the other hand to the objections stated by Mr. Perceval to an entire separate Establishment for the Queen, entrusted as she is with the care of the King's person, it appears that by allotting a gross sum for the Establishment of the King, Queen and Princesses under the general head of a vote to his Majesty alone, subject to being appropriated in such portions as may be hereafter arranged, the public discussion of the detail of the expences of the Royal Family, always to be deprecated, and more especially under the present circumstances, will be completely avoided, and the Civil List returned in its full integrity to the King, if it should please Divine Providence to restore his Majesty's health whilst it is enjoyed in the meantime, equally unimpaired by the Prince Regent.

The amount of this gross sum may be estimated thus:

The King £110,000, which will include the services which Mr. Perceval meant to be discharged out of the Privy Purse appertaining to the Civil List.

The Queen in addition to her Civil List allowance, £50,000.

The four Princesses, each £9000 in addition to their Civil List allowance £36,000 making in the whole, one vote to his Majesty of £196,000 either inclusive or exclusive of the Duchy of Lancaster as may be thought proper.

It cannot but be supposed that such a sum not wide of that afforded with cheerfulness to support the *State and Court* of an Allied Sovereign will not with tenfold alacrity be supplied by the people to their own, endeared to them by a reign as unexampled in its length as in its popularity.

Adverting further on the one hand to the claim of the Prince of Wales to the arrears of the Duchy of Cornwall, supported as that claim is by the opinion of almost every law authority of the country, and on the other hand to the anxiety he feels not to press any question of personal advantage to himself from which the general difficulties of the country have induced his Royal Highness hitherto to abstain and to the statement of his pecuniary affairs delivered by Mr. Adam—it appears that the continuance of the Prince of Wales's Exchequer income for a time will fully enable his Royal Highness not only to discharge those various claims upon him recognised and sanctioned by Parliament in 1803, and which are now in train of liquidation, but for the encreased expences attendant upon the Regency.

His Royal Highness's anxiety to devote as much of his income as could be withdrawn from his immediate wants, induced his servants to apply a sum which left but enough to meet those wants in the most oeconomical manner.

Within a few months the income tax was unexpectedly demanded for the first time, and the creditors continuing to receive undiminished instalments, that part of his Royal Highness's income retained for his own use, has in eight years fallen £96,000 short of what it has naturally been calculated at, by the King's Ministers and the nation, and has by so much in fact been less a burthen upon the people.

To this diminution of revenue from the public is to be added £49,000 for the Princess of Wales's debts, so unexpectedly called for, and an increase of £5,000 to her allowance during the last three years, the particulars of which, and of the arrangements which took place upon this subject, must be fresh in the memory of the Lord Chancellor and Mr. Perceval. If these sums are withdrawn from the total amount of the debts recognized in 1803 abstracting also the smallest sum that can be proposed to be granted to the Prince in remuneration for Regency services, there would be no remainder, or if any it would not equal in amount to a quarter of the Prince's Exchequer income.

This detail has been entered into in answer to the Minute of Mr. Perceval's interview with Mr. Adam, and in explanation of facts which appear to have been misunderstood by Mr. Perceval, to prove that with encreased calls upon the Prince for public, private, and family largesses—without means of reducing his Establishment below that of splendid privacy no exceeding beyond three months over the letter of the Act would have existed had not these events taken place—in the one instance the public directly benefitted by the reduction of the Exchequer allowance from £120,000 to £108,000, in the other, indirectly by the Prince charging himself with debts which must otherwise have been thrown in the whole or in part on some public fund.

Upon this plan then, the vote intended to be proposed by Mr. Perceval for Regency services will not be necessary and by this arrangement, one vote for the specific gross sum required for the King, to be allotted in manner before stated, will alone be necessary to be proposed to Parliament and that the amount of this vote may be subject to such further reduction as may arise from the aid which the revenues of the Duchy of Lancaster as stated by Mr. Perceval, or other funds may afford (Perceval MSS.).

3277   COLONEL MCMAHON TO THE DUKE OF NORTHUMBERLAND
York House, 11 Dec. 1811
The Prince Regent being indisposed & confined to his bed by a spasmodic complaint in his arms, hands, & feet, has honor'd me with his command to make your Grace his most affectionate regards, & to acknowledge the receipt of your kind letter,[1] which nothing should possibly have prevented his Royal Highness himself from instantly replying to, but the indisposition which, for the present, precludes him the power of answering with his own pen; and H.R.Hss. could not delay for a moment longer the pleasure of conveying to your Grace the extreme happiness & satisfaction he feels in assuring your Grace of the flattering gratification he has in promising that Lord James Murray shall be one of the Lords of his Bedchamber whenever his Royal Highness's Establishment of Regent shall be formed. An infinite variety of pleasing circumstances combine to make such an appointment most highly fitting & desireable to his Royal Highness in the person of Lord James Murray; but high as all those most justly are, the greatest to H.R.Hss.'s mind is the happiness of meeting your Grace's wishes on this occasion.

The Prince Regent requests his kindest regards to the Duchess & your daughters (Alnwick MSS.).

1. No. 3267.

3278 PRINCESS SOPHIA TO THE PRINCE REGENT

From the Nunnery, No. 3, Castle Court, 12 Dec. [1811]

As I know how difficult it is to you, my ever dearest brother, to read my scrawls, I am determined to send you a few lines in a legible hand, trusting to your kindness to forgive my troubling you at this busy time, but my heart overflows with gratitude for all your noble & generous intentions towards us which, should you succeed in or not, our gratitude *must be the same.* The only things that *frets* & worries me is the idea that your kindness to *four old cats* may cause you any *désagrémens* with the Ministers. I could forfeit everything sooner than that we should be the cause of this. How good you are to us, which, however imperfectly expressed, I feel most deeply. *Poor old wretches* as we are, a *dead weight* upon you, *old lumber* to the *country*, like *old clothes*, I wonder you do not vote for putting us in a *sack* & *drowning us* in the Thames. *Two* of us would be fine food for *the fishes*, & as to *Mimy & me*, we will take our chance together.

Thank God that you got safe to town; how vexed I am that I did not see you again before you left Oatlands. All here goes on the same, quiet days do us no good, it only shews the mind more completely gone. God bless you. (Add. Georgian 13/51)

3279 DR BAIRD TO COLONEL MCMAHON, AND AN ENCLOSURE

9 Upper Baker Street, 12 Dec. 1811

Herewith I have the honor to enclose an account showing the decline of ship diseases in his Majestys Navy from the year 1790 up to the beginning of the present year. (18898)

[Enclosure] AN ACCOUNT shewing the number of SEAMEN and MARINES annually voted by Parliament in four distinct and equal portions of War, with the number sent to HOSPITALS and HOSPITAL SHIPS on the HOME STATIONS during those periods—Vizt.

	Years	Number of SEAMEN and MARINES		
		Voted by PARLIAMENT	Sent to HOSPITALS	
	1779	70000	24226	
	1780	85000	32121	
1st PERIOD	1781	90000	23812	
Lemon juice not issued	1782	100000	22909	
	1783	110000	13577	
		455000	116645	or about 1 in 4
	1794	85000	19248	
	1795	100000	20579	
2nd PERIOD	1796	110000	16860	
Lemon juice partially	1797	120000	20544	
supplied	1798	120000	15713	
		535000	92944	about 1 in 6
	1799	120000	14608	
	1800	111538	17747	
3rd PERIOD	1801	131538	15082	
Lemon juice in general use	1804	100000	7650	
	1805	120000	8083	
		583076	63170	about 1 in 9
	1806	120000	7662	
	1807	130000	6535	
4th PERIOD	1808	130000	7630	
Lemon juice continued in	1809	130000	7971	
general use	1810	145000	9965	
		655000	39763	1 in about 16½

1st In the first five years it appears that out of 455,000 men voted for the service 116,645 were sent to hospitals and hospital ships on the Home Station, equal to about 1 man in 4.

2nd In the second period of five years when the beneficial effects of the distribution of lemon juice, partial as it then was, in the service, began to appear, it is found that out of 535,000 men voted for the service only 92,944 were sent to hospitals and hospital ships on the Home Station, equal to about 1 man in 6.

3rd In the period between 1799 and 1805, lemon juice was generally directed to be distributed in the proportion of one ounce of lemon juice to two ounces of sugar p. man p. diem, but the proportion of sugar was reduced to one ounce at Doctor Baird's recommendation of the measure to Lord St. Vincent, producing a saving in that article of £12,000 a year in the Channel Fleet alone in the year 1801, and it was to Dr Baird's recommendation of the efficacy of lemon juice as a specific in the prevention as well as cure of scurvy that it was introduced into general use. Excluding the years 1802 and 1803 considered as years of peace, out of 583,076 men voted, no more than 63,170 appear to have been sent on shore on the Home Station, equal to about 1 man in 9.

4th In the fourth period out of 655,000 men voted for the service, only 39,763 were sent to hospitals and hospital ships at home, equal to one man in about $16\frac{1}{2}$, a proportion falling short of the first period by no less a number than 128,154 men, the expense of whom, if sent to an hospital, taking the average amount of hospital charges for every man sent on shore (exclusive of all salaries and other standing expenses) at the very moderate rate of £5 a cure, would have amounted in this last period to an additional expenditure in hospital charges to no less a sum than £640,770.

Taking the total number number of men sent sick in the three last periods short of the proportion sent on shore in the first period, and which appear to have amounted to no less a number than 259,672 men, at the aforesaid very moderate calculation of £5 for the expense of every hospital case, and it will appear that the hospital expenses in Great Britain and Ireland have been less in those periods than they would have been had the proportion of sick been the same as in the first period by no less a sum than (£1,298,360): one million, two hundred and ninety eight thousand, three hundred and sixty pounds.

Whilst the great advantages of lemon juice cannot be too highly appreciated in relieving the Navy of a disease formerly the most destructive to seamen, yet it cannot be denied that to the great improvement in discipline begun and perfected under Lord St. Vincent the prevention of ship fever and other diseases equally fatal is to be ascribed. (18899–900)

3280   SAMUEL PEPYS COCKERELL TO MAJOR–GENERAL T. H. TURNER

Saville Row, 12 Dec. 1811

Having troubled you in August last with the particulars of a discovery of statues in the Island of Ægina which through your obliging communication was honored with the Prince Regent's particular attention, & was attended with so fortunate a result to my son & others of his company; I beg leave again to communicate the further accts. which I have received concerning them, and to lay before his Royal Highness the enclosed sketches of the Marbles in the state they were discovered, which will give some idea of the heroic character of the sculptures.

It appears from my son's letters dated in August from Zante, that having very great apprehensions of interruption from the Turks to their removal from Athens, the gentlemen concerned had the address to convey them privately from thence to Zante; and not having then any idea of the very gracious patronage bestowed upon them here, or of the prompt & decisive measures adopted by the Prince Regent's command for their conveyance to England, the discoverers had made an arrangement for their continuance at Zante for fifteen months, and had united the mutilated parts, and they now form a splendid collection.

I have no doubt that it would be known at Malta that the statues were so removed and that the Topaze would in consequence proceed to Zante instead of Athens; and I presume the parties interested in them will readily embrace the arrangement which has been made here for bringing them to England, so that they may be expected to arrive in a few weeks.[1]

I presume to request that you will have the goodness to return the sketches to me, being the only copies I have of them. (18901–2)

3281   WILLIAM ADAM TO SPENCER PERCEVAL, AND AN ENCLOSURE

York House, 3.30 p.m., 12 Dec. 1811

Your letter found me here—and I have received the Prince's commands to whom I have had the honour to read it, to say that his Royal Highness does not think that the present position of the business requires that his Royal Highness should give me any farther directions upon that part of the subject, especially as H.R.H. has commanded me to convey to you a plan which he conceives supercedes every difficulty, Parliamentary and other, and which consequently must bring this matter to conclusion.

A plan which is meant to supercede what his Royal Highness read to you on Tuesday, and which I afterwards transmitted by his command—

1. 'News of the arrival of the *Topaze* frigate at Malta, with the statues lately dug up at Ægina' (Colchester, ii. 353 [11 January 1812]).

which places the only vote required upon its proper ground—by being a vote for his Majesty's service—and limits that to a sum, in point of annual amount, the same with that which you proposed to both as a Privy Purse for the Prince Regent—and at the same time embraces the object which his Royal Highness has so much at heart for the Queen and the Princesses —while it secures the means of discharging the obligations on his Royal Highness as Prince of Wales, and after all making a considerable contri- bution from his income to the Civil List revenue—in retribution of what will be taken away for the purpose of providing for his Majesty, the Queen and the Princesses.

If (as will appear from the paper) the sum of £45,500 is sufficient as a contribution from the Prince to the Civil List—there will be no necessity to vote anything for the services of this year of Regency. But if it is thought requisite to add to that contribution, then it will be necessary to vote a suitable sum for those services, to be applied in satisfaction of claims which must otherwise be diminished by instalments —as specified in the paper.

It is farther proposed but not stated in the paper (because it is matter of private arrangement with the departments of the Household) that such things as are required by each department of the Household should, where the Prince is provided with the article, be taken from his Royal Highness at its just value—the sum paid by the department to be applied in the payment of claims upon the Prince of Wales of a similar nature. (Perceval MSS.)

[Enclosure] PLAN SENT BY MR. ADAM ON 12 DECEMBER

The sum required [according to the intention of the Prince Regent]—for the King—the Queen and the Princesses—is £196,000 a year.

His Royal Highness proposes, instead of the manner suggested in the paper, which he delivered himself to Mr. Perceval on Tuesday last, that this sum should be provided for as follows—

To vote for the King £60,000 a year—to be applied to the payment of the pensions on his Privy Purse [the result of the bounty of a long reign] and to provide for the expence of medical attendance on his Majesty.

To take from the Duchy of Lancaster £10,000 a yr., from the Civil List £126,000. These sums making a total of £196,000 to be allotted in the manner proposed by H.R.H. in his paper delivered on Tuesday— viz: to his Majesty £110,000—to the Queen £50,000—to the Princesses £36,000.

To replace the sum to the Civil List—there would be the Prince's Exchequer income of £108,000, the Duchy of Cornwall £13,000—the property tax, to be released as to the Prince's Exchequer income—£12,000—rent, taxes, rates & insurance not to be paid for the King's Palace or Carlton House any more than for the Queen's Palace or St. James's—£4500. These sums together making £137,500 replace the Civil List advance and leave a balance over of £11,500.

But the obligations upon the Prince of Wales require that there should be applied of this sum of £137,500—the following sums—to the Princess 17,000; to her Royal Highness's creditors 10,000; to the appropriation made by the Prince to liquidate claims upon his Royal Highness £30,000; to arrange other claims—£35,000 more than has yet been set apart (viz. £20,000 for the claims in England—£15,000 for those of the Landgrave); these sums, amounting to £92,000, would leave £45,500 of the sum of £137,500 unapplied. This it is proposed to pay over regularly to the Civil List, as a sum to be administered in the general & regular course of that portion of the Civil List revenue, which is applied in payment of Household expences & Establishment, which will now be kept up for the Regent.

If the contribution of £45,500 from the Prince's Fund to the Civil List Fund is thought insufficient—then that sum may be augmented to £65,500 by paying thereto the sum of £20,000 (viz. that proposed to liquidate claims in England to the Civil List)—and voting for this year of services, as Regent, a proper sum for the discharge of that duty, which sum would go so far in liquidating claims in England, that it would be easy to settle the remainder by means of the £10,000 a year now engaged in paying off the debts of the Princess of Wales.

In one view and by one arrangement the Civil List would be abridged £80,500 of its annual amount—in the other to the extent of £60,500.

According to this plan the Prince Regent's Privy Purse will be derived from the Civil List (Perceval MSS.).

3282   OUTLINE OF A PLAN FOR THE SETTLEMENT OF THE REGENCY

No. 1 *Memorandum drawn up in consequence of a conversation with the Prince Regent at Oatlands, 28 Nov. 1811*
His Majesty to be secured by recital and enactment in restoration to his authority, and all that belongs to the Royal Power and Civil List precisely as it has been enjoyed by the most effectual, the most simple and most public mode—The Establishment to be formed upon the following plan and principle, which keeps the present Constitution of the Monarchy entire and perfect—so that when the Royal power should revert by complete recovery to the King, all the parties would be restored to their

proper place; the Queen and Princesses be again under the King, and the Prince would again receive his income as Prince of Wales.

1st   His Majesty to have an ample Establishment for his present condition and suited to his most illustrious rank—viz.

A Grand Master of the Household

A Deputy to the Grand Master

Eight Equerries to be called Gentlemen of the Household attendant upon the King as there would would [sic] be no Equerry duty to discharge.

All these officers with full and ample salaries.

The fully complement of Pages

Do. of footmen

Do. of stable people

The stables to consist of two sets of horses, proportionable carriages and saddle horses for grooms & servants

A kitchen &c ample & suitable for his Majesty and for the Establishment.

2nd   The Queen to be on the Establishment of a Dowager Queen.

The Princesses to be put on an independent Establishment such as would suit them on the decease of the Crown.

The Prince Regent to have the full enjoyment of the entire amount of the Civil List revenue, and the whole state, dignity and place of the person exercising the Sovereign power.

The effect of this will be to disturb nothing of the system of the Royal Establishment, but suspend the income which the Prince receives from the Exchequer. This will probably cover or nearly cover the new Establishment to the King, Queen and Princesses, taking into the account of these Establishments what the Queen and Princesses now receive.

The obligations upon the Prince's income of Prince of Wales leads to details which the Prince Regent leaves to be discussed by his own Chancellor Mr Adam, who is alone acquainted with them, and who will enter upon that part of the business with Mr Perceval, and will likewise communicate with him upon the whole subject.[1] (18903–4)

No. 2   HEADS OF GENERAL OBJECTIONS TO MR. PERCEVAL'S PAPER

1st   The appropriation of a small portion of his Majesty's Household consisting of officers of subordinate rank must by the comparison excite a feeling of inferiority.

2nd   The Establishment which has been uniformly considered as necessary to the person exercising the Royal authority cannot be

1. This plan was sent to Perceval on 4 December.

Henry Petty-Fitzmaurice,
3rd Marquess of Lansdowne

by H. Walton, 1806

Henry Temple, 3rd Viscount
Palmerston, at the age of
eighteen; a water-colour by
Thomas Heaphy, 1802

The West Front
from *The Royal Pavilion at Brighton* by John Nash, 1827

The Banqueting Room
from *The Royal Pavilion at Brighton* by John Nash, 1827

maintained by the Regent upon the fund proposed to be granted to him.

3rd   The detailed quotations of the amount & fitness of the expenditure must according to the outline of Mr Perceval come repeatedly under the discussion of Parliament, a circumstance which has always been particularly obnoxious to his Majesty, and must be injurious to the interests of the Crown.

4th   The retention by the Prince Regent of his income from the Exchequer accompanyd with the suggestion as to its application holds out to the public one course of expenditure, when in fact, another is intended, and it is necessary further to observe that the addition of a Privy Purse to the amount proposed will not be sufficient to answer all the objects of applications direct & indirect.

5th   There being no certain or fixed appropritures [*sic*] of the income, according to the different heads of expenditure, it is not easy to ascertain such reasonable arrangements as will direct what sum ought to be applied to each.

6th   The Queen appears to be placed in a very embarrassing situation by being to share in or to be maintained out of the fund allotted for the King's Establishment, and by having the superintendance and direction of that common fund, together with the care & custody of the King's person.

Her majesty will thereby find it difficult to regulate her own expenditure from an apprehension that it may encroach upon the fund as applicable to the King.

The Prince Regent has in addition to the foregoing general observations, made some marginal remarks upon Mr Perceval's paper, and in addition to a sketch drawn up before he received that paper (which sketch he now transmits) adds another, in which he endeavours to point out more at large

1st   What he conceives to be consistent with the true dignity and real comfort of the King, and at the same time free from any comparison which might beget a sense of inferiority.

2nd   He attempts to shew what may enable the Regent to maintain the full Royal Establishment, calculated to give effect to the exercise of the Royal authority, by means of the state & splendour which has always belonged to it.

3rd   A further object is to have the different allowances estimated so as to prevent Parliamentary discussions on the details of management, the danger of which it is not necessary here to repeat.

4th   To avoid the application of the funds to any but their specified & avowed purposes is a main object of the Prince Regent's outline, for which reason and to render that part of the case more distinct, he has in a separate paper suggested the means of supplying the demands upon him as Prince of Wales from funds arising out of his rights in that character.

5th To secure regularity of expenditure by fixed appropriations and certain given funds made applicable to such distinct object, has likewise engaged his particular attention.

6th It has been a principal consideration with him to secure to the Queen the utmost facility, and the most unembarrassed means, of regulating what belongs to her Majesty's situation in discharging the anxious duties attached to the care and custody of the King's person, to relieve her Majesty therefore from the possibility of imputation which must destroy her comfort if the expenditure on account of his Majesty and the Queen were drawn from the same fund. He earnestly proposes that they should form distinct appropriations. (18905–6).

No. 3 *Outline of a plan for the regulation of the Civil List, drawn up by the Prince Regent, subsequent to the rect. of Mr. Perceval's paper.*

Outline of a plan for the regulation of the Civil List, and for the Establishment of the Royal Family under the present circumstances, transmitted by the Prince Regent to Mr. Perceval.

It is proposed to recite & enact in the most unequivocal terms his Majesty's return to Regal authority when he shall be capable of discharging its duties, and to provide the most solemn, the simplest and most public mode of declaring his Majesty's restoration to that capacity, with the clearest understanding that his Majesty is entitled, in the first instance, to have his provision made out of the Civil List revenue.

It is proposed that a sum should be directed to be taken from that revenue, upon such full and ample estimate as will cover whatever expenditure may be necessary for the dignity & comfort of his Majesty.

That this sum should be paid quarterly to the great officer who shall be placed at the head of the King's family.

That the Household of the King during his Majesty's continuance in his present situation should not be formed by withdrawing a portion of the Establishment of the Crown because that mode of forming the King's Establishment would produce contending & inconsistent duties and create confusion in accounting, & seems irreconcilable to the system of the Civil List as regulated by Act of Parliament.

N.B. There are a variety of other objections to this part of Mr Perceval's plan some of which are stated in the observations on his Memorandum.

His Majesty's family should consist of persons to be selected from those who are known to have been honoured with his Majesty's regard, and whom he would therefore wish to find near his person.

The Household thus established to be under the controul, management & direction of the Queen, who, as now, should have the care & custody of the King's person, and the regulation of all the Establishment which has relation thereto with a Council, the first great officer of the King's Household to be one of that Council.

The Household to be composed as follows:

The King's Lord High Stewart [sic] and
Deputy High Stewart
Four Lords attendant
Four Gentlemen attendant
Six Equerries to be called Gentlemen attendants, one of this number to be Secretary to the Establishment. Two of the Gentlemen attendants to be always in waiting at the Palace where the King may reside.

The detailed part of the Establishment is stated in an Appendix from which estimates may be made with accuracy and the sums required are proposed to be specifically appropriated to their respective purposes. The amount of the permanent charges on the King's Privy Purse likewise to be ascertained.

All the above mentioned sums to be issued to the principal officer of the King's Household under their distinct heads who shall in the same manner account for their expenditure in the proper Office.

An annual sum to be granted to the Queen for the support of her Majesty, in a style of splendour & dignity suited to her illustrious rank.

This may be properly measured by her Majesty's allowance of jointure as fixed by Act of Parliament.

Her Majesty to administer this by her own establishment of officers & servants.

The whole & full amount of the sums thus to be withdrawn from the Civil List, to be made good to that revenue, and when thus reinbursed [sic] & made up to its full amount to be given to the Prince Regent as essential to the proper discharge of the duties of Soverignty [sic].

The provisions for the Princesses not to rest as hitherto upon allowances from the King & Queen but to be placed on the footing on which they are established by Act of Parliament on the demise of the Crown, with such an addition as the lapse of thirty years & the difference of the times may make adviseable.

This completes the system by placing the Establishment for the King in every respect suited to the present calamitous circumstances, and ensure to his Majesty the being served by officers high in rank and ample in number, without breaking in upon that order of State office which has been established to give dignity to the Soverign authority, or disturbing in any respect the regular administration of the Civil List revenue.

By this system the Prince Regent's income from the Exchequer as Prince of Wales would [be] sunk during the continuance of the Regency and would indemnify the public for the advance to make the revenue of the Civil List & Compl. [*sic*] By this arrangement too, mixing the Prince of Wales's income with the Prince Regent's in his Sovereign character would be avoided and at the same time no confusion would arise from having a portion of the Prince Regent's expenditure as Regent subjected to the Act of Parliament which regulates the expenditure of his income as Prince of Wales.

If it shall please Providence to restore his Majesty to health and to a capacity again to resume the regal functions and duties of his station, all these provisions & regulations will cease of themselves, his Majesty will again enjoy the full revenue of the Civil List, the Queen, the Princesses will be replaced in their situation under his Majesty, & the Prince Regent will return to his income as Prince of Wales.

APPENDIX

The full compliment of Pages

A sufficient number of servants of all descriptions

Two setts of horses

A proper number of carriages

A proper table for the Gentlemen of his Majesty's family who might be permitted to have each day at their table a certain number of guests, as well as the physicians & medical gentlemen in attendance on the King.

The great officers of the family would likewise be entertained there when business might require their presence.

There should likewise be the means to provide everything suitable & handsome for a table for his Majesty.

A sufficient number of physicians.

A sufficient number of other medical attendants. (18907–10)

3283 MEMORANDUM

Memdm. of certain heads of arrangements for his Majesty's Household to be submitted to the view and consideration of H.R.H. the Prince Regent for the purpose of receiving H.R.H.'s suggestions (if H.R.H.

262

should be graciously pleased to communicate the same) previous to such arrangements being finally discussed and considered by his confidential servants. The principles on which Mr. Perceval humbly submits the following arrangements are

1. That his Majesty is entitled in the first instance to have such provisions made for him out of the Civil List which was granted by Parliament to his Majesty for his life in exchange for his hereditary revenues, as may be sufficient for securing to his Majesty all the comforts and dignity which are compatible with his present calamitous situation.

The Civil List being the fund out of which any provision for his Majesty should be made is acceded to in the most ample sense in which that proposition is capable of being stated, and it does not seem that it could have been doubted at any time by any person who respected his Majesty and his rights, or who knew the nature of that fund.

2. That subject to such charge and deduction as may be necessary for the above purposes, the whole remainder of the Civil List as enjoyed by his Majesty should accompany the exercise of the royal power and authority and devolve on H.R.H. the Prince Regent.

This proposition does not admit of any doubt, nor does the next. The three propositions amount to this and no more, vizt., that his Majesty's provision should be made from that part of the public income called the Civil List. That what is not applied to his Majesty should be left to the Prince Regent as enjoying the full powers of Sovereign; and lastly, that what is abstracted from the Civil List to provide for the King must be supplied to the Regent from some other fund. It is not therefore upon the propositions that the question of differences arise, but upon the mode of carrying them into execution.

3. That as these charges and deductions will necessarily diminish the amount of the Civil List in the hands of H.R.H. the Prince Regent, the deficiency thereby arising should be supplied by some other means.

Under the first head it is submitted that it having been declared by the Preamble of the 13th clause of the Regency Act, that the care of his Majesty's person should be committed to the Queen, together with the sole direction of such portion of his Majesty's Household as shall be deemed requisite and suitable for the due attendance on his Majesty's sacred person, and the maintenance of his royal dignity.

The part which under the present circumstances it may be deemed necessary and proper to assign for this purpose, and to continue under her Majesty's controul, should consist of the Groom of the Stole—4 Lords of the Bedchamber—4 Grooms of Do.—the Privy Purse—the Master of the Robes—the Equiries [sic]. That the general management and controul of the whole of this arrangement should be placed under the Groom of the Stole, who would require a Secretary or some officer of that description. That the Groom of the Stole should be required and authorized to call upon the Lord Steward, the Lord Chamberlain, and the Master of the Horse for such and so many of the servants and inferior officers under their respective departments as may be necessary for the accommodation of that part of his Majesty's family and attendants, which may be in attendance on his Majesty at the Palace where he may from time to time reside, and to draw upon the several heads of those depart-

It is agreed that the sole direction should remain under the Queen, but it is not agreed that the terms of the Preamble to the thirteenth section of the Regency Act, taken according to the letter, should be the rule: but it is thought that the spirit of the Preamble should be the guide—vizt., that his Majesty should have the persons about him in sickness whom he was known to prefer when in health.

The selection of officers from the Household is objectionable on several grounds.

1st. The officers who are selected are inferior in rank, which will mark a distinction arising from the incapacity of his Majesty to govern, which appears degrading and will be felt as mortifying by his Majesty, should he be restored to a situation capable of weighing and judging of such things, though still not restored to a capacity to enable him to govern. 2nd. It seems much more dignified to have a distinct office filled by a person of great rank to discharge this high trust of superintending the King's separate Household by which all comparison between the state of the King and that of the Prince Regent is avoided.

By these means the regal state and official arrangements for the support of the Monarchy in the person of the Regent will be preserved, but if the system which pervades Mr. Perceval's memorandum is adopted, the preservation of the antient Establishment is impracticable.

ments for such money as may be required to defray the expences of such Establishment not exceeding (   ) a certain sum.

It is suggested that the blank should be filled up with a specific sum to be calculated upon estimate of the probable expence, and that any exceeding beyond that sum (if any such should occur) should not fall upon the Civil

This introduces a new system of accounting, quite inconsistent it should seem, with the Civil List regulations.

The Groom of the Stole is only First Lord of the Bedchamber, and has no character which renders him an accountant to the public or to any officer of the Household or of the State. The officers who are to supply the attendants or the money cannot account for an expenditure which they do not superintend, so that a new law must impose new duties on the Groom of the Stole, which is virtually creating a new office. There would be more dignity and propriety in doing this directly. A further effect of this system will be to defeat in a great measure the regulations connected with the Queen having the controul of all that belongs to the King's person, as the appointment of the attendants on his Majesty in the Palace where he may from time to time reside will rest with the great officers to be placed under the Prince Regent, so that in effect the great officers of the King's Household appointed by the Queen will not name the attendants on the King, but those attendants will be named by the great officers appointed by the Prince Regent.

An application to Parliament for any deficiency will bring all the particulars respecting the King's situation and the Queen's administration of the fund into discussion, like the items in the extraordinaries of the Army or of

List, but should be brought before Parliament.

It is estimated upon reference to an account of the actual amount of the salaries of the servants at Windsor and of the expences under the several departments for the year ending the 5th July last (which account is annexed to this paper) that the expences of an Establishment so framed need not exceed £100,000 pr. annum, as it is assumed that although there may be some expences to be added to this account, particularly those incurred at the Queen's House in St. James's Park, and some other articles which may not appear in the account as actually paid at Windsor: yet such deductions will of course be made from the expence of last year as will bring the whole within the compass of the above sum.

As the expences of the King's physicians must be provided for, it is thought that for that purpose the Privy Purse allowance should be continued, and put under her Majesty's disposal, subject to such annual charges as are now upon it, and also the payment of his Majesty's medical attendance.

If this fund should not be thought sufficient an addition must be made to it for that purpose either from the revenues of the Duchy of Lancaster, from the droits of Admiralty or by some distinct provision.

Under the second head, it is not any other account laid before Parliament.

Whatever relates to the estimated or conjectured amount of the sums to be taken from the Civil List, and again to be replaced for the support of the state of the Prince Regent, has so close a connection with the application of his income as Prince of Wales, that it is thought better to leave all that part of the subject to the separate paper which relates to his Royal Highness's situation as Prince of Wales.

This should not be left loose but fixed by estimate, and a separate appropriation made for it. The same observation applies to those pensions and allowances which are paid from the King's Privy Purse. The demand upon it should be ascertained and a sum should be specially appropriated from the Civil List revenue to make good that sum.

This mode of supplying the deficiency seems more exceptionable than even a direct application to Parliament, as the droits of Admiralty have become a particular subject of jealousy, dispute and investigation.

thought that any additional remark will be necessary.

Under the third head it is to be considered in what manner the deficiency occasioned in the Civil List by the provision for the King should be compensated. This may be done two ways. The simplest and easiest would be to vote a sum to the Civil List, equal to the deduction, to be applied towards supplying to the Regent the salaries for the additional Lords of the Bedchamber &c. &c. in the room of those taken for attendance on the King, and for repaying the amount of the expences incurred by the provision for his Majesty and his family. Under this arrangement it is conceived that the allowance to the Regent as Prince of Wales would be expected to cease.

The other way would be by continuing to H.R.H. his allowance as Prince of Wales.

The latter it is humbly suggested would be found preferable.

The effect of the first would be to restore indeed to the Civil List what would be taken from it for the King's use, but then the sum so restored would necessarily be appropriated to the same uses, and would not afford a Fund which would be capable of being applied in any other manner than to the expences of the departments to which it would by the very nature of the grant be assigned.

Whereas it is conceived that the allowance as Prince of Wales or such part of it as is free, might be employed in the maintenance of

This head relates peculiarly to the question arising out of the Prince of Wales's income payable at the Exchequer. It will therefore only be necessary to remark in this place that the principle of directness and simplicity seems to be wanting in the first part of Mr. Perceval's outline, and that the object he has in view of applying the income to other objects than those of the Civil List, cannot be attained without reducing the splendour which ought to accompany the Regent.

such part of H.R.H.'s Establishment as Prince of Wales, or of his expences connected with the same as H.R.H. might be desirous of providing for.

It is conceived that it will be necessary further to provide H.R.H. with a Privy Purse. It would be desirable to procure a vote of Parliament for that purpose *to the same amount as his Majesty's*.

And it is thought that the object of obtaining a vote to such an amount would be much facilitated provided the general arrangements in its other branches should not create an additional burden on the public.

It is further humbly submitted that a sum of money should be voted to H.R.H. to enable him to defray the expences which he must have incurred by the Regency— the amount of which sum is left for consideration.

With regard to her Majesty as it is understood that she has certain debts which are extremely pressing and inconvenient, it is conceived that some plan may be devised for their immediate or gradual liquidation. But Mr. Perceval, conceiving that the idea of creating a separate Establishment for her Majesty independent of his Majesty's would not be consistent with the principles on which the custody of his Majesty's person has been consigned to the Queen, and that not only on account of the increased expences but from a variety of still more important considerations, it would

The separate paper to be submitted on the subject of the income of the Prince Regent as Prince of Wales will shew that the addition here proposed of a Privy Purse equal to that of the King will not answer the purposes in view.

The custody of the King's person being vested in the Queen, and the object in view being to form a permanent Establishment, it is conceived to be more consistent with principle that there should be a separate and distinct appropriation of funds for the King and Queen, than that they should be united, because in such a case their pecuniary interests should not be blended, and the Queen should not be brought into the distressing predicament of being possibly supposed to withdraw from the comforts of the King, in providing for her domestic and personal arrangements. The

throw great additional difficulties in the way of the proposed arrangement [*sic*].

With regard to the Princesses, it is humbly conceived that it would not be prudent to embarrass this arrangement of the Household with any subject not necessarily forming a part of these discussions, but that any gracious consideration which H.R.H. may be pleased to give to the situation of their Royal Highnesses, would be much better reserved till after the new arrangements should have been carried into effect.

force of this observation is greatly encreased when it is considered that any deficiency of the fund is to be made up by application to Parliament.

What relates to the Princesses is fully and amply enforced in the separate paper or outline transmitted by the Prince Regent to Mr. Perceval. (18911–20)

3284 WILLIAM ADAM'S MEMORANDUM AS TO WHAT PASSED AT A CONFERENCE AT YORK HOUSE ON 13 DEC. [1811] [draft]

Statement of the proposal as it stood on Mr Perceval's Memorandum shewing the points which have been varied by the communications and discussions which have taken place.

Present:

H.R.H. The Prince Regent
H.R.H. The Duke of York
Mr. Perceval and Mr. Adam

Mr. Perceval having received the commands of the Prince Regent to attend H.R.H. on the subject of the pecuniary arrangements necessary to form an Establishment for the King, the Queen and the Princesses as well as for H.R.H. the Prince Regent,

The discussion took place on the last mentioned paper made out under the direction of the Prince Regent and delivered by

Mr. Adam to Mr. Perceval in the afternoon of the preceding day, as basis for the arrangement with reference to Mr. Perceval's first memorandum, and generally to all which had been the subject of communication in writing or otherwise since the matter was introduced by Mr. Perceval in the conference he had with the Prince Regent at Oatlands on the 29th Novr.

1. After a full discussion it was agreed that the sum of £60,000 a year should be proposed to be added to the Civil List to defray the Privy Purse pensions of the King, and the expence of medical attendance upon his Majesty, and that the Prince's Privy Purse like that formerly enjoyed by the King should come from the Civil List.

1. By Mr Perceval's memorandum a sum of £60,000 was proposed to be voted for a Privy Purse to the Prince Regent —and the Privy Purse which is allotted to the King out of the Civil List was proposed to be appropriated to the payment of the pensions upon the King's Privy Purse—the residue to be applied to the payment of the medical attendance upon his Majesty, and in case of any deficiency the Duchy of Lancaster or some other fund was to be resorted to.

2. It was agreed that £10,000 a year should be taken from the Duchy of Lancaster in aid of the proposed provision for the King and Queen.

2. The Duchy of Lancaster was by Mr Perceval's memorandum considered as a fund to be called in aid of deficiencies if wanted.

3. That a further sum should be taken from the Civil List and made a distinct fund, sufficient for the purpose of the King and Queen's Establishment at Windsor or such other Palace as his Majesty may reside at; but it was not finally conceded by Mr. Perceval that it was advisable to separate

3. Mr Perceval's memorandum proposes to take £100,000 from the Civil List, and to apply that sum to the Establishment at Windsor under the direction of the Queen and the management of the Groom of the Stole, who according to that Memorandum was to draw on the heads of the

the funds into one for the King's support, and another for the Queen's. It was understood to be an arrangement of a domestic nature—but it was understood as distinctly implied that the services to be performed by the application of those funds were to be separately and distinctly managed by the Establishment to be formed for the King and Queen. And that officers to be appointed to the King's Household were not to draw their services from the several Household departments remaining with the Regent. It was understood that this sum including the £60,000 to be voted as an addition to the Civil List should amount to £170,000.

departments of the Household for the services, servants and attendants required for the King.

The memorandum did not contain any additional provision for the Queen, but proposed that her Majesty's debts, suppose about £25,000, should be got from the droits of Admiralty.

The sum to be taken from the Civil List (as stated above) by Mr. Perceval's Memorandum was £100,000. The plan sent by the Prince Regent on the 13th instant was to take £126,000 from the Civil List—£10,000 from the Duchy of Lancaster and £60,000 for his Majesty by special vote—making £196,000 in which was to be included £36,000 for the Princesses. Taking off this provision for the Princesses there would remain £160,000 for the King and Queen. This Mr Perceval by his statement made to the Prince at the Conference makes £170,000.

4. It was understood that the Princesses were to continue to enjoy the income out of the Civil List which they now receive, and likewise that which they receive from the Queen; and that as soon as the Regency should be established, it was understood to be decided that the Prince Regent should communicate by Message to Parliament his desire that the Princesses should be provided in £9000 a year more from the Consolidated Fund in addition to their present income. But that this should not be mixed up now with the question of settling the

4. The Princesses were not included in Mr Perceval's memorandum—but he now adopts a provision for their Royal Highnesses varying it from the Prince's proposal—1st, as to the time of bringing it forward—2ndly, as to the fund out of which it is to be paid.

He proposed that it should be brought forward by Message to the Houses when the Regency is settled and the restrictions expired and that it should be charged on the Consolidated Fund.

271

Regency, but be so completely understood as a measure decided upon, that any Administration which H.R.H. should chuse to name to carry on the affairs of the Kingdom should consider to be a pledge.

5. It was understood that the income of the Prince of Wales was to remain with the Prince Regent, augmented by relief from the property tax and from the taxes, rates, &c. for Carlton House or by some sufficient mode to £137,000 and that the sum taken from the Civil List for the purpose of the Establishment of the King and Queen was to be so far replaced by the sum of £50,000 a year to be paid from the income of the Prince of Wales to the Civil List. That the remainder of the Prince of Wales's income was to be applied to the amount of £87,000 a year to discharge the obligations on his H.R. and upon that income.

6. That the idea suggested originally by Mr. Perceval of a sum to be voted for this year of Regency should be adopted in preference to the providing any sum (as suggested in Mr. Adam's letter) to be applied to the Prince's objects, by supplying to the departments such articles as H.R.H. might possess, and they might reserve for his service as Prince Regent.

7. It was stated by Mr. Perceval, and slightly discussed, how far taking a portion of the Household to put about the King, or the plan

5. By Mr. Perceval's memorandum there would have remained of the Prince's Exchequer income the balance over £100,000 a year, vizt. £8,000. The Duchy of Cornwall £13,000. The proposed Privy Purse to the Prince £60,000, making £81,000 charged with the Princess's income of £17000, her Royal Highness's debts £10,000, appropriation for other claims on her Royal Highness £30,000, making together £57,000, leaving £24,000 for all purposes of Privy Purse, pensions, charities &c. &c— and a further provision for the claims and arrears not yet put in liquidation.

suggested by the Prince was best. In that discussion Mr. Perceval proposed that the Groom of the Stole must be made a responsible officer, and that the Act of Parliament could also give him rank above the other officers of the Household.

Just at taking leave Mr. Perceval said that if any circumstance or particular object required that the Prince should pay less than £50,000 a year to the Civil List, suppose £40,000, that he should think the latter a very fair sum.

There was in the course of the conference a good deal said about the annual deficiency of the Civil List—that this should be made apparent so that it might not be ascribed to the Prince—And a good deal about the introduction of œconomical arrangement; neither necessary for statement here. (18929–34)

3285 THE DUKE OF NORTHUMBERLAND TO COLONEL MCMAHON

Alnwick Castle, 14 Dec. 1811

Confidential. As your letter, my dear Colonel, which I received last night, was official, I have written you an answer in the same style which may be shewn to H.R.H.

I now here acknowledge the receipt of your former letter of the 6th. You must have been surprised at the Regent's return to town after the determination he had taken to remain some time longer at Oatlands, as mentioned in your letter of the 6th. I dont at all like these spasms of which H.R.H. complains, & shall be quite uneasy till I learn they are removed. I shoud fear they were somewhat connected with gout, than which he cannot have a more cruel disorder.[1] Every word in the official

1. Princess Charlotte wrote to Mercer Elphinstone on the 18th: 'The Prince is better, & had *more sleep* last night; I have not seen Sr. Walter today but Bloomfield brought me the account,

273

letter written by his order shews the goodness of his heart, & he may rest assured I shall never forget them.

I am sorry the Queen & Princesses further Establishments are to come on just now. This will greatly increase Mr Perceval's embarrassments. He must apply to Parliament on this subject, & bringing forward such an additional charge upon the publick just at this time when, in addition to the great national demand for the war, he will have to provide a proper Establishment for the Regent, will frighten him, & probably make him very anxious to avoid these new & unexpected demands if possible. All this I shoud think very likely to bring on disagreable discussions which if possible shoud be avoided just as the Session is opening. Any change at the moment cannot fail to be attended with great inconvenience not only to the nation but to the Regent himself.

I take it for granted all power restrictions will now be taken off from the Regent, & that we shall see the Blue & Red Ribbands gracing the shoulders of those who will do credit to the two Orders, & that we shall not again see the Red Ribband bestowed on an illegitimate child,[1] contrary to the express statutes of that Order. Some years ago I mentioned to H.R.H. that I shoud sollicit him whenever he had the power, if I was alive, to call Lord Percy up to the House of Peers by our old Barony in fee as Baron Percy. I shall be much flattered to find that H.R.H. still retains this in his memory, when he has the power.[2] I trust H.R.H. will be sparing at first in his creation of new Peerages. This will give him great popularity and he will be the better able to create them afterwards without any animadversions. I hear that Lord Wellesley is gaining

I promised in my last to tell you all Sr. W. Farquar confided to me, & as it is upon so interesting a personal subject I thought I would do what you would wish & what my feelings dictated —communicate the same to you. The fact was this, when Sr. Walter left him at Oatlands he was to take some medicine, wh. however he did not do & *would not* [*in spite of*] *all that could be said* to him; the consequence was that a stoppage took place wh. lasted for 4 or 5 days & began to have those pains & that sort of sickness that is the forerunner of an inflammation. As I mentioned to you before, the old *doctor* was sent for instantly, & upon his arrival *insisted positively* upon an immense dose of castor oil being taken, wh. he did *at last*, but not till after much persuasion. He was after that, I *may say*, very obstinate & *would* come to town when he was totally unfit to be moved, & when the great thing was to keep him quiet. However he arrived as you know, & has been *very weak* & poorly since, suffering extreme pain from his elbows to hands, from the *constant* resting upon them for 26 days, & he feels much pain in using his hands. They therefore give him what they do for the "tic douloureux", *hemlock*, & this he takes a great quantity of mixed in laudanum & in pills, wh. has already eased him. They are not now afraid of giving it him as it is the only thing for him to sleep, & besides he takes medicine, so there is not the same danger likely to occur again; but Sr. Walter says tho' all danger is over, yet he *cannot* declare when he will be *quite recovered*, as he has retarded it himself so much owing to his playing with his constitution. His frame however is quite restored to its former good state, & things look much more favorable' (Bowood MSS.).

1. Sir William Carr Beresford. K.B., October 1810.

2. See Nos. 2134*n*., 2139 (v. 334, 338).

much of H.R.H.'s confidence. I know very little of that noble Marquis, & hope if this is true that he may be a person of great abilities, honour and one of decisive character. Our foolish half measures will I fear draw on a war with America, which I know woud have been avoided had proper determined measures been pursued I know the character & disposition of the Americans as well, or perhaps better than anybody, having had much to do with them, at the very first begining of the Rebellion, & I am certain half measures will never succeed where they are concerned. Buonaparte has given you a lesson how to treat them. An Admiral, with 12 sail of the line, was the only proper Embassador to have sent there in the begining, & I will answer for it everything woud have been settled the moment he appeared, without the least danger of any war.

We all unite in compliments to you & Mrs Mac-Mahon. Tomorrow Ld Algernon being 19, will pass for a Lieutenant.[1] God however only knows when he will get a Lt.'s commission, Mr. Yorke being very much disinclined to oblige me. (18954–5)

3286   SIR CHARLES HASTINGS[2] TO COLONEL MCMAHON

Willesley Hall, Atherstone, 16 Dec. 1811

Have the goodness to present to my Royal master and Sovereign the Prince Regent (if I may so presume to call him) my humble duty, and respectfully assure him that he has not bestowed the 12th Infy. to one ignorant of its value. For, tho' seemingly living quietly in the country I have not been idle about the Regt. I have had my Lt. Col. here to consult, got him leave to superintend the depot, and discipline the detachment at Maldon, recalled all the scattered offrs. who had been recruiting these two or three years to little or no purpose, and have so new organized the whole system as to leave me no doubt but I shall be able to furnish a sufficient number of recruits thoroughly disciplined, to complete the Regt. when it comes home, thereby entitling it to be called again the old Steady Twelfth. Several militia regts. have promised us a great number of recruits, and the old spirit of the corps seems to have revived itself amongst the detachment at Maldon, for I have received

1. Lord Algernon Percy (1792–1865), the Duke's second surviving son, succeeded his brother as 4th Duke on 11 February 1847. Created Baron Prudhoe, 27 November 1816. His date of birth is given as 15 December (Burke); as the 19th (G.E.C.). Lieutenant, 1812; Commander, 1814; Captain, 1815; Rear-Admiral, 1850; First Lord of the Admiralty, February-December 1852.

2. See No. 1350.

several letters from the Field Offrs. and Capts., assuring me of their zeal to promote the good old cause. (18957–8)

3287 MRS JORDAN TO [?] COLONEL MCMAHON
Bushy, Monday [*16 Dec. 1811*]
I yesterday saw Mr Adam—and you may imagine my surprise—when he declared he knew nothing of the proposed *arrangement* or even of the Duke's wish that the children should live with me 'till they attained the age of 17. He had seen the Duke *the Thursday before.* All this, my dear Sir, you will allow must appear strange to one who has acted so fairly and openly as I have done. If they will *decidedly* say they cannot meet my fair demands—I should make up my mind on the subject and do the best I could for myself and children, but this is trifling most cruelly with my feelings and unfortunate situation. I now begin to feel the value of the advice of not quitting Bushy till something decided is done—but as a friend to both parties, you will, I am sure, feel the *advantage* of an early *decision* in consequence of our last conversation, I told all those who are anxious about me that it was finally settled; judge then of my disappointment.

Mr Adam had not *seen* or *heard* of MY statement. (42507–8)

3288 THE DUKE OF YORK TO THE PRINCE REGENT, AND AN ENCLOSURE
Horse Guards, 6.45 p.m., 18 Dec. 1811
I have this instant received the enclosed and lose no time in transmitting it to you. (44254)

[Enclosure] THE REV. CYRIL JACKSON[1] TO THE DUKE OF YORK
Felpham, 8.30 a.m., Wednesday morning [*18 Dec. 1811*]
Yr. R.H.'s letter has just reached Felpham.

I have no doubt of my brother's[2] liking Oxford because I know that

1. He had resigned the Deanery of Christ Church in 1809 and retired to the Manor House at Felpham, near Bognor.

2. William Jackson (1751–1815). Prebendary of Southwell, 1780; of York, 1783; of Bath and Wells, 1792. Regius Professor of Greek at Oxford, 1783; Dean of Bath and Wells, 1799; Bishop of Oxford, February 1812 (nominated 30 December 1811).

on a former illness of the poor Bishop,[1] before the time of the Regency, he did actually write to Mr. Ryder[2] to beg that he wd. mention his wishes to Mr. P.[3] & forward them, but the recovery prevented, I believe, Mr. R. from saying anything on the subject.

When the Regent first mentioned to me his gracious intentions, I remember certainly to have spoke en badinant of Llandaff as the one that had the least business to do & wd. leave a person most at liberty, but next to that I do not know whether there be any better in those respects than Oxford.

So much, Sir, it seemed right that I shd. say upon the subject & send it back without the least delay by express, and I add therefore at present not one word more. Everything else that I feel I will reserve for the post. I know that both the Regent & yourself will give me credit for it till then. (44255)

3289   CHARLES FOX CRESPIGNY[4] TO COLONEL MCMAHON
Aldborough, 18 Dec. 1811
As I find that the middle of next month will be the time most convenient to the greatest number of my distant friends to attend at Aldborough I will thank you to have the writ for the seat you have vacated moved for as soon as possible after the ensuing meeting of Parliament.

I beg leave to observe that the last Act[5] having made it ineligible to employ agents or bankers in any arrangements concerning elections I shall be under the necessity of receiving from you alone the sum necessary to defray the expences of your next return.

I will have the honor of waiting on you for that purpose about the time of the meeting of Parliament. (18962)

1. Charles Moss (1763–1811), Bishop of Oxford, 1807–11, died 16 December 1811.

2. Richard Ryder had been Home Secretary since 1 November 1809.

3. Perceval.

4. His family had been patrons of Aldborough for over forty years. For McMahon's re-election, see No. 3267n., and also *Letters of George IV*, i, 40.

5. Curwen's Act, 1809.

Downing St., Thursday evening, 19 Dec. 1811

Mr. Perceval presents his humble duty to your Royal Highness, and has the honor to transmit to your Royal Highness the statement of a plan for the Royal Household under the unrestricted Regency which has been digested by Mr. Perceval and his colleagues after his having laid before them all the papers which have passed upon this subject,[1] as well between your R. Highness & Mr. Perceval as between Mr. Adam & Mr. Perceval, together with the substance and result of the conversation with which your R. Highness was graciously pleased to honor Mr. Perceval upon it in the last week. Mr. Perceval, conceiving that your Royal Highness may wish to see him, and may require some explanation upon the plan, will be happy to wait upon your R. Highness for that purpose tomorrow[2] (Blair Adam MSS. and Perceval MSS. (draft)).

1. Ryder had written to his brother, Lord Harrowby, on the 17th: 'Thornton has written to say that negotiation [i.e. with Sweden] is broken off and that he has been civilly desired to go away. He is now on board the *Victory*. [No. 3232*n*.] Ld. Wellesley was to go to York House with the contents of these dispatches. Yorke was too busy to leave the Admiralty. The remainder of the Cabinet met and approved of Perceval's paper' (Harrowby MSS.).

2. 'Mr Perceval has the satisfaction to inform your Royal Highness that the plan as now transmitted has received the sanction of the unanimous approbation of all your Royal Highness's confidential servants.' This sentence, at the end of Perceval's draft, was scored through in pencil. Also, at the head of the draft, the following was added in pencil: 'Add clause about Princesses.'

Ryder's letter to his brother, Saturday the 21st, explains the omission of the last sentence of Perceval's letter to the Regent: 'At the Council on Wednesday Perceval received back from Wellesley the paper upon the Regency which he had sent him . . . with a private letter from W. stating that he could not agree to the plan, that he thought the Prince ought to have 150,000 instead of 100,000 for Regency services . . . but that he did not wish to dissent hereafter from what appeared to be settled before it; . . . that he should not notice on any occasion hereafter that disagreement, but only wished Perceval to communicate that letter to the Prince. Perceval, who was to have laid the plan before the Prince at an audience after the Council, determined on receiving that, to summon the Cabinet next day, that we might understand what that meant, as it had been before taken for granted, from W. making no objection, that he agreed to the plan and had waived his objection, and at all events that if he dissented the dissent should not be communicated in a manner so strong as a private letter. By the by, the whole of us have but one opinion that that was a most shabby proceeding of the Grand Lama. The next day I was in bed with a headache, but I find from Perceval, Bathurst and Liverpool that the private letter was withdrawn by Wy. and the word "unanimous" struck out of Perceval's statement . . . On the whole it went off well though they tell me that Yorke was very near letting off against the Lama.

'Pl. has been with the Prince today and the whole arrangement for the Regency is settled with him as we would wish. The Prince wished us to reconsider the question of £100,000 or £150,000 for Regency services but yielded to Pl.'s persevering obstinacy that it was in vain to rediscuss it. But you will be glad to hear that the Prince said he would still return the £50,000 instead of the £45,000 to the Civil List and thus does not take all we had offered. This is creditable and Adam says it is now all as it should be.

3291 COLONEL MCMAHON TO THE DUKE OF NORTHUMBERLAND

Carlton House, 19 Dec. 1811

Private. I enclose for your Grace's confidential perusal three plans or projets of a Civil List Establishment, which have been convers'd upon by the Prince Regent and Mr. Perceval, but the last of which has only nearly approximated a mutual understanding. It is the wish of Ministers to agree to some plan which may be made preparative in Parliament to the extinction of the Restrictions; however, the Prince is not very sanguine whether any arrangement of a Civil List Establishment shall either precede or follow their expiration.

I have great joy in telling your Grace that I had the honor to lay your *ostensible* letter before H.R.Hss. who was delighted with it & has kept it, and H.R.Hss. has commanded me to make your Grace his love and to assure you that all his pains & aches are gradually & quickly subsiding, that he can lay his whole foot to the ground, & is quite well in general health[1] (Alnwick MSS.).

3292 THE EARL OF LIVERPOOL TO THE PRINCE REGENT

Fife House, 20 Dec. 1811

Lord Liverpool has the honour to acquaint your Royal Highness that in consequence of your Royal Highness's permission he has had a conversation with Mr Percival respecting Lord Minto, and Mr Percival agrees with Lord Liverpool in opinion that the compleat success which has attended all the measures which have been so judiciously adopted by the Govr.-Genl. of India for extinguishing the remains of the French power in that quarter, appear to give his Lordship a fair claim to some mark of your royal favour, and that conferring upon Lord Minto an additional step in the Peerage by creating him a Viscount (as soon as the restrictions upon the Regency shall have expired) may be considered as

'R[ichard] W[ellesle]y is to come to the Treasury but this was not acceded to till Ld. W. had taken the Prince's pleasure. So many points in the Foreign Department remain undecided that it is determined the Grand Lama is to have Cabts. every day that we may be prepared with answer in Parlt. to the questions which are likely to be put very soon after the meeting. They are endless and to many of them no satisfactory answer can be given. Bathurst advises and is wholly delighted with that plan, because he says it will prove to the Lama his own utter inefficiency and that he also grows frightened when Parlt. meets (Harrowby MSS. A decoded cypher letter).

1. Princess Charlotte said on the 20th, referring to her father's health: 'The spasms have been very violent and his hands continue still very weak, but his left is rather stronger, however. He is not yet able to sign papers' (Bowood MSS.).

under all the circumstances of the case the most adviseable mode of effecting the purpose.

Lord Liverpool humbly therefore submits to your Royal Highness whether you will be graciously pleased to permit him to inform Lord Minto that as soon as the restrictions on the Regency have ceased it is your Royal Highnesses intention as a mark of the sense which you entertain of his publick services, to confer upon him the rank of a Viscount of the United Kingdom.[1] (18966–7)

3293 THE MARQUESS WELLESLEY TO THE PRINCE REGENT
Apsley House, 21 Dec. 1811
Lord Wellesley has the honor to submit to your Royal Highness a letter[2] received from Colonel Macleod, proposing to entertain Lucien Bonaparté at Cheltenham. It is unnecessary to state to your Royal Highness the impropriety of this request & the impossibility of granting it without great public inconvenience.

With these sentiments Lord Wellesley hopes that your Royal Highness will be graciously pleased to approve the inclosed draft of an answer to Colonel Macleod.

It is humbly requested that your Royal Highness will direct this box to be returned as soon as possible in order that the answer may be dispatched today. (18969)

3294 COLONEL MCMAHON TO THE DUKE OF NORTHUMBERLAND, AND A REPLY
Carlton House,[3] 21 Dec. 1811
Most Private. I have great delight in coming to the knowledge (without being empower'd to impart it) that immediately on the expiration of the Restrictions it is the Prince Regent's determination to call up Earl Percy

1. It was not until 24 February 1813 that Lord Minto was created, not a Viscount, but an Earl.

2. Missing.

3. Princess Charlotte wrote on the 21st: 'The Prince had not quite so good a night the night before last, but he went over Carlton House and I understand was not much fatigued. He goes into it today, I fancy, his own rooms not being the least affected with paint, and the rest of the house very little' (Bowood MSS.). And on the 23rd: 'The Prince has got into Carlton House, but since his establishing himself there I have not heard one word about him' (ibid.).

280

to the House of Lords by your Grace's old family Barony of Percy, and that I have reason to believe this step will lead in such Peerages (not many) as his Royal Highness may be induced to create. I have great happiness in assuring your Grace the *P.R.* is nearly completely well, and that we have been all this day in the act of removing official boxes, State papers &c. &c. &c. from York House to Carlton House, which has hitherto kept us & still keeps us in the greatest hurry & confusion imaginable, & from the last ring of the bell forces me to conclude with paying my most respectful regards [etc.][1] (Alnwick MSS.).

FROM THE DUKE OF NORTHUMBERLAND
Alnwick Castle, 21 Dec. 1811

I shoud not have troubled you with this letter merely to have thanked you for yours of the 16th containing the good news of the capture of Batavia, in which no man can rejoice more than myself. But having seen in the newspaper that the Regent had not removed from York House into Carlton House at the time he intended, in consequence of H.R.H. having had a return of the spasms in his arms, I shall not be easy till I hear from you that either there was no foundation for the paragraph or that his Royal Highness's spasms have entirely left him. I am sure, my dear Colonel, you will excuse the trouble I give you on this occasion, & attribute it to its true cause, the anxiety which my attachment to the Regent must naturally occasion me whenever I hear that he is any way indisposed.

I am truly happy to learn that our Aldborough friend is at last willing to fullfill that agreement by which, as I have always acted up to it, he indisputably ought to look upon himself as bound. Add to all this, that the breach of the agreement just at this time coud not but be looked

1. The Duke wrote to his friend Lord Strangford on the 27th: 'I hear W[e]ll[esle]y wants to go again to India, being over head and ears in debt, but the Directory will not agree to it. I should think that the Regent may possibly introduce two or three of his particular friends into the Administration, and that will be all. The Prince has plenty to give away when the restrictions are taken off—3 Garters—a Lord Chamb.—together with Bishopricks, &c. H.R.H. has been particularly kind to me. Lord James Murray, my son-in-law, is to be one of the Lords of his Bedchamber, and I have some reason to believe H.R.H. intends calling Lord Percy up to the House of Lords: this last unsolicited, nor have I heard it directly from the Prince himself. The Lords Grey and Grenville are certainly not such favorites as they have supposed themselves to be, having displeased H.R.H. very much by their conduct towards him on the first establishment of the Regency. New establishments must be formed for the King, Queen and Princesses as well as the Regent, and it was imagined these woud produce discussions which might possible [*sic*] shake the present Cabinet, but I believe these are now all adjusted and settled' (Alnwick MSS.).

upon as a marked piece of disrespect to the Regent, who, when he coud command a seat from the Treasury for his Secretary, was willing to permit him to accept of it as a favour done him by Mr. Crespigny. Some people however are not only inclined to be uncivil but are even blind to their own interest.

I had yesterday a letter from the Prince of Brazil filled with expressions of kindness similar to those with which I am honoured from our Regent. I find he still feels sore at the same compliment not having been paid him which he paid to this Court when he appointed Souza Embassador & which he understood had been promised thro' Mr. Canning, who was then Secretary of State for the Foreign Department. He fully acquits H.R.H. the Regent, in consequence of his conviction of the great difficulty in which H.R.H. was placed after Lord Wellesley had informed him of his Majesty's determination; but he by no means thinks he has been properly treated by the Administration, who he seems to imagine have deceived him. Princes of the second order take these kind of things more to heart than those of the first order, as they always suppose they were intended purposely to mark their inferiority. H.R.H. however does not desire me to mention this to the Regent, & therefore I shall say nothing about it, only I can perceive he is a good deal hurt at it, & probably the more so from what has happened with respect to Mr Wellesley's new dignity to the Regency in Spain.[1]

I am sorry to learn that Ld. W. & Sr. W. C. B—[2] do not at all agree, & that they complain mutually of each other.

I will trouble you no longer, my dear my Colonel [sic], but to desire you to offer to H.R.H. the compliments of the season, together with my most humble duty. (18974–5)

3295 SPENCER PERCEVAL TO THE PRINCE REGENT
Downg. St., 22 Dec. 1811
Mr. Perceval returns to your R.H. the copy of his paper respecting the Household arrangement, after having made two marginal notes upon it in consequence of what passed at his Audience with your R. Highness at York House yesterday—together with a copy of the same prepared by your R.H.'s commands for her Majesty. (18976)

1. See No. 3190.

2. Sir William Carr Beresford, who had been sent out to reorganise the Portuguese army. Wellington was far from satisfied with the way in which he had commanded at the battle of Albuera on 16 May.

Oatlands, 22 Dec. 1811

Private. You are, I trust, too well convinced of my sincere friendship and regard for you and of the desire which I have ever felt to forward, as far as was in my power, whatever could prove agreeable to you, not to give me credit for feelings of sincere regret at being under the necessity of making a communication which can possibly make any other than a satisfactory impression. I think it nevertheless incumbent upon me to give you thus confidentially the earliest intimation of an arrangement to which the Government are about to give effect in regard to the Staff in Ireland, which will unavoidably remove you from the Command of the Forces there.

I have understood it to be their object to place it, under present circumstances, in the hands of an officer from whose state of health they shall be justified in expecting great personal exertions, and whose rank in the Army shall at the same time authorize the removal from the Staff of Ireland of such Lieut.-Generals as are senior to him.

I have received the Prince Regent's sanction to give you private intimation of this intended measure of his Government and his commands to assure you, at the same time, of his entire approbation of your conduct and his high estimation of your character, of which and of his personal friendly regard, he will, upon your return from Ireland, be most happy to give you every proof in his power.[1] (44256)

1. Sir John Hope succeeded Harrington as Commander-in-Chief in Ireland. Lord Bathurst wrote to the Duke of Richmond on 6 January 1812:

'When Pole's letter was read to the Cabinet in which he strongly pressed for a complete & immediate change in the military staff of Ireland, adding that you no longer wished to have the command yourself; it did not certainly strike me that under these circumstances it was of any consequence to you whether the Commander-in-Chief was above or below you. What I had originally felt was that as Lord Harrington had the command, when you were appointed, it was not necessary for you to insist upon his being taken from it: but that if any thing should occur in the change, it would be very unpleasant for you to have any body put over your head, if you wished to have the command yourself. The Union certainly makes a greater difference in the question than I was at first aware. Before the Union, the army was the army of Ireland: it is now only part of the British army. It is in fact under the command of the Commander-in-Chief here; and the first on the Staff in Ireland is in fact subject to him, and under his command.—I wish I had been aware of your feels as to the point whether the person to be sent was above or below you: for I am not sure whether I was not as forward as any of them in the Cabinet except those to whose department the question belongs, in deciding in favour of Hope, instead of Lord Cathcart, who was the other person thought of. I had often heard you speak of Hope with praise: and I understand him to be a very manageable man; but I had heard so many things to the disadvantage of Lord Cathcart's temper, that I am afraid you could not have gone on well with him. I suppose you know, (if not, you must not repeat it) that Lord Hutchinson was the person proposed by H.R.H. the Regent and that we put a flat negative upon it' (Richmond MSS.).

3297   THE EARL OF LIVERPOOL TO MAJOR-GENERAL T. H. TURNER

Monday night [? *23 Dec. 1811*]

Private. I have sent a note to the Prince Regent in a box tonight to which it is material that I should receive an answer tomorrow morning, as it relates to Lord Minto, and there are ships which will be dispatched in the course of tomorrow, by which we are obliged to answer the publick dispatches respecting the capture of Java.

The Prince is already prepared for this communication,[1] and if his Royal Highness continues therefore to approve of the suggestion, it will be only necessary for him to trouble himself with saying so.

The box belongs to my Department is marked *private*, and dated this day.

I have written to Sir Saml. Auchmuty to acquaint him that he will have the Red Ribbon, but after what passed I did not feel it necessary to trouble the Prince *again* upon that point. I wish however that you would have the goodness to inform him that I have written to Sir S. Auchmuty to that effect.[2] (19152–3)

3298   THE QUEEN TO THE PRINCE REGENT

Windsor, 24 Dec. 1811

Having just received an account from Madrass that Sr. Thomas Strange[3] is likely to return to England, I am requested by Sr. John Newbolt[4] to

1. See No. 3292.

2. Auchmuty was rewarded for his services in capturing Java (August 1811). Minto himself accompanied the expedition. Liverpool wrote to Auchmuty on 21 December: 'My public letter of this day will convey to you the Prince Regent's approbation of your conduct, and that of the army under your command in the late operations in the island of Java. I am desired by his Royal Highness to acquaint you that he is very desirous upon this occasion to confer upon you some distinguished mark of the Royal favour. Though the Regency Act has not imposed any restriction as to granting the several Orders of Knighthood, his Royal Highness has thought it proper to impose a restriction upon himself in this respect until the period when by the determination of Parliament all the restrictions imposed upon the Regency shall have ceased. He has in conformity to this rule been under necessity of suspending the grant of the Order of the Bath to General Graham and General Hill, who from their distinguished conduct in Spain and Portugal during the last campaign are considered as justly entitled to such a mark of Royal favour. It is probable that in the course of the month of February all difficulty on this subject will cease and his Royal Highness has desired me to assure you that as soon as this shall be the case it is his intention to confer the Order of the Bath upon you at the same time as upon Lieutenant-General Graham and General Hill. As I feel the most sincere personal gratification at the distinguished manner in which you have executed the important services which have been entrusted to you, I have great pleasure in being the channel of this communication to you, and you may rely upon no exertions being wanted on my part for carrying his Royal Highness's intentions into effect as soon as possible.' (Add. MSS. 38246, f. 35)

3. Sir Thomas Andrew Lumisden Strange (1756–1841). Chief Justice of Nova Scotia, 1789; Chief Justice at Madras, 1800–15. Knighted, 1798.

4. Sir John Henry Newbolt (*c.* 1768–1823), M.P. for Bramber, 1800–2. Commissioner of

apply that he may be advanced in his situation as perhaps a younger person than himself, being named, may prove disadvantageous to him. The present Lrd. Chancellor as well as Lrd. Erskine always befriended him, & will, I am sure, give you a satisfactory account of him & his abilities.

I beg pardon for this trouble but as those places cannot be long without being filled up I thought it at least but justice to him to be early in my application.

I rejoice to hear you are better & flatter myself to hear very soon of yr. perfect recovery. (36594)

3299   THE DUKE OF CLARENCE TO COLONEL MCMAHON

King's Row, Tuesday night [? *24 Dec. 1811*]

I received your letter of yesterday too late to save post: I now therefore take up my pen to express thro' you my thanks to the Prince Regent for the very handsome and unexpected manner in which my brother has had the kindness to appoint me Commander-in-Chief of the Fleet or rather the Admiral of the Fleet. The Marines will follow whenever it pleases God to take some of the old and hard bargains.[1] (45003)

Bankrupts, 1796–1811; Auditor of Duchy of Lancaster, 1800; Judge at Madras, 1810; Chief Justice at Madras, 1815–21. Knighted, 17 April 1810. On 18 February 1794 he married Julia Digby, Maid of Honour to the Queen. He had been one of Canning's Christ Church friends. He informed Canning (President of the India Board) in 1817 that if he would procure for him a pension he would return home in 1820: he had already asked friends at home to purchase for him a cottage in the Isle of Wight, 'a situation I have coveted from my youth up.' 'I mean a *bona fide* cottage and not a cottage ornée such as a real Nabob would order. I shall at best be but a Naboblet' (Harewood MSS.).

1. The Duke invited himself a second time during the latter part of 1811 to Purbrook Park, Lord Keith's country home, and Princess Charlotte commented (25 December): 'Indeed I think the D. of Clarence is *over & above agreable* in his intended visit, & that there is very little feeling of good breeding in thus *forcing himself* upon people; but when *things are* so *very glaring*, it is astonishing to me how he can *pursue*. I suppose he thinks himself at liberty to do so, now he is Fleet Admiral. I heard from very good authority that he *has ideas* of going across to Ireland, but I fear he will not finde it answer his expectations. His great friends & cronies are Lady Mayo & her sister Mrs Smith—both very vulgar people, I fancy. The best thing I think that ever was, is his *denying positively* his *ever having* proposed to Miss Long, & saying that it was *all* the D. of Cumberland's *mischief* & *idea*' (Bowood MSS.).

The Princess wrote again on 6 January: 'Why the D. of Clarence should be so anxious to obtain the place of Port Admiral is what I do not comprehend. It seems to me so *grasping*, after being made Admiral of the Fleet, a place of 3 thousand a year. Besides I should really think it would not be a *popular nomination*, as it *should* be given to some *weather beaten* sailor, wh. we cannot compliment his Royal Highness upon; & *perhaps* it *might* make people fancy that the Prince *meant* to give things away to his family, *overlooking* others in the same

285

Alnwick Castle, 24 Dec. 1811

I have had the pleasure of receiving your letter of the 19th safe, with its accompanying papers. It is very plain that Mr Perceval's great object is to apply to Parliament as little & as late as possible, & indeed it must be confessed that this wish of his is a very natural one for any person placed in his situation. I was extremely happy to find that H.R.H. has persisted in not giving up his claim to the arrears due to him for the revenue of Cornwall during H.R.H's minority. This has always appeared to me an object of such magnitude that it ought never to be lost sight of, and it is by no means disadvantageous to the Prince's interest that some circumstance shoud bring it on the tapis from time to time. If I may be allowed to judge, I confess it appears to me to be better that the King & Queen's Establishments shoud both be included in *one* sum than that they shoud be separately apportioned in the first instance. Being made a domestic arrangement, it will be settled with less discussion & without any of disagreement & animosity which it might possibly otherwise occasion. Indeed, upon a consideration of the whole matter, I hope it is now so arranged in the third paper that, with the explanations which attend it, it will afford as general satisfaction to all the parties as it is possible for a transaction of that nature to do. It is certainly one of the most delicate subjects that coud be offered to Mr Perceval's consideration, & I am glad to perceive that he has been inclined in most instances to arrange it agreably to the Prince's wishes. With respect to the exact time when these Establishments shoud take place, it appears to me that they ought rather to follow than precede the extinction of the present restrictions because shoud they precede, & H.R.H. shoud think proper to continue the present Administration, those who are desirous to find fault with everything may insinuate that this Establishment so arranged was the price which Ministers paid for their continuance in office. Whereas if these arrangements follow it will be more the act of the Regent himself, & can never be liable to the misconstruction above mentioned. I have no doubt but Mr Perceval will be of the contrary opinion, for reasons which must be obvious.

I have had the pleasure of receiving yours of the 21st & am happy to have so good an account of the Regent's health, about which, from the paragraphs I saw in the papers, I was very anxious till your letter relieved me. (18979–80)

profession who *certainly* would have a prior claim from their services, age, experience &c. Does it strike you so?' (Bowood MSS.).

3301 GEORGE COLMAN TO [?] COLONEL MCMAHON

4 Melina Place, Westminster Road, 24 Dec. 1811

The proposed period has nearly arrived when the different questions arising from my memorial are to be fully consider'd, & I trouble you with my thoughts upon the subject with the highest deference & gratitude for the suggestions which the Prince Regent has condescended to communicate; but as it appear'd to me that the persons who were thought on, at the first impulse, were not actually decided upon to investigate the various points, I trust I shall not be thought deficient in duty to his Royal Highness, nor disrespectful to any individual whatever, by expressing my feelings relative to the appointment of parties who are to examine a case in which my future interests are so very materially involved.

I must be thoroughly confident of the purity of principles attach'd to any whom the Prince may think proper to select—but there is an involuntary bias, imperceptible even to men's own bosoms, which sways on particular occasions. Long continued intimacy & habitual modes of acting & of thinking, with a gentleman who, on this occasion, may imagine that my theatrical speculations may clash with his own, might occasion a predilection for his arguments & his eloquence fatal to my cause. There are irradicable inclinations towards particulars, *quo humana parum cavit natura*, & to which men of the nicest honour are subject. I hope, however, it will be clearly understood that, although Mr Sheridan may argue against my memorial I am most fully sensible that he would argue (*ex parte*) with as much liberality as ingenuity, & that he is incapable of using undue influence on other minds—nor could I have the shadow of an objection to Mr. Sheridan, himself, being (as in a former instance) one of those sitting to consider the rights of theatrical patents, &c.—but surely the less *other* investigators are in the habits of intercourse with ANY of the parties interested, the better, on the score of impartiality.

Might I presume to offer an opinion, I would submit that a part if not the whole, of those of his Majesty's Privy Council who met last year on the subject of 'A Petition for a third Theatre in this metropolis' should compose the Committee intended for the present questions. The ground would not be new to them as to others; they have already listened to the pleadings of lawyers upon the subject; much which they know & have heard will apply, & clear the way to points which may now be brought forward; & much time & trouble may thus be saved which could not be the case with other persons.

The new third Theatre speculators are, I have heard, high in hope, & making great preparations to come with all their strength before Parliament in the ensuing Session. It is a matter, therefore, of great importance to the present case that the proposed investigation should take place *before Parliament meets.*

287

At the end of this week, I shall have prepared all the further observations which I propose to submit to the investigators who may be appointed. (18981–2)

3302   SPENCER PERCEVAL TO THE PRINCE REGENT

Downg. St., Tuesday evg., 24 Dec. 1811

Mr. Perceval presents his humble duty to your Royal Highness, and in obedience to your R. Highness's commands, communicated to him by Mr. Adam, has laid before your R. Highness's confidential servants who are in town the paper containing your R. Highness's reasons for thinking that £150,000 was the sum to be proposed to Parliament to be granted to your Royal Highness for the past year of the Regency, instead [of] £100,000. And Mr Perceval has to acquaint your Royal Highness that the strong impression of your servants is that it will not be without difficulty that the sum of £100,000 will be obtained; that the attempt to procure more would be extremely hazardous, very likely to fail in Parliament, and even if it were to be obtained there, yet most injurious in impression upon the public to your Royal Highness. And with this feeling and opinion your Royal Highness's servants consider it to be their duty, tho with great reluctance, humbly to submit to your Royal Highness that a sum larger than £100,000 cannot with propriety be asked for from Parliament on this head.

Mr Perceval thinks it necessary to add that altho' this is the general opinion of your Royal Highness's servants, he cannot represent them as unanimous upon this point, for Lord Wellesley continues to think as his Lordship did think before, that it would be preferable to ask from Parliament the larger sum of £150,000, not conceiving that there would be that difference in public impression between the two sums which your Royal Highness' other servants apprehend, and feeling that less than £150,000 would not enable your Royal Highness adequately to meet the expences of the former year and of the necessary Establishment for the permanent Regency.

Those of your Royal Highness' servants who are out of town are Lord Camden, Lord Westmoreland & Lord Harrowby; and altho Mr Perceval has not been able to collect their opinions on this point since the receipt of yr. R. Highness's paper, yet he has no doubt from the manner in which they viewed that subject when it was first before the Cabinet, that they would concur in opinion upon it with the majority of their colleagues.

Mr Perceval transmits to your R. Highness a copy of the proposed arrangement, as ultimately settled, according to your R. Highness's commands, for the purpose of its being forwarded by your R. Highness to the Queen. He also returns to your R. Highness the copy of it which he had transmitted before, with those alterations in the margin which had been introduced in consequence of his last Audience—Mr Perceval conceiving that your R. Highness's desire that the paper to be presented to her Majesty should be altered did not extend to that copy which was to be left with your Royal Highness. (18983–4)

3303   WILLIAM ADAM TO COLONEL MCMAHON

Woburn Abbey, 10.30 p.m., 25 Dec. 1811

I have examined the papers with great care—and have compared them. That in the envelope indorsed in my hand is the original paper sent by Mr Perceval after the conference with the Regent at which the Duke of York & myself were present. It has on it the two marginal notes which were inserted after the conference of the 21st between Mr Perceval and myself—and his subsequent Audience—More annotations are in the state in which they were when I delivered that paper back to Mr Perceval on the 23d. accompanied with the paper drawn up for the Queen with the same annotations. The paper now sent for the Queen omits those annotations and presents the paper for her Majesty in the shape of a finished paper—inserting the 100,000 as the sum for outfit and inserting the rank to be given to the Groom of the Stole likewise in the body of the paper—so that this paper may now be sent to the Queen as a perfect paper.

It is proper to remark however that the terms in which it expresses the matter of precedence—is positive as to the fitness that the precedence should be granted by the Regent—but not positive as to the power. This, however, is merely because until looked into with more care it may be thought not right to express positively that it can be done by the Prerogative. This, however, does not render the paper less perfect or less fit in its *now* state to be conveyed to her Majesty.

Mr Perceval's note to the Prince shews that, Marquis Wellesley dissentient, the Cabinet decided for the £100,000. From the clear tenor of his Royal Highnesses opinion, as well as from what is expressed in your note to me—with these papers—his Royal Highness will now relieve Ministers from any farther deliberation upon the subject and permit them to proceed to draw up the Bill.

I have digested a breviate of it in my mind which I will put to paper & send to you—that his Royal Highness may have the substance shortly correctly & distinctly before him without the jargon.

You will have the goodness to put Perceval's paper with the others on this subject—that we may have it to compare the draft of the Bill with when it comes.

I am sorry that by not having had the papers returned to Carlton House sooner there should have been the trouble & delay of sending after me here.

The servant arrived ¼ before nine.

If there had been any thing [to] require my personal attendance on the Prince or farther personal interview I wd have returned immedy.— but the matter is now completely closed.

I have inclosed ye paper of which I delivered the duplicate to Mr Perceval on Monday the 23d.[1] (18985–6)

3304   THE DUKE OF YORK TO THE PRINCE REGENT

Windsor, 28 Dec. 1811

I lose no time in acquainting you according to my promise with the result of my embassy here.

I read to her Majesty the whole of Mr. Perceval's paper, and explained to her very fully its contents and the kind part you had acted towards her in endeavouring as far as possible to have the arrangement made according [to] her wishes, and that therefore no blame attached to you if the plan proposed did not meet them. She listened with great attention to it, and after expressing herself very handsomely, concerning you, she objected very much, as I expected, to the idea of the King's and her Establishment being continued as one, and stated the great difficulties it would throw her into, and the impossibility of correcting the many abuses and inordinate expences that she is fully aware are going on here.

With regard to our sisters she made no remark whatsover, though I took care to make her thoroughly sensible that there would be a considerable saving of expence by their Ladies, servants &c being hereafter at their own expence.

As her Majesty expressed very naturally a wish to read over and consider well Mr. Perceval's paper before she made any remarks or

1. Princess Charlotte wrote to Mercer Elphinstone on Christmas Day: 'I am sure you will say that I have done right in writing to the Prince today & offering my wishes on the day. If it *does no good*, at least it will prove to him that I wish to be *attentive upon all occasions*. He went out today in the carriage & by that I should hope he was better, tho' I have not heard anything about him since he became our neighbour. I am wholly ignorant whether he intends going to the House of Lords or not. They are making great alterations & improvements, & I intend to go & see them as soon as they are finished. Should the Prince really go, I own it would give me infinite pleasure were I to be allowed to go; & as he gave his consent last year I should suppose he would not object this, but as yet I know nothing about the plans' (Bowood MSS.).

remonstrance upon it, I offered if she pleased to return tomorrow morning here to receive her commands, which seemed to please her. I therefore trust to be able on Monday to lay before you the Queen's general sentiments.

I afterwards read the paper again to our four sisters and explained to them generally their situation, and cannot express to you how much they seemed pleased and sensible of your kindness towards them in considering their comfort and interest as you have done. (44260–1)

3305 MRS JORDAN TO THE PRINCE REGENT

Bushy, Saturday [? *28 Dec. 1811*]

I need not inform your Royal Highness that the arrangements for the future provision of myself and dear children are intirely settled, and (independant of any selfish *feelings*) I am happy to add in a manner that does high honor to the Duke of Clarence, but it is not in H.R.H's power to relieve ME from some *immediate* pecuniary difficulties that at this moment *press heavy on me*, with the addition of having a house to *furnish* and a large family to provide for, and to commence this *establishment*, destitute of *ready money*. The consequences appear frightful to me—and under these apprehensions I have this day addressed myself to some of your Royal *brothers*,[1] and tho' thoroughly conscious of the *liberty* I am taking I now offer myself to *your kind consideration*, highly and truly grateful for *any* assistance your Royal Highness's goodness may urge you to *afford* me. As this is most probably the last time I shall ever have the honor of addressing you, allow me to express my most sincere thanks for

1. The following is one of these letters: the recipient is unknown. 'Nothing but the most cruel pecuniary distresses, at this time pressing hard on me, could have forced me to the liberty of appearing before your Royal Highness as a petitioner to your generosity and well known munificence. Allow me, Sir, to do justice to your Royal brother the Duke of Clarence in saying he has in his arrangemts. for me and his children done everything worthy of himself, but it is *not* in his Royal Highness power to relieve the PRESENT difficulties I must labour under, in having a *house* to *furnish*, to commence *housekeeping* with a *large* family without any ready money to begin with. I mean therefore to throw myself at the feet of yourself and Royal brothers, *gratefully* acknowledging ANY assistance your humanity may urge you to afford me.' (42509)

Mrs Jordan received no assistance from any of the Royal Dukes to whom she appealed.

McMahon wrote to William Adam on 30 December: 'I send you, by desire of H.R.Hss., a letter I had on Saturday from Mrs Jordan, and which he thinks a very extraordinary proceeding, especially as she has written a circular one to the same effect to all the royal brothers she is most acquainted with. The P. has consider'd that in the late arrangement with the D. of Clarence, it was an understood thing that a quarter or half year's allowance was to be made her as an outfit, and this I know the Prince would be gratified in having done, if circumstances will at all admit it' (Blair Adam MSS.).

the many marks of kindness I have received from you and more particularly at a time when I was most in need of it. May every blessing of health and happiness attend your Royal Highness is the truest wish of [etc.]. (42510–11)

3306   RICHARD BRINSLEY SHERIDAN TO MAJOR-GENERAL T. H. TURNER

Cavendish Square, Sunday evening [*29 Dec. 1811*]

I wish'd very much for an opportunity to have spoken to the Regent on the subject of the Police, conceiving the present to be an occasion when great popularity may *originate* from him—but I have not left my room & scarcely even my bed since I saw you on Friday last. I find you have seen Arnold. I send you his letter to me & his plan. I hope to be able to get out on Tuesday when I will come to Carlton House. (18993)

3307   GEORGE WALKER TO MAJOR-GENERAL T. H. TURNER

Pall Mall, No 81, 30 Dec. 1811

Mr Walker presents his most respectful compliments to General Turner. The paper he took the liberty to send last for General Turner's perusal was the substance of what he had drawn up about two years since when Lord Keith was pleased to honor the undertaking with his Lordship's countenance.

In this arduous task he is anxious to avoid what may be considered as presumptuous;—instead of the word *essays* he has been advised to substitute that of *history*—but this, besides being too pompous, would imply at least a volume or two on the subject. *Essays*, it is true, are now given on almost every subject; however, after all that can be done either in art or in science, the utmost effort is but an essay.

The strictures, or essays in question, are intended to be addressed to *nine-tenths* of the *connoisseurs* and to be read, if read at all, previous to entering on the descriptive account of the pictures, & consequently should precede it in the arrangement. The list given contains the names of those noblemen and gentlemen who have honored the undertaking with their countenance. On this score he is under great obligations to Lord Moira, Lord Keith and General Turner. He begs to state that he has no intention of publishing the work by *subscription*. He had calculated on the sum of twelve or fifteen hundred pounds, covering the expence of the portraits alluded to, but he now finds it would require a much larger sum—which circumstance has led to the abandonment of that part of his plan.

In a day or two he shall have an opportunity of sending to Woburn for the purpose of recording the Duke of Bedford's pictures, a volume bound up similar to that which the Earl of Moira was pleased to charge himself with the transmission of to Carlton House for his R.H. the Prince Regent's pictures; and as he shall have occasion to refer to his Grace's letters he requests General Turner will have the goodness to cause the portfolio & papers [to] be returned to him along with those specified on the other side, and which, from a note of the Earl of Moira, he understands were transmitted to General Turner for his perusal.

Regarding his R.H. the Prince Regent's valuable pictures he shall say nothing till he has the pleasure of hearing further on the subject from General Turner. Unless it may be permitted him to express his admiration of the *Vandyck*[1]—*Ostade*[2]—*Wouvemans*[3]—*Both W. & A. Van de Velde*[4] and also of the *Rembrandt*, which are all of the highest class of their respective masters. Respecting the *Ostade* & *Wouvemans* he is inclined to think they have both been engraved from.

In his extensive collection of prints & etchings, he has, at Hunter Square, Edinburgh, a large assemblage of the latter by *Rembrandt*, which he intends to bring to town next summer. In the meantime, he requests General Turner will be so good as to give house room to the accompanying portrait till an opportunity be afforded him of describing his R.H. the Prince Regent's pictures—as it is interesting to compare an artist with himself, even to the paraphernalia of his painting-room or study. He has another duplicate of a fine portrait by Rembrandt which, so soon as returned by a friend who has a sight of it, he shall have to request of General Turner to allow it to remain in his hands till the period alluded to.

The papers above referred to & transmitted to the Earl of Moira are as follow—

a letter from Mr Byres regarding the Raphael;
a note from Sir W. Forbes[5]—on Mr Byres's return from Rome;
a description of the portrait of Sir Kenelm Digby[6] by Vandyck, and a note on the subject from Lord St. Helens. (18997–8)

1. Sir Anthony Van Dyck (1599–1641).

2. Adriaan Van Ostade (1610–85), the Dutch painter.

3. Philip Wouwerman (1619–68), the Dutch painter.

4. Both Willem Vandevelde (1610–93), the Dutch painter and his son Willem (1633–1707) painted in England. Adriaan (1636–72) was the younger Vandevelde's brother, a pastoral painter.

5. He succeeded his father, Sir William, in the baronetcy on 12 November 1806, and died in 1828.

6. Sir Kenelm Digby (1603–65), author, naval commander, and diplomatist. Van Dyck painted several portraits of him.

Windsor, 31 Dec. 1811

Colonell Taylor, who is the bearer of this, will deliver you also a copy of the paper for Mr Perceval in answer to the one I received on Saturday by the hands of the Duke of York. You will of course be so kind as to talk it over with C. T. who in many respects can inform you of such minutia[e] which I was unacquainted with when I saw you, & I am sensible that you will upon due consideration see at once that the specifyed sum stated in Mr. P.'s paper will not answer by any means, for independant of what is called *living*, the outgoings in pensions etc. are much more extensive than I fear the sum allotted for it will come up to. I will fairly own that the sum for the Kg. & myself being combined, it makes me very uneasy, whereas if a certain sum was stipulated for me I should not feel that I might be either suspected or accused of incroaching upon the King, & the very idea of either being attached to me would render my situation most deplorable. Under these circumstances you will not be surprised that as it stands now I must decline to agree to this arrangement, & flatter myself that Mr. P. upon reflecting over what I have said will arrange matters in a manner that I can fullfill both my duty to the King & to myself without concurring [*sic*] the censure of the world.

As to yourself I feel no words are adequate to express my gratitude for the liberality you have shewn upon this occasion towards me; it will ever be engraven on the heart of [etc.]. (36595)

[Enclosure] THE QUEEN TO SPENCER PERCEVAL [copy, in Sir Herbert Taylor's hand]

Windsor Castle, 30 Dec. 1811

The Queen has received from the Duke of York the paper presented to the Prince Regent by Mr. Perceval for the purpose of being forwarded to her Majesty. She has given due consideration to it, and she will now proceed to communicate to Mr. Perceval her sentiments upon its various parts, in as regular succession as the general subject and her feelings upon certain prominent features will admit.

She laments that those feelings should unavoidably have produced very strong and irrevocable objections on her part to the general principle and to many of the details of Mr. Perceval's proposal, but she considers it due to herself as well as to Mr. Perceval to put him at once in possession of her sentiments and to enable him to give such early and serious attention to them as shall induce him to weigh thoroughly the means & expedients which may appear to him best calculated to meet her Majesty's objections, and to reply to them in writing for her information; after which the Queen will be prepared to see him and to discuss the points upon which they may still differ.

The first part of Mr. Perceval's paper relates to the arrangement of the superior part of the *King's* Household and the nomination of the individuals who are to compose it. To this arrangement the Queen has no intention of objecting, presuming that the actual melancholy circumstances require that the King's Establishment should be placed upon the proposed reduced scale. She wholly approves of the choice of Lord Winchelsea to preside over the King's Establishment as Groom of the Stole, and of that of Lord John Thynne[1] to be his deputy. Her Majesty considers this selection to be already made, as well as that of the Master of the Robes[2] and the Privy Purse to which she cannot object, and she highly approves of the continued attendance of his Majesty's actual Equerries.

The selection however of the Gentlemen and of the Grooms of the Bed Chamber, whose number is to be respectively limited to four, is made to rest with the Queen, and her Majesty does not deny that she has felt much embarassed in the adoption of the principle upon which the selection is made. She has not indeed hesitated in preferring to retain individuals who actually hold those situations to the nomination of others who have not the same claims, but she has felt the difficulty which attends a selection from which two thirds of the number must unavoidably be excluded. If her Majesty had named the four eldest in each rank, her choice would have fallen upon those who are either unable to attend or who have attended very little at Windsor. If she had named the two eldest & the two youngest, the same objection would have applied, or the greater proportion of those would have been omitted who have made a point of attending here often & have in consequence been frequent members of his Majesty's private circle. The Queen therefore has upon full reflection determined to consider those as having the best claim and as offering a continuation of attendance most agreable to his Majesty and best suited to the circumstances under which his family will be placed who have most frequently been members of his Majesty's private circle at Windsor. According to this principle the Gentlemen would be—Lord Somerville,[3] Lord

1. Lord John Thynne (1772–1849). M.P. for Weobley, May–December 1796; for Bath, 1796–1832. Vice-Chamberlain of the Household, 1804–12. Succeeded his brother Lord George Thynne (1770–1838), who was Comptroller of the Household, 1804–12, as 3rd Baron Carteret, 19 February 1838.

2. Henry Sedley.

3. John Southey, 14th Baron Somerville (1765–1819) succeeded his uncle in the peerage on 16 April 1796. Scottish Representative Peer, 1796–1807; a Lord of the Bedchamber, 1799–1819.

Rivers,[1] Lord Arden,[2] and Lord St Helens.—The Grooms—Mr. Greville,[3] Admiral Legge,[4] Sir Harry Neale and M.-Genl. Campbell.[5]

The Queen concludes that it is not intended to make any reduction in the number of the King's Pages in usual attendance at Windsor, the greater proportion of whom have either passed the best part of their lives in his Majesty's service or have by zealous and faithful attendance established strong claims to his regard and confidence, and to the consideration of those whose attachment to the King must produce in them an anxious desire to promote the interests of servants whose services his kindness would not have left unrewarded. Besides the regular Pages there are other individuals who have been employed during many years by the King in various situations and whose claims to due consideration cannot in justice be set aside. This observation must apply equally to the retention of inferior servants of every description 'in the proportion necessary for the accomodation of the King and his family.'

The principle of extreme economy which seems to pervade the proposed plan will necessarily limit the selection of inferior servants of every description to a small proportion of the most efficient and of those who, being the youngest, have the least salaries, and the consequence will be that the oldest servants, those who are encumbered with families, who cannot hope for provision or support in any other quarter, will be thrown upon the wide world without bread for themselves or their families.

The Queen has been prematurely led to an observation upon the principle of economy which pervades the plan, and which in its execution must necessarily exclude all liberal and, she may add, all just consideration of the services of his Majesty's old servants. She appeals to Mr. Perceval, she would appeal to the whole country whether the sum of £100,000, proposed to be granted for the support of the Establishment,

1. George, 2nd Baron Rivers (1751–1828) succeeded his father in the peerage, 7 May 1803. M.P. for Dorset, 1774–90; a Lord of the Bedchamber, 1804–19. He told the Speaker on 19 January following that the King believed that they meant to poison him (*Colchester*, ii. 356).

2. Charles George Perceval (1756–1840) succeeded to his mother's peerage as 2nd Baron Arden [I.] in 1784. M.P. for Launceston, 1780–90; for Warwick, 1790–6; for Totnes, 1796–1802. Created Baron Arden [U.K.], 28 July 1802. A Lord of the Admiralty, December 1783–February 1801; Master of the Mint, 1801–2; Commissioner of the India Board, 1801–3; a Lord of the Bedchamber, 1804–12.

3. Robert Fulke Greville.

4. Sir Arthur Kaye Legge (1766–1835), a brother of the 3rd Earl of Dartmouth. Lieutenant, 1789; Commander, 1790; Captain, 1793; Rear-Admiral, 1810; Vice-Admiral, 1814. K.C.B. 1815.

5. Sir Henry Frederick Campbell (1769–1856). Lieutenant-Colonel, 1796; Colonel, 1803; Major-General, 1810; Lieutenant-General, 1814; General, 1837. K.C.B. 1815. M.P. for Nairnshire, 1796–1802 and 1806–7.

can, after providing for the salaries of the individuals, high and low, who are to form part of it, and for the various items of Household expence, afford the means either of maintaining an adequate or respectable number of inferior servants, or a fair and liberal provision for such as must be discharged after long and faithful services, incapacitated from age and habits for any other employment.

Much has indeed been said in regard to the indirect advantages which have been derived by the individuals forming part of the Establishment, exclusively of their salaries. The Queen admits the fact and she does not question the prevalence of many abuses which may be corrected and checked, but she must observe that perquisites have been authorized and have been considered as forming part of the salary which would otherwise have been so inferior, so inadequate, as to offer no inducement to respectable individuals to accept or continue in these situations. The smalness of the general provision made must necessarily lead to strict reform in every branch of expenditure, and to the abolition of every indirect advantage, and the natural consequence (if the King and his family are to be served by proper persons in the several inferior situations) must be a considerable encrease in their respective salaries, thus producing a further diminution of the means from which any provision can be made for those who are dismissed.

The Queen is unwilling to extend this paper to unreasonable length, and therefore omits many observations and arguments by which she might enforce the remarks which she has already made upon the inadequacy of the proposed provision, but she cannot avoid stating her confident belief that the narrow principle upon which it is proposed to form an Establishment for the King and his Family, and the inevitable distress which must result from it to the old servants of a beloved Sovereign who, though secluded under the pressure of the greatest calamity which can befal man, is still in existence, cannot be consistent with the feelings which generally pervade the country towards that Sovereign and his Family. Her Majesty is indeed persuaded that this country would consider itself disgraced if it were recorded in its history that less liberality had been shewn by it in the provision made for its own Sovereign, under misfortune, and towards the support of his attendants and servants, less regard for his dignity and that of his family than had been so frequently manifested in its consideration of the necessities of other Sovereigns and Princes whom Revolutions and other causes had driven to the alternative of seeking a refuge and support in England.

Mr. Perceval cannot be surprized that, with these feelings upon this subject, the Queen should positively decline to have any controul whatsoever over an Establishment which she has declared to be so objectionable in principle and in detail, and equally refuse to interfere in any manner in its arrangements and execution, whether at the outset or in its further course beyond that sanction which she has already given to the nomination of the persons proposed to fill the higher offices. Her Majesty cannot, by her acquiescence in this proposal place herself in a situation in which the incessant complaints of individuals whom she may not be able to relieve, the restrictions upon reasonable expenditure, the fear of incurring responsibility and reproach by exceeding in a trifling degree the expences which must be so strictly regulated and limited, if to be brought within the proposed scale, would subject her to continual uneasiness & worry & add to the anxiety and distress already created by other more serious causes. She has not health nor spirits to engage in such an undertaking, and she feels that, although she has not the power of prescribing what should be the arrangement, she cannot be denied the option of declining to sanction by her assumption of the controul and interference that which has been so proposed.

The Queen had hoped that, under all the circumstances of the present moment, and with due regard to the King's dignity & to her comfort & that of her family, an arrangement would have been proposed which should provide for separate and distinct Establishments of the King's & her own Households. She solemnly declares that she had not flattered herself with this expectation from any view to personal advantage beyond the immediate comfort resulting from the means and the facility of regulating her own arrangements & expenditure, and from being responsible to herself alone for the application of the provision made for that purpose; above all she had fondly looked forward to such an arrangement as securing her from any concern, direct or indirect, in the management of a mixed Establishment, in the arrangement & consequences of which she foresaw so many sources of distress & embarassment. Her Majesty equally declares that her expectations of a provision for such separate Establishment have not been formed upon an unreasonable scale, and that she is thoroughly disposed to admit of such as shall be considered limited as far as it can be, consistently with her station & dignity, aware as she is that, when the utmost amount shall be fixed, her arrangements and calculations must be made in conformity to that amount and that her expences must strictly keep pace with the funds assigned.

The Queen cannot but hope that this candid and unreserved exposition of her sentiments & wishes will prove a sufficient motive with Mr. Perceval to consider of the propriety & expediency of framing such an arrangement as may satisfy the only feelings which she can ever entertain on this subject.

The only remaining point in Mr. Perceval's paper which the Queen feels herself called upon to notice at any length is the proposed appropriation of the sum of £60,000 issued in lieu of his Majesty's Privy Purse allowance & that of £10,000 per annum from the Duchy of Lancaster.

It is stated that this sum of £70,000 per annum 'and such parts of the King's revenue as remain at his Majesty's disposal' shall defray the private pensions charged on the Privy Purse to their full amount and also such expence of the medical attendants as has hitherto been incurred or as shall arise in future.

The Queen considers it probable that the claims upon the King's Privy Purse will greatly exceed Mr. Perceval's expectation, various annual sums or pensions having been paid by his Majesty in person or by separate drafts on the Privy Purse, which have not usually been specified in the Privy Purse books, nor probably in the statements given in by Mr. Braun. There are also debts remaining unpaid which must absorb a proportion of the funds actually in the hands of the Privy Purse; and the Queen is persuaded that Mr. Perceval will see with her the propriety of directing that these various claims should be ascertained and specified, and that they should be liquidated before any other appropriation takes place of the sum in hand, and that provision should be made for such additional payments as are annual and progressive.

The Queen very much doubts whether, after discharging the debts and other claims and the current payments, a balance in any degree sufficient will remain towards defraying the expences of the medical attendance up to the present period, although the sum assigned may hereafter prove equal to meet those expences and the current disbursements.

The arrangements proposed for the management of the King's private property appear to the Queen unobjectionable.

Upon the proposed grant of £70,000 towards defraying her Majesty's extraordinary expences of removal from place to place, and of keeping up her house in town or elsewhere, the Queen forbears to make any remark, as it has reference to the general arrangements to which she has so strongly objected.

The Duke of York has explained to the Queen the nature & extent of the provision which it will be proposed to Parliament to make for the Princesses, and the principle upon which it is now granted, and her Majesty cannot but highly approve it. At the same time she conceives that the adoption of this principle by which the Princesses are placed upon an independent footing, furnishes a strong ground for her own claim to a separate and distinct Establishment at the present period.[1]
(36596–601)

1. McMahon wrote to William Adam on the 30th: 'The P.R. is in general health perfectly good, and all unpleasant remains of his sprain are entirely gone, but the spasmodic tinglings of his hands and arms are not as yet quite removed, but still they are so far recover'd as to have enabled him (for the first time this fortnight) yesterday evening to sign and knock off a dozen office boxes, which were much wanting. He has not express'd a syllable since you return'd Mr. P[erceval]'s papers, on the subject of that arrangement, nor has he seen a Cabinet

Minister' (Blair Adam MSS.). Princess Charlotte wrote on the 30th: '1 saw the D. of Cambridge yesterday . . . He had just come from the Prince, who, he said was *very sore* about *himself*, his hands being so *weak* he could *hardly hold* a pen, wh. put back very much the business & signatures he has to do—that the P. fancies it is paralasis in his hands. Now between friends I should not think that very *unlikely*, as from the quantities of opium it is *very apt* to cause that. I should be *hung* were I to give that as my opinion to any of *the learned* doctors. Sr. Walter promised to call upon me today if the P. had a 3rd good night *without artificial* sleep, but as he has not been I confess I fear it has not been the case' (Bowood MSS.).

11 The Last Weeks of the Restricted Regency, January–February 1812

Ever since the autumn of 1811 the Regent had been free to change the Ministry. The King's recovery was then seen to be hopeless, and the Prince could no longer claim that he was retaining Perceval as Prime Minister solely in the interests of his father's health. The whole ground on which the continuance of the Administration had been excused, if not defended, fell away, and other considerations henceforth caused the Prince to keep the Tories in office. Perceval necessarily profited from the Prince's fear of committing himself, his anxiety for a quiet life, his painful state of indecision. The longer Perceval remained Prime Minister after the autumn of 1811 the less reason there would seem to be for turning him out. They agreed on the necessity for a vigorous prosecution of the war in Spain and the Prince had identified himself with Perceval in the measures pursued in Ireland to suppress the illegal Catholic Convention.

If the Regent chose to consider himself in fetters until the restrictions expired, he was deceiving himself, but he decided to postpone a decision until it could no longer be avoided. This policy of inactivity (it can hardly be described as masterly, inspired as it was by extreme timidity if not downright cowardice) had the advantage of keeping the Opposition more than usually quiet during the first six weeks of the parliamentary session which opened on 7 January 1812. In any case, even those Whigs who believed that Perceval would probably be retained, had no stomach for a fight, and the leaders deprecated anything like a declaration of war against Carlton House.

At the beginning of January Wellesley, who alone of the Ministers possessed any degree of the Regent's confidence, was fairly sure that there would be no 'total' change: the Prince would not wish to throw himself entirely into the hands of the Opposition. On the other hand he had given Ministers no assurance of continuing them in office, and still less, an assurance of continuing them *as they were*.

Wellesley's diagnosis of the situation was accurate. Towards the end of December the Prince had informed his friend William Adam that his object was 'to unite as many persons of talent in the Government of the country under its present difficulties, as possible.' When Grey and Grenville had last seen him at Carlton House in January 1811 Moira had been present, and the Prince now intended that Moira and the Duke of York should go see Lord Grey after the Duke had informed Perceval that he was to be sent on this mission.

Moira had seen little of the Prince since the failure of the *pourparlers* in January 1811, and for the most part he had kept to himself in the country. He was reported to be out of humour, knowing nothing of what was going on at Carlton House, and not being consulted. When, in September, Lord Grenville's friend Lord Auckland urged him to go to London to be near the Prince, he replied, 'Feel how unconstitutional the situation would be if I thwarted the counsel of his Ministers by secret advice; how mischievous, if by being on the spot and silent I appeared to concur in their policy!' By adopting an unconciliatory tone towards the Prince the Grenville Whigs had given Ministers the opportunity of insinuating that he would put himself in thraldom if he persevered in his original idea of forming a Whig Administration; and the opposition of Lord Grenville's friends in the Commons to the reinstatement of the Duke of York had been most impolitic. 'Can you wonder,' Moira asked Auckland, 'that a man should be estranged by procedures so calculated to revolt him? . . . You should advert to the share which [you] yourselves have had in producing the continuance of the present Ministry, and you should not fix upon the Prince an unqualified charge of inconsistency.'

The proposed mission was timed for 8 January, the day after the meeting of Parliament. William Adam and the Duke of York again saw the Prince that day, but the situation had been changed by the notice which Grenville had given the previous evening during the debate on the Lords Commissioners' Speech, to raise the Irish question during the next few days. The decision had been a difficult one. On the one hand it was felt that great care would have to be taken during the early days of the Session not to furnish the Prince with a pretext, much less to give him a motive, for throwing himself into the hands of the Tories. They should avoid as much as possible any appearance of distrust or anything like impatience at his dilatoriness in coming to a decision. On the other hand the Whigs felt that it was necessary for their character and consistency as well as for the safety and welfare of Ireland to show that their forbearance was the result of their confidence and their hopes, not of their weakness or shabbiness; they must not shrink from a firm adherence to constitutional principles and advocacy of a policy of conciliation for Ireland.

Grenville's notice was the subject of much discussion and was much regretted by the three in conclave at Carlton House as ill-judged and premature, but the Prince continued to think that there was a case for carrying out his plan after the Catholic question had been disposed of.

On the 16th Lord Wellesley had an audience at Carlton House and 'begged to have permission to retire.' He meant it to take effect only if Perceval was confirmed in the Premiership. Their differences had become so pronounced that the retirement of one or the other was now inevitable, though there was no open quarrel as there had been between Canning and Castlereagh. Perceval was jealous of the Marquess's influence at Carlton House. Wellesley considered him quite unfit for his situation. 'He is an able man, an honest man (in the ordinary sense of the word—that is, he does not actually tell lies though he occasionally gives *lying impressions*), but he is not fit to be Prime Minister of England. He is the most *unfit* man of *any* of the same or nearly the same capacity that I ever met with.'

Wellesley had decided to go out as far back as October 1810, but, he said, something had then happened which had prevented him from doing so, and the King's illness which had quickly followed had further made it impossible. 'I am weary of the whole thing,' he said, 'and when the time comes, must speak my mind quite plainly to the Regent. I cannot go on with Perceval as he is.' On several occasions he had expressed his willingness to give up his office to Canning and to agree to Castlereagh's return to the Cabinet along with Canning but not without him, unless a 'fair and honourable' offer had been made to Canning and rejected. Canning himself never acted on the principle that hatreds were never to be forgotten or forgiven, and he was willing to act with Castlereagh once more provided that Castlereagh was not again placed in the War Department.

Although the Prince said nothing to Wellesley about the Premiership, Wellesley left Carlton House after his audience with the distinct impression that he would be sent for as soon as the restrictions expired, and he was actually planning to offer the Admiralty to his brother Wellesley-Pole, even though they were politically unconnected. Pole thought his brother was most foolish to imagine that he might be the next Prime

Minister: any Government that he could form would not last a week. Many of his colleagues would have refused to serve under him (as the events of June 1812 were to show), and it was far from certain that the 'interior Cabinet' at Carlton House would be favourable to his pretensions. There, Lord Yarmouth and his mother were working for the return to office of their relative Castlereagh. Yarmouth rightly believed that if Wellesley were to become Prime Minister he would bring Canning into the Cabinet, and that might be the end of Castlereagh politically. Yarmouth, however, was under a misapprehension; he was told that Wellesley had no wish to proscribe Castlereagh: it was merely his fixed determination not to sit in a Cabinet with Castlereagh from which Canning had been excluded.

Wellesley complained that he had not that weight in the Cabinet which he had expected to have when taking office; that he was frequently carrying out a policy not of his own choosing; and that more should have been done to aid his brother's campaign in the Peninsula. Discussing the matter with Perceval shortly afterwards, the Regent gave him the impression that the Catholic question was another most important factor. Wellesley, like Canning, was always an advocate of Catholic relief, though he had accepted Pitt's view that substantial concession would have to be postponed during the King's reign. Perceval and other members of the Cabinet were of the opinion that the door should be closed more or less permanently against it, and it was understood that they were distinctly to separate themselves from him on this aspect of the Irish question during the coming debate. When Perceval informed his colleagues of this development Lord Bathurst commented, 'It struck us all that this circumstance must fully justify the Regent in changing the Administration.'

In India the 'Grand Lama' (Canning often referred to him as 'the Mogul') had possessed virtually autocratic power; at home he was temperamentally unfitted to be in anything but a commanding position in the Cabinet. He had little desire to meet his colleagues and to have his dispatches scrutinized and criticized (Canning, with whom he was much more intimate, had always been willing to amend *his* drafts provided the changes were not fundamentally contrary to his own views); and he probably attended fewer than half the Cabinet meetings which took place whilst he was Foreign Secretary.

Wellesley communicated his intention to resign to Perceval indirectly—through Bathurst, on the 17th. There were meetings of Perceval, Wellesley, Eldon and Liverpool at Carlton House on the 18th and 19th. The result was a declaration by Wellesley that he could not continue in office, and a declaration by the Prince that he should mediate between them in the hope that the Government could remain precisely as it was until the restrictions came to an end.

On the 21st Perceval was again received in audience whilst the Duke of York and William Adam were at Carlton House. He told the Prince privately that it was the wish of all his Cabinet colleagues that he, the Prince, should not take the trouble to mediate between them and the Marquess; the wounds were too deep to be healed: clearly, they had had enough of him. The Prince wanted to know what was to be done, explaining that he understood that the Opposition considered they had claims on him—claims which he could not admit. They knew that when they were in office (1806–7) he had expressed the hope that the Catholic question would be kept back; that Fox had agreed with him, but that others had insisted on its being brought forward, with disastrous results. Now, the Whigs were again bringing it forward, regardless of his feelings and situation, and they seemed disposed to force him in a manner to which he felt no disposition to submit. They meant to force him in another way. They sent Canning a message through his friend Lord Granville Leveson-Gower pointing out the advantage of reducing the Prince to the necessity of choosing between Perceval and the supporters of Catholic emancipation, and imploring him not to spoil the game by giving him a third choice—by dividing the pro-Catholics into two parties, Whigs and liberal Tories. Canning was wholly contemptuous: 'Independently of my principle . . . that the Crown *should have* a choice, a real effective choice of Ministers (in opposition to the Whig system of choosing *for* the Crown) I could not reflect on the transactions of this time twelvemonth, when the Prince Regent proposed me, and they excluded me, without marvelling at their impudence in now calling upon me to side *with them against* him.'

Perceval insisted on acting on Wellesley's conditional resignation as a positive one, and asked for permission to offer the seals to Castlereagh and also to open negotiations with the Sidmouths. The Prince said he had no personal objection to Castlereagh. 'I hardly know him, indeed. I think I never spoke to him but once in my life, coming out of his house at a rout of Lady Castlereagh's last year. He asked me some question about the King, which I answered. But I have no sort of objection to him. He is a man of honour and of talents, I believe. Whether there is any inconvenience belonging to him, you are the best judge. You can best judge what will best suit your own Government . . . But if you do what you intend, I will tell you what will happen. Wellesley will consider the bringing in Lord Castlereagh in his place without an offer to Mr Canning as an insult to him and a proscription of Canning; and instead of going out (as he intended to do) in perfect good humour, he will go into d——d furious opposition. You know Wellesley's opinions upon the Catholic question are *the same as mine*. Canning's, I suppose, are the same too. At present they will do you no mischief, but if you put this insult (as they will conceive it) upon them, mark my words—Grenville, whose heart will presently soften towards Wellesley upon his going out of office, will make overtures of reconciliation, and Wellesley and Canning will join with the Opposition, and then you may judge what you will have to stand against. But I repeat, it is your own affair. I have nothing to do with it. If you choose to have Lord Castlereagh you are very welcome. Judge for yourself.' The Prince remarked that Castlereagh was the worst War Minister the country had ever had, and that it would be most inadvisable to place him in the Foreign Office, a Department so nearly connected with the War Department where he had planned the disastrous Walcheren expedition. 'Do you not see that the very first disaster would raise such a clamour as must overturn him and you and your whole Government?'

Both Richard Ryder and Charles Yorke were anxious to retire from the Cabinet on account of ill health. Perceval went on to suggest that Sidmouth should succeed Ryder as Home Secretary. The Prince gave Wellesley a highly coloured account of his reaction to this proposition. 'The Doctor! By God, that scoundrel the Doctor.' And he was alleged (surely most improbably) to have quoted a line from Virgil:

Obstupui, steterant comae et vox faucibus haesit

(I stood amazed. My hair stood on end and my voice stuck in my throat). 'As soon as I could utter I told Mr Perceval my mind about that fellow. "No, Mr Perceval, that is too bad—that d——d scoundrel, that fool. No! Never shall he come into my Councils with my good will. No, No, anyone else. Strengthen yourself as you will from any other quarter, but not the Doctor, if you please."' It was too bitter a pill to swallow. Sidmouth had deceived him and had been largely responsible for the break-up of the 'Talents' in March 1807. If he were in the Cabinet the Prince would no longer find it possible to be open and unreserved in his communications with the Prime Minister. Perceval commented that it would be most distressing if there were to be proscriptions, and he seemed to imply that, if the Prince felt like that, the only thing to do would be to 'go to the other side.' The Prince admitted that he had thought of sending the Duke of York to Lord Grey to propose an extended Administration, but that 'the violence' of the first day of the parliamentary session, when notice was given that the state of Ireland was to be debated in both Houses, had made this impossible. The Prince also told Perceval that Wellesley had not offered to form a Government. 'I do not think he could, but he did not offer, so I must come to you.' Lord Bathurst, on receiving an account of this audience, said that he would not have been at all surprised if the Prince had said that Wellesley's resignation must oblige him to 'look elsewhere.'

Returning to Downing Street after this audience, Perceval consulted with his colleagues, and, according to Wellesley, wrote a very pressing letter to the Prince recapitulating all his difficulties and again pressing for an overture to Sidmouth. There is no copy of this letter either in the Perceval Papers or at Windsor, and Wellesley may have been mistaken, especially since Perceval had frequent audiences during these days.

Perceval's proposals alarmed William Adam, and after a sleepless night he again saw the Prince early in the morning. In effect, the Regent was proposing to abandon Ireland; to allow Sidmouth in particular to join the Government would be a decisive proof of abandonment, and the resignation of Wellesley, which might well be followed by a speech in favour of Catholic relief, would naturally create the impression that he had been dismissed because of his pro-Catholic opinions. And if Tyrwhitt and McMahon were to vote against the Whig motion, that impression would be confirmed beyond question. The Government would be too weak to withstand the united forces of the Opposition, and then the Prince would be in fetters.

On the 23rd Perceval saw Castlereagh and asked him whether he would come in alone to replace Wellesley, or, if not, whether he would join in company with Sidmouth and his friends. He was told that the Cabinet, with the obvious exception of the Marquess, unanimously approved these suggestions. Next day Castlereagh was ready with his reply. He must decline coming in alone as a mere stopgap, not knowing how the Government would eventually be constituted. He said he had great respect for the Sidmouths and that they could not properly be excluded from any arrangement to be made, but that in view of all the difficulties the Government would have to encounter in Parliament, the proposed basis was too narrow. And if the Prince was 'decided as to his own system' he ought to try to persuade some of 'his own friends' to join. 'He owed the attempt both to his Ministers and himself. Without this, the political world would not suppose his Royal Highness's decision taken to stand by the Government.'

Perceval had already consulted his colleagues about Wellesley's offer of resignation, and they all agreed that he should tell the Prince that he need not take the trouble to mediate between them and the Marquess. But, in spite of Perceval's entreaties that he would not do so, the Prince interfered to stop Wellesley's resignation. It would be mischievous; it would give rise to false constructions against him, the Prince. Wellesley said that he had no wish to cause embarrassment and that he would continue in office for the time being.

On the 24th Perceval reported to the Prince the result of his overtures to Castlereagh, and they agreed that, for the moment, the matter should go no further. Then Perceval asked the Regent to authorize him to declare that he possessed his entire and exclusive confidence. The Prince later told Wellesley what he had said in reply. 'No, Mr Perceval. I have never said anything to you that warranted such an assumption, and I have no thoughts of saying anything to that effect now. You know perfectly well the relation in which you and your Government stand to me. I have never said or done anything to alter that original relation, and will not now. You will do what you think right. I will object to nothing that you propose for strengthening your Government to carry on the public service, but I will not say or do anything, and you are in a great mistake if you think I have said or done anything to authorise you to consider yourself as possessing my exclusive confidence.' Perceval declared that if this fact was revealed he would find it very difficult to negotiate further. The Prince, however, repeated he could do nothing. He could write no letters. Perceval then asked whether the required effect might be produced if offers of place were made to the Prince's particular friends such as Moira. The Prince wondered how he could imagine that an offer to Moira could be accepted since Moira was more pledged on the Catholic question than any other of his friends, and even on the Peninsular War his views were not identical with those of the Cabinet. Perceval then mentioned Lord Holland. The Prince replied that although Holland agreed with Wellesley on the war in Spain and disagreed with Grenville on the Catholic question and on America he differed widely from the Government.

Wellesley's resignation, which had been only temporarily postponed, filled Canning with dismay. If only he had stayed in, seeking to strengthen the Government and leaving Perceval where he was, all would have been well. As it was, he had thrown himself overboard and, probably, brought Castlereagh in, and Castlereagh alone. Canning rightly believed that Wellesley's remaining in was better for him, Canning, than any change without him. 'As to Perceval,' said Canning, 'his power is confirmed for ever (so far as any politics are for ever) and without balance or control, whereas Wellesley and I together in office and the Catholic question for a ground of difference—and all might in six months have been well. One thing to be sure I did not foresee—that the Prince Regent would consent to put Castlereagh in my office. That is an affront beyond what I thought even my support of him against the restrictions, at the expense of all my Pittite following (which that lost me) could have merited of his gratitude, and this at a moment, too, when I am about to act for his benefit at his immediate wish, is peculiarly piquant. No matter. I will go my own way still—happen what may, but as to office, adieu to it for this reign!'

Canning was writing on 2 February, the day before Lord Morpeth brought forward his motion on the state of Ireland. It was not a straightforward debate on the Catholic question, the Whigs criticizing the Government for its policy of repressing the Catholic Convention. Canning's speech on the first day of the debate was designed deliberately to benefit the Prince Regent in the first place, himself and

Wellesley in the second. In pursuing their agitation the Irish Catholics had taken an extreme line, and it would be madness in any Government, no matter how well disposed towards them, to concede everything they demanded without securities for the Constitution in Church and State, 'when the Catholics were behaving so ill, and when their behaviour has irritated all the sober people of this country against them; at a moment, too, when, if given, it must be given unconditionally without any securities.' If the Whig motion were carried the Prince would either have to surrender at discretion or go over to the side of the Protestant 'bigots' and so become odious to the Catholics for ever. He would feel most keenly the pain and disgrace of this alternative. Canning felt he could help him out of this dilemma by showing that it was possible both to support Catholic relief in substance and to oppose its being granted at that particular moment. Canning made sure that the Prince knew of the line he was going to take by getting Wellesley to explain it to him.

Canning was immensely satisfied with the success of his speech which followed the line of Wellesley's in the Lords on 31 January. The Prince had been freed from the necessity of surrendering either to the demagogues on one side or to the Protestant fanatics on the other. 'He has a person in each House of Parliament who has spoken what he must *wish* to be considered as *his* opinions—and if he NOW chooses to put the Government into mine and Wellesley's hands I should not *now* hesitate to undertake it.'

Morpeth's motion was defeated by 229 votes to 135. Canning and his friends voted with the Government. Sheridan, one of Sidmouth's friends (Benjamin Hobhouse), one of Canning's (Mildmay) and two friends of Administration (Marryat and Odell—Odell, indeed, being a placeman in Ireland) voted with the Whigs. The division was not primarily on the Catholic question but on the Government's record in Ireland. In spite of the numbers Canning was now confident that the Catholic question would soon be carried. 'My speech,' he said, 'has carried it'. 'Perhaps in justice to the Mo[gul] I ought to say *our* speeches, for his had a great effect too—but it was rather from the shewing the *fact* that such were *his* opinions, and the inference . . . that such also are the opinions of the Regent—than from the development of those opinions in the speech itself. Be that, however, as it may, the question is, in effect, carried, and the Prince Regent is relieved from a weight of anxiety and agitation by what has been done for him by *us*.' Even Wellesley-Pole, the Irish Secretary, had to admit that the debate had been more favourable to the Catholic cause than any former discussion. 'It has shown that there is a very general inclination to consider their claims and to grant them further indulgences if they do not prove themselves unworthy of them.' After he had read the speeches the Duke of Richmond, the Lord Lieutenant, commented, 'Almost everyone who has

spoken in either House talks of it [emancipation] as a probable measure.'
For the first time it was debated as a non-party measure.

The division, Canning thought, was much more unfavourable to Perceval than appeared on the surface. If he and his friends had voted the other way, Perceval's majority would have been 82 instead of 94, or 76 if six more who had been absent had attended and voted with him against the Government. If Castlereagh's four friends had voted the other way, as they would probably do on a division on the Catholic question, the 76 would further have been reduced to 68; and if the Prince's four personal friends ('but they are at least 10') had voted with the Opposition, the 68 would have been only 60. If those who had voted with Perceval in defence of his Administration but who would not vote against the Catholic question, were also deducted, the majority of 60 would dwindle to between 40 and 50, and if half of those 40 or 50 changed sides on the Catholic question, Perceval's majority would vanish. Canning declared, 'This, considering the exertions which Perceval naturally would make and certainly *did* make, to bring up all his forces upon a question which if triumphantly carried, would have constituted him Minister in spite of the Prince Regent—is in fact no majority at all—for further is to be taken into account that manifest inferiority in the debate of which even his friends complained, and which, if the Prince Regent's countenance had been withdrawn from him, would have contributed to lose him the question.'

So Canning's gloom had been dispelled by the division and the great success of his speech, and he was now full of confidence. If the Prince chose to call upon Wellesley to form a Government rather than put himself in fetters by choosing either Perceval or Lord Grenville, Canning would be quite ready to take the management of the House of Commons and make headway against the combined forces of Whigs and Tory bigots. The Prince would have parted from Perceval on a public ground, not on a mere ground of liking and convenience; and the Opposition would lose numbers from their having refused a reasonable arrangement. Consequently the Prince, now that he was King *de facto*, would have the support of that numerous body of King's Friends who had always been ready to support the Minister of the King's own choice.

So the Catholic question had now to be considered, said Canning, as 'carried in principle—and only time and mode remaining to be arranged.' He and Wellesley began to explore the possibilities of Cabinet making. Canning still had no objection to sitting in Cabinet with Castlereagh provided that he was not in the War Department. It would suit Canning best if Castlereagh were given a peerage. Canning inquired whether Lord Liverpool could be induced to join them. Wellesley replied: 'Liverpool was very ill with the Prince Regent. I have laboured to reconcile them, and I *believe* Jinky feels his obligation to me in this respect. I judge from his countenance which, when he is sulky and suspicious, you know, is turned down like a pig's. Now it is up in the air whenever he meets me, and one of his best grins on it. He would be very valuable for the House of Lords.' 'That,' said Canning, 'is just what I was thinking. Supposing the Prince Regent [were] to place you at the head of the Treasury and of the Government, could you undertake for the daily business of the House of Lords? Your speech the other day shews that you can make a speech when you please—but have you nerves and temper and health for the daily work? I doubt it.' 'I doubt it too,' Wellesley replied, 'and at all events I am quite sure that I would rather a thousand times only have to come down and take my part in the debate on great occasions, and leave Jink in his present province.' Canning wondered whether Liverpool's opinions on the Catholic question might prevent his joining. Wellesley reassured him: 'I doubt whether his objections go like Perceval to the Virgin Mary. I apprehend the King's scruples were his.' Canning observed: 'I doubt that—and though I should wish of all things to have Jink, as I think him an able and honourable man, and think too that he acted with peculiar fairness in all the affair of 1809—yet it is essential in such an undertaking as we are now contemplating that there should not be any one man reckoned upon by us whose refusal would reduce us to stand still. If Jink, feeling his own importance, would not take the House of Lords, what is the resource? Could Lord Melville do it?' Wellesley thought not, and suggested Castlereagh—a solution which would take him out of Canning's way in the House of Commons, and in so honourable a manner as to avoid the appearance of a removal for Canning's convenience. In view of his having been Irish Secretary at the time of the Union, the Home Secretaryship, thought Canning, might be the most suitable office for Castlereagh at a time when they hoped to carry the promises of the Union into effect. Wellesley thought that Eldon was not closely attached to Perceval and not too vehement about the Catholic question. 'The King's scruples were his.' 'I know him but little,' commented Canning.

The conversation, which Canning reported to his wife, necessarily went no further. They had to see whether the Opposition would accept an invitation to form part of a new Government, whether, in the event of a refusal the Prince would have the courage to try 'the middle course' or whether he would fall back, frightened, into Perceval's hands.

Meanwhile, on 5 February the Prince had discussed the situation further with William Adam. He then thought that, since the restrictions would expire in less than a fortnight, the best thing to do would be to revert to the original plan of sending the Duke of York and Moira to Lord Grey, and Grenville might be called in if Grey, as was likely, refused to negotiate without him. Adam thought it might be better to send the Duke to Grey and Moira, but the Prince said that that would never do: Moira might think that he was to be the Minister. Moira should accompany the Duke because he was the person who was present when Grey and Grenville had their last conversation with him at Carlton House in January 1811. The Prince said he should speak fully on the subject, first to the Lord Chancellor and then to Perceval. He had no intention of inviting his old Whig friends to form a pure Whig Government: that would be to put himself in their power. He favoured the formation of a Broad Bottom Ministry. But in view of the Whig attitude to the Catholic question the Prince must have deceived himself if he genuinely hoped or expected that they would coalesce with Protestant 'bigots' like Perceval. In January 1811 they had rejected the idea of a junction with Canning, and there was no reason to suppose that their proscription of him had been modified.

The Prince was fearful of exposing himself to the charge of broken faith if he repudiated his pledges to the Catholics (Wellesley said that he was in absolute horror of mind), and he was equally afraid of the load of unpopularity he would bring on himself if he abandoned the Whigs, with whom he had acted politically during much of his life. If, on the other hand he kept the Tories in office their Government would probably be too weak to survive. Both Wellesley and Canning would go into opposition, and take at least twenty votes with them. Contemplating a Broad Bottom as a reasonable compromise, the Prince looked to both parties to make concessions. They ought to consider his own position. Though he had not taken the coronation oath he now professed to entertain a certain opinion about it. He maintained that he was still persuaded of the justice of the Catholic claims, but he now thought of a means of evading the issue by alleging that, though he himself had not taken the oath, the King had, and he was only administering the Government in the name of the King who, before his illness, had considered himself restrained by this oath. So, though in principle, he still favoured Catholic relief, it must be conceded at a time of his own choosing—in other words, not before the King died. The Whig Lords naturally regarded this as a trumped-up, disgraceful excuse, and they decided they could take office only if they were given authority to introduce and carry a Relief Bill. From the first, Grenville had been most reluctant even to consider the idea of taking office: a disinclination grounded on his 'total want of confidence in the Prince's steadiness and good faith.'

On Thursday the 6th the Prince saw the Lord Chancellor and said he was satisfied with his Ministers and much dissatisfied with the conduct of the Opposition in declaring against the system which the Government had been pursuing. After these declarations he thought it impossible that a Broad Bottom could be formed, and he intended to write to Lord Grey to this effect. Nevertheless, not very consistently, he proposed to invite his old Whig friends to coalesce with the existing Ministers.

Next day Perceval saw the Prince, who spoke in similar terms and showed him the draft of a letter to Grey. Perceval said that if he was satisfied with the Ministry, was determined not to change his system of policy, and thought it impossible that the Whigs could join the Government after the declarations which had been made, the offer of a junction would expose him to the charge of insincerity, and the Prince ought to inform the Opposition that in view of their declarations no offer to them could be made.

On Saturday the 8th McMahon saw Moira and asked him to postpone his projected visit to Cambridge, as the Prince meant him to accompany the Duke of York to see Lords Grey and Grenville. McMahon told him that it was the Prince's view that nothing could be done for Ireland so long as the King lived. Moira was therefore confident that the overture would be rejected. William Adam, however, disagreed: he thought that there was a possibility that Perceval might not remain Prime Minister, in which case the great difficulty over Ireland might be overcome, and, if the Whig veto against Canning could be removed, an Administration united in support of Catholic relief might be formed with the help of Wellesley. In that case the Prince would have to have second thoughts about the coronation oath.

After two conferences with Perceval, Eldon and the Duke of York on the 9th and 10th the Prince agreed that Perceval's advice was the most suitable. Perceval prepared a letter to this effect, and it was accepted on the 11th. But the Prince changed his mind, sent for Perceval and the Chancellor and told them that he must after all make the offer, though he knew it would be rejected. He showed then the draft of his own letter which contained an approbation of the Government's system of policy, especially with regard to the Continent, and declared his wish to have the friends of his early youth form part of the Government. He remarked that this last phrase was meant to exclude Lord Grenville, to whom, however, he was desiring Grey, in the letter, to communicate its contents. Perceval and Eldon repeated their objections, but the Prince merely replied that he knew nothing would come of it; that having promised (in January 1811) to give them the whole loaf, the least he could do would be to offer them half.

The Prince was persuaded not to send Moira with the Duke of York to Lord Grey, though it was obvious that Moira would be greatly mortified at being left out since he had been mixed up in the business a year earlier, and his absence would create an unfavourable impression in connection with the Catholic question, which was not referred to in the letter. The Prince later alleged that he had selected the Duke of York to convey the communication in order to show the Whig Lords that no one was then considered by him as the head of the Government that was to be formed.

On the 13th the Duke received the Prince's letter between 4 p.m. and 5 p.m. and he immediately set off with it to Lord Grey. At the same time Lord Yarmouth delivered a copy to Perceval who was on the point of going to the House of Commons, and Wellesley soon received one which he was authorised to give to Canning. Grey seemed pleased with the mode of communication. The Duke asked him whether it would be more agreeable to him if they went together to Grenville's house. Grey replied that he would like the communication to be made to them together, and it was arranged that they should attend the Duke at 11 a.m. the next morning, the 14th. The Duke offered to read the letter to Grey, but Grey said he preferred that it should be shown to him for the first time in Grenville's presence.

Seeing the Duke on the 14th they said they would bring him their written reply the next day. Grenville wrote: 'I certainly never read a paper drawn in terms less conciliatory, or, to speak more properly, I never saw one so highly offensive. Our answer will of course be short and decisive. There is evidently an attempt in it to create disunion among ourselves. This has entirely failed. The rest is all written for popular effect—how successfully time alone can show.' Canning commented: 'The matter is not ill stated, but there is more of the figure called rigmarole in it than a practised writer would have thought necessary.' He thought that the offer would not be peremptorily refused. 'They will put themselves much in the wrong if it is.'

Knowing that Grey and Grenville were engaged to meet the Duke of York at 1 p.m. on the 15th, Wellesley decided to seek an audience of the Prince early in the morning in order to urge the necessity of his empowering the Duke to declare that Perceval was not to be considered by them as Prime Minister; that they were not to consider themselves as called upon to join Perceval or anybody else, but that the office of Prime Minister as well as every other office, high and low, was open to arrangement if they would accept his proposition. Finding that he could not see the Prince so early, Wellesley wrote to him. Unfortunately the letter seems not to have been preserved, but there is no doubt that he did write. He pointed out that Perceval had received his copy of the Prince's letter to the Duke just as he was going down to the House of Commons, and that Perceval, replying to some observation from Curwen, had made a statement which was taken to mean that he was to be confirmed in the Premiership. Wellesley therefore told the Prince that this speech had created a strong impression of the insincerity of the Prince's offer. He further urged that it should be made clear that the Whigs were not to consider Perceval as confirmed in the Premiership. Finally, Wellesley offered to take the Premiership himself *pro tempore*, or in any other situation to conduct the negotiation with Grey and Grenville if they agreed to enter into it—knowing that they would refuse to treat with Perceval directly on the Catholic question or with Perceval as Prime Minister at all. Wellesley made it clear, however, that he had no wish to be in permanent possession of the Treasury: he was ready to serve under any suitable person except Perceval when the arrangements were completed. The letter was apparently received and acted upon, the Duke being empowered to give the assurance which Wellesley had recommended.

So, on the 15th, when Grey and Grenville brought their written reply to him, the Duke told them that it was by no means the Prince's intention that they should join the existing Government. 'His idea was to form an Administration upon a broad basis by a union of different parties of which he should consider himself the keystone and as a centre round which their Lordships and others might rally,' and that this was one of the reasons why he had chosen to employ the Duke on this over-ture. It had, he said, been generally considered as a piece of political etiquette that the person who was employed in such negotiations was considered as the prospective head of the new Administration. They had not known, they replied, that it was the Prince's intention first to dissolve the existing Government and then to form it anew. Would they then reconsider their answer?, the Duke inquired. Grenville gave a negative reply. A written paper could only be answered on paper according to the terms in which it was expressed. There were many other measures besides the Catholic question on which they differed fundamentally from the Ministers that it was quite impossible they could ever act together. If they came in only for a fortnight they must introduce a Catholic Relief Bill immediately.

The Prince never thought of adopting the third alternative, the middle course, which Wellesley had suggested to him. As soon as he received the Whig reply he sent for Perceval and told him that he must consider himself as his Minister. It was understood that the Catholic claims were to be postponed during the King's life and were never to be granted without adequate security for Church and State. On the 17th[1] the Regency restrictions expired. The real reign of George IV had begun.

1. Presumably at midnight. The 17th was a Monday; the Session had begun six weeks earlier, on Monday, 6 January.

3309 PRINCESS ELIZABETH TO THE PRINCE REGENT

1 Jan. 1812

As I shall not have the pleasure of seeing you I take the liberty of sending a ridiculous dab of a seal which I hope will make you laugh & believe that I wish you every blessing this world can possibly give. This time is an anxious one for you but you have acted so fine a part that all must love & respect you for it. Your kind intentions towards us is engraven on my heart, & tho' I do not expect to be *happy*, believe me, I shall be *content*; my spirits are sadly broken but I am sure you will ever be our friend.

Will you do me the favour to send me AS A PRESENT two silk pocket handkerchiefs as I wear yours constantly as a turban, its being the only comfortable thing I have to keep me *warm*. I have had a violent attack of rhumatism which has made me very unwell for the last few days, otherwise I would not have made this request. I can hardly hold my pen from pain & cold. (Add. Georgian 11/201)

3310 SPENCER PERCEVAL TO THE QUEEN [copy]

Downing Street, 1 Jan. 1812

Mr Perceval presents his humble duty to your Majesty and has to acknowledge the receipt of your Majesty's observations upon Mr Perceval's proposed arrangement for the Household during the continuance of his Majesty's indisposition, which were presented to him yesterday by Colonel Taylor.

Mr Perceval humbly hopes that your Majesty will have the gracious indulgence to pardon him if, before he enters upon any remarks on the detail of your Majesty's papers, he feels himself unable to repress the extreme concern which he has experienced from perceiving that your Majesty has been, even for a monent, impressed with the opinion that the proposed arrangement has been calculated upon principles of such extreme economy and reform as to render the plan itself incapable of being carried into execution with any due feelings of liberality or justice to the old servants of his Majesty, or indeed with any proper regard to the dignity of his Majesty's exalted character and station.

Mr Perceval is persuaded that this impression would never have been taken by your Majesty if it had not been from his own fault in omitting to give such an explanatory view of the result of the arrangement, and of the adequacy of the means of supporting it as would have rendered it impossible for your Majesty so to have misconceived it.

Mr Perceval is so far from 'being surprised that, with these feelings upon the subject, your Majesty should positively decline to have any control whatsoever over an Establishment which your Majesty declares to be so objectionable in principle and detail,' that he is only surprised at your Majesty's condescension in thinking the person who could present to your Majesty an arrangement which your Majesty conceives to be so incompatible either with the dignity or comfort of his Majesty, to be deserving of the notice which your Majesty has been graciously pleased to give to him by your observations on his paper.

But Mr Perceval begs most confidently to assure your Majesty that no such principles of extreme economy and reform have ever entered into his imagination upon this subject, nor indeed of any reform beyond what he is convinced your Majesty would yourself think absolutely necessary to be carried into execution upon this occasion. Mr Perceval was so anxious upon this part of the subject, and thought it so important to his own credit and character to remove as soon as possible this misconception that he lost not a moment in furnishing Colonel Taylor with the items of those calculations upon which Mr Perceval formed his estimate, and which he has the satisfaction of feeling convinced will, when explained to your Majesty, remove that deep impression against the arrangement, which, while it remained would render it hopeless to Mr Perceval that your Majesty should be ever reconciled to any part of it.

With regard to what your Majesty remarks upon the arrangement, and the persons to be selected to form a part of it, Mr Perceval begs to state that the arrangement proposed is certainly made under the hope and with the impression that it was suitable in point of quality, and ample in point of extent, for the purposes which, in the state to which disorder has unhappily reduced his Majesty, can either contribute to his comfort or to his dignity.

With respect to the selection of the persons to fill the respective stations Mr Perceval has nothing to say. Were it his duty to suggest anything upon that selection he certainly should be obliged to say that he thought that the choice could not be directed by more correct principles of selection, nor fall upon any individuals more properly than those named by your Majesty. Mr Perceval thinks it necessary merely to advert to this part of your Majesty's observations lest the principle of the arrangement should be misunderstood. That principle intends to leave to your Majesty to select these servants in the first instance, and to remove and replace them, afterwards, entirely at your Majesty's discretion.

With respect to what is observed as to the number of pages and inferior servants Mr Perceval begs humbly to state that it is intended to be left entirely to your Majesty to determine what number of pages and footmen and servants of all descriptions below that of the higher classes, which are specifically mentioned, shall be continued not only about his Majesty's person but about his Household; and Mr Perceval humbly submits, but most confidently believes, that the income proposed to be appropriated to this service will be found ample for the purpose of retaining all that your Majesty can upon any principle wish to retain. But beyond this consideration, Mr Perceval understands your Majesty has had it explained to you that it was no part of his intention that any persons should be turned adrift from his Majesty's Establishment. Your Majesty was to select the description of servants which your Majesty wanted, and the remainder would be to be transferred over with the Civil List to his Royal Highness the Prince Regent, to whom it would necessarily belong to consider what individuals he would retain, and on what terms he would be disposed to dismiss those, if any, for whose services he would have no occasion.

Mr Perceval in the first instance confines himself to these few observations, and refers to such further explanation as Colonel Taylor will be enabled to give to your Majesty in consequence of the full conversation Mr Perceval had with him yesterday afternoon; and Mr Perceval cannot but entertain a confident hope that the above remarks, with Colonel Taylor's explanation, will reconcile your Majesty to a plan which he feels confidently certain will be found infinitely more suitable to the station of your Majesty and the King, as well as more convenient to your Majesty than any separate Establishment could be, which it would be possible to prevail upon Parliament to sanction, if, indeed, Parliament could be prevailed upon (which Mr Perceval much doubts) to sanction any separate Establishment at all.[1] (19037–41)

1. Colonel Taylor wrote, in his diary on 31 December: 'He [Perceval] discussed the subject fully, explained the principle upon which he had prepared the arrangements proposed, refuting the Queen's objections to the prominent features of it, proved to me by various documents that his calculations had been liberal, and that it had been his object to pay every attention to the comfort of the Queen and her family, and desired me to explain this to the Queen, whose letter he would answer to the same effect.

'He also explained to me fully the footing on which it had been his object, in conformity to the wishes of the family, to place me; in fact, to create any office or situation, which would would authorize my continuation in the King's Household. . . .'

'*1 Jan.* [*1812*]. On my return to Windsor I reported to the Queen and explained all that had passed, but was disappointed in finding her so wedded to the idea of a distinct and separate establishment for herself, as not to be disposed to admit that Mr. Perceval's proposal was reasonable or such as would relieve her from difficulty or embarrassment; and she laid great stress on the preference given to the Princesses, to whom separate establishments were to be granted *now*, although the King never meant they should have them until after his death.

'I did not attempt any direct argument, but thought it best to meet her Majesty's objections, loose and ill-founded as they were, by observations given as *matter of information*, which were calculated to refute them. The Queen was friendly and gracious, but evidently not pleased with the result of my negotiations, nor did the Duke of York, who was with her afterwards, succeed in removing her objections. The Prince Regent as well as the Dukes of York and Cambridge and the Princesses in general, admitted the propriety and liberality of Mr. Perceval's plan.'

'*2 Jan.* Waited upon the Queen by her commands; found her Majesty still averse to the plan, but in consequence of a letter just received from Mr. Perceval, disposed to think he

3311 COLONEL MCMAHON'S MEMORANDUM RESPECTING HIS SEAT IN PARLIAMENT, ON BEING APPOINTED SECRETARY TO THE PRINCE REGENT[1]

2 Jan. 1812

Private & Most Confidential.

To first ascertain whether the acceptance of such office does or does not vacate a seat in Parliament.

To put such re-election (if it does) to the advantage of guarding against another, by whatever arrangement may be made hereafter for me as 'Private Secretary to the Prince Regent.'

When the Regency first took place in Feby. 1811 H.R.Hss. told me the salary of his Private Secretary as Regent would be precisely the same as the King's, namely £2000 a year. Soon after this, Mr. Perceval sent for me & with great kindness, in a very frank & satisfactory manner, stated the objections to this arrangement, & more especially as considering the King's illness would be in all human probability of a very short duration.

In this view of the subject I not only acquiesced with Mr Perceval but observ'd that I would not vacate my seat in Parliament (were such a step a preliminary

To move the writ for Aldborough in the Co. of Suffolk, in the room of John McMahon, who since his election hath accepted the place or office, of 'Receiver & Pay Master of the Royal Bounty of Widows' Pensions' so soon after the meeting of Parliament as may bring on the election Wednesday the 15th of January next.

A prospectus of a Secretarial Department was in the month of February 1811 either laid before, or convers'd upon with Mr Perceval by Col. Gordon with the authority of the P.R.

would not make any change. I strengthened this impression by the opinion I gave, and after some further discussion on the subject, and very detailed explanation on my part of the principle of the plan, its various features and circumstances which applied to its adoption and execution, had the satisfaction to find that the Queen seemed disposed to view it more favourably, and I concluded from all that passed that her objections, though not removed, were nevertheless so much weakened that on further reflection she would probably acquiesce in the propriety of what was proposed.

'Her Majesty had answered Mr. Perceval's letter to a certain extent, but agreed to appoint him to come here on Sunday next that she might have a personal communication with him, and desired me to write a note for her signature to that effect' (*Taylor Papers*, p. 74).

1. Given to Perceval, 12 January 1812.

necessary) for the appointment, but rather continue to do the duties gratuitously. Mr Perceval then remark'd that if his Majesty's illness should unhappily be prolong'd and the Regency grow into any length of time, then certainly I ought to have a salary as such, & it would then become necessary to see in what way it should be done.

As the Prince Regent would not burthen the country with any charge for exercising the Sovereign duties I must conclude that I could only be paid for mine during the past year out of H.R.Hss.' own private funds & therefore I wish for no remuneration for that period, only to be placed on a different footing for the future as a public servant. (19042–3)

On the 5th of February next, I shall have serv'd one year as Private Secretary to the Prince Regent.

3312   THE QUEEN TO THE PRINCE REGENT

Windsor, 2 Jan. 1812

Col. Taylor having received yr. orders to come to London I take this opportunity of informing you that I have received this morning an answer from Mr. Perceval to the paper I sent him on Tuesday, in which he has explained very circumstantially what he intends to propose. I shall make no comment upon the subject excepting that notwithstanding all the trouble he has taken it must & will ever remain unpleasant upon one subject which nobody can judge of but myself.

I hope you will agree with me that Mr. Perceval, whom I now will see on Sunday, should speak to Lrd. Winchelsea to know whether or not he will accept of the proposed situation intended for him.

I am sorry to hear you are not so well since Sr. Henry[1] left London. He will attend you at the stated hour & I beg you will if possible not detain him very long, as his presence is of great consequence here this

1. Halford.

day on account of the consulting physicians who will be here on account of Saturday. I trust Sr. H. H. will bring us a good account. (36602)

3313   RICHARD RYDER TO THE PRINCE REGENT
Whitehall, 3 Jan. 1812
Mr Ryder presents his humble duty to your Royal Highness and respectfully requests to be honoured with your Royal Highness's commands as to the hour and place which your Royal Highness may be graciously pleased to appoint for the Council on Monday next on your Royal Highness Speech upon opening the Session.

Mr Ryder presumes to conclude unless he should receive your Royal Highness's commands to the contrary, that your Royal Highness would be attended by the members of the Council on this occasion in full dress. (19044)

3314   THE MARQUESS WELLESLEY TO COLONEL MCMAHON
Apsley House, 3 Jan. 1812
Private. I am anxious to assure you that I am very sensible of your obliging attention to my wishes respecting Doctor Knighton,[1] whose valuable qualities are already well known to you although you have not yet had the opportunity of ascertaining them by so many proofs as I possess. The Prince Regent received my thanks yesterday with his usual

---

1. Sir William Knighton (1776–1836). In 1809 he had attended Wellesley as his physician on his Embassy to Spain, and after his return Wellesley recommended him to the Prince. Physician to the Prince, 1810; created Baronet, November 1812; Auditor of the Duchy of Cornwall, December 1817, and Secretary and Keeper of H.R.H.'s Privy Seal and Council Seal. He made himself indispensable to the Prince Regent and became his confidential friend and adviser after McMahon's death in 1817.

One of the Marquess of Buckingham's correspondents wrote to him on 5 January: 'The appointment of Knighton is of more consequence, I apprehend, than at first meets the eye. He is, without exception, one of the most accomplished and by far the most insinuating man of his class or profession, and very soon obtains influence where he becomes intimate. In his quality of *accoucheur*, which, in fact, is his trade, he is now at the head of his profession and has the keynote of every family almost, of distinction in the country . . . His devotion to Lord Wellesley is extreme, and as the Prince has resisted Lady Melbourne and other female favourites for these last two years, in recommendations for this place—in the naming to which it seems the Prince is more particularly fastidious than to any other in his gift—the appointment of Knighton to it is looked upon as a great achievement and likely to keep all matters steady in future' (Buckingham, *Regency Memoirs*, i. 174).

condescension & gracious indulgence; & I am led to hope that Doctor Knighton's name may appear in the Gazette of tomorrow night.

I request you to receive my grateful acknowledgments for your kindness on this occasion, in which I am satisfied that you have afforded a fresh instance of your stedfast attachment to our Royal master, by recommending to his notice a person of the most sound professional knowledge, of the most correct judgment, & of the warmest & purest heart.

It may be necessary to apprise you that any article intended for the Gazette, should be sent to Mr Rolleston[1] before two o'clock tomorrow. (19045–6)

3315   LIEUTENANT-COLONEL BUNBURY[2] TO COLONEL MCMAHON

War Department, 4 Jan. 1812

Colonel Bunbury is desired by Lord Liverpool to recall to Colonel McMahon's recollection the letter from his R.H. the Prince Regent to the Dey of Algiers. It was sent to Carlton House on Friday the 27th ultimo, and as the object presses, Lord Liverpool requests Colonel McMahon will take the earliest opportunity of soliciting the Prince Regent's signature to the letter. (19047)

3316   JOHN CHAMBERLAINE[3] TO MAJOR-GENERAL T. H. TURNER

Paddington Green, 4 Jan. 1812

I beg leave to trouble you with two portraits which I am desirous of the honor of having presented to H.R.H. the Prince Regent with my humble duty.

I published the whole collection of portraits after Holbein's[4] drawings

---

1. Chief Clerk in the Foreign Office.

2. Sir Henry Edward Bunbury (1778–1860), 7th Bart. Under-Secretary of State for War and the Colonies, 1809–16. Lieutenant-Colonel, 1803; Colonel, 1812; Major-General, 1814; Lieutenant-General, 1830. M.P. for Suffolk, 1830–2. Succeeded his uncle as Baronet, 1821.

3. John Chamberlaine (1745–1812), antiquary. Succeeded Richard Dalton as Keeper of the King's Drawings and Medals, February 1791. He published *Imitations of Original Drawings by Hans Holbein, in the Collection of His Majesty, for the Portraits of Illustrious Persons of the Court of Henry VIII. With Biographical Tracts*, 2 vols., folio, London, 1792–1800; and a quarto edition in 1812.

4. Hans Holbein (1497–1543).

in his Majesty's Cabinet, of the size of the originals, which are folio, and some years ago H.R.H., meeting me in the Park, was so gracious as to suggest the first idea to me of a quarto edition; and that he thought it would be a very fine and curious work if I were to publish the portraits in quarto, adding that he would allow me the honor of affixing his Royal Highness's name to the dedication.

I have therefore had those which accompany this letter engraved, and if my health should permit I hope to proceed with them, but at present I am so extremely low and weak as not to be able to leave my room.

It has occurred to me (unless you consider it to be an improper measure) that my son Frederick might have the honor of being in the room when they are presented to H.R.H., in which case you would perhaps favour me with a line, but I by no means wish it unless it entirely meets your ideas on the subject, and I shall consider myself indebted to you to present them. (19048)

3317 SPENCER PERCEVAL TO THE PRINCE REGENT

Downg. St., 4 Jan. 1812

Mr Perceval presents his humble duty to your Royal Highness and takes the liberty of inclosing for your Royal Highness's perusal an extract from a most handsome and proper letter which he received yesterday from the Earl of Cardigan,[1] expressing his Lordship's desire that his pensions should be cancelled from the 5 of July last. They are three—two of £131, and one of £150 pr anm. Mr Perceval requests to have your R. Highnesses authority for directing that they should be cancelled accordingly.

Mr Perceval takes this opportunity of acquainting your Royal Highness that he is now enabled, from the diminutions which have taken place in the pension list since he last had the honor of communicating with your Royal Highness on that subject, to carry into effect your Royal Highness's pleasure with regard to the contingent pension to Lady Dundas to the amount of £1000 pr anm. if your R.H. should be graciously pleased to approve of his so doing. (19050)

---

1. Robert, 6th Earl of Cardigan (1769–1837) succeeded his uncle as Earl, 24 February 1811. M.P. for Marlborough, 1797–1802.

Alnwick Castle, 4 Jan. 1812

Your letter of the 31st of last month giving an account of the spasmodic affections with which the Prince has been lately affected makes me very anxious to hear from you again, & I hope in God you will be enabled to assure me that they have entirely left High [*sic*] Royal Highness. I own I shoud fear that they proceeded from some nerve in the foot having been hurt when he met with his accident at Oatlands. I remember a case somewhat similar when the injury was removed perfectly, but the recovery was tedious. I shoud be ungratefull indeed if I did not feel more than I can express upon the occasion, when I am receiving fresh proofs every day of his Royal Highness's gracious favour & goodness. His consideration for my feelings in case Lt.-General Grey had been appointed to the command of the Northern District in the place of General Dundas, is such an instance of H.R.H.'s kind attention as calls for my most dutifull and gratefull acknowledgements, as the correspondence which must have been carried on between us from our official situations must have proved disagreable to both.

The papers last night brought us down the brevet promotion, which I perceive is a large one. The Hills are particularly fortunate, for I see there are three of the brothers who have got promotion in it. They are all three very deserving of it, & excellent officers.[1]

Lord Percy intends setting off for London tomorrow. I hope you may be allowed to tell him what line he shoud take in Parliament, or perhaps if you woud write *me* a line from yourself on that subject it might be as well, for else my friends, if not spoken to or written to by me may sometimes unintentionally err.

As I have no doubt but you must have a great deal of business upon your hands just now, I will not detain you any longer than to desire you to assure the Regent that I am most truly sensible of his unbounded goodness towards me; and as I think this will reach you on the 7th I beg leave to add, if his Royal Highness will permit me, my most sincere congratulations upon the return of this day, together with my most ardent prayers that every revolving year may produce a fresh accession of happiness to that most amiable Princess,[2] whose birthday it is as well as to himself. (19051-2)

1. Rowland Hill was gazetted a Lieutenant-General on 30 December; his brother Robert a Lieutenant-Colonel. Robert and Clement (A.D.C. to his brother the General) were both in the Duke of Northumberland's Royal Regiment of Horse Guards.

2. Princess Charlotte.

3319 RICHARD RYDER TO THE PRINCE REGENT

Great George Street, 5 Jan. 1812

Mr Ryder has the honor of humbly submitting to your Royal Highness the draught of the Speech which your Royal Highness's servants have drawn up for your Royal Highness's gracious consideration. (19055)

3320 SPENCER PERCEVAL TO THE PRINCE REGENT

Downg. St., 7 Jan. 1812

Mr Perceval presents his humble duty to your Royal Highness & has the honor to acquaint your Royal Highness that as soon as the Speech was read by the Speaker Sir Francis Burdett anticipated Lord Jocelyn, and proceeded with a long speech to move an Address containing all the perverted views of policy which he so frequently brings forward. He was seconded by Lord Cochrane. Lord Jocelyn then rose to move his Address in the shape of an Amendment to Sr. Francis Burdett's Motion—and he was seconded by Capt. Vyse. Mr Perceval had been apprehensive that the very unexpected course of proceeding adopted by Sir Francis would have discomposed Lord Jocelyn & Capt. Vyse and prevented them from executing their purpose, but they were not at all put out by it, and both of them made very good speeches. Mr Whitbread then said that he could neither vote for the Motion nor the Amendment. Mr Ponsonby said the same. The Atty. General & Mr Perceval said a few words as did Mr Dillon[2]—and the House divided against Sir Francis Burdett's Address, *238[3]* to *1*.

Mr Ponsonby gave notice of the intention of some friend of his, he did not mention his name, to move for a Committee to enquire into the state of Ireland but did not say when.[4] (19064)

1. Richard William Howard Vyse (1784–1853), M.P. for Beverley, 1807–12; for Honiton, 1812–18. Entered the army, 1800; Lieutenant, 1801; Captain, 1802; Major, 1813; Lieutenant-Colonel, 1819; Colonel, 1837; Major-General, 1846.

2. Henry Augustus Dillon-Lee (1777–1832) succeeded his father as 13th Viscount Dillon, 9 November 1813. Colonel in the Irish Brigade, 1794; Colonel in the army, 1806. M.P. for Harwich, 1799–1802; for Co. Mayo, 1802–13.

3. Wrongly given as 243 in Colchester, ii. 351.

4. *Parliamentary Debates*, xxi. 17–49. Ryder had written to the Lord Lieutenant on the 1st: 'Whether the Opposition are to begin with violent hostilities, or whether they will wait till the new Regency Bill is passed we do not know; and the reports on this subject are contradictory. Lord Jocelyn's moving the Address, and T. Tyrwhitt's circular to the Prince's friends to desire their attendance on the first day, which I take it for granted will be known, though it should not appear to come from authority, will puzzle some people' (Richmond MSS.). Michael Angelo Taylor was one of the Whig M.P.s to receive a circular from Tyrwhitt: he

3321   SIR JOHN DOYLE TO COLONEL MCMAHON

Govt. House, Guernsey, 7 Jan. 1812

From my heart do I thank you for your kind & efficient aid in poor dear Carlo's[1] promotion, because full well do I now know you work for your friends, though you do not chuse to say anything of it yourself; you know how I feel those things, & therefore will imagine what I would wish to say to you.

I congratulate you upon the attacks which have been made upon your place, because it has brought forth from all sides such gratifying as well as just testimonials to your character. If you lost your place I think you would be a gainer. What I should like would be that *you* should, with the concurrence of our illustrious master, in a short speech resign the office, 'finding that it was the sense of Parliament that it should be abolished' & then be indemnified by a better situation in the new order of things, at which the nibblers could not carp.

I hope your wife & you are proud of the conduct of your old comrades of the *Prince's Own Irish*, and I hope his Royal Highness will see that the glorious appellation with which he honored them has not been misplaced.

The recruiting serjeant who called them heroes though it was at the time a vulgar anticipation, does not seem to have been a bad prophet. (19066)

3322   THE EARL OF LIVERPOOL TO [?] COLONEL MCMAHON

Downing Street, 8 Jan. 1812

I send with this note the Prince Regent's answer to the Address of the House of Lords if his Royal Highness shall be pleased to approve of it. It is material that the answers of the Prince Regent to the Address of the two Houses should be delivered to their respective messengers tomorrow in order that they may be reported at the meeting of the two Houses at four o'clock. (19067)

wrote to Lord Grey on the 4th: 'I have refused coming up to give my vote favourable to the present Government. The intimation to me was strongly though kindly conveyed. I imagine that my future seat, if not my present one, is gone. Be assured, all is settled and Ministers are triumphant' (Blair Adam MSS.).

1. Carlo Joseph Doyle was a Captain (1807) in Sir John Doyle's Regiment (the 87th, or Prince of Wales's own Irish Regiment of Foot). In January 1812 he was transferred to the 4th Garrison Battalion and promoted Major.

327

Downg. St., 8 Jan. 1812

Mr Perceval presents his humble duty to your Royal Highness and acquaints your Royal Highness that the Committee was appointed for examining his Majesty's physicians, & that the same persons were appointed members of it as were upon the former Committee, with the exception of two or three who are not now in town.

Nothing particular occurred in the debates of the House this evening except a Motion by Mr Creevy[1] to postpone the consideration of the Supply for the purpose of considering the number of placemen in the House of Commons. On this Motion he took occasion to animadvert on some late appointments, that of Mr Rob. Thornton to the Marshalship of the Admiralty, but most particularly that of Col. McMahon. He did every justice to Col. McMahon himself, represented him as a most honorable man & faithful servant of your Royal Highness and as deserving any act of remuneration which your R. Highness could bestow, but he found great fault with your R. Highness' Minister for having advised the grant of this particular office—as an act of injustice to Col. McMahon, as bringing your Royal Highness into discredit, and as insulting the Parliament. Mr Perceval defended himself from this charge and explained the manner in which yr. Royal Highness had distinctly directed that upon conferring the office upon Col. McMahon, he should be apprized of the opinion which had been given upon different reports of Comsers. that the office should be abolished, in order that there should be no impediment to Parliament taking such measures with regard to it as they might think proper. Mr Creevy was supported by Mr Brougham & Mr Whitbread and was opposed by Mr Stephen, Mr Montagu[2] & Mr Croker. The House, not expecting any possible opposition to the Motion for a Supply, was very thin, but Mr Creevy's Motion was rejected by a very considerable majority.[3]

1. Thomas Creevey (1768–1838), Whig M.P. for Thetford, 1802–6 and 1807–18; for Appleby, 1820–6; for Downton, 1831–2. Supposed to be the natural son of Charles William, 1st Earl of Sefton. Secretary to the Board of Control in the 'Talents' Ministry, 1806–7; Treasurer of the Ordnance, 1830–4; Treasurer of Greenwich Hospital, 1834–8.

2. Matthew Montagu, 4th Baron Rokeby [I.] (1762–1831). M.P. for Bossiney, 1786–90; for Tregony, 1790–6; for St. Germans, 1806–12. Succeeded his brother as Lord Rokeby, 21 May 1829.

3. The numbers were 54 v 11 (*Parliamentary Debates*, xxi. 124). McMahon wrote to Sir Walter Farquhar on 12 January 1812: '. . . The flattering & consoling balm to my feelings which the H. of Commons, on all sides, so generously gave to me on the debate of the former night, together with the congratulations of such friends as you, upon such an occasion, would to my mind, more than remunerate the loss of ten times such a place, were it the pleasure of Parliament for ever to extinguish & abolish it; and become what may of it, the office *now* owes me nothing, thank God . . .' (Farquhar MSS.).

Col. Hutchinson then gave notice of a Motion for repealing the *Union* of England & Ireland for the first Tuesday in March. (19068–9)

3324   JOHN WILSON CROKER TO COLONEL MCMAHON

9 Jan. 1812

May I remind you that our weekly box has not been returned to the Admy. since his R. Highness has come to town & as tomorrow (Friday) is the day on which you expect it I should thank you to give directions to have it sent to me today. (19070)

3325   THE QUEEN TO THE PRINCE REGENT

Windsor, 9 Jan. 1812

Talking over with Col. Taylor the present arrangement by which of course some expences must fall upon me which are most just to those of my servants who would suffer by it, I thought it right to send for Mr. Mathias,[1] who is quite *au fait* of my affairs, to have an interview with Col. Taylor who very kindly informed him of everything, & as Mathias' report to me appears not to coincide with Mr. Perceval's provision for me, he will by my orders state to Mr. P. the difficulties which seem to arise upon that subject tomorrow who I trust will give him a fair hearing.

I think it but justice to you who have been so very liberal upon this subject, to make you acquainted with the step I have taken, feeling there was no time to be lost, & also being convinced that what is in your power to promote it, you will with yr. affection for me do what you can [*sic*].

I beg to be understood that I do not mean to ask what is unreasonable, as you very well know that I am always desirous to pay my servants myself. I send this by Mr. Mathias. Should you be at liberty to see him he will obey yr. orders & explain whatever you wish to know. I have taken this liberty as no time is to be lost to represent it to Mr. Perceval.

I beg pardon for this additional trouble & subscribe myself [etc.].[2] (36603–4)

1. See No. 3152.

2. Colonel Taylor wrote on the 5th: 'Another long conversation with the Queen, who appeared to me more reconciled to the general arrangement' (*Taylor Papers*, p. 75. On page 76 there is an inaccurate copy of part of the Queen's letter).

3326 RICHARD RYDER TO THE PRINCE REGENT
Great George Street, 10 Jan. 1812
Mr Ryder has the honor of humbly submitting to your Royal Highness
the dispatch which he has just received from the Lord Lieutenant of
Ireland together with the documents to which it refers, relative to the
enquiries that have taken place in consequence of a communication made
to the Attorney General by Mr Grattan and Mr Fitzgerald[1] respecting
the existence of a treasonable conspiracy in Dublin. (19073)

3327 CHARLES FOX CRESPIGNY TO COLONEL MCMAHON
Aldbro, Suffolk, 10 Jan. 1812
I have the pleasure of receiving your letter this morning with all its
inclosures. You will be re-elected on the 15th between eleven and
twelve. (19074)

3328 THOMAS JAMES MATHIAS TO THE PRINCE REGENT
Queen's Treasury, Middle Scotland Yard, Whitehall, 10 Jan. 1812
I feel myself much honoured and gratified in your Royal Highness's
gracious permission to present to you a volume of which I have printed
privately a *very few* copies.

I have humbly but zealously attempted to to [*sic*] promote & recommend the attention of the enlightened & cultivated in this country to the
literature and poetry of Italy, & I am convinced that your Royal Highness
will not disapprove my endeavour, as no person can be better acquainted
with the productions of that auspicious era than yourself,

'When the Muses rose,
And, wildly warbling, scattered, as they flew,
Their blooming wreaths from fair Valclusa's bowers
To *Arno's* myrtle border, & the shore
of soft *Parthenope*.' (19075)

1. Probably Maurice Fitzgerald, Knight of Kerry (?1771–1849). See No. 1655.

3329   SPENCER PERCEVAL TO THE PRINCE REGENT

Downg. St., 10 Jan. 1812

Mr Perceval presents his humble duty to your Royal Highness and has the honor to acquaint your R. Highness that the vote of thanks to Genl. Achmuty, Genl. Abercrombie & the naval officers concerned in the capture of Batavia and the Mauritius was carried this evening in the Ho. of Commons unanimously; and to Lord Minto for superintending & directing the expeditions. The vote of thanks was carried without a division but not without an opposition—Mr Sheridan, Mr Whitbread & Sir Henry Montgomery opposing it.[1] (19076)

3330   EARL CAMDEN TO MAJOR–GENERAL T. H. TURNER

Arlington Street, 10 Jan. 1812

Lord Camden presents his comps. to Major-Genl. Turner & in order to save that time which the sending this representation to Mr Secy Ryder might retard, he takes the liberty of sending it to him. From the circumstances stated Major Genl. Turner will perceive that it is very desirable the Proclamation alluded to should be signed this evening or tomorrow morning. (19077)

3331   SPENCER PERCEVAL TO THE PRINCE REGENT

Downg. St., Sat. morning [11 Jan. 1812]

Mr Perceval presents his humble duty to your Royal Highness & has the honor herewith to transmit a copy of the examination of his Maj.'s physicians, taken before the Committee of the Ho of Commons yesterday morning. The attendance of the other physicians who were not then examined being required at Windsor this day, the Committee adjourned till Monday to take the remainder of the examinations.[2]

Mr Perceval has the satisfaction to inform your Royal Highness that the examination went off very satisfactorily, no attempt having been made by anyone to enter into any enquiry which was not strictly connected with the present state of H. Majesty's health, and the probability of his recovery. (19078)

1. *Parliamentary Debates*, xxi. 131–46.

2. The Select Committee's Report, dated the 13th, is in *Parliamentary Debates*, xxi. 84–99.

Alnwick Castle, 11 Jan. 1812

I shou'd not have troubled you with this letter but to enquire after the Prince's health, & to inform you that I had safely received yours of the 7th with its accompanying papers. A paragraph likewise in a letter I have received inclines me to make it known to you. A person of the name of Goodwin relates, I am told, to everybody, 'that he received a letter from Lord Grey informing him that the Prince Regent wou'd in proper time fullfill the expectations of himself & his friends, & that he wished (this Mr. Goodwin) to make it publick.' Now tho' I am not as partial to Lord Grey as our friend Colonel Gordon, yet I [think] his Lordship has more understanding than to commit himself in this manner. But yet Mr. Goodwin persisting in the fact, which I understand he does, will do equal harm, in the effect it will have on the publick mind.[1] I am sure you see, my dear Colonel, the mischievous intention with which this report is propagated. It is ment to convey the idea that H.R.H. is playing a double game, & that whilst he is apparently approving & supporting the measures of the present Ministers he has pledged himself to engagements with Lord Grey & his Party. This, if it cou'd be credited, must give the greatest uneasiness to the minds of the present Cabinet & fill them with distrust & suspicion. The man I am assured persists in his story, & I really think you ought to get somebody who is acquainted with him to insist upon seeing the letter. The truth then must come out. Talking of Lord Grey reminds me that I received a letter the other day from Colonel Gordon pressing me in the strongest manner to consent to Lt.-Genl. Grey's being appointed to the command of the Northumberland District, & that he was permitted by the Duke of Y. to make this application to me. I was in hopes, my dear Colonel, from your letter that the Regent had already been so gracious as to have settled this point, & that Lt.-Gen. Grey was certainly to be placed on the Staff in Scotland. I am sorry to find on more occasions than the present one the unaccountable partiality which my good nephew has for the Grey family. But when he comes to put their interest against mine, & seems to think that ought to give way on all occasions to their wishes, & thus wou'd wish me & my family to play second fiddle to the Grey family in this county I cannot say I feel much flattered by the preference he appears to give them. I trust however the Regent will carry his intended arrangement into execution, notwithstanding this secret interference (Alnwick MSS.).

1. This person is mentioned in one of Tierney's letters to Grey (13 December 1811): 'Maitland tells me you do not leave Howick till the 29th, which will discompose poor Goodwin very much, as he made sure of an opportunity to unburden all his grievances to you before Christmas' (Howick MSS.) and see No. 3340.

3333 THE QUEEN TO THE PRINCE REGENT

Windsor, 12 Jan. 1812

By a letter Col. Taylor received this morning from the Duke of York I perceive that his interview with Mr. Perceval has not been able to produce any change in his arrangements respecting myself, & by a letter I received from Mathias he only says that he has seen the Minister but gives no particulars of their conversation. I therefore take the first moment to state to you that if Mr. Perceval means to put those expences relating to the board wages upon the Windsor Establishment I fear it will not be sufficient, & on the other hand it cannot well be mix'd, at least I think so, with any other. To take it away from the Maids of Honours [*sic*] would be shabby as they have a right of time immemorial to a table, & the sum of £470 was given in lieu of that, & to my lower servants it was given in lieu of lodging money from the first of my arrival in England, as there could be but one of my Pages allowed to be an inhabitant of the Castle. I feel Mr. P. difficulties most strongly & can only lament that he did not collect before he framed the Bill all the information necessarily belonging to a King's Establishment which, differing so essentially from that of a private family, might have induced him to make the provisions upon a larger scale. As to myself I must submit but will not deny that I expected upon the representation made to him by the Duke of York & the information Mr. Mathias has given him, of whose integrity he can have no doubt, I did hope he would have given it a more favourable consideration.

I will not any longer trespass upon yr. time.[1] (36605–6)

3334 RICHARD RYDER TO COLONEL MCMAHON

Whitehall, 12 Jan. 1812

Private. I am just informed that a Council is necessary to be held to-morrow for the purpose of passing the Navy Estimates, which will not admit of any delay.

I will beg the favor of you to lay this circumstance before his Royal Highness with my humble request to be honoured with his Royal Highness's commands at what hour & place & in what dress his Royal Highness will be graciously pleased to direct that the members of the Council should attend his Royal Highness.

---

1. Tyrwhitt told the Speaker on the 16th 'that the arrangements for the Queen's Household would excite great clamour, and that she was *voracious*, and had tormented the Prince in his worst illness, at Oatlands, with a visit to prevent his giving the Princesses an independent establishment' (*Colchester*, ii. 354).

I will only add that it would be desirable that the summonses for the Council should be sent as soon as you have the means of receiving his Royal Highness's pleasure and can signify it to me. (19101)

3335 SAMUEL WHITBREAD TO COLONEL MCMAHON, AND AN ENCLOSURE

Dover Street, 12 Jan. 1812

When the committee for rebuilding Drury Lane Theatre had obtained the gracious permission of his Royal Highness the Prince Regent that they might adopt the likeness of his Royal Highness as the subject of the common seal of the Company of Drury Lane proprietors, I was directed by the committee to request the favour of the President of the Royal Academy to prepare a design suitable to the subject and the occasion.

The committee were yesterday favoured with a letter from Mr West of which I take the liberty to send a copy inclosed by their direction, together with the drawing which accompanied the letter and the medal struck by order of the Highland Society in commemoration of the taking of the standard from the Invincibles in Egypt as a specimen of the talents of Mr. Pidgeon the artist recommended by Mr. West to cut the seal.

The design for that medal was given by Mr West.

The Committee have directed me to address you and to forward to you the design, begging that you will have the goodness to take an opportunity of submitting it to the consideration of the Prince Regent for the approbation of his Royal Highness together with their humble duty. (19109)

[Enclosure] BENJAMIN WEST TO SAMUEL WHITBREAD [copy]

Newman Street, 10 Jan. 1812

The subject of the sketch which will accompany this letter to you represents his Royal Highness the Prince Regent reanimating the harmony of Shakespear, in tragedy, comedy and memory of Garrick,[1] on the ruins of Drury Lane Theatre.

Should the design meet the concurring approbation of yourself and the gentlemen of the committee for rebuilding of Drury Lane Theatre as appropriate for the seal to be employed in the concerns of that Theatre, I shall hold myself fortunate in giving the device, and making

1. David Garrick (1717–79).

334

the drawing agreeable to it on the occasion as well as of assuring you that I am with great respect [etc.].

P.S. Should the design be accepted for the Seal the likeness of the Prince Regent and Garrick can be given when the model is made in wax for cutting the Seal. I have shewn the drawing to Mr. Pidgeon, and I find he is every way qualified to cut the seal from it, should it be agreeable to yourself and the committee to employ it. (19110)

3336 GEORGE COLMAN TO [?] COLONEL MCMAHON
4 Melina Place, Westr. Road, 13 Jan. 1812
I can easily conceive how much you must be press'd by immediate business; & were not the matter in which you have already had the kindness to take so much trouble of very great importance to me I would not now intrude upon your time.

I sent you that hideous bore, call'd a long letter, on Christmas Eve.[1] Do me the favour to let me know whether anything has been done, or is likely soon to be done, relative to its contents. Pardon my anxiety; relieve, if you can, my suspense. (19111)

3337 SPENCER PERCEVAL TO THE PRINCE REGENT
Downg. St., 14 Jan. 1812
Mr Perceval presents his humble duty to your Royal Highness & has the honor of forwarding the remaining part of the examination of the physicians before the Comee. of the House of Commons.[2] (19114)

3338 THE MARQUESS WELLESLEY TO COLONEL MCMAHON
Apsley House, at night, Tuesday, 14 Jan. 1812
Private. The Prince Regent, when I had the honor of seeing H.R.H. yesterday, was pleased to command me to attend at Carlton House at *one* o'clock tomorrow (Wednesday). This evening I have received a summons to a Council at *two* o'clock tomorrow. May I request you to learn

1. No. 3301.
2. Folios 19115-23.

335

from the Prince Regent whether H.R.H. wishes me to attend at *one*, or after the Council tomorrow?[1] This messenger will wait for your answer. (19124)

3339   CHARLES FOX CRESPIGNY TO COLONEL MCMAHON
Aldbro, [*15*] *Jan. 1812*
I have the pleasure to inform you that you were unanimously elected Member of this borough at eleven oclock today upon my nomination. (19126)

3340   COLONEL MCMAHON TO THE DUKE OF NORTHUMBERLAND
Carlton House, *16 Jan. 1812*
To your Grace's unequal'd generosity & to the noble & princely munificence of your splendid bounty I have again to pour out the gratitude of my heart & soul for another return to one of your Grace's seats in Parliament, as will appear by the enclosed letter this instant received from Mr. Crespigny: and the Prince Regent commands me to add, besides his admiration of, & his indelible obligation for the distinguish'd honor and benefits you have thus repeatedly bestow'd upon me the very great sense of further kindness which his Royal Highness feels for your Grace's consideration in having caused my re-election without requiring the necessity of a personal attendance, at a time when he was so anxious for my being so immediately within his reach, from the great pressure of business which so critically awaited him, & when his hands & fingers unhappily continued still to perplex & embarrass him. Such greatness & magnificent generosity as your Grace has shewn to me has no parallel, & it in truth so entirely overpowers me that I have no vent to my feelings but in silence & devout gratitude.

The Prince, I can assure your Grace, in *strict confidence* was more angry than I have almost ever seen him at the idea that anyone should have presumed to attempt the changing of Lt.-Genl. Grey's destination in command after H.R.Hss. had *himself* for cogent reasons in his own words ('Looking to my loved friend the Duke') directed him to be placed

1. This is Wellesley's last letter to the Prince Regent before the restrictions expired. He tendered his resignation of the Foreign Secretaryship on the 16th, but the Prince pressed him to remain.

on the Staff of Scotland, & *upon no account* to be sent into Northumberland, and your Grace may rely that General Grey will *never* be put upon the Staff for Northumberland unless *specifically applied for by the Duke of Northumberland*. I have enquired about, & search'd after this Mr. Godwin [*sic*] to whom it is stated Ld. Grey had written, & find him to be an impudent, maddish kind of fellow, whom, notwithstanding, Lords Grey & Lauderdale are in the habit of trusting in political experiments, but not I believe to the length, in this instance, that this man has asserted, because we know that Lds. Grey & Grenville have declared their intention to lay by & steer clear until the expiration of the Restrictions. I fee at this moment of encreased kindness a fresh impetus for being anxious to offer my sentiments of respectful good wishes to the Duchess, & the Ladies Percy, & to assure your Grace, with what unbounded sentiments of affectionate attachment, & obligation, I shall be thro' life [etc.] (Alnwick MSS.).

3341   SPENCER PERCEVAL TO THE PRINCE REGENT
Thursday evening, 16 Jan. 1812
Mr Perceval presents his humble duty to your Royal Highness and has the honor to acquaint your Royal Highness that he proposed the Resolutions necessary to introduce the Bill to provide for the Household arrangement, in a Committee of the House of Commons this evening; and that those Resolutions were carried without a division. In moving them Mr Perceval opened the whole plan with as much distinctness as he could. No one made any comments upon it but Mr Ponsonby & Mr Tierney, and their observations were upon the whole of such a general nature as to leave them pretty much at liberty to make their observations in future to any part of it. Upon the whole the tendency of their observations was to express an opinion that the arrangement was complicated when it might have been simple, and as far as regarded the attendance on his Majesty it was too costly, and also that it was establishing a second Court the influence of which might be prejudicial. Mr Ponsonby also seemed to object to the £10,000 for her Majesty, to which Mr Tierney said he would make no objection.

As to the £100,000, the specific vote not being capable of being proposed except in a Committee of Supply, the necessity of discussing it in detail at that time was disclaimed and Mr Tierney expressly witheld his opinion as not being prepared to say whether it was necessary or not, stating, however, as Mr Perceval understood him, that he would not object to it if Mr. Perceval should state on yr. Royal Highness's authority that it was necessary either for the assumption of the restricted Regency or for making preparation for the more permanent one. The whole was urged in terms of perfect respect to all the branches of the Royal family.

Some conversation arose upon a question put by Mr Ponsonby, with regard to the claim of your Royal Highness for the arrears of the Duchy of Cornwall; and whether that claim was to be renounced on this arrangement. Mr Perceval answered that he had nothing to urge on the subject of that claim; that it was well known that he had always been of opinion against that claim, and that his view & interpretation of what passed in in [sic] 1803 on that subject was that the claim was abandoned; but that he had received no commands from your R. Highness on that subject, could speak therefore with no authority, & only expressed his individual opinion on it. Upon this Mr Sherridan contended that Mr Perceval was quite wrong; & reading the Message of your Royal Highness, delivered to the House of Commons by Mr Tyrwhitt from the Journal, contended that the claim was not abandoned, but the suit only discontinued. Mr Perceval maintained his construction of the Message which Mr Sherridan persisted in representing to be erroneous.

The Resolutions are to be reported tomorrow, and the Bill cannot be brought in till Saturday if the House meets on that day, or till Monday.

Mr Perceval moved to reappoint the Secret Committee for examining into the amount of small payments made by his Majesty out of his Privy Purse.[1] (19128-9)

3342 VISCOUNT PALMERSTON TO MAJOR-GENERAL T. H. TURNER
War Office, 18 Jan. 1812
I must take blame to myself for the irregularity of the inclosed paper because I omitted to mention to you the result of an explanation which I had upon a similar case some little time ago with Colonel O'Loghlin.[2]

The irregularity I allude to is the circumstance of the paper having received the Regent's signature before it was sent to H.R.H. by the Secretary at War.

The manner in which promotions in this Corps have hitherto taken place is as follows. The Commanding Officer takes to the King or the

1. *Parliamentary Debates*, xxi. 151-77. The Speaker wrote: 'Tierney delivered a violent invective against the Queen's Court, which would grow out of the numerous offices about the King, which were to be under her appointment. Sheridan endeavoured to revive the Prince's right to the arrears of the Duchy of Cornwall, but without success' (*Colchester*, ii. 354).

2. Terence O'Loghlin (*c*. 1764-1843). Lieutenant-Colonel, 1801; Colonel, 1805; Major-General, 1812; Lieutenant-General, 1825. He was the Lieutenant-Colonel of the 1st Life Guards.

Regent a memorandum of the proposed exchange or promotion to which the Royal Assent is *verbally* signified; the Commanding Officer then gives or transmits the memorandum to the Secretary at War who submits it to the King or Regent for the Royal *signature*.

The first deviation from this practise occurred about two months ago, & upon communicating with Colonel O'Loghlin it appeared to have arisen from his not having fully explained to you the former mode of proceeding. You were out of town at the time & the circumstance had since escaped my recollection till this paper again brought it to my mind; unless therefore, his Royal Highness should wish to alter the practise which has hitherto prevailed, these memoranda should not be signed by H.R.H. in the first instance when submitted to him by the Commanding Officer, but sent to H.R.H. afterwards in the regular manner by the Secretary at War.

This matter seems so little important that I ought almost to apologize for troubling you on the subject, but it is as well to adhere to official practise & forms unless there is any good reason for departing from them. (19132–4)

3343   THE DUKE OF NORTHUMBERLAND TO COLONEL MCMAHON

Alnwick Castle, 19 Jan. 1812
Confidential. I cannot delay one moment, my dear Colonel, congratulating you on your re-election & assuring you that I feel the greatest possible gratification in having been able to contribute to the success of your wishes. To be any way instrumental towards the accomplishment of what I know to be the wish of his Royal Highness, as it is my duty so will it ever be my most ardent desire, & any success with which my endeavours may be crowned on such occasions will constantly afford me the highest & most unfeigned satisfaction.

A singular circumstance came to my knowledge yesterday which I think it right to mention to prepare you for what is coming. A person came to me & brought with him a large sheet of parchment on which nothing was written, prepared for the signature of names. To the top of this parchment was affixed by a single pin a small printed piece of paper, in two parts. The one to the Lords Spiritual & Temporal—& the other to the Commons being Petitions for the repeal of all the restrictions against Catholicks & claiming the right of enjoying all the advantages of other subjects with perfect freedom of conscience. This paper, so printed, I was then informed was sent down by a noble Lord to a friend, who desired it might be left at some proper place & as many signatures procured as possible, & that the friends to Catholick Emancipation, having

339

found that there woud not be time for engrossing the different skins of parchment with the Petitions, as they wished to bring on the question as soon as possible, had directed their being printed off, & forwarded in that manner, by which means they had been able to transmit them to every market town throughout G. Britain, & the words of the Petitions might afterwards be written on the parchment when the skins were returned. The one I saw was yesterday left at a stationer's, being market day. This is quite a new & most dangerous mode of procuring signatures for a Petition to Parliament. The printed paper, passed on, may be varied to suit the opinions of different persons, & indeed people under the idea of signing a respectfull Petition, may unfortunately, when the Petition is written & presented, find their names annexed to treason or rebellious threats. This proceeding does not quite accord with the intentions of laying by untill the expiration of the restrictions. At all events I thought it proper to communicate this circumstance to you. (19135)

3344   LETTERS FROM SPENCER PERCEVAL TO THE PRINCE REGENT
Downing Street, Monday evening, 20 Jan. 1812
Mr Perceval presents his humble duty to your Royal Highness and has the satisfaction to acquaint your Royal Highness that, after some little conversation between Mr Perceval, Mr Tierney, Mr Adam,[1] Mr Ryder & Mr Whitbread the vote for a grant of £100,000 for the expences incident to the assumption of the Regency passed in the Committee of Supply this evening without a division.[2] Mr Tierney suggested that it should be expressed to be for the expences *incurred* & *to be incurred* in consequence of assuming the Regency, and Mr Perceval's acceding to those words was the occasion of preventing a division which would otherwise have taken place.

Mr Ponsonby was not in the House, but Mr Tierney said that the Motion which was to have been made next Monday by Lord Geo. Cavendish respecting the Roman Catholics, would be put off and probably not come on before Monday sev'nnight.[3] (19136)

1. Princess Charlotte wrote to Mercer Elphinstone on 6 January: 'I sincerely regret Mr Adam quitting Parliament upon many accounts, and there are *too many* who are inclined to the Ministers, & *every* vote *against them* is of consequence; yet I *can see* that it would have been *very awkward* for him to vote. He *could not* in his *conscience for* these men, then he votes against the Prince; so that all this considered, he is relieved from a thousand embarrassments' (Bowood MSS.).

2. The Speaker said that some observations were made 'upon the Prince having formerly declined and now desiring an advance upon this occasion' (*Colchester*, ii. 357).

3. *Parliamentary Debates*, xxi. 227–34. The Motion was put off on account of the death of Lord George's son William on the 14th.

Downing Street, Wednesday morning, 22 Jan. 1812

Mr Perceval presents his humble duty to your Royal Highness and has the honor to acquaint your Royal Highness that Mr Brougham's Motion respecting the Droits of Admiralty came on last night and has continued till about one o'clock this morning. The substance of the Motion was to declare the existence of such a fund in the hands and at the disposal of the Crown to be unconstitutional, and after describing at length the amount and danger of the Fund, to resolve that the House would forthwith proceed to take measures for putting it under the immediate controul of Parliament.

His speech was long & in many parts very able & eloquent, but he was decidedly wrong in his law, & as Mr Perceval thought, extremely unfair in his exaggerated statement of the amount of the Fund and the possible danger to the Constitution from the abuse of it. The actual application which had taken place Mr Brougham likewise condemned with great asperity. The payments in aid of the Civil List, the advances to the younger branches of the Royal family, and some two or three particular items he particularly objected to. He was met by an exposure of his errors in point of law, by shewing that as the Civil List Act left the Fund with the Crown on the arrangement of the hereditary revenue at the beginning of the reign, it was not open to us now to take it away; that there was no manner of impropriety in the application of the funds, that all Governments in succession had so applied them, except indeed that as to the payments in aid of the Civil List, it had not been so applied till Lord Grenville's & Mr Fox's Administration, which application however was contended to be as unexceptionable as any—that as to any particular cases, they were all decided upon by a previous enquiry before the proper officers, and the whole case should be produced if any genln. thought that any one of them required explanation.

The speakers were

For the Motion	Against it
Mr Brougham	
Mr Brand[1]	
	Mr Courtney[4]
	The Atty. Genl.
	Mr Stephen
Mr D. Giddy[2]	
Mr Herbert[3]	Mr Rose

1. Thomas Brand, 20th Baron Dacre (1774–1851). M.P. for Helston, 1807; for Hertfordshire 1807–19. Succeeded to the peerage, 3 October 1819.

2. Davies Giddy (1767–1839). M.P. for Helston, 1804–6; for Bodmin, 1806–32.

3. Henry Arthur Herbert (*c.* 1756–1821), M.P. for East Grinstead, 1782–6; for Co. Kerry, 1806–12; for Tralee, 1812–13.

4. Thomas Peregrine Courtenay (1782–1841), M.P. for Totnes, 1811–32. Deputy Paymaster

Mr Abercrombie could not concur with Mr Brougham in his law nor in his idea of breaking in now upon the Civil List arrangement, but only in declaring the sense of Parl. with regard to its danger & as to what ought to be done with it at the commencement of a new reign.

Mr Tierney & Mr Ponsonby concurred with Mr Abercrombie, & moved an Amendment accordingly. Mr Perceval would not agree to any Amendment, He had no difficulty in concurring in any vote for the production of the further account of the application of the Fund, but he thought the language of the Motion & the nature of the argument by which it had been supported so objectionable that he would not consent to get rid of it any other way than by a direct negative.

The numbers were for the Motion 38
against it 93[1] (19138–9)

of the Forces, 1807–11; Secretary to the Board of Control, 1812–28; Vice-President of the Board of Trade, 1828–30.

1. *Parliamentary Debates*, xxi. 241–77. John Whishaw wrote to Creevey on the 22nd: 'You will be glad to hear that Brougham's speech last night was completely successful, and made a considerable impression. Horner and others, from whom I have had an account of it, all agree that, although not exempt from Brougham's usual faults, it was less strongly marked with them than any former speech that he has ever made, and upon the whole it is thought that he has done very great things both for himself and the question. With respect to the latter, Horner is confident that the discussion has produced a great effect, and that whenever a new arrangement of the Civil List comes to be considered at the commencement of a new reign, the subject of the *droits* will inevitably form a part of the discussion and will be very fully considered in any new bargain with the Crown. Brougham had collected a great quantity of materials in a very short time, and I was only afraid that he would be embarrassed by the information he had got together, and that he would fatigue and exhaust the House, but this seems by no means to have been the case. He was perfectly well listened to throughout, and even Lord Yarmouth observed to Abercromby that he spoke with great ability and great knowledge of the subject. This was towards the commencement of the speech; but when Brougham talked afterwards of the possibility, at other times and under other circumstances, of private funds being squandered in favour of a *mistress* or a *minion*, Yarmouth was distinctly embarrassed, and probably altered his opinion of the merits of the speech. By the way, it may be observed that the term 'minion' is a very good one, and if brought into use may have a considerable effect upon public opinion, and ultimately upon the politics and secret Cabinet of Carlton House. Whitbread was prevented that night from speaking from a very violent headache, and he was prevented by the same reason from saying much on Monday. I met Whitbread on Sunday at Lord Holland's, and thought him out of spirits, and I am afraid that he is out of health. Blachford voted last night with the minority, but I do not know for what reason. Calcraft was not there, and I believe he is *gone out of town*. There may probably be other defaulters, but I have not heard of them. William Lamb went away, as did Ward' (Creevey typescript).

Brougham himself wrote to Creevey on the 22nd: 'In the House last night the droits business went off as well as could have been expected, or indeed rather better. I had a d——d sore throat which obligingly broke out a few hours before the debate began, and has not been much mended by speaking. This annoyed me much, for it had the effect of *blowing* me very early, that is, I was jaded in the first ¾ of an hour, which in general never happens to me till the middle of the second hour; so I soon lost the command of my voice, and my first hour must have been very harsh and loud, and therefore tiresome. I recovered by degrees as I got into the *fat* parts of the subject, and I laid it on unsparingly. My illness did not prevent me from saying everything I intended to say, and I went (as you know I had resolved) fully and honestly through the whole subject. There was no other way of doing, and I felt that its real importance and the greatness of the occasion made it absolutely incumbent on me to do so at all risks of being tiresome. I must add, in justice to the Hon. House, that tho' I began at a ticklish time (about six o'clock when dinner is thought of) they all remained and listened very patiently, and latterly with great cheering to the whole matter. Indeed they clearly went along with me, especially for the last hour.

'These things you may like to know, as the reports can't, of course, have them. I fear they will also suppress my repeated attacks on Kings, Prinnies, and Yarmouths. I fired twice distinctly into Y.

'Let me mention what I recollect of the expressions because I am sure no notice will be taken in the papers.

'In speaking of the probable secret uses of the fund—I supposed it were the wish of some Prince, having a favourite, to reward a person who had no merits; nothing to show the public in his behalf—deriving his influence from hidden causes unknown to the people, or odious to them—some minion whose very sight was disgustful to them, or words to that effect; which brought Old Y'.s praises to a close. He had before that being crying me up to Aber[cromby]. In the end, taking your hint t'other night, I gave it him more in detail—supposing the case of America, I described a Minister or a secret favourite unimbued with the spirit of the Constit'n, or careless of it, so he walked safe within its forms, unacquainted with the feelings and character of the people, or insolently regardless of their rights—desperate from his own rapacity, or the blind pander to his Master's necessities, with just talent enough to be aware that boldness, as it is always the safest, is generally the surest avenue to power; and so forth, and I showed how the funds in question, if fenced by the doctrines of the prerogative lawyers armed the rapacity of the favourite, and surrounded with temptations the weakness of the Prince. During this there was a general looking towards Y. I learn that he flung out of the House and did not return for $\frac{1}{2}$ an hour.

'Our Resolutions having been sent to Tierney, Ponsonby and Whitbread, and shown to others, they made no objection, and proposed no alteration; but this was because they had not time given them. Sam would have gone all lengths, but T. and P. had *constitutional* doubts, and wanted me to withdraw, and move an Amendment on my own Motion. This I refused, so Tierney moved one, and admitted in his speech all our principles, only differing as to the time. I felt it necessary in my reply (which was devoted to the Citizen's peculiar use) to drive pretty stiffly at him; so we divided on his Amendt. Having explained that we (of the Mountain) approved of it as far as it went, but as it did not go far enough we should divide again upon our last Resolution, which leaving out a word, we accordingly moved and divided on . . . Nothing could have prevented our dividing first on our own strong Resolutions but that Tierney, Ponsonby &c. threatening to go away, and the temptation of a larger division on their milk and water Amendment made Burdett and some others come into the idea of taking the division on that; above all, because Romilly had let P. and Aber. wheedle him into a rash expression that he would not vote for our first Resol'n . . . However, these are minute particulars; the main point is, we were quite successful on the whole, no fight on t'other side.

'Perceval is in a fury at my inflammatory language from its effects out of doors. Courtenay (the pamphleteer) broke down in a maiden speech, and every one of them—Atty. Gen., Stephen, Nichol, &c. treated me with much courtesy notwithstanding the inflammatory topics with other passages too long to mention. Then, their tone is lowered mightily on the droits as a matter of separate right, and the general impression that we have done for them, on a demise' (ibid.).

3345 THE QUEEN TO THE PRINCE REGENT[1]

Windsor Castle, 23 Jan. 1812

You will see from the letter which I have written to Mr. Perceval and of which I send you a copy that I have not hesitated in acquiescing in the propriety of the suggestion which you conveyed to me through the Duke of York, and I hope that you will approve of the manner in which I have expressed myself upon this occasion.

I am too well assured of your disposition to consult my feelings and too well convinced, as I have stated to Mr. Perceval, that yours coincide with mine under the present circumstances not to be persuaded that those wishes which have already been made known to you in regard to the immediate appointment of the proposed Establishment for the King, and those which I may express to you in the event of future vacancies will experience from you that kind attention for which I have so often felt indebted.

Although I am surprised that Mr. Perceval under the expectation of such serious Opposition difficulties, should not have thought proper to communicate with me upon the subject, I must repeat to you that I make no sacrifice by surrendering the appearance of patronage, and I trust you are convinced that if I had attached any importance to this object I should most readily forego such personal consideration when placed in competition with the unequivocal success of any measure of your Government, for the prosperity of which I shall ever feel most anxiously solicitous. (36607)

[Enclosure] THE QUEEN TO SPENCER PERCEVAL[2]

Windsor, 23 Jan. 1812

The Queen, having reason to believe from a message which she has received from the Prince Regent, that considerable opposition may be made to that part of the King's Household Bill which provides for her Majesty's nomination to the superior offices in the proposed Establishment, has determined to relieve the Prince's Government from any difficulties under which they might be placed from a desire of carrying into effect that provision of the Bill.

The Queen is sensible of the regard which has been shewn by Mr. Perceval, under the Prince Regent's sanction, to her situation and feelings, in proposing that the nomination to the situations in question

1. In Colonel Taylor's hand, with the Queen's signature
2. Copy in Colonel Taylor's hand.

should be vested in her Majesty, but she assures him that her disposition has never led her to court either patronage or political influence, and that she makes no sacrifice by waving her pretensions to a circumstance from which, on the contrary, she had expected more embarassment than gratification; such embarassment indeed as the sole desire of doing her duty towards the King by selecting the individuals who, if it should please God that his Majesty should recover would be most agreable to him, could possibly induce her to incur.

Her Majesty trusts that, if any proof were wanting of her firm conviction that the Prince Regent is actuated by the same principle in his consideration of the King's situation, it will be found in the readiness with which under this feeling she has relinquished appointments to the *nature* of which she attaches so much consequence. (36608)

3346 SIR PHILIP FRANCIS TO COLONEL MCMAHON

23 Jan. 1812

Tho' I should be as happy as ever to see you now and then, I do not trouble with my visits, for reasons for which I am sure you will give me credit. Indeed my own limping state makes me incapable of any exertion. The object I am going to recommend to your attention will not give you much disturbance if you will only have the goodness to bear it in mind. A project for making a canal on the north side of the town is now on foot. The undertakers, for the honour of the name, but much more to get favour & protection, are pleased to call it the Regent's Canal. Now this canal is intended to cut directly thro' the estate of our friend Harry Eyre, and will do him a most essential injury. His trustees are now in treaty to let the very ground, which they want to cut thro', on building leases. The value of it of course would be reduced to very little, nor is it possible to give him a compensation at all proportioned to his loss. What I have to intreat of you is that you will, if you find that attempts are made to prejudice his Royal Highness's mind in favour of the canal, give us your assistance by explaining the case to him, so far forth at least that his name or authority may not be allowed to act against us, and that the parties may be left to fight it out on the strength of their respective interests in the case, and the merits of the questions.

Do not give yourself the trouble to write; only keep the thing in your memory. (19143–4)

Carlton House, 23 Jan. 1812

Most Private. Language has no expression which can acknowledge the grandeur & generosity of your Grace's acts of bounty & munificence, and the mode in which you have cover'd this last instance of so many such noble acts towards me before, by only naming it in congratulations, illustrates at once the greatness & splendour of the heart which induces the hand that confers them.

The Prince Regent commands me to reassure your Grace of his love & admiration, & to say 'that the world has no such goodness & dignity of soul as belongs to the Duke of Northumberland'. The parchment for signature to a projected but unexpress'd Address to both Houses of Parliament on the subject of Catholic Emancipation the *P.R.* thinks to be a most curious proceeding, but of a nature so obvious as to quickly disclose the 'cloven foot,' as it keeps pace with the political designs of the Opposition in forcing that question not only out of all course in Parliament, but not even in conformity with the instructions of the Catholic body itself, who had previously determined to take no further steps until after the restrictions had expired, but it would seem that as they knew of this determination on the part of the Catholics, the Opposition Junta chang'd their ground, & instead of waiting, as they had previously resolved, the arrival of this event, were at once induced to declare immediate war. *In great confidence*, I have to acquaint your Grace that a misunderstanding has got to a great heigth in the Cabinet, and chiefly from a difference of opinion on the Catholic Question, besides which Lord Wellesley complains that the inducements held out to him for joining the present Administration have not been fulfill'd, & that he cannot endure to continue longer to act under Mr. Perceval, who solicits to be permitted to give the Foreign Seals to Lord Castlereagh in his stead. This Catholic Question is obviously brought on at this juncture to embarrass the Prince by forcing him to declare himself before any imperative occasion even calls for it. I have also *in confidence* to tell your Grace that whether the *P.R.* keeps in the present Ministers or not, Mr. Yorke has announced his intention of quitting public office so soon as the restrictions are over, & Mr. Perceval looks for further support in Lord Sidmouth & his friends. The Opposition has been so impatient & has acted so unhandsomely to the P. that it requires great judgement and nicety to steer clear & with safety. There is nothing from the Peninsula, Sicily, or America; & nothing new at home (Alnwick MSS.).

The Lodge, Castle Hill, near Great Ealing, 23 Jan. 1812

I have a million of thanks to return you for your most kind and affectionate letter of Friday last which I found on my return home from Windsor on Sunday evening, and would have immediately acknowledged had business left me one half hour's leisure to have done so, but I really have been so unavoidably engaged for the last 3 days that, in the whole of them, I have not had a single moment I could call my own. Today however I am determined shall not pass without my endeavouring to prove by my punctuality in answering you how much I value your friendship and how highly *I* appreciate your kindness in writing to me. You make me quite wretched at the little prospect you hold out of my seeing you soon, tho' I cannot but applaud your repugnance to come nearer to the Metropolis at present, which God knows is the focus of everything that is odious. You enquire with so much interest about my health and happiness that I feel I may without incurring with *you* the reproach of egotism speak of both: the former thank God remains as unimpaired as I have a right to expect from the life I have ever led, but much alas! is wanting to the *latter* from *many* causes, but from none so much as from the disappointment I experience at no intimation being given me of an intention to consider me, when the restrictions are over, a circumstance to which, as *you* know, I have the best founded pretensions; and after all I have suffered, to see that I am neglected at that moment which I was always taught to look up to for the compensation of my long unmerited disappointments, is heart breaking in the extreme. However I may be premature in thus expressing myself, and therefore I am unwilling to say more on the subject; were *you* at this time so situate as to be able to remind my brother of those promises which you yourself witnessed in 1801 & 4, I am sure I should *not* want an advocate in you to urge him to fulfill them, but alas! I fear I dare not hope that you can now feel yourself warranted in interfering, and therefore I cannot think of being so indiscreet as to press you to write to him, even if you are still in the habit of so doing. The P——'s health has certainly been very much shaken since the accident which confined him so long at Oatlands, but I *do* really hope that he is now beginning to rally again, for I was far better pleased with his appearance yesterday than I had been for a very long time preceeding. I believe when the tendons snapped he suffered fresh acute torture; that he was compelled, for fear of the worst consequences, to take a most immoderate quantity of laudanum, and that *that* so affected his nervous system that it will be some time before the debility produced by it is removed, but *that* is, I apprehend,

---

1. The Duke's letter to her, dated 30 December 1809, is in W. H. Wilkins, *Mrs. Fitzherbert and George IV*, ii. 111.

the whole extent of the evil, and if *other* reports have got any credit we *well* know *here* from what quarter they come; I mean *one* to which neither you nor I are particularly partial: but thank God, that trait and a couple of others have operated a great *refroidissement*, at which a very universal joy is expressed. Could but the P—— see as clearly the character of the *other* individual, then indeed would there be grounds for rejoicing; as yet however there is no appearance of so fortunate an event taking place. All this I say to *you* in the fullness of my heart, well knowing that you won't betray me and that we have but one object in our way of viewing this matter, my brother's happiness and honor and the salvation of the country.

The poor Duke of Sussex feels most grateful for your recollection of him and your kindness during his illness; I fear his heavy pecuniary difficulties and the failure of all his expectations of relief thro' the P. often press hard upon him, and are the occasion of the recurrence of these attacks. With regard to yr friend Mr Bowen, we had better not enquire whether my list of chaplains is full or *not*, but direct him to send me his warrant for signature, and I shall be most happy to sign it, as nothing can afford me greater pleasure than to do anything that is agreable to *you*, from whom I have uniformly received every mark of the most affectionate kindness. I am still, as you will perceive from the date of this, resident at your old favorite spot, but as, after inhabiting the house without intermission for nearly four years, it requires a little whitewashing, painting and papering, I must necessarily submit to passing 10 or 11 weeks at Kensington, where fortunately there is little probability at present of the early return of my great female neighbour.[1] And now I am sure you will think, it is high time that I should take my leave of you, as I must nearly if not wholly have exhausted your patience by this long epistle. I shall therefore only add that neither time, nor distance ever can alter the sentiments of attachment, friendship and esteem with which I shall ever be proud to subscribe myself [etc.]. (45288–92)

3349   PRINCESS AUGUSTA TO THE PRINCE REGENT

23 Jan. 1812

I am commanded by the Queen to inform you that being most anxious to meet with your wishes in consequence of a message she received from you by Frederick, she sent immediately for Col. Taylor and communicated to him the purport upon which she was to write, and, equally desirous of being very clear and explicit, she caused him to write the

1. The Princess of Wales.

letter for her. She would have copied it but she really had a bad headache and therefore hopes you will excuse her only having *signed* the letter addressed to you.

So far I have executed her commands. Now I think it candid and *due* to you to tell you that she mentioned the subject to us after dinner, but not one word till Col. Taylor brought her the letters to sign, and she then expressed herself with great irritation at Mr. Perceval not having written to her saying, 'he wrote to me last year when he felt himself embarrassed and I answered him in very *handsome terms*, therefore it was an attention *he ought* to have had now, and I feel it very much'. She then asked my sister and myself if we did not think so. I said that it appeared to me *being your servant* it was more *delicate & proper* in Mr. Percival to speak to *you* upon the subject and that I made no doubt he had written last year *previous* to your being *Regent*. She looked very steadily at me and said with a kind of suppressed anger, '*That may be*, but still I think *I ought* to have been *addressed strait to myself*'; these were her words. Since the letter has been signed she has been very chearfull & good humoured so that I hope tomorrow she will have *forgot* all this *fantom of indignity*.

I am happy to hear you are better: Sir *Henry*[1] *really* has given me a very comfortable account of you.[2] The King has passed a more quiet day but both Sir Henry and Doctor John[3] say he is considerably *more weak* than at any period of this long and sad illness.[4] (Add. Georgian 10/50)

3350 SPENCER PERCEVAL TO [?] COLONEL MCMAHON

Downing St., 24 Jan. 1812

I had promised the Archbishop of Canterbury to enquire today of his R.H. whether he had any wish that the 30th of Jany.[5] should be observed this year by the two Houses of Parliament going to Church.

1. Halford.

2. On the 20th Princess Charlotte wrote to Mercer Elphinstone: 'The Prince is in *good spirits*, but his *hands still remain feeble*, but Sr. W. [Farquhar] is *not without* hopes of his *soon getting* the better of *that also*. His hands are to be *put into a warm bath* tonight, wh. he expects will do *a great deal* to ease the P. He told me, & I *declare* without having led to the subject, that he *often meets* the P. at diner at Ld. Hertford's, where he generally (always) *dines*; that there are but *few people* at these dinners, & that Ld. Yarmouth he only saw 2 [i.e. twice] there, but that he *frequently* is invited to join the *family circle*' (Bowood MSS.).

3. Willis.

4. On the 19th Tyrwhitt told the Speaker that the King was in great danger, 'and it was not impossible that any hour might put an end to his life. He would take no sustenance. Willis had attempted to give him milk and water, but had even been unable to approach him or persuade him' (*Colchester*, ii. 356).

5. The anniversary of Charles I's execution.

349

It had been for some years customary not to observe it, but in 1806 the King expressed a wish that it should be observed—and it has been so ever since—but the fact that the two Houses attend so very scantily that the pretence of their attending defeats the object of paying attention to the day by making the real neglect of it more apparent.

The Speaker & two Members or at most three are the whole Parliamentary congregation of the Lower House, and the Chancellor and a couple of Bps. is pretty nearly the whole congregation of the Lords. There seems also an additional reason for not requiring the two Houses to attend this year, as the General Fast is within 3 or 4 days of the 30th of Jany.

Under the circumstances I should rather think it would not be adviseable and would request you (in order to save the Prince the trouble of seeing me upon the subject) to state these circumstances to him, adding that I would not determine against the Houses of Parliament attending without first receiving H.R.H.'s pleasure.

If the two Houses do not attend, the two Houses will adjourn over that day, and no notice will be taken of it in Parliament. (19145–6)

3351   VISCOUNT STRANGFORD TO COLONEL MCMAHON
Rio de Jano, 24 Jan. 1812
Confidential. Notwithstanding your long tried friendship for me I should not think of troubling you upon this occasion did I not conceive that it involved matters of far greater importance to the country in general than to myself as an individual.

After nine years of successful and honourable service at the Court of the Prince of Brasil, I find that I have incurred my Lord Wellesley's displeasure, and that he has proposed my recall as a matter of absolute necessity. It is quite impossible for me to divine the grounds of his Lordship's dissatisfaction; it cannot arise from my want of success or consideration at this Court, for I am not conscious of having failed in any one negotiation that I have ever undertaken.

It may be that I have acted without instructions in the affair of Spanish South America. I did act without instructions, because Lord Wellesley never deigned to send me any or to take notice of a single dispatch of mine on that most important question: and if I acted on my own responsibility in consequence of his Lordship's extraordinary silence I have the satisfaction of knowing, and of possessing means to *prove*, that I & I alone was the means of preventing Buenos Ayres from throwing off her allegiance to Ferdinand VII and from openly declaring her independence under the guarantee of France. This I am ready & able to demonstrate. The position in which I was placed was most cruel—& if I have extricated my country from the inconveniences which must have arisen from Lord Wellesley's silence I shall never regret the loss of my employment, fatal as it must be to all my future pursuits in life. It is a hard thing for a man to sacrifice his profession; but that sacrifice is really great when he is so fondly attached to it as I am to mine.

All that I supplicate of you in the most earnest manner is that you would kindly endeavour to prevent the enmity of my Ld Wellesley towards me from injuring me in the opinion of H.R.H. I do humbly but confidently hope that H.R.H. will not condemn me unheard. I think that I may not unreasonbly expect this from such a character as the Prince of Wales. And if occasion should serve, may I beg you to lay me at H.R.H.'s feet, & to renew to him the expression of my never failing gratitude & duty, together with my respectful but earnest prayer that H.R.H. previously to taking any step which must consign me to actual ruin, would graciously be pleased to listen to my justification against any charge that my enemies may have brought against me.

But enough of myself. The main object of this letter is to beg that you will take an opportunity (if you should think fit) to intimate to H.R.H. the real state of affairs at this Court. It is to be lamented that the indifference of the British Ministry towards the Prince of Brasil has begun to produce in H.R.H.'s mind sentiments the most opposite to those which he formerly entertained towards England. It is absolutely necessary that something should be done to put him in good humour. He complains of unanswered communications, & of a systematic neglect on the part of our Minister on any point not absolutely and mainly connected with the extension of Lord Wellington's authority and influence in Portugal. But the great cause of dissatisfaction is the omission to pay him the compliment of an Embassy at this Court; he having an *Embassador* in London, & there being only an *Envoy* here: while we have lately sent Mr Wellesley as *Ambassador* to Spain. You know that this Court cannot brook the slightest appearance of preference to Spain; & this circumstance of the difference of rank in the Missions at the two Courts has renderd the Prince of Brasil more indignant & more seriously indisposed against us than it would be proper for me to describe. Something really ought to be done in this business, and I have no hesitation in saying that if the present state of the Prince's feelings be permitted to subsist we shall for ever lose his friendship. I am sure you know me too well to suspect me of a desire to exaggerate the Prince's ill-humour merely for the sake of recommending a measure which, if I were to stay here, might be personally advantageous to myself. I do most solemnly & upon my honour disclaim such intention, and I declare that I have no other motive for making this confidential communication to you than a hope that it may tend to the adoption of a different system towards the

Prince of Brasil, and one more calculated to maintain our interest at this Court.

I fear that you can hardly decypher this wretched writing. I have seriously injured my wrist by a violent sprain, & I can hardly hold my pen.

May I beg to know whether you have received my letters respecting Sir Walter Farquhar's nephew? This Court behaved with the greatest liberality in that affair. (19147–51)

3352 THE DUKE OF NORTHUMBERLAND TO COLONEL MCMAHON
Alnwick Castle, 27 Jan. 1812

In my last letter I mentioned a curious circumstance relative to the steps taken by certain persons to procure a multitude of signatures in support of their favorite plea of Catholic Emancipation, and which, as you justly observe in your letter of the 23d, is of a nature so obvious as quickly to disclose the 'cloven foot'. I now send you a paragraph out of the Globe newspaper[1] of Thursday the 23d the very mischievous intention of which cannot be mistaken. I cannot help being myself convinced that there is not a word of truth contained in this paragraph, because I can never bring myself to believe that Lord Granard woud have thus publickly committed the Prince in such an assembly; much less can I ever be brought to imagine that Lord Moira woud have authorised him to have done so. The evil design however with which this paragraph has been published is not one bit the less, because the account is false, and proves too plainly the purport of their eagerness for bringing on this Catholic question in such a hurry, & with so much indelicacy towards the Regent's feelings. It is done with no other view than that of committing the Prince in the strongest manner either one way or the other, & thus ensuring the loss of H.R.H.'s popularity either amongst the Protestants or the Catholics, and by so doing they hope to weaken his strength & enable them to dictate to him or force themselves into power as his masters. What however surprises me the most is that this article shoud appear in the Globe, a paper not only devoted to the interest but under the controul of the Lords G. & G. and their party. Surely if they have that dutifull regard for the Prince which they pretend to have, they shoud not have allowed such a paragraph to have appeared in their paper, & have taken such a liberty with the names of the Prince and Lord Moira. It will tend

1. 'The Earl of Granard, on Saturday last, added another to the names of distinguished and leading Protestants of Ireland, who have enrolled their names in a supplication to Parliament, for the emancipation of their countrymen. It was announced, by the same Noble Lord, that it was the anxious wish of the Earl of Moira that every Protestant who approved the great measure in contemplation should not be diverted by any ordinary impediment or difficulty

to do an incalculable deal of mischief. Excuse me, my dear Colonel, for treating this subject so much at length, but I am so much alive to everything which in any degree is connected with H.R.H.'s dignity, honour and happiness that I cannot help endeavouring to tear the mask from the face of those who, whilst they are pretending to be attached to H.R.H. are only occupied by their own interest; & to let H.R.H. see their undisguised characters & intentions. It is frequently the object of those who style themselves the friends of a Prince, to deceive him for their own advantage, or for that of their connections. It shall always be mine to speak the truth, & to clear away the mist with which they woud endeavour to encircle him.

By what you mention of the complaints of Ld. W[ellesley], his Lordship has very unwisely for himself let the P. into his true character, & proved to H.R.H. that it was solely his own interest & not any regard for the publick welfare which induced him to join the present Administration & continue to act with them; & the moment he found his expectations disappointed he was determined to leave them, let the consequence be what it woud either to H.R.H. or the publick. The services of such a person are hardly worth having. When zeal for the Prince & welfare of the State animates a man to devote himself to their service in any line or any profession, I honour & respect him. But when a man is induced to take such a step prompted merely by considerations of his own private advantage and interest, and pretends to bargain for what he is to get before he will accept of office or commission, making entirely a matter of profit & loss of the business, I confess I look upon him in the opposite light; and instead of esteem & respect I can only entertain a secret contempt for him. As for Mr Y.'s intended resignation, I do not imagine either the affairs of the P. or the publick will suffer much from it. He was one of the two of whom the late Mr Pitt used to say 'that he never coud determine whether it was more disadvantageous to have them connected with or in opposition to him. They were so violent & unmeasured in their opposition that they were very troublesome; & so very wrongheaded & opiniatre that, when connected, they generally did more injury than service to their friends.' I remember Sr Charles Saunders,[1] Lord Rodney & the late Admiral Barrington used always to tell me the affairs of the Admiralty were never so well conducted for the advantage of the State & of the Service as when a nobleman (not a seaman) of great rank, fortune & weight, so as to make him perfectly independent, was at

from subscribing the Petition. In this wish, we have some reason to be certain, all the friends of the Prince Regent strenuously concur.'

1. Sir Charles Saunders (c. 1713–75). M.P. for Plymouth, 1750–4; for Hedon, 1754–75. Entered Navy, 1727; Lieutenant, 1734; Captain, 1741; Rear-Admiral, 1756; Vice-Admiral, 1759; Admiral, 1770. A Lord of the Admiralty, 1765–6; First Lord of the Admiralty, August–December, 1766.

the head of that Board, assisted by two old Admirals, as Junior Lords, to act as his Council in matters merely professional, & who, by being two, woud prevent partialities & jobbs in granting commissions & commands. A professional man, as First Lord, coud not help entertaining partialities to or prejudices against certain persons, both perhaps ill founded, which did great injury to the Service. But the worst of all (the whole agreed) was when the Irish Lord had two captains or very young Admirals for his Council, for then they never remained quietly at the Admiralty to give him the assistance he wanted, but were always getting themselves employed at sea; & when in a Fleet were always disputing with the Admiral who commanded as to what were the intentions of the Admiralty, instead of obeying his orders. The situation of Secretary of State for Foreign Affairs is undoubtedly best filled by a person in the habit of being concerned in great publick correspondence & negotiations with foreign Courts, by having filled the previous situations of Minister in the diplomatic line. He is well acccustomed beforehand with the mode of carrying on business with foreign Courts, & probably personally acquainted with some of the principal persons at those Courts; which must always give him a great advantage over others in all negotiations. In this respect, from his station as Govr. General in India, Lord Wellesley always has appeared to me as well adapted to the situation he holds. Lord Sidmouth I believe to be a most perfectly honest & honourable man; most zealous & well inclined to act for the benefit of his Sovereign & the State to the utmost of his abilities. I have very little personal acquaintance with his Lordship, but from some of his particular friends I understand he is a person of a most amiable character in private life. I only wish his publick abilities were equal to those of the late Mr Fox. With Mr Fox's head & his own heart his Lordship woud indeed be a most valuable acquisition to any Administration.

The times are very delicate, my dear Colonel, and the present situation of the R– requires great caution & prudence on the part of those who are really & truly attached to him. I am not yet able to go up to town, & Lord Percy, with the very best intentions, is yet a young man. Confiding in that sincere regard which I am convinced you are so good as to entertain for me, I most earnestly beg of you that you will favour him with your advice how to act upon particular occasions so that he may conduct himself, & persuade his friends to do the same, in the manner most satisfactory & agreable to the person whom above all others I would wish to please. I know Lord Percy will be happy to receive your advice & act accordingly. Shoud he be hampered by any former declarations he can always retire on particular subjects when so embarrassed. Give him likewise a hint as to the general line he ought to pursue, In doing this I shall feel myself more obliged to you than it is possible for me to express.

It affords me great satisfaction to be able to say that my daughter

Isabella, Marchioness of
Hertford
by Sir Joshua Reynolds, 1781

Charles Philip Yorke

by an unknown painter

Julia is daily advancing towards health.[1] As for myself, I have been so weakened by long confinement that I improve but slowly & have for this last fortnight been tormented with a cold & cough of which I cannot get rid. The rest of the family are quite well; only the Duchess is naturally much afflicted by the death of her sister, Lady Beverley,[2] of which we got the acct. last night. We all unite in the best of wishes to you, & Mrs Mac-Mahon. I had an account of Lord Algernon's health a few days ago, & we are all here much rejoiced of course, at finding that Sr. Edward Pellew's kindness towards me, added to my young man's own good conduct, had induced him to appoint Lord Algernon[3] a Lieutenant, on the very day after he had passed his examination, on the vacancy of a Lieutenant by death of which Sr. E., fortunately for Algernon, got the official report from Malta, the day before.

Be kind enough to say everything proper for me to H.R.H. of the sincerity & fervour of my attachment to him. I trust this letter is a convincing proof. (19154–7)

3353   RICHARD RYDER TO THE PRINCE REGENT

Whitehall, 28 Jan. 1812

Mr Ryder has the honor of humbly submitting to your Royal Highness the accompanying Petition from Edward Phillips, one of the convicts whose sentence is to be carried into effect tomorrow.

Mr Ryder has the honor of respectfully stating to your Royal Highness that he has communicated this Petition to the Lord Chancellor and the Recorder,[4] and that their opinion concurs with his own that there is nothing in the circumstances disclosed in the case which can justify him in humbly recommending the prisoner to the Royal mercy. (19161)

1. Lady Julia Percy (1783–1812) died on 20 March.

2. Algernon Percy, Lord Lovaine (1750–1830), who was created Earl of Beverley, 2 November 1790, married, 8 June 1775, Isabella Susanna (1750–1812), sister of Peter, 1st Baron Gwydyr. She died on 24 January.

3. Lord Algernon Percy.

4. Sir John Silvester (1745–1822).

355

3354 SPENCER PERCEVAL TO THE PRINCE REGENT

Downg. St., 28 Jan. 1812

Mr Perceval presents his humble duty to your Royal Highness and has
the satisfaction to inform your Royal Highness that the Household Bill
went thro' the Committee this evening with very little further debate, &
no division.[1] (19163)

3355 COLONEL MCMAHON TO THE DUKE OF NORTHUMBERLAND

Carlton House, 1 Feb. 1812

Your Grace's most kind & invaluable letter of the 27th ulto. I had not
the honor & good fortune to receive so in time as to give me the opportunity of communicating its contents to the Prince Regent until this
morning, when H.R.Hss. rapturously confess'd that if it were possible
to entertain so sacrilegious a thought as to doubt the enthusiastic sincerity of your Grace's affection & attachment towards him this letter
was indeed a complete & convincing proof of its never-ceasing zeal &
fervour. His Royal Highness, fill'd with love & regard, commands me to
make your Grace his heartfelt acknowledgements & to assure you of the
indelible impression your constant kindness has made upon his mind &
memory.

The paragraph which your Grace had the goodness to cut out of the
Globe & enclose, is certainly a very curious proof of the various &
indefatigable operations of the political *miners* & *underminers*, but I am
sorry to observe to your Grace that there is still something more in this
paragraph than meets the eye, as I find that Lord Granard has actually
sign'd & been promoting this Address from the Protestants in Ireland
in favor of the Catholics, in which I fear he has brought forth the
insidious insertion of Lord Moira's name, & at which Lord Moira is
deeply vex'd & affected. It is quite impossible for me to express how
overjoyed & delighted I have been with the gracious, flattering, &
precious mark of kindness & confidence which your Grace has honor'd
me with in granting your permission that I might, without the imputation of venturing too great a presumption, take the liberty of offering my
opinions & information from time to time to Lord Percy on the prevailing
subjects in which the Prince may happen to take a particular or more
than ordinary interest, & I had yesterday the honor to wait upon his
Lordship with my first essay, who received it with all that sweetness &
kindness which so peculiarly characterises his manner, & you may rest
assured that with the attachment & gratitude which binds my whole

1. *Parliamentary Debates*, xxi. 381–99.

heart & soul to your Grace I must ever feel an unshaken love & fidelity to Lord Percy. The attempt last night in the H. of Lords to force the Prince Regent to make some uncall'd for or premature declaration, was baffled by a large majority,[1] & which I have no doubt will serve to give a tone & complexion to the debate on the same subject on Monday night in the House of Commons, where I congratulate myself upon finding that the Prince's wishes for the fate of the motion are in unsought-for unison with Lord Percy, as I have long known them to be with your Grace's sentiments on the score of Catholic emancipation.

I am inexpressibly happy at Lady Julia's advance to health, & truly concern'd to hear of your Grace's cough which is tedious to shake off at this season of the year. I sincerely hope from my heart that the Duchess is recover'd from both her illness & affliction for the loss of Lady Beverley. I must beg leave to offer my best respects & best wishes to her Grace, & the Ladies Percy, and have the honor to remain [etc.].

P.S. A Mr. Dodd[2] who is a Chaplain to the Prince Regent, has caus'd an application to be made to H.R.Hss. praying to be favourably recommended to your Grace, & I beg leave merely to lay his papers before your Grace, as I am no judge of the prayer of his petition (Alnwick MSS.).

3356   THE QUEEN TO THE PRINCE REGENT

Windsor, 2 Feb. 1812

I send a servant to London to obtain some account of yr. health, of which Sr. Henry Halford gave a better account on Fryday than I expected, but cannot feel easy to be any longer without hearing how the new remedies have answered, & I hope to hear that your health improves.

Just as I was going to write I had a message from Robert Keate the surgeon who wished to see me. He came owing to a report that you as Regent were to have two Household surgeons instead of one, & supplicates to be remembered upon this occasion. His attendance upon poor

1. *Parliamentary Debates*, xxi. 408–77. (Lord Fitzwilliam's Motion on the State of Ireland: rejected by 162 to 79.) 'The Opposition speeches will do mischief,' wrote Wellesley-Pole to the Duke of Richmond (1 February), 'but I think the mischief will act both ways. Lord Grey and Lord Grenville have given up the Veto!! Lord Wellesley's speech has, I hear, excited much discussion and conjecture. His saying that the question should be taken *early* into consideration was laid hold of by the Opposition and was not approved of by our friends. His defence of the Irish Government was very good' (Richmond MSS.).

2. The Rev. Philip Stanhope Dodd (1775–1852), the Prince's Chaplain since 29 October 1810. Rector of St. Mary Hill, London, 1807–12; of Aldrington, Sussex, 1812–52; of Penshurst, Kent, 1819–52.

Amelia for near two years, which he did with loss to himself, & likewise the four month constant confinement with Mary during the operation upon her foot, give him a right to expect *my making interest* for him. He also attends I believe your daughter & is a very attentive young man in every respect to his patients. I have now said all I can say & know to his advantage, more if necessary you may learn from others, & I only beg that you will be so good when you have determined what to do to let him know that I have kept my promise of acquainting you with his request.[1]

I shall long to hear that you are better. (36609)

3357   THE EARL OF LIVERPOOL TO THE PRINCE REGENT

Fife House, 6.30 p.m., 4 Feb. [1812]

Lord Liverpool has the honour to send your Royal Highness the dispatch of Lord Wellington with the satisfactory intelligence of the capture of Ciudad Rodrigo by storm on the evening of the 19th of Jany.

Lord Liverpool took the liberty of calling at Carlton House with Major Gordon as soon as he received the dispatches, but as your Royal Highness was from home Lord Liverpool has humbly conceived that your Royal Highness would not disapprove of the guns being fired, particularly as this has been done in all cases of a similar nature, and as this most important operation has been terminated in much less than half the time which the French spent in taking the same place from the Spaniards in 1810.

Lord Liverpool is concerned to be under the necessity of adding that besides the loss of Major-Genl. Mackinnon[2] who was killed in the assault there is very little prospect of the recovery of Major-Genl. Robt Craufurd who was wounded on the same occasion.[3] (19171)

3358   LETTERS FROM SPENCER PERCEVAL TO THE PRINCE REGENT

Downg. St. Tuesday morng., 4 Feb. 1812

Mr Perceval presents his humble duty to your Royal Highness and acquaints your Royal Highness that the House of Commons was engaged in debate upon Lord Morpeth's Motion for a Commee to enquire into the

1. Keate was the Queen's Surgeon, and, in 1812 Surgeon to the Prince's Household.

2. Henry MacKinnon. Lieutenant-Colonel, 1799; Colonel, 1809; Major-General, 1812.

3. He died of his wounds on 24 January. A monument was erected to him and MacKinnon in St. Paul's Cathedral.

state of Ireland till between two & three o'clock this morning, when the debate was adjourned till this day. The speakers were

For the Motion	Against it
Lord Morpeth	
Lord Tavistock[1]	Sr. J. Nicholl
	Mr Canning
Mr Hutchinson	
	Mr Peele
Ld. G. Grenville[2]	
Mr Herbert	
Sr. A. Piggott	Mr W. Pole
Mr Sherridan	

Lord Morpeth confined himself very much to the Rom. Cath. question passing over very lightly the late transactions of the Governt. in Ireland. Sr. J. Nicholl followed him with a very good speech, but going further into the Rom. Ca. question than merely stating what the present state of things required. Mr Canning took very much the same line which Lord Wellesley had done in the House of Lords; he spoke with very great ability and eloquence, but was charged by Mr Hutchinson who followed him with having made a speech which should have led to another vote— Sir Arthur Piggott attacked the late legal proceedings in Ireland, and made his observations on them a very considerable part of his speech. Mr W. Pole defended the Irish Governt. at much length, and seemed to carry the House completely with him in that part of his speech in which, describing the nature & proceedings of the Irish Convention, he repre- sented the Irish Governt. as having had no option but either to have done what they did or to have basely relinquished their duty. There remain still a great many persons who probably will speak, & Mr Perceval would not be surprised if the debate were to be continued into a third night tho' he hopes it will not.[3] (19173-4)

1. Francis, 7th Duke of Bedford (1788–1861). Styled Marquess of Tavistock from 2 March 1802, when his uncle, the 5th Duke, died, until 15 January 1833 when he was summoned to the House of Lords, *v.p.*, in his father's Barony of Howland. M.P. for Peterborough, 1809–12; for Bedfordshire, 1812–32. Succeeded his father as Duke, 20 October 1839.

2. Lord George Nugent-Grenville (1789–1850), second son of the 1st Marquess of Bucking- ham (1753–1813). He succeeded to his mother's peerage as 2nd Baron Nugent [I.], 16 March 1812. M.P. for Buckingham, 1810–12; for Aylesbury, 1812–32 and 1847–50. A Lord of the Treasury, 1830–2; Lord High Commissioner to the Ionian Islands, 1832–5.

3. *Parliamentary Debates*, xxi. 494–601. Canning wrote to his wife on the 4th about the debate: 'Yes, dearest love, I am perfectly satisfied with the success of yesterday: which, I believe, was as brilliant as my own love could desire, and, (considering that my speech and my vote taken together could please *neither* Party) more generally acknowledged than could have been expected.

Downing Street, Wednesday, 5 Feb. 1812

Mr Perceval presents his humble duty to your Royal Highness and humbly acquaints your Royal Highness that the House of Commons proceeded yesterday with the debate on Lord Morpeth's Motion which lasted till about 5 o'clock this morning. The speakers were

For the Motion	Against it
Sir J. Newport	Mr Adams
	Mr W. Fitzgerald
Mr Wms Wynn	
	Mr Mans. Sutton
Mr Parnell	Ld Castlereagh[1]
Mr Whitbread	Mr Ryder
	Mr Atty. General
Mr Ponsonby	
	Mr Perceval
Mr Grattan ×	
	Mr Croker
Mr Tierney ×	
Mr Odell × a Lord of the Irish Treasury[2]	
Mr Eliot ×	
Sir G. Warrender × [3]	
Lord Morpeth ×	

'I spoke early, and I hope very temperately, and with more than my usual slowness (or rather I should say with less than my usual rapidity) so that I ought to have a chance of being well reported. But I have seen no paper yet, and cannot tell. One thing I know that I left out a third of my speech—at least a fourth—which generally happens when I prepare myself too much—but preparation on this occasion was absolutely necessary. The policy and the propriety of the line which I took consist in this—the propriety in that it would be real madness in anyone, even a Government, however well disposed, to give the Cath. everything at a moment when they are behaving so ill, and when their behaviour has irritated all the sober people of this country against them—at a moment when too when if given, it must be given unconditionally without any securities, arrangements &c.—the policy—in that the Opposition, furious against the P. R., determined to press him upon this point now, when he could not yield—and to mix the question with that of the conduct of the Governmt. in Ireland which they well knew he had approved—in order to force him either to surrender at discretion (which however they could not hope he would do) or to marry himself once for all and thoroughly to Perc[eval] and his prejudices, and so become odious to the Cath. for ever . . .' (Harewood MSS.).

1. 'Lord Castlereagh declared himself for concession with securities; Grattan for concession unconditionally' (Colchester, ii. 366).

2. William Odell (*c.* 1752–?), M.P. for Limerick County, 1797–1800 [I.], and 1801–18. Lieutenant-Colonel Limerick Militia, 1793—death; a Lord of the Treasury [I.], 1810–17; [U.K.] 1817–19. He died some time after 1826.

3. Sir George Warrender, 4th Bart. (1782–1849). M.P. for the Haddington Burghs, 1807–12; for Truro, 1812–18; for Sandwich, 1818–26; for Westbury, 1826–30; for Honiton, 1830–2.

Those gentlemen whose names your Royal Highness will observe to be marked in the above list with a cross all declared that their vote was not given on the ground of imputing blame to the Irish Government, Mr Tierney & Mr Eliot indeed saying that they thought the conduct of the Irish Government should be enquired into, but the others declaring that they considered it unexceptionable and proper.

The numbers were, for the Motion, 229; against it, 135.[1] (19177–8)

3359 THE REV. JAMES HOOK TO COLONEL MCMAHON

Conduit Street, Wednesday, 5 Feb. 1812

I have always found you so attentive to my requests that I feel the less abashed at making one which originates in a feeling that always meets consideration at your hands. I mean a loyal attachment to the Prince Regent.

My object is to ask whether w[ith] your friendship you cannot contrive to attach to me some *nominal* office in the new Household of the P.R. I mean really *nominal*, and of course without emolument or income. Might not for example after the office of 'Private Chaplain' might not be given to me in addition the title '*Secretary for Foreign Literature*' or Secretary in the Literary Department or anything of the sort that your better judgement may suggest? I wish to be identified with the arrangements of his Royal Highness's Establishment but not to interfere when I know so much difficulty in selection must exist. Pray pardon this and turn it in your mind for me.[2]

I have never heard from Mr. Perceval about the Irish paper. Have you?[3] (19175–6)

Succeeded his father, 14 June 1799. A Lord of the Admiralty, 1812–22; a Commissioner of the Board of Control, 1822–8. He had been in opposition, but joined the Government as a placeman in 1812. Later he was a Canningite. His friends styled him Sir George Provender, on account of his good dinners.

1. *Parliamentary Debates*, xxi. 605–69. Wellesley-Pole wrote to the Duke of Richmond on the 5th: 'Nothing can have been more triumphant than the debate for your Grace's Administration. Not one of the Opposition attempted to grapple with any part of my argument, and Ponsonby made a wretched figure against us; Grattan very moderate, and rather approving of our conduct than otherwise; Tierney the same. In short, no one attacked us but Piggott, Parnell, Wynn, Ponsonby, Newport, and in some degree Whitbread' (Richmond MSS.).

2. The suggestion seems to have been unacceptable.

3. The following letter from Mr. Hook to McMahon is dated merely 28 March, but it was obviously written in 1813, Dr. Whittington Landon being appointed Dean of Exeter in 1813 in succession to John Garnett (died 11 March 1813).

Winchester, March 28

'I am sure you will be as much surprized as I am at finding that Lord Liverpool has given

361

3360 LORD ELDON TO THE PRINCE REGENT

Wednesday evening, 6 [5] Feb. [1812]

The Lord Chancellor offers his humble duty to your Royal Highness the Prince Regent—and takes leave to mention that he has had an opportunity of seeing Mr Perceval, to whom he has stated, with as much fidelity (as his recollection would enable him to state it) the conversation or the substance of it with which he was honoured this morning. He understood from Mr Percival that he was likely to have the honour of waiting upon your Royal Highness upon some other subject tomorrow morning. The Lord Chancellor will not fail very anxiously to consider what advice he can with propriety himself humbly offer to your Royal Highness upon the subject with reference to which your Royal Highness condescended to converse with him today, whenever he may again be honoured with an interview by your Royal Highness. (19179)

3361 THE DUKE OF NORTHUMBERLAND TO COLONEL MCMAHON

Alnwick Castle, 7 Feb. 1812

I coud not help being a good deal surprised, just after reading your letter of the 1st, in which you mentioned Lord Moira's being deeply vexed & affected at his name having been brought forward by Lord Granard in support of the Petition for Catholick Emancipation, to perceive by the newspapers that our friend had spoken himself in the House most strongly in favour of the Catholick cause. This I can assure you will have a very great effect in the country. People have been so long used to look upon Lord Moira as a nobleman the most favoured by H.R.H., &

---

the Deanery of Exeter to Dr. Landon of Oxford, having, as I concluded from the beginning, found it impossible to place so young a man as Mr Lowther in a situation of that nature in the Church.

'After the truly gracious manner in which you represent the Prince Regent to have entertained my request upon the subject I am sure you will feel regret with me upon the present disposition of that piece of preferment to a person who never could have had a pretension to it but as an electionering partizan of Lord Eldon.

'I am fully aware of the avidity with which Ministers at all times avail themselves of Church preferment, but if Lord Liverpool had been disposed to attend to the implied wishes even of his Royal Highness he might in the event I had contemplated have provided both for Mr Lowther and myself by allotting this Stall, which in point of value (under all circumstances) is fully equal to the Deanery of Exeter, to that gentleman.

'You are always so kind and considerate that I am satisfied you will pardon my breaking upon you even with my feelings upon this interesting subject; *doubly so* as the locality of Exeter in Devonshire air for Mrs Hook's health would be no less beneficial, than the step itself in my profession.' (17826-7)

one who was the channel thro' which the sentiments of the Prince were conveyed, that it will in this instance be a very difficult matter to convince the publick that he woud have ventured to take so strong & active a part in the debate if he had any reason to think he might incurr the Regent's displeasure by so doing. They naturally say had this not been the case, whatever his private inclination might have been, he woud have staid away; at least he never would have ventured to have shewn himself so zealous an advocate in the cause. This you must allow is very natural reasoning, & will I fear do a great deal of harm in the country. It is exactly what I am sure every true friend to the Regent woud wish to avoid at this moment; it is apparently committing the Prince, unless H.R.H. woud submit to enter into explanations which it woud be unbecoming in H.R.H. to do. Indeed, our worthy & good friend Lord Moira shoud consider his situation, and be much more guarded.

Knowing it was Lord Percy's wish to act in such a manner as woud give the greatest satisfaction to the Regent, I was certain that he woud feel himself most particularly obliged to you for any communications which you woud be so kind as to give him.

The Duchess, tho' severely grieved at the loss of her sister, endeavours to bear the misfortune with tranquil and patient resignation, the surest sign of real, internal grief.

I have returned you Mr Dodd's papers, who seems to understand making out his own story as well as any man with whom I have ever met. He certainly appears to be as keen & anxious to add to his Church preferment as ever his uncle was. The plain matter of fact is this. He is the Rector of a parish in the city of London of very considerable value, the presentation to which is alternate in my family & the trustees for the parish. Mr Dodd was presented by the trustees in their turn. The ecclesiastical law says, a Rector possessed of a Living to such a value ought not to hold a second Living. Mr Dodd therefore says, if I can secure to myself that I can be re-presented to this Rectory in case I resign it, I will do so. I then hold no Living at all, & can be presented to the little College Living, & then this Living being under the value mentioned, I will cheat the law by this fraud, & being re-presented to the great & valuable Rectory afterwards, I will thus hold them both in spite of the law. For this purpose he first began to endeavour to persuade me to forego my right, & consent that a resignation shoud not be deemed a vacancy. This of course, contrary to every rule & full of every mischief & injury to the person having the next right of Presentation, I positively refused. He then had the effrontery to propose to me to join with him in a simoniacal transaction; & to finish the business he has now the impudence to endeavour to draw H.R.H. if he can into being inadvertently a participator in this pretty transaction: for all persons concerned in simony are equally guilty. This I know, from the instance of a clergyman, an acquaintance of mine, who agreed to accept the presentation to a Living, to hold it for a short time, till another clergyman coud take it, & it was determined that accepting of the presentation under such or any promise of resignation was absolute simony, & rendered all the parties concerned subject to the punishment for simoniacal contracts. So much for the modest Parson Dodd! I perceive to the Bp. he has told the truth, but not the whole truth. (19182–3)

3362   LORD ELDON TO THE PRINCE REGENT

7 Feb. 1812

The Lord Chancellor takes leave dutifully to state to your Royal Highness the Prince Regent that Mr Justice Lawrence,[1] being advised by his physicians that it is of importance to the restoration of his health that he should not go the next Circuit, has humbly requested that the Chancellor would submit to your Royal Highness his humble prayer that Mr Sert. Marshall[2] may officiate in his room upon the Circuit. The Lord Chancellor presumes to express his hope that your Royal Highness will be graciously pleased to grant the request of this most excellent Judge. (19190–1)

3363   SPENCER PERCEVAL TO THE PRINCE REGENT

Downing Street, Friday evening, 7 Feb. 1812

Mr Perceval presents his humble duty to your Royal Highness and has the satisfaction of informing your Royal Highness that he succeeded beyond his expectation in his resistance to Mr Bankes's Reversion Bill. Mr W. Dundas began the debate by opposing it; he was answered by Mr Bankes. Mr Perceval followed Mr Bankes, and Mr Whitbread, Mr W. Elliot, Mr Ponsonby, Mr Davis Giddy followed Mr Perceval in support of the Bill. The House divided 56 against the Bill and 52 for it.[3] (19184)

1. Sir Soulden Lawrence (1751–1814), Justice of the Common Pleas, and knighted, 1794; King's Bench Judge, 1794; returned to the Common Pleas, 1808; retired, 1812.

2. Samuel Marshall.

3. *Parliamentary Debates*, xxi. 691–700. Romilly said that Perceval opposed the second reading, without giving any previous notice of his intention to do so, although on former occasions the Bill had passed the Commons almost without opposition. (Romilly, *Memoirs*, iii. 9).

3364 SPENCER PERCEVAL TO COLONEL MCMAHON

Downg. St., 8 Feb. 1812

His Royal Highness commanded me yesterday to acquaint the Lord Chancellor that H.R.H. would see his Lordship & me at Carlton House tomorrow, but I carelessly came away without settling the hour. I wish you therefore to be so good as to present my duty to his R.H. and desire to know whether he would have us wait upon him after Church at *one* o'clock or at what other hour.[1] (19193)

3365 LADY HONYWOOD[2] TO THE PRINCE REGENT

Westbourne Farm, 8 Feb. 1812

There was a period in my life in which I frequently had the honor of seeing your Royal Highness and when I could have addressed you without embarassment. The case is now widely different! I now look up to you as my Sovereign!, the father of your people and the particular protector of the orphan and the widow, in which latter character *I* now present myself before your Royal Highness.

The person your Royal Highness has more than once honored with the name of *friend* now addresses you from the confines of a prison! Feeling and good as is the heart of your Royal Highness you will be shocked to hear that it is the award of an unnatural and unprincipled son (who by breaking the most solemn promises and engagements made to his dying father, and not by any extravagance or misconduct of mine) obliges me to submit to this decree. From particular circumstances in the late Sir John Honeywood's affairs my provision was obliged to depend, and rest in a great measure on the honor of my son; and my husband not being able to make me independent of him (I can safely affirm) shortened his days. Next week by the orders of my son I am to be submitted to confinement! In this wretched situation, Sir, allow me to interest your Royal Highess in favor of my unfortunate girl, my orphan Louisa. She has no friend to look up to but myself, and my imprisonment will most

---

1. The Speaker wrote on the 9th, 'Rose told me that Perceval was to see the Regent again today, but in the meantime he had thought himself at liberty to communicate to the Cabinet anything that had passed' (*Colchester*, ii. 368).

2. Sir John Honywood (*c.* 1757–1806), 4th Bart., M.P. for Steyning, 1784–5, 1788–90; for Canterbury, 1790–6, 1797–1802; for Honiton, 1802–6, married, 13 December 1779, Frances, daughter of William, 2nd Viscount Courtenay (1742–88). She had one son and six daughters. The son, Sir John Courtenay Honywood (1787–1832), succeeded as 5th Bart., 29 March 1806. The unmarried daughter Louise Catherine (*d.* 1822) married the Rev. Henry R. Quartly in 1820.

probably soon terminate my miserable existence! I have applied to my own family for redress but in vain.

One gleam of hope presents itself to me which *is* to obtain the patronage of your Royal Highness to support my claim to the Barony of Redvers to which there is a small income attatched and which had my father lived six months longer would have been mine. If through your Royal Highness's interference I should be permitted to obtain this Peerage (which I only ask for my natural life) the emolument which appertains to it would enable me to overcome my present calamity and peacably to end those days which distress of mind will otherwise speedily destroy.

Redvers is a female Barony attatched to the eldest daughter of the house of Courtenay by Ethelred King of England, but which was attainted by Queen Mary with the other honors of my noble house in the person of Henry Marquis of Exeter.[1] I must also further take the liberty of requesting to be allowed to present a memorial I have written which will explain to your Royal Highness my precise situation. This is a duty I owe to the memory of Sir John Honeywood, my husband, and the zealous and attatched friend of your Royal Highness. I went to London yesterday to have the honor of an interview with his Royal Highness the Duke of York, my motive for which was to solicit his good offices in procuring for me if possible an Audience from your Royal Highness which would be of the most essential service to me in my present situation. After seeing his Royal Highness yesterday I had an intimation from the Under-Sheriff that I must be at Maidstone on Monday. Under such circumstances might I implore your Royal Highness to give me an Audience of a few minutes at any hour tomorrow, but should your present situation, Sir, render this request impossible may I beg and beseech that you will bear this my petition in your mind and before it is too late grant me the redress I have presumed to solicit. (19197–8)

3366 SAMUEL PEPYS COCKERELL TO MAJOR-GENERAL T. H. TURNER
Saville Row, 9 Feb. 1812
In the last note I had the honour to receive from you, returning to me the sketches of the Egina Marbles, you express'd a desire to hear any further intelligence which might be received of them. I therefore beg leave to

1. Henry Courtenay, 10th Earl of Devon (*c.* 1498–1539), was created Marquess of Exeter in 1525. His second but only surviving son, Edward (1526–56) was created Earl of Devon in 1553, but was implicated in Wyatt's rebellion and imprisoned. His estates were divided among his heirs. After his death the title was considered extinct for nearly three centuries, and was conferred in 1603 and again in 1618 on quite different families (G.E.C.).

acquaint you that by a letter receiv'd yesterday from Mr. C. R. Cockerell at Athens dated 25th Novr. my expectations of their early arrival in England are very much disappointed.

It appears that at the time arrangemts. were forming here for bringing them to this country, provided they were not previously disposed of, the owners of them had mutually entered into written obligations for their being publickly sold in November *1812* & issued notices to that effect in the Continental papers, whereby they feel themselves for the present precluded from the benefit of the liberal terms of the British Governt.

To secure them however from the hazards of war by remaining at Zante they had by letter dated 25 Novr. requested Captn. Percival[1] of the Paulina brig of war, who had been dispatch'd to Zante on that service, to convey them to Malta for protection.

I am therefore not without confident hope that they may yet be added to the collections of antient art in this country.

At the date of my son's letter he was in the hurry of embarking for Egypt with the Honble. Mr F. North & his nephew Mr. Douglas,[2] from whence they expected to return to Greece in April, so that he did not know whether Capt. Percival could receive & convey the marbles to Malta upon the terms requested, vizt., for safe custody only. (19199)

3367   THE EARL OF DERBY TO [?] COLONEL MCMAHON

The Oaks, 10 Feb. 1812

Some weeks since I did myself the honor of transmitting to you a Petition which I had been desired by some of the most respectable gentlemen of Liverpool to present on their behalf to his Royal Highness the Prince Regent upon the subject of certain Orders of Council, and at the same time I took the liberty of addressing a note to you in which I requested you would lay this Petition before his Royal Highness in the way you thought most likely to call his attention to the subject. I immediately informed the gentlemen interested in the fate of this Petition with what I had done, & told them that whenever I was honoured with any answer the same should be communicated to them. This day's post has brought me a most urgent letter to know how far I had been able to obtain any answer or notice of their Petition. I am therefore under the necessity of again troubling you to request you will favor

1. Westby Perceval. Lieutenant, 1800; Commander, 1808; Captain, October 1813.

2. Frederick Sylvester North Douglas (1791–1819). M.P. for Banbury, 1812–19. His father was Lord Glenbervie; his mother, Catherine Anne North, daughter of the 2nd Earl of Guilford (the Prime Minister), was the sister of Frederick North (1766–1827), who succeeded his brother Francis as 5th Earl of Guilford on 11 January 1817.

me with some answer or acknowledgement that you have received this Petition from me that I may stand excused to those who entrusted it to my care, so far as may convince them I have not neglected any thing which was in my power to facilitate the conveyance of their Petition to the feet of his Royal Highness.

Pray send your answer to Grosvenor Square.[1] (19200)

3368   COLONEL MCMAHON TO THE DUKE OF NORTHUMBERLAND

Carlton House, 12 Feb. 1812

Most Private. I have again, since I last had the honor of writing to your Grace, such a severe & heavy return of my cold that I have undergone an illness not less acute than before, & have been obliged to confine myself to my bedroom for several days, otherwise I should have sent you the particulars of Ciudad Roderigo before they made their appearance in the Gazette, but I was really so unwell at the time as not to have known of them myself.

It having occur'd to the P.R. that the Restrictions being now on the eve of expiring, it would be not only consolatory to the country but expected in candour & fairness that H.R.Hss. should evince some disposition, founded in sincerity, for not proscribing any set of men, from political differences, against discussing, & if possible agreeing on certain measures which might enable him to form a vigorous & firm Administration on a broad basis. He has accordingly prepared a sort of State Paper or Manifesto, which I herewith *confidentially* transmit to your Grace, & which no eye but those concern'd in the mere writing of it has yet seen, a copy of which it is his present intention to give the

1. The Earl of Carlisle wrote to the Prince Regent on 10 February 1812, from Grosvenor Place: 'With a most grateful recollection of the flattering protection, with which you honoured my son Frederick, and under the strong conviction that neither in thought, word, or deed, he has ever intentionally done anything to forfeit your good opinion and favour, I feel courage when I advance his name to your R. Highness's notice, and humbly suggest the advantage that will accrue to him should you, Sir, condescend to place him upon the list of your Aides-de Camp; conceiving his rank in the Army does not preclude him from this honour, it having been acceded to the pretensions of Lord Forbes.

' In order to render this interruption as little irksome as possible, I confine myself to this single point, and only add that I press this request on your indulgence with the anxious, but I trust pardonable, eagerness of a father' (Historical Manuscripts Commission, Carlisle MSS., p. 740).

Frederick Howard (1785–1815), Lord Carlisle's third son, was killed at Waterloo; he was a Major in the 10th Hussars. George John Forbes, styled Viscount Forbes (1785–1836) was the first son of the 6th Earl of Granard (1760–1837). Whig M.P. for Co. Longford, 1806–32, and 1833–6. Lieutenant-Colonel, 1812; Colonel, 1815; Major-General, 1825.

Ministers tomorrow, & to have another communicated, thro' the Duke of York to the Lords Grenville, & Grey, Altho' I had no other news worth troubling your Grace with at this moment I thought it too important not to send this paper immediately.

I am quite miserable that the notorious simonist, the Revd. Mr. Dodd, should have made me the instrument of conveying to your Grace the papers on which he grounded his audacious application. I have return'd them to him with 'a flea in his ear,' & I will not fail to represent him in his proper colours to H.R.Hss. (Alnwick MSS.).

3369 HENRY GOULBURN TO MAJOR-GENERAL T. H. TURNER

Whitehall, 12 Feb. 1812

Private. As Mr Ryder wishes to ascertain whether it will be necessary for him to attend the Council on Friday in full dress or half dress I am under the necessity of troubling you to obtain the necessary information on this subject & to communicate it to me. (19202)

3370 WILLIAM [RICHARD] HAMILTON TO MAJOR-GENERAL T. H. TURNER

12 Feb. 1812

I do not observe any part of Mr. Cockerell's letter[1] that wants further explanation than that the liberal offers which were made from this country were grounded, on a loose kind of valuation which Robt. Cockerell had put upon them when first discovered—not upon any direct *proposal* from the owner to give up the Marbles for the particular sum mentioned. Consequently untill they had learnt & accepted our proposals, they were of course at liberty to make any other arrangement they thought proper—and I have no doubt they already heartily repent them of that which has precluded them from agreeing to the liberal offers sent from hence. I am rather inclined to suspect that the French Consul at Athens, an intriguing designing man, was at the bottom of this arrangement in order to create a delay which might offer some chances for Bonaparte's getting possession of the Marbles.

I enclose to you Mr Cockerell's letter to me on the subject—and take this opportunity of giving you the consoling intelligence that the Paulina, tho' she will not have brought home the Egina statues, will probably

1. No. 3366.

bring between 90 & 100 cases containing the remainder of Ld. Elgin's magnificent collection—amongst other relics the urn which once contained Aspasia's ashes, & in which was found a sprig of myrtle of solid gold—certainly dug out of a large tumulus, long known by the name of the Tomb of Aspasia.[1] (19203)

3371   THE PRINCE REGENT TO THE DUKE OF YORK[2]

Carlton House, 13 Feb. 1812

As the restrictions on the exercise of the royal authority will shortly expire, when I must make my arrangements for the future administration of the powers with which I am invested, I think it right to communicate to you those sentiments which I was withheld from expressing at an earlier period of the session by my earnest desire that the expected motion on the affairs of Ireland might undergo the deliberate discussion of Parliament, unmixed with any other consideration.

I think it hardly necessary to call your recollection to the recent circumstances under which I assumed the authority delegated to me by Parliament. At a moment of unexampled difficulty and danger I was called upon to make a selection of persons to whom I should entrust the functions of Executive Government. My sense of duty to our royal father solely decided that choice, and every private feeling gave way to considerations which admitted of no doubt or hesitation. I trust I acted in that respect as the genuine representative of the august person whose functions I was appointed to discharge, and I have the satisfaction of knowing that such was the opinion of persons for whose judgment and honourable principles I entertain the highest respect. In various instances, as you well know, where the law of the last Session left me at

1. For Lord Elgin's proposals to sell his famous collection to the public, see *Colchester*, ii. 326–30; and ii. 348–50. It was purchased by the nation for £35,000 in 1816, and deposited in the British Museum. It is said that the acquisition cost the Earl £74,000. He was a Scottish Representative Peer, 1790–1807, and 1820–41. In 1811 he vainly asked for promotion in the peerage, Perceval writing to him on 7 May of that year: 'I have had the honor of receiving your Lordship's letter to me of the sixth of this month, respecting your Lordship's collection of Pieces of ancient Sculpture, etc., and I beg leave to acquaint your Lordship that I previously had had some conversation with the Speaker and Mr. Long upon the subject. If your Lordship therefore will allow me to refer you to those gentlemen, they will be ready to communicate with you as to the terms upon which it may be thought advisable for the public to become purchasers of the collection. In reply to the observations conveyed in your Lordship's letter respecting the peerage, I must candidly say that I should feel it quite impossible to recommend any arrangement of that nature as connected in the remotest degree with the purchase of your Lordship's collection.' (Add. MSS. 38191, fo. 198)

2. This is the letter in its final shape (*Dropmore Papers*, x. 212).

George Ponsonby, M.P.

engraved by J. Godley from an original drawing by A. Pope

Sir Benjamin Bloomfield

engraved by C. Turner from a painting by T. C. Thompson, 1819

William Wellesley-Pole

from an original picture
by W. Owen, R.A.
Drawn by J. Wright,
engraved by C. Picart

full liberty, I have waived any personal gratification in order that his Majesty might resume on his restoration to health every power and prerogative belonging to his Crown; I certainly am the last person in the kingdom to whom it can be permitted to despair of our royal father's recovery.

A new era is now arrived and I cannot but reflect with satisfaction on the events which have distinguished the short period of my restricted Regency. Instead of suffering in the loss of her possessions by the gigantic force which has been employed against them, Great Britain has added most important acquisitions to her Empire; the national faith has been preserved inviolate towards our allies, and, if character is strength as applied to a nation, the increased and increasing reputation of his Majesty's arms will shew to the nations of the Continent how much they may still achieve when animated by a glorious spirit of resistance to a foreign yoke. In the critical situation of the war in the Peninsula I shall be most anxious to avoid any measure which can lead my allies to suppose that I mean to depart from the present system. Perseverance alone can achieve the great object in question, and I cannot withhold my approbation from those who have honourably distinguished themselves in support of it. I have no predilections to indulge, no resentments to gratify, no objects to attain but such as are common to the whole Empire. If such is the leading principle of my conduct, and I can appeal to the past as evidence of what the future will be, I flatter myself I shall meet with the support of Parliament and of a candid and enlightened nation.

Having made this communication of my sentiments on this new and extraordinary crisis of our affairs, I cannot conclude without expressing the gratification I should feel if some of those persons with whom the early habits of my public life were formed, would strengthen my hands and constitute a part of my Government. With such support, and aided by a vigorous and united Administration formed on the most liberal basis, I shall look with additional confidence to a prosperous issue of the most arduous contest in which Great Britain was ever engaged.

You are authorised to communicate these sentiments to Lord Grey, who I have no doubt will make them known to Lord Grenville.

P.S. I shall send a copy of this letter immediately to Mr Perceval.

3372   THE DUKE OF KENT TO THE PRINCE REGENT
The Lodge, Castle Hill, Friday, 14 Feb. 1812
The moment being now near at hand when those Restrictions will expire, which, notwithstanding the united zealous exertions of all your

friends, this time twelvemonth, the formidable phalanx of the Ministerial Party succeeded in imposing upon you, I am sure you will forgive me if, previous to *that* day, so anxiously looked forward to by all *those* who (*like myself*) can have *no* expectation but from *you*, I once more obtrude my personal situation upon *your* attention, and sollicit your favorable recollection of those pretensions which your goodness to me led me to form successively in the years 1801 & 1804, in the event of your having *then* assumed the Regency of the country, and by the change of Administration (which you *then* had in contemplation) the Master Generalship of the Ordnance consequently becoming vacant. In thus venturing to recall this to your recollection, I trust it can scarcely be necessary for me to declare that nothing is farther from my thoughts than entertaining the most distant apprehension of your having forgotten the circumstances under which, with a degree of spontaneous warmth and kindness which greatly enhanced the value of the promise, you were pleased to communicate to me the highly flattering views you had in my favor; but I have in truth suffered so much anxiety of mind ever since the year 1803, when, notwithstanding *your* best exertions to ward off the blow, my professional character was so cruelly, and (as *you well know*) so unjustly stigmatized, that it is more than I am capable of, under the extreme agitation I experience, as the moment approaches which I am looking forward to for the accomplishment of all my hopes, to remain silent, and I hope it is not presuming too far on your indulgence thus candidly to avow the impression under which I am prompted to address you. Indeed, I am sure, that possessing *that* high sense of honor *you* do, it cannot have escaped *your* attention how much more important to me the attainment of this object must be at *this*, than any *other* moment of *my* life, the events, that occurred in 1809, having attached at least a latent stigma on my character, the confirmation, or removal of which, now wholly depends upon the manner in which *you* may be pleased to distinguish me in the new arrangements. The Duke of York already owes to *your* protection *his* restoration to that distinguished active situation in the service of the country which, but for *your* support, must have been lost to him for ever; may *I* not *then* confidently hope that *I* shall not be *less* fortunate, and that the auspicious moment which places you at the head of the British Empire with unshackled powers will be *that* of restoring to my deeply wounded mind *that* comfort, and tranquillity to which for the last *nine* years it has been a stranger. Forgive me if I have said more than I ought, but you have taught me from my earliest infancy to look upon *you* as my first friend and protector, and my heart is too full at this moment to admit of my drawing that distinction which I am nevertheless fully sensible I ought between the Prince of Wales and the Prince Regent, for tho' our relative situations are now changed, nothing *can* alter the fervor of that devotion and attachment which thro' life it has been my greatest pride to profess towards you, and which never *can* cease but with the existence of *him* who now subscribes himself with all these sentiments [etc.].[1] (46519–20)

1. On the 17th G. Merrifield wrote to Robert Gray from 16, Albemarle Street:

G. MERRIFIELD TO ROBERT GRAY

16 Albemarle St., 17 Feb. 1812

I am desired by the Executors of the late Duke of Queensberry to request you will appoint a time for my waiting upon you to receive the 300 gs. due from H.R.H. the Prince Regent for the Opera Box the 25 Decr. last. (30025)

III Some Undated and Additional Letters

3373 LETTERS FROM THE PRINCE OF WALES TO CHARLES JAMES FOX
Wednesday evening, 10 o'clock [April 1783]
Dear Fox, Nothing would give me more satisfaction than the message yt. you was so good as to send me this morning. You know how sincerely you have my good wishes, & therefore will be convinced yt. I shall rejoice not a little if I again see you in Administration, as I look upon it as the most fortunate event yt. can happen to us all, I mean not only to myself in particular but to the nation in general. With respect to yr. friendly kindness to me I shall ever be happy to acknowledge it with the gratitude it so justly deserves. I will not take up any more of yr. time at present than merely to ask you whether it will be convenient to you or not my calling upon you between Court (if it is over in proper time) & dinner tomorrow; you may depend upon my coming the moment I am released. I can assure you no one can be more anxious than I am to see you at the present moment, as no one has yr. interest more sincerely at heart, & I hope you will ever look upon me as your most affectionate friend.[1] (Add. MSS. 47560, f. 1)

1. See i. 103n. The subsequent letters begin 'Dear Charles'.

12.30 a.m., Thursday [April 1783]

When I left the Queen's House this evening Weymouth[1] was with the King. I wish you wd. tell me in a short note how you interpret his frequent visits & let me know whether you have heard anything fresh this evening. (Add. MSS. 47560, f. 3)

Queen's House, 4 o'clock [?April 1783]

I am now returned home, & if you have anything particular you wish to say to me I am ready either to come to you or receive you at ye Queen's House, whichever is most convenient to you. But if you shd. have anything to say to me I intend going out of town early this evening. (Add. MSS. 47560, f. 5)

2.45 [p.m.] [?April 1783]

I am waiting for you at yr. own house. Pray come directly if you can as I wish very much to speak to you. I will not detain you three minutes.

[*P.S.*] If you have not got yr. own carriage you had better take anybody else's. (Add. MSS. 47560, f. 7)

Queen's House, 12 o'clock, 30 April 1783

I did not return home till it was too late to answer your kind letter last night. I cannot express to you how very happy you made me by the contents of it; as I have always entertained the highest opinion of Dr. Cyril Jackson & have always had the greatest friendship for him you may easily conceive how much pleased I shall be at seeing him in so eligible situation & in a situation he must so much wish for himself. Before I conclude allow me to thank you, my dear Charles, for your kind attention to me on this & every other occasion.[2] (Add. MSS. 47560, f. 9)

1. Thomas Thynne, 3rd Viscount Weymouth and (1789) Marquess of Bath (1734–96). Succeeded his father, 1751. A Lord of the Bedchamber, 1760–3; Master of the Horse to the Queen, 1763–5; Lord Lieutenant of Ireland, April–July 1765; Secretary of State for the Northern Department, January–October 1768, and for the Southern, 1768–70 and 1775–9; Groom of the Stole, March–November 1775 and 1782–96. K.G., June 1778; created Marquess, 18 August 1789. See No. 326.

2. See Nos. 73, 76.

Queen's House, 1 o'clock, 31 May 1783
I have a thousand excuses to make to you for not having answered yr.
letter immediately but I am only this instant awake & therefore have only
just had time to read yr. letter. I saw ye. Dss. of Rutland yesterday &
took ye. liberty of desiring her Grace to deliver a message from me to ye.
Duke of Portland, desiring him if it was not inconvenient to him to
allow me to come to him tomorrow at eleven instead of today. I ought to
have explained this to you at Carlisle's when I desired you to meet me in
Downing Street on Sunday at eleven o'clock, but it really quite slipped
out of my memory. I must therefore entreat of you to clear up the matter
to the Duke of Portland & make all proper apologies for me. I cannot
however conclude without seizing this opportunity of thanking you for ye.
part you have taken in bringing this essential business to me so near a
conclusion, wh. I can assure you I shall never forget as long as I live.[1]

P.S. You may depend upon seeing me tomorrow at eleven. (Add. MSS.
47560, f. 11)

Cumberland House, 9.15 [16 June 1783]
I have this instant received yr. kind letter & am most exceedingly
sensible of the kind & friendly attention you have shewn me thro' out the
whole of the business wh. is of so much importance to my happiness.
Should anything arrive yt. you wish me to be immediately apprised of,
pray send it to the Queen's House. I shall leave a servant there to bring
me any letter that may come from you, wherever I am. James Luttrell[2]
I sent an express for immediately but have not as yet sent to Lord
Herbert,[2] & according to yr. advice the step not being as yet taken, I
shall not send for him at all.[2] (Add. MSS. 47560, f. 15)

Queen's House, 18 June 1783
After what has already passed I did not require this additional proof of
yr. friendship & attachment, & you will see by a letter I have this instant
written to the D. of P[ortland] how ready I am to take yr. advice, & yt. I
leave it entirely to the Cabinet.[3] (Add. MSS. 47560, f. 13)

1. See No. 77.
2. See No. 84.
3. See No. 92.

Carlton House, 19 Nov. 1783

I have but this instant received yr. letter owing partly to my not being at home & partly to the negligence of my servant, or I most undoubtedly wd. have answered it before. I am afraid it is totally out of my power to see you today as I am this moment going to Buckingham House to dinner & then immediately to see Mrs Siddons[1] *in town*. I am exceedingly anxious to know what yr. business with me is & if it cannot be postponed till I have ye. pleasure of seeing you at the Drawing Room tomorrow I must trouble you to write me a letter. (Add. MSS. 47560, f. 17)

Brighton, 19 July 1786

I am more obliged to you than I can possibly express for the contents of ye. letter[2] I yesterday received from you, & am more and more convinced of the necessity of pursuing that plan wh. I assure you I never should have adopted had I not intended to have gone thro' with it. With regard to the other plan you mention I approve most highly of it but shall not touch upon it at all at present as I mean to be in London for a few hours on Monday next when I hope to have the pleasure of seeing you & of discussing the matter fully at length. At twelve o'clock I shall be ready to receive you at Carlton House. I will not tresspass any further upon yr. patience at present but conclude with assuring you that no one can feel more sensibly every mark of yr. friendship & regard than [etc.].

P.S. My best compliments to Mrs. Armitstead. (Add. MSS. 47560, f. 19)

Monday night, 12 p.m., 30 Apr. 1787

I beg to see you for five minutes tomorrow after I have seen Marsham[3] & Powis[4] whom I beg you will desire to be at Carlton House *at one o'clock tomorrow*. When I see you I will relate to you what has passed between *my friend & me* relative to yr. seeing *ym*. I feel more comfortable by

1. Sarah Siddons (1755–1831), the actress. She had a highly successful season at Drury Lane in 1783.

2. No. 191.

3. Charles Marsham, Earl of Romney (1744–1811), son of 2nd Baron Romney. M.P. for Maidstone, 1768–74; for Kent, 1774–90. Created Earl of Romney, 22 June 1801. An independent country gentleman, a leading member of the St. Alban's Tavern group of independents who tried to bring about a coalition between Fox and Pitt during the opening weeks of 1784.

4. Thomas Powys, Baron Lilford (1743–1800). M.P. for Northamptonshire, 1774–97. Peerage, 26 October 1797. Like Marsham, an independent country gentleman.

Sheridan's & Grey's account of what has passed today. I have had a distant insinuation that some sort of message or terms are also to be propos'd to me tomorrow. If you come a little after two you will be sure to find me.[1] (Add. MSS. 47560, f. 25)

3374   LETTERS FROM PRINCESS AUGUSTA TO THE PRINCE OF WALES
Wednesday evening [? 1811]
The Queen commands me to inform you that she would have written yesterday to have returned her thanks to you for your very kind message, but that she delayed it for the chance of seeing you today: she hopes that you have not worried yourself *sick* with all the anxiety you must have on your mind & she ardently hopes (as I hope I need not add I DO) that all things will soon be settled to your mind.

The Queen would be much obliged to you if it is not very inconvenient if you would send the same *person* to Windsor who was *here a fortnight ago*, who has the care of cleaning your plate. I believe his name is Boulter or Bolton, & she will send him back again on Friday unless you wish him to return sooner.

Charlotte is quite well and enjoyed this ride of all things this morning. God bless you.[2] (Add. Georgian 10/44)

[? Jan. 1812]
Mary and I have had a long & private and *confidential* conversation with Sir Henry Halford; he will be kind enough to make you a faithfull report of it, & you will turn your mind to assist us if you can.

Of all things don't let us be separated from the King's roof; we need not see him if it is thought wrong, but if we don't stop under his roof its encouraging a *bad delusion*. I have not time to add any more. (Add. Georgian 10/49)

1. The reference is to the Parliamentary discussions regarding the payment of the Prince's debts. See i. 272 and *Memorials and Correspondence of Fox*, ii. 288.

2. Early November 1811 is a possible date. Princess Charlotte visited Windsor during that month.

[*1 June*]¹
The Queen commands me to inform you that she has received a message
from Madame de Mehrfeldt asking to be presented to her tomorrow.
She thinks it would be too early for you if this took place *before* the
Drawing Room, therefore she wishes to know if you don't think it will
be just as well for her to be introduced after it is over. The Queen is
obliged to send to Mr. Chester² this evening, which is the reason of my
writing to you at this hour. Will you just send me an answer to York
House? (Add. Georgian 10/40)

*Thursday evening, 2 June*³
The Queen not having received your answer to the message I delivered
to you from her yesterday evening about Countess Mehrfeldt's presentation, commands to inform you that if she does not hear from you she
shall put off the receiving Countess Mehrfeldt to another day.

I am much more comfortable about poor Eliza since the account
Baillie brought us last night; she was quite certain you sent Baillie to her
and she was all gratitude for it. God bless you. (Add. Georgian 10/41)

3375   LETTERS FROM PRINCESS MARY TO THE PRINCE OF WALES
Saturday night [*1810*]
I am most thankful to be able to say that the phyans. inable me to give
you a better *report* than I ventured to hope this morning, though this
last attack has been most *violant* & is not over yet. Yet they are decided,
though in a much more suffering state than when they saw her⁴ last, that
she is not *materially worse* & hope in a few days we may see a great
change for the better. She desires her most affe. love to you & thanks you
for the coffee which she likes very much. No words can discribe what a
week of anxiety I have passed & how alarmed I was part of yesterday &
early this morning as the violance of the pain in the side was very frightful to witness attended with fever which was very painful to witness. The

1. For the year, see the next letter.

2. Robert Chester was Assistant Master and also Marshal of the Ceremonies in the Lord
Chamberlain's Department of the King's Household.

3. If the letter is correctly dated the year must be either 1808 or 1814. Merveldt came to
England as Austrian Ambassador in 1814.

4. Princess Amelia.

cold weather, added to the distress of mind she suffers on the subject of the Villiers,[1] has certainly helped to make her much worse & her nerves have been much affected & I fear will remain so for some time as I think she is only now begining to feel the affects of this long illness. I hope you are quite well. (Add. Georgian 12/151)

Sunday night [1810]

I am most thankful to be able to say that the phyans. found Amelia's pulse better yesterday than they have yet & in many respects went away more satisfied; however they will not allow me to go so *far* as to *call* her *better*. The same plan is to go on. The cold weather affects her very much & for fear of takeing cold they advise her keeping as much in bed as possible. I wish I could add she was in a less suffering state for the pain in the side continues *much* the same & at times she has violant pains in her head. She desires her love to you & is very sorry to find you have suffered so from your eyes;[2] she hopes as well as myself you are much better. This unfortunate business of the Villiers[3] affects her very much & though she hopes & trusts all may turn out well, yet the anxiety and suspense is most painful to all those who love them.

Amelia wishes you to have the kindness to send her some more coffee & as soon as you can.

Poor Gasken [*sic*] is very ill; we are very uneasy about her, more so than we venture to tell Amelia.[4] She has kept her room nearly three weeks with a bad cough & much fever & I fear has no chance of seeing Amelia in a hurry & indeed, ill as she is, it is better they should not meet. Sophy is quite well. (Add. Georgian 12/150)

Friday morning [?*1810*]

As I have had nothing new to say concerning Amelia for the last three days I have not troubled you with one of my scrawls, but as I think you

1. See No. 2718.

2. See the reference to the Prince's eyes in 2718 (9 May 1810).

3. See No. 2718.

4. See No. 2694 (1 January 1810). It was on 15 January 1810 that Perceval informed the King that George Villiers had resigned his office of Paymaster of the Marines (*Later Correspondence of George III*, v. 484). Consequently, Sunday, 21 January 1810 is a possible date; but if something of the 'unfortunate business' of Villiers was known at Windsor before his resignation, then the 14th is a possibility, and this date would be appropriate for the 'nearly three weeks' illness of Mary Anne Gaskoin. And see *Later Correspondence of George III*, v. 486.

may begin to get anxious I take up my pen to say that Amelia's cough has continued much the same, but Milman, who came down today, says the inflammation in the lungs for the present is over & he thinks the cough is turning to nerves; he says everything depends on her mind being *kept* as quiet as possible & she ought to be *considered* in *everything* to make her as comfortable & *happy* as possible, in short to be *worried* about nothing, which entre nous in our house is very *dificult*, and with such a fine creature as she is who possesses such very strong feelings it requires great care to manage her well.

The Queen is better but not out of her room yet; she hopes to do without a blister as the warm bath has done her a great deal of good.

God bless you. I was sorry to hear from Ernest you was not well. (Add. Georgian 12/164)

Thursday [*?Nov. 1810*]

In consequence of a long conversation I have had with Gaskin [*sic*][1] concerning Mary Anne, I trouble you with these few lines as he is anxious I should take the earliest opportunity of representing to you his feelings on her subject, & as I have desired him to give you this letter himself, perhapes [*sic*] you will have the kindness to talk the matter over with him, & should you be of the same opinion it would be a great comfort to him, feeling all your kindness & deeply impressed with *gratitude as he* is for the unbounded fairness he and his children have ever received from you makes him the more difident to explain his *wishes* about his daughter. The looking forwards to her being one of Charlotte's attendants is most gratifying to him as it brings her more immediately under his own eye, and a proof that you are satisfied with her conduct in her trying *situation* about poor Amelia, but it strikes Gaskin the King having been so good as to promis to make Mary Anne one of his *pensioner* [*sic*] that it would be more respectful of him not to let Mary Anne move to Carlton House or Warwick House till the King is in a situation to be informed of his future plans for his daughter & of your kind intentions towards her. It will prove to the King her gratitude by accepting of no new situation untill his Majesty has approved of it. I have promised as long as Mary Anne remains at the Castle to be her friend & keep her so far in employment in assisting Byerly that she shall not loose her time. Of course if you still are of opinion that she had better go to Charlotte without loss of time you have but to say so & she is at your *commands* as pray understand it is not Gaskin's *wish* she should *not belong* to Charlotte *in time*, only he feels a delicacy in her leaving the Castle before the King is made acquainted with it.

1. Mary Anne's father was Clerk of the Stables in the Prince's Household.

I have not time for more but must just say that it strikes me things go on much as when I saw you last, quiet but under great delusion at times. I hope to see you soon.

[*P.S.*] Sophy is better but not well.[1] (Add. Georgian 12/167)

8 Dec. [?*1810*]

We were here delighted to hear so good an account of you from Lady Harcourt and she is full of gratitude for all the kindness she has received from you during her stay at Brighton, which she says she never can forget.

Sophy is tolerable & the dear King quiet & composed.

[*P.S.*] What do you say to Mr. Perceval?[2] (Add. Georgian 12/180)

[*c. 8 April 1811*]

I have just received the enclosed letter which I beg you to read, & if you have not time to give me an answer yourself do have the kindness to order one of your gentlemen or somebody to give me a line as soon as you can on the subject.

The Queen has been so kind as to offer to make Col. Desbrowe go to Monsieur de Clermont *pour lui recommander* Montmollen *de sa part* but a word from you *will* have much more affect & therefore I send this by the coach that you may either speak to him or read him a message to beg of *him to take* Montmollen *with him to Paris*. Montmollen has had a letter today which informes her Clermont is going in less than 10 days, therefore if *you* are so kind as to manage that he should *take her* she must be informed of it as soon as possible. I told the Queen how kind you had been to her in offering to find out the best way for her to go & upon nameing Clermont she said if you *would* recomend Montmollen she would make *Desbrowe* go & do so as from her likewise.

I am just come up from the King; he is not as free from plans as last night but very *composed*, but grieved am I to add, *dressed in black*. (Add. Georgian 12/172)

1. See No. 2763 (18 November 1810). The letter may have been written on 15 November 1810.

2. The paper is watermarked 1804, but the references to the King and Perceval seem to indicate that this is an 1810 letter. The reference to Brighton apparently rules out 1811, as the Prince had not been there for several weeks on account of his injured foot.

[*?Jan. 1812*]

Baillie is just returned & assures us Eliza is as well as can *ever be* & that he sees no reason to doubt the attack is going off finally, at the same time she is not without fever & the pulse was still a hundred & six when he left Windsor; they had put on leeches on her side.

[*P.S.*] Augusta has wrote you a note which the Q. is anxious you should send an answer too [*sic*]. (Add. Georgian 12/183)

[*?Jan. 1812*]

Soon after my letter went off the Queen I *suppose* thought *better* & she told Augusta she would allow her & Sophy to go to Oatlands tomorrow & that as she *wanted* to speak to you on BUSINESS she should go with Eliza & me next Monday. I took this opportunity of giveing my mind strongly to my two elder sisters & this time must prove to them how *decided* we *must be* for nothing would have CARRIED this point of my sisters *going* but my being so DECIDED in telling her I WOULD HAVE AN ANSWER TO SEND YOU immediately & that at all EVENTS if she refused our GOING she must do so herself. I WILL NOT SAY A WORD about not comeing myself or my own severe disapointment (I cannot say) because I felt SURE she would not let me go, but I will say no more.

As to the poor King, he has passed a bad day, not quite as violent as yesterday *because* no *restraint* was CALLED FOR, but a violent storm took place this evening at 4 o'clock that was dreadful in *every respect*. He went to bed quietly, quite fatigued & complaining of cold; he was not asleep when Sir Henry came up.

[*P.S.*] As the Queen knows poor Sophia is in a most delicate state & *really* quite unfit to undertake so long a drive as to Oatlands & back again it is the more provoking that she would not out of charity spare her & have sent me. Sophia of course delighted to go, but sensable she is quite *unfit* to go so far, & if you ask Sir Henry when you see him he will tell you *how* out of *health she is*. Of course this is quite for yourself. (Add. Georgian 12/184)

PRINCESS MARY TO THE PRINCE REGENT

Windsor, 24 Feb. [*?1812*]

I think I need not say the pleasure it gives me, the thoughts of seeing you next Monday, & I sincerely hope to find you *much better*.

The King was *shaved* yesterday after having refused to be *shaved* for

16 months; he looks well in health but I understand much *older in the face* & much thiner. Sophy tolerable. (Add. Georgian 12/181)

PRINCESS MARY TO THE PRINCE REGENT

[*24 March 1812*]

My *heart* is so full I have not *words* to express half what I want to say & half how *deeply* I feel all your kindness concerning *us*, but how my happiness is damped at *our* being the innocent cause of such an unpleasant subject being *brought forth* as was last night in the House. Nothing could be so *greating* [*sic*] to my feelings than all I have read in the newspapers *today*, but God grant your steadiness of conduct & angelic behaviour may be rewarded at last are ardent prayers of your [etc.].

[*P.S.*] I shall write again to night.¹ (Add. Georgian 12/182)

PRINCESS MARY TO THE PRINCE REGENT

11 Nov. [*?1812*]

This has been a perfect quiet, silent, composed day; the King has eat his dinner well, went to bed at six o'clock & droped asleep at 9. Lord Bathurst came today & returned to town; the very moment after he left the Q. the Queen told me Lord Bathurst perfectly UNDERSTOOD HER that her object was to have it clearly made out her daughters *were not to prevent* the Pss. of Wales comeing into the Prince's private box (if she was so mad as to attempt it) & that Lady de Clifford and the gentlemen who will attend upon Charlotte *must have all the responsibility*. She beged Lord Bathurst to try to persuade you to name some lady to assist Lady de Clifford should she be ill, she did not *wish* her ladies to have anything to do with Charlotte. She said she had told Lord Bathurst she saw no *use* in his WRITEING to *you* on the *subject* as it would be quite time enough to *settle* it all when you returned *to town*. I think that is word for word what *she told me* as she hoped all these plans would not take place for some time yet. My answer was that if it was proposed in a political point of *view* the *sooner it took place the better*.

1. *Parliamentary Debates*, xxii. 122–46. The Opposition criticized the proposed grant of £9,000 to each of the Princesses (exclusive of the grant of £4000 each from the Civil List). By letters patent dated 2 February 1802, the King had granted the five Princesses an annuity of £6,000 each, to date from the King's demise. The Government considered that in view of the King's insanity the House should consider the situation of the four surviving Princesses in the same way as if the King had actually died. See *Letters of George IV*, i. 51–3.

I thank God the accounts from Lord Cathcart are so good.[1]

[*P.S.*] Of course this letter is for yourself; pray don't shew it William but you have my love. (Add. Georgian 12/179)

[?*May 1813*]

I am commanded by the Queen to ask you what she is to say, for her Ladys who have received invitations for Tuesday at Carlton House have been with her to inquire if they are to appear out of mourning?[2] The cards don't say it is an Assembly or party in honour of the Queen's birthday & takeing place so immediately after makes people suppose it is in honour of that day; therefore the Q. begs you will give your orders accordingly as people only wish to do what is most respectful & untill it is clearly understood we one & all don't know what answer to give.

[*P.S.*] If your cards had said in honour of the Q.'s birthday everybody would have known at once no black could have been *admited*; as it now stands it is but *understood*; for a common assembly at your house the Court mourning would not of course be put off. An answer yes or no is all that is requested by Bloomfield tomorrow, or any body. (Add. Georgian 12/174)

3376   THE DUKE OF CAMBRIDGE TO THE PRINCE OF WALES

Berkeley Square, Thursday morning [?*1810*]

I return you the enclosed with my best thanks & tho' I find by it that Dr. Baillie thinks poor Amelia better than when he last saw her, yet I really do feel so miserable about her that I have given up the inspections and shall set off for Windsor at eleven o'clock. Should dearest Minny not write, you may depend on hearing from me. (48616)

1. Lord Cathcart had been appointed Ambassador to Russia in July 1812. He arrived at Abo on 27 August and had an audience of Alexander I two days later. He arrived at Petersburg with the Tsar on 4 September.

2. Possibly mourning for the Duchess of Brunswick, who died on 23 March 1813.

Richmond, Saturday night[1]

It was my intention to have wrote yesterday in consequence of what passed between me and MacMahon: but I was prevented by other business: till now: I believe you must have received a letter from him relative to Stuart the newspaper writer. Macmahon and I are both of the same opinion relative to this man and I rejoice to find Lord Moira thinks alike: any money and any trouble ought to be given to find out those servants in Carlton House who have had any hands in the papers: but more [I] believe is dangerous: for I have already seen in the *Morning Herald* that somebody is employed in the *Morning Post* by you to write against the Princess:[2] besides I am sure that Stuart has not the abilities to write a pamphlet. I really think the matter is best buried in oblivion or else you will provoke answers and the whole affair may be brought up again.

I have just received a letter from Lady Jersey desiring to see me and I shall attend her Ladyship next Monday if convenient at twelve: I shall certainly at my interview strongly recommend no publishing but to let the thing drop. I am confident this advice is the most for your interest.

I understand the Duke of York goes on Monday to Bath for a fortnight which I hope will do him good: I saw him last Tuesday and he was very far from being well. (45237–8)

Bushy House, Thursday night [?*Dec. 1810 or early 1811*]

As you must be anxious to know how our interview went off today and the Duke of Kent intends seeing you on the subject next Saturday I will write my statement which you will compare with his.

We saw the King alone and remained with him from one till half-past two: we were present at his dinner and I understand this is the first day he was waited on by his own servants. I did not see any keeper. Halford introduced us. He was very civil and kind, and particularly considering what I know to be the opinion of the doctors relative to the health, I thought he looked much better and clearer in the face than I could have expected, but certainly feebler on his legs. He eat with appetite roast mutton, took his broth with turnips and bread and cheese with pleasure. I never saw him out of an illness of this kind but in 1801. He certainly was not so much hurried: his thoughts however flew from one subject to another tho' he conversed rationally on the point. Dress, plans and schemes for going to Kew, Weymouth and even again to St. James's, with the most detailed minutiae as to rooms and servants, were the chief

1. The internal evidence shows that this letter was probably written on 9 July 1796.

2. The Princess of Wales.

topicks of conversation. He talked of you in the kindest manner and enquired about the arrangements at Carleton House, at which he seemed delighted. Halford in going over to the Castle said this was a good day: if so, I do not understand what a bad one can be: in short, the mind appeared to me to be amused by absolute trifles: there was not any obscurity or any tendency to it, but an absolute vacuum of mind. To detail a whole conversation of this kind for an hour and a half with such rapidity would be as impossible as uninteresting, and I trust with this letter the Duke of Kent will relate all that passed and everything that was said. We compared notes and think alike. I shall be perfectly able to state everything that occurred this day at Windsor when I see you. The Queen of course was curious to know my sentiments. I told her the King looked much better in the face than I could have expected, and there I left the subject as I would not and could not tell a lie. In a few days I shall repeat my visit and so on occasionally: only I must be informed the days Halford is at Windsor that I may be sure of being admitted. Tho' the manner is not so hurried it is my decided opinion the mind is full as deluded as it was in October when I last saw him. Examine the Duke of Kent with this letter and you must be master of everything. (44982–3)

Bushy House, Saturday night [Aug. 1812]
You may very easily believe that I cannot be an unconcerned spectator of public events and rejoice therefore at the peace being signed between this country and Sweden[1] and that Mr. Thornton has transmitted a treaty between us and Russia which I make no doubt will also be signed: you will not I am sure forget my private concerns which I trust may eventually prove the means of bringing the British and Russian alliance closer together.

You will of course do as you choose: but if it is your intention to go by water up and down the Channel I must observe that it is time you would give your directions to Lord Melville:[2] in whatever ship it may be expedient for you to embark it will require some days to prepare her and collect a proper set of officers: the full moon in this month is on the twenty second[3] and I should trust you would not make it later than the

1. Thornton was sent to Stockholm in 1812, arriving there on 6 April, to negotiate a peace treaty with Sweden. It was signed on 18 July, and on this day was signed at Stockholm a treaty between Great Britain and Russia, the signatories being Thornton and Van Suchtelen, the Russian Minister to Sweden.

2. Lord Melville had become First Lord of the Admiralty on 24 March 1812 in succession to Charles Yorke.

3. This proves conclusively that August was the month.

twenty fourth to sail for Plymouth: I would strongly recommend beginning by that place for as in September we are sure of a westerly wind you have only to name your day and hour and I can always bring you to your own time into Torbay to Weymouth and to Southampton, Portsmouth and the Isle of Wight: one night with a fair wind will run you from Portsmouth to the Downs where you will find Lord Liverpool at Walmer Castle[1] and where a Council might be held: then I conceive the weather would determine your going by water or by land to Sheerness: at all events I should recommend leaving the ship entirely at Sheerness and going in your barge to Chatham and from thence to London by land.

Should you adopt the measure of embarking to prevent trouble and all dispute I suggest the cabin being fitted for your accommodation by the Lord Chamberlain[2] and that the table should be kept by the Lord Steward.[3] (44998–9)

3378 LETTERS FROM THE DUKE OF CLARENCE TO COLONEL MCMAHON

St. James's, 5 p.m., Monday [1811]

I write for two reasons: first to account for my not calling on you this morning and I have been so busy respecting the Berkely Peerage[4] I could not spare time and since which I have been engaged with the Countess. My other reason is to explain to the Prince Regent my inability to go tomorrow to Oatlands: as I must be in the house for the sake of what you know is dearest to my happiness[5] I may not see my brother till Wednesday and request you will tell the Prince that my mind is so entirely engaged with this cruel and unjust persecution of the most perfect and injured woman that I really have not spirits to be present at the fête of tomorrow and I should only be a wet blanket to the company assembled at Oatlands. I shall of course write to the Dutchess of York and indeed request the Regent to carry my letter.

I have much to say to you on the point in which not only my happiness

1. Lord Liverpool, who had become Prime Minister on 8 June, was Lord Warden of the Cinque Ports.

2. The Marquess of Hertford had succeeded Lord Dartmouth in March 1812.

3. Lord Cholmondeley had succeeded Lord Aylesford in February 1812.

4. Mrs. Jordan said on 16 June that the Duke had been spending a lot of time on the Berkeley peerage case (*Mrs. Jordan and her Family*, p. 193), which was disposed of by the House of Lords on Tuesday, 2 July (*Parliamentary Debates*, xx. 782).

5. Apparently a reference to his wish to marry Lady Berkeley. See No. 3231n. The Prince Regent evidently (not surprisingly) refused to allow his brother to marry her. Mrs. Jordan said on 17 July that Lady Berkeley had gone to Madeira.

388

but eventually my life and existence⁻may be concerned: it will be hard indeed when my other brothers are in search of honours, employment &c &c that I, more attached than any one to the Prince, should be refused the *only humble* request I *shall ever* make and in which believe me not only my future comfort but even my very existence is concerned: the wound is deeper, much deeper than my brother imagines, and with my life only can it be eradicated. (45269–70)

Sudborn,[1] *Tuesday noon* [?*17 Nov. 1812*]

I have this morning received the enclosed from Lord Moira which I am to request you will forward to Mrs. Jordan that she may see what I have done with his Lordship relative to Alsop: on my return to town I will do what I can to get him out and let me know to whom I ought to apply.[2]

The Prince is quite well and seems pleased with his journey: hitherto it has gone off very well and I trust for my brother's sake we shall remain out of town till the last moment:[3] no people can be more attentive than Lord and Lady Hertford and you know I particularly like the conversation of the Marquis. Henry[4] is very much improved in every way. The news from Russia is excellent[5] and you know I am both publickly and privately interested in the events of that country:[6] I hope we shall soon have good accounts from Lord Wellington and then we shall come to Parliament with éclat. Adieu till we meet. (44992)

Bushy House, Thursday night [?*early Jan. 1814*]

I know no person so perfectly disagreeable and even dangerous as an author: I enclose a letter and several pamphlets I have this evening

1. The Duke went to Sudbourne on Saturday, 14 November 1812, so the letter may have been written on the 17th.

2. The reference is to the Duke's efforts to provide for Mrs. Jordan's son-in-law, Thomas Alsop who, hopelessly in debt, was facing ruin. When Moira was appointed Governor-General of Bengal in November 1812 he agreed to take Alsop with him to Calcutta in the hope that Alsop would retrieve himself.

3. The Prince Regent did not open the Parliamentary Session in person on the 24th.

4. Henry FitzClarence.

5. Napoleon's retreat from Moscow had begun.

6. The Tsar had then only one unmarried sister, the Grand Duchess Anne (1795–1865); on 21 February 1816 she married the Hereditary Prince of Orange (1792–1849), later King of the Netherlands—the young Prince to whom Princess Charlotte had momentarily become engaged in 1814. It was not until the end of 1813 that the Duke decided to offer himself in marriage to the Grand Duchess Catherine (1788–1819), the widow of the Grand Duke of Oldenburg who had died on 27 December 1812.

received from a man I have not any knowledge of and to whom I do not mean to put pen to paper: but it may be as well to watch the gentleman and I therefore send his papers.

My return to town depends on the Prince Regent's motions entirely. I shall be in London on Sunday at whatever hour you choose and shall be ready to accompany you either on that day or Thursday to settle with Lord Castlereagh about the manner of my expenses being paid during my excursion.[1]

Barton[2] informs me there are difficulties started by the Insurance Offices which I think ought to be got over as I may have occasion to return again even this year to the Continent. I am going to write to him. (45240)

3379   LETTERS FROM WILLIAM ADAM TO THE PRINCE OF WALES

House of Lords, 4 o'clock, Monday, 15 May [?1809]

I have not got my interview with the Chr.[3] till this moment, and it has consisted merely in his Ldp.'s discovery that I might see him & Mr. Perceval together tomorrow morning as they both attended at Kensington. His Ldp. wishes both to report, stating generally that the matter was brought to a more favourable point than he at first expected. I have fixed tomorrow at ten to be at Downing Street, and will from thence go to attend your Royal Highness at Carlton House[4] (Blair Adam MSS.).

1. This probably refers to the Duke's visit to Holland in January 1814, undertaken with the idea of meeting the widowed Grand Duchess Catherine of Russia and proposing marriage to her. The Cabinet refused to pay his expenses, but the Prince Regent, with his usual generosity, gave him £1000. The Grand Duchess found him too rough in his manners, 'awkward, not without wit, but definitely unpleasant'; she said she hated his vulgar familiarity and want of delicacy. He escorted her to England on a visit to the Prince Regent, at the end of March, in the *Jason* frigate.

2. Sir John Barton (1771–1834), the Duke's Secretary and Treasurer.

3. Eldon.

4. This letter apparently refers to the negotiations for the settlement of the debts of the Princess of Wales. See vi. 382.

9.40 p.m., Thursday [?*1809 or 1811*]

The Chancellor was gone before I recd. your Royal Hss.'s letter, but he is to be here again tomorrow morning & then I am to see Perceval. I will then attend your Royal Hss. Had there been anything conclusive to state I would have disregarded the fatigue I am under (from having been in motion on bss. ever since four this morning) & gone to Carlton Hse. As it is I hope you will pardon me for not attending your Royal Hss.'s command till after I have seen Perceval which will be at ten tomorrow. When I see the Chr. I will add the suggestions in your Royal Hss.'s letter to those I have already communicated.

The Chr. assures me that he has not varied the expressions in the paper as the original will shew, & he will put in writing his observations tomorrow morning on each head (Blair Adam MSS.).

3380   LORD ELDON TO THE PRINCE REGENT

Sunday morning [?*1811*]

The Lord Chancellor, offering his humble duty to your Royal Highness the Prince Regent, takes leave to mention that, understanding that your Royal Highness was from home last night, he did not call at Carleton House upon his return from Windsor. The whole Council attended, & went, as the Chanr. believes, with a determination to state to his Majesty the circumstances which your Royal Highness is aware that many of them were anxious should be represented. This, however, had been done on the Friday by Dr. Willis, who read to his Majesty the paper which had been signed by all the Council, directing him so to do. The Council, and particularly some individuals, are greatly out of favour—the whole of them very much so; but, though they cannot yet appretiate the effects of this communication, they entertain hopes that it may do good.

The Council took into a very anxious consideration whether they should personally *yesterday* in a body, or any individuals should address the King on the same subject. Upon this question there was a great difference of opinion among the medical advisers. Sir H. Halford thought that step *would do good*. Dr Baillie thought that there would be no disadvantage in it, & that there was a CHANCE *of benefit*, but that nothing would be either gained or lost by postponing it for a week. Dr Willis thought it would be *prejudicial*. Dr Heberden thought it would *do harm*. Mr Dundas thought that, if it was tried at the end of another week, it would *do good*, but would not advise it to be *adopted yesterday*. Sir H. Halford was again called in, & expressed an opinion that there would be *no disadvantage in postponing it for a week*. The Council were unanimous in postponing it. Their reasons appeared to be these—that a communication so painful to the King, on Saturday, following a communication made only on Friday, might & probably would greatly irritate the King—that the communication on Friday was, in truth, made *as from the Council*, THEIR paper being read to the King, and his Majy. having ordered Dr Willis to read it to him whenever he saw occasion to put him in mind of its contents; that the effect of this communication was not ascertained, &, if the personal interposition of the Council was supposed to have more weight than their written communication from Dr W—there seemed to be a degree of prudence in husbanding this, their last means of persuasion, till it could be known from the effects of Friday's communication whether it was necessary to resort to it. They left a paper directing the physicians individually & collectively whenever a departure from right appeared, to bring to his Majesty's recollection the effect of the paper already communicated. His Majesty received the Chief Justice, the Master of the Rolls and the Chancellor, tho so angry with all, & so peculiarly so with one of them, in an interview so well regulated that there was nothing in his manner or conversation but what was good. The word 'Sir' struck the Lord Chancellor's ear a little oftener than it seems to have been noticed by the others. Of his Majesty's bodily health the Council have not had any reason to be apprehensive: and the Chancellor believes all the Council were relieved as to apprehensions created by reports of trifling conversations. (17647–8)

3381   THE EARL OF LAUDERDALE TO THE EARL OF MOIRA

Warrens Hotel, Friday [?*Feb. 1811*]

Lord Lauderdale presents compts to Lord Moira—he sends him a copy of the Commission 10th March 1789—& also a copy of a Commission for opening the Session in the usual form.

Lord Moira will at once perceive that the former pledges the King or Regent who signs it to approbation of the measures that have been pursued in opening Parliament—indeed it has been argued both by the Chancellor & Perceval that his Majesty's approbation of the measures of 1789 were to be inferred from the Commission of the 10th of March.

This proceeding must appear the more extraordinary from the recollection that Mr. Perceval has recently told the Prince, in the following paragraph of his letter, that he knows he disapproves what he is now proposing he should sanction.

'Mr Perceval humbly trusts that whatever doubt your Royal Highness may entertain with respect to the Constitutional propriety of the measures which have been adopted &c.'¹ (19027)

3382 CHARLES STUART TO COLONEL MCMAHON

Tuesday morning [?1796]

Inclosed I have the honour to return you the Address which I have inserted in the M[orning] P[ost] and O[racle] of today, and it will be in the chief evenings of to-night, and the mornings of to-morrow. You will see other articles in the M. P. and O. of to-day, which I hope will please.²

Be assured that I shall be unremitting in all my exertions, and I have no doubt of success. You and your friends, I hope, perceive that I have at least stemmed the tide of calumny greatly, and I am confident that I shall soon do more. In all this business,³ it is a great happiness to me to have been introduced to a gentleman of your zeal for his Royal Highness's service. Your many hints and particular attention to his fame, by advising me, has enabled me to do several good things of great utility to the cause. Would to heaven he had had always such fidelity and zeal surrounding his person as you. He would not then have been calumniated by those very people who have so well thriven by his bounty. (41552)

3383 LETTERS FROM HENRY FREDERICK, DUKE OF CUMBERLAND TO THE PRINCE OF WALES

Great Lodge, Wednesday, 6 Sept. 1780

I enclose you a key of the Park; desire you will be so good as not to leave it in the hands of your livery servants when you have done riding. Shall be happy at all times that the Park may afford you every amusement you can wish.

When the Queen is brought to bed if you will be so good as to send word to the Great Lodge it will be forwarded to Brighthelmstone.⁴

[*P.S.*] My best wishes and love attend upon Prince Frederick. I have had a fine hunt this morning. (54451)

1. This paragraph gives the clue to the approximate date of the letter. *See* Perceval's letter to the Prince, 5 February 1811 (No. 2836). For the Commission issued under the Great Seal for opening the Parliament, *see Parliamentary Debates*, xviii. 1146 (12 February 1811).

2. See Nos. 1171, 1185, and also references to Peter and Daniel Stuart.

3. Relating to the Princess of Wales.

4. Prince Alfred (1780–2) was born on 22 September.

Brighton, Wednesday, 11 Oct. 1780

I have had some very good hunting in this country but it is very hilly & hard work for the horses. I wish you & Prince Frederick had been of the party. I wish you would let me know whether you go to Court of the Accession which is next Wednesday fortnight[1] & whether you hunt that week of the Monday or Tuesday, because I would do myself the pleasure of attending you if you send your answer to the Great Lodge ither [*sic*] Friday or Monday. I have a conveyance from thence that will bring your letter safe.

My love to Prince Frederick; all health and happiness attend you both. (54452)

Brighton, 17 Oct. 1780

I beg my best love to Prince Frederick; tell him how hurt I am at the accident but hope it will be of no bad consequence. I shall certainly do myself the pleasure of waiting upon you next Sunday soon after one o'clock. I hope by that time you will have your Establishment fixed.

We have had great sport here. You need not give yourself the trouble of writing to me again as there will [be] no way of conveying here time enough for me before Sunday. I hope we shall have some good hunts together as I shall devote my time to you whenever I am not thought troublesome. I have given your compts. & they are much flattered with your goodness, never doubting your good intentions.

I can easily conceive your feelings for your brother; indeed he is a delightful fine fellow & I am sure nothing has made me happier in my acquaintance with you both as that perfect harmony that subsists between you. Tell poor Frederick I have some curious anecdotes about Osnaburg to communicate to him when we meet from a person who is just come from thence.

Permit me to conclude with assuring you how sincerely & unalterably I am attached to you & that nothing in life can ever make me differ in these sentiments. (54453)

Great Lodge, 18 July 1782

I have heard from London this morning & find the tide will suit at two o'clock. I have sent Lord Melburne, Ly. Melburne, Charles Fox, John Townshend & St. Leger to be at Cumberland House Thursday at one to go on the water & to dine.

1. George II died on 25 October 1760.

Forgive my hurry or else it would be too late for you to hear from me. (54457)

Brighthelmstone, 2 Sept. 1782
I have been very uneasy here at a report that Prince William was dead of the accident in breaking his arm, but not hearing from you made me discredit the report. I hope the K., Q. & the rest of the family have got their spirits up again since their return to Windsor. Garth[1] mentions to me that Man.[2] should have hinted at the Levée last Friday that next Wednesday fortnight, I mean the 18, is to be the day for holding a Chapter of the Garter to invest the Duke of Rutland;[3] if that is a fact I beg you will be so kind as to let me know it, as being at Brighthelmstone I shall have some necessary orders to give, & also whether the D. of Rutland intends on the day of receiving the Garter to invite us to dine, as I mean to come back here again as I shall have but one week after that to bath[e].

I hope you have had good sport & shooting, but I fear the birds are very scarce. (54458)

Brighton, 8 Sept. 1782
I am just favoured with your [letter], tho' very sorry at your accident of having strained your wrist. If there is no order for the Chapter I shall be at the Lodge next Thursday fortnight; if there should be, you will be so good as to let me know in time & also a line to Daly at the Lodge to say what day the Chapter is to be, as he has my orders to send some things up in consequence of it.

I am glad you have had good sport & shooting. The Ds. is much flattered with your attention, as is *C*. (54459)

1. Major-General George Garth was the Duke's Treasurer.

2. Probably the Duke of Manchester (1737–88), the Lord Chamberlain, April 1782–April 1783. He had been a Lord of the Bedchamber, 1762–70, and, before he succeeded his father (10 May 1762) he was M.P. for Huntingdonshire, as Viscount Mandeville (1761–2). He was a Rockingham Whig.

3. The Duke of Rutland was invested with the Order of the Garter on 3 October. Shelburne, the Prime Minister, recommended him for this honour.

Paris, Sunday, 30 Nov. 1783

We arrived here last Thursday, the Duke & Dutchess of Manchester have shewn us every mark of civility;[1] we have seen the French Opera & Play, the musick noisy & bad, fine shew & the dancing very good, Gardel exceedingly improved but I hear he is in a decline therefore does not dare to dance much. I gave yours safe to St. Leger who has dined with me & sups here tonight, a party of about 18 at my house. I leave this place on Tuesday for Strasbourg & do not now go to Dijon at all. I have just seen the Duke of Chartres;[2] a visit passed from him at my door & I waited on him yesterday morning; very civil but no offer to entertain nor mentioned the Ds. of Chartres. So far for his civility to us after our amusing him in London! The Ds. desires me to express her most respectful good wishes to you. I hope you are diverting yourself. I feel very severely the loss of you, my dear friend, & indeed after such an acquaintance as I have had with you I find nothing that anywhere can resemble you.

I find a safe hand to whom I have confided this; send your letters without a cover directed to me, to Miller[3] at Cumberland House.

I have no kind of news to tell you here & I fear my letters to you, who live in a very gay world, will appear but dull. I hope your *friend* will not be scrupulous & come & partake of your agreable parties at your house. Be happy my dear Sir is my greatest wish. You must allow me when I write to put it without a cover as I shall always direct it under cover to somebody who will give it safe at your house. (54462)

Strasbourg, Sunday, 28 Dec. 1783

How much am I flattered by your kind letter of the 16th which I recevd. last Friday (the post from the badness of the roads did not arrive as it ought to have done on the Wednesday or I should have answer'd yours on the Thursday, which is our constant day to write to England). With what words can I express your ever repeated goodness to me; now, God knows, it is but in words; may ever a time arrive in which I may prove to you how sincerely I am attatched to you. The Ds. joins me in her most sincere wishes for your welfare & happiness & we both lament that the present critical situation of publick affairs does by no means assist in making you happy.

1. The 4th Duke of Manchester (1737–88) was Ambassador to France, April–December 1783. On 23 October 1762 he married Elizabeth (c.1741–1832), daughter of Sir James Dashwood, 2nd Bart.

2. See No. 76.

3. One of the Duke's pages.

The post of this day is not as yet come in & as I am promised by you, my dear friend, another letter, I am in great expectation for the event altho' I fear that the determination was taken previous to Ld. T——e[1] visit to [illegible] *our friends* if there was a possibility; should it succeed it cannot last; you know best whether Nh.[2] is steady: if he does not join the other side they will find it a very hard struggle indeed, & yet how will Ld. *Te.* with *St.*?[3] I know they will try to get at Loughborough. I suppose Th——w[4] will be Chancellor. He is the *great favourite* of all. I must own I was not at all surprized to hear about the House of Lords. I suppose if the change has not happened yet that all the wheels will be at work during the recess, yet, Sir, I must feel most sincerely as every event that makes so many changes at home does *us* the greatest harm abroad & shews that when we have not other ennemies to cope with we must quarrel among ourselves. I was always sorry at St.[5] being in the last Administration; I knew he would act double whenever he could, as he certainly was not cordial with *your friends*: he had been too long used to bear to act an underpart & I suppose with the change will be made Secretary of State for the Foreign Department. I do not fancy much Te. & Mr. Pitt together; I think they will not like to act together or give way to one another. S——e[6] may act in the House with them but I think he has had enough of Government not to venture again, but if he does all will soon be in confusion again.

With regard to this place, we have just been here three weeks & got into our new habitation last Tuesday sevennight. The house belonged to Princess Christine-Chanoinese of Remiremont who has been dead about a twelve month. We have two rooms to see company in & a dining room which can hold but 20 upon occasion. We had an Assembly last night for the first time. The hours here are very early as you know everything is abroad; company came at six and as we had no supper the house was clear of them about eight as that is the time people go to play cards at houses where they are invited to sup; supper on table at half pt. nine and part soon after eleven. The rule is to be about three quarters of an hour at supper & then finish the game of cards that were begun in the evening. We have a French Playhouse open four times in a week; begins at half pt. five, over soon after eight. We dine at three, but only our own family. The natives on acct. of the garrison dine at one. I hear it reported here

1. ?Lord Temple.

2. ?Lord North.

3. ?Lord Stormont.

4. Thurlow.

5. Lord Stormont (1727–96), who succeeded his uncle as 2nd Earl of Mansfield in 1793, was President of the Council in the Fox–North Coalition Ministry, 1783.

6. Shelburne.

as if Prince Frederick was to come over this winter to England. I have this morning seen a Monsieur Frederick who is Judge Advocate to the German troops at Gibraltar; he is going Wednesday to Hannover. I shall write to Frederick by him.

I shall now conclude this, but not before I ask you after the *M.s.* Are they in favour? for you do not mention their names. As for Madame Future¹ who I saw at Paris, I cannot by any means say she would suit you; she is thin and did not appear to me to be sprightly enough. I suppose you have seen the D—— M——r. as I desired him to call upon you & tell you everything relative to us. Be on your guard if the D. C[hartre]s comes to England & do not be too civil, for I think, considering the attention I shewed him, he ought to have given us a fete or at least as much attention as to a private English gentleman how [*sic*] goes a hunting.

I want much to know *your* reception after Monday vote; you need not write names out, I fancy we understand each other enough without being too explicit. I assure you it is great charity during my abscence to hear from you. I write this today for fear I should not have time enough tomorrow when the post goes from here & shall wait till the latest hour tomorrow, which is eleven in the morning. If I say nothing, depend upon it the post is not arrived. (54465–6)

Strasbourg, 11 a.m., Monday, 29 Dec. 1783
The post arrived yesterday eve. owing to the badness of the roads, which ought to have been in at twelve o'clock, but brought nothing from you. I see by letters I recevd. as well as by the papers that *our friends* are out: I am sorry also to hear you have not been well owing to heat & fatigue you caught at the Hs. of Commons, but am glad² [to] hear you are well. I can easily conceive how chagrined [you] must have been at this sad change.² Various [are the] conjectures of the change; some [say] that, St. is to be³ [   ]. My letters do not mention his name³ [I] wish a *certain person* would again wish to have him of the Party.

1. The reference is obscure: she was probably some German Princess. The Duchess of Cumberland's letter to the Prince of Wales on 27 December from Strasbourg evidently refers to the same person. See No. 3384.

2. Paper torn.

3. Paper torn.

By chance the post of today may bring me yours as I have sometimes not received all my letters together.

[*P.S.*] If I hear from you before the next post goes out from here, which is Thursday, by that day's post I will certainly answer it. (54467)

Strasbourg, Wednesday, 14 Apr. 1784

I am exceedingly sorry to hear you have been ill;[1] the weather having been so bad I fear has hinder'd your taking that exercise which is so benefitial to your health.

Our life here is pretty much the same; the Marquis de la Salle, the Commandant, is at home three evenings in the week, at a little after eight, after the Play, parties of cards are made; everybody plays at a very moderate price & indeed in a garrison town it is of the greatest consequence that play for any great sum should be forbid. Supper is over & everybody retires by half pt. eleven. Every Sat. the Ds. has company to supper & we at our house just do the same as the Commandant. The Ds. desires to be kindly remembered by you as well as [illegible].

Sr. Thomas Fouke[2] is obliged to come to England as he has a disagreable lawsuit with his vicar & therefore will not return to me: he will have the honor of leaving this at Carlton House in case you do not see him.

I find by the paper the Duke of Chartres is come to England; he is quite done up at Paris & has been obliged to leave the Ds. of Chartres but £4,000 a year after the great fortune she brought him. He is in very bad repute in his own country. The papers mention your having supped with him at the French Ambassador's.

The weather here is getting rather finer but the spring is most exceedingly backward owing to the hard frost. How goes on musick? [*sic*]. I have not had an answer to the letter I wrote to Prince Frederick just before Christmas. (54468)

1. See No. 109.
2. Sir Thomas Fowke, the Duke's Groom of the Bedchamber (*d.* 1786).

Monday, 23 Aug. 1784

I had the pleasure of receiving your kind & affectionate letter last night. Sr. Godfrey[1] having spent some time at Nancy in Lorraine has made yours be so long in hand. I am very glad you are on your guard what you write, yet if ever you have anything to communicate, Garth will let me know without mentioning your name. The Ds. is extremely sensible of your attention to her & begs me to assure you of her best compliments & good wishes. We mean the 1st of Octr. to go to the South of France in order to pass a warmer winter then the last. This climate is changeable beyond measure, hot & cold the same day. Our life here is pretty much alike; when the troops exercise of a morning I go out to see them. The Comte de Cogny that you remember in England is Inspector of the Cavalry.

I recevd. a letter yesterday from Heyman from Conflans just at his return from Brighton, where he mentions the very gracious manner you had treated him & the house you have given him. Both in your letter as well as in his the same mention is made of my *friend's* intention to come abroad. I beg you will be so good as to assure him how happy I should be if it were practicable, but without his getting leave I forsee disagreable consequences.

As for politicks, I receive these from different quarters as well as what is in the newspapers; therefore on that score I am not in the dark. With regard to yourself, the manner of passing your time or anything you wish to communicate altho' you may think trivial cannot be to me who am always glad to know what you are about; if therefore when you write you will send it to Miller only sealed, without a cover, he will put it up safe under cover of my newspapers.

Ld. & Ly. Clive[2] have been here for a few days; she talks in raptures about the balls & parties you have given them . . .[3] (54469–70)

Thursday, 3 Jan. 1788

I have just had a letter from my brother who desires I will acquaint you he has wrote to the K. to make his excuse for his not attending Court this day; he means to keep quiet in No. 1, Park Street. I wrote him for

---

1. ?Webster.

2. Edward Clive (1754–1839), son of the famous Lord Clive (1725–74), and M.P. for Ludlow, 1774–94, succeeded his father as 2nd Baron Clive [I.], and was created Baron Clive [G.B.], 13 August 1794, and Earl of Powis, 14 May 1804. On 7 May 1784 he married Lady Henrietta Antonia Herbert (1758–1830), daughter of the 1st Earl of Powis. He was Governor of Madras, 1798–1803.

3. For the remainder of this letter, *see* i. 154*n*.

answer that I was happy to find in those two places he met a more friendly reception que chez lui. (54487)

3384   THE DUCHESS OF CUMBERLAND TO THE PRINCE OF WALES

Strasbourg, 27 Dec. 1783

I never can forget any thing yr. R.H. wishes me to remember & had it so much at heart that I stay'd a day longer at Paris on purpose to see —— [*sic*] for half an hour at the Duke of Manchester's. The first coup d'oeil is not striking, but yr. R.H. knows that a little beauty accompany'd wth. strong sensibility & a thousand agréments constitutes the tout en semble capable of inspiring a forte passion rather than symmetry of form or features; of these however I had no opportunity of judging, but if (as intend'd) they stop here some days in their way home, I shall be very observing & yr. R.H. shall know the pour e[*sic*] contre. A print I had given the D. of M. excited the curiosity of all his company as to the mental qualitys &c. & I gave them my sentiments very fully without having the fear of the D. of G. commentary's before my eyes.

Here we are at Strasbourg for the winter, much feté by all the commandants & not ill lodged; the Duke de Crillion offer'd his magnificent house at Avignon but the Duke's penchant for Germans & music gave the preferance to Strasbourg. As to myself, when I had taken leave of yr. R.H. my difficulty's were at an end, or having exausted every painful sensation I felt not at all the fatigues of the journey. The Duke & Dutchess of Manchester did everything that depend'd on them to make Paris agreable to us; they are both much esteem'd there. The Spanish Ambassadour's dinner everybody say'd was superb, but I recollected the Friday before I left England & thought I had seen a better.

I am more grieved than surprised at this fresh proof of great objects sacrificed to the gratification of private pique in the fate of the India Bill.[1] You know, my dear Prince, I ever was of opinion that the prerogative of the Crown ought not to be diminish'd & every struggle for power in the present inauspicious season of republicanism is dangerous to monarchy.

My sister[2] was extremely flatter'd by yr. R.H. gracious remembrance of her: she is now perfectly recover'd. Tonight is the first Masquerade at the Theatre but I have no friar to dress or inducement to join the throng. (54463–4)

1. Fox's India Bill, thrown out by the House of Lords. The King then dismissed the Coalition. See i. 100.

2. Lady Elizabeth Luttrell. See No. 158.

Carlton House, 3 Apr. 1802

In the late discussion which took place in the House of Commons respecting my claim to the revenues of the Duchy of Cornwall accumulated between the 12th of August 1762 & the twelfth of August 1783, it appears to have been thought that the question could be decided only by a judicial proceedure. I must be necessarily solicitous to accomodate my steps to that which seemed the prevailing opinion of the House. I know not however any avenue to a proper tribunal unless a Petition of Right may afford it to me, & on that point I must feel some deficiency of confidence. I did some years ago deliver a Petition of Right to Lord Chancellor Loughborough, requesting him to lay it before the King. But his Lordship declined to present that Petition, alledging that it was not his function, but without indicating to me what would be the regular channel. Under this doubt I think it expedient to send to your Lordship the copy of the Petition of Right which I wish should be offer'd to the King, & you will allow me to ask for your answer whether you will take his Majesty's pleasure upon it. The explanation is requisite, because, in case your Lordship should deem it not to be within your province to present this Petition & cannot suggest any other person whose duty it may be, a Motion in Parliament to define or establish a proper officer for the purpose would become immediately indispensible.

I am, My Lord, with esteem, yours sincerely[1] (Eldon MSS.).

1. For the Prince's claim to the arrears of the revenue of the Duchy of Cornwall, see iv. 248–51.

iv   Some Additional Letters, 1812–1830

3386   LETTERS FROM THE PRINCE REGENT TO THE MARCHIONESS OF HERTFORD

Windsor, Thursday, 27 Aug. 1812

With all, my ever dearest Lady B., my best desire to scribble a line today I have hardly a minute's time to do so, I am so hurried with one plague or another, but it is of less consequence & I feel less vex'd & annoy'd by it than I should at another time, as I am to have the happiness of seeing you the day after tomorrow, & which, notwithstanding, appears an age to come. Your kind letter of yesterday has just reach'd me, & as I know him a little I shall be most anxious to know how you will have lik'd your visitor Dr. Parr,[1] who, if he will chuse at all to let himself out, I think you will have found, though a very serious one, yet, at the same time not an unentertaining beast, for notwithstanding all his learning & talents, I cannot help in many other respects considering him as a very great brute, not to mention his Jacobinism, & his great respect & private friendship for Burdett, &c., &c., &c. As to news, I unfortunately have none to write for Lord Hertford by this post, & all I can say, if for yourself, is that my hand today is weaker & more unsteady than ever, as you will perceive from the badness of this scrawl, but neither this nor any thing else do I mind at this moment. I am so happy at the thought of seeing you, my best & ever dearest friend, & Lord Hertford on Saturday; I really do feel quite like a young colt going to be turn'd out to his first grass, as gay as a

1. Samuel Parr (1747–1825), 'the Whig Johnson'.

lark & as light as a feather, & pray tell Lord Hertford (with all that is kindest from me) that I shall be quite content if you are only half as glad to see me, as I shall be rejoic'd to see you. Tho' this will be my last letter for some time at least, I have neither the means, the power or the time to spin it out to a greater length; I can only think of the happiness of presenting my uggly phizz to you on Saturday which really is my only thought just at present. Now then adieu, my ever dearest Lady B., & never cease to beleive me, your ever & most affectionate (Egerton MSS. 3262, f. 83).

Carlton House, Tuesday, 10 Nov. 1812

First, my ever dearest Lady B——, before I step into my carriage to begin my travels, I take up my pen to scribble a line, & really but a line, which you must be very glad of after the long scrawl I tired you with by the last evening's post. I have no intelligence to communicate but what is so much better & ampler detail'd in all the papers of this day that I shall not trouble either you, my best & ever dearest friend, with any of my remarks upon it, except that in the general & upon the whole, everything & everywhere seems to bear the most favorable & auspicious aspect. The last Bullitin [*sic*] of Bonaparte (which reach'd me about an hour after I had put my yesterday's letter to you, to the post) & which I now inclose, is the grossest of all possible fanfaronades, & is evidently fram'd merely to furnish a colouring for his return to Paris, after having fail'd in all his plans, & we are the more confirm'd & strengthen'd in this opinion, for by most private & secret intelligence receiv'd last night, we are inform'd that there have been very general risings throughout all the provincial cities & towns in France, similar to what we heard of a fortnight ago having taken place at Paris; that they in general shewn themselves [*sic*] in the night time, by cries 'La Paix, la Paix, la Paix, et point de conscription;' that this had occasion'd great alarm, that the Police had become extremely vigilant, that numberless devastations [?] had taken place, that the Government had taken great alarm, & were circulating innumerable half-fabricated false reports & bulletins of what they would call good news from their armies, of partial advantages & of a prospect of peace with Russia, the whole of which are void of all foundation, merely to temporize, gain time, & as far as they can to mitigate & assuage the immediate ferment of the public mind against Bonaparte, & which has been carried beyond all manner of doubt, to a much greater extent than we can ourselves form any very correct or accurate idea of (here I was interrupted by the sudden arrival of Castlereagh), there being not an attom, no, not even a particle more of news with which I could stay Lord Hertford's rapacity & voraciousness for intelligence & which I beg that you will tell him, accompanied with my best regards, I shall now my ever dearest Lady B——, take my leave of you until Friday, when I look forward with certainty to the heartfelt happiness of presenting myself in person to you at Sudbourne, & when I cannot help hoping that you will be better pleas'd with that apparition, than with one of my long & dull scrawls. My cold, though somewhat better today than it was yesterday, is still very heavy, notwithstanding which, Farquhar, who I have also just seen, is very desirous that I should set off. I therefore shall throw myself into my carriage & set out upon my travels as soon as I have seal'd & inclos'd this scrawl. God for ever bless you, my ever dearest Lady B, until we meet, which is all that I can add more at present, except that I am most unalterably [etc.].

[*P.S.*] There was so little to be done this week, that it was not worth while to send a servant down (Egerton MSS. 3262, f. 85).

Carlton House, 1.30 a.m., Tuesday, 15 Dec. 1812
What a day of punishment this day has been, but, however, now & then everything has its ending, thanks be to Providence, & therefore, & altho' my poor paw is hardly able to hold a pen, still I cannot resist sending you the glorious intelligence that has just reach'd me. All you know has gone not only quite quietly but quite well, domestically speaking, but only judge of my inexpressible joy at hearing Castlereagh announc'd, out of his bed, with despatches from Lord Cathcart[1] dated not the very latest date, but the exact hour or day; my mind is so puzzled at the present moment I cannot tell with any degree of exactitude but I believe so late as the 25th, stating a bull[e]tin from Stuttgard to the Emperor late as the 18th, in which he informs him that he had come up with Bonaparte's army, completely routed him in Saxony, taken 20,000 prisoners & 200 pieces of cannon, that Bony was there in person, who owed his safety intirely to the fleetness of his horse in flight; all this is accompanied with a personal message from the Emperor to me assuring me in the strongest & firmest of language that no proposal whatsoever *from any quarter* shall induce him to listen to anything like a peace until he has exterminated Bonaparte, & can enter into one with us & our sanction, & such a one as to liberate *all Europe from the tyranny of this monster or that he & everyone in his country will be & shall be first exterminated*, & of which, thank God, there is now but very little appearance or probability, quite on the contrary. This is the bulk of the whole,

1. Cathcart, our Ambassador to Russia, 1812–19, was at Petersburg until 12 February 1813 when he accompanied the Tsar to Germany, Switzerland and France during the 1813–14 campaign.

accompanied by many other circumstances & even of a very interesting nature, but which are of too voluminous a nature to attempt to detail at this late hour, but all excellent in their nature & which I will have the happiness of relating to you verbally tomorrow when I have the happiness of seeing you tomorrow. But however late, I cannot & could not help sending you for Ld. Hertford's information, the glad, joyous & most glorious tidings; N.B. This makes up the whole of the French bulletins as discrib'd per papers of today & yesterday.

I am really almost quite out of my mind (in a certain way that cannot be express'd) with joy. Pity my scrawl, recollect that I am dying to see you & to tell you everything else of this day. If I am too late pardon my intrusion, which for such news I dare say Lord Hertford will do, & only remember in addition to my sad scrawl, & in addition to the good news I send, I am to the end of my existence, my ever dearest Lady B., most invariably & unalterably your ever & most affectionate.

P.S. Pardon blotting, hurry & all other encomiums. I inclose a little note from Cork to *prove* the authenticity of the rest. Alas! my poor hand is quite at [illegible] very near [?] (Egerton MS. 3262, f. 89).

3387 THE PRINCE REGENT TO THE EARL OF LIVERPOOL

Carlton House, 7.30 p.m., Thursday, 11 Feb. 1813
Private. Nothing in my opinion can be so honorable to your feelings or so agreable to mine *in every respect*, as the appointment of young Mr. Percival[1] to the vacant Tellership of the Exchequer. (Add. MSS. 38190, fo. 23)

3388 LETTERS FROM THE PRINCE REGENT TO WILLIAM ADAM

[15 Feb. 1813]
Most private. I have seen Ld. Sidmouth, who brought me for my approbation previous to its being sent out, the sketch of the circular letter of summons to the different members of the Privy Council who are in-intended to compose the Court of Inquiry, with the latter part of the wording of which, I am by *no means either satisfied or pleas'd*, for, after

1. Spencer Perceval (1795–1859), son of the Prime Minister. M.P. for Ennis, 1818–20; for Newport (Isle of Wight), 1827–31; for Tiverton, 1831–2. The Tellership, a lucrative sinecure, had been held by the Marquess of Buckingham, who died on 11 February. Perceval had died almost penniless, leaving a large family.

mentioning and asserting my atribute right to the complete management of my daughter in every respect, and adverting to the Princess's letter and publication upon which I inform them that I have order'd all the papers relating to the former Investigation, and all subsequent papers and documents of every sort that are in my possession, and that have at any time pass'd between the Princess and me, from that time down to the present moment, for their information and for them to report to me upon;[1] it then goes on to *draw their attention only* in limine to *my* management of my daughter, of late, as if I was asking their sanction for what *is and ever must be* '*my undisputed and establish'd right*, and after having claim'd and establish'd *that*, by assumption in the previous part of this letter, a circumstance which, I need not, I am sure, state to you, is quite *infra dignitates* [*sic*], and therefore quite *inadmissible*. Thus it narrows entirely (and I should be assur'd, almost quite turns in a manner) the grounds of all further and other general investigation, giving the entire go by and that too in the shabbiest of all possible ways, also, to the Princess's call for fresh investigation of the pass'd, and as such therefore *must ultimately fall upon me*,' and be incalculably prejudicial to to [*sic*] me in the public view and opinion when it comes to be known and canvass'd over; furnishing the Princess with every advantage from non-investigation, and subjecting me to the obloquy of the whole world and to its being twisted by her and her colleagues into any shape they please, to my disadvantage, by arguments and reasonings which are so much too obvious that it is quite unnecessary for me to take up your time with mentioning them or detailing them, as they must both naturally and necessarily occur to you from all you know of the case. Further I have to observe that there is also this to be added, the not taking the smallest notice of any of the various and infamous aspersions and allegations thrown out upon me in her letter, such as subornation of witnesses &c. &c. &c., which ought not, can not, must not, *and shall not* be pass'd over unnotic'd, so long at least as I have any thing to do with the business, or that *I have breath in my body*, for that is what neither publicity nor privately, as a man, a gentleman, or a Prince, I either ever can or will submit to, or can or ought to be expected to do so, and I think that no man or set of men can be so base, so unfeeling in themselves, so impudent, or so totally dead to all sense of honor of whatever discription

---

1. On 14 January the Princess of Wales wrote a letter to the Regent complaining that additional restrictions had been lately imposed upon her intercourse with Princess Charlotte. The letter was returned unopened, and after it had been published in the *Morning Chronicle* on 10 February, the Regent decided to submit the matter to his Ministers and other members of the Privy Council for his own justification. Having examined the evidence on which the 1806 charges had been based, they reported on the 27th that the intercourse between the Princess of Wales and her daughter should continue to be subject to restraint.

(not to mention their being perfectly devoid of all sentiment or feeling of regard for myself personally, and for my character, in every possible light) if they could or can for one single instant entertain in the first place so preposterous a notion, and, much more, in the second, to submit it to me. I therefore have stopp'd the letter and order'd Ld. Sidmouth instantly to summons another Cabinet and to draw their attention to this point, the total erasure and the entirely leaving out the whole of the latter part of the intended circular letter, as the former part is quite sufficient of itself, for it can not *rest better* than upon the first part of the statement, namely, of my having summoned them together for this particular purpose, in consequence of the Princess's letter, her complaints therein contain'd, her assertions, her allegations against me, and that I having therefore furnish'd them with the whole of all papers and documents and materials in my possession that bear any relation to any part or parts connected in any shape with the different transactions and events, and that I finally do therefore call upon them to report to me upon the whole mass of business contain'd in the Princess's letter, in the most circumstantial manner. Having now (though in great haste) express'd myself in the fullest, but at the same time I hope in an intelligible manner to you, you will, my dear [Adam] . . .[1]

(Here in my hurry I have pass'd over a page, therefore proceed on to the other sheet) (Blair Adam MSS.).

Carlton House, Monday night, 15 Feb. 1813
Only one line, just to say that *we* have just receiv'd a *fresh communication* through Lord Liverpool, since the letter which I wrote to you this day, and which *is invaluable* (according at least to my ideas) *in itself*, and which makes it doubly necessary for me to see you at *a very early hour tomorrow, at any rate before you* go to any interview with anybody whatsoever. Depend upon it, that it is *most pressing*, and I will be visible, however early, at any time that may suit you to call at Carlton House; and I think that you will be *most astonished*.

P.S. *You must come at any rate* (Blair Adam MSS.).

1. The third sheet, which was probably the outside cover, does not seem to have been preserved.

Colonel McMahon wrote to William Adam from Carlton House at 6.30 p.m. that day: 'I am charg'd that you should get the enclosed letters as soon as possible, and if you feel it difficult to read (which I am sure you must, for besides the interlineations and marks, the sheets are not regularly placed) that you may call upon me to explain it before you go to Lord L[iverpool] and the Chancellor, as H.R.Hss. has read it to me. I find that no report from Cabinet has reach'd him since he sent Ld. Sidmouth back this forenoon to reconsider it. I am truly sorry you are thus broke in upon, but am always [etc.].'

Carlton House, Sunday night, 21 Feb. 1813

Most private. I merely scribble a line tonight to prepare you for a visit at an early hour tomorrow morning from the Ld. Chr., who told me that he meant to call upon you to have a long conversation with you upon the further proceedings in this business, and relative to many other matters relating to it and connected with it. I rather suppose that you will find this to arise from a notification which Cochrane Johnstone has given or sent to the Government, to apprize them that he means to give a notice in the House tomorrow, of an intended motion for the next day, or upon the most immediate possible day, for not only all the papers that are now before the Committee, but for a long list of others, many of which I never have not only not possess'd, but never even heard of, and amongst the rest, for all the evidence that has been taken or sworn to before a magistrate, independant of that that was taken upon oath before the Commissioners during the Investigation. Out of this it is possible that much good may come, as it may compel the Government to go into the whole of the evidence of the past investigation at once; at least I am sure they may be able certainly to avail themselves (if they please) from what may drop, of the substance of this as an excuse or reason for entering into the full investigation of every part of the business from the very earliest period down to the present moment, which (I do not know what you may think) I cannot but help thinking, as it appears to me at this moment, as matters are now standing, would be, and cannot fail to be most fortunate and desirable in every point of view, that I either can or do consider it or turn it over in my mind. At any rate I hope you will lay the *most distinct and unbounded* stress on the positive, absolute and imperative necessity there is, paramount to every other consideration whatsoever, for the Government to hold the most decided language; and in the plainest, most distinct and most direct words and terms, they should give it to be understood that so far from flinching, hesitating, or trying to evade inquiry, I am ready, desirous, and even most anxious to meet it in all and every shape that it can come in, be propos'd or offer'd, and ready to grant it and to forward it by every means in my power. Pray press the absolute necessity of this upon the Chr. in the strongest and most forcible manner that is possible and that you are able.

I think upon the whole, from what pass'd between him and me this evening, you will find him much less averse to going into the thorough investigation of the past, than he has hitherto been, that is object [*sic*] is to collect your ideas upon that head, to settle him in this new view of things, and that what he will throw out to you by way of doubt or objection, is more for you and for the purpose of your reasoning him out of his old system, and confirming him, or rather converting him to this change of sentiment, than for you to give any support to the former considerations and opinions he had entertain'd and express'd. This I believe

410

(unless he should change again before tomorrow morning) I believe you will find pretty correct; at any rate it is worth your knowing and being appriz'd of, to put you upon your guard and to feel your way accordingly. After you have had your interview with the Chr., if it be possible and without any risk to yourself in coming out, I am most anxious to see you, and indeed it is most important that I should see you, as I have many notes that I have made, and much further intelligence of importance which I have come at this evening, and which therefore I am most desirous of giving you and explaining to you viva voce, and in person, than through any third person or other channel. Good night. I can hardly see enough even to finish this scrawl, which I hope you will be able to decypher and understand. All I beg is one line of answer to say whether you can or will come, and if you do, at what hour tomorrow morning I may expect you (Blair Adam MSS.).

3389   THE PRINCE REGENT TO THE EARL OF LIVERPOOL
Carlton House, 10.30 p.m., Tuesday, 23 Mar. 1813
Sir Henry Halford has this instant come to Carlton House to inform me that he was desir'd by Dr. Baillie to hold himself in readiness, should he be sent for, to attend with him upon the Dss. of Brunswick, who had within this few days [*sic*] an attack of the present epidemick complaint, in addition to her habitual asthma; that about an hour ago, Dr. Baillie not being able to be found, he was suddenly sent for, and that when he reach'd the Dss.'s bedside, which was almost immediately, he found [her] expiring, and she died within a few minutes afterwards. Sir Henry Halford will write you the *official account* presently. I need scarcely add that I shall command in all the papers of tomorrow the Levée's being postpon'd till further orders. I desire to see you in the course of tomorrow morning. (Add. MSS. 38190, fo. 24)

3390   THE PRINCE REGENT TO THE DOWAGER DUCHESS OF RUTLAND
C.H., 9 a.m., Saturday, 3 July 1813
The glorious news is this moment arriv'd;[1] the cavalry from the nature of the country were *not at all engaged, & all safe & well*. We have

1. By Wellington's despatch to Lord Bathurst from Salvatierra, 22 June, brought to London by his A.D.C., Captain Fremantle. Wellington was raised to the rank of Field-Marshal after the battle of Vitoria (21 June).

411

entirely demolish'd that whole French army having taken upwards of 10,000 prisoners, 157 peices of cannon, four hundred & upwards baggage waggons & the whole of the rest (of the depot) of the ammunition & stores for that whole army in Vittoria which they were unable to destroy previous to their retreat or rather flight; they did not dare stop at Pampeluna notwithstanding the strong fortifications they had thrown up there, & were flying into France as fast as possible, having no one further strong place left them in that part of the country; & Lord Wellington has sent me Marshal Jourdan's baton de maréshalle [*sic*] which is now laying upon my table whilst I am scribbling to you this very hasty scrawl. Your mind I hope now will be, my dear Duchess, quite at ease (Belvoir MSS.).

P.S. No officer of any note kill'd except, I am sorry to say, poor Lt. Col. Cadogan.

3391 LETTERS FROM THE PRINCE REGENT TO THE EARL OF LIVERPOOL

Brighton, Tuesday night, 10 Aug. 1813

I have this moment receiv'd Dr. Jackson's answer declining the See of London upon the score of ill health. You are therefore at full liberty to keep your appointment tomorrow morning with Dr. Howley[1] and to close with him if he should accept, as I have no doubt, and indeed as I hope that he will. (Add. MSS. 38190, fo. 25)

Ragley, 1 Sept. 1813

The Prince Regent has receiv'd Lord Liverpool's note for which he returns him many thanks, and at the same time desires that Lord Liverpool will give the Professorship according to the wish he has expressed, to Mr. Van Mildert.[2] Nothing can be more agreable to the Prince Regent than to learn from Lord Liverpool how strongly this nomination will be approved of by the highly respected and respectable persons he has mention'd on this occasion.

P.S. The P. Rt. most heartily congratulates Ld. L. on the flattering turn which events seem to be taking upon the Continent. (Add. MSS. 38190, fo. 27)

1. William Howley (1766–1848). Nominated Bishop of London, 12 August 1813 (consecrated, 1 October); Archbishop of Canterbury, August 1828–48. He was Regius Professor of Divinity at Oxford, 1809–13.

2. William Van Mildert (1765–1836), Regius Professor of Divinity at Oxford, 1813–19; Bishop of Llandaff, 1819–26; Dean of St. Paul's, 1820–6; Bishop of Durham, 1826–36.

3392 THE PRINCE REGENT TO THE DUKE OF RUTLAND

Ragley, 11 Sep. 1813

I do not delay a single instant acknowledging your Grace's very kind letter which has this moment reach'd me, & endeavouring to express to you how truly flatter'd I feel myself for your recollection of me upon the present occasion, in which I trust that you will do me the justice to beleive that there is no one of the whole circle that surrounds you who does more cordially participate than myself. I am therefore most happy in undertaking the responsibility for the little Marquis[1] which you have been so kind as to impose upon me, with the warmest wishes for the Duchess's speedy re-establishment & for the prosperity of every branch of your Grace's family (Belvoir MSS.).

3393 THE PRINCE REGENT TO THE DOWAGER DUCHESS OF RUTLAND

Carlton House, 30 Sep. 1813

I can hardly express to you the happiness I feel at having it now in my power to offer you my most sincere & hearty congratulations upon the recovery of our dear Bob.[2] I have felt most truly for you for many days past, ever since I first heard of his indisposition, & most anxiously have I, I do assure you, made my enquiries daily at your house in Sackville Street, trembling at the re-appearance of my servant lest the intelligence he brought me might not be as favorable as the warmth & sincerity of my affection for you & him led me to hope & to pray that it might be. However, now, thank Heaven, you & I & all his friends have every reason & prospect to be quite at ease; never mind the rest, my dearest friend, & do not now plague & torment yourself so completely un-necessarily as you appear to do with (you really must forgive me) a parcel of conundrums which you conjure up to yourself without the smallest shadow of reason to support them. Do (I once more repeat) pray, I do conjure you & charge you to make yourself quite tranquil & comfortable & leave it all to me. I will keep a constant eye upon the darling & never lose sight of him a single moment, & you may depend upon nothing happening to him or about him, at least that is at all within my compass or management that either can or need in the most distant degree affect or distress your feelings. Now, after this declaration & assurance will you for once compose yourself & make yourself easy & curb all (you must

1. The Duke's eldest surviving son, George John Frederick Manners, Marquess of Granby (*b.* 20 August 1813, *d.* 15 June 1814). He was baptized on 4 January 1814. The Duke's eldest son, the Marquess of Granby, died in 1807 when only a few weeks old.

2. Her son, Lord Robert Manners.

413

allow me to say) those your very unnecessary worries & alarms about him. My very affectionate feelings towards yourself, my dearest friend, I am sure you can have been no stranger to for many many years, & therefore I am satisfied that you will not take offence at my venturing upon so great a liberty as this is in writing to you with such liberty & frankness & which I am perfectly aware no other but such a motive could entitle me to do unless it be one other, & that is my anxiety for your health, & which must materially & inevitably & most essentially suffer if you do not determine & resolve upon allaying, aye, & upon crushing, at once, whenever they attempt to obtrude themselves, irritations which will get the better of you if you do not contrive to keep them down & extinguish them. After having given you this little bit of a scold I will now answer the other part of your kind letter by telling you that by this very same post I write a letter to the Duke (& which I could not think of doing during the state of uncertainty & alarm your whole family must have been in concerning poor dear Bob) to make my best acknowledgments to him for his flattering invitation either to Cheveley or subsequently to Belvoir, the latter of which I have ventured to prefer, having previously made another allottment [*sic*] of my time, which I could not without considerable inconvenience have differently disposed, added to which I am in the daily expectation of the arrival from abroad of a very near relation who I have not seen for many years & who is to take up his abode chez moi. I therefore look to the first week of the recess of Parliament to set me free when I hope we shall meet & enjoy as hearty a laugh together as we did when last under the hospitable roof of the old chateau. The only remark I shall make upon this is, would that I were as young as I was then. I am quite ashamed of the length of this scrawl & therefore I hasten to subscribe myself, at all times, my dearest Duchess's most sincere friend & humble servant.

P.S. I hope our friend Miss Finch has not fancied herself of late either a hare or a glass bottle; perhaps *you can* best inform me what *it is* that she does *just now fancy* (Belvoir MSS.).

3394   THE PRINCE REGENT TO THE MARCHIONESS OF HERTFORD

Cottsmore,[1] *31 Dec. 1813*

The post, my ever dearest Lady B—— comes in, at such a very awkward hour here, & goes out again so very immediately again [*sic*] that I have hardly time to scrawl one short line to thank you for the kind letter I have just receiv'd. You are very good to think so much of our little faux

1. Lord Lonsdale's seat near Oakham, Rutland.

pas of the other evening, but indeed from your great kindness you over-rate very much, & it has not been attended to me in its consequences with anything but a very slight cold in the head, & which is now almost already gone by. We perform'd our journey here yesterday most prosperously, & I am lodg'd here pas grandement but what is much better really most comfortably & warmly, especially this very very very severe & hard frost, at which I am sure my best & ever dearest friend, if you do not rejoice, at least you do not repine, as you know that at any rate it must preclude all possibility of hunting & even of riding, by which means (for I know just as well as if I was sitting by you), you think that my neck is quite safe. Our party, besides Lord & Lady Lonsdale,[1] the three young ladies, & my companion de voyage, consists only of a few old hunting friends of mine, Forrester, Lord Robert Manners, & old Ned Perceval, & there dined also yesterday with us, the young Marquis of Exeter,[2] Lord Winchelsea, who has already set off this morning for London, to return on Sunday, & Mr. Fludyer[3] le beau frère de la maison. The first & last of these three, I beleive, did not sleep here, but return'd to their own homes, which are at no great distance from hence. The servant is already pressing for my box to carry it to Greetham for the mail coach. I therefore, having given you my whole budget of news, such as it is, shall only add that I inclose for Lord Hertford some details from the Northern Continent, & which, though not very interesting, yet as in all probability they may not appear in the papers, except perhaps by driblets, I have thought best to send you for him. I must now say God bless you, my ever dearest Lady B till tomorrow when I shall again scribble. Would to Heaven you were as tired of the country as I am, as I think that if you were, you would quit it with less *reluctance*, & come the *sooner* to London. With regard to Mrs. Hancock I will write you fully tomorrow (Egerton MSS. 3262, fo. 93).

3395   THE PRINCE REGENT TO THE EARL OF YARMOUTH

Carlton House, 4 p.m., Saturday, 12 Mar. 1814

Dst. F., It has just occurr'd to me upon turning over in my mind one part of our conversation of this morning whether it might not be more adviseable to suspend for a day or two your letter to the Quarter Master

1. Lord Lonsdale (1757–1844) married Augusta (1761–1838), daughter of the 9th Earl of Westmorland, in 1781.

2. The 11th Earl and 2nd Marquess of Exeter (1795–1867). Styled Lord Burghley until he succeeded his father on 1 May 1804.

3. George Fludyer (1761–1837), M.P. for Chippenham, 1783–1802; for Appleby, 1818–19. In 1792 he married Lady Mary Fane, daughter of the 9th Earl of Westmorland.

Serjeant of your corps respecting Berenger[1] until the matter is clearly made out against him, especially as the Bow Street officers are now after him, & one cannot tell, in his present apparent state of delinquency, of distress & of dispair [*sic*] what the scoundrels with whom he is connected might from pique, resentment & disappointment induce him or persuade him to invent against you, for these reasons as well as for party views (Egerton MSS. 3262, f. 40).

3396   THE PRINCE REGENT TO THE EARL OF LONSDALE

Carlton House, 6.30 p.m., Monday, 16 May 1814

I was in the greatest hopes of paying my respects to Lady Lonsdale & yourself this evening, but a most unexpected & melancholy event has taken place in my family (the death of my mother's brother),[2] which though not as yet announced to be in the official form, yet is too circumstantially authenticated to admit of any doubt as to the loss we have sustain'd. I trust that both Lady Lonsdale & yourself are too well aware of how truly sensible I am of your kindness and attention to me at all times to doubt how sincerely I feel this disappointment & how anxiously I do look forwards to a very early opportunity when you will allow me to make for it. With my best and kindest remembrances to all in your house, I remain, my dear Lord [etc.] (Lonsdale MSS.).

3397   THE PRINCE REGENT TO VISCOUNT SIDMOUTH

Carlton House, Friday evening, 22 July 1814

I am much concern'd that it was not in my power to see you this morning, but I was very much indispos'd & too much fatigued with the bustle of yesterday evening to allow of my admitting any Lord. I regret this the

1. Captain de Berenger, a French refugee and officer in one of the foreign regiments. On 20 February 1814, whilst at Dover, he sent word to the Admiral at Deal—and the news was transmitted to London—that news had arrived from Paris that Napoleon had been killed, that the Allies were marching on Paris, and that peace was imminent. Government stocks rose heavily on the news and reacted sharply when the news was contradicted. Lord Cochrane's uncle, Andrew James Cochrane-Johnstone, made a big profit, and it was alleged that Lord Cochrane himself was one of the swindlers. The three were arrested and convicted of fraud. Cochrane himself was sentenced to pay a fine of £1000, to stand in the pillory for an hour, and to be imprisoned for twelve months. Charles Random de Berenger was sentenced to one year's imprisonment and to stand for one hour in the pillory, facing the Royal Exchange in the City.

2. The Duke of Mecklenburg-Strelitz died only on 6 November 1816.

more as I had intended to desire you without *loss of time* to give *the most positive directions & caution, in my name, that none of the trees in either of the Parks* should be *lopp'd, trimmed, mutilated,* much less CUT DOWN, under the pretence of seeing the fireworks to better advantage. I have chanced to learn that this is intended at least to be done, if it has not *already* in more than one instance been put in[to] practice. This therefore requires from *you* the most immediate & peremptory order to the Rangers in order to prevent all possibility of its happening[1] (Sidmouth MSS.).

3398   MRS. FITZHERBERT TO THE PRINCE REGENT
14 Aug. 1814
After the very ill success of my former applications it is with much painful reluctance (and from the absolute necessity of my situation only) that I am again forced to address your Royal Highness upon the subject of my income—feeling as I do that all the pecuniary difficulties I have endured originated from the very scanty allowance you made me for several years, yet you must do me the justice to allow that I never uttered a complaint or asked your assistance at that time because I knew your income was then so limited that you had it not in your power, and to prevent your suffering uneasiness on that score, I was frequently driven by necessity to borrow money, and about nine years ago, as you know, mortgaged my house to procure *absolute necessaries* both for yourself and me. It is true that the last four years you have increased my income to £6000 per annum, a sum which is not now as much as £3000 was about nine or ten years ago. But this income I have not yet enjoyed having been obliged to apply it as far as I could towards the paying of the old debts of former times, debts from which with the most rigid economy I have not been able to extricate myself. These debts Sir, have never been increased by any ostentation or extravagance of mine; *the whole of them* were *incurred when we were living together.* I will not pain your Royal Highness by reminding you for *whom these* debts *were contracted.* You will, I am sure, Sir, do me the justice to acknowledge that I never was an interested person; that I never (which I certainly might have done) solicited for, or benefitted either my family or friends at your expense. I confess I have a degree of pride which makes me revolt at the idea of asking assistance from anyone, but I do not feel this in addressing your Royal Highness for the performance of a promise of what is due to

1. The Prince Regent's Fête in honour of the Queen and of the Duke of Wellington was on the 21st at Carlton House. The Queen stayed until 5 a.m. See the card of invitation in *Letters of George IV*, i. 472, and Colchester, *Diary and Correspondence*, ii. 512, for the reference to Wellington.

me, is not degrading for me to receive, though extremely painful to be obliged to ask, and what I wish your Royal Highness had done yourself and have allowed me to have felt gratitude to you for. But not to trouble you with more details let me briefly add that I have no desire for riches; *comforts* at my time of life and *under my unfortunate circumstances* become necessary. It is *creditable* to *yourself*, Sir, that I should not be without them; I can add no stronger motive. Yet one other my heart leads me to name, that under your Royal Highness's sanction I have made myself responsible (and I have never for a moment regretted it) for the proper education and maintenance of my beloved child.[1] She is, thank God, everything I could wish, nothing is spared as far as I am able and I should grieve as her expenses increase with her age if I had it not in my power to finish her education as she deserves. Allow me, Sir, to request and implore you will pay some little attention to this letter. It is most probably the last you will ever be troubled with from me, it being my intention to go very soon to the Continent. I am not certain what my creditors may do when they hear I am leaving the country. It is through your enabling me to pay them that many distressing discussions may be stopped which *we* ought *both on every account* to prevent becoming public.

I am very well informed, Sir, that your ear has been frequently assailed by malignant insinuations against me. I have been accused of entering into cabals against your Royal Highness and doing you all the mischief in my power. No asseverations are necessary on my part; I disdain the charge. I thank the Almighty that through all my bitter trials and persecutions I hitherto have had forbearance enough never to utter one syllable that could have affected your interests, made you an enemy or given you cause for resentment. You ought to know me better, Sir, than to believe such representations. There can be no stronger proof of their falsehood than what you can yourself give, that aware as you are of *how much* I have in my power, that power has remained *unused by me*.[2] I have always acted from principles of honour and feeling towards you. I ought and do apologise for the length of this letter, but I am going away. I am not in good health and life is uncertain and the derangement of my affairs torment me sadly. Let me once more implore you will consider my situation and let me have a few lines *from yourself*, whom, Sir, notwithstanding all your prejudices against me and the misery and wretchedness you have entailed upon me, I shall ever rejoice to hear of your health, happiness and prosperity (Wellington MSS.).[3]

1. Mary Seymour.

2. Her power to ruin him by revealing their marriage.

3. The MS. is in the possession of the Duke of Wellington because the great Duke was one of George IV's executors.

3399 THE PRINCE REGENT TO LORD ELDON

[?*1814*]

The solution of the present question appears to me to be compriz'd within a very narrow compass, & the plain common sense of it is neither more nor less than this, that she chuses to be married according to her own tenets & fashion, contrary to all decency, usage & the moral spirit of the act; to emancipate herself from her father & to make a complete cypher of her husband; in short, to put herself at once at the age of eighteen upon the footing of a widow, just like the Duchess of Oldenburgh,[1] who has no one's pleasure to consult but her own (Eldon MSS.).

3400 THE PRINCE REGENT TO WILLIAM ADAM[2]

3 May 1815

Most private and confidential. I write in the Prince's name. You will see the extreme importance of the present object, and it is quite unnecessary, informed as you are, to add any animadversion upon the few words which the Prince is now dictating to me for your information.

Princess Charlotte (by the report of Princess Mary to his Royal Highness the Prince Regent) has at length assented, in the letter intended to be addressed by her to the Prince Regent, to use the expression that 'she agrees with him perfectly in the impropriety that there wou'd be in her ever seeing her mother again after what she has revealed to the Prince,[3] consequently, in the propriety of his interdicting all intercourse between

1. The Grand Duchess Catherine (1788–1819), the Tsar's favourite sister, had married the Duke of Oldenburg on 3 August 1809, and he died on 27 December 1812. She remained a widow until 24 January 1816 when she married the Hereditary Prince of Wurtemberg (1781–1864) who succeeded his father as William I on 30 October 1816.

The letter, then, was written sometime between 1813 and 1816, and if it refers to Princess Charlotte (and this seems to be the only possibility) the obvious date is 1814, when she was eighteen. Her father practically tricked her into consenting to an engagement to marry the young Prince of Orange, but in April 1814 she refused to entertain the idea of a compulsory residence in Holland (which would mean subjecting herself, the heiress-presumptive to the British throne, to a foreign husband), and though Lord Liverpool reminded her of the duties of a wife, she declined to give way, and quickly broke off her engagement.

2. The first three paragraphs, and the postscript, were written by Sir Benjamin Bloomfield.

3. The reference is to Princess Charlotte's disclosure to her family on Christmas Day, 1814 of the extraordinary attempt by her mother to corrupt her. The young Princess had formed an imprudent friendship with Lieutenant Charles Hesse of the 18th Hussars, the reputed son of the Duke of York by a German lady of rank, and in 1812, at the age of sixteen, she fell in love with him. They often met at her mother's house in Kensington, and one day her mother left them together in her own bedroom, turned the key upon them, and, in effect, invited the young man to seduce her daughter. ('À present, je vous laisse, amusez vous.')

her and her mother, and thanking him for so far consulting the delicacy of her feelings by his not insisting upon her being herself the channel of such information to the Princess.'

The Princess Charlotte is to be at the Queen's House by twelve to-morrow to dress for the Drawing Room, and she has told the Princess Mary that she means to see Lord Keith and perhaps the Bishop of Salisbury, to signify these her intentions, and possibly to write such a letter in consequence to the Prince to this effect. However satisfactory this may appear from what you must know, the Prince can put no reliance whatever upon it. However he thinks it most essential that you should have the earliest communication possible with Lord Keith if not with the Bishop, to acquaint them, without naming Princess Mary, that you have certain information to this effect, previous to their seeing Princess Charlotte, in order that if there shou'd be any change or prevarication of language on her part, they may adhere most strenuously to this point, as the only one, as you well know, by which either she can be saved from the past and secured against all future misery. You will please to observe that this is quite confidential, and that it must be communicated at the earliest moment to Lord Keith, at the same time that he must act with the greatest resolution, and he must be enjoin'd to preserve the greatest secrecy as to any previous knowledge whatever of this information. Shou'd you be able to see the Bishop,[1] the same injunction must be laid upon him.

3 May 1815
Dear Adam—I am too fatigued to be able to add a line to this, written under my own eye and under my own dictation, further than to desire you *most punctilliously* to adhere to the injunctions contain'd in the preceding pages. Always sincerely yours, George P.R.

P.S. An acknowledgment of this by the servant if you please for the Prince's satisfaction (Blair Adam MSS.).

3401　LETTERS FROM THE PRINCE REGENT TO THE MARCHIONESS OF HERTFORD
Carlton House, 2.30 a.m., Thursday, 22 June 1815
I have, my ever dearest Lady B—, to acquaint you of my having this instant receiv'd the intelligence of the most glorious victory atchiev'd by our arms under our immortal Wellington, that has perhaps ever yet been

1. Dr. Fisher, Bishop of Salisbury.

recorded in the page of history. The tyrant Bonaparte in person, being entirely defeated & routed, after the most sanguinary battles ending the eighteenth at night; the carnage most shocking; our loss calculated at least at ten thousand men,[1] & that of the enemy, at upwards of thirty thousand men, together with the loss of two hundred & ten peices of cannon, with all their baggage & ammunition, & the Prussians came up quite fresh, & were in pursuit of this completely routed host when the officer came off with his dispatches. The accounts state that nothing can surpass the conduct of our troops of every discription; or, of the undaunted heroism with which they resisted the most daring & persevering attacks of the enemy. You will be sorry to learn that my dear & gallant friend Uxbridge[2] has lost his leg, but thank God is doing well. The Duke of Brunswick,[3] Sir Thomas Picton & Sr. Wm. Ponsonby[4] kill'd, as well as my poor élève & servant Frederick Howard;[5] & the Hereditary Prince of Orange dangerously wounded. It does not appear that Pack[6] is even touch'd, but the list of kill'd & wounded is Alas! so sadly extensive that I must reserve that & other details till I see you tomorrow. It is not beleiv'd that the French Army *can ever assemble again, but certainly not till it reaches Laon.* I am so fatigued & so overpower'd with all the circumstances & all the consequences depending upon them, glorious & melancholy at the same time as they are, that to you alone, my ever dearest Lady B—, I could have written so much, & that I have not strength to add another word now, except that I am always & most unalterably [etc.].

P.S. It has just occur'd to me that as Ly. Wm.[7] is with you, that she will be glad to know that her nephew L.-Col. Woodford is safe, his name not being mention'd in any of the lists. *I will be with you* as soon as I can (Egerton MSS. 3262, fo. 95).

1. Killed and wounded: British and Hanoverians, 11,678; Prussians, 6,999; Netherlanders, 3,178; Brunswickers, 687; Nassau contingent, 643. Total, 23,185.

2. Lord Uxbridge, who commanded the cavalry at Waterloo, was created Marquess of Anglesey on 4 July following.

3. The Duke was killed at Quatre Bras on the 16th.

4. Sir William Ponsonby (1772–1815), second son of the 1st Baron Ponsonby, and a great-grandson of the 1st Earl of Bessborough. Major, 1794; Lieutenant-Colonel, 1800; Colonel, 1810; Major-General, 1813; K.C.B., January 1815.

5. Major Frederick Howard, of the 10th Hussars (1785–1815), third son of the 5th Earl of Carlisle. Equerry in the Royal Household, 1813–15.

6. Sir Denis Pack (*c.* 1772–1823), Major-General, 1813; K.C.B., 1815; commanded a Brigade of Picton's Division at Waterloo.

7. Lady William Seymour Conway.

Stud House, 4 p.m., 14 Oct. 1815

I have, my ever dearest Lady B—, an excuse, & one which, before I mention it, I am sure you will approve of & think a very good one indeed, for not scribbling many lines again today, & that is that I have but just dismounted my horse, after a ride of between four & five hours, & after making half a dozen visits to old Mrs. Grimes (I hope no scandal) & to [illegible] Thomas, &c. &c. &c., at & in the neighbourhood of the Palace at Hampton Court, & if I delay many minutes longer, I am afraid that my servant will be too late in London for this evening's post. The day has been most beautiful & I feel less bilious than I have for some time past. With respect to your new correspondent, though she may be white, I shall rate her black, & I think her so dangerous that I hope, though you may not place her quite on your black list, still that you will not let her have a place quite at the head of your white one, in short, that you will not encourage the correspondance [*sic*]. As to all the b——dash stuff she may hear or write, I care not a fig (or as Miss Tabitha Runt[?] more politely terms it, not three skips of a louse) for it all; in the first place, the whole at present is a complete lie, & as to what may happen, that I cannot answer for, but one thing, thank God, is sure & that is that no one *here* either can, or has any right to interfere with anything, or whatever I may chuse, or be pleas'd to do with or at or in Hannover, & I desire, & I shall desire no better fun than to see such a hare started, for, by whoso-ever it may be, it will & must be to their utter confusion & disgrace. I do assure you, my best & ever dearest friend, *upon my honour*, that ever since I had the happiness of last seeing you, I have never open'd my lips to any individual whatever upon that particular subject, & what is more, I never will again, unless I am compell'd so to do, & I have not heard even an allusion to it ever since. I have not time to add another line except to say how I rejoice to hear your excellent accounts of Lord Hertford's perfect convalescence, & upon which I entreat that you will offer him, together with my best regards, my most sincere congratula-tions, being myself at all time most unalterably, my ever dearest Lady B—s [etc.].

P.S. Still no news. You may depend upon hearing again by Monday's post (Egerton MSS. 3262, fo. 97).

Stud House, 4 p.m., 16 Oct. 1815

The carriage, my ever dearest Lady B— is at the door & I am just going to start for Brighton, where I shall only stay over tomorrow & return on Wednesday to town, for an odious Council which is to take place on Thursday. Yesterday I was at Windsor where all was *mum* upon a certain subject, & the wind bearing much more to the South than to the East;

as you may easily imagine I did not open my lips, & kept steadily my resolution, of observing the strictest silence with respect to everything that has already pass'd, as well as to what it is possible may arise hereafter; in short, everything went off perfectly well, much better than I expected, & I think that things are all getting back into their usual course again, as the bile subsides, & perhaps also, as reflexion leads them to consider that their conduct has not been quite correct, & certainly in many instances not what it should & ought to have been throughout this disagreable & odious transaction.[1] Yesterday I heard from Neumann, the Austrian Secretary, that the Archdukes[2] cannot be here till the twentieth, but upon which day they will most surely arrive, so that I must, alas! remain a complete prisoner at any rate till two or three days after that date, which Bloomfield has written to my friend Anglesea to acquaint him with, & which, by the bye, I beleive he is not very sorry for, for it grieves me to inform you that I have learnt that he has of late, especially since his last journey to Yorkshire been tormented to death with worse spasms than ever in his poor stump, & that in consequence, he has been under the necessity of throwing aside for the present at least & indeed for some time to come, all thoughts of his wooden leg, but I am afraid that he has only himself, poor fellow, to thank for all this, as he has undoubtedly brought it all on himself, for he has been sporting & riding upon a horse or poney, not being able to walk, for four & five hours together, then travelling & taking long journeys to & from Yorkshire; in short, doing everything he ought not to do, when he ought to have kept for a length of time as quiet as possible. There is also another peice of news I heard yesterday which has given me great & sincere pain & regret, & which, from the manner in which it reach'd me, I fear is but too true, & that is the report of the death of our worthy & excellent friend Lord Scarborough.[3] A more loyal & a better subject than him, never did, & never can exist, nor one, I beleive, as a man that was more personally attach'd to myself. He is really a loss, for there are not many such worthy men now to be met with nor reckon'd in the world, & I do feel & regret him, my best & ever dearest friend, most sincerely & truly than I can find words to express to you.

Your scrap of a letter has this moment reach'd me whilst scribbling the last line, & I hope that the sermon which you was going to hear, & which

1. The reference is to the Queen's refusal to receive at Court her niece and daughter-in-law, the Duchess of Cumberland, who had married the Duke on 29 May 1815. See No. 1515 (iv. 108), iv. 3, and *Letters of George IV*, ii. 129.

2. The Archdukes John and Lewis, the Emperor Francis I's brothers, arrived in London on the 23rd, after a tour through Great Britain. They were received by the Prince Regent.

3. The report was untrue: Lord Scarbrough died on 17 June 1832. He had succeeded his brother as 6th Earl on 5 September 1807.

prevented your writing more to me, was a sufficient reward to you for inflicting such a mortification upon poor me, & that it was sufficiently enlighten'd to produce the usual effects of such discourses, either that of affording you a good nap, or perhaps afterwards of procuring you a good appetite to your dinner; at any rate I am sure if it had not in the first instance that effect upon you, it did not fail upon Lord Hertford, who I know never could resist the calls of somnus, in a comfortable pew. My best regards always attend his lordship, & I am sorry that I have no intelligence of any interest to communicate for his information, excepting one morsel which I am sure that will delight him, & which came to me en droiture from the fountain head, Mr. Vansittart, & that is that the revenue of this country this year does exceed by many, many, many, millions that of any former year ever yet known, & that it will leave after all & everything else is paid, war, & every other establishment & call possible included, an unapropriated sum of no less than eight millions,[1] & which I could not help telling him & proposing to him, should be transferr'd by the country to my private coffer, in consideration of my exertions & all I have done for the country as well as for the whole world.[2] Such are my deserts, at least such I feel them to be. What say you to this, my best & ever dearest friend? & pray do tell Lord Hertford that whenever this is brought forward he will not omit to insure the attendance of all his members, in particular of McNaghton & Lord Henry Moore.[3] I think you must now be quite tired to death of all my scribbling & all my garrulity which I dare say you will think that I have been infected with & caught during my stay here, from old Mrs. Wally; however, it is high time to take compassion upon you, & to set you at liberty again for the present; & therefore I now take my leave of you, subscribing myself what, with the best feelings of my heart, I must & ever & shall most invariably & must unalterably do, my ever dearest Lady B.'s ever & most affectionate.

P.S. I am afraid I shall not be able to scribble again till Wedy.'s post, but when you may depend upon hearing from me again. Pray write constantly & do not be bob short (Egerton MSS. 3262, fo. 99).

---

1. The total gross income for Great Britain for the year ending 5 January 1815 was £77,887,336, and the total expenditure was £112,917,042 (a figure which does not include the cost of servicing the national debt, i.e. £30,004,659). The Budget was balanced by borrowing (£92,934,267, from which sum £59,013,967 should be deducted on account of debt repayment). During the next year the gross income was £79,101,126, and the total expenditure £99,456,546. The Prince Regent's figures are obviously bogus.

2. A most extraordinary suggestion, now revealed for the first time.

3. Lord Henry Seymour Moore (*c.* 1784–1825), M.P. for Orford, 1806–12; for Lisburn, 1812–18. His mother, Anne, Marchioness of Drogheda, was one of Lord Hertford's sisters.

Carlton House, 10 p.m., Saturday, 31 May 1817

Pray tell me, my dear Lord, who it is thought most adviseable should offer himself for the now vacant seat for the University of Oxford?[1] (Sidmouth MSS.)

1. Peel, the Irish Secretary, was elected for the University on 10 June 1817, the by-election being caused by the retirement of Charles Abott, the Speaker, who was then created Baron Colchester on 3 June.

For two reasons, the death of Sir John McMahon on 12 September 1817 deserves mention here. In the first place, he was succeeded as Secretary and Keeper of His Royal Highness's Privy Seal and Council Seal in December 1817 by that remarkable man Sir William Knighton, who made himself indispensable to the Regent and became his confidential friend and adviser. In the second place, Knighton, as McMahon's executor, came into possession of documents relating to 'all those secret concerns which a life of pleasure and sensuality had exposed him [the Prince] to'. See A. Aspinall, *George IV and Sir William Knighton* (*English Historical Review*, January 1940, pp. 57–82). There is a reference to these private papers in Knighton's letter to the Prince Regent, Hanover Square, 18 August 1817: 'I have the honor to approach your Royal Highness with a detailed account of the several transactions which you have been graciously pleased to commit to my care. In obedience to your Royal Highness's most gracious commands I proceeded on Saturday to visit my poor friend Sir John McMahon at his cottage. On my arrival, to my great surprise, I found he had unexpectedly left it for town, but fortunately accompanied by Mrs. Milford. The delay occasioned in waiting for his return made it impossible for me to give any account of him to your Royal Highness on that day. I found him very feeble in body, and his head *quite* gone. This temporary state of insanity had then existed for several hours. I believe it to have arisen from the great depletion which of necessity was used at Salt Hill and which had been followed for several days by the entire absence of all stimuli, for on giving him a small quantity of strong brandy & water his mind, though feeble, gradually returned to its usual state and has *remained* so ever since.

'Yesterday I repeated my visit, Sir, to his cottage. I remained with him five hours, for the purpose of accomplishing my object respecting the papers, and I have now the honor and satisfaction to state to your Royal Highness that in this I have completely succeeded. I have the honor to inclose the key, and all your Royal Highness's private letters, early correspondence and other documents are now safe in my possession in Hanover Square.

'Agreeably to your Royal Highness's most gracious instructions, I am proceeding with all diligence to look through every letter and paper, to memorandum and number such as it may seem fit for your Royal Highness to preserve, so that on your return to town, without any trouble, time or inconvenience, your Royal Highness will be brought acquainted with what you preserve and I shall have the opportunity of destroying the remainder in your Royal Highness's presence.

'Nothing can have been more secret or more satisfactory than the accomplishment of this desirable object, for no second person has been or need be, unless it should be your Royal Highness's pleasure, brought acquainted with any part of your early correspondence or early documents of any description. It was so managed that my poor friend directed Mr. Marrable in my presence, who has behaved with great propriety of conduct, to put himself entirely under my instructions on this occasion and to give and deliver up whatever I call'd for. Under those circumstances everything has rested with myself and I humbly hope & trust will meet your Royal Highness's most gracious approbation' (RA Box 8).

THE PRINCE REGENT TO LORD ELDON[1]

Pavillion, Brighton, 1 Jan. 1818

... I will now briefly enter upon the real reasons for my summoning you to pay me a visit here for four & twenty hours, if it had been in your power to do so; in truth they had but little to do with the holding a Council, & only just so much in this respect, for the present, to enable me under the shew of a Council being held at the Pavillion, to throw a mask to the public over the real object, & to assemble such of my confidential servants about me as I wish'd, to whom I meant to state my intention of shortly laying before them a paper, accompanied by other papers & vouchers respecting the unparalell'd conduct of the Princess of Wales since her residence on the Continent; a conduct so atrocious as well as so universally notorious as to have not only shock'd almost every Court over the whole Continent of Europe, but such as, in one particular instance, to have drawn upon her a public censure for that conduct from the highest & most respectable of all those Courts & of their Sovereigns, the Court of Vienna, by a flat & positive refusal of receiving her or any of her disgraceful associates & servants. You cannot, therefore, be surpriz'd (much difficulty in point of delicacy being now set aside in my mind by the late melancholy event which has taken place in my family)[2] if I therefore turn my whole thoughts to the endeavouring to extricate myself from the cruellest as well as the most unjust predicament that ever even the lowest individual, much more a Prince, ever was plac'd in by unshackling myself from a woman who has for the last three & twenty years not alone been the bain & curse of my existence, but who now stands prominent in the eyes of the whole world characteriz'd by a flagrancy of abandonment unparalell'd in the history of woman, & stamp'd with disgrace & dishonour. Is it, then, my dear friend, to be tolerated that such a monster is to be suffer'd to continue to bear my name, to belong to me & to the country, & that that country, the first in all the world, & myself its Sovereign, are to be expected to submit silently to a degradation under which no upright & honorable mind can exist? This, then, was my main object for collecting certain of my confidential servants here.

I have communicated the matter to Lord Liverpool & Lord Castlereagh who have since gone through a full discussion by my command with Sr. John Leach,[3] & both he & I have every reason to be satisfied with the

---

1. Parts of this letter were published in Twiss, *Life of Lord Eldon* (2nd ed., 1844), ii. 304–6. The result of the Cabinet's deliberations which followed this letter was the appointment of the celebrated 'Milan Commission' to investigate the conduct of the Princess of Wales after her departure from England for the Continent in 1814.

2. The death of Princess Charlotte, in childbirth, on 6 November 1817.

3. The Prince Regent's confidential legal adviser; appointed Vice-Chancellor of England, and knighted, 1818. M.P. for Seaford, 1806–16.

impression they have receiv'd. Sr. John Leach has left me this morning for London, & I trust that by the time this will have reach'd you, he will already by my order have laid everything before you, & that he will have taken your advice upon every point & detail connected with the further progress of this, to me, vital question . . . (Eldon MSS.).

3404 THE PRINCE REGENT TO THE DUKE OF NORTHUMBERLAND[1]
Brighton, 23 Jan. 1818
Private and Confidential. Lord Liverpool has communicated to me your application for the next Blue Ribband which might become vacant.

I need not, I hope, say how much I must desire to confer that distinction upon your Grace at the first opportunity which may be in my power, and although I feel the strong objections which in general exist to prospective promises in matters of this nature, yet, under all the circumstances, and with *an anxious desire*, to meet your wishes, I have no difficulty in saying that the second Blue Ribband which may become vacant shall be conferred on your Grace. Indeed I do truly assure you that I should have felt a *personal* satisfaction in acceding to your wishes upon the first occasion if I had not held out strong expectations to the Marquis of Anglesey very long since, when he receiv'd the Order of the Bath;[2] that I considered his distinguished services at the Battle of Waterloo particularly, and the loss he sustain'd there, to deserve from me this further mark of my approbation so soon as I should have fullfilled what I felt due to my Government, in the person of the Earl Bathurst,[3] and to his long and arduous political services, in his laborious Department, during the late most severe and gloriously terminated contest. I have only now to add that I must be at all times happy to embrace any favorable opportunity of manifesting that friendly disposition which I have ever borne towards you from your infancy[4] (Alnwick MSS.).

1. The Duke had succeeded his father on 10 July 1817.

2. G.C.B., 2 January 1815; K.G., 19 February, 1818.

3. Bathurst, Secretary of State for War and the Colonies, 1812–27, was made a K.G., 24 July 1817.

4. The Duke was made a K.G. on 25 November 1819.

3405 THE PRINCE REGENT TO THE DUKE OF WELLINGTON

Carlton House, 14 Feb. 1818

My dear friend, I cannot resist writing to you a few lines to endeavour to express to you, however faint the attempt may be, the happiness I experience at the accounts I have just receiv'd of the providential escape you have so lately had; as well as the sentiments of horror & indignation with which I am impress'd by the infamy & baseness of the foul attempt.[1] I have only in common with the rest of the nation to return my most grateful acknowledgements of the superintending goodness of divine Providence in having protected a life so important to the best interests of your own country, as well as to the preservation of the tranquillity of Europe; that you may long continue to enjoy that life so invaluable to us all, is the most earnest prayer, of your very sincere & affectionate friend (Wellington MSS.).

3406 LETTERS FROM THE PRINCE REGENT TO THE MARCHIONESS OF HERTFORD

Stud House, 4 p.m., Saturday, 29 Aug. 1818

It is, my ever dearest Lady B., quite impossible for me to express to you how gratefully I feel Lord Hertford & your kind invitation to dear Ragley, or the real pleasure, indeed I may say with great truth, the real delight with which I avail myself of the most kind proposal & with which I do also look forwards to making one in your society & to be once more an inhabitant of that dear & most beautiful mansion. I must unfortunately be guided at this moment a little in my motions by Lord Castlereagh's, or possibly I might, as I have little or nothing upon my hands just at present, have begun my journey & have gone part of my way this very evening, but this I am prevented from doing by his having just told me that it is possible that he may have occasion to see me again before he sets out for the Continent, but that his departure is finally & positively fix'd for next Monday or for Tuesday at the very latest; according to this I shall regulate my own little matters & I trust that I may be able thus to present myself at Ragley to you & Lord Hertford certainly on Wednesday, though perhaps it may be a day earlier if Lord Castlereagh's business is wound up in time to suffer me to do so. You may tell Lord Hertford from me that I can confidently assure him, after the interview I

1. On 10 February, about midnight, the Duke was fired at in his carriage outside his hotel in Paris. The conspiracy was organised by French refugees in the Netherlands, but Cantillon, an ex-sergeant of dragoons, who was alleged to have fired the shot, was subsequently acquitted by the French jury. The Duke was instructed to quit Paris and withdraw to the comparative safety of Cambrai, the Allied headquarters.

have had with Castlereagh this morning, & which by the bye lasted full if not more than four long & entire hours (he had so many points & so much ground to discuss & to go over) that everything, & in all quarters looks most auspicious & promising respecting the approaching Congress,[1] & that Lord Castlereagh who, as Lord Hertford well knows, is at no time a very or an over-sanguine person, seems perfectly content & augurs every possible good in the result. Castlereagh has detained me so very long & so very unconscionably late that I am under the necessity, my best & ever dearest friend, of bringing my epistle to a very speedy close, & that I may not be too late for the post, which you know as well as Old Time waits for no one. Here then I must bid you adieu & probably till I have the inexpressible pleasure & happiness of seeing you at Ragley when I hope in person to be able to assure you how unalterably & how irrevocably I always remain [etc.].

P.S. Pray remember me in all that is kindest to Lord Hertford & tell him that I propose to bring with me no one but little Col. Thornton[2] who, I hope, will not be disagreable to him, nor a nuisance to anyone else, nor any more than I hope to be myself. You are both very kind to think of me & indeed it is *quite* & *a great charity to me just now* (Egerton MSS. 3262, f. 103).

Carlton House, Tuesday, 15 Sept. 1818
I am, my ever dearest Lady B., really most affected by the death of poor Dyke, although there has been such reason to expect the intelligence for some time past, from day to day. I do assure you, with the greatest truth, that this house has put on a face of mourning; not a servant as I have seen as yet that has not a tear in his eye, so universally loved & esteem'd was this excellent creature amongst all his comrades & fellow servants; & as for me, in him, I am sure that I have an almost irreparable loss, for a better, a more sober, a more dilligent or intelligent, a more attentive or more attach'd servant never came into any family. In short, he is universally, & what is very rare indeed, most sincerely regretted by all those who have known him & served with him. The D. of Y[ork] has this moment only left me, after a very long visit indeed, but from him I have learnt no news of any sort, as the object he had to treat was the arrangements that will be necessary respecting the troops when they return from

1. At Aix-la-Chapelle. The representatives of the Powers considered, *inter alia*, the propriety of withdrawing the allied army of occupation from northern France. This was the main achievement of the Congress.

2. Charles Wade Thornton, who had formerly been Equerry to the Duke of Cumberland. See No. 2726.

the Continent, & he has detain'd me so very late that I have hardly time to scribble these few lines. I am now going to Kew, where, alas! I have reason to fear that I shall find matters nearly in the same distressing state as I left them yesterday.[1] I cannot take my leave, my best & ever dearest friend, of you without offering with my best regards, my congratulations also to Lord Hertford upon the fine soft falling rain which I now see out of my window pouring delightfully, which notwithstanding brings a gloom with it, which is not much out of character with the state of my own mind at the present moment. Now then adieu, my ever dearest Lady B., & always beleive me most unalterably & most irrevocably your ever & most affectionate [etc.].

P.S. Bloomfield has amus'd me very much with the account he has given me of my friend Addenhoff changing his appearance like a camelion, first as Van Butchell & then transmogrofying [*sic*] himself into Petersham. What has happen'd to him, poor soul! I suppose that he frightens not only all the servants but all the ghosts likewise from Ragley (Egerton MS. 3262, f. 105).

3407   THE PRINCE REGENT TO THE EARL OF LIVERPOOL
Carlton House, 16 June 1819
Most private and confidential. The Prince Regent, regarding the subject of the annex'd communication, only in its public and national view, refers the same to the consideration of his confidential servants, with this observation, that it appears to the Prince Regent that it might be useful to the public interests that the ultimate purpose of divorce should be effected rather by arrangement than by adverse proceedings.[2] (Add. MSS. 38190, fo. 31)

3408   THE PRINCE REGENT'S MEMORANDUM, 29 JULY 1819 [copy]
The Prince Regent considers the sum of £150,000 as altogether inadequate to the arrangements necessary for converting the Queen's House

1. The Queen died at Kew on 17 November.

2. Brougham, the Princess of Wales's legal adviser, advised her to agree to a formal separation in order to avoid a public scandal: she should renounce the right to be crowned in the event of a demise of the Crown, and should from that time take some title other than that of Queen; and her existing annuity should be granted for life instead of ceasing with the King's death. On 17 June the Cabinet informed the Prince that a divorce 'never could be accomplished by arrangement' (Yonge's *Liverpool*, iii. 17).

into a Palace for the habitual town residence and Court of the Sovereign.

This object H.R.H. conceives cannot be accomplished for a sum much short of £500,000, namely for the building from £150,000 to £200,000—for fitting up fixtures and internal decorations, the like sum—for furniture £100,000.

The whole expense may probably be kept within £400,000—but it will be safer to reckon upon £450,000.

The Prince Regent approves of the proposal to bring the whole subject before the House of Commons in the mode and upon the principles stated in the Memorandum,[1] and wishes Lord Liverpool to settle in Cabinet all the preliminary steps for this purpose.

The Prince Regent regrets that from the necessity of applying to Parliament nothing material can be done towards forwarding the intended improvement till next year, but he fully acquiesces in that necessity, and hopes that the subject will be brought forward at an early period of the next Session.[2] (Add. MSS. 38278, fo. 358)

3409 THE PRINCE REGENT TO THE EARL OF LIVERPOOL

Brighton, 7 Aug. 1819

I cannot embark without conveying to you that, after the *fullest* consideration of the subject which you mention'd to me yesterday, and of your intention to send me within a few days a copy of the paper which you then shew'd me, my mind is so *completely* settled upon the inexpediency of

---

1. The Memorandum referred to is as follows:—

   Memorandum respecting the expense of converting the Queen's House into a Palace

   £150,000 the utmost sum that can be raised.

   Three years will be requisite to realize this sum.

   In case the original estimate should exceed £150,000, it must necessarily and in the first instance be submitted to Parliament.

   In case the actual expense should materially exceed the estimate of £150,000, the deficiency could only be raised by Parliament, and such a proceeding would be subject to insurmountable objection.

   The alternative, therefore, is, would it be more advisable to apply to Parliament in the first instance for power to expend a sum to be limited by their authority, submitting to them the estimate and plans as the ground of such application, with a statement of the mode in which the £150,000 is to be raised, and a proposal to procure the remainder by the sale of other Crown property—or firmly to resolve to confine the whole expense within the sum of £150,000, and to complete the whole arrangements (externally and internally) for that sum, without the interference of Parliament? (Add. MSS. 38278, fo. 357)

2. Lord Liverpool's reply is in Yonge's *Liverpool*, ii. 402–3. 'It would be quite impracticable to look to any grant of public money by Parliament for this purpose.'

431

that measure, that I am sure that you will feel it to be your duty to relieve me from the repetition of that application.[1] (Add. MSS. 38190, fo. 32)

3410 THE PRINCE REGENT TO VISCOUNT SIDMOUTH

Brighton, 24 Oct. 1819

Notwithstanding that the Archbishop of Cashel[2] is not willing to place the living held by Mr. Gough in his Grace's Diocese at the disposal of the Lord Lieutenant,[3] & that his Excellency in consequence hesitates to bestow the Deanery of Derry upon that gentleman, notwithstanding that by much the most valuable of his Livings is given to Government, my interference for the advancement of Mr. Gough has now become matter of such notoriety that your feelings, my dear Lord, I am sure, will immediately concur in the necessity of closing this transaction. The zeal & integrity with which Sr. B. Bloomfield attends to the concerns of the Government claim *our* favor & protection, exclusive of his long & faithful services to *myself*; added to which, the Lord Lieutenant has, under his own hand, borne testimony to the high character & eligibility for preferment of Mr. Gough.

Every effect which has been produc'd by our late measure connected with Yorkshire, as far as I learn, has prov'd most satisfactory.[4] The language of this place, which you know contains Jews & Gentiles of every discription, is strongly in praise of the measure. Even that most eccentric & vinegar old gentleman Lord Carhampton[5] swears that *it alone* could save us & our properties, & that now he sees the Government dispos'd to take firm & resolute measures, that he shall to the utmost of his means & by his vote give them his support, in the hope to crush all those Radicals & their system. I have likewise heard it pretty confidently

1. See Yonge's *Liverpool*, iii. 19, for the Cabinet Minute of 24 July 1819 (there wrongly dated 1820), which advised against the introduction of a Divorce Bill into Parliament.

2. Charles Brodrick.

3. Lord Talbot had succeeded Lord Whitworth as Lord Lieutenant of Ireland on 9 October 1817.

4. Lord Fitzwilliam was dismissed from his office of Lord Lieutenant of the West Riding of Yorkshire after he had agreed to sign a requisition for a county meeting to discuss the 'Peterloo' affair at Manchester on 16 August.

5. Henry Lawes Luttrell, 2nd Earl of Carhampton (?1737–1821) succeeded his father, 14 January 1787. Adjutant-General [I.], 1770–83; Colonel, 1777; Major-General, 1782; Lieutenant–General of the Ordnance [I.], 1787–97; and Master-General, 1797–1800; Lieutenant-General, 1793; Commander of the Forces [I.], 1796–7; General, 1798. M.P. for Bossiney, 1768–9 and 1774–84; for Middlesex, 1769–74; for Plympton, 1790–4; for Ludgershall, 1817–21.

affirm'd that Mr. Drummond Burrell, who is here, has refus'd to sign one or two Reform requisitions, & expresses his regret that Lord Fitzwilliam should have drawn upon himself his dismissal by lending his sanction to such proceedings.

Of course if anything occurs you will not fail to write & inform me of it.

P.S. Is nothing to be done with the [*sic*] respect to Lord Grosvenor[1] & the Duke of Hamilton,[2] the subscribing Lords Lieutenant to the Manchester sufferers?—for I cannot dismiss from my mind the *offensive* letters which accompanied their subscriptions (Sidmouth MSS.).

3411   THE KING TO LORD ELDON

Carlton House, Wednesday evening, 4 Nov. 1820

Private. I send you what I am convinc'd you will consider should claim your most *minute* & *careful* attention. If the law as it now stands has not the power to protect the Sovereign against the licentious abominations of this description,[3] it is *high time* that the *law* should be *amended.* I feel that I cannot leave it in safer or more able hands than yours.

P.S. I have sent duplicates to the Attorney Genl.[4] (Eldon MSS.).

3412   LETTERS FROM THE KING TO THE EARL OF LIVERPOOL

Brighton, 5 Jan. 1821

The King has receiv'd Lord Liverpool's letter, and under the existing circumstances approves of the arrangement therein proposed that Mr. Bathurst should perform the duties of the Board of Controul, in addition to those of his present office.[5] (Add. MSS. 38190, fo. 33)

1. Lord Lieutenant of Flintshire, 1798–1845.

2. Lord Lieutenant of Lanarkshire, 1802–52.

3. Possibly indecent or malevolent caricatures.

4. Sir Robert Gifford, 1st Baron Gifford (1779–1826), M.P. for Eye, 1817–24; Solicitor-General and knighted May 1817; Attorney-General, July 1819; Chief Justice of the Common Pleas, January–April 1824. Peerage, January 1824. Master of the Rolls, April 1824–6.

5. Disapproving the Government's proceedings with respect to Queen Caroline after the abandonment of the Bill of Pains and Penalties, Canning resigned his office of President of the Board of Control on 13 December 1820. Peel, who had been out of office since 1818, declined Liverpool's offer of the India Board (Parker's *Peel*, i. 298), and Bragge Bathurst reluctantly accepted it as a temporary arrangement, retaining his office of Chancellor of the Duchy of Lancaster (*Letters of George IV*, ii. 401n.).

433

Brighton, 16 Jan. 1821

The King has receiv'd Lord Liverpool's letter, with the enclosures from Mr. K[eppe]l Craven,[1] and the draft of Lord Liverpool's proposed answer. With that answer the King is perfectly satisfied, as far as the matter of business to which it relates, but the King so highly disapproves of the character of indecent interrogating in Mr. Craven's first Address to Lord Liverpool, that the King feels it to be quite impossible that Lord Liverpool should, in the answer now propos'd to be sent, not *confine* himself to state to Mr. Craven that he had submitted to the King the *substance only* of his letter, as Lord Liverpool could not fail to consider the language in which they were couched to be such as to render it impossible for him to lay the correspondence *itself* before the King. (Add. MSS. 38190, fo. 35)

3413   THE KING TO VISCOUNT SIDMOUTH

Carlton House, Friday morning, 26 Jan. 1821

Most Private. My Dear friend—I directed Bloomfield to speak to you on the subject of a presentation to the Charter House which I at this moment *particularly* want. I am sorry if this should interfere with any arrangements which you might think yourself authoriz'd to make, and am oblig'd to propose that you will state to your friend that the *next presentation* shall be *his*, but as I have made *a promise* on the subject, I am sure that with *your* personal feelings *you* will see the *impropriety* that the *King's word should be broken*. Be so good, *therefore*, as to forward the nomination to me for my signature (Sidmouth MSS.).

3414   THE KING TO LORD ELDON

Carlton House, 10 May 1821

Many thanks for the draught of the Bill,[2] which I now return, as well as for your letter which accompanied it. I feel fully sensible of the care & attention you have given to my interests in the formation of this Bill, & I

---

1. Richard Keppel Craven (1779–1851), the youngest son of the 6th Baron Craven. In 1814 he accompanied the Princess of Wales to the Continent as her Chamberlain, but resigned the appointment six months later. He was her Vice-Chamberlain in 1820, and on her instructions he wrote letters to Lord Liverpool demanding for her a royal residence and all the other rights of a Queen Consort.

2. A Bill concerning the disposition of certain real property of his Majesty, his heirs and successors.

434

entertain no doubt that my Cabinet will feel it to be its duty to carry it through Parliament with the whole of its provisions (Eldon MSS.).

3415 THE KING TO VISCOUNT SIDMOUTH

Carlton House, Sunday night, 13 May 1821

The King has read with attention the letter inclos'd by Lord Sidmouth relative to the scheme of the Litterary Society lately recommended to the King by the Bishop of St. David's.[1]

What is stated in this letter may be all very true, but the King would have relied with more confidence in the opinions there suggested if the writer had not been an author by profession.

Under these circumstances, the King is more dispos'd to rely on the judgment of learned men, not professedly authors, & more especially when such men are alone influenced by motives of pure piety & true benevolence.

The King however is ready to submit the consideration of the whole affair to Lord Sidmouth, the Bishop of St. David's, & the King would also add the name of Sr. Wm. Scott (Sidmouth MSS.).

3416 LETTERS FROM THE KING TO THE EARL OF LIVERPOOL

Carlton House, 10 p.m., Friday, 1 June 1821

Secret. The King has given his serious attention to the communications which Lord Liverpool made to him yesterday.

That part which relates to the propos'd retirement of Lord Sidmouth is most painful to the King. If however it must be so, the King cannot consent to the retirement of this distinguish'd servant of the Crown and of the public without such remuneration as shall mark to the public the great regard and estimation in which he was held not only by the late but by the present King, and to which his long and *very meritorious* services have so justly entitled him.[2] (Add. MSS. 38190, fo. 43)

1. Thomas Burgess (1756–1837), Prebendary of Durham, 1794; Bishop of St. David's, 1803; of Salisbury, 1825–37. Author of sermons and pamphlets; founder of St. David's College, Lampeter, for the education of Welsh clergy, 1822.

For an account of the foundation of the Royal Society of Literature, see *Gentleman's Magazine*, 1823, i. 543–6.

2. Lord Liverpool proposed that Sidmouth should be given a pension of £3000 a year (Yonge's *Liverpool*, iii. 142).

Brighton, Monday, 7 Jan. 1822[1]

Most secret and confidential. [The King has the pleasure to acknowledge to Lord Liverpool the communication of his correspondence[2] with the Marquis of Hertford.[3] The King feels most sensibly the delicacy of Lord Liverpool upon this occasion, and highly approves of Lord Liverpool's answer. The King will be ready to receive the Council at Brighton whenever Lord Liverpool will give the King *timely* information of his wishes for that purpose.] But as Lord Liverpool seems to think that the Council at the very soonest cannot be held till on or about the 16th of this month, the King is desirous that Lord Liverpool should come for a few hours to Brighton on *Wednesday next*, in order that the King may have *some private and confidential* conversation with him. The King will not detain Lord Liverpool a moment longer than may be quite convenient to him, and the King desires that Lord Liverpool will *not say* that he has been *expressly* sent for.

P.S. The correspondence with the Marquis of Hertford the King returns inclos'd. (Add. MSS. 38190, fo. 53)

3417 LETTERS FROM THE KING TO VISCOUNT SIDMOUTH

Brighton, Monday, 7 Jan. 1822

Private. The King has receiv'd Lord Sidmouth's letter containing the request that the King would receive Lord Talbot at Brighton, soon after his Lordship's return to London.[4] The King will with great pleasure receive Lord Talbot, and hopes that Lord Sidmouth will accompany him. The King desires Lord Sidmouth to acquaint him of Lord Talbot's arrival in town, and the day, to which the King may look forwards, for their intended visit (Sidmouth MSS.).

1. That part enclosed within square brackets is printed in *Letters of George IV*, ii. 490, and there dated the 5th (inaccurately, because it is only a copy and the day of the week does not appear).

2. *Letters of George IV*, ii. 488–9 (2 and 4 January 1822).

3. Lord Hertford, very old and infirm, had been persuaded to resign his office of Lord Chamberlain in July 1821 (*Letters of George IV*, ii. 447). The Marquess had asked for a Dukedom after the Marquess of Buckingham had been promised one as part of the arrangement whereby the Grenville party joined the Government.

The Dukedom was refused: the influence of the family had waned. Lady Hertford had been supplanted as the King's favourite by Lady Conyngham in 1819.

4. Lord Talbot was deemed incapable of dealing effectively with the disturbed condition of Ireland and he was recalled at the end of 1821, being replaced on 29 December by Lord Wellesley.

Brighton, 12 Jan. 1822
I return you the dispatches from the Marquis of Wellesley [*sic*] which are most ably drawn up, & most interesting to read; nevertheless, I cannot help deeply lamenting the *painful* picture which it has been his *painful* duty to submit to my Government but, according to what the old adage says, *nec aspera terrent*.[1] We have seen as thick clouds as these, they have been with energy & firmness dispers'd; & therefore we will hope that this may be the same now. I shall be glad to receive you & Lord Talbot to dinner on Monday next (ibid.).

3418   THE KING TO THE DUKE OF DEVONSHIRE [copy]
Brighton, 16 Jan. 1822
My dear Hart, As Lady Cowper and some other friends of yours have promised to be with me on Thursday the 24th to pass a few days, I am very anxious that you should join our party, and I shall be most happy to see you at that time should it be quite convenient to you (Chatsworth MSS.).

3419   THE KING TO THE EARL OF ELDON[2]
Friday night, 12.30 a.m. [after Jan. 1822; watermark, 1821]
Pray read the inclos'd in the box which I have just receiv'd by messenger from Peel. I think it important that you should see it before your interview with Sr. David Scott,[3] as it will, I should think, enable you to throw new lights upon the advice you may have to give him. I suppose that you have the kea [*sic*] of the box with you; should you not only send down to me, never mind how early the hour, & I will immediately send it to you. The letter, I think establishes *the fact* most decidedly & conclusively.

P.S. Perhaps you will give me a minute before you return to town (Eldon MSS.).

1. 'Difficulties do not dismay us'—the motto of the Royal Hanoverian Guelphic Order, founded by the Prince Regent in 1815.

2. Eldon was rewarded with an Earldom on 7 July 1821 (a 'Coronation' peerage).

3. Sir David Scott (1782–1851), M.P. for Yarmouth, Isle of Wight, 1806. He succeeded his uncle, Sir James Sibbald as 2nd Baronet in September 1819, in conformity with the limitation of the patent.

Brighton, 8 Mar. 1822

Private. It is only this morning that I have receiv'd answers from several individuals who I had invited in the beginning of the last week to meet here as tomorrow [*sic*] & to pass a few days with me. My wishes being gratified in this respect, & hoping that the party would be such a one as might be agreable to you, I do not hesitate a moment in naming it to you, & expressing how gratified I shall be, if your avocations will admit of your coming & adding one more to the number under my roof. If I could have ascertain'd my success with any degree of certainty, sooner, I should not have delay'd so late as the present moment, my present request. (Wellington MSS.).

Brighton, 12 o'clock, Friday night, 14 [15] Mar. 1822

Most confidential. I have the pleasure of returning you Lord Stewart's letter, & I thank you for the trouble you have taken in this affair. I am ready to agree to the proposals contain'd in Lord Stewart's letter, but as the object of the Mission seems to be for the purpose of Bloomfield's advancement, I am very anxious, if by any means practicable, that it should be done immediately.[1] Pray urge Lord Londonderry to this, as strongly as possible. At any rate, I must desire, that this business be now concluded (Wellington MSS.).

Brighton, 21 Mar. 1822

Confidential. In consequence of your last letter,[2] I have finally made my intention known to Lord Liverpool respecting Sr B. Bloomfield & as you have kindly interested yourself in this matter, I beg that you will [make] a point of seeing Lord Liverpool for the purpose of being made acquainted with what I have written (Wellington MSS.).

1. Bloomfield's influence was now waning, and his presence was no longer necessary to the King. He had been supplanted by Lady Conyngham's second son, Lord Francis Conyngham, and he was deprived of his office of Private Secretary. He demanded, as compensation, but was refused, a U.K. peerage. He declined the Governorship of Ceylon, and Castlereagh (who had succeeded his father as 2nd Marquess of Londonderry on 6 April 1821) made an effort to open a diplomatic situation for him. Bloomfield was more or less promised an Irish peerage whenever there was a vacancy, and a diplomatic appointment when a Mission fell vacant. There is much correspondence on this subject in *Letters of George IV*, ii. *passim*. He was given a G.C.B. on 1 April, and appointed Minister to Sweden in 1822.

2. *Letters of George IV*, ii. 513 (18 March).

Brighton, 30 Mar. 1822

Most private. I should take great shame to myself did I not immediately acknowledge your very affectionate and kind attention towards me. This has been lately so strongly, so sincerely evinc'd that I have no words to convey to you the warmth of my feelings on the occasion.

This latter circumstance, which gave rise to your able and circumstantial dispatch to Mr. Peel[1] shews at once how much your heart is involv'd in real attachment and devotion towards your Sovereign and your friend.

I have but two observations to make on the extraordinary circumstance relative to the man Percy.

If he is insane, his insanity should be ascertained my [*sic*] medical agency, and dealt with, as the melancholy circumstances of his situation would necessarily call for; and it would indeed be a question of great delicacy to decide, even when his sanity should return, at what period of time the unhappy man should again be entrusted with the care of his own conduct. I have no personal apprehensions, but to entertain a stratagem against the life of a Sovereign involves so much of peril to others that it is impossible to look at it, however obscur'd it may be with improbabilities as to the practical result, without serious apprehension.

If the man is sane, there must be a motive, and that motive must be founded on wickedness. The man must therefore not be let loose until the matter is fairly made out to your satisfaction. Whether Percy should be kept where he is, or sent to this country, I leave entirely to your own judgment and that of Mr. Peel.

God bless you, my dear Wellesley, and may you be as happy and as successful in all your arduous and great undertakings as I wish you.

Always your affectionate friend.

P.S. I can assure you that your beautiful poplin is much admir'd. Your amiable attention is well bestow'd and appreciated. (Add. MSS. 37414, fos. 38–9)

Carlton House, 4 May 1822

Most private and confidential. I can judge of the severity of your illness by your having been prevented from acknowledging my last letter. I am myself under the influence of a severe attack of the gout, and write with difficulty and in pain.

You will have receiv'd by this time Col. Burton's[2] resignation of the

1. Peel had become Home Secretary on 15 January 1822.

2. Sir Francis Nathaniel Burton Conyngham (1766–1832), Lord Conyngham's twin brother. M.P. for Co. Clare, 1801–8; Lieutenant-Governor of Lower Canada, 1808–25. Peel, in his

command of the Clare Militia, and I am *very desirous* that Ld.MtCharles,[1] who is the Lt.Col. of that Regt., should be his successor.

This is on many accounts very desireable, and a great object to the family, and your difficulty, if any should arise, will be immediately got rid of, because it is the natural promotion, and therefore an act of justice. Let me add to this, also, should it be necessary that you are at liberty to state that it is *my particular desire*. I know your own kind feelings, and merely mention this to relieve you, should any other strong applications be made to you. Pray let me have the satisfaction of hearing from you as soon as you can write. (Add. MSS. 37414, fos. 41–2)

3422   THE KING TO THE BISHOP OF ST. DAVID'S[2]
Carlton House, 17 May 1822
The King acknowledges with great pleasure, the Bishop of St. David's letter relative to his pious & useful scheme[3] for the benefit of those who are in future to constitute the great body of the Welch [*sic*] Clergy. The King can not express, in terms of *sufficient commendation*, this most laudable effort of the Bishop of St. David's. Whenever the money is wanted, the King has order'd his Privy Purse to transmit one thousand pounds in aid of the Bishop's benevolent intentions (Windsor MSS.).

Memorandum on the state of the Irish Representation, 1818–20, noted that the Conyngham family held most of the Co. Clare honours. 'Governors, Hon. F. N. Burton . . . [and] Rt. Hon. Fitzgerald. Custos Rotulorum, M[arquess] Conyngham; Colonelcy of Militia, Hon. F. N. Burton' (Add. MSS. 40298). His father's name was Burton, and in 1781, he, the father, took the surname Conyngham in lieu of that of Burton on inheriting the Barony of Conyngham from his uncle (1705–81).

1. Henry Joseph Conyngham, Earl of Mount Charles (1795–1824), first son of Lord Conyngham, the Lord Steward. M.P. for Co. Donegal, 1818–24.

2. This letter was presented in August 1940 to King George VI by Mr. Alfred L. Marriott, whose grandfather (George Wharton Marriott) was Chancellor of the diocese of St. David's.

3. The building of St. David's College at Lampeter. See *Letters of George IV* iii. 42.

3423 THE KING TO THE DUKE OF WELLINGTON

R[oya]l G[eorge] Y[acht], Leith R[oads], 9 p.m., 15 Aug. 1822
Private. The melancholy event has just reach'd me.[1] You know well my
feelings for that distinguished individual; I lov'd him as my friend, I
esteem'd him as a statesman, & I respected him as my servant. Do not
commit even your *own private* thoughts until *you* see *me* respecting any
new arrangements, for I need not tell *you* who are so *well* capable of
judging, how *deep* the consideration must be, which involves the direction of the foreign politicks (Wellington MSS.).

3424 THE KING TO CHARLES ARBUTHNOT

Pavilion, Brighton, 28 Nov. 1822
Secret. Our friend Sir William[2] has told me of your kind and affectionate
conduct towards me. This is not new, because I have always found it to
be the case. I do not choose however to let it pass without assuring you
of my regard and warm esteem. Sir William will have many things to talk
to you about, and that which relates to Windsor, I put into your hands
for *myself*[3] (Arbuthnot MSS.).

3425 LETTERS FROM THE KING TO THE EARL OF LIVERPOOL

Thursday, 2 Jan. 1823
Private. Sr. Herbert Taylor has mention'd to me the distress of poor
George Villiers. You may remember that Taylor was one of my father's
trustees, who was oblig'd to examine his accounts, and notwithstanding
the unfortunate conduct of George Villiers,[4] I felt a good deal for him at
the time. He has two grown up sons, unprovided for; if you would help
one of them by a situation in any of the Offices it would be an act of
charity, and very agreable to me. (Add. MSS. 38190, fo. 62)

1. Castlereagh committed suicide on 12 August, the result of mental overstrain. On the 10th
the King had embarked at Greenwich for Edinburgh: his first and only visit to Scotland.

2. Knighton.

3. The reference is probably to the financing of the building works at Windsor. Arbuthnot,
who had been Joint Secretary of the Treasury since 1809, was appointed First Commissioner
of Woods and Forests at the end of the year in succession to Huskisson.

4. See No. 2740.

Pavilion, Brighton, 27 Feb. 1823

I fully intended to have spoken to you when in town upon two or three points, and therefore it is that I now write to you.

I find that Sr. Bn. Bloomfield's pension can no longer for the present be paid, in consequence of his appointment to Sweden,[1] from the Civil List. This is hard upon me, but as it cannot be help'd, I must provide for it from my Privy Purse.

Mr. Watson,[2] you may remember I mention'd to you for an appointment about two years since, in consequence of his own desire, dependant upon Sr. Ben. Bloomfield's temper, as they could not then go on together; Mr. Watson reminded me of this request some months ago, then wishing also to be plac'd in some situation, *for life*. He is a very good man, as you know, and it is a question of strong feeling with me that he should be advanc'd to a superior situation, both on his account as well as my own. I therefore do wish for many reasons that you would make him Auditor of the Civil List, for which he is most competent. This will save me the expense of his salary which will thus defray the expense over to be incurr'd, relative to Sr. Ben. Bloomfield. I have mention'd this to Sr. Wm.,[3] who with his usual affection and zeal towards me, has kindly undertaken with the assistance of Mr. Marrabel[4] who, you know, has been with me more than ten years, to regulate everything relative to the boxes and my papers, so that I shall not, by this means, require any new or additional servant and consequently save a thousand pr. an. We all very much regard Watson, and it will give me personally great pleasure to give him this proof of it.

Now, I must remind you respecting my Bill,[5] and as it is only an Act to amend and render effectual, that formerly passed for my father, there can be no reason, I should think, for a *message* but give it quietly to the Attorney General, and let him bring it in. Sr. Wm. cannot proceed in my affairs without this, and I am paying heavy interest (for some absurd bargains formerly made by Sr. B. B——d) in consequence of the want of the passing of this Bill.

1. His appointment as Minister to the Court of Sweden was gazetted on 9 September 1822. He received his credentials on 24 April 1823.

2. Sir Frederick Beilby Watson (*d.* 1852). In 1815 he was the Duke of Cumberland's private secretary. On 1 July 1815 he was appointed Assistant Secretary to the Prince Regent. Knighted, and appointed Master of the Household, 1827. In September 1823 was he appointed a Commissioner of the Customs (see Liverpool's reply to the King's letter, in *Letters of George IV*, iii. 1).

3. Knighton.

4. Sir Thomas Marrable, Secretary of the Board of Green Cloth. Knighted 6 March 1840.

5. Liverpool informed the King that a Message from him to the two Houses of Parliament was essential 'in point of form to the introduction of the Bill relative to your Majesty's private property.' The Message is in *Letters of George VI*, iii. 2n.

I expect the D of Yk. here today. You seem to be going on very well in Parliament. I thank God I am daily improving in my health, though still very lame. I send Sr. Wm. to London either tomorrow night or Saturday, if you should wish to see him. (Add. MSS. 38190, f. 67)

3426   THE KING TO THE DUKE OF WELLINGTON

Pavilion, Brighton, 23 Mar. 1823
Private. I have written to Francis Conyngham,¹ and desir'd him to invite Mr. Canning² to come down here to me on Saturday next, & to remain until the following day, or Monday. I wish on every account that you would be here at that time. The longer *you* stay the more agreable it will be to me, but I do not wish to interfere with any plans which you may have already form'd. Your propos'd appointment of Sr. Henry Harding,³ has my entire approbation (Wellington MSS.).

3427   THE KING TO LORD ELDON

Pavilion, Brighton, 26 Mar. 1823
When you have the opportunity you will oblige me much if you will make Mr. Wm. Brent, Brent [*sic*], a Commissioner of Bankrupts. He is a very worthy man & the nephew of one [of] my best & most meritorious servants;⁴ to his zeal & services I am much indebted.

1. Lord Francis Nathaniel Conyngham (1797–1876), first surviving son of the Marquess Conyngham. Succeeded to the courtesy title of Earl of Mount Charles on the death of his elder brother, 26 December 1824. Page of Honour to the Prince Regent until 1820, when he entered the Army. M.P. for Westbury, 1818–20; for Co. Donegal, 1825–31; Groom of the Bedchamber and Master of the Robes, 1820–30; Under-Secretary of State for Foreign Affairs, 1823–6; a Lord of the Treasury, 1826–30; Postmaster-General, July–December 1834, and May 1835; Lord Chamberlain, 1835–9.

2. Canning had succeeded Castlereagh as Foreign Secretary and Leader of the House of Commons on 16 September 1822.

3. Sir Henry Hardinge, 1st Viscount Hardinge (1785–1856). Joined the army, 1799; Major, 1809; Lieutenant-Colonel, 1811; Colonel, 1821; Major-General, 1830; Lieutenant-General, 1841; General, 1854. K.C.B., 1815. M.P. for Durham City, 1820–30; for St. Germans, July–December 1830; for Newport (Cornwall), 1830–2; for Launceston, 1832–44. Clerk of the Ordnance 1823–7 and February–August 1828; Secretary at War, 1828–30, and 1841–4; Irish Secretary, July–November, 1830 and 1834–5. Governor-General of India, 1844–8. Peerage, May 1846. Master-General of the Ordnance, 1852; Commander-in-Chief, 1852–6. Field-Marshal, 1855.

4. Sir Timothy Brent (*d.* 1833). Groom and Clerk of the Robes and Deputy Comptroller of the Household. Commissioner of Bankrupts, 1823.

P.S. I put this in writing in order that it may not escape your recollection (Eldon MSS.).

3428   THE KING TO THE EARL OF LIVERPOOL

Pavilion, Brighton, 6 Apr. 1823

Although the Bishop[1] is not dead I may as well write and give my approbation to the promotion of the Bishop of Chester,[2] and the elevation of the Dean of Chichester,[3] whenever the event of the demise of the Bishop of Bath and Wells shall happen. The name of Chichester reminds me of a wish that I have long had, and which I beleive I have before mention'd to you, namely, that whenever that diocese shall become vacant, to promote the Dean of Hereford to that See.[4] You know him to be an excellent and exemplary man, and is much esteem'd, respected and look'd up to by all our most respectable friends in this country, and I confess I take a great interest in this. In reference to the preferment of Bath and Wells, and likewise of Dr. Bethell, I think you have judg'd rightly.[5] (Add. MSS. 38190, fo. 70)

3429   THE KING TO GEORGE CANNING

Carlton House, 4 p.m., Thursday, 17 Apr. 1823

Most private. The King desires to draw Mr. Canning's most *serious* attention to the contents of several of the inclos'd interceptions, & most *earnestly* recommends to Mr. Canning to be *extremely cautious* of the language he holds as Minister of the Crown, upon the present crisis[6] (Harewood MSS.).

1. Richard Beadon, Bishop of Bath and Wells, 1802–24, died on 21 April 1824. Master of Jesus College, Cambridge, 1781; Bishop of Gloucester, 1789–1802.

2. George Henry Law (1761–1845), son of Edmund Law (1703–87), Bishop of Carlisle. Bishop of Chester, 1812–24; of Bath and Wells, June 1824–45.

3. Christopher Bethell (1773–1859), Dean of Chichester, 1814–24; Bishop of Gloucester, April 1824; of Exeter, June 1830; of Bangor, October 1830–59.

4. John Buckner, Bishop of Chichester since March 1798, died on 1 or 2 May 1824, and was succeeded by Robert James Carr (1774–1841), Dean of Hereford, 1820–4; Bishop of Chichester, 1824–31; of Worcester, 1831–41.

5. Part only of this letter is quoted in a footnote in *Letters of George IV*, iii. 2.

6. The French invaded Spain on 6 April in order to destroy the liberal Constitution of 1812 and restore Ferdinand VII to absolute power, of which the Revolution of 1820 had deprived

[Royal] Lodge, Windsor, 26 June 1823
Private. The King has read with great attention Sr. Wm. A'Court's[1] interesting dispatches; who seems to have acted with great judgment in the critical situation in which he has been plac'd. As soon as this self-created, mad Regency is dissolv'd, Sr. Wm. Acourt [*sic*] will of course proceed immediately to Cadiz, or even before, should the safety of the King require it. Under these circumstances it will be wisest & safest to place everything in the discretionary power of Sr. Wm. Acourt (Harewood MSS.).

3430   THE KING TO THE EARL OF ELDON
King's Lodge, Windsor Great Park, 1 July 1823
Do you recollect when you were last at Brighton I put into your hand a memorandum requesting you to make my faithful servant, Mr. Brent's nephew (a most proper person) a Commissioner of Bankrupts? I see by the newspapers that there are two vacancies. Let me have the pleasure of hearing that you have nominated him to one of them. Bis dat qui cito dat[2] (Eldon MSS.).

3431   THE KING TO FREDERICK JOHN ROBINSON[3]
Royal Lodge, Windsor Great Park, 1 July 1823
The King cannot help thanking Mr. Robinson for his earnest and effective attention relative to the arrangement that has taken place for the

him. Canning, speaking in the House of Commons on the 14th, strongly criticised the French Government and expressed the hope that the Spanish people would come triumphantly out of the struggle. The King was afraid that Canning's breach with the Continental Powers would involve England in war.

1. Sir William A'Court, 1st Baron Heytesbury (1779–1860). Secretary of Legation at Naples, 1801–7; Envoy to the Barbary States, 1813, and to Naples, 1814–22. Succeeded to the Baronetcy, 22 July 1817; Envoy to Spain, 1822–4; Ambassador to Portugal, 1824–8; to Russia, 1828–32. Lord Lieutenant of Ireland, 1844–6. Peerage, 23 January 1828.

2. See No. 3427.

3. Frederick John Robinson, Viscount Goderich and Earl of Ripon (1782–1859), second son of 2nd Baron Grantham. M.P. for Carlow, 1806–7; for Ripon, 1807–27. Private Secretary to Hardwicke, Lord Lieutenant of Ireland, 1804–6; Under-Secretary of State for War and the Colonies, 1809; a Lord of the Admiralty, 1810–12; Vice-President of Board of Trade, 1812–1818; a Lord of the Treasury, 1812–13; Joint Paymaster-General, 1813–17; President of Board of Trade, 1818–23, and 1841–3; Treasurer of the Navy, 1818–23; Chancellor of the Exchequer, 31 January 1823–27; peerage, 28 April 1827; Secretary of State for War and the

completion of the purchase on the part of the Crown of the property at Kew. The King feels such dutiful conduct very sensibly. (Add. MSS. 40862. fo. 96)

3432   THE KING TO THE EARL OF HARROWBY
Royal Lodge, Windsor Great Park, Friday evening, 4 July 1823
The King is much gratified by Lord Harrowby's communication, & desires Lord Harrowby to accept of his most sincere congratulations. The King has great pleasure in signifying to Lord Harrowby his entire acquiescence respecting his intended journey to Switzerland.[1] (Harrowby MSS.).

3433   LETTERS FROM THE KING TO THE DUKE OF WELLINGTON
Carlton House, 17 July 1823
I am induc'd to write you this from the anxiety entertain'd by Lord Londonderry relative to the filling up the Colonelcy of the Militia in Ireland, so long held by his late excellent brother, our much lamented friend.

It is very disagreable to my private feelings to be thus disturbed for the want of that spirit of accomodation so necessary even in the ordinary affairs of life, and consequently much more so on questions which have relation to the unanimity which should always prevail where the good government of the country is concern'd. As this is the only true principle upon which a Government can be satisfactorily carried on, I feel the interruption of it very sensibly. The *great* and *just* confidence I repose in you, my dear friend, makes me desirous that you should communicate these sentiments to Sr. George Hill;[2] at the same time informing both

Colonies, April–August 1827 and 1830–3; First Lord of the Treasury, 31 August 1827–January 1828; Lord Privy Seal, 1833–4. Earldom, 13 April 1833. President of the India Board, 1843–6.

1. The reference is to the engagement of Lord Harrowby's son and heir, Viscount Sandon (1798–1882) who succeeded to the Earldom on 26 December 1847. On 15 September 1823 he married, at the English Embassy at Berne, Frances (1801–59), daughter of the 1st Marquess of Bute.

2. Sir George Fitzgerald Hill (1763–1839). M.P. for Londonderry Co., 1801–2; for Londonderry City, 1802–30. Lord of the Treasury [I.], 1807–17; Vice-Treasurer for Ireland, 1817–30. Succeeded his father as 2nd Baronet, 31 January 1795. Governor of Trinidad, 1833–9. His appointment to the command of the Londonderry Militia led to great bitterness between Lord

him and Lord Londonderry that my feelings towards whatever Government I may support will never admit of half friends. I have always held a good opinion of Sr. G. Hill; it is however but justice to both, distinctly to state what I feel upon the present subject (Wellington MSS.).

Carlton House, 17 July 1823
Most private and confidential. If the letter which I send relative to Sr. G. Hill should not entirely meet your views, send it back with any alterations that you may suggest and I will re-write it.

I need not tell you of the warm affection I entertain towards you; *you are indeed my much valued friend.*

It is right I should say something on your very kind conduct relative to my friend Sr. Wm.[1] No man ever deserv'd more from the Government or from myself in providing him for their use; and the return is, Lord Liverpool's *usual* absurd, weak, and disgusting conduct. Depend upon it, that Lord Liverpool, if he lives till Doom's Day, will never be corrected, or made fit for the high office, to which I rais'd Him, and I should consider it a mercy to be spar'd the irritations to which he continually subjects me. I value Sr. Wm.'s feelings as I ought, more than I can express, and I therefore desire him to take no further step in this measure. He will continue to manage my private affairs, which are beginning, thank God, to be most prosperous, but, as to Lord Liverpool, he must manage *his* interests and the Govt. business, as he can[2] (Wellington MSS.).

3434   THE KING TO GEORGE CANNING
Windsor Castle, 8 Oct. 1823
Private. The King sends his kind regards to Mr. Canning & the King quite approves of Mr. Canning's proposal of writing to Lord Clancarty[3]

Londonderry and Lord Liverpool. Castlereagh had been Colonel of the Regiment, and his half-brother considered that *he* should have inherited it. See *Letters of George IV*, iii. 7.

1. Knighton.

2. Lord Liverpool declined to have Knighton called to the Privy Council (George III had placed Colonel Taylor on the same footing as an Under-Secretary of State, who was never a Privy Councillor. See *Letters of George IV*, iii. 9, and *English Historical Review*, January 1940, pp. 66–9.

3. Richard Le-Poer Trench (1767–1837). Styled Lord Dunlo from 11 February 1803 when his father was created Earl, until he succeeded his father as 2nd Earl of Clancarty [I.] on

on Friday. The King is much satisfied with Lord Clancarty's conduct, & to make the correspondence complete, the King writes Lord Clancarty another letter which Mr. Canning may seal & send. The King hopes Mr. Canning will have a pleasant excursion[1] (Harewood MSS.).

3435   THE KING TO THE EARL OF ELDON
Pavilion, Brighton, 15 Dec. 1823
I was glad to see by the papers that you were in your Court, for I was very much afraid, from what Mr. Beckett[2] told me, that you were likely to have a fit of our old & inveterate enemy, the gout. I should have written to you before had I not thought it likely for some days past that I should have sent Sr. Wm. Knighton to London. Pray let me know how you are (Eldon MSS.).

3436   THE KING TO THE ARCHBISHOP OF CANTERBURY
23 Dec. 1823
Private. The King sends his very kind regards to the Archbishop of Canterbury. The King at present believes that a presentation to the Charter House would be a matter of great convenience to him in about three or four months; now if the Archbishop could obligingly manage to find a nomination for the King at the time specified, the King will be happy to place one at the disposal of the Archbishop, in the ensuing year, when the King's turn of nomination will come round (Windsor MSS.).

27 April 1805. M.P. for Co. Galway, 1801–5; for Rye, 1807. Created Baron Trench [U.K.], 1815. Irish Representative Peer, 1808–37. A Commissioner for the Affairs of India, 1804–6; Joint Postmaster-General [I.], 1807; Postmaster-General [I.], 1807–9; Master of the Mint, October 1812–September 1814; President of Board of Trade, 1812–18. Ambassador at The Hague, 1813–15, and 1816–23; Joint Postmaster-General, 1814–16. Created Viscount Clancarty [U.K.], 8 December 1823.

Canning's close friend Lord Granville succeeded Clancarty as Ambassador at The Hague in February 1824. See *Wellington (Civil) Despatches*, ii. 143–5 for the reasons for his recall.

1. To Cirencester, Lord Bathurst's seat.

2. Sir John Beckett (1775–1847), M.P. for Cockermouth, 1818–21; for Haslemere, 1826–32; for Leeds, 1835–7. Under-Secretary of State, 1806–17. Judge Advocate General, 1817–27, and 1828–30. Succeeded his father as 2nd Baronet, 1826.

3437   THE KING TO THE EARL OF ELDON

Pavilion, Brighton, 14 Jan. 1824

Private. Lord Liverpool has propos'd to hold a Council here on Monday next for the purpose of swearing in as Privy Councillors the two new Judges.[1] I wish *you* to signify my pleasure that they both dine with me on that day. Now, my good friend, if your health or your convenience enable you to do it, I shall be *truly happy* to see *you* either on Saturday, Sunday or Monday, or all these days, but do exactly in this matter as you like. Should you not come, our friend Sr. William will call on you on Sunday morning with a little message from myself (Eldon MSS.).

3438   LETTERS FROM THE KING TO THE DUKE OF WELLINGTON

Pavilion, Brighton, 11 Feb. 1824

Private. I agree to every word in your letter. I am glad that you have decided under all the circumstances, in giving Sr. Benn. Bloomfield the Battalion.[2] I shall have the comfort of seeing you on Sunday (Wellington MSS.).

Windsor Castle, 24 Feb. 1824

Private. I entirely approve and sanction your arrangments respecting the succession of Sr. George Murray[3] to Lord Beresford,[4] and a further provision to be made for Sr. G. hereafter. I would have answer'd your letters yesterday, but I was much indispos'd then with a very sharp

---

1. Sir William Alexander, Chief Baron of the Exchequer, and Sir Robert Gifford, Chief Justice of the Common Pleas.

2. Bloomfield had been removed from his commission of Lieutenant-Colonel of the Artillery as a Major-General under the operation of the warrant of 8 August 1814. In 1824 he was the senior Major-General of the Artillery Officers without the command of a battalion, and in view of that circumstance and of his services to the King, Wellington recommended this promotion, in his letter to the King of the 10th (*Wellington* [*Civil*] *Despatches*, ii. 198).

3. Sir George Murray (1772–1846). M.P. for Perthshire, 1824–32 and 1834. Entered the army, 1789; Captain, 1794; Lieutenant-Colonel, 1799. Assistant Quartermaster-General at the Horse Guards, 1803; Deputy Quartermaster-General in Ireland, 1804–5. Colonel, 1809; Major-General, 1812. K.B., 1813. Governor of Sandhurst, 1819–24. Lieutenant-General of the Ordnance, March 1824–5; Commander-in-Chief in Ireland, 1825–8. Lieutenant-General, 1825; Secretary of State for War and the Colonies, May 1828–November 1830; Master-General of the Ordnance, December 1834–5 and 1841–6; General, 1841.

4. Beresford was Lieutenant-General of the Ordnance, 1823–4.

449

attack of rheumatism (not gout) and which I am sorry to say, is not very much better this day. I most sincerely hope that you continue quite well (Wellington MSS.).

3439   THE KING TO GEORGE CANNING

Windsor Castle, 4 Apr. 1824

Private. The King sends his regards to Mr. Canning. The King is very anxious that Mr. Canning should make a point, that Lord Francis Conyngham does not quit his present office,[1] upon his marriage, until another be found for him suitable in every respect. The King does not doubt that Mr. Canning will see the propriety of this suggestion (Harewood MSS.).

3440   THE KING TO FREDERICK JOHN ROBINSON

Carlton House, 25 May 1824

The King sends his very kind regards to Mr. Robinson and thanks him for his note. Whatever the result may be, the King desires to assure Mr. Robinson how truly satisfied the King is with that affectionate and dutiful zeal which he constantly evinces for the King's interests. (Add. MSS. 40862, fo. 114)

3441   THE KING TO THE DUKE OF WELLINGTON

Royal Lodge, Friday night, 17 Dec. 1824

Most private. I have but just receiv'd the enclos'd, and dispatch it off to you that you may receive it if possible the very first thing in the morning, and so as to enable you to furnish me with an answer, and with *your advice and sentiments upon it, previous* to my leaving the Lodge tomorrow for Windsor Castle to hold the Council and which *at latest must be at one o'clock.* I have put in pencil some queries, which you will have the goodness to reply to *in your answer,* and *not* in Lord Liverpool's document, in which I have put my pencil'd interrogatories. Should you think it

1. That of Under-Secretary of State for Foreign Affairs (1823–6). On 24 April 1824 he married Lady Jane Paget (*d.* 1876), daughter of the Marquess of Anglesey.

desireable to see me upon this business there can surely be no reason why you should not come to Council and meet me at the Castle, but upon this I would have you consult your own convenience and what you really think is best at the present moment and under the present circumstances. Should I not either hear from you, or see you previous to the Council, I shall be very short, and *very peremptory* with the Secretary for Foreign Affairs upon the answer which I receiv'd from Ld. Liverpool, and which when you have done with I will desire you to send me back. I am very sorry to be the occasion of giving you so much trouble, but, as I already have told you, in my letter of this morning, you are the only person in whom I can completely confide, and the only one upon whom I do, and that I can, *entirely depend*[1] (Wellington MSS.).

3442   THE KING TO FREDERICK JOHN ROBINSON
King's Lodge, 6 p.m., 27 Mar. 1825
The King sends his kind regards to Mr. Robinson and assures him that the King does not, and did not even upon the first perusal of Mr. Robinson's letter,[2] impute any blame to him. When the King has settled his mind upon the business, he will acquaint Mr. Robinson.[3] (Add. MSS. 40862, fo. 133)

3443   THE KING TO THE EARL OF CHATHAM
St. James's Palace, 7 p.m., Monday, 4 July 1825
By mere chance I have only this moment learnt that you are arriv'd & at Thomas's Hotel. There is a Dress Ball at St. James's Palace this evening, & I am so truly rejoic'd to hear of your safe arrival, & so impatient to have the pleasure of seeing you that I cannot resist the writing you a line myself to express my desire that you will give me the satisfaction of presenting yourself to me, at the Ball this evening. Your Audience of Ceremony shall be postponed till $\frac{1}{2}$ pt 4 tomorrow after the Privy Council (Hoare MSS.).

1. For the struggle between the Cabinet and the King on the question of recognizing the independence of the former Spanish American colonies, see *Wellington Civil Despatches*, ii. 364 sqq., and Temperley's *Foreign Policy of Canning*, pp. 145–7.

2. *Letters of George IV*, iii. 107. This, and the King's letter of the 26th to Robinson, refer to the proposed grant to the Duke of York of mineral rights in Nova Scotia (ibid., iii. 106).

3. On 19 April Robinson informed the Duke of York that the King had consented to the proposal to grant him the lease of the mines in Nova Scotia. [f. 134]

3444 THE KING TO GEORGE CANNING

Royal Lodge, 13 Sept. 1825

Secret & confidential. The King sends his very kind regards to Mr. Canning.

The King writes for the purpose of renewing his communication with Mr. Canning upon the subject of Lord Albert Conyngham,[1] whom the King has decided on sending to Vienna for the purpose of being plac'd as an Attaché with Sr. Henry Wellesley.

The King's great affection & regard for his young friend will naturally suggest to Mr. Canning's mind the great anxiety which the King feels respecting him.

Under these circumstances the King has resolv'd to send his friend Sr. William Knighton to Vienna with Lord Albert for the purpose of explaining to Sr. Henry the King's entire wishes on this subject.

It has occurr'd to the King that if Lord Albert was fix'd at Vienna, as a paid Attaché, it might make his conduct & application of a more responsible discription, by being the first step as it were to future promotion; but the King leaves this with great confidence to Mr. Canning's own judgment & prudent discretion.

The King would of course wish that Sr. Wm. Knighton's absence should be as little known as possible (Harewood MSS.).

3445 THE KING TO THE MARQUESS WELLESLEY

Royal Lodge, 20 Oct. 1825

Private. The King sends his affectionate regards to Lord Wellesley and desires to express the real pleasure the King feels at the communication of an event which promises so much happiness.

The King has always felt the greatest respect towards the distinguished lady on whom Lord Wellesley has bestow'd his hand and his heart, and the King desires Lord Wellesley will present his congratulation and kind compliments on the occasion.[2] (Add. MSS. 37414, fo. 50)

1. The youngest son of the Marquess Conyngham (1805–60), created Baron Londesborough, 1850. The King, said Lord Aberdeen, the Foreign Secretary, in July 1829, 'is very desirous for Lord Albert to go to Berlin as Secretary of Legation, in order that he may be with [Sir Brook] Taylor. He pressed this very strongly; and as Lord Albert has been Secretary of Legation at Florence for a year and a half, he may be moved without any impropriety.' He was Secretary of Legation at Berlin, 1829–31.

2. Lord Wellesley's first wife had died in 1816. On 29 October 1825 he married, at the Vice-Regal Lodge, Dublin, Mrs. Patterson, a wealthy Roman Catholic widow. Her husband, Robert Patterson, had been a merchant of Baltimore, Maryland. She became a Lady of the

3446 THE KING TO THE DUKE OF DEVONSHIRE

Brighton, 9 Nov. 1825

Mme. De Lieven,[1] who arriv'd here to dinner, has *just* inform'd me that she has had the pleasure of seeing you upon your return from the Continent, and intimated to me, from the kind enquiries you made after me, that it might not be unpleasant to you were I to propose to you to make a visit here for a few days; if this should not interfere with any previous engagements you may have form'd, I cannot express to you how glad I shall be to see you. I name the earliest day possible, which is Tuesday. I am, my dear Hart, ever very afftly yrs (Chatsworth MSS.).

3447 THE KING TO THE EARL OF LIVERPOOL [copy]

Royal Lodge, 4.30 p.m., 28 Dec. 1825

Private. I forward to you the extraordinary inclosure, which I have only just now recd. from the Duke of Buckingham. It is not necessary for me, I am sure, to add any comment or observation of my own upon it, further than this, that I consider it as a very indelicate & improper communication to me, both as to its matter, as well as to the mode in which it has pleased the Duke of Buckingham of stating *that* matter to me.

As your name, together with that of the Duke of Wellington & of Mr. Canning, are so often brought forward in this curious composition, I desire that you will (with as little loss of time as may be convenient to you) communicate it to them, & consult with them what sort of notice should be taken of it, & what sort of answer (if any) *you* will jointly recommend *me* to make to it.

At the same time I must state to you my opinion that I think it is quite impossible to suffer so very strange a paper, as it is, to pass entirely *sub silentio* & without some sort of notice & reply[2] (Harewood MSS.).

Bedchamber to Queen Adelaide and died in 1853. Lord Liverpool described it as a 'very strange and awkward event'.

1. Princess Lieven (1785–1857), the wife of Count Lieven (1774–1839), the Russian Ambassador in London.

2. The Duke of Buckingham had been pressing his claims to office (he wanted either the Governor-Generalship of Bengal or the Lord Lieutenancy of Ireland) in a persistent and absurd manner, and had hinted that unless his ridiculous pretensions were recognized, Government might lose the support of his members in the Commons.

3448 THE KING TO FREDERICK JOHN ROBINSON

Royal Lodge, 19 Jan. 1826

Private. The King sends his very kind regards to Mr. Robinson and is highly sensible of the promptitude, the zeal and the attention which Mr. Robinson has manifested in the arrangement he has made in all the matters relative to Windsor Castle, and the new Palace[1] now building in St. James's Park, which are so intimately connected with the King's future comfort and convenience. The manner in which Mr. Robinson has express'd his personal feelings towards the King also calls for the King's best acknowledgments. (Add. MSS. 40862, fo. 156)

3449 LETTERS FROM THE KING TO THE EARL OF LIVERPOOL

Royal Lodge, 9 Mar. 1826

The King thinks it right to state, in justice to Mr. Canning, that every word, which he, Mr. Canning, mentions to have passed on the subject of India and the Duke of Buckingham in the King's closet, is most *honestly, correctly & fairly* stated, and that the whole converstion arose, as Mr. Canning truly says, from the King's *own* enquiries (very natural) and not from any *previous* mention or putting forth of the subject by Mr. Canning. The King gave *no approbation* to Mr. Wynn,[2] on the subject of the Duke of Buckingham's proposed appointment, and for this *obvious reason*, that the Duke's name was *never officially* submitted to the King.

The King had yesterday thus far written with his own hand, but the King had no longer strength to finish this note to Lord Liverpool and today the King is obliged to dictate.

The King considers the Duke of Buckingham to have no cause of complaint whatever; but the King cannot refrain from observing that Mr. Wynn has no right to disclose any political transaction or conversation, passing in the King's closet, to any individual not a member of the Cabinet (Harewood MSS.).

1. Buckingham Palace was eventually to replace Carlton House.

2. Charles Wynn, the Duke's nephew, was the leading member of the Duke's small group in the House of Commons, and, when the Grenvilles joined the Government at the end of 1821, he was brought into the Cabinet and appointed President of the India Board as the representative of that 'connexion' in the Cabinet.

Royal Lodge, 11 Mar. 1826

The King is unable to sit up in his bed to write to Lord Liverpool with his own hand; the King is obliged therefore to dictate this note.[1] The King has no objection that Lord Liverpool should propose to the Bishop of Llandaff to take the Bishopric of Durham, should it unhappily become vacant; and the King desires to know the result of the Bishop's answer.[2] The King consents to Dr. Sumner's nomination to the Bishopric of Llandaff and the Deanery of St. Paul's, under the circumstances anticipated, in the first instance; but the King thinks it right distinctly to state to Lord Liverpool that no consideration will induce the King to suffer Dr. Sumner[3] to remain in a subordinate Bishopric. (Add. MSS. 38190, fo. 99)

3450   THE KING TO THE EMPEROR NICHOLAS I[4] [copy]

Carlton Palace, 5 May 1826

Sir My Brother, I cannot allow the period of your Imperial Majesty's Coronation to arrive, without manifesting the lively interest which I take in whatever concerns your Imperial Majesty, by the appointment of an Ambassador Extraordinary for the special purpose of assisting at that auspicious ceremony, and of offering to your Imperial Majesty my cordial congratulations thereupon. In nominating a person to proceed to your Imperial Majesty's Court on this occasion, I have been above all things desirous that my choice should be agreeable to your Imperial Majesty. For this reason, knowing the high regard which your Imperial Majesty entertains for the character of the Duke of Devonshire, I have thought that I could not better prove the sincerity of my sentiments towards your Imperial Majesty, than by confiding the expression of them to that distinguished nobleman. I request your Imperial Majesty will give entire credence to whatever the Duke of Devonshire shall say

1. It is in Knighton's hand.

2. William van Mildert was translated from Llandaff to Durham in April 1826: Shute Barrington died on 25 March.

3. Charles Richard Sumner (1790–1874) owed his rapid advancement to the friendship of the King, and the Conynghams, to whose two sons he had been tutor. Lord Liverpool resisted the King's attempt to have him made a Canon of Windsor in 1821 on the ground that he was then a mere curate. Appointed Bishop of Llandaff in April 1826 he was soon translated to Winchester (December 1827).

4. Nicholas I (1796–1855) succeeded his brother Alexander I on 1 December 1825. Wellington had been sent to Petersburg on a special mission of condolence and congratulation on the Tsar's accession, and the Duke of Devonshire, despite his Opposition politics, was sent on this subsequent mission. He attended the coronation in Moscow on 3 September.

to you on my behalf, more especially when he shall renew to your Imperial Majesty the assurances of my unalterable esteem and attachment, and of my ardent wish that your Imperial Majesty may be destined by Divine Providence to reign long and prosperously over your mighty Empire. I am Sir my Brother, Your Imperial Majesty's Good Brother (Wellington MSS.).

3451 THE KING TO VISCOUNT GRANVILLE

Royal Lodge, 30 June 1826

Private. The King sends his very kind regards to Lord Granville.[1]

This letter will be put into the hands of Lord Granville by Sr. Wm. Knighton, whom the King in conjunction with the opinion of Mr. Canning has sent to Paris as his confidential friend for the purpose of communicating with Lord Granville on a subject upon which the King is most deeply anxious; & the King has no doubt that Lord Granville will give his most anxious attention to this matter.[2] The King desires his very best & most affectionate remembrances to Lady Granville (P.R.O., G.D. 29/16).

3452 LETTERS FROM THE KING TO GEORGE CANNING

Royal Lodge, 4 Oct. 1826

Most Secret. The King sends his most kind regards to Mr. Canning, & writes with great difficulty having the gout in his right hand.

The King can therefore only add that much to the King's personal inconvenience the King has sent his confidential friend to Paris, who will explain the King's *increas'd anxiety* to Mr. Canning on a subject which need not be nam'd.

Many thanks for your two highly interesting & satisfactory letters.[3]

The King's very kind remembrances to Lord Granville (Harewood MSS.).

1. Granville had been Ambassador to France since November 1824.

2. The King was worried about the blackmailing activities of the courtesan Harriette Wilson and her 'hellish gang'. These people were placed under the surveillance of the Director of the Paris Police (*Letters of George IV*, iii. 501).

3. Canning was visiting his friend Granville in Paris. His letters to the King whilst there are in *Letters of George IV*, iii. 157–76.

Royal Lodge, 16 Oct. 1826

Most Private. The King sends his most kind regards to Mr. Canning & desires to express the great satisfaction the King has deriv'd from the whole of Mr. Canning's correspondence during his present residence in Paris.

The explanation which the King has receiv'd from his confidential friend, is indeed most agreable to the King's feelings, & the earnest & dutiful attention which Mr. Canning has evinc'd on the occasion demands from the King the warmest acknowledgements.

The King desires everything most kind to Lord Granville (ibid.).

3453 THE KING TO THE DUKE OF WELLINGTON

Royal Lodge, 17 Oct. 1826

Private. I return you many thanks for the box and its contents which I have receiv'd by the messenger, and I shall regulate myself according to your recommendation. Berresford wrote to Conyngham desiring to see me, and as it is important that he should delay his departure as little as possible, I have appointed to receive him here tomorrow[1] (Wellington MSS.).

3454 THE KING TO GEORGE CANNING

Royal Lodge, 14 Dec. 1826

Private. The King sends his very kind regards to Mr. Canning.

The King, as Mr. Canning will readily beleive, feels most deeply the melancholy intelligence convey'd in Mr. Hill's[2] last dispatch. In the Marquis of Hastings, the King has to deplore the loss of one of the best & most attach'd of friends.[3] Here the subject must close.

The King sincerely hopes that Mr. Canning has shaken off his recent indisposition, & that his health has not suffer'd from his great & splendid

---

1. Lord Beresford had been invited to resume the command of the Portuguese army, but, being refused powers necessary for rendering his command efficient, he returned home early in 1827.

2. William Noel Hill was at this time Minister to Sicily.

3. The Marquess of Hastings (Moira had been given a Marquessate in February 1817) died on 28 November 1826 on board H.M.S. *Revenge* in Baia Bay, off Naples. He had been Governor of Malta since March 1824.

exertions the other evening in the House of Commons[1] (Harewood MSS.).

3455   THE KING TO THE DUKE OF DEVONSHIRE
Royal Lodge, 15 Dec. 1826
The melancholy event of the death of my lamented friend the Marquis of Hastings has occasion'd a vacancy in the Order of the Garter. But it is a matter of some consolation to me that I have it in my power to gratify my own feelings in nominating you, my young friend (the son of my very dear old friends the late Duke & Duchess) to fill up the vacancy upon the present occasion.

It is but justice to Lord Liverpool, to state to you that he most cordially enters into my feelings upon your nomination[2] (Chatsworth MSS.).

3456   LETTERS FROM THE KING TO THE DUKE OF WELLINGTON
Royal Pavilion, Brighton, 24 Jan. 1827
As Sr. Andrew Barnard[3] will naturally succeed to the command of the 1st Bn. of the 95th Foot, now vacant by the death of Lt. Genl. Sr. Wm. Stewart,[4] I desire, that you will nominate Major Genl. Sr. Sydney Beckwith[5] to the battalion of the 95th. Regt. which will be thus vacant by the promotion of Sr. Andrew Barnard[6] (Wellington MSS.).

1. It was in the course of this speech, on the 12th, that Canning used the famous phrase, 'I called the New World into existence to redress the balance of the Old'.

2. See Liverpool's letter in *Letters of George IV*, iii. 188, and the Duke's reply to the King's, iii. 190.

3. Sir Andrew Francis Barnard (1773–1855). Captain, 1794; Lieutenant-Colonel, 1808; Colonel, 1813; K.C.B., 1815; Major-General, 1819; Lieutenant-General, 1837; General, 1851. A Groom of the Bedchamber, 1821.

4. Sir William Stewart (1774–1827), second son of John, 7th Earl of Galloway. Entered the army, 1786; Captain, 1791; Lieutenant-Colonel, 1795; Major-General, 1808; Lieutenant-General, 1813; G.C.B., 1815. M.P. for Saltash, 1795–6; for Wigtownshire, 1796–1802 and 1812–16; for the Wigtown Burghs, 1803–5.

5. Sir Thomas Sydney Beckwith (1772–1831). Captain, 1794; Major, 1802; Lieutenant-Colonel, 1803; Major-General, 1814; K.C.B., 1815; Lieutenant-General, 1830. Commander-in-Chief at Bombay, 1829–31.

6. The Duke's reply on the 26th is in *Wellington (Civil) Despatches*, iii. 568.

Royal Pavilion, Brighton, 31 Jan. 1827

Private. As there is to be a Council held here before dinner, on Monday next the fifth, I write a short line to say merely that I hope you will come here to me on that day, and that if you can stay at least another day with us it will give me great pleasure. As the matters concerning which you have written to me, do not immediately press, I shall postpone what I have to say to you, till I have the pleasure of having you here (Wellington MSS.).

3457   LETTERS FROM THE KING TO GEORGE CANNING

Pavilion, Brighton, 8.45 p.m., Saturday, 17 Feb. 1827

The King sends his very kind regards to Mr. Canning, with *the greatest pain & difficulty having the gout all over him* but particularly *in both his hands* the King attempts this short scrawl to Mr. Canning accompanying the two enclos'd notes this moment only receiv'd from Mr. Peel. The King is so surpriz'd, so shock'd & so petrified, that he cannot at this moment add a word more or of comment to Mr. Canning[1] (Harewood MSS.).

Royal Lodge, 16 Mar. 1827

The King sends his kind regards to Mr. Canning & thanks him for his note, conveying the intelligence of the *friandise* which the King's old acquaintance Madame de Beurke, has been so obliging as to forward for him. The King feels that somehow or other he ought to offer some little *galanterie* to Mme. de Beurke as an acknowledgement, & by way of expressing his thanks for these repeated marks of her attention & good-will. The King will therefore in a few days, forward a small parcel to Mr. Canning for Mme. de Beurke, which he will desire that Mr. Canning will have deliver'd to its destination, accompanied by a few lines from Mr. Canning expressive of the King's thanks.

The King wishes that Mr. Canning had not omitted the mentioning the state of his health, which the King sincerely hopes by this time is quite re-establish'd. The King will write to Lord Granville in the course of a day or two[2] (Harewood MSS.).

1. Lord Liverpool's apoplectic seizure on the 17th ended his political life. For the struggle for power between Canning and Wellington which ended in Canning's becoming Prime Minister on 10 April, see A. Aspinall, *The Formation of Canning's Ministry* (Royal Historical Society, Camden Third Series, vol. LIX [1937]).

2. Granville returned home on leave for a short period, and was offered but refused the Foreign Secretaryship.

Royal Lodge, 31 Mar. 1827
Private. The King sends his very kind regards to Mr. Canning. The King quite approves of the course Mr. Canning has taken in the communication which Mr. Canning has made to the Cabinet.[1]

The King proposes to be in town on Thursday (Harewood MSS.).

Royal Lodge, 11.30 p.m., Tuesday, 3 Apr. 1827
Private. The King sends his very kind regards to Mr. Canning.

The King is most truly gratified with the intelligence convey'd in Mr. Canning's note[2] that the Court of Spain appears, at last to have open'd her eyes as to her real & true interests, & it cannot be less pleasing to Mr. Canning *personally*, as it is quite evident, & beyond all power of contradiction, that this result is alone to be attributed to the *correct view* which Mr. Canning has taken of the relative situations of the different Powers interested, & to the ability, steadiness & firmness with which he has conducted the whole of this most intricate & difficult negotiation in all its branches, to its present most fortunate issue.

The King laments that owing to a misapprehension on the part of one of the King's servants respecting Mr. Canning's messenger, the King has unavoidably been prevented from giving an earlier acknowledgement of Mr. Canning's very wellcome note of the last evening (Harewood MSS.).

St. James's Palace, 3.30 p.m., Tuesday, 10 Apr. 1827
Private. The King sends his very kind regards to Mr. Canning, & desires to see him at St. James's Palace, as soon as he can conveniently come after this note shall have reach'd him[3] (Harewood MSS.).

1. The King wished to evade his responsibility for choosing a new Prime Minister by leaving to the Cabinet the choice of a Premier from among those Peers holding Lord Liverpool's views on general questions. Peel and Canning agreed that such a proceeding was unconstitutional and objectionable in principle, and Canning informed the King on the 31st that he had withheld from the Cabinet the King's communication on this point.

2. *Letters of George IV*, iii. 213 ('arrangements for the settlement of all difficulties between Spain and Portugal, & for the general tranquillization of the Peninsula').

3. The King then instructed Canning to plan the reconstruction of the Government.

St. James's Palace, 3.30 p.m., 1 May 1827

Private. In regard to the office of Woods & Forrests [*sic*], I have no particular objection that Mr. Charles Grant,[1] although I do not know him, should *temporarily* hold it, until Lord Lowther[2] can take it. The Lonsdale interest is too great an object to be put aside. The more you can strengthen yourself by the Tory Party, the greater security I feel, in the stability & permanency of my present Government. You see that I am all sincerity towards you. One word more on the subject of the Woods & Forrests. My comfort & tranquillity, are so intimately mix'd up in this office, that I must consider myself, & myself only in whatever arrangements are made.[3] If the Duke of Montrose[4] cannot come here tomorrow at three o'clock, let him send his & Lord Graham's[5] keas [*sic*] & wands by Mr. Mash of the Chamberlain's Office.

P.S. Pray do not forget Lady Glenlyon's[6] ticket to pass through the Horse Guards & Park (Harewood MSS.).

1. Charles Grant, Lord Glenelg (1778–1866). M.P. for the Inverness Burghs, 1811–18; for Inverness-shire, 1818–35. A Lord of the Treasury, 1813–19; Irish Secretary, 1818–21; Vice-President of the Board of Trade, 1823–7, and President (and also Treasurer of the Navy), September 1827–June 1828; President of the Board of Control, 1830–4; Secretary of State for War and the Colonies, 1835–9. Peerage, 11 May 1835.

2. William, Viscount Lowther (1787–1872) had this courtesy title from 7 April 1807 when his father was created Earl of Lonsdale, to 19 March 1844 when he succeeded as 2nd Earl. M.P. for Westmorland, 1813–31 and 1832–41; for Dunwich, 1832. A Lord of the Admiralty, 1809; a Commissioner of the India Board, 1810–18; a Lord of the Treasury, 1813–27; Chief Commissioner of Woods and Forests, 1828–30; Vice-President of the Board of Trade and Treasurer of the Navy, 1834–5. Summoned to House of Lords in his father's Barony of Lowther, 8 September 1841. Lord President of the Council, 1852.

3. Charles Grant remained Vice-President of the Board of Trade. Lord Lowther resigned his seat at the Treasury Board, and he was appointed Chief Commissioner of Woods and Forests by Wellington in June 1828—the office which Arbuthnot resigned in April 1827, and to which Lord Carlisle succeeded at the end of May.

4. The Duke of Montrose was succeeded as Lord Chamberlain by the Duke of Devonshire on 15 May.

5. The Marquess of Graham (1799–1874) was so styled from 1790, when his father succeeded as 4th Duke of Montrose, until 30 December 1836 when he succeeded as 5th Duke. M.P. for Cambridge, 1825–32; Vice-Chamberlain of the Household, 1821–7; Commissioner of the India Board, 1828–30; Lord Steward of the Household, 1852–3; Chancellor of the Duchy of Lancaster, 1858–9; Postmaster-General, 1866–8.

6. On 19 May 1810 Lord James Murray (1782–1837), who was created Baron Glenlyon on 17 July 1821, married Lady Emily Frances Percy (1789–1844), daughter of the 2nd Duke of Northumberland.

St. James's Palace, 6 May 1827

Private. I thank you for your note[1] of last night relative to Lord Mansfield, but you must remember, that *my* letter[2] is, to the ArBp. of Canterbury, next to myself the Head of the Church, & absolutely necessary for the purpose of putting aside a foul calumny on my Protestant faith conduct & honour. I have mention'd what I have done without reserve, & I care no more what Lord Mansfield or any of those with whom he acts, or advizes, if the object be the aspersion of *my* character, their Sovereign, than I do, for the most contemptible individual in the country[3] (Harewood MSS.).

St. James's Palace, 8 p.m., 27 May 1827

Pray come to me about ten o clock this eveg. I will not detain you five minutes (Harewood MSS.).

St. James's Palace, 11 a.m., Friday, 1 June 1827

Private. What could your note yesterday mean to Sr. William, stating that Ld. Albert Conyngham was arriv'd with dispatches from Vienna? The messenger will wait your answer (Harewood MSS.).

Royal Lodge, 13 June 1827

Private. I will talk to you on the subject of the Sheriffs & Address when I have the pleasure of seeing you here tomorrow. Pray acquaint Mr. Sturges Bourne[4] with this when you see him, as it will obviate the

1. *Letters of George IV*, iii. 228 (5 May).

2. Ibid. (4 May).

3. Mansfield, speaking in the Lords on the 2nd, implied that George III, had he then been King, as a staunch 'Protestant', would never have consented to the formation of a Cabinet in which advocates of Catholic emancipation were in a majority. And he pointed out that George IV had consented to these appointments after he had assured the Archbishop of Canterbury of his 'determination to exclude from a preponderance in his councils those who supported a measure which he could not conscientiously support'.

Lord Mansfield (1777–1840) was styled Viscount Stormont from 1793 to 1 September 1796 when he succeeded as 3rd Earl. He was an ultra Tory.

4. William Sturges-Bourne (1769–1845), M.P. for Hastings, 1798–1802; for Christchurch, 1802–12 and 1818–26; for Bandon, 1815–18; for Ashburton, 1826–30; for Milborne Port, 1830–1. One of Canning's close friends. Joint Secretary of the Treasury, May 1804–January 1806; a Lord of the Treasury, March 1807–October 1809; Commissioner for the Affairs of India, September 1814–February 1822; Home Secretary, 30 April 1827–July 1827; First Commissioner of Woods and Forests, 23 July 1827–January 1828.

necessity of any further correspondence to all parties upon this matter[1] (Harewood MSS.).

Royal Lodge, Friday, 6 July 1827
Private. I shall be quite ready to receive you on Monday next the 9th int. at one oclock p.m. I sincerely hope that you have recruited your health, not a little since the Prorogation took place (Harewood MSS.).

Royal Lodge, 25 July 1827
Private. I am very sorry for the delay I fear that I have been apparently the means of creating in the appointment of the Duke of Buccleugh[2] (which I entirely approve of) owing to my having return'd the box to you again without having answer'd its contents. It is alone to be attributed to the mistake of one of my servants who, finding that the box was lock'd, fancied therefore that it was done with, & therefore, packed it off, with a great number of others, of which I had just completed the signatures. As to the Deanery, & the vacant Canonry, you have my entire approbation to appoint Mr. Baggott,[3] to the first, & the Revd. Mr. Markham,[4] who is the grandson of my Preceptor, the late Archbishop of York, to the Canonry of Windsor, vacated by Dr. Baggott's advancement to the Deanery of Canterbury. I have heard the highest possible character of Mr. Markham; to render him more distinct to you, as to who he is, perhaps I had just better further add that he is either the second or third son (but which of the two I am not quite positive) of the late William Markham, the late Archbishop's eldest son, to whom he left whatever estates he had purchas'd in the county of York. I shall certainly be very glad to see you any morning at the end of the week, that may be convenient to you, but I wish that you had said a little more, of your approach to convalescence (Harewood MSS.).

1. The Sheriffs of London and Middlesex wished to see the King to learn H.M.'s pleasure as to the time of receiving an Address from the City (*Letters of George IV*, iii. 250 [12 June]).

2. The 5th Duke of Buccleuch (1806–84) succeeded his father in 1819. He was to be appointed Lord Lieutenant of the County of Edinburgh as soon as he became of age (Canning's letter of the 22nd, in *Letters of George IV*, iii. 271).

3. Richard Bagot (1782–1854), brother of Lord Bagot and of Sir Charles Bagot. Dean of Canterbury, 1827–45; Bishop of Oxford, 1829–45; of Bath and Wells, 1845–54.

4. The Rev. David Frederick Markham (1800–53), Vicar of Addingham, 1825; of Stillingfleet, 1826; Canon of Windsor, 1827; Rector of Great Horkesley, Essex, 1838; Rural Dean of Dedham, 1850. There is a memorial brass to him in St. George's Chapel, Windsor. He dined with William IV and Queen Adelaide every Sunday during their residence at Windsor Castle; and he arranged the burial of Queen Adelaide on 13 December 1849.

Royal Lodge, Saturday night, 28 July 1827

Private. The stray box has at last been found & I now return it, & I shall take good care that a similar blunder shall not again in a hurry be repeated. I shall hold myself in readiness to receive you on Monday & hope that you will be at the Royal Lodge not later than one o'clock (Harewood MSS.).

3459   THE KING TO THE MARQUESS OF LANSDOWNE

Royal Lodge, 1 Aug. 1827

The King sends his kind regards to Lord Lansdowne, and the King having had a communication with Lord Goderich and some members of his Cabinet this morning, it would be a satisfaction to the King to have the pleasure of seeing Lord Lansdowne at the Royal Lodge tomorrow (Saturday) at one o'clock[1] (Bowood MSS.).

3460   THE KING TO THE EARL OF HARROWBY

Royal Lodge, 9 Aug. 1827

Private. The King desires that Lord Harrowby will be persuaded that if anything could add to the deep regret which the King feels at the great loss the country & himself have sustained by the death of poor Mr. Canning, it would be, the knowledge that he was to be depriv'd of the assistance of Lord Harrowby at so critical a moment, & after so many years of faithful service.

The King assures Lord Harrowby of the continuation of his best regards whether in or out of office[2] (Harrowby MSS.).

3461   THE KING TO MRS CANNING[3]

Royal Lodge, 17 Aug. 1827

Private. I must break in upon your deep sorrow for the purpose of expressing to you my sincere condolence upon the severe affliction with

1. Canning was dying. He died on the 8th.

2. Lord Harrowby was feeling the burden of his increasing years, and the Duke of Portland, Mrs. Canning's brother-in-law, succeeded him as Lord President of the Council.

3. Joan Canning (*c.* 1777–1837), who married Canning on 8 July 1800, was the youngest

which it has pleased the Almighty to visit you by the death of your lamented husband. It is in vain at this moment to hold out the language of consolation that can only be obtain'd through the mercy of God & in bowing with resignation to His Divine Will.

I can, now only shew what my opinions of Mr. Canning's splendid talents really were, *through you*; & in confirmation of that, I desire to offer you, (if it should suit your own private views) a Peerage in your own person (Harewood MSS.).

3462 THE KING TO THE MARQUESS OF LANSDOWNE

Royal Lodge, 22 Aug. 1827
Private. The King sends his regards to Lord Lansdowne.

There is a poor old man of the name of James Mansells whom the King would wish Lord Lansdowne to place in the situation of a Poor Brother of the Charter House, and which is now vacant. The poor man is to be found at Mr. Roberts's, King's Mews, Pimlico (Bowood MSS.).

3463 LETTERS FROM THE KING TO WILLIAM HUSKISSON

Royal Lodge, 20 Sept. 1827
Secret and Confidential. The King sends his very kind regards to Mr. Huskisson.

The King was desirous to have spoken to Mr. Huskisson (if he could conveniently have done so, previous to Mr. Huskisson's leaving London) upon a matter of great interest to the King, and which will contribute much to the King's comfort.

The King is very desirous not to interrupt Mr. Huskisson's short relaxation from the labours of office, and which is so necessary for the re-establishment of his health, and which the King feels is so very important both for his own as well as for the service and best interests of the country, at this very critical moment. The King therefore prefers communicating his wishes to Mr. Huskisson through the medium of his pen, to the putting Mr. Huskisson to all the trouble of a journey to the Royal Lodge merely for the sake of a short interview of a few minutes.

But now to the point. The appointment of Governor to the Island of

daughter and co-heir of Major-General John Scott. On 22 January 1828 she was created Viscountess Canning. Difficulties with regard to income had to be surmounted before she felt able to accept the honour (*Letters of George IV*, iii. 289).

Jamaica, being now finally vacant, by the Duke of Manchester's[1] acceptance of the Post Office, the King is most anxious that Sr. Francis Burton, who has been for some years Lt. Govr. of Canada, and universally and most justly esteem'd and belov'd there, should be *now* appointed, as the Duke of Manchester's successor in the Island of Jamaica; and that then, Lt. Genl. Sr. Hilgrove Turner, now Governor of the Bermudas, should follow Sr. Francis Burton in the situation of Lt. Govr. of Canada. This will place the Govt. of the Bermudas entirely at Mr. Huskisson's disposal, and contribute very materially and essentially to the comfort and gratification of the King's feelings.

The King sincerely hopes to receive from Mr. Huskisson a good report of his speedy, if not complete re-establishment of his health.[2] (Add. MSS. 38751, fos. 32–3)

Royal Lodge, Tuesday night, 25 Sept. 1827

Private. The King sends his very kind regards to Mr. Huskisson and regrets that he should have sent a box of which Mr. Huskisson had not the kea. But it is a matter of no consequence, for if Mr. Huskisson will come to the Royal Lodge either tomorrow (Wednesday) or the next day (Thursday) at one o'clock, it will answer every purpose. (Add. MSS. 38751, fo. 68)

Royal Lodge, Thursday, 11 Oct. 1827

The King sends his very kind regards to Mr. Huskisson.

The King highly approves of the Govt. of Canada being propos'd to the Duke of Gordon upon Lord Dalhousie's[3] being nominated to succeed Lord Combermere[4] in the command of the Army in India.

1. The 5th Duke of Manchester (1771–1843), styled Viscount Mandeville from the death of his elder brother, 23 February 1772, to 2 September 1788 when he succeeded his father as Duke. Governor of Jamaica, 1808–27; Postmaster-General, 1827–30.

2. Huskisson, who was now Secretary of State for War and the Colonies, replied next day, saying that he would communicate with the Prime Minister on the subject (fo. 39, and *Letters of George IV*, iii. 312).

3. The 9th Earl of Dalhousie (1770–1838). Joined the army, 1788; Lieutenant-Colonel, 1793; Major-General, 1808; Lieutenant-General, 1813; General, 1830. Succeeded his father, 15 November 1787; Scottish Representative Peer, 1796–1806 and 1807–18. Lieutenant-Governor of Nova Scotia, 1816–19; Governor-in-Chief of Canada, 1819–28; Commander-in-Chief in India, 1 January 1830–2. Created Baron Dalhousie [U.K.], 11 August 1815.

4. Sir Stapleton Cotton, Viscount Combermere (1773–1865). Entered the army, 1790; Colonel, 1800; Major-General, 1805; Lieutenant-General, 1812; General, 1825. M.P. for

Sr. Lowry Cole[1] having signified his preference for the Govt. of the Cape, to the remaining at the Mauritius, by a letter to Mr. Huskisson, the King considers that appointment as fix'd, and therefore the King highly approves also of Mr. Huskisson's idea of leaving that Govt. vacant for the present, subject to its being offer'd to Sr. Wm. Clinton, whenever his command in Portugal shall have ceas'd, and in lieu of the Lt. Gen[ship]. of the Ordnance, which he now holds; and the King need hardly express to Mr. Huskisson how entirely the King's sentiments are in unison with Mr. Huskisson's in the further object of appointing Sr. Herbert Taylor to the Lt. G[l]. of the Ordnance, so soon as Sr. Wm. Clinton shall have receiv'd the appointment to the Mauritius.[2] (Add. MSS. 38751, fos. 194–5)

Royal Lodge, 20 Oct. 1827
Private. The King sends his very kind regards to Mr. Huskisson, and incloses a letter which the King has receiv'd this day from the Duke of Gordon.

The King is not quite clear from the singular wording of the letter, whether the Duke's feeling as to employment or service is to be consider'd as referring to the specifick object upon which Mr. Huskisson has written to him, or whether it means to embrace every sort of connexion with office at the present moment.

The King desires that Mr. H[n]. will preserve the letter, and that when he shall have read it over, that he will then, at his leisure, acquaint the King with his sentiments upon it, and with what Mr. Huskisson may suggest as best to be done in consequence. (Add. MSS. 38751, fo. 273)

Newark, 1806–14. Succeeded father as 2nd Baronet, 24 August 1809. K.B., 1812; G.C.B., 1815. Created Baron Combermere 17 May 1814. Governor and Commander-in-Chief of Barbados, 1817–20; Commander-in-Chief in Ireland, 1822–5; Commander-in-Chief in East Indies, 1825–30. Created Viscount, 8 February 1827. Field-Marshal, 1855.

1. Sir Galbraith Lowry Cole (1772–1842). Entered the army, 1787; Major, 1793; Lieutenant-Colonel, 1794; Colonel, 1801; Major-General, 1808; Lieutenant-General and K.B., 1813; Governor of Mauritius, 1823–8; of Cape Colony, 1828–33. General, 1830. M.P. for Fermanagh, 1803–23.

2. Clinton did not go to Mauritius, and Sir Herbert Taylor consequently was not appointed Lieutenant-General of the Ordnance.

3464 THE KING TO THE MARQUESS OF LANSDOWNE

Royal Lodge, Saturday evening, 10 Nov. 1827

Private. The King sends his kind regards to Lord Lansdowne.

The King will, in consequence of Lord Lansdowne's letter, come to St. James's Palace on Friday next, the 16th, to hold the Council for receiving the Recorder's report, *punctually* at one o'clock p.m.

It will always be a matter of pleasure to the King to receive Lord Lansdowne whenever he has any matters of business to communicate (Bowood MSS.).

3465 THE KING TO THE EARL OF HARROWBY

St. James's Palace, Friday, 14 Dec. 1827

Private. The King sends his very kind regards to Lord Harrowby.

The King desires that Lord Harrowby, upon the receipt of this, will be so good as to come to the King, to Windsor Lodge, but, in his way thither, to pass through London, for the purpose of seeing Mr. Huskisson.

The King most *urgently desires* that Lord Harrowby will *not mention* the contents of this note *to any one*[1] (Harrowby MSS.).

3466 THE KING TO WILLIAM HUSKISSON

Royal Lodge, 11.30 a.m. Saturday, 15 Dec. 1827

Most Private. The King sends his kind regards to Mr. Huskisson.

The King desires that Mr. Huskisson will inform the Lord Chancellor[2] that the King does entirely unite with the opinion and the sentiments express'd in Mr. Huskisson's letter[3] (which has just reach'd the

---

1. Goderich, unfit for his situation, had in effect invited the King to find another Prime Minister. But Harrowby refused the Premiership on account of his declining health, and Goderich remained Prime Minister until 8 January 1828, by which time the Government was on the point of breaking up.

2. Sir John Singleton Copley, Lord Lyndhurst (1772–1863). Chief Justice of Chester, 1818–19; Solicitor-General, 1819–24. Knighted, October 1819. Attorney-General, 1824–6; Master of the Rolls, September 1826–April 1827. M.P. for Yarmouth (Isle of Wight), 1818; for Ashburton, 1818–26; for Cambridge University, 1826–7. Peerage, 25 April 1827. Lord Chancellor, April 1827–November 1830; Lord Chief Baron of the Exchequer, 1831–4; Lord Chancellor, 1834–5, and 1841–6.

3. *Letters of George IV*, iii. 350.

468

King) that the thrice propos'd communication should be made to Lord Goderich.

The King thanks Mr. Huskisson for the communication of the intelligence contain'd in Lord Lansdowne's note, and which corroborates entirely accounts of a similar nature which had already reach'd the King some days, and which also comes from a quarter which the King thinks may be well relied upon, both in point of its correctness as well as its veracity.[1]

P.S. The King has commanded the messenger to return immediately to Mr. Huskisson. (Add. MSS. 38752, fo. 248)

[*Undated, endorsed, 16 Dec. 1827*]
Private. The King sends his kind regards to Mr. Huskisson, and, in the box, returns Lord Harrowby's note.

The King will be prepar'd to receive Lord Harrowby at the Royal Lodge at two o'clock tomorrow p.m., and the King suggests to Mr. Huskisson that it is very desirable that Mr. Huskisson either should accompany Lord Harrowby or at least should come to the Royal Lodge much about the same time, as there is no foreseeing with any degree of certainty whether there may not be some circumstance or other which may arise out of or in consequence of the interview of tomorrow which may call for immediate attention in some shape or other. The King desires therefore that Mr. Huskisson will communicate this to the Lord Chancellor and then settle with him as to the expediency of the proposal of Mr. Huskisson's attendance at the Royal Lodge tomorrow. (Add. MSS. 38752, fo. 268)

3467   THE KING TO THE MARQUESS OF LANSDOWNE
Royal Lodge, 18 Dec. 1827
Private. The King sends his kind regards to Lord Lansdowne.

Though the King is but little acquainted with the names of either of the gentlemen laid before him for the situation of Head Librarian to the British Museum, the King thinks that considering the length of service

1. It was rumoured that Lord Grey, who had opposed the Whig junction with Canning in April and May, had coalesced with the ex-Tory Ministers with the object of defeating the Goderich Ministry at the beginning of the Parliamentary Session, and of forcing the King to take them back. The King told Huskisson that he would not submit 'to have a Government of Ultra Tories, formed upon the Whig principle of being forced upon him by this sort of combination'.

in the British Museum under the late Mr. Planta[1] and the tabulated works published by Mr. Ellis,[2] his pretensions and claims are by far the best and most just, and that therefore Mr. Ellis must have the preference, and Lord Lansdowne in consequence will be so good as to notify Mr. Ellis's nomination accordingly to those persons whose duty it is to carry it into effect.

The King desires that Lord Lansdowne will return his acknowledgments to the members of the Thames Tunnel Company for the very beautiful model which they have been so good as to transmit to the King through the medium of Lord Lansdowne[3] (Bowood MSS.).

3468   THE KING TO THE DUKE OF DEVONSHIRE

Royal Lodge, 14 Jan. 1828

Private. I write to you from my sick bed. You must have heard what has happen'd in the Govt.; and my object in writing to you is to express my sincere hopes that you will remain as you now are, in my Family and about my person, and that my friend Carlisle will decide, to continue in the Cabinet. I cannot help looking upon you both as my personal and attach'd friends.

I desire to add, that to the Marquis of Lansdowne, I have nothing but the kindest feeling[4] (Chatsworth MSS.).

3469   THE KING TO THE MARQUESS OF LANSDOWNE

Royal Lodge, Thursday, 17 Jan. 1828

Private. The King sends his very kind regards to Lord Lansdowne.

The King has given the title of Durham to Mr. Lambton,[5] as the King understands that Mr. Lambton propos'd it.

1. Joseph Planta, senior (1744–1827), Assistant Librarian, 1773; Keeper of the MSS., 1776; Principal Librarian, 1799–1827.

2. Sir Henry Ellis (1777–1869). Keeper of the Printed Books, 1806–27; Principal Librarian, 1827.

3. See Lansdowne's letter to the King on the 17th (*Letters of George IV*, iii. 352).

4. The leading Whigs who had joined Canning in 1827, refused to serve under Wellington, an anti-Catholic Prime Minister. As Lansdowne's views were known, no offer was actually made to him. Carlisle resigned his office of Lord Privy Seal, and the Duke of Devonshire his office of Lord Chamberlain.

5. John George Lambton, 1st Earl of Durham (1792–1840). M.P. for Co. Durham, 1813–28; created Baron Durham, 29 January 1828. Lord Privy Seal, 1830–3; Ambassador to Russia,

The list the King desires thus to stand:

Mrs. Canning
Sr. Hy. Wellesley
Sr. Chs. Stuart
Sr. Wm. A'Court
Ld. Rosebery[1]
Ld. Clanwilliam[2]
Mr. Lambton
Mr. Bootle Wilbraham.[3]

(Bowood MSS.).

3470   THE KING TO THE DUKE OF DEVONSHIRE

Royal Lodge, 6.30 p.m., Wednesday, 23 Jan. 1828

Prince Lieven has this instant left me, and I lose not a moment in forwarding to you a pacquet containing the Order of St. Andrew (and a very gracious and explanatory letter from the Emperor[4] himself to you) which I authorize you to wear; indeed, through Prince Lieven, I had convey'd to the Emperor my desire that this mark of distinction should be conferr'd upon you and I therefore I [*sic*] feel highly pleas'd that it is through me that this mark of the Emperor's regard is transmitted to you (Chatsworth MSS.).

1835–7. Earldom, 23 March 1833. Governor-General of Canada, January–December 1838. Joint author of the famous Durham Report on Canada.

1. The 4th Earl of Rosebery [S.] (1783–1868) had been styled Viscount Primrose until 25 March 1814 when he succeeded his father. M.P. for Helston, 1805–6; for Cashel, 1806–7. Representative Peer, 1818, 1820 and 1826. Created Baron Rosebery [U.K.], 26 January 1828.

2. The 3rd Earl of Clanwilliam [I.] (1795–1879) succeeded his father, 3 September 1805. Castlereagh's private secretary, 1817–19; Under-Secretary of State for Foreign Affairs, 1822–3; Minister to Prussia, 1823–8. Created Baron Clanwilliam [U.K.], 26 January 1828.

3. Edward Bootle-Wilbraham, 1st Baron Skelmersdale (1771–1853). M.P. for Westbury, 1795–6; for Newcastle-under-Lyme, 1796–1812; for Clitheroe, 1812–18; for Dover, 1818–28. His father's family name was Wilbraham; his mother's, Bootle. In 1814 he took the name of Bootle before instead of after, that of Wilbraham. He was one of Canning's friends.

For these peerages, promised whilst Goderich was still Prime Minister, see *Letters of George IV*, iii. 353, 357.

4. Nicholas I.

3471 THE KING TO LORD FORESTER[1]

[Royal Lodge, 1 Feb. 1828]

Private. You do me but justice in beleiving that I do most sincerely participate in every event which takes place in your family, & it is therefore that I do most cordially congratulate you upon the present occasion, as it seems to afford you all such general satisfaction. I beg that you will express these same sentiments for me to Lady Kate, together with my best & kindest regards & remembrances. After all the trouble you was so good as to give yourself respecting the grey horse I could not bear to plague you with any more letters upon that head; but I am sure that you will be pleas'd to learn that he completely answers in every respect; he is certainly as yet, being a very high-courag'd horse, a little warm & eager in company, but this is a trifling defect which is mending every day.

I am sorry to say I am still a cripple in my chair from the remains of gout in my knee; the first attack which I had of it is now nearly two months ago, one month of which I have been entirely confin'd to my bed as it was mix'd up with violent rhumatick seizure & spasms in my chest, shoulders & loins, at the same time that I was completely laid upon my back with the gout in both my feet, ankles & right knee. As you say nothing of yourself, I do most sincerely hope that you are not only well at the present moment, but that you have for some time past been entirely free from this most cruel visitation. I am looking forward with great pleasure to the hope of seeing you quite in force when you come to London (Earl of Bradford MSS.).

3472 LETTERS FROM THE KING TO THE DUKE OF WELLINGTON

Royal Lodge, 3 Feb. 1828

Private. I will, according to your request,[2] hold a Council on Tuesday next, here, at the Royal Lodge at three o'clock p.m. With respect to the Recorder's Report, I have already written to Mr. Peel, that in my present state of debility, that that is quite impossible, *now*, but that I will then, (if *he* should attend the Council) have further conversation with you and him upon that subject.

As to the elevation of Dr. Laffan[3] (for I believe that is the way he spells

1. Cecil Weld-Forester, 1st Baron Forester (1767–1828). M.P. for Wenlock, 1790–1820; Peerage (a Coronation one), 17 July 1821. On 16 June 1800 he married Katherine Mary (1779–1829), daughter of 4th Duke of Rutland. He died on 23 May. The reference may be to him in No. 3394 (the King spelt his name Forrester on both occasions).

2. The Duke's letters of the 2nd are in the *Wellington Civil Despatches*, iv. 253–4.

3. Sir Joseph de Courcy Laffan (1786–1848), Physician to Lord Anglesey, the Lord Lieutenant

his name) to a Baronetage, Anglesey's health is a matter of too much importance in my opinion, for me not to give my cordial assent to it (Wellington MSS.).

Royal Lodge, 9 Feb. 1828
Private. I will with great pleasure receive Lord Goderich on Tuesday next, as well as Lord Hill to be sworn of the Privy Council.[1] Perhaps, as you will have to announce this to Lord Goderich you will at the same time, either yourself, or through him, acquaint Mr. Wynn that I will take the same opportunity of receiving him, for he has also applied for an audience, in retiring from office (Wellington MSS.).

Royal Lodge, 10 Feb. 1828
Private. Wednesday at the same hour will be quite as convenient to me for the Council as Tuesday would be, therefore let it be so; and you must be so good as to notify the change of day accordingly to the different individuals who are to come down, or otherwise they will be put to unnecessary inconvenience (Wellington MSS.).

Royal Lodge, 14 Feb. 1828
Private. I lose no time in forwarding to you the inclos'd letter which I have just receiv'd, and I am the *more desirous* of doing so because I cannot help taking no inconsiderable share of blame to myself in not having mention'd the subject to you some time ago, when I first heard of Dr. Hook's death,[2] and as I feel myself not only interested, but also strongly committed upon the present occasion. Nothing but the multiplicity of business and the innumerable important and interesting topics which I have had of late to discuss with you could have made me forget, (even temporarily) this matter. I can vouch not only for the truth of every word contain'd in this letter but for the excellent character and unceasing

of Ireland, 1 March 1828–March 1829 (when the Duke of Northumberland succeeded him). The letter shows the incorrectness of the *D.N.B.* statement that the doctor owed his baronetcy to his successful treatment of an illness of the Duke of York.

1. The Duke's letters of the 8th are in the *Wellington Civil Despatches*, iv. 258–9. The Duke's Cabinet, on its formation, had refused to allow him to remain Commander-in-Chief of the Army after his appointment as Prime Minister.

2. The Dean of Worcester died on 5 February.

473

exertions, now for years, of this individual, but as a clergyman and zealous supporter of the Establish'd Church, and as a most active magistrate in the districts surrounding his residence, and which have so strongly intitled him to my protection. I should not have written so much at length to you, did I not, as I now repeat, feel that it is entirely owing to my forgetfulness that I did not mention to you before my intentions with respect to the Deanery of Worcester[1] (Wellington MSS.).

[1]. The following letter from the Rev. Townshend Forester (1772–1841), was enclosed. Written from Rectory Broseley, Shiffnal, it was dated the 11th: 'Sire, Crippled as my poor brother, Lord Forester, at this moment is, from a severe attack of gout in both his hands; and fearing it might be too late to delay writing 'till he is able to do so himself I have ventured upon this unusual and I fear presumptuous method of conveying my humble petition to your Majesty's Royal ear.

'I have now resided upwards of 25 years in the centre of a working population of nearly a hundred thousand persons, during which period of unexampled difficulty and danger I have by my own personal exertions and watchfulness been able to maintain the peace and quiet of the neighbourhood, and to cause the laws to be duly respected and obeyed without ever once having had occasion to call in the assistance of the military; notwithstanding in the two years immediately preceeding my residence in this neighbourhood military aid was had recourse to not fewer than fifteen times. I have letters by me now from Lord Sidmouth, the late Duke of Portland, and Mr. Perceval thanking me for my public services in language too flattering for me to mention; and I can safely aver without the fear of contradiction that no common workman who earns his daily bread by the sweat of his brow has ever laboured harder than I have done night and day both in body and mind to make myself serviceable to my country, and useful to my fellow creatures: and it was upon these grounds that my brother in the year 1817 applied to your Majesty, when the Deanery of Worcester became vacant by the death of Dr. Onslow, for my appointment to that Deanery, when your Majesty was most graciously pleased to signify it as your Royal will and pleasure that I might be appointed thereto: but the Earl of Liverpool making it a particular point at that time to nominate his own relation Dr. Jenkinson to the Deanery of Worcester, your Majesty was most graciously pleased to acquiesce in his, Lord Liverpool's, wishes, but upon this express condition: viz. 'That Lord Liverpool should promote his relation with as little delay as possible in order to make room for Dr. Forester at the Deanery at Worcester'. In the year 1825 when Dr. Jackson was promoted to the See of St. David's etc., I never heard of his promotion 'till after the Deanery was filled by the appointment of Dr. Hook; therefore no application was at that time made in my behalf. The Deanery I am sorry to say has again become vacant by the lamentable decease of Dr. Hook.

'I do therefore most humbly implore your most gracious Majesty to issue your Royal mandate that the vacancy caused in the Deanery of Worcester by the death of Dr. Hook may be filled up by the appointment thereto of your most gracious Majesty's most devoted, most faithful and obedient servant and subject.

P.S. The only piece of preferment I covet or shall ever ask at your Majesty's Royal hands is the Deanery of Worcester.'

3473 THE KING TO WILLIAM LAMB[1]

Royal Lodge, 16 Feb. 1828

Confidential. There is a Captn. Fitzgerald that I am desirous from particular circumstances to have made in Ireland, either an Inspector General of Police or local Magistrate of Police. He has sat upon the Middlesex Bench of Justices, so that he is competent. Write to me, as soon as you can do this.

Your aff[te] friend (Panshanger MSS.).

3474 LETTERS FROM THE KING TO THE DUKE OF WELLINGTON

Royal Lodge, 16 Feb. 1828

Private. I write for the purpose of communicating with you on the subject of Windsor Castle, Buckingham Palace etc. etc., etc. It has been clearly explain'd to me what your intentions are on all the points. I understand that you will ask for a further grant this year of one hundred and fifty thousand pounds to be appropriated to Windsor Castle. This is very satisfactory to my feelings. Pray *guard* the Chancellor of the Exchequer,[2] against making any promise in the House that Windsor Castle will not require a further grant, as I fear that this sum will not complete it. Not the slightest alteration has ever been made in the original plan of architecture, and the additional expense incurr'd has entirely arisen from the age of the Castle. God knows, at my time of life, the nation has a much greater interest in this Royal edifice than I can have, but I should be truly sorry not to see it completed. I find that the Commissioners are embarassed respecting the ormoulu furniture which I thought it right to have bought under the circumstances of Mr. Watson Taylor's[3] sale; it is quite appropriate for Windsor Castle, and worth double what it cost, but, my friend,[4] who manages my private affairs, will from some fund or other relieve the Commission from this expense. I may however, as well take this opportunity of observing that there is now *already* in Windsor Castle twenty thousand pounds worth of my *own private property*, the estimate of which is now at the Treasury, and *this* was made under the cognizance of the present Chancellor[5] (then

1. Then Irish Secretary.

2. Henry Goulburn.

3. George Watson Taylor (*c.* 1770–1841). M.P. for Newport (Isle of Wight), 1816–18; for Seaford, 1818–20; for East Looe, 1820–6; for Devizes, 1826–32.

4. Knighton.

5. Lyndhurst.

Attorney-General) and Mr. Herries (then Secretary of the Treasury) and under the authority of Lord Liverpool and Mr. Robinson, (then Chancellor of the Exchequer). This money, I shall some day call for, which I propose to lay out on my present habitation. I find that the present embarassment of the Woods and Forests will not permit the stables at Cumberland Lodge to be thought of this year, but that the Board of Works will set aside, a sum, to complete the other little things connected with the ornament and comfort of my Park, and which in truth, is my only recreation and amusement. I find that you have had the goodness to manage one hundred thousand pounds this year for the new Palace in St. James' Park, and that we may calculate on the similar sum the next year. I am much oblig'd to you for this attention as it is so intimately connected with my comfort. By this detail you will perceive the whole arrangment, has been faithfully explain'd, with which I am quite satisfied[1] (Wellington MSS.).

Royal Lodge, 22 Feb. 1828
Private. I return you according to your desire the warrant for the new Bishop[2] in Ireland, with my signature *now affix'd* to it, for I think (after the Petition which you sent for my satisfaction, presented to Parliament, from the Archbishop of Dublin,[3] sign'd by the Clergy of his diocese and to which the Dean of St. Patrick has also inscrib'd his name) it is impossible to entertain any further doubts respecting his feelings or intentions of supporting to the fullest extent our Establish'd Church. With respect to the gentleman who you have propos'd to me, to succeed to the Deanery of St. Patrick's,[4] I am not even acquainted with his name, and therefore I neither do nor can know anything of what his merits are or what his pretensions are which may entitle him to the present recommendation; but, I have that *entire reliance in your feelings being in complete unison with mine on this great and vital question,*[5] that I cannot hesitate a moment in giving my assent to your recommendation of this gentleman, for I am sure that you would never think of laying his name before me if he were not fully competent to, and qualified (according to

1. See Wellington's reply on the 21st in the *Wellington Civil Despatches*, iv. 269.

2. The Hon. Richard Ponsonby (1772–1853), son of the 1st Baron Ponsonby. Bishop of Killaloe, 1828; of Derry, 1831–53.

3. Dr. William Magee.

4. The brother of George Robert Dawson, M.P. for Londonderry Co. and Secretary of the Treasury.

5. The Catholic question.

my understanding upon these matters) for the dignified station in which he is about to be plac'd.

I shall say but one word upon the other matter, at present, as I shall have other opportunities of discussing it over at length and in all its different bearings with you. I therefore shall content myself with saying, that you are already in possession of my sentiments in my former letter upon it, and that they continue the same, and that they are not likely to alter, although for the *present* I may concur in the policy in not immediately meeting the subject.[1]

P.S. Before the estimates for the Castle at Windsor are carried to Parliament I do desire to see you and to have some further conversation with you (Wellington MSS.).

Royal Lodge, 1 Mar. 1828
Private. As I intend being in town on Monday evening, and as I trust to your calling upon me in the course of Tuesday's afternoon, I shall postpone all the little I have to say to you upon the arrangments propos'd in your letter of this day, until our meeting[2] (Wellington MSS.).

Royal Lodge, 23 Aug. 1828
The Council is appointed to meet at the Royal Lodge (according to your desire) on Monday next the 25th inst. at 2 o'clk. p.m. (Wellington MSS.).

Windsor Castle, 8.45 a.m., 30 Jan. 1829
Most Private. I have not the smallest objection to your offering the Privy Seal to the Duke of Beaufort, and in the event of his declining it, to Lord Westmorland, to whom, I have every good feeling—But here I must remark, that in *my* opinion, in the Duke of Beaufort, you will gain nothing but *the name*. Perhaps, before you quite fix your determination, you will turn your thoughts for a moment to Lord Eldon upon the present occasion, for I cannot help thinking that he would carry much weight at this particular crisis in the House of Lords upon the public business that is likely to occur, as well as aid and alleviate in all private

1. For the Duke's reply on the 23rd see the *Wellington Civil Despatches*, iv. 273.

2. The Duke endorsed the letter: 'In answer to my letter recommending for the Church preferments.'

and Law business that immense burthen which the Lord Chancellor has to wade through, for as the Lord Chancellor is situated at present, he is quite alone, without any assistance whatsoever.[1]

P.S. I had totally forgotten to send you (as I now do) the name of the very respectable gentleman to whom I gave the vacant Stall here a couple of months ago. His name is Richard Adolphus Musgrave, and he married a Lowther, a distant relation of Lord Lonsdale's (Wellington MSS.).

3475 LETTERS FROM THE KING TO THE DUKE OF CUMBERLAND

Windsor Castle, 1 Feb. 1829

I wish you to take this letter to the King of Prussia, in your hand, to convey to his Majesty the warmest feelings of my personal friendship & attachment to his person.

Upon the death of our poor brother the Duke of York,[2] the late King of Prussia, father of the late Duchess of York[3] (& also of his present Majesty) by a private treaty would have become entitled to the restoration of 40,000 crowns. Now our poor brother, the Duke of York, died as you know, *positively insolvent*. With these matters, Parliament, as you are well aware, can have nothing to do. I have therefore resolv'd to make it a personal affair of my own towards my friend the present King of Prussia, & I have sent over by my confidential servant, my Privy Purse,[4] the said sum of 40,000 crowns, which you will deliver, my dear brother, to the King, with every kind feeling from me, & which you know how so well to express. God bless you.[5] (Add. Georgian 15/24)

1. Lord Ellenborough, who had been Lord Privy Seal since the formation of the Ministry, became President of the Board of Control on 24 September 1828. It was not until 10 June 1829 that Lord Rosslyn, who had been a Whig, became Privy Seal. Wellington's views are in the *Wellington Civil Despatches*, v. 476 (writing to the King on 29 January). The Duke of Beaufort declined office, and so did Westmorland, and the Duke made no offer to Eldon, who had been left out of the Cabinet in January 1828. The Government was now faced with the critical situation in Ireland and the King's hostility to Catholic relief.

2. He died on 5 January 1827.

3. She died on 6 August 1820.

4. Knighton.

5. The Duke and Duchess of Cumberland were then in Berlin.

Windsor Castle, 1 Feb. 1829

Private. I have sent our friend to Berlin, for the purpose of explaining to you the position in which I am at this moment plac'd relative to Ireland.

The affectionate & zealous attachment that you have shewn towards me, in the present crysis I feel most sensibly & be assur'd is deeply engraven on my heart.

You will hear by the same hand that delivers this letter to you, from the Duke of Wellington,[1] & you will find that the Duke is most strongly impress'd that your coming over to England had better be deferr'd for the present. He has given me some sensible reasons for this opinion, which will be stated to you; & knowing as I do the personal friendship & kind feelings the Duke entertains towards you, I feel the more confident, in concurring in the Duke's considerate judgment, in respect to this matter. Nevertheless, I must say that it is a great disappointment to me, but I look forward to the happiness of seeing you, the dear Duchess, & my beloved George,[2] in the Spring.

In the Duke of Wellington's ability to administer the affairs of this country, I have every reason to place the greatest reliance, & I have an equal reliance, that what will happen, such is his integrity, & upright zeal towards me, that no considerations will induce him to suffer the glory of my reign to be tarnished.

I never can say enough to you, upon the strenuous & admirable exertions you have made in the affairs of the Duke of Brunswick.

P.S. Best love to the dear Dss. & to my dear George. (Add. Georgian 15/25)

3476   THE KING TO THE DUKE OF WELLINGTON

Windsor Castle, 7 p.m., Sunday, 8 Feb. 1829

Private. Lord Conyngham[3] has just sent me your letter, and I take up my pen to tell you that I am very sorry to say that he has been really

1. Wellington's letter of the 2nd to the Duke of Cumberland is in *Wellington Civil Despatches*, v. 482. He was afraid that the violent ultra Tory party, in its opposition to the Catholic Relief Bill which was about to be introduced into Parliament, would put forward the Duke of Cumberland as their leader in the House of Lords, if he came over at that critical moment.

2. The Duke's son (1819–78) who succeeded his father as King of Hanover in 1851, with the title George V.

3. Henry, 1st Marquess Conyngham (1766–1832), succeeded his father as 2nd Baron Conyngham [I.] on 22 May 1787. Major-General, 1808; Lieutenant-General, 1812; General, 1830. Created Viscount Conyngham [I.], 6 December 1789; Earl Conyngham [I.], 27 December 1797; Marquess [I.], 15 January 1816; and Baron Minster [U.K.], 17 July 1821.

very *seriously indispos'd* for the last three days; to stir out of the house, much less to go up to town for the present for him is therefore quite out of the question. If he should be able to present himself at the Council on Wednesday next, I am quite sure that it is the very extent of what he will be equal to. He is anxious to make the attempt himself, but I will not suffer him (Wellington MSS.).

3477   THE KING TO THE DUKE OF CUMBERLAND[1]
Windsor Castle, 1 Mar. 1829
Private. My dst. Ernest, I have hitherto refrain'd from expressing myself strongly to you upon the subject of your present position here, because the desiring you [not] to return even for a time, is so strongly oppos'd to all my best feelings and affection. Nevertheless I will not disguise from you that I have always thought the Duke of Wellington right (and which I wrote to you at the time, by the same opportunity that the Duke wrote to you) in wishing you not to come over at *this particular* crisis, especially as your proxy was here. You may suppose how anxiously I must have felt this, or I could never have brought myself to write to you upon the subject, for you know how much I love and value your society, and what a positive comfort I derive from the presence of your brotherly and affectionate attachment. My Minister feels, and I beleive justly, that in discussing this momentous question for which I have given permission, everything should be avoided that by interpretation might by possibility give the appearance of a separate opinion existing between myself and my Government, in the *present* stage of this business. Now, when I say this, I do not mean that I am pledged to the Bill about to be propos'd; *my* mind can only be finally made up in the progress of the discussion, and *my* settled opinion form'd, by what I hear from the Bench of Bishops and the high legal authorities of my kingdom. *My situation* is *most* painful and difficult; I am therefore naturally desirous that the brother whom I love and value above all my other brothers, should not be involv'd in any proceeding against my present Government; and why, because I feel satisfied that my difficulties may be such that I may have to call upon *that* brother for his best affections and assistance. You may ask me why your single voice is to produce such inquietude in the mind of my Government. The answer is obvious. It is well known, my dearest Ernest, that you stand with me in the same relative situation as you did

Representative Peer, 1801–32. Lord Steward of the Household, 1821–30. On 5 July 1794 he married Elizabeth (*c.* 1769–1861), daughter of Joseph Denison, banker.

1. Endorsed by the Duke of Wellington: 'This letter was never sent.'

with our revered and excellent father, for our political sentiments have for many years been entirely in unison, and I may say blended together. Besides, they all know your great talents, your perseverance, your activity; and above all your experience in these matters.

I know that I am calling upon you to make a great sacrifice for me. Indeed, I am making a *very great* one *myself* by desiring it; but you shall state to Lord Eldon, leaving your proxy with him, if you please, that I have desired you, under the present circumstances, to do this. With the King of Prussia you shall have no difficulties, for I shall write to the King, as *my private* friend, fully on the subject. I shall again send over my private confidential servant, with you, for the purpose of settling the domestic pecuniary affair that has been entail'd upon me by the unfortunate state in which our late poor brother Frederick left his affairs.

Once more, my beloved Ernest, beleive in my affection, and I shall consider, by your making this sacrifice, you will have the highest claims on my gratitude as well as the best affections of my heart (Wellington MSS.).

3478   THE KING TO THE DUKE OF WELLINGTON[1]
Dated from my bed, Windsor Castle, at 7.15 a.m., 5 Mar. 1829
I am wak'd by the arrival of your messenger with your letter, and as I know how much press'd you are for time, I send him off again immediately. *You are certainly correct in the construction you have put upon my letter.* But at the same time I cannot disguise from you that this has given rise to feelings within me, under which I hardly[2] know how to support myself[3] (Wellington MSS.).

1. The letter is endorsed, in the King's handwriting: 'Copy (to the best of my recollection) of my answer to the D. of W.'s letter to me on the 5th of March 1829, and which I wrote immediately after the messenger was dispatch'd, as I did not wish to detain him any longer whilst I open'd my letter again to take a verbatim copy of it.' There is a very different version of the letter in the *Wellington Civil Despatches*, v. 518.

2. 'Scarcely' is written above; 'hardly', however, is not scored through.

3. The King's letter of the 4th, reluctantly abandoning his opposition to the introduction of the Catholic Relief Bill, is in *Wellington Civil Despatches*, v. 518. On the same page is the Duke's letter, written at midnight on the 4th.

[?c. June 1830]

After many repeated struggles with myself from the apprehension of appearing troublesome or intruding upon your Majesty after so many years of continual silence, my anxiety respecting your Majesty has got the better of my scruples & I trust your Majesty will believe me most sincere when I assure you how truly I have griev'd to hear of your sufferings: from the late accounts I trust your Majesty's health is daily improving, and no one can feel more rejoiced to learn your Majesty is restor'd to complete convalescence, which I pray to God you may long enjoy, accompanied with every degree of happiness you can wish for or desire.

I have enclos'd this letter to Sr. H.H.[1] as your Majesty must be aware there is no person about him through whom I could make a communication of so private a nature attended with the perfect conviction of its never being divulged.[2] (50227)

3480 LORD ELDON'S MEMORANDUM RESPECTING GEORGE IV'S WILL

1 Apr. 1823

Some short time before Good Friday Sir William Knighton brought me a message from the King, desiring to see me at Brighton on Good Friday upon the subject of a Will.

When I got to Brighton, his Majesty took me into his private room. He was at that time a good deal disturbed by the conduct of a man, I think of the name of Griffith, who had written some letters imputing crimes to him and the Duke of York, and that conduct tending to make him uneasy by some circumstances relative to loaded pistols, from which danger to his person might be apprehended. Sir David Scott was in the room, and the conversation for some time turned upon the subject of this man's conduct.

The Bill for enabling his Majesty by will to devise and bequeath certain property had been some years in contemplation. His Majesty had been again and again assured, year after year, that this Bill should be brought into Parliament, but some reason had occurred at the beginning, in the course of, and towards the close of every Session, which postponed the measure, and Lord Londonderry died not having introduced it.

In the meantime, I think about a year or perhaps two years ago, his

1. Halford.

2. Mrs. Fitzherbert later endorsed the letter: 'Written a short time before the death of the King.' He died on 26 June.

Majesty, as I understand, had made a Will, and I drew, what I was now told, he had introduced into that Will viz. some words, submitting to the wisdom of Parliament whether it might not be pleased to give effect to that Will, as if the meditated Bill had passed. When his Majesty made this will, he did not, in a single word, communicate to me what disposition he had made of any one article of his property, nor, previous to making it, did he communicate to me, any disposition which he meant to make of any one article of it.

After Sir D. Scott had left the room on Good Friday his Majesty said that he might have a Will drawn with blanks as to the names of persons, and could fill them up himself—but that he thought it better to communicate his intentions as to persons as well as intended bequests. He then mentioned that he had granted an annuity of £6000 a year to Mrs. F——t, that he had been strongly urged to make it £10,000—that he had positively refused so to do by grant amounting to obligation—but that he thought himself bound to charge the property he could devise or bequeath with the whole annuity of £10,000 a year to her for life, and he said the £6000 a year was charged on the Brighton property. Note—I found from a conversation hereafter adverted to, that this must mean such part of the Brighton property only as he had at the time of making the charge of £6000.

He then mentioned that he had a natural son, an officer in the East Indies, to whom he thought himself bound to give a legacy of £30,000.

He mentioned an annuity of about £400 a year, which I think he said he had granted to a person for life, whose name I don't remember. I think it began with the letter G.

I understood him also to say he owed Weltjie, or some other person, £1,100.

He did not mention a debt of £45,000 due to Mr. Coutts, which I heard of in the conversation hereafter mentioned, and for which Coutts's House had all his title deeds.

I mentioned that I suppose he meant to charge all his property, that he could devise or bequeath, with all his debts generally—he said that must be done.

Note. I *think* in the conversation hereinafter mentioned—Sir William Knighton said his debts would be paid in two years and half. If a Will was to operate immediately, debts, that would only be paid, if he lived, in two years and half, must be a material charge.

He then mentioned that he should, he thought, give legacies to different persons, but he neither mentioned what legacies, or any of the persons.

He then spoke of a residuary legatee. He said the Duke of York would succeed to a station which made it unnecessary to make him residuary legatee. I think he said his Royal Highness had had about £50,000 from him. He said, I think, that the Duke of Clarence had had £30,000 from him—that it could not be expected he should look to the family of the Duke of Kent, or that he should to the Duke of Sussex—that the Duke of Cambridge wanted nothing—and he added, naming his several sisters, that he did not think there was a necessity to attend to them as residuary legatees. This, I understood, as relating to who he meant to be residuary legatee—he not explaining what legacies he should give, or to whom he should give such legacies. He then said he should make *a friend* residuary legatee, *not naming the person*, but he certainly meant Lady C[onyngham].

His Majesty then said he should name several Executors—and he named the Chancellor, the Duke of Wellington, Sir Charles Long, Mr. Dennison, Sir William Knighton, the Attorney-General I think and two more whose names I dont recollect, [Hart Davis was one of the two][1]—and that he should empower only three or four of them to examine his papers.

It was quite clear when he desired me to draw out an instrument for these purposes in proper form, that, without much information as to the particulars of his property, which he had power to bequeath or devise, this could not be done. The nature of his property real, leasehold or personal—the nature of the charges upon it—the difficulty of distinguishing between personal chattels in his possession, which were or were not affected by the Jus Coronæ, and which he could or could not affect by will—the nature of his debts to be charged—the description of his different sorts of property as to its locality, etc. etc.—the manner in which it was to be enjoyed whether specifically—whether all or any and what plate, pictures, jewels etc. was to be converted by sale and made beneficial in bequests *of the produce of* sale—all this was necessary to be known, and of course His Majesty could not be looked to for the requisite information. His Majesty therefore proposed that Sir William Knighton should bring Mr. Bicknell to me on Monday morning, Mr. Bicknell being the King's man of business.

I made no observation at the time upon the nature of all or any of the proposed dispositions. They were such, however, as appeared to me to call for observations to be submitted to his serious attention. My judgement was that this could not be done, either so usefully or so respectfully at that very moment, as it might be after time should appear to have been employed in considering the subject, and I was to see his Majesty next morning, when I thought the opportunity would offer. It, however, did not offer. His Majesty, when I saw him between eleven and twelve, was in bed—complained of a bad night occasioned by spasm in his breast—and of a return of gout in his knee, and his mind was much engrossed

1. An afterthought.

with what was to be done with the monies upon the Solicitor of the Treasury coming down that day. I told his Majesty therefore that the matter would be further discussed and considered when I saw, as it was settled I should see, Mr. Bicknell and Sir William Knighton on Monday in town.

On the Monday morning I saw that gentleman. It appeared very clearly to me that Mr. Bicknell was not able to give the information necessary to be collected before any disposition by Will, which his Majesty might finally be determined to make, could be drawn. After this was settled, Mr. Bicknell withdrew and left Sir William Knighton with me. He informed me that, upon his Majesty's having mentioned to him that he should desire me to frame a draft of his Will with blanks for the names of the persons who were to take [?] by virtue of it, he had desired his Majesty to disclose to me in confidence what he meant to do, and who these persons were, whose names were to fill up blanks. (Note. I had seen Sir William at Brighton alone before I saw the King, but he made no mention of what on the Monday he told me in London)—that the King objected to that, saying that the Chancellor might be making objections to what he proposed to do—that he, Sir William told his Majesty that, notwithstanding that, he advised him to communicate names, and give the Chancellor his full confidence (Note: the King described his proposed residuary legatee not by name, but by the words 'A friend'). On the Monday Sir William mentioned to me that the King had told him, *on the Friday I think*, that the Chancellor had not stated objections. I told Sir William why I did not state them at the moment, or on the Saturday when I found his Majesty ill in bed, but that I felt the necessity of stating much, that had occurred to me, which required serious attention before he executed any instrument, that should be prepared. I now learnt or at least so I understood Sir William Knighton, that the above mentioned Will, which the King had executed, written by himself was, as to the effect of the dispositions what he proposed to effectuate by the Will, which he was preparing to execute, and which Sir William strongly expressed his own uneasiness about. I believe I made him fully understand what was of less consequence than the other point (i.e. the nature of the intended dispositions) the impossibility of executing his Majesty's intentions by making different bequests and any individual whomsoever a residuary legatee—that, in making the Will of such a personage, one ought so distinctly to understand the nature of every article of the property to be given to each legatee, and of every article, constituting a part of the residue given to a residuary legatee as to be able to offer one's humble opinion upon the propriety as well as efficiency of every gift in the Will. That this might be of still greater importance, public importance, as A or B happened to be chosen as a residuary legatee—that his Majesty distinctly stated to me his purpose of not altering the Jure Coronæ property by gift inter vivos, whatever his power might enable him to do by such a gift, though he could not do it by a Will. But, notwithstanding that, the nature of what he meant to do and could do by Will was of great importance not only to himself and his memory, but to the public, as interested in the character of all a King did. Passing over the Crown and his family as residuary legatee was a consideration of great moment even as to impression—but that there was a great difference between making any individual the residuary legatee of the King, and making that individual, if the individual ought so to be, the legatee of any specified sum, and some part of the family as residuary legatee—even if the same benefit remitted to the other individual. Whatever might be what that individual took as residuary legatee, be it little or much, it would, because the quantum of it and nature of [it] was not known, be represented to be enormous, and especially considering what would be supposed to be the reason why it was given—that it also seemed to me to be a matter likely to be of evil public impression, not making the members of the family objects in the disposition, and the principal or some member of it residuary legatee—or the Crown [?].

Before therefore an instrument of Will should be drawn, much further information was wanted, and much consideration was necessary.

Sir William Knighton seemed to feel very strongly all this, and all that was said.

I then wrote to the King that I had entered into much detail with Sir William Knighton—that he would relate it to him—and that progress could not be made till his Majesty's return to town. See my letter.*

Sir William left me expressing strongly his belief that much good might be done by representation to his Majesty—and I understood him as intending to relate to him what had passed.

I remarked upon a King's Will
            the principal objects—Mrs. Fitzherbert, a natural son—
the Friend (Eldon MSS.).

* Dated 31 March 1823.

486

Appendix
Select List of Officeholders,
October 1809–February 1812

SPENCER PERCEVAL'S MINISTRY, OCTOBER 1809 TO FEBRUARY 1812[1]

	Oct.–Nov. 1809	6 Dec. 1809	1 May 1810
First Lord of the Treasury } Chancellor of the Exchequer }	*Perceval*[2] (4 Oct.)	*Perceval*[2]	*Perceval*[2]
Lord Privy Seal	Earl of Westmorland	Westmorland	Westmorland
Lord President of the Council	Earl Camden	Camden	Camden
Lord Chancellor	Lord Eldon	Eldon	Eldon
Home Secretary	*Richard Ryder* (1 Nov.)	*Ryder*	*Ryder*
Foreign Secretary	Earl Bathurst (11 Oct.)	Marquess Wellesley	Wellesley
Secretary for War and the Colonies	Earl of Liverpool[5] (1 Nov.)	Liverpool	Liverpool
First Lord of the Admiralty	Lord Mulgrave	Mulgrave	Charles Yorke
President of the Board of Control	*R. S. Dundas*[4] (13 Nov.)	*Dundas*	*Dundas*[4]
Master-General of the Ordnance	Earl of Chatham	Chatham	Lord Mulgrave[6]
President of the Board of Trade	Earl Bathurst[3]	Bathurst[3]	Bathurst[3]
Ministers without portfolio	Duke of Portland (d. 30 Oct.) Earl of Harrowby (Nov.)	Harrowby	Harrowby

1. To the close of this Correspondence. Perceval was assassinated in May 1812.

2. Also Chancellor of the Duchy of Lancaster. Cabinet Ministers in the Commons are italicised.

3. Bathurst retained the Presidentship of the Board of Trade whilst Foreign Secretary *ad interim*, the duties of the office being performed by George Rose, the Vice-President. On 7 Oct. Perceval told the King that Harrowby would go to the Board of Trade whilst Bathurst was temporarily at the Foreign Office, but this proposal was in fact not adopted. Bathurst was also Master of the Mint.

4. A seat in the Cabinet, about 4 November 1809. Succeeded his father as 2nd Viscount Melville, 29 May 1811.

5. He kissed hands, along with Ryder, on 1 November, which seems a better date than 31 October (*Handbook of British Chronology*, p. 118 [1961 ed.], Royal Historical Society).

6. Denis Gray wrongly says March (*Perceval*, p. 471). On 28 April Perceval wrote to the Duke of Richmond: 'Mulgrave goes to the Ordnance and Charles Yorke to the Admiralty' (Richmond MSS. 66/885).

Junior Lords of the Treasury[1]	John Foster, Wm. Brodrick, Wm. Eliot, Earl of Desart, Snowdon Barne
23 June 1810	Foster, Brodrick, Eliot, Barne, Berkeley Paget
31 Dec. 1811	Brodrick, Barne, Paget, Richard Wellesley, Wm. Wellesley-Pole
Secretaries of the Treasury	Charles Arbuthnot and (8 Dec. 1809) Richard Wharton, *vice* Huskisson[2]
Junior Lords of the Admiralty	Sir Richard Bickerton, Robert Ward, James Buller, Wm. Domett, Robert Moorsom, Visct. Lowther
4 May 1810	Bickerton, Ward, Buller, Domett, Moorsom, Lowther
3 July 1810	Bickerton, Ward, Buller, Domett, Sir Joseph Sydney Yorke, Frederick John Robinson
17 June 1811	Bickerton, Buller, Domett, Yorke, Robinson, Lord Walpole
Secretary of the Admiralty	John Wilson Croker
Under Secretaries of State	
Home Department	John Beckett and (to *c.* end Oct. 1809) Chas. Cecil Cope Jenkinson
27 Feb. 1810	Beckett and Henry Goulburn
Foreign Department	George Hammond and William Hamilton
13 Dec. 1809	Wm. Hamilton and Chas. Culling Smith
War and the Colonies	Chas. Cecil Cope Jenkinson and Lieut.-Col. Henry E. Bunbury
12 June 1810	Bunbury and Robert Peel
Commissioners of the Board of Control	
13 Nov. 1809	Lord Lovaine, Lord Teignmouth, Thos. Wallace, Lord Francis Almeric Spencer[3]

1. The composition of the Treasury Board in 1809–10 requires comment. According to Denis Gray, John Foster resigned his seat when Perceval became Prime Minister (*Perceval*, page 269), but the *Complete Peerage* and also the *Royal Kalendar* list him as a member until 1811. He could not have resigned, changed his mind and been re-appointed, because there was no consequential by-election in Co. Louth. On page 472, however, Gray states that Foster was a Lord of the Treasury until July 1811 (according to *Haydn* the new Treasury Commission was not issued until 31 December 1811).

On 13 November 1809 it was stated that Lord Desart had declined a Lordship of the Treasury (Barne was already a member of the Board). There is no doubt that Desart changed his mind, for on 1 February 1810 he was re-elected for Bossiney after appointment to the Board (so was Barne for Dunwich on 29 January 1810).

2. Huskisson had resigned with Canning in September but, according to custom, remained in office until the appointment of his successor, and he received his salary, apparently, until 7 December. There were similar delays with other appointments.

3. The case of Lord Francis Almeric Spencer illustrates the difficulty occasionally experienced in compiling these Lists and the necessity of detailed research in the Public Records. According to the *Complete Peerage* he was never a member of the India Board; according to Haydn's

7 July 1810	Ld. Lovaine, Ld. Teignmouth, Wallace, Visct. Lowther
Secretary to Board of Control	George Peter Holford
	Sir Patrick Murray (from 6 Jan. 1810)
Secretary at War	Visct. Palmerston
Lieut.-Gen. of the Ordnance	Sir Thomas Trigge
Surveyor-Gen. of the Ordnance	Lieut.-Col. James Murray Hadden; Robert Moorson (from July 1810)
Clerk of the Ordnance	Cropley Ashley Cooper
	Robert Ward (from June 1811)
Principal Storekeeper of the Ordnance	Mark Singleton
First Commissioner of Woods and Forests[1]	Lord Glenbervie
Paymasters-General	Ld. Chas. Henry Somerset and Chas. Long
Treasurer of the Navy	George Rose
Postmasters-General	Earl of Sandwich and Earl of Chichester

Book of Dignities and the *Royal Kalendar* for 1810 he was a Commissioner. He refused office when Perceval formed his Ministry. Lord Binning then declined to be included in the new Commission, 'as, from the battling in the newspapers lately about Lord F. Spencer, my friends might be led to imagine that I had been thrown out to make room for a man who, after all, did not choose to have anything to do with the place.' On 5 December (i.e., six days later) Binning wrote: 'My coming in again after the refusal of Lord F. Spencer would convey an idea that I had either resigned or been turned out to make way for him, and was very happy to come back on his decision not to accept.' The India Office Records (Board of Control, Compilations and Misc. F/5/1) kindly supplied by Miss S. R. Johnson, explain the situation. The copy of the Commission 50 Geo. III, No. 18, dated 13 November 1809 (gazetted 7 November) has the following docket opposite Lord F. Almeric Spencer's name: 'Never attended the Board, of course was never sworn,' and, on the opposite page: 'It has been said that his name was inserted in the Patent without his consent.' Had he been sworn in he, like Lord Teignmouth, would have been unsalaried.

These records elucidate George Johnstone's position as a Commissioner for the Affairs of India. Denis Gray, in his usually accurate *Life* of Perceval (1963) states that he remained in office until June 1810 (page 473). This is incorrect: the Commission dated 13 November 1809 excludes him. And Lord Binning wrote to Lord Harrowby, the new President of the India Board, on 7 July 1809: 'I am much flattered by your having thought of me to succeed Mr Johnstone.' This Commission is docketed: 'Lord Harrowby retired in consequence of the very ill state of his health.'

Gray omits Binning's name as a Commissioner during the last few weeks of the Portland Ministry (from 17 July 1809). This Commission, incidentally, is docketed very curiously: 'On the 11th of July the Commissioners were gazetted as above, omitting, by accident, the name of "The Right Honble. Robert Dundas," in consequence of which they were *re-gazetted* on the 15th of July, including Mr. Dundas's name, which was inserted between the names of Mr. Perceval and Lord Lovaine.' This reference to Dundas will remind readers that the *ex-officio* members of the Board (President, Lord President of the Council, the Secretaries of State, the First Lord of the Treasury and the Chancellor of the Exchequer) are not given in the present volumes.

1. With effect from 31 July 1810 the offices of Surveyor-General of the Land Revenues of the Crown, and the Surveyor-General of Woods and Forests were united under a Board of Commissioners, named the Commissioners of Woods, Forests and Land Revenues.

Vice-President of Board of Trade	George Rose
Judge Advocate General	Chas. Manners-Sutton
Master of the Rolls	Sir William Grant
Attorney General	Sir Vicary Gibbs
Solicitor General	Sir Thomas Plumer
Lord Advocate of Scotland	Archibald Colquhoun
Solicitor General [S.]	David Boyle; David Monypenny (from *c.* Feb. 1811)

THE IRISH GOVERNMENT

Lord Lieutenant	Duke of Richmond
Chief Secretary	Wm. Wellesley-Pole
Lord Chancellor	Lord Manners
Chancellor of the Exchequer	John Foster
	Wm. Wellesley-Pole (from June 1811)
Attorney General	William Saurin
Solicitor-General	Chas. Kendal Bushe
Under-Secretaries of State	
Civil Department	Sir Charles Saxton
Military Department	Sir B. Littlehales
Irish Office (*in London*)	Chas. William Flint

Corrigenda and Addenda; Volumes I to VIII

VOLUME I

p. 12 Note 2: *read* Scarbrough.
p. 230 Line 5 from end: *read* unfavourable.
p. 247 No. 190, line 3: *read* weeks ago.
p. 277 Line 11 from end: *read* investigate.
p. 312 No. 240, line 3: *read* His R.H.

VOLUME II

p. 142 Note 2, line 1: *read* 1718.
p. 142 Note 2, line 3: *read* Vice-Admiral, 1776.
p. 142 Note 3, line 1: *for* 1787 *read* 1786.
p. 142 Note 3, line 2: *for* 26 *read* 14.
p. 166 No. 593, line 3: the illegible name must be Turner, as in No. 598 (p. 172, *n.* 2).
p. 242 Note 1: *for* 1774–6 *read* 1774–5, and in line 2, *for* 1779 *read* 1770.
p. 276 Note 1, last line: *for* Stewart (the Royal family's spelling) *read* Steward. See iv., p. 567.
p. 525 Note 2: *after* Princess *read* Charlotte's.

VOLUMES III and IV

For additional information about Nathaniel Parker Forth *see* Marion Ward, *The Du Barry Inheritance* (Chatto, 1967).

VOLUME IV

p. 465 Line 16 from end: *read* procured.
p. 513 Note 6, line 2: delete the sentence beginning *See.*

VOLUME V

p. 176 Note 2: *for* mother *read* wife.
p. 353 Note 1: *read* 2204.

VOLUME VI

p. 20 Line 1: *read* in the.

VOLUME VII

p. 105 No. 2783: a further examination of this letter shows that the 15th, as given, is correct. Therefore '[? 19]', together with note 2, should be deleted.

493

p. 105 Note 1: *add to end*: 'What a desperate defence the *Néreide* must have made,' wrote Grey. 'I know nothing like it, at least as to the proportion of killed and wounded' (Howick MSS.).

p. 434 Under Grey, Charles, 2nd Earl: *insert 2784n.*

VOLUME VIII

Princess Mary's undated letter (3375) on page 385, and the Prince Regent's (3396) on page 416 require an additional comment.

One cannot be quite certain that the Princess's letter was written in May 1813. Was the Court still in mourning for the Duchess of Brunswick in mid-May (the Queen's birthday was on 19 May)? The Queen wrote to the Prince Regent on 21 April 1813: 'I received last night the order for the change of mourning on the 25th Sunday next. The mistake arises from our putting it on the Thursday before the funeral which the Kg. did frequently, but it can only be reckoned from that day. Therefore you must have the order altered for the 2d of May and I advise this the more as very little trifle in the conduct of the Royal family is at present so severely censured. Pray let McMahon send only one line that we may know what to do on account of our dress for Mary's birthday [25 April]' (36643). Did the Queen mean that the Court was coming out of mourning on the 2nd, or did she mean that it would not be in such deep mourning from that date?

In mid-May the *Morning Chronicle*, and subsequently the *Gentleman's Magazine*, reported that the Prince of Mecklenburg-Strelitz, 'the Queen's nephew', had been killed at the battle of Lützen on 2 May; but this information was obviously inaccurate (Prince Leopold of Hesse Homburg was killed in that battle). Prince Augustus Ferdinand of Prussia, the son of King Frederick William I and of Sophia, daughter of George I, died on 2 May 1813, but one would have thought that the relationship to George III and Queen Charlotte was too remote to warrant Court mourning for him.

Princess Mary's letter cannot refer to the death of Prince Ernest of Mecklenburg-Strelitz, whose demise (27 January 1814) was known in London within three weeks. On 14 February 1814 the Queen wrote to the Prince Regent thanking him for his 'kind attention upon this melancholy occasion for having sent the Duke of York, accompanied by Sr.H.H., to acquaint me with the loss of a most amiable and beloved brother' (36683-4). On 18 May 1814 the *Morning Chronicle* stated that the news of the death of the Duke of Mecklenburg-Strelitz had been received on the 17th. Was it not this unfounded rumour to which the Prince referred in his letter of the 16th?

It may be useful to note here that the undated letter from Lord Liverpool to the King (*Letters of George IV*, ii. 452) was written at 5 a.m. on 8 August 1822. There is a copy in the Liverpool MSS. in the British Museum.

Index to Volumes I to VIII

Index to Volumes I to VIII

© *Cassell and Company Limited* 1971

To facilitate reference to the appropriate volume, the numbers of the letters which comprise each volume are given at the foot of each right-hand page of the index.

A few dates misprinted in earlier volumes are here corrected, and a few other changes embody recent research.

Vol. I: 1–444; Vol. II: 445–942; Vol. III: 943–1416; Vol. IV: 1417–1865; Vol. V: 1866–2287; Vol. VI: 2288–2693; Vol. VII: 2694–3056; Vol. VIII: 3057–3480.

497

Adam, William—*cont.*
  letters from, 627, 627n., 1673, 1945, 2135,
  2268, 2376, 2454, 2463n., 2471, 2477, 2477n.,
  2510, 2513, 2559, 2564, 2571, 2571n., 2573,
  2573n., 2575, 2577, 2579, 2581, 2583, 2642,
  2679, 2841, 3031, 3049n., 3054, 3135, 3179,
  3180n., 3255, 3272, 3281, 3303, 3379, 3400
  letters to, 419, 1673, 1682, 1695n., 1707n.,
  1832n., 2135, 2135n., 2167n., 2171n., 2224n.,
  2273–4, 2289n., 2308n., 2322n., 2355–6,
  2362, 2367, 2372n., 2376n., 2463n., 2476,
  2477n., 2478, 2507, 2513, 2518, 2551, 2557,
  2564, 2568, 2571, 2573, 2575, 2578n.,
  2579n., 2583, 2682n., 2693, 2769n., 2792,
  2809, 2826, 2841, 2859, 3135, 3305n., 3308n.,
  3388, 3388n., 3400.
  memo by, 2742n., 2801, 2811, 2840n., 3284
  his sisters and daughter, 2135
  pressed to take office of President of the
  Court of Session [S.], 3179, 3179n.
Adams, 492
Adams, Charles (*c.* 1753–1821), 2562n., 3074,
  3358
Adams, John, 3228
Adams, William (*c.* 1752–1811), 2582n.
Adams, William Dacres (1775–1862), 2153n.,
  2582n.
  letters to, 1671n., 2299n.
Adamson, 1883
Addenhoff [*sic*], 3406
Addington, Dr. Anthony (1713–90), 321n.,
  335–6, 424, 1761
Addington, Henry, 1st Visct. Sidmouth
  (1757–1844), 1126, 1495, 1507, 1552n.,
  1594–5, 1597, 1598n., 1601, 1601n., 1621,
  1621n., 1625, 1628, 1635, 1661, 1682, 1689–
  1690, 1697, 1697A, 1701, 1702n., 1705, 1724,
  1728, 1736, 1738, 1749, 1755, 1761, 1764,
  1767, 1772, 1775, 1780, 1783n., 1804n.,
  1806n., 1810, 1810A, 1819, 1830n., 1837–8,
  1842, 1844, 1854–5, 1861, 1866, 1877,
  1889, 1896, 1955n., 1971, 1992, 1996n.,
  1998, 2010, 2016, 2025, 2052, 2056, 2058,
  2072, 2092, 2092n., 2120, 2123n., 2125, 2134,
  2140, 2150, 2153n., 2209n., 2229n., 2258n.,
  2338n., 2363, 2498, 2622n., 2704n., 2756n.,
  2983, 3081, 3084, 3143, 3244, 3347, 3352,
  3388, 3388n., 3472n.
  letters from, 657, 1608n., 1626, 1720, 1723,
  1725–7, 1758, 1980n., 1996n., 2236n.,
  2237n.
  memo by, 1591n.
  minute by, 2385n.
  letters to, 1474, 1474n., 1588n., 1591, 1598n.,
  1608, 1616n., 1626, 1629n., 1695n., 1720,
  1723, 1725–6, 1758, 1806, 1815n., 1835n.,
  1854, 1854n., 2113n., 2123n., 2125n., 2415n.,
  3397, 3402, 3410, 3413, 3415, 3417
  his bereavement (1811), 3081
  list of his friends (1810), 3244n.
  proposed retirement of (1821), 3416
Addington, Henry, jun. (1786–1823), 2092,
  2092n.

Addington, John Hiley (1759–1818), 1631, 2120,
  2258n., 2498, 2779
  letters to, 1631n., 1980n.
Addingtonians, the, 1958, 2800n., 3347
Additional Force Bill (1804), 1882n., 1887n.,
  2287
Additional Force Act Repeal Bill (1806), 2170,
  2173
Adjutant-General, the, *see* Calvert, Sir Henry
Admiralty, Court of, 3029
  droits of the, 2347, 2571n., 2572, 2715n.,
  3283–4, 3344, 3344n.
  sessions, 2899
  office of Marshal of the, 3168, 3174, 3176
Adolphus Frederick, Duke of Cambridge
  (1774–1850), 161, 259, 581, 581n., 584, 651,
  750, 766, 771, 778–9, 782, 784, 812, 819,
  876n., 881, 889, 896, 900–1, 903, 992, 1267,
  1437n., 1598n., 1603, 1609, 1615, 1615n.,
  1665, 1693, 1716n., 1719, 1731, 1734, 1770,
  1787, 1789, 1791, 1800, 1806, 1901, 1923,
  1929, 1932, 1935, 1956, 1968n., 2032, 2055,
  2074, 2080, 2080n., 2084, 2111, 2147–8,
  2171n., 2197, 2288, 2292, 2322n., 2347, 2490,
  2515, 2552, 2552n., 2570, 2603, 2616, 2627,
  2629, 2639, 2639n., 2692, 2696, 2722, 2740,
  2746, 2770n., 2789, 2791, 2837, 3006,
  3009n., 3201, 3308n., 3310n., 3480
  letters from, 652, 778, 795, 797, 801, 803,
  818, 850 856, 862, 872, 889, 905, 995, 1016,
  1063, 1068, 1269, 1437, 1515, 1598, 1604,
  1624, 1632, 1647, 1662, 1667, 1710, 1712,
  1718, 1747, 1863, 1961, 2051, 2068, 2075,
  2077, 2086, 2421, 2659, 2661, 2710n., 2768,
  2789, 3376
Adultery Bill, the, 1543n.
Advocate, the, *see* Hope, Charles
Ægina Marbles, the, 3141, 3145, 3280, 3366,
  3370
Affari, M. d', 690
Affleck, Admiral Philip (1726–99), 732
Afflick, William, 3228
Africa, a 64-gun ship, 2443
Agamemnon, a 64-gun ship, 780n.
Agra, capture of (1803), 1757
Ailesbury, Anne, Countess of (1753–1813),
  1269, 1274, 1373, 1881, 1884, 1898, 2001,
  2014
Ailesbury, 1st Earl of (1729–1814), 278, 492,
  492n., 1373, 2957
  letters from, 72, 106, 134
  diary quoted, 1270n.
Ainslie, Sir Robert (*c.* 1730–1812), 2161
Aiton, J. T., 2598n.
Aiton, William Townsend (1766–1849), 2598
Aix-la-Chapelle, Congress of (1818), 3406
Alba, House of, 1829
Alba [Alva], Duke of (1508–82), 1829
Albemarle, Elizabeth, Countess of (1776–1817),
  2436n.
Albemarle, 4th Earl of (1772–1849), 1264
  letter from, 2264
  letter to, 2264

Albert, Louis, 879
his father, 879
Albuera, battle of (1811), 3059
Albuquerque, Duke of (*c.* 1775–1811), 2881, 2892, 2910
Alcudia, Manuel de Godoy, Duke of (1767–1851), 1916, 2338n.
Aldborough, 3rd Earl of (*d.* 1823), 2305n., 3146n.
Aldborough (Suffolk), election (1806), 2128, 2276, 2288, 2369n., 2747, 2747n., 2776n.; (1812), 3289, 3294, 3311, 3327, 3339–40
Alderney, its smuggling industry, 3094
Alexander, 2154
Alexander the Great, 722
Alexander I, Tsar (1777–1825), 1662, 1667, 2031, 2031n., 2092, 2119–20, 2264, 2326, 2419, 2524n., 2537n., 3114, 3142, 3142n., 3386
Alexander, Henry (*c.* 1763–1818), 2323
Alexander, Sir William, appointed Chief Baron of the Exchequer and knighted, 3437
Alfred, a 74-gun ship, 732
Algerine Ambassador, the, 3144
Algiers, Dey of, 3315
Ali Ibrahim Khan, 520
Alien Office, the, 3114
Aliens Act, the, 1243
Aligarh, capture of (1803), 1757
Alkmaar, Convention of (1799), 1457n., 1499
Allan, 2012
Allan, David, 2771
letters from, 2319, 2771, 3162
Allen, 5th Visct. (1728–1816), 783
Allen, Mrs., 1444
Allen, John (1771–1843), 2811n.
Allerton, Duke of York's estate at, 251n., 271n.
All Souls, Oxford, 2666
Almon, John (1737–1805), 36, 324
Alost, battle of (1794), 3094
Alsop, Frances (1782–1821), Mrs. Jordan's daughter, 3140, 3140n.
Alsop, Thomas (*d.* 1826), 3140, 3140n., 3378
Althorp, Visct., later 3rd Earl Spencer (1782–1845), 2230n., 3065n.
Alting, Governor-Gen. of Batavia, 492
Alvensleben, Baron (*d.* 1795), Hanoverian Minister in London, 40, 43
letter to, 330
Ambler, Charles (1721–94), 334n.
Amelia, Princess, daughter of George II, (1710–86), 96n., 162n., 2398
letter to, 162
Amelia, Princess (1783–1810), 76n., 876n., 987, 1187, 1217, 1220, 1226, 1371, 1378–9, 1381–3, 1385, 1389, 1391–2, 1401, 1415, 1420, 1426n., 1471–2, 1478, 1511–12, 1514, 1558, 1604, 1620, 1665, 1668, 1670, 1678, 1687, 1731, 1734, 1747, 1789–90,

Amelia, Princess—*cont.*
1796, 1823–4, 1826, 1828, 1831, 1833, 1836, 1857, 1901, 1915, 1925, 1958, 1968n., 1970, 2067, 2090–1, 2202, 2292, 2390n., 2470, 2472, 2521, 2556, 2560, 2570, 2585, 2587, 2589, 2592, 2595, 2597–8, 2605, 2611–12, 2620, 2623, 2629, 2635, 2638, 2641, 2643, 2646, 2651–2, 2656, 2659–63, 2670–2, 2675, 2677, 2685–6, 2694, 2696, 2702–3, 2705, 2710n., 2720, 2722, 2724, 2729, 2734, 2737, 2740–1, 2740n., 2744, 2746–8, 2751n., 2755, 2759, 2759n., 2763–5, 2765n., 2768, 2772–3, 2775n., 2777, 2780, 2780n., 2837, 2837n., 2849–50, 2855, 3356, 3375–6
letters from, 1258, 1267n., 1291, 1372, 1372n., 1380, 1386, 1390, 1395, 1439, 1441, 1477, 1501, 1503, 1511, 1533, 1552, 1609, 1669, 1759, 1856, 1859, 1910, 1920, 1968, 2066, 2066n., 2200, 2263, 2263n., 2309, 2390, 2409, 2488, 2490, 2494, 2553, 2584, 2592, 2603, 2606, 2616, 2627, 2630, 2636, 2639, 2650, 2671, 2673, 2676, 2684, 2684n., 2696, 2710, 2718, 2732, 2740, 2743
letter to, 2635n.
Amelia Lodge, Windsor, 600n.
Amerson, 914
Amherst, Jeffrey, Lord (1717–97), 26, 157, 673n., 723, 770, 785, 789, 799, 800, 813, 838, 883, 954, 954n., 969, 980n., 1462n.
letters from, 434, 753, 763, 788
letters to, 788, 791
Amherst, Miss, 1462n.
Amherst, William Pitt, Earl (1773–1857), 1462n., 2892, 2964
Amiens, Peace of, 2120, 2632, 2983, 3143
Amon, Mrs. (*d.* 1797), 1025
Amphion, a 32-gun frigate, 247
Ancaster, Mary, Duchess of (*d.* 1793), 274
Ancient Britons Society, the, 1596, 2912
Ancient Music Concerts, the, 2702n., 3038
Anderson, William, 1901
Andréossy, Antoine François, Count (1761–1828), 1690, 1877
Andrewes, Dr. Gerrard (1750–1825), 2527
Andrews, Mrs., 1632
Andrews, Miles Peter (*c.* 1742–1814), 1861
Andromeda frigate, 156, 264, 266, 405, 855n.
Angellelli, 1375
Angerstein, John (1774–1858), 2449n.
Angerstein, John Julius (*c.* 1735–1823), 3270
letter to, 2449
Angier, a speech therapist, 1721
Anglesey, Marquess of, *see* Paget
Anglo-Swedish treaty signed at Stockholm (1812), 3377
Anglo-Russian treaty signed at Stockholm (1812), 3377
Angoulême, Louis Antoine de Bourbon, Duc d' (1775–1844), 885n., 1021, 1215, 1215n., 3025
Anguishes, the, 1389

Vol. I: 1–444; Vol. II: 445–942; Vol. III: 943–1416; Vol. IV: 1417–1865; Vol. V: 1866–2287; Vol. VI: 2288–2693; Vol. VII: 2694–3056; Vol. VIII: 3057–3480.

499   33—C.G. IV

Augusta Sophia, Princess—*cont.*
  letters from, 463*n*., 485*n*., 762, 772, 826,
  828, 967, 998, 1090, 1183, 1285, 1298, 1306,
  1345, 1364, 1371, 1378, 1383, 1415, 1472,
  1502, 1513, 1594*n*., 1649, 1687, 1734, 2071,
  2090, 2400, 2410, 2567, 2850, 3013, 3123*n*.,
  3254, 3349, 3374
Augustine, 2207
Augustus, Emperor (63 B.C.–A.D. 14), 298
Augustus I, King of Saxony (1750–1827),
  2983, 3084
Augustus Frederick, Duke of Sussex (1773–
  1843), 261, 385, 471*n*., 532, 585, 652, 683*n*.,
  710, 728*n*., 777, 781, 794*n*., 802*n*., 863, 1475,
  1478, 1481–2, 1506*n*., 1509, 1528*n*., 1536,
  1536*n*., 1539, 1555–7, 1559, 1569, 1577,
  1600*n*., 1639, 1643, 1643*n*., 1644, 1652–3,
  1657, 1660, 1666, 1668, 1671*n*., 1682, 1747,
  1915, 1920, 1925, 1932, 1935*n*., 1942, 1958,
  1968*n*., 1971, 2032, 2080, 2086, 2099, 2113*n*.,
  2147, 2168, 2171, 2171*n*., 2197, 2253, 2263,
  2275, 2285, 2287, 2292, 2299*n*., 2305–6,
  2315, 2320, 2322, 2326, 2347, 2390, 2409,
  2421, 2423, 2425, 2429*n*., 2442, 2498, 2501,
  2514–17, 2519*n*., 2565, 2570, 2635, 2770*n*.,
  2789, 3098*n*., 3155*n*., 3158, 3480
  letters from, 255, 263, 273, 409, 570, 570*n*.,
  595, 595*n*., 615, 639, 658, 683, 683*n*., 714,
  714*n*., 728, 747, 802, 804, 860, 876, 876*n*.,
  892, 933, 947, 982, 1004, 1022, 1037, 1085,
  1093, 1465, 1488, 1490, 1492, 1494, 1539,
  1593, 1600, 1642, 1671, 1698, 1809, 1809*n*.,
  1935, 2033, 2263*n*., 2296, 2299, 2307, 2323,
  2325, 2331, 2345, 2504
  letters to, 198*n*., 251*n*., 259, 280*n*., 339,
  463*n*., 485*n*., 600*n*., 1071*n*., 1480
  illness of (1812), 3348
  financial worries, 3348
  his daughter, *see* D'Este
  his son, *see* D'Este
Aust, George, 113*n*.
Austen, Mr. and Mrs., of Fowey, 631
Austen and Maunde, banking house, 2098
Austerlitz, battle of, 2119
Austin, Mrs. Sophia, 2196, 2199
Austin, William (1802–49), 2196, 2388*n*.
Austrian Netherlands, revolution in the (1789),
  493
Axen, M. van, 62
Aylesbury Election Bill (1804), 1958
Aylesford, 4th Earl of (1751–1812), 3128*n*.,
  3201, 3217, 3238
  letter to, 2897*n*.
Ayr Burghs election (1794), 883
Ayrshire election, 2649, 2985
Ayton, *see* Aiton

Baden, 1877
Baden, Electorate of, 1839

Baden-Durlach, Charles Frederick, Margrave
  of (1728–1811), 1877
Baden-Durlach, William Louis, Prince of
  (1732–88), 382
Bagnion (?), Mr., 514
Bagot, Emily, Lady (1770–1800), 1444
Bagot, Dr. Lewis (1740–1802), 73
Bagot, Rev. Richard (1782–1854), 3458
Bagot, 2nd Lord (1773–1856), 1444
Bagwell, John (*c.* 1754–1816), wants a peerage,
  3180*n*.
Bailey [Baily], 1280
Baillie, Lieut.-Col., 883
Baillie, Sir Ewan (*c.* 1743–1820), 2271, 2745
Baillie, Matthew (1761–1823), 2198*n*., 2676–7,
  2694, 2710*n*., 2720, 2722, 2740, 2746, 2749*n*.,
  2751*n*., 2756, 2757*n*., 2758, 2764, 2787,
  2837*n*., 2897*n*., 3064, 3100, 3117, 3123,
  3129, 3217, 3217*n*., 3374–6, 3380, 3389
Baillie, William, Lord Polkemmet (*d.* 1816),
  3230
Baird, General Sir David (1757–1829), 2195
Baird, Dr., *letter from*, 3279
Baker, 465, 482, 484, 484*n*., 508, 2287
Baker, Sir George (1722–1809), 283, 287, 289*n*.,
  293, 321*n*., 335, 424.
  letter to, 344
Baldwin, the Duke of Portland's secretary,
  1633, 1651, 1656
Baldwin, William (*c.* 1737–1813), 531, 549–50
Ball, Rear-Admiral Sir Alexander John (1757–
  1809), 2601, 3124
  letter from, 2601
Ballard, John, 1708*n*.
Bampfylde, Sir Charles Warwick (1753–1823),
  2161
  letter from, 542
Banbury, Corporation of, 2076
  Freedom of, for Prince of Wales (1808),
  2516*n*.
Bank of England, the, 3091
Bankes, Henry (1756–1834), 3055, 3091, 3109,
  3112, 3115, 3363
Bankes, Meyrick, Sheriff of Lancashire, 2259
Banknote Bill, *see* Gold Coin
Bannister, John (1760–1836), 1477–8, 1665
Bantry, Visct. (1767–1851), 3146*n*.
Barber, Mrs., 879
Barclay, Robert (1732–97), *letter from*, 681
Barclay, Sir Robert (1755–1839),
  letter from, 2313, 2313*n*.
  letter to, 2313
  his infant son, 2313*n*.
Barclay, Thomas, 2313
Barère (1755–1841), 856–7
Barfleur, a 98-gun ship, 160, 2530
Barham, Joseph Foster (1759–1832), 1253,
  2204
  letter from, 2152

Vol. I: 1–444; Vol. II: 445–942; Vol. III: 943–1416; Vol. IV: 1417–1865; Vol. V: 1866–2287;
Vol. VI: 2288–2693; Vol. VII: 2694–3056; Vol. VIII: 3057–3480.

501

Bolingbroke, 2nd Visct. (1734–87), 145
Bolton, 2053
Bolton, an attorney, 2542, 2671, 2673, 2675–6, 2696, 2740
Bolton, 6th Duke of (1720–94), 716, 729
Bolton, Katherine, Duchess of (c. 1736–1809), 1412n., 2004n., 2357
    letter from, 716
Bolton, Petition from weavers of, 2922, 2924
Bonaparte, *see* Napoleon
Bonaparte, Joseph (1768–1844), King of Naples (1806), King of Spain (1808), 2264, 2556n., 2591n., 2599, 2711
Bonaparte, Lucien (1775–1840), 3293
Bond, Nathaniel (1754–1823), 1955n., 1958
'Book, The', 2304n., 2337n., 2338n., 2351n., 2362n., 2380, 2380n., 2384–5, 2463n., 2476–7, 2477n., 2583n.
Boose [*sic*], 587
Bootle Wilbraham, Edward, 1st Lord Skelmersdale (1771–1853), 3469
Bootle Wilbraham, Mrs., *letters from*, 614n., 669n.
Boreas frigate, 216
Boringdon, Lord, later 1st Earl of Morley (1772–1840), 1604, 1609
Borrow, Mr., 2259
Bosanquet, Jacob, 2935
Bostock, John (1773–1846), a Liverpool doctor, *letter from*, 2231n.
Bosville, Thomas (d. 1793), 776
Bosville, William, 1908n.
Bott, J., 3009n.
Boudé, M. de la, the French banker, 686
Boughton, 1317
    his son, 1317
Bouillé, Marquis de (1739–1800), 604, 604n.
Boulton, Matthew (1728–1809), 991
Bourbon, conquest of island of, 3092
Bourbon, Louis Henry Joseph, Duc de (1756–1830), 14, 1565, 1692n., 3025
Bourchier, Margaret, 3035
Bourgogne, Antoine de (1421–1504), 2046
Bouverie, 143, 562n.
Bouverie, Edward (1738–1810), 1375
Bouverie, Edward (1760–1824), 1375n.
Bouverie, Mrs. (c. 1750–1825), 1345, 1345n., 1375
Bowater, Captain Edward (Admiral, 1819) (?1752–1829), 919
Bowen, Rev. Mr., 3348
Bowers, Mrs., 1025, 1045, 1072, 1179, 2117, 2739
    letter to, 1025n.
Bowes, George, 2348
Bowes, Miss, 'the great heiress of the north,' 39n.
Bowlby, Thomas (1721–95), 770
Bowles, John, 2818
Bowles, Major Thomas, 2554

Bowyer, Sir George (1739–99), 535
Boyd, 2505
Boyd, Capt. (d. 1807), 2505, 2738n.
Boyd, John, of the Beef Steak Club, 1520, 1520n.
Boyd, General Sir Robert, Governor of Gibraltar (1710–94), 563
Boyd, Walter (c. 1754–1837), 593n.
Boyne, a 98-gun ship, 732
Braddyll, Thomas Richmond Gale (1776–1862), 1751
Braddyll, Wilson (1756–1818), 1037n., 1770, 2279
    letters from, 1520, 2269
    letter to, 2153
Bradford, 2nd Baron and 1st Earl of (1762–1825), 2299n.
Bradshaw, Augustus Cavendish (1768–1832), 1752n., 2078, 2083, 2098
    letters from, 1820, 1822, 1827, 2209, 2814
Bradshaw, Colonel, 2098, 2209
Bradshaw, Mrs., 2209
Bragge, *see* Bathurst
Braham, John (c. 1774–1856), 2305n., 2903
Braine, George, 1615n.
Brand, Thomas, 20th Baron Dacre (1774–1851), 1908n., 3344
Brande, Dr., 1275
Brandenburg-Schwedt, Margrave of (d. 1788), 382
Brandes, Baron, 1693
    letter from, 1693
Brandish, 2423, 2425, 2430
Brandon, 1769
Brathwaite, Sir John (1739–1803), 158
    his father, 158
Brawn [Braun, Braund], R., 255, 259, 1668, 2296, 2763, 3118, 3308
Brawn [*sic*], Miss, Princess Elizabeth's maid, 2517, 2763n.
Braymeyer, Mrs., 1275
Brazil, Prince of, *see* Portugal, John, Prince of Brazil
Breadalbane, 4th Earl and 1st Marquess of (1762–1834), 517, 608, 613, 2266, 2302, 2308n., 2561
Brennier, General, 3028n.
Brent, Sir Timothy (d. 1833), 1070, 1280, 1451n., 1521, 1523, 3427, 3430
    letter from, 1525
    letter to, 1526
Brent, William, 3427, 3430
Brent, Mrs., 1525
Bretagne, Jean de Montford, Duke of (1339–1399), 2046
Bridge, 1773
Bridge, the London jeweller, 2390, 2651
Bridport, Visct., *see* Hood, Alexander
Brighton, the Prince's estate at, 913n.
    barracks, 2035

Vol. I: 1–444; Vol. II: 445–942; Vol. III. 943–1416; Vol. IV: 1417–1865; Vol. V: 1866–2287; Vol. VI: 2288–2693; Vol. VII: 2694–3056; Vol. VIII: 3057–3480.

505

Buckingham, 1st Marquess of—*cont.*
2483*n.*, 2519*n.*, 2798*n.*, 2801, 2816*n.*, 3065*n.*,
3314*n.*, 3383
letters from, 1215*n.*, 2052, 2288*n.*, 2519,
2596, 2798, 2868
Buckingham, Duke of, *see* Temple
Buckingham House, 1958
Buckingham Palace, 3474
Buckinghamshire, 4th Earl of (1760–1816),
1868*n.*, 2052, 2125*n.*, 2649
letter to, 2237*n.*
Buckinghamshire election (1807), 2380
Buckley, Edward Pery, 2390*n.*
Buckley, Lady Georgiana (?1767–1832), 1958,
1968*n.*, 2390
Buckner, John (1734–1824), Bishop of Chiches-
ter, 3428*n.*
Budd, John, bookseller, 2477*n.*
Budé, General J. (*c.* 1736–1818), 6, 22*n.*, 62,
104, 109–10, 110*n.*, 111, 113, 116, 140, 249*n.*,
519, 599, 601
Budget, the, 1811, 3036
Buenos Aires, capture of, 2195, 2262*n.*, 2422,
2443, 2680
loss of, 2262*n.*
Buffa [*sic*], 1775, 2347
Buffon, George Louis Leclerc, Comte de
(1707–88), 2067
Bulkeley, 7th Visct. (1752–1822), 489*n.*,
2672*n.*
Bulkeley, Elizabeth, Viscountess (*c.* 1759–
1826), 489*n.*
Buller, Sir Francis (1746–1800), 1544
Buller, James, Clerk of the Privy Council
(1772–1830), 613
Bullion Report (1810), the, 3030
Bullock, 665
Bullock, George, artist, 3029*n.*
Bunbury, Sir Henry Edward (1778–1860),
letter from, 3315
Bunbury, Lieut.-Col. Henry William (1750–
1811), 273
Groom of the Bedchamber to Duke of York,
249*n.*
Bunbury, Mrs., 1380, 1464
Bunbury, Sir Thomas Charles, 6th Bt. (1740–
1821), 664, 677, 1183*n.*
letter from, 2064
letter to, 632*n.*
Bunnell, a tradesman, 230
Burchell [?], 1861
Burdett, Sir Francis (1770–1844), 1660, 1660*n.*,
1908, 2230, 2308*n.*, 2311*n.*, 2415*n.*, 2545,
2609, 2704, 2711, 2711*n.*, 2761*n.*, 2820*n.*,
2861, 2893, 2966, 3015, 3060*n.*, 3091, 3219,
3320, 3344*n.*, 3386
letters from, 3228
demands abolition of flogging in the Army,
3074
Burges, Sir James Bland (1752–1824), 910

Burgess, Henry, 2308*n.*
letter from, 2311*n.*
Burgess, Thomas (1756–1837), Bishop of St.
David's, 3415
letter to, 3422
Burgoyne, Lt.-Gen. John (1723–92), 404, 410
Burgundy, Charles the Bold, Duke of (1433–
1477), 2046
Burke, Edmund (1729–97), 564, 564*n.*, 777,
2229, 2536
letters from, 349, 473, 602
address by the House of Commons drafted
by, 331, 331*n.*
memo etc. by, 356, 356*n.*, 397
letters drafted by, 373, 375
Burlington House, meeting of Opposition
Peers at (1790), 545
Burney, 1259
Burney, Dr. Charles (1726–1814), 1799*n.*
letter from, 2112
Burney, Fanny, Mme. d'Arblay (1752–1840),
6*n.*, 16*n.*, 65*n.*, 984*n.*
Burr, Mr., 3209
Burrard, Rev. Sir George (1769–1856), 1501
Burrard, Sir Harry (1755–1813), 2530, 2534*n.*,
2639, 2641
Burrard, John Thomas (1792–1809), 2639,
2641
Burrell, Sir Charles Merrik (1774–1862), 3091
Burrell, Drummond, 3410
Burrell, Sir Peter, Lord Gwydir (1754–1820),
274, 274*n.*, 1077, 1094*n.*, 1167*n.*
his wife, *see* Willoughby
Burroughs, Sir William (1753?–1829), 487
Burrows, one of Sheridan's friends, 578
Burt, Rev. Robert (*c.* 1761–91), 630
letter from, 574
Burton [Barton], Captain, 684
Burton, Sir Francis Nathaniel, *see* Conyngham
Burton, General Napier Christie (1758–1835),
1786–7, 1791
Burton, Sir Robert (?1738–1810), 307, 333
letter from, 333
Burton, William (1739–1818), 410
Busaco, battle of, 2747
Busche, Charles Kendal (1767–1843), 2905
Busche, General William von dem (*d.* 1794),
896, 914, 1031
Bus[s]che, 37, 39*n.*, 40, 42–3, 45, 47
Bushy Park, 2171*n.*, 2504
Bute elections, 472
Bute, 4th Earl of and 1st Marquess of (1744–
1814), 1087, 1695, 1702*n.*, 1866, 1959*n.*
letter from, 1589
Butler, Charles (1780–1860), 1820
Butler, Fanny, 1425, 1427
Butler, Lieut.-Gen. James (*d.* 1836), Com-
mandant of the Royal Military College, 2682
appointed Lieut.-Gov. of the College, 3136,
3155

Vol. I: 1–444; Vol. II: 445–942; Vol. III: 943–1416; Vol. IV: 1417–1865; Vol. V: 1866–2287;
Vol. VI: 2288–2693; Vol. VII: 2694–3056; Vol. VIII: 3057–3480.

507

Canterbury, Archbishop, of, *see* Moore, John; and Manners-Sutton
 election, 443
Canton, Viceroy of, 2932
Capel, Sir Thomas Bladen (1776–1835), 1389
Cape of Good Hope, Governorship of, 2149, 2158, 2292, 2331, 2345, 2347, 2691
 its charms, 3166
Capper, Col. Francis, 2554
Capuchins, the, 32
Caracciolo, Prince Francesco, Neapolitan Admiral (1732–99), 1470
Caradoc [Cradock], Lieut.-Gen. Sir John Francis, Lord Howden (1759–1839), 2459, 3094
 letters from, 2249, 2393, 3166
Carden, Dr., of Truro, 539, 565
Cardigan, 5th Earl of (1725–1811), 873, 1860, 1958, 2879, 2879n.
Cardigan, 6th Earl of (1769–1837), 3317
Cardigan, Elizabeth, Countess of (née Waldegrave) (1758–1823), 894, 1153, 1884, 2001, 2879n.
Cardinal, the, *see* York, Henry Benedict
Carew, Reginald Pole (1753–1835), 1980n.
Carey [Cary], Mrs., 2545n.
Carey [Cary], Lieut.-Col. Thomas (*d.* 1824), 2347
Carhampton, 1st Earl of (1713–87), 29n., 537n.
Carhampton, 2nd Earl of (?1737–1821), 3410
Carignan, Louis, Prince de (1721–78), 684n.
Carignan, Marie Josèphe Thérèse (1753–97), sister-in-law of Princesse de Lamballe, 639
Carleton, Hugh, Visct. (1739–1826), 3085
Carletons, the, 2519n.
Carlisle, Bishop of, *see* Harcourt
Carlisle, Margaret Caroline, Countess of (1753–1824), 2534n.
Carlisle, Georgiana, Lady Morpeth, later Countess of (1783–1858), 208, 484, 696, 1578, 2163, 2251n., 2287, 2534n.
 letter from, 2287n.
Carlisle, 5th Earl of (1748–1825), 188, 1190, 1448, 1546, 1546n., 1599, 1601n., 1735, 2268n., 2289n., 2324, 2324n., 2327, 2333, 3373
 letters from, 189, 1593n., 1601, 2198n., 2358n., 3367n.
 memo by, 1598n., 1601
 letters to, 2327, 2387n., 2534n.
Carlisle, 6th Earl of (1773–1848), 1735, 1968n., 2251n., 2289n., 2291, 2291n., 2324n., 2534n., 3358
 letters to, 2163, 2287n., 2315n.
 refuses office under Wellington, 3468
Carlisle, 7th Earl of (1802–64), 2287
Carlisle election (1790), 573
Carlton House, building operations at, 2729
 the Regent's Speech at, 2857

Carlton House Party, the, 2206, 3097n.
Carmarthen, Marquess of, later 5th Duke of Leeds (1751–99), 11, 14, 28, 254, 321, 332n., 447n., 460, 861, 878n., 1105n., 1115n., 1118n., 1153, 1153n.
Carmarthen, Marquess of, later, 6th Duke of Leeds (1775–1838), 1046, 1187, 1187n.
Carmarthen, Amelia, Marchioness of (1754–1784), 11, 15
 letter from, 14
Carnac, Capt., 2992, 2994–5
 letter from, 2993
Carnarvon, Elizabeth, Countess of (1752–1826), 1007n., 1014, 1094n., 1118n., 1119n., 1153, 1194, 1455, 1607, 1607n., 1615n., 2448n.
Carnarvon, Henry, 1st Earl of (1741–1811), 1014, 1735
Carnatic, the, 487, 520, 2977
Caroline, Queen, wife of George II (1683–1737), 1067
Caroline, Princess of Wales, later Queen (1768–1821), 859, 863–5, 871, 873, 878, 882, 887, 892, 894–5, 897, 899, 903–4, 910–11, 914–16, 918, 920, 922–5, 927, 931, 935n., 945–6, 950, 955, 963, 965n., 967–8, 971, 974, 977, 980n., 983–5, 986n., 987–9, 991, 997–9, 1000, 1004–9, 1012–18, 1020, 1024–6, 1028, 1032, 1034, 1040, 1044–5, 1050, 1056–9, 1059n., 1061, 1063–73, 1080, 1082, 1086, 1090–1, 1094n., 1097–8, 1099n., 1100, 1103, 1107, 1116–20, 1122, 1124, 1127, 1130–2, 1134, 1136–7, 1139–42, 1145, 1147, 1149–50, 1152–4, 1157, 1159–61, 1163, 1166, 1168, 1170, 1175, 1178, 1181, 1187, 1194, 1200–2, 1204, 1208, 1218, 1231–2, 1242, 1260, 1294, 1301, 1304–5, 1307, 1310, 1314, 1336, 1345, 1359, 1405–6, 1408, 1410, 1415, 1452, 1459–60, 1493, 1499n., 1603, 1607, 1610, 1612, 1615, 1618, 1620, 1621n., 1622, 1648, 1650, 1665n., 1674, 1697, 1697A, 1702, 1745, 1906n., 1910, 1919, 1923, 1926, 1929–31, 1933n., 1935, 1937, 1941, 1978, 1994–5, 1995n., 1996, 1996n., 1998, 1999n., 2010, 2013, 2017n., 2025, 2028, 2032–3, 2055, 2113n., 2157, 2171n., 2183n., 2196, 2196n., 2198–9, 2205, 2214, 2216, 2221, 2225, 2258, 2263, 2268, 2275, 2298, 2300, 2302–4, 2317n., 2330, 2337n., 2338, 2338n., 2351, 2351n., 2352n., 2353–4, 2355n., 2357, 2358n., 2362, 2373, 2376, 2378, 2381, 2385, 2388n., 2389, 2392, 2396n., 2398, 2455, 2475–6, 2477n., 2484n., 2491, 2548, 2559, 2564, 2564n., 2568n., 2571, 2571n., 2572, 2573n., 2576–8, 2578n., 2579n., 2581, 2583n., 2642, 2678, 2678n., 2682, 2684, 2689, 2723, 2777n., 2801n., 2818, 3238n., 3348, 3375, 3377, 3379n., 3388
 letters from, 886, 1094, 1096, 1104–5, 1113, 1115, 1143, 1158, 1164, 1167, 1184, 1197,

Chambers, 1751, 1770

Chambre, de, 2161

Champagné, Major-Gen. Forbes (*d.* 1816), 2894, 2894n.

Champagné, Lieut.-Gen. Sir Josiah (*c.* 1753–1840), 2894

Chanceaux, M. de, 198

Chancellor, Lord, *see* Thurlow, Loughborough, and Scott, Sir John

Chancellor, Lord [I.], *see* Clare, and Manners-Sutton, Lord Manners

Chapman, Charles (*c.* 1754–1809), 1842

Charette, M. de (*d.* 1796), 1019n., 1029n.

Charlemont, 1st Earl of (1728–99), 410, 1215, 1334
  letter from, 1239

Charlemont, 2nd Earl of (1775–1863), 3146
  letter from, 3085
  letter to, 3085

Charles, Archduke of Austria (1771–1847), 1091, 1112, 1240, 1437, 1440, 1442, 1470, 1505n., 1507, 1645, 2120, 2586, 3401

Charles I (1600–49), 1485

Charles II (1630–85), 1485, 3026

Charles III, King of Spain (1716–88), 382

Charles IV, King of Spain (1748–1819), 382, 2108, 2441

Charles XIII, King of Sweden (1748–1818), 529

Charlotte, Lady, *see* Bruce, Lady Charlotte, *and* Belasyse, Lady Charlotte

Charlotte, Queen (1744–1818), 15, 22n., 26–7, 29, 31–3, 36, 39, 41, 43, 47, 49, 51, 57, 61, 64, 69, 71–2, 76, 79, 79n., 94, 99, 106, 116, 118–20, 125, 134, 140, 157, 266, 278, 280, 287, 289, 309, 312, 316, 331, 332n., 338–9, 350, 352, 368, 371, 373, 380n., 384, 388, 390n., 397, 412n., 421, 433, 446n., 449, 457n., 464, 467, 477, 479, 484n., 591, 599, 605, 620n., 621n., 642, 690–1, 697, 706n., 735, 740, 742, 782, 792, 826, 835, 858–9, 871–2, 876n., 877, 891, 899, 903n., 920, 942, 945n., 958, 968, 972, 977, 977n., 979, 981, 981n., 983, 977–8, 1000, 1007, 1009, 1013–14, 1018, 1024, 1032, 1042, 1044, 1050, 1057, 1059n., 1060, 1065, 1067, 1072–4, 1090, 1094, 1100, 1106, 1111n., 1114, 1117, 1119, 1121, 1127, 1131, 1135, 1143, 1157, 1161, 1165, 1169, 1175, 1179, 1183, 1187, 1205, 1212, 1217, 1231, 1249, 1254, 1259n., 1260, 1272, 1275–6, 1288, 1292, 1303, 1335, 1337, 1344–6, 1359, 1362, 1369, 1371, 1375n., 1377–9, 1382–4, 1388n., 1390, 1392, 1405, 1407, 1416, 1421n., 1431, 1433, 1439, 1441, 1447, 1454n., 1458–9, 1471–2, 1477, 1493, 1501, 1511, 1513–14, 1531, 1558, 1560, 1563, 1567, 1594, 1594n., 1598n., 1603–4, 1609–10, 1614, 1617–18, 1620, 1621n., 1623, 1637, 1643, 1649, 1660n., 1678, 1685, 1687, 1690, 1694, 1696, 1702, 1702n., 1713, 1721, 1742, 1744, 1749, 1763,

Charlotte, Queen—*cont.*
  1769, 1777, 1789, 1796, 1802, 1806–7, 1809, 1810A, 1813–14, 1818, 1823–4, 1826, 1828, 1831, 1833, 1836, 1836n., 1839, 1843, 1853, 1859, 1869, 1880, 1897, 1901, 1910, 1913n., 1915, 1919–20, 1923, 1925–6, 1929–30, 1935, 1937, 1942n., 1958, 1960, 1966, 1968n., 1971, 1996n., 2010, 2014, 2022, 2032, 2055–6, 2058, 2065–6, 2077, 2081, 2085, 2091, 2128n., 2173, 2200n., 2263, 2263n., 2288, 2292, 2383, 2390, 2390n., 2398, 2400, 2470, 2491, 2493–4, 2511, 2517, 2521–2, 2556, 2560, 2565, 2567, 2570, 2572A, 2585, 2587, 2606, 2611, 2616, 2627, 2629–30, 2639, 2648, 2650, 2660–1, 2670, 2676–7, 2682, 2684–5, 2702, 2705, 2714, 2721–2, 2727, 2731, 2734, 2737, 2740–1, 2756–8, 2757n., 2765, 2775, 2777, 2781, 2783, 2786–7, 2790–2, 2800, 2800n., 2803, 2807, 2826n., 2833, 2849–50, 2855–6, 2877, 2879, 2897n., 2948, 2952, 2970, 2984, 2986, 2989, 2991, 3006, 3009n., 3011, 3013, 3030, 3034, 3038, 3044, 3047, 3047n., 3053, 3069, 3088, 3098–9, 3115, 3117–18, 3127, 3129, 3139, 3152, 3185, 3194–5, 3201, 3205, 3217, 3224, 3246, 3254, 3254n., 3268, 3276, 3281–5, 3295, 3300, 3302–4, 3308, 3349, 3374, 3383, 3396
  letters from, 2, 3, 26n., 28, 29n., 30n., 65, 114, 131, 161, 198n., 220, 222, 269, 274, 332, 340n., 341, 351, 360, 371n., 396, 396n., 412, 455, 600, 610, 619, 642n., 663, 667, 678, 686, 688, 698, 705, 718, 722, 730, 741, 749, 767, 773, 781, 790, 867, 873, 879, 894, 897, 900, 907, 942, 945, 970, 985, 987, 991, 1006, 1008, 1012, 1017, 1025, 1030, 1040, 1045, 1059, 1064, 1071, 1076, 1110, 1134, 1142, 1153, 1162, 1178, 1194, 1198, 1201, 1211, 1219–20, 1222, 1227, 1263, 1277, 1283, 1289, 1312, 1385, 1389, 1391, 1401, 1420, 1432, 1434, 1444, 1448, 1452, 1455, 1471n., 1478, 1512, 1542, 1542n., 1553, 1581, 1585, 1646, 1648, 1650, 1663, 1668, 1795, 1872, 1881, 1898, 1913, 1918, 2070, 2201, 2348, 2384, 2392, 2404, 2463, 2569, 2729, 2751, 2825, 2837, 2837n., 2848, 2886, 2897n., 2957, 3045, 3064, 3080, 3128, 3201, 3224n., 3227, 3238, 3238n., 3243, 3246, 3298, 3308, 3312, 3325, 3333, 3345, 3356, 3377
  memo by, 1810
  letters to, 1, 96n., 102, 131, 220, 241, 248, 274, 341, 360, 396, 406, 412, 414, 437, 446, 448, 617, 678, 684, 686, 694, 705, 722, 741, 773, 781, 873, 879, 894, 900, 921, 928, 932, 945, 987, 1006, 1012, 1028, 1033, 1040, 1045, 1059, 1064, 1071, 1079, 1083, 1103, 1116, 1118, 1124, 1134, 1142, 1153, 1176, 1178, 1194, 1198, 1201, 1211, 1217n., 1219–20, 1315, 1381, 1387, 1389, 1410, 1420, 1432, 1444, 1448, 1455, 1463, 1481, 1516, 1518, 1535, 1585, 1648, 1650, 1660, 1666, 1795,

Vol. I: 1–444; Vol. II: 445–942; Vol. III: 943–1416; Vol. IV: 1417–1865; Vol. V: 1866–2287; Vol. VI: 2288–2693; Vol. VII: 2694–3056; Vol. VIII: 3057–3480.

511

Cumberland, Anne, Duchess of (1743–1808), 29, 29*n*., 30*n*., 105*n*., 148, 158, 165, 168, 196, 198, 202, 265, 507, 518, 528, 530, 534, 537, 537*n*., 579, 607, 609, 1502*n*., 2483, 2483*n*., 3025, 3383
letters from, 200, 536, 537*n*., 854, 934, 989, 3384
letters to, 85, 953
Cumberland, Frederica, Duchess of (1778–1841), 740, 745, 1437*n*., 3475
her first husband, 636*n*.
Cumberland, Duke of, *see* Ernest Augustus
Cumberland, Henry Frederick, Duke of, (1745–90), 29–31, 35–6, 39, 41–2, 44, 49, 51, 79, 103, 140, 148, 156, 191, 218, 264, 322*n*., 388, 395, 468, 474*n*., 507, 516, 530, 534, 534*n*., 536, 537*n*., 580*n*., 600*n*., 3025
letters from 36*n*., 46*n*., 90, 103, 105*n*., 112*n*., 118*n*., 156, 158, 165, 198, 200, 202, 395, 395*n*., 518, 526, 3383
letters to, 85, 168, 196, 528
Cumberland, Richard (1732–1811), 2903*n*.
Cumberland, Richard, son of the dramatist, 2390*n*.
Cumberland, William Augustus, Duke of (1721–65), 39
Cumberland Lodge, 1958
stables at, 3474
Cuningham [Cunningham], Colonel, 2227
Cuninghame, John, *letter from*, 1899
Cunliffe, William, 3005, 3008
Cunynghame, Sir William Augustus (1747–1828), 486*n*.
Curran, John Philpot (1750–1817), 2156*n*., 2614
Curtis, Corporal Robert, 2896, 2896*n*.
Curwen, John Christian (1756–1828), 2832
Curwen's Act (1809), 2573*n*., 2832, 3289
Curzon, 1st Visct. (1730–1820), is refused an Earldom, 3180*n*.
Curzon, 2nd Visct., later Earl Howe (1796–1870), 3180*n*.
Cuyler, General Sir Cornelius (*d.* 1819), 1381
Czartoryski, Prince Adam (1734–1823), 2031, 3114

D'Aguine [*sic*], 1411
Dalhousie, 9th Earl of (1770–1838), 2102, 3463
Dalkeith, Lord, *see* Buccleuch, 4th Duke of
Dallas, Sir George (1758–1833), *letters from*, 2318, 2977
his sons, 2977
Dalrymple, 771
Dalrymple, 1886
Dalrymple, Mrs., 935
Dalrymple, Sir Hew Whitefoord (1750–1830), 1730, 1754, 1761, 2347, 2529–30, 2534*n*., 3124

Dalrymple, Admiral John (*d.* 1798), 935
Dalrymple, Col. William, 89, 111, 113, 116, 118, 140, 152, 614, 1034, 2171*n*., 2682
letters from, 990, 1207, 2682*n*.
letter to, 2171*n*.
Dalrymple, William, Duke of Kent's Treasurer, 1487, 1699
letter to, 1388*n*.
Dalrymple, Lieut.-Gen. William (*c.* 1736–1807), 789, 1770, 1838, 1841, 1949, 2074
Dalrymple-Hamilton, Sir Hew (1774–1834), 2649*n*., 2969, 2985*n*.
Daly, 3383
Daly, Denis Bowes (*c.* 1745–1821), 410, 1820, 2161
letter from, 1976
letter to, 1987
Daly, Richard, the Dublin theatre proprietor (*d.* 1813), 624*n*., 3140*n*.
D'Ama [*sic*], Comte Charles, 198
D'Ameland [De Ameland], Lady Augusta, *see* Murray
Damer, Lady Caroline (1752–1829), 1187*n*., 2085, 2470
Damer, Lionel (1748–1807), 439*n*., 1187, 1385
Damer, Mrs., 1187
Damers, the, 1277, 1289, 1379
Danish fleet, capture of (1807), 2422, 2456, 2588
Danloux, M., 1300
Danost, Messrs., 469*n*.
Danser, Major, 1700
Darby, 2059
Darby, Captain Frederick J. (*d.* 1809), Lady Lade's nephew, 2544–5, 2695
Dardanelles, expedition to the (1807), 2785
Darell, Sir Lionel (1742–1803), 1511, 1809
Darlington, 3rd Earl of (1766–1842), 2023, 2299, 2299*n*., 2582, 2801
letters from, 2023, 2064, 2582
Darnley, 4th Earl of (1767–1831), 956*n*., 1118, 1411*n*., 2015*n*.
letters from, 959*n*., 1834, 2481
letter to, 2481
Darnley, Elizabeth, Countess of (*d.* 1831), 2372*n*.
Dartmoor, plans to cultivate, 608, 613, 693, 712, 2561
prisoners of war at, to be enlisted in Army, 3245
Dartmouth, 3rd Earl of (1755–1810), 1607, 1613, 1923, 2015, 2116–17, 2123, 2183, 2392*n*., 2803*n*., 2903, 2914, 3192, 3218
Dartmouth, 4th Earl of (1784–1853), 2914
Dashwood, Helen, Lady (*d.* 1796), 1018, 1018*n*., 1024–5, 1032, 1050, 1057, 1071–2, 1076, 1176, 1178–9, 1197–8, 1211, 1219, 1231
letter from, 1179

Dashwood, Sir Henry Watkin (1745–1828), 1211

Dauphin, the, *see* Louis XVII

Davaray [*sic*], 471

Davenport, Mrs., 1025*n*.

David, 1063

Davidson, 2031

Davidson, Dr., 3031

Davies, a tradesman, 230

Davies, Dr. Jonathan (1736–1809), 65

Davis [Davies], 52–4, 57–8, 60, 62

Davis, Edward, 1615*n*.

Davis, Major, 1517

Davis, Richard Hart (1766–1842), 3480

Davison, 1039, 1842, 2210

Davison, Alexander (*c.* 1750–1829), 2642, 2680, 2680*n*.
letter from, 2108
letter to, 2109

Dawson, 1656, 1773

Dawson, Thomas, Dean of Clonmacnoise (*d.* 1811), 3252, 3273

Day, M., 2294–5
letter from, 2290

Daynes, Dawson & Co., 2112*n*.

Deane, Captain (*d.* 1794), Lord Moira's A.D.C., 832*n*., 834

Deamers, the, *see* Damers

De Beaune, John James (*d.* 1793), 524, 524*n*., 549*n*., 552*n*., 2642*n*.

Deboign, 1757

Debrett, John (*d.* 1822), 1343

De Camp, Miss, 1942

De Chambre, 2161

Decies, Lord (1743–1819), Archbishop of Tuam, 3273

Decken, Major-Gen. F., *letter from*, 3169A

Decken, Capt., 1598, 1710, 1712

De Clifford, *see* Clifford

De Coucy, Ingleram, husband of Edward III's daughter Isabella, 2046

De Crespigny, *see* Crespigny

De Foix, Gaston, Comte de Benauges, Captal de Buch, 2046

De Foix, Jean, Earl of Kendal (*d.* ?1485), 2046

De Lancey, General Oliver (1749–1822), 1077

Del Campo, Marquess, 382, 1211

Delhi, capture of (1803), 1757

'Delicate Investigation', the, into the conduct of the Princess, 2179, 2193, 2196, 3388

De Ligne, *see* Ligne

Delpini, *memo by*, 1849

Delvin, Lord (1785–1871), 1785

Demosthenes, 578*n*.

Dempster, George (1732–1818), 366

Denain, Princesse de, 611

De Neufchastel, Jean, Seigneur de Montagu, 2046

Denham, Sir John (1615–69), 1006

Denison, William Joseph (1770–1849), banker, and Lady Conyngham's sister, 3480

Derby, Earl of (1752–1834), 653, 1520*n*.
letters from, 2922, 2924, 2943, 2955, 3367

Derrit, 230

Desnoyer, 69

Despard, Edward Marcus (1751–1803), 1690, 3219

Desperate, a 14-gun brig, 2350

D'Esquerdes, Philip de Crevecoeur, Seigneur, 2046

D'Este, Augusta Emma, Lady Truro (1801–66), 728*n*., 1643, 1809

D'Este, Sir Augustus Frederick (1794–1848), son of the Duke of Sussex, 728*n*., 947, 1093, 1465, 1480, 1482, 1488, 1490, 1492, 1494, 1600*n*., 1643, 1643*n*., 1809, 1809*n*., 2299, 2322

D'Estifania, Duc, a Spanish nobleman, 1657

Dettingen, battle of (1743), 1189

Devaynes, Dawes, Noble and Co., bankers, 2112

Devaynes, John (*c.* 1725–1801), 1587

Devaynes, William (*c.* 1730–1809), 1587*n*.

Devon, Lord Lieut. of, 2395

Devon, Edward Courtenay, Earl of (1526–56), 3365

Devonshire, Elizabeth, Duchess of (*c.* 1760–1824), 132, 208, 504, 599*n*., 877*n*., 1118*n*., 1452*n*., 1966*n*., 2287, 2560, 2644*n*., 2881*n*., 3126
letter from, 3249
letters to, 2163A, 2560, 2644
in a sad state, 3132, 3249, 3249*n*.

Devonshire, Georgiana, Duchess of (1757–1806), 132*n*., 145, 148, 357*n*., 364*n*., 371*n*., 379*n*., 518*n*., 611, 616, 671, 683*n*., 708*n*., 728, 728*n*., 860, 1684, 1690, 1913*n*., 2163A, 2163, 2165, 2251*n*., 2644, 3126, 3132, 3455
letters from, 91, 208, 465, 469, 471, 482, 484, 484*n*., 504, 506, 508, 533, 559, 603, 629, 668, 860*n*., 877*n*., 1861, 1959*n*., 1966*n*., 1968*n*., 2287
memo by, 1777
letters to, 115, 696, 714*n*., 1467*n*., 1566*n*., 1578, 1592, 1748, 1865, 1865*n*., 2286

Devonshire, 5th Duke of (1748–1811), 91*n*., 115, 148, 208, 341*n*., 439*n*., 469*n*., 482, 484, 484*n*., 508, 533, 559, 599*n*., 603, 1264, 1578, 1660*n*., 1684, 1697A, 1861, 2163, 2163A, 2251*n*., 2287, 2311*n*., 2560, 2644, 2881*n*., 3249, 3249*n*., 3455
his death, 3125–6, 3130, 3132

Devonshire, 6th Duke of (1790–1858), 506*n*., 533, 696, 1861, 1865*n*., 2287, 2560*n*., 3125
letter from, 3132
letters to, 3126, 3418, 3446, 3455, 3468, 3470
succeeds father as Ld. Lieut. of Derbyshire, 3125–6
his special mission to Russia (1826), 3450
his Garter (1826), 3455
his Russian knighthood, 3470
resigns Household office (1828), 3468*n*.

Devonshire family, the, 402, 3244
Devonshire House, 1948, 2010, 2305n., 2560, 2644
Dewar, Lieut., 764
Dibden, Charles (1745–1814), 1500
Dickenson, 1782
Dickenson, John, 37n.
Dickson, Rev. William, Bishop of Down (1745–1804), 1690, 2287
Diepbrock, Col., 66
Digby, 1st Earl (1731–93), 688
Digby, Julia (d. 1807), 3298n.
Digby, Sir Kenelm (1603–65), 3307
Digby, Mary, Countess (d. 1794), 688
Digby, Robert, Admiral (1732–1815), 69
  letter from, 467n.
Digby, Stephen (1742–1800), 31n., 54, 54n., 790n.
  letter from, 396n.
Dilkes, W. T., 2639
Dillon, 12th Visct. (1745–1813), 1321, 1326–7
Dillon, Henry Augustus Dillon Lee, 13th Visct. (1777–1832), 3320
Dillon, John Joseph, letters from, 2498, 2565, 2609, 2609n.
Dingwall, Mr., 611n.
Directory, the French, 1211, 1223, 1270n., 1355
Disbrowe, Col. Edward (c. 1754–1818), 2014, 2684, 3375
Dissenters, electoral influence of, 473n.
Dobinson, a creditor of Georgiana, Duchess of Devonshire, 465n.
Dod, 2161
Dodd, 1462n.
Dodd, Mrs., 2347
Dodd, Rev. Philip Stanhope (1775–1852), 3355, 3361, 3368
Dodd, Captain Thomas, the Duke of Kent's A.D.C. and Secretary, 1462n., 1699–1700, 1704, 1709, 1749, 1775, 2347n., 2550n., 2670n., 2674, 2736n.
  letter from, 1709n.
  letters to, 2080n., 2347
Dodington, George Bubb, Lord Melcombe (1691–1762), 422, 971, 1185
Doherty, 2453
'Dolly', see Adolphus Frederick
Domeier, Dr. William, 1557, 1559, 1652–3, 1660–1, 1663, 1668
Domett, Admiral Sir William (1754–1828), 3212
'Domini', see Keate, Thomas
Dominica, Collectorship of, 3140
Don, General Sir George (1754–1832), 1515
  letter to, 2035
Donahoe [sic ?Donaghue], 1457
Don Gabriel, see under Spain
Donnelly, Sir Ross (c. 1761–1840), 2195
Donnithorne [Donnythorne], 539

Donoughmore, 1st Earl of (1756–1825), 2819n.
  letters from, 2375, 2819
Donovan, Captain Jeremiah, 2550
Donovan, Lawrence, 2607n.
Dorchester, Sir Guy Carleton, Lord (1724–1808), 254, 800, 954, 954n., 1379
Dorchester, Joseph Damer, 1st Earl of (1718–1798), 2470n.
Dorchester, 2nd Earl of (1746–1808), 1955, 1955n., 2066, 2085, 2470
Dorker, J., 2112n.
Dormer, of Fowey, 631
Dornberg, Colonel, 3167, 3256
  letter from, 3256n.
Dornford, Prince Augustus's friend, 385, 570
Dorset, 3rd Duke of (1745–99), 156, 999, 1012 1444
  letters from, 925, 925n.
  letters to, 361n., 390n.
Doublet, Francis, of Groenveldt, father of Lady Holdernesse, 9n.
Douglas, Capt., 3096
Douglas, Sir Andrew Snape (?1763–97), 1268
Douglas, Andrew Snape, diplomatist, 2892
Douglas, Charlotte, Lady, 2099, 2113n., 2183, 2183n., 2196, 2198, 2304, 2338, 2351, 2385, 2389, 2678
Douglas, Frederick Sylvester North (1791–1819), 3366
Douglas, Sir Howard (1776–1861), 3136
Douglas, John, Bishop of Salisbury (1721–1807), 1768, 2914
Douglas, Sir John (d. 1814), 2099, 2113, 2113n., 2183, 2196, 2296, 2304, 2389, 2678
  letter to, 2183n.
Douglas, Marquess of, later 10th Duke of Hamilton (1767–1852), 2302, 2709, 3410
Douglas, Sylvester, Lord Glenbervie (1743–1823), 761n., 769n., 864n., 978n., 1092n., 1186n., 1198n., 1239n., 1266n., 1345n., 1454n., 1468n., 1518n., 1537n., 1570, 1603n., 1620n., 1643n., 1665n., 1670n., 1786n., 1805n., 1807n., 1812n., 1835n., 1836n.
Dover, Collector of the Customs at, 426
  election (1784), 426n.
Dover, Joseph, Lord (1724–92), Col. of the first Life Guards, 447
Down, Co., election (1805), 2074, 2289n.
Downes, William, Lord (1751–1826), 2156
Downing, a mason, 1215
Downpatrick, 2289n.
Downs, William Augustus, 2679
  letters from, 2427, 2465
Downshire, 2nd Marquess of (1753–1801), 1338
Downshire, 3rd Marquess of (1788–1845),
  letter from, 2707
Downshire, Mary, Marchioness of, and Baroness Sandys (1764–1836), 2002–3, 2203, 2289, 2289n., 2600n., 2707, 2707n., 3231n.

Vol. I: 1–444; Vol. II: 445–942; Vol. III: 943–1416; Vol. IV: 1417–1865; Vol. V: 1866–2287; Vol. VI: 2288–2693; Vol. VII: 2694–3056; Vol. VIII: 3057–3480.

Vol. I: 1–444; Vol. II: 445–942; Vol. III: 943–1416; Vol. IV: 1417–1865; Vol. V: 1866–2287; Vol. VI: 2288–2693; Vol. VII: 2694–3056; Vol. VIII: 3057–3480.

521

Edward, Duke of Kent—*cont.*
2670*n.*, 2674, 2736, 2736*n.*, 2802, 2807, 2847,
2929, 2953, 3124, 3348, 3372
memo by, 1810, 1855, 3124
letters to, 1487*n.*, 1607, 1635, 1708, 1809,
1814, 1818, 1840, 1994*n.*, 2015*n.*, 2126,
2168, 2194, 2267, 2317*n.*, 2401, 2462
asks for a command in the Mediterranean
(1811), 3124
would like office of Master-Gen. of the
Ordnance, 3124, 3372
Edward Augustus, Duke of York and Albany
(1739–67), 3218
Edwards, Mrs. A., 2284
Edwards, Bryan (1743–1800) ,1317
Edwards, J., of Truro, *letter from,* 539
Edwards, Richard, printer, 2385
Edwin, John (1768–1805), actor, 1385
Egerton, Mrs. Ariana Margaret (*c.* 1752–1827),
2775
letter from, 2775
her mother, 2775
Egg [Egge], gun-maker, 57, 230
Egle, 803
Eglintoun, 11th Earl of (1726–96), 517–18,
1213–14
Eglintoun, 12th Earl of (1739–1819), 1213,
1844, 2302*n.*, 2649, 2803*n.*, 2969
Egmont, 2nd Earl of (1711–70), 970
Egremont, Countess of (*d.* 1794), 28
Egremont, 3rd Earl of (1751–1837), 341*n.*, 591,
1183*n.*, 1278*n.*, 1287, 1370, 1375, 1468*n.*,
1697A, 1861*n.*, 3233
letters to, 1468, 1505, 1733
Egypt, office of Consul-General of, 2601
Elboeuf, Duke of (1596–1657), 2046
Eld, George (*d.* 1793), 792
Eldon, Lord, *see* Scott, Sir John
Eldon, Elizabeth, Lady (*d.* 1831), 2482*n.*
Elections, parliamentary, see under Alborough,
Antrim, Appleby, Aylesbury, Ayr Burghs,
Ayrshire, Barnstaple, Bedford, Bodmin,
Buckinghamshire, Buteshire, Caithness-
shire, Callington, Cambridge University,
Camelford, Canterbury, Carlisle, Cornwall,
Coventry, Dover, Down Co., Dublin City,
Dublin Co., Dumbartonshire, Durham,
Exeter, Eye, Fowey, Gloucester, Gloucester-
shire, Haslemere, Helston, Honiton, Hor-
sham, Huntingdon, Huntingdonshire, Ilches-
ter, Kilkenny Co., Kincardineshire, Kirk-
cudbright, Knaresborough, Launceston,
Leicester, Linlithgowshire, Lisburn, Lis-
keard, Middlesex, Newport (Cornwall),
Newtown (I. of Wight), Nottinghamshire,
Okehampton, Orford, Petersfield, Plymouth,
Poole, Portsmouth, Shropshire, St. Ives,
Southwark, Stafford, Steyning, Stirlingshire,
Stockbridge, Sudbury, Totnes, Tregony,
Wells, Wendover, Westminster, Wilton,
Winchelsea
Eley [*sic*], 280

Elford, Sir William (1749–1837), 2153, 2153*n.*,
2301
letter from, 2153*n.*
his son, 2153*n.*
Elgin, 5th Earl of (1732–71), 1025*n.*
Elgin, 7th Earl of (1766–1841), 492, 1398*n.*,
1438, 1694, 1721, 1931, 1941, 1981*n.*, 2167A,
3180*n.*, 3370, 3370*n.*
letter to, 3370*n.*
wants promotion in the peerage, 3370*n.*
Elgin, Martha, Countess of (1740?–1810),
1025, 1229, 1231–2, 1275, 1301*n.*, 1384–5,
1389, 1434, 1458, 1467, 1470, 1477–8, 1547,
1551, 1623, 1637, 1645, 1660, 1663, 1668,
1678, 1696, 1792, 1839, 1857, 1933*n.*, 1935,
1940, 1981, 2115–7, 2119, 2692
letters from, 1025*n.*, 1622, 1665*n.*, 1721, 1919,
1926, 1931, 1933, 1941, 1981*n.*
memo by, 1706*n.*
letters to, 1249, 1261, 1266, 1273, 1276, 1278,
1288, 1290, 1293, 1296, 1299, 1335, 1344,
1374, 1417*n.*, 1438, 1447, 1459, 1472*n.*,
1473, 1493, 1502*n.*, 1503*n.*, 1505*n.*, 1508,
1510*n.*, 1550*n.*, 1560, 1563, 1567, 1569*n.*,
1572, 1660*n.*, 1678*n.*, 1681, 1694, 1927, 1933,
1933*n.*
Elgin, Mary, Countess of (*d.* 1855), 1438,
1721
Eliot, Edward, Lord (1727–1804), Receiver-
Gen. of Duchy of Cornwall, 475, 475*n.*, 476,
512, 515, 631
Eliot, William, later 2nd Earl of St. Germans
(1767–1845), *letter from,* 2484*n.*
Elizabeth I, Queen (1533–1603), 564, 777,
1593*n.*, 2046
Elizabeth, Princess, later, Landgravine of
Hesse-Homburg (1770–1840), 43, 156, 280,
280*n.*, 741–2, 790, 897, 921, 945, 967, 1006,
1025, 1028, 1030, 1033, 1040, 1064, 1103,
1135, 1153, 1169, 1174, 1187–8, 1198, 1211,
1220, 1249, 1276, 1309, 1335, 1379, 1385,
1389, 1405, 1420, 1510, 1603, 1818, 1839,
1856, 1958, 1970, 2071, 2357, 2402, 2409–10,
2491*n.*, 2502, 2522, 2532, 2542, 2552, 2605,
2616, 2627, 2650, 2676, 2722, 2737, 2740*n.*,
3038, 3254, 3254*n.*, 3375
letters from, 600*n.*, 790*n.*, 891, 920, 942,
968, 977, 981, 983, 997, 1000, 1007, 1009,
1014, 1018, 1024, 1032, 1044, 1050, 1057,
1060, 1065, 1071*n.*, 1073, 1106, 1114, 1121,
1131, 1144, 1165, 1169, 1174, 1187, 1217,
1224, 1226, 1229, 1231, 1254, 1260, 1272,
1275, 1284, 1292, 1303, 1313, 1337, 1346,
1359, 1382, 1400, 1405, 1407, 1431, 1433,
1458, 1471, 1514, 1614, 1618, 1702, 1813,
1815, 1824, 1826, 1828, 1831, 1833, 1836,
1843, 1857, 1874, 2053, 2065, 2067, 2081,
2085, 2091, 2174*n.*, 2200*n.*, 2343, 2358, 2365,
2386, 2391, 2398, 2470, 2472, 2484A, 2491,
2493, 2502, 2511, 2515, 2517, 2521, 2532,
2542, 2552, 2556, 2572A, 2587, 2589, 2648,
2663, 2692, 2702, 2705, 2724, 2731, 2734,
2737, 2775, 2777, 2781, 2783, 2786, 2791,

Elizabeth, Princess—*cont.*
2856, 2879, 3006, 3037, 3044, 3098, 3195, 3309
letters to, 1433, 1926, 2383, 2775, 2877
Elizabeth, Lady, *see* Devonshire, Elizabeth, Duchess of
Ellenborough, Anne, Lady (*c.* 1769–1843), 2678
Ellenborough, Lord (1750–1818), 2123*n.*, 2148*n.*, 2179, 2183*n.*, 2259, 2303, 2338, 2338*n.*, 2363, 2678, 2681, 2933, 2974*n.*, 2984, 3127, 3128*n.*, 3129, 3194, 3238, 3380, 3474*n.*; *letter from*, 1629*n.*
letters to, 2147*n.*, 2148*n.*
Ellice, Edward (*c.* 1783–1863), 2230*n.*
Elliot, Sir Gilbert, 1st Earl of Minto (1751–1814), 170*n.*, 218*n.*, 221*n.*, 306*n.*, 310*n.*, 316*n.*, 331*n.*, 335*n.*, 340*n.*, 341*n.*, 374*n.*, 375*n.*, 393*n.*, 403*n.*, 415*n.*, 416*n.*, 432*n.*, 459*n.*, 460*n.*, 531*n.*, 1156*n.*, 1198*n.*, 1805*n.*, 2128*n.*, 2155, 2419*n.*, 3143, 3292, 3297, 3329
letters from, 330*n.*, 370*n.*, 412*n.*, 446*n.*, 462*n.*, 467*n.*, 554*n.*, 761*n.*, 1259*n.*, 1301*n.*, 1499*n.*, 2091*n.*, 2198*n.*, 2204*n.*, 2264*n.*
letters to, 885*n.*, 2156*n.*
Gov.-Gen. of Bengal, 3092, 3292
promotion in peerage for, 3292, 3297
Elliot, Hugh (1752–1830), 148, 170*n.*, 445, 445*n.*, 611*n.*
letters from, 148*n.*, 170
Elliot, Lord, *see* Eliot
Elliot, Mrs. (*d.* 1823), 1435
Elliot, Sir John (1736–86), 532, 1435
Elliot, William (1766–1818), 2156, 2156*n.*, 2917*n.*, 2966, 3358, 3363
letter from, 2156*n.*
Ellis, Charles Rose, Lord Seaford (1771–1845), 1861*n.*
Ellis, George, soldier, 3228
Ellis, Sir Henry (1777–1869), 3467
Ellis, Welbore, 1st Baron Mendip (1713–1802), 576
Elliston, Robert William (1774–1831), actor, 1665, 1942, 1958
Elphinstone, George Keith, Visct. Keith (1746–1823), 69, 157, 166, 212, 216, 239, 247, 250, 254, 258, 262, 264, 266, 268, 284, 343, 388, 567, 948, 1213, 1216, 1237, 1245, 1382, 1642, 1652, 1660, 1660*n.*, 1690*n.*, 1695, 1697, 1697A, 1942, 2024, 2054, 2350, 3085, 3220, 3231*n.*, 3307, 3400
letters from, 213, 566, 738, 751, 796, 1241, 1695*n.*, 2029, 2040, 2044, 2049
letters to, 405, 746, 1236, 1238, 1246, 1250
Elphinstone, 11th Lord (1737–94), 518
Elphinstone, 12th Lord (1764–1813), 1695*n.*, 1697A, 1942, 1956, 2029, 2049
letters from, 1954, 2024
Elphinstone, Margaret Mercer, Baroness Keith (1788–1867), 3231*n.*

Elphinstone, Margaret Mercer—*cont.*
letters to, 3098*n.*, 3100*n.*, 3110*n.*, 3155*n.*, 3195*n.*, 3217*n.*, 3246*n.*, 3263*n.*, 3285*n.*, 3291*n.*, 3294*n.*, 3299*n.*, 3303*n.*, 3308*n.*, 3344*n.*, 3349*n.*
Duke of Clarence wishes to marry, 3231*n.*
Elphinstone, William Fullarton (1740–1834), 2040, 2155
Elrington, Thomas (1760–1835), 3222
Elven, a sloop, 2928
Ely, 1st Marquess of (1738–1806), 2167
Emily, *see* Amelia
Emperor, the, *see* Leopold II and Francis II [I]
Ende, Capt., 818
Engerström, M. d', 3232, 3248
Enghien, Duc d' (1772–1804), 1841
Epernon, Duke of (1554–1642), 634
Epsom Races (1806), 2277
Ernest Augustus, Elector of Hanover, father of George I (1629–98), 570
Ernest Augustus, Duke of Cumberland, later King of Hanover (1771–1851), 11, 161, 259, 581, 581*n.*, 584, 750, 766, 771, 778–9, 792, 819, 849–50, 856, 859, 872, 876*n.*, 882, 889, 892, 898, 900, 903, 995, 1016, 1063, 1067, 1079, 1079*n.*, 1083, 1111*n.*, 1124, 1131, 1144, 1148, 1151, 1153, 1157, 1187, 1237, 1267, 1400, 1403, 1420–1, 1421*n.*, 1425–6, 1426*n.*, 1432, 1437, 1439, 1444, 1448, 1454*n.*, 1457, 1461, 1474, 1474*n.*, 1487, 1490, 1512, 1514–5, 1531–3, 1548, 1548*n.*, 1583, 1597, 1597*n.*, 1598*n.*, 1609, 1617, 1643, 1660, 1663, 1665, 1668, 1670, 1701*n.*, 1702*n.*, 1718, 1769, 1802, 1806, 1810, 1814, 1901, 1912, 1937, 1968*n.*, 1971, 2065, 2073, 2080, 2147–8, 2169*n.*, 2171*n.*, 2173, 2197, 2258, 2263, 2288, 2288*n.*, 2292, 2347, 2357, 2362*n.*, 2398*n.*, 2406, 2479*n.*, 2493*n.*, 2498, 2515, 2550*n.*, 2570, 2605–6, 2611, 2616, 2651, 2672*n.*, 2676, 2725–34, 2737, 2741, 2743, 2756, 2763, 2770*n.*, 2775, 2783, 2789, 2801, 2825*n.*, 2826*n.*, 2879, 2879*n.*, 3155*n.*, 3174*n.*, 3195*n.*, 3242, 3247, 3299*n.*, 3375
letters from, 261, 385, 425, 651, 675, 750*n.*, 760, 808, 810, 812, 815, 817, 820, 827, 829, 829*n.*, 836, 852, 858, 863, 871, 877, 881, 885, 890, 896, 901, 904, 906, 912, 914, 950, 963, 976, 992, 1005, 1031, 1038, 1051, 1062, 1111, 1135, 1161, 1199, 1403*n.*, 1413, 1416, 1421*n.*, 1474*n.*, 1806, 2169, 2196*n.*, 2598, 3099
letters to, 876*n.*, 1482, 2285, 3013, 3475, 3477
his strong support of Perceval, 3225
Errington, Henry, Mrs. Fitzherbert's uncle (1740–1819), 148, 1454, 2682*n.*
letter from, 3233
Erroll, Elizabeth Jemima, Countess of (*d.* 1831), 1916
Erskine, Miss, a Maid of Honour, 1094*n.*
Erskine, Cardinal, 532, 777, 3026

Fitzroy, George Ferdinand, 2nd Baron South-ampton (1761–1810), *letter from*, 174
Fitzroy girls, the, 3263*n*.
Fitzwarine, Barony of, 3035
Fitzwilliam, 2nd Earl (1748–1833), 357, 469*n*., 473, 490, 1320*n*., 1601*n*., 1709*n*., 1735, 1861, 2123, 2123*n*., 2229, 2237, 2246, 2273, 2338*n*., 2341*n*., 2351*n*., 3065*n*., 3094, 3410*n*., 3355*n*.
letters from, 975, 1895*n*., 2246, 2273, 2302*n*., 2351*n*.
letters to, 439*n*., 706*n*., 720*n*., 885*n*., 1046*n*., 1783*n*., 1955, 2123*n*., 2246, 2311*n*., 2337*n*.
and the Garter, 3065*n*.
dismissal of (1819), 3410
Fitzwilliam, Charlotte, Countess (1747–1822), *letter to*, 2678*n*.
Fitzwilliam, General John (1714–89), 447*n*.
Fleeming, Charles Elphinstone (1774–1840), 2024, 2029, 2029*n*.
Fleet Prison, the 1643*n*.
Fleischer, Major de, 2450
Fletcher, Sir Henry (*c.* 1727–1807), 2324*n*.
Flint, Sir Charles William (1777–1834), 2632
Flogging in the Army, 3074, 3171, 3228
Floyd, General Sir John (1748–1818), 541
Fludyer, George (1761–1837), 3394
Fogg, 2585
Folch, Colonel, 2910
Folkestone, William, Visct., later 3rd Earl of Radnor (1779–1869), 2293–4, 2318, 2468*n*., 2545, 2896*n*., 2966, 3091
letters from, 3102–3
Fondbrune [*sic*], M. de, 683
Fontana, Dr. Felix (1730–1805), 532
Fontiny, M., 543
letter to, 544
Fontiny, Mme., 544
Fonty [*sic*], Mrs., 3188
Foord, Mrs., 2327
Foord, Rev. T. Fyshe, the Prince's Chaplain (appointed 1806), 2324, 2327, 2339
Foote, Samuel (1720–77), 3218
Forbes, 18th Lord (1765–1843), 2082, 2588
Forbes, Visct. (1785–1836), 3367*n*.
Forbes, C., 3093*n*.
Forbes, Frederick (1776–1817), 3172; his wife, 3172
Forbes, Maj.-Gen. Gordon (*d.* 1828), 1499; his son, 1499
Forbes, John, Recorder of Drogheda, 470*n*.
letters from, 470, 853
Forbes, Admiral John (1714–96), 395
Forbes, Sir William (*d.* 1828), 3307
Ford, Dr. John, *letter from*, 1436*n*.
Ford, Sir Richard (?1758–1806), 624, 624*n*.
Fordice [?], 1403*n*.
Fordyce, John (*c.* 1728–1809), 1621*n*.
Fordyce, Lady Margaret (1753–1814), 148, 864, 1198, 1198*n*.
letter from, 864
Forest, Captain, 1385
'Forest, Monsieur', 1448

Forester, Lady Katherine Mary (1779–1829), 2165, 3471
Forester, 1st Baron (1767–1828), *letter to*, 3471
crippled with gout, 3472*n*.
Forester, Rev. Townshend (1772–1841), 3472, *letter from*, 3472*n*.
Forrester, 3394
Forster [?Foster], 2407, 3222
Forster, a solicitor, 2172, 2172*n*., 2227
Forster, B. M., 2449
Fortescue, Hugh, Earl (1753–1841), *letter from*, 2395
Forth, Rev. John (*c.* 1764–1816), 2324, 2327, 2333, 2339
Forth, Nathaniel Parker (*d.* 1809), 531*n*., 579, 579*n*., 1192, 1541, 1574
letters from, 579*n*., 1540, 1544, 1550, 1571, 1571*n*., 1573, 1575, 1575*n*., 1633
his wife, 1571
Fortt, *see* Forth
Foster [Forster], a forger, 2918, 2933
Foster, Sir Augustus John (1780–1848), 2881, 2900, 3004, 3029
Foster, Lady Elizabeth, *see* Devonshire, Elizabeth, Duchess of
Foster, Frederick Thomas Hervey (*b.* 1777), 3249
Foster, John, 1st Baron Oriel (1740–1828), 1735, 2881*n*., 3036
Foster John (*c.* 1787–1846), architect, 3141
Fosters, the, 1861
Foudroyant, an 80-gun ship, 258
Foulston, Cabanel and Robinson, Messrs., 3214
Fowey politics, 571–2, 631, 633, 637, 641, 641*n*.
Fowke, Sir Thomas (*d.* 1786), 3383
Fowler, Duke of York's dentist, 249*n*.
Fox, Charles James (1749–1806), 73, 86, 91, 91*n*., 191, 218*n*., 221*n*., 291*n*., 303, 310–11, 323*n*., 331*n*., 335*n*., 354*n*., 357*n*., 365*n*., 366, 374*n*., 375*n*., 384, 398–9, 402, 439, 462–3, 473–4, 492*n*., 532, 551, 564, 578, 592, 599*n*., 635, 701, 704*n*., 706*n*., 720, 877*n*., 1056*n*., 1153, 1153*n*., 1270, 1270*n*., 1274, 1329*n*., 1396, 1590*n*., 1601*n*., 1690, 1697A, 1707*n*., 1735*n*., 1780, 1802, 1812, 1812*n*., 1830*n*., 1835*n*., 1842, 1842*n*., 1844, 1866, 1868, 1868*n*., 1871, 1871*n*., 1882*n*., 1886, 1892, 1908*n*., 1929*n*., 1937, 1939, 1966*n*., 1987, 2027, 2031, 2052, 2083, 2123, 2123*n*., 2127–8, 2127*n*., 2128*n*., 2130, 2131*n*., 2132, 2134, 2134*n*., 2139, 2141, 2143, 2145, 2147*n*., 2148*n*., 2149–50, 2156, 2158, 2161–2, 2167A, 2171, 2173*n*., 2175, 2179, 2196*n*., 2198*n*., 2218, 2218*n*., 2220–1, 2223–6, 2229–31, 2232*n*., 2236*n*., 2237, 2239, 2241, 2243–4, 2248, 2250, 2252, 2253, 2256, 2261–2, 2273, 2283, 2287, 2288*n*., 2297*n*., 2301*n*., 2302, 2305*n*., 2311*n*., 2313*n*., 2318, 2322*n*., 2327, 2329, 2329*n*., 2334, 2340, 2341*n*., 2373, 2415*n*., 2448*n*., 2467*n*., 2501, 2555, 2561, 2679, 2680*n*., 2760, 2780, 2794, 2816, 2818, 2833, 2919, 3094, 3115, 3244, 3344, 3352, 3383

Vol. I: 1–444; Vol. II: 445–942; Vol. III: 943–1416; Vol. IV: 1417–1865; Vol. V: 1866–2287; Vol. VI: 2288–2693; Vol. VII: 2694–3056; Vol. VIII: 3057–3480.

Garrick, David (1717–79), 3335
Garrow, Sir William (1760–1840), 2135, 2232n., 2417, 2477n., 2564, 2571, 2918
letter from, 2135n.
Garter, Order of the, 39, 161, 165, 490, 1085, 1422n., 1468, 1468n., 1761, 1768, 1998, 2032, 2046, 2123, 2125, 2321, 2341, 2341n., 2349, 2349n., 2621, 2704, 2803, 2803n., 2889n., 2914, 3026, 3065n., 3285, 3294n., 3383, 3404, 3455
Garth, Miss Frances (*b.* ? 1772), 1071–2, 1176, 1178, 1198, 1211, 1231–2, 1263, 1266n., 1301, 1603, 1607n., 1615n., 1620, 2182–3, 2185–6, 2189, 2189n., 2448n.
letter from, 2184
letters to, 1179.
Garth, General George (*d.* 1819), 158, 534, 537n, 609, 953, 1071, 1071n., 3383
Garth, General Thomas (1744–1829), 1071, 1071n., 1187n., 1325, 1328–9, 1384, 1583n., 2051, 2185–6, 2189, 2597, 2646, 2659–60, 3013
Garthshore, William (1764–1806), 1013n., 1236, 1387, 1528n., 1599n., 2097, 2562n.
Garton, 1187, 1473
Gascoigne, J., *see* Gaskoin
Gascoyne, Isaac (1770–1841), 906, 912, 1419, 2979
Gaskoin, J., Clerk of the Prince's Stables, 1419, 1519n., 2553, 3375
Gaskoin, Mary Anne (*c.* 1779–1811), 2605, 2627, 2694, 2710, 2718, 2763, 2765, 2768, 3375
Gates, Horatio (1728–1806), 1586
Gaubert, M., 128–9, 232, 236
Gazette, the, see *London Gazette*
Gazetteer, the 632, 1279
Geddes, Capt., 3066
General Advertiser, the, 36n., 324, 340n.
General Election (1806), 2288, 2288n., 2298, 2329, 2329n.
General Fast Days, 3350
Geneva, 19, state of, in 1774, 18
a dull place, 479
George I (1660–1727), 102, 1693
George II (1683–1760), 31, 79n., 80–1, 102, 235n., 970, 1067, 1189, 1347, 1462n., 1998, 3218
George III (1738–1820), *passim*
letters from, 26–7, 29, 29n., 31, 44, 61, 71, 76n., 79, 79n., 80–2, 87, 89n., 110n., 119, 122–3, 135, 137–8, 142, 159, 167, 225, 229, 231, 238, 265, 461, 655, 719, 766, 780, 865, 980n., 1058n., 1059n., 1082, 1117, 1128, 1160, 1305, 1308, 1325, 1347n., 1475, 1619, 1726, 1728, 1906n., 1919n., 1923, 1964n., 1966, 1968n., 1975, 1977, 1981, 1988n., 1991n., 1995, 1999, 1999n., 2002, 2005n., 2015, 2017, 2017n., 2019, 2026, 2105, 2180, 2182, 2185, 2189n., 2351, 2353, 2355n., 2362n.,

George III—*cont.*
2378n., 2448, 2462, 2482, 2484, 2576, 2578, 2717
memo by, 704
letters to, 24–5, 26n., 27, 27n., 29, 30n., 31, 36n., 39n., 46n., 54n., 55n., 56n., 61, 64n., 69n., 78n., 80, 83, 88, 95n., 96n., 97n., 104n., 119, 121, 124, 133, 136, 141, 159, 163, 169, 182, 234, 240, 265, 321n., 395n., 445n., 449, 461, 467, 512, 534n., 537n., 589, 595n., 621n., 655, 703, 709, 719, 721, 766, 780, 865, 973, 980, 1022, 1059n., 1082, 1105, 1108–9, 1117, 1119–20, 1122, 1128, 1133, 1136, 1140, 1143, 1157–8, 1160, 1167, 1254n., 1307, 1310, 1314, 1325, 1347, 1369n., 1406, 1475, 1479, 1539, 1543, 1600n., 1619, 1726, 1728, 1739, 1792, 1800, 1906, 1919n., 1923, 1929, 1966, 1969, 1972n., 1974, 1977, 1981n., 1988n., 1994n., 1995, 1995n., 1996n., 1999, 1999n., 2001n., 2002, 2005n., 2009n., 2015n., 2017n., 2022n., 2026n., 2033n., 2047, 2105, 2107n., 2114n., 2180, 2180n., 2182, 2184–5, 2198, 2330, 2381, 2385, 2388n., 2396, 2448, 2482, 2484, 2576, 2578, 2619, 2714, 2717, 2725, 2735
memo by, 1981, 2001, 2005, 2116
reports about his health, 3064, 3070, 3098n., 3099, 3100, 3100n., 3110, 3113, 3117, 3120, 3123, 3123n., 3138, 3185, 3194–5, 3217, 3224, 3254, 3331, 3337, 3349, 3375, 3377
eats hasty pudding, 3100n., 3110n., 3113
no money for payment of his doctors, 3199
his Household establishment (1812), 3260, 3268, 3276, 3281–4, 3294n., 3300, 3304, 3308, 3310, 3345
George, Prince of Wales, later George IV (1762–1830), *passim*
Patron of Linnæan Society, 3058, 3222
his Fête (1811), 3064, 3068–9, 3074n., 3135
final separation from Mrs. Fitzherbert, 3074n.
living at York House, 3160, 3184
and Drury Lane Theatre, 3214, 3216, 3237
fears of his hostility to Cath. Eman., 3244
sprains his ankle, 3246, 3246n., 3249, 3270, 3273n., 3308n., 3318, 3348
question of his debts, 3269, 3272, 3275
memo by, 3276, 3408
returns to Carlton House, 3268n., 3294n.
his pictures, 3307
claims arrears of revenue of Duchy of Cornwall, 3275–6, 3300, 3341, 3341n., 3385
his offer of office to Grey and Grenville, 3371
is sent Marshal Jourdan's baton, 3390
his fantastic suggestion to Vansittart, 3401
presses for a divorce (1819), 3407, 3409
Bill relating to his private property, 3425, 3480
and Catholic Relief Bill (1829), 3478
his Will, 3480
his natural son, 3480

530

Gordon, Jane, Duchess of (1748–1812), 472, 472n., 1440, 3084

Gordon, Sir James Willoughby (?1772–1851), 1462n., 1531, 1915, 2030, 2074, 2082–3, 2089, 2111, 2178, 2347, 2416, 2422, 2442, 2445, 2617, 2621, 2625, 2634, 2645, 2739, 2764, 2803, 2813, 2823, 2928, 2947n., 2952, 3011, 3048, 3095, 3120, 3148, 3169, 3242, 3311, 3332

letters from, 2171, 2370n., 2610, 2823, 2835, 2919, 2956, 3001, 3169n., 3183n., 3244

letters to, 2171, 2658

appointed Quarter Master General (1811), 3110, 3120, 3148n.

his wife, *see* Gordon, Mrs. Julia

Gordon, Lord William (1744–1823), 472n.

Gore, William John (1767–1836), 2814

Gorton, 907

Gosford, 2nd Earl of (1776–1849), 3085, 3085n.

his Representative Peerage, 3146, 3146n., 3172, 3231n.

Gosselin, Admiral Thomas Le Marchant (1765–1857), 966

Gott, Sir Henry, 562n.

Göttingen, 255, 263, 339, 581n.

Gottorp, Count de, *see* Gustavus IV

Gough, Rev. Mr., 3410

Gough, 1847

Goulburn, Henry (1784–1856), 3474

letters from, 2942, 3005, 3175, 3369

Gould, Sir Charles (later, Morgan) 1st Bart. (1726–1806), 364

Gould, Sir Charles (later, Morgan) 2nd Bart. (1760–1846), 364

'Goully', *see* Goldsworthy, Miss

Gower, Lord, *see* Stafford, Marquess of

Gower, Earl, later 2nd Duke of Sutherland (1786–1861), 686, 2800n.

Graaff, Van der, 492

Grafton, 3rd Duke of (1735–1811), 1971, 2936

Grafton, 4th Duke of (1760–1844), 502, 1692, 2276, 2941n.

letters from, 1675, 1683, 1683n., 3073

letters to, 1675, 1683, 1683n., 1688, 3086

Graham, 1504, 1588, 1942

Graham, auctioneer, 2222

Graham, Marquess of, later 5th Duke of Montrose (1799–1874), 3458

Graham, Messrs. of Lincoln's Inn, 542

Graham, Sir Robert (1744–1836), 761n., 1338, 1361, 1446, 1504, 1588, 1842

Graham, Sir Thomas, Baron Lynedoch (1748–1843), 2954n., 2960–1, 2966, 3266

letters from, 3053, 3066, 3096

his K.B., 3297n.

Grahame, Robert, Scottish reformer, *letter to*, 466

Gramont, Antoine Heraclius, later 9th Duc de (1789–1854), 2286, 2497

Gramont, Capt. de, 3228

Granard, Selina Frances, Countess of, Lord Moira's sister (1759–1827), 1035n., 1365, 2512, 2514

Granard, 6th Earl of (1760–1837), 562n., 1035, 1234, 2012, 2621, 3172, 3352, 3352n., 3355, 3361

Granby, Marquess of (1813–14), 3392

Grandison, 2nd Earl (1751–1800), 262, 1187

Grandisons, the, 1277

Grand Junction Canal, the, 2000

Grange, the, near Alresford, 1033, 1089, 1187n., 1207, 1212, 1412, 1412n., 1523, 1563

Grant, Charles (1746–1823), 2040, 2049, 2054

Grant, Charles, Lord Glenelg (1778–1866), 3458

Grant, Capt. James, R.N., 1992, 1998, 2146

Grant, Sir William (1752–1832), 1385, 1998, 2779, 3031, 3128n., 3238, 3380

Granville, Lord, *see* Leveson-Gower

Granville, Henrietta Elizabeth (Harriet), Countess (1785–1862), 208, 484, 696, 3451

Grassini, Guiseppa (1773–1850), the Italian singer, 2305, 2504

Grattan, Henry (1746–1820), 499, 1233n., 1354, 1735, 2483, 2483n., 2609n., 2888, 3057, 3057n., 3326, 3358, 3358n.

Graves, Admiral Lord (1725–1802), 262, 738, 755

Gravina, Admiral, 2176

Gray, 13th Lord (1754–1807), 1825

Gray, Richard, 1523, 1526, 1528, 2469n.

letter to, 1525

his wife, 1525

Gray, Robert, the jeweller (d. 1788), 39, 41–2, 51, 57, 96, 98, 110, 230,

Gray's, the jeweller's, 1467

Gray, Robert (d. 1823), Deputy Auditor of the Duchy of Cornwall, 515, 637, 712, 1282, 1519n., 1525, 1607, 1610, 1612, 1615, 1628, 1852, 1931, 2117, 2469, 2469n., 2478n., 2513, 2559, 2572n., 2573

letters from, 1180, 1526, 1534, 2449, 2557

letters to, 748, 1451, 1521–3, 1527–8, 1532, 1621, 1687n., 1706, 1852, 1883, 1951, 1999n., 2003n., 2018n., 2112, 2160, 2405, 2436n., 2474, 2525, 3007, 3372n.

Gray, Mrs. Robert, 1523, 1528

Gray, Thomas, a seaman, 160

Gray, William, jeweller, 39n., 465n., 484, 2959

Gray, William John, Lord (d. 1807), 1959n.

Gray, William, house-steward, 2117

Greaves, 1773n.

Green, General Sir Charles (1749–1831), 1790

Green, Lieut.-Col. Nuttall, 3266

Green Ribbons, *see* Thistle, Order of the

Green, Thomas, 538, 869, 2025, 2097

Greenwich Hospital, 1469n., 1612

Greenwood, Charles (c. 1747–1832), 692n., 1287, 1499, 1741, 1744, 1749, 1756, 1772,

Vol. I: 1–444; Vol. II: 445–942; Vol. III: 943–1416; Vol. IV: 1417–1865; Vol. V: 1866–2287; Vol. VI: 2288–2693; Vol. VII: 2694–3056; Vol. VIII: 3057–3480.

531   35—C.G. IV

Vol. I: 1–444; Vol. II: 445–942; Vol. III: 943–1416; Vol. IV: 1417–1865; Vol. V: 1866–2287; Vol. VI: 2288–2693; Vol. VII: 2694–3056; Vol. VIII: 3057–3480.

535

Haverkam, Lieut. James, 2687
Haversham(?), 758
Hawke, an 18-gun cutter, 1992, 2146
Hawker, Colonel Sir Samuel (1763–1838), 2204
Hawkesbury, Lord, *see* Jenkinson
Hawkins, Charles, surgeon, 528*n*.
Hawkins, Charles, 822, 824, 857
    his son, 822, 857
Hawkins, C., 528*n*.
Hawkins, Sir Christopher (1758–1829), 2083, 2679, 2679*n*.
Hawkins, Pennell, 528*n*.
Hawley, Mary, 2116
Hay, Charles, Lord Newton (*d.* 1811), 3230
Hay, Edward (*c.* 1761–1826), 2819*n*., 2888, 2888*n*.,
    letter to, 2819
Hayes, 832, 1270
Hayes, Sir John Macnamara (1750–1809), 2292*n*.
Hayman, Miss, 1266, 1273, 1275, 1301, 1301*n*., 1335, 1607*n*., 1615*n*., 1620, 1620*n*., 2448*n*., 2572*n*.
Haymarket Theatre, the, 1849, 2305, 3186, 3191–2, 3218
Haynes, *see* Hague
Haytor [Hayter], 1528*n*., 1546*n*.
Head, Isaac, 460
Headfort, 1st Marquess of (1757–1829), 2162, 2167, 2299, 2305, 2974*n*.,
    letters from, 2876, 2974
Heard, Sir Isaac (1730–1822), 1403
    letter from, 2046
Heath, John (1736–1816), 693
Heathcote, 2464
Heathfield, 2nd Lord (1750–1813), 2194, 2194*n*., 2534*n*.
Heaton, 2287
Heberden, Mrs. (*c.* 1776–1812), 2781
Heberden, William (1710–1801), 287, 289
    fees for attending the King, 424
Heberden, William (1767–1845), 287, 289, 289*n*., 1806*n*., 1894, 1895*n*., 1935, 2033, 2650, 2684, 2749*n*., 2751*n*., 2756, 2756*n*., 2757*n*., 2758, 2764, 2769*n*., 2830*n*., 2897*n*., 3013, 3113, 3185, 3217, 3238, 3380
Helder, expedition to the (1799), 1464, 1472, 1481, 1483, 1487*n*., 1497, 1499
Helston, borough of, 460, 460*n*.
Henderson, 2500
Henderson, Mrs., 1448*n*.
Henley, Charles, 597
Henry III (1207–72), 2020
Henry IV, King of France (1553–1610), 564, 634, 647
Henry VI (1421–71), 2046
Henry VII (1457–1509), 153, 1593*n*.
Henry VIII (1491–1547), 1485, 2046, 2278, 2842
Henry, Kitty, 1576
    her brother, 1576
Hepburn, Sir George Buchan (1739–1819), 3211, 3225, 3242

Herald, see Morning Herald
Herbert, Lord, *see* Pembroke, 11th Earl of
Herbert, Mrs. Georgiana (*d.* 1799), 1455
Herbert, Henry Arthur (*c.* 1756–1821), 3344, 3358
Hereford, 14th Visct. (1777–1843), 2050
Hereford, Bishop of, *see* Luxmoore
Hereford, Deanery of, 2550
Herries, John Charles (1778–1855), 3097, 3097*n*., 3148, 3474
    letter to, 3148*n*.
    appointed Commissary in Chief, 3148, 3148*n*.
Herries, Sir Robert, & Co., bankers, 593
Hertford, Isabella, Marchioness of (1760–1834), 147, 200, 959, 1119*n*., 1528*n*., 1802, 2213, 2423, 2430*n*., 2438, 2442, 2444, 2511, 3006, 3064*n*., 3378, 3416*n*.
    letters to, 2167A, 2254, 2289, 2297, 2328, 2425, 2430, 2437, 2537, 2590, 2593, 3138, 3257, 3386, 3394, 3401, 3406
Hertford, 1st Marquess of (1718–94), 108*n*., 659, 661, 959, 3218
    letter from, 660
    letters to, 108, 215
Hertford, 2nd Marquess of (1743–1822), 200, 215, 660–1, 949, 1118, 1683, 1688*n*., 1958, 2032, 2043, 2167A, 2254, 2272, 2288*n*., 2289, 2289*n*., 2297, 2328, 2349*n*., 2421, 2425, 2430, 2437, 2511, 2537, 2590, 2593, 2600*n*., 2637, 2637*n*., 2737, 3138, 3257, 3349*n*., 3378, 3386, 3394, 3401, 3406
    letters from, 215*n*., 951, 959, 959*n*., 1036
    letters to, 147, 951, 959, 1692, 2213, 2379, 2423, 2434, 2438, 2442, 2444
    appointed Lord Chamberlain, 3377, 3377*n*.
    his Members in the Commons, 3401
    resignation (1821), 3416
    wants a Dukedom, 3416*n*.
Hertfords, the, 3244
Hervey, John Augustus, Lord (1757–96), 258
Hervey, Mrs., a Woman of the Bedchamber, 1094*n*.
Hervey, Mrs., Lord Thurlow's mistress, 2227
Hervilly, Comte d' (*d.* 1795), 847, 1007*n*., 1019*n*.
Heseltine, 1146, 1215
Heseltine, James, 2102*n*.
Hesse, Captain Charles (*d.* 1832), 3400*n*.
Hesse, George (*d.* 1788), 269*n*.
Hesse-Cassel, Princess Caroline of (1771–1848), 1499*n*.
Hesse-Cassel, Prince Charles of (1744–1836), 66
Hesse-Cassel, Princess Frederica of (1768–1839), 66, 69
Hesse-Cassel, William, Hereditary Prince, and (1785), Landgrave of, later Elector of (1743–1821), 66, 161, 217, 591, 597, 611, 1499, 1499*n*., 1534, 1537, 1549, 1673, 1697, 1832, 1832*n*., 1854, 2557, 3135, 3275, 3281
    letter from, 687
    letter to, 3135
Hesse-Darmstadt, Prince Charles of (1757–95), 981

Hungerford, John Peach (1719–1809), 2574, 2580

Hunt, Miss, Sub-governess, 1721, 1861, 2117n.

Hunt, Thomas (c. 1723–89), 333

Hunter, a courier, 148

Hunter, John, surgeon (d. 1809), 1564, death of, 2590

Hunter, Brig.-Gen. Peter, 823

Hunter, William, a messenger, 1068, 1528n., 1599n., 1890
    letter from, 1891
    his sick daughter, 1891

Huntingdon elections, 422

Huntingdonshire, political state of (1788), 357, 422

Huntingfield, Marquess of, see Gordon, 5th Duke of

Huntingfield, Maria, Lady (d. 1811), 2357

Hurd, Richard, Bishop of Worcester (1720–1808), 26, 26n.

Hurd, see Heard

Hurst, Mr., 1451

Huskisson, William (1770–1830), 1039, 1077, 1182, 1216, 1375, 2171n., 2574, 2657, 3465–6
    letters from, 1935n., 2642n.
    letters to, 3463, 3466

Hussey, William (c. 1725–1813), 215n.

Hutchinson, Christopher Hely (1767–1826), 2869, 2888, 3074, 3323, 3358

Hutchinson, John Hely-Hutchinson, 1st Baron, later 2nd Earl of Donoughmore (1757–1832), 1714, 1735, 1738, 1741, 1796, 1819, 2058, 2082, 2128, 2252, 2307, 2307n., 2325, 2419, 2869n., 3012, 3085n., 3094, 3166,
    letters from, 1729, 1772, 2074, 3012
    letter to, 1772
    not to be Com.-in-Chief in Ireland, 3296n.

Hyde, an artist, 2807

Ilchester elections, 2415
    seats at, 3165

Ilchester, Maria, Countess of (d. 1842), 2001, 2775
    letters from, 2015n., 2017n.
    letter to, 2015n.

Illegitimacy not a bar to a K.B., 3285

Income tax, Royal family and, 1419, 3275–6, 3281, 3284

Income Tax Bill, Pitt's (1798), 1419, 1850

Inconstant, a 36-gun ship, 758

India Bill, Fox's, 384, 399, 462, 3384
    Pitt's, 156

Infantado, Duchess Dowager of, 3158

Infantado, 13th Duke of (d. 1841), 2520, 3150–1, 3158

Inglis, Sir Hugh (c. 1744–1820), 2935

Ingram, John, 2289n.

Ingram, Captain Nicholas, R.N., 268, 1385

Invasion, an, still thought possible, 2801

Inverary, borough of, 2829

Ireland, state of (1797), 1233, 1255, 1286, 1300, 1302; (1811) 3153, 3164

Irish Catholics, Petition of (1793), 774

Irish Commercial Propositions (1785), the, 153

Irish Convention Act (1793), 3108n., 3159

Irish Melodies, Thomas Moore's, 2440

Irish Parliament, Address of, to the Prince of Wales, 410, 416, 418n., 449
    the Prince's reply, 418

Irish Rebellion (1798), 1365, 3164

Irish Representative Peers, election of, 3085, 3146, 3146n.

Ironmongers Company, the, 3022

Irvine, Viscountess (1734–1807), 2213, 2254, 2289, 2328, 2425, 2430, 2437–8

Isle of Wight, Governorship of, 2499n.

Jacko, see Payne, John William

Jacobin Club, 570

Jacoby, Mrs., 1275

Jackson, a servant, 200

Jackson, Rev. Cyril (1746–1819), 23n., 73, 76, 2751n., 3155n., 3219, 3288, 3373, 3472n.
    letters from, 1545, 3288
    declines See of London, 3391

Jackson, 2574, 2580

Jackson, Francis James (1770–1814), 2881n., 2887n., 3010

Jackson, Sir George (1785–1861), his Diaries quoted, 2392n.

Jackson, William, Bishop of Oxford (1751–1815), 3288

Jacobi, Constans Philipp Wilhelm, Baron von Klösst (1745–1817), 1440, 1507, 1667

Jacobi, Miss (or Mrs.), 1275

Jacombe, General, 1775

Jaffray, Dr., of Glasgow, 712

Jago, Rev. Mr., 2111

Jamaica, Governorship of, 2292, 2299, 2306, 2315, 2320, 2331, 2345, 2347, 2347n.

James, 1785, 1794, 1842, 1844, 1870

James I (1566–1625), 153

James II (1633–1701), 1485

Jarnac, Comte de (1740–1813), 822

Jarri, M., 650

Jarry, General (c. 1733–1807), 2370

Jarvis, 1396, 1412

Jason frigate, 1027n., 1029n., 3378n.

Java, capture of, 3297, 3297n.

Jebb, Sir Richard (1729–87), 42, 47, 131, 235, 437

Jecole (?), the Sœur, 32

Jeffery, John (c. 1751–1822), 2145
    his son, 2145

Jeffreys, Nathaniel, jeweller, 230, 465n., 601, 611, 611n., 711, 1576, 1584, 1621, 1621n., 1638n.
    letters from, 1621n., 1638

Jeffreys, Miss, 2542n.

Jeffries, see Jefferys

Le Clair [Le Clerc], Mlle., 1432
Le Commerce de Marseilles, a French warship, 409
Leda, a 38-gun frigate, 2034
Lee, *see* Leigh
Lee, Rev. Francis (1766–1826), 1659
Lee, George, 1134–5, 1172n.
Leeds, Catherine, Duchess of (1764–1837), 11n.
Leeds, Duke of, *see* Carmarthen, Marquess of
Lefebvre, François Joseph, Duke of Danzig and Marshal of France (1755–1820), 2586
Lefebvre-Desnouette, C., 2747, 2990, 3020, 3228
Le Fevre, 268
Legge, Sir Arthur Kaye (1766–1835), 3308
Legge, Lady Charlotte (1774–1848), 894
Legge, William (d. 1784), 2nd son of 2nd Earl of Dartmouth, 31n., 1528n.
Legh, George John, Sheriff of Cheshire, 2259
Legh, Thomas Peter (c. 1755–97), 1287, 1287n.
Leicester election (1800), 1574, 1576
Leicester, Sir John Fleming, 1st Baron de Tabley (1762–1827), 663n.
Leigh, 257, 1052
Leigh, Mrs. Augusta, *letter from*, 2420
Leigh, Lieut.-Gen. Charles (d. 1815), 148n., 760, 764, 776, 784, 1324, 1486, 2499, 2499n., 2546
Leigh, Major, 1173, 2249
Leigh, Lieut-Col. George, son of General Leigh, 562n., 1486, 1491, 1519n., 1528, 1611, 1617, 1943, 1952, 1960, 2059, 2062, 2074n., 2204, 2286–7, 2420, 2429, 2546
his father, 1486
Leigh, Mrs., Canning's aunt and wife of Rev. William Leigh, 1253n.
Leinster, 2nd Duke of (1749–1804), 404, 410, 1363, 1735
letter from, 389, 1239
Leith, Major, of East India Company's service, 2249
Leith, Lieut.-Gen. Sir James (1763–1816), 3110
Leitrim, 1st Earl of (1732–1804), 198
Leitrim, 2nd Earl of (1768–1854), 3085, 3085n.
letter from, 3146
and an Irish Representative peerage, 3146, 3146n.
Le Marchant, Major-Gen. John Gaspard (1766–1812), 3089, 3136
Le Mesurier, Paul (1755–1805), 1455
letters from, 1456, 1485
letter to, 1456n.
Lemon, Major, 539
Lemon, Jack, 521, 523, 525, 1705
Lennon [*sic*], 183
Lennox, Col., *see* Richmond, 4th Duke of
Lennox, Lord George Henry (1737–1805), 1855
Lenthe, Ernst Ludwig Julius von (1744–1814), 1624
Leominster election (1797), 1426n.

Leopard, frigate, 3004n.
Leopold II, Emperor (1747–92), 532, 564, 585, 592, 612, 623, 626, 650, 1877, 2983, 3084
his wife, Maria (1745–92), 532
Le Roux, M., 544
Leslie, Lieut.-Gen. Alexander (d. 1794), 883
Leslie, Col. Charles Powell (c. 1767–1831), 1822
Leslie, John, Bishop of Dromore (d. 1854), 3273, 3273n.
Les Lois de Minos, 14
Less, Professor Gottfried, 581n.
L'Estrange, Col. Thomas (c. 1755–1845), 2709
Lethbridge, Mr., 2329
Lethbridge, Rev. Charles (c. 1763–1840), 713, 1690, 1690n.
Lethbridge, Sir John (c. 1746–1815), 3180n.
letters from, 193, 3035
letter to, 3035n.
Lethbridge, Sir Thomas Buckler (1778–1849), *letter from*, 3035n.
Leven, 9th Earl of (1749–1820), 1949n.
Levery, Mrs., 2347
Leveson-Gower, Lord Granville, 1st Earl Granville (1773–1846), 1690, 1735, 1812n., 2031, 2031n., 2415n., 2770n., 3452, 3457, 3457n.
letter from, 2315n.
letter to, 3451
Leveson-Gower, Rear-Admiral John (1740–92), 444, 513
Lewes, Races at, 518, 1666, 1668
Lewis, Island of, its desolate appearance, 613
Lewis, Matthew, Deputy Secretary at War, 1259
Lewis, Matthew Gregory (1775–1818), 2881n.
Lewis, Major-Gen. Robert Mason (d. 1800), 1034
Lewisham, Lord, *see* Dartmouth
Leycester, Ralph (1764–1835), 2161
Lichtenberg, Professor, 581n.
Liddell, Sir Thomas Henry, 1st Baron Ravensworth (1775–1855), 2289, 2289n.
Lieven, Prince (1774–1839), 3446n., 3470
Lieven, Princess (1785–1857), 3446, 3470
Life's Vagaries, a play, 987
Light, Captain, 2558n.
Ligne, Charles Joseph de, Austrian Field Marshal (1735–1814), 695
Lille, peace negotiations at, 1274
Lille, Comte de, *see* Louis XVIII
Lima, Don Lorenzo de, 1600, 1861
his brother, 1600
Limerick, Bishop of, *see* Warburton
Lindeman, 1499, 1549, 1710
Lindemann, Frederick, 2539, 2575, 2577, 2579
Lindenau, Baron, 695
letters from, 672, 672n.
Lindsay, Lady Anne, *see* Barnard
Lindsay, Charles Dalrymple (d. 1846), 3137
Lindsay, Lady Charlotte (1770–1849), 2484, 2484n., 3231n.

Vol. I: 1–444; Vol. II: 445–942; Vol. III: 943–1416; Vol. IV: 1417–1865; Vol. V: 1866–2287
Vol. VI: 2288–2693; Vol. VII: 2694–3056; Vol. VIII: 3057–3480.

545

McMahon, Sir Thomas (1779–1860), 3182, 3222

McNaghton, Edmund Alexander (1762–1832), 2272, 2289, 3041

Macnamara, Arthur (1783–1851), 2048, 2050

Macnamara, John (*c.* 1756–1818), *letters from*, 2048, 2050

Macnamara, 2599

Macpherson, James (1736–96), *letters from*, 497, 505, 547, 568, 575

Macpherson, Sir John (1745–1821), 99, 99*n.*, 401*n.*, 487*n.*, 658, 714, 714*n.*, 2150
letters from, 436, 463–4, 488, 492, 532, 564, 585, 592, 626, 644, 666, 807, 842, 996, 1084, 1507, 1631, 1631*n.*, 1877, 2120, 2983, 3084, 3143
minute by, 201
letters to, 379, 384, 1507*n.*, 1631

Macquainon [Mecquinien], a cook, 2928, 2952

Madison, James (1751–1836), 2785

Madocks, William Alexander (1773–1828), 1908*n.*

Maffoli, 639

Magdalene Asylums, 2058

Magee, William, Archbishop of Dublin (1766–1831), 3222, 3474

Magicienne, a 36-gun frigate, 2782*n.*

Magna Carta, 2130, 2134*n.*, 2562

Mahomet, 2536

Mahon, Lord, *see* Stanhope

Maida, battle of, 2960

Maidstone, a frigate, 212

Mainwaring, Lieut. Jemmett, 157, 266*n.*, 268

Maitland, Lieut.-Gen. Sir Thomas (1759–1824), 2371, 2424, 3011, 3110, 3144

Maitland, Visct., later 9th Earl of Lauderdale (1784–1860), 1697A

Majendie, Rev. Henry William (1754–1830), Bishop of Chester, 1629, 2570

Malcolm, William, 2538*n.*

Malden, Lord, *see* Essex, 5th Earl of

Maling, Capt. Thomas James, R.N., 1747

Malmesbury, Lord, *see* Harris

Malortie, Col. von, 581*n.*, 750*n.*

Malsch, 1549

Malta, Governorship of, 2331
capture of, 3130

Manby, Paymaster of the 10th Light Dragoons, 1947, 1952, 2008*n.*

Manby, Capt. Thomas, R.N. (1769–1834), 2196, 2304, 2304*n.*, 2338*n.*

Manchester, Elizabeth, Duchess of (*c.* 1741–1832), 3383–4

Manchester, 4th Duke of (1737–88), 3383–4

Manchester, 5th Duke of (1771–1843), appointed Postmaster-General, 3463

Manchester, a ministerial meeting at (1788), 369, 402

Manchester Mercury, the, 369*n.*

'Manchester Square, the Lady of', *see* Hertford, Isabella, Marchioness of

Manesty, 2452

Mann, Sir Horace (1744–1814), *letter from*, 443

Manners, Lady Catherine (1779–1829), 1385

Manners, Lord Charles Henry Somerset (1780–1855), 1398, 1402, 1427, 1513, 1611*n.*, 3130

Manners, Lieut.-Col. Frederick (*d.* 1803), 753

Manners, John, 1574

Manners, General Robert (1758–1823), 396*n.*, 776

Manners, Major-Gen. Lord Robert William (1781–1835), 1398, 1402, 1513, 1603*n.*, 1611*n.*, 1947, 3130, 3393–4

Manners, Sir William (1766–1833), 2415*n.*, 3165, 3180*n.*,
his father, 3165*n.*

Manners-Sutton, Charles, Archbishop of Canterbury (1755–1828), 2032, 2753, 2970, 3117, 3128, 3157, 3201, 3205, 3217, 3224, 3227, 3238, 3243, 3246, 3251, 3350
letter from, 3223
letters to, 3224*n.*, 3227, 3436

Manners-Sutton, Charles, 1st Visct. Canterbury (1780–1845), 2896, 3074, 3358, 3458
letters from, 3090, 3239

Manners-Sutton, Sir Thomas, Lord Manners (1756–1842), 1621, 1629*n.*, 1655, 1785, 2874, 2975, 3093*n.*, 3153, 3159, 3164

Manning, William (1763–1835), 3091

Mansells, James, 3462

Mansfield, 1st Earl of (1705–93), 90, 698

Mansfield, Lord Stormont, later 2nd Earl of (1727–96), 82–3, 87, 93, 319, 517, 1046, 1550, 3383
letter from, 1046*n.*

Mansfield, 3rd Earl of (1777–1840), 3458

Mansfield, Sir James (1734–1821), 1186, 1338, 1361, 1629*n.*, 1738, 2123, 2565
his *Opinions*, 1538, 1538*n.*

Mansfield, Louisa, Countess of (1758–1843), 3081

Mantua, capture of (1799), 1470

Marathas, the, 487, 520, 541, 1517*n.*, 2318

Marceau, General (1769–96), 1189

March, General James (*d.* 1804), 950

Marchesi, opera singer (*d.* 1792), 639, 1063

Maria, wife of Emperor Leopold II (1745–92), 532

Marie Antoinette, Queen of France (1755–93), 686, 688, 690, 696, 2709

Marienswerder, 3202

Marrion, General, 3094

Markham, Rev. David Frederick (1800–53), 3458

Markham, William (1719–1807), Archbishop of York, 3093*n.*, 3458

Markham, William (*d.* 1815), son of the Archbishop, 3458

Vol. I: 1–444; Vol. II: 445–942; Vol. III: 943–1416; Vol. IV: 1417–1865; Vol. V: 1866–2287; Vol. VI: 2288–2693; Vol. VII: 2694–3056; Vol. VIII: 3057–3480.

547   36—C.G. IV

Marlborough, 4th Duke of (1739–1817), 2229n., 3180n.
his Members in the Commons, 2229n.
Marmont, Marshal, Duc de Raguse (1774–1852), 3039n.
Marrable, Sir Thomas, Secretary of the Board of Green Cloth, 3402n., 3425
Marrell, 2287
Marriott, Sir James (c. 1730–1803), 1381, 1383, 1385
Marschalck, Baron, 728
Marsden, 1192
Marsden, Alexander, Under-Sec. of State [I.], *letter from*, 1980n.
Marshall, Samuel, Serjeant, 1751, 3362
Marsham, Charles, Earl of Romney (1744–1811), 215n., 3373
Martens, G. F. von, 581n.
Martin, the jeweller, 230
Martin, a creditor of Georgiana, Duchess of Devonshire, 465n.
Martin, Major-Gen. Anthony George (d. 1800), 857
Martin, Sir Henry (1733–94), Bart. (1791) and M.P. for Southampton, 150, 152, 157
Martin, Mrs., 157
her daughter, Eliza Anne, 150
her daughter, Sarah Catherine, 150, 157, 207
Martin, James (1738–1810), 1429
Martindale, a club manager, 1504, 1546
Mary, Queen (1516–58), 3365
Mary, Princess, later, Duchess of Gloucester (1776–1857), 43, 584, 597, 765, 782, 790, 795, 803, 818, 872, 876n., 891, 899, 940, 977, 977n., 1067, 1091n., 1187, 1226, 1372, 1381, 1386, 1387n., 1390, 1439, 1441, 1447, 1477, 1501, 1503, 1511, 1515, 1604, 1624, 1660n., 1663, 1669, 1670n., 1685, 1694n., 1731, 1796, 1836, 1859, 1915, 1970, 2063, 2065, 2202, 2292, 2390–1, 2410n., 2433, 2470, 2490, 2493–4, 2517, 2521, 2556, 2592, 2595, 2612, 2616, 2620, 2627, 2630, 2635, 2639, 2639n., 2641, 2643, 2650–1, 2670–1, 2684, 2686, 2696, 2710n., 2718, 2720, 2722, 2740, 2747, 2762, 2764, 2768, 2781, 2783, 2786, 2791, 2793, 2948, 2958, 3009n., 3011, 3100n., 3217n., 3227, 3254, 3254n., 3278, 3356, 3374, 3376, 3400
letters from, 1379, 1384, 1392, 1665, 1670, 1678, 1789, 1807, 1853, 2570, 2585, 2597, 2605, 2611, 2623, 2629, 2638, 2652, 2675, 2677, 2685, 2694, 2703, 2741, 2744, 2763, 2765, 2775n., 2849, 3070, 3088, 3088n., 3375
letters to, 2729, 2773
Mash, Henry T. B., 3458
Mason, Sir Francis, 2350
Mason, T., *letter from*, 2443
Mason, Mrs., 2443
Mason, Rev. William (1724–97), 473
Masons, the, *see* Freemasonry
Massena, André, Duc de Rivoli, Prince d'Essling, and Marshal of France (1758–1817),

Massena André—*cont.*
1440, 2747n., 2767, 2776, 2960, 2989–91, 3039
Master of the Mint, office of, 2933, 2990
Mathew, Montagu James (1773–1819), 3057n.
Mathew, Visct., later 2nd Earl of Landaff (1768–1833), 1820, 1827
Mathew, William, 2587, 2589
Mathews, Charles, the comedian (1776–1835), 1382
Mathews, Henry, 1615n.
Mathias, Thomas James (c. 1754–1835), 3152, 3325, 3333
letter from, 3328
Matthias, Emanuel (d. 1790), 254
Mattocks, Mrs. Isabella (1746–1820), 1385
Maude, Messrs. T. and W., of Westminster, 258
Maule, Captain, 1749
Maule, Dr., 3187
Maule, William, 1st Baron Panmure (1771–1852), 2308n.
Maupeou, Nicholas Augustin de (1714–92), the French Chancellor, 11
Mauritius, capture of, 2863, 2866, 2870n., 3092, 3329
Maximilian Joseph, King of Bavaria (1756–1825), 2119
Maynard, Anne, Viscountess (d. ?1815), 570
Maynard, Charles, 2nd Visct. (1752–1824), 570
Maynooth College, parliamentary grant to, 2480
Mayo, 4th Earl of (1766–1849), 3231, 3231n.
and an Irish Representative Peerage, 3085n., 3146n., 3231n.
Mayo, Arabella, Countess of (1766–1843), 3299n.
Meade, Colonel John (c. 1775–1849), 2289n.
Mecklenburg-Schwerin, Frederica, Duchess of (1722–91), 66
Mecklenburg-Schwerin, Frederick, Duke of (1717–85), 66, 95
Mecklenburg-Schwerin, Frederick Francis, Duke of (1756–1837), 68–9, 95
Mecklenburg-Schwerin, Louisa, Duchess of (1756–1808), 68–9, 95
Mecklenburg-Strelitz, Adolphus Frederick, Duke of (1738–94), 835
Mecklenburg-Strelitz, Charles, Duke of (1741–1816), 15, 39, 39n., 43, 64, 101, 105, 162, 2088, 3098
Mecklenburg-Strelitz, Princess Charlotte of (1755–85), 64n.
Mecklenburg-Strelitz, Prince Ernest of (1742–1814), 39–40, 43, 57, 64, 111, 1054, 1054n.
letter from, 955
letters to, 958, 1053
death of, 3396
Mecklenburg-Strelitz, Princess Frederica of (1752–82), 15n., 64, 64n.
Mecklenburg-Strelitz, Prince Frederick of (b. & d. 1774), 15
Mecklenburg-Strelitz, Prince Frederick of (1781–3), 39

Montagu, Mrs., 1840
Montagu, Rev. John (c. 1750–1818), 2666
Montagu, Matthew, 4th Baron Rokeby (1762–1831), 3323
Montem, the Eton, 3069
Montfort, 3rd Baron (1773–1851), 2483, 2682
Montgomerie, Col. Hugh, 12th Earl of Eglintoun (1739–1819), see Eglintoun
Montgomerie, Major-Gen. James (c. 1756–1829), 2969, 2985
Montgomery, Bob, 1420n.
Montgomery, Sir Henry Conyngham (1765–1830), 2888n., 3074, 3329
Montgomery, Sir Thomas, 2046
Montjoye Frohberg, Comte de, 2296, 2321, 2321n.
Montmollin, Mlle. Julie de, 2765, 2775
Montmollin, 3375
Montpellier, Bishop of, 2287
Montpensier, Antoine Philippe, Duc de (1775–1807), 1769
Montrose, 643
Montrose, Duke of (1755–1836), 2362n., 2803n., 3128, 3185, 3201, 3217, 3224, 3238, 3458
Moore, Mrs., 2740
Moore, 1584
Moore, Francis, Deputy Secretary at War, 2347
Moore, Lord Henry Seymour (c. 1784–1825), 2637, 2637n., 3401
Moore, Lieut.-Col. James (d. 1848), 1742
Moore, Dr. John, Archbishop of Canterbury (1730–1805), 311n., 1085, 1093, 1490, 1511
 letter from, 514
Moore, Lieut.-Gen. Sir John (1761–1809), 2074, 2347, 2545n., 2682, 3228
Moore, Peter (1753–1828), 2469, 3214
Moore, Stephen, letter from, 2273
Moore, Thomas (1779–1852), 2308n., 2440
 letter from, 3068
Moorfield, George, 2461
Morand, 1546n., 1599n.
Mordaunt, Lieut.-Gen. Thomas Osbert (c. 1730–1809), 2554
Moreau, Jean Victor, General (1761–1813), 1240
Morgan, John (1742–92), 364
Morier, John Philip (1776–1853), 3004, 3190
Morland, William, 531n., 583, 1540–1, 1584
Morning Chronicle, the, 36, 44n., 302, 1320n., 1338, 1738, 1779, 1850, 2477n., 2622n., 2895, 3388n.
Morning Herald, the, 36, 47, 1154, 1209, 1333, 1333n., 1338, 1375, 1779, 2261, 2982n., 3377
Morning Post, the, 913n., 1171, 1171n., 1185, 1193, 1209, 1218n., 1333, 2338n., 2357, 2547, 2547n., 3377, 3382
Mornington, Lord, see Wellesley, Marquess
Morocco, Emperor of, 548, 1680, 2347
Morpeth, Visct., see Carlisle, 6th Earl of
Morpeth, Viscountess, see Carlisle, Georgiana, Countess of
Morres, Lodge Evans, 1st Visct. Frankfort (1747–1822), 410

Morrice, Charles, 2089n., 2374
 letters from, 871n., 2175
Morris, Edward (c. 1769–1815), 2305, 2305n., 2369n.
Morris, George Colman's partner, 3218
Morris, Mrs., a nurse, 1198, 2117
Morrison, 1886
Morrison, surgeon, 3171
Morschalck (d. 1793), 778
Morshead, Rev. Edward, 569
Morshead, Sir John (1747–1813), 249n., 539, 1225, 1228, 1230, 1235, 1522n., 1783n., 2485n.
 letters from, 565, 569, 598, 631, 633, 637, 641, 734, 1522
 letter to, 593
Mortier, Edouard Adolphe Casimir Joseph, Marshal of France, and Duke of Treviso (1768–1835), 3202
Moseley, Benjamin (1742–1819), the Duke of York's physician, 461
Moseley, William Henry, physician, 2292n.
Moss, a porter, 1935
Moss, Charles, Bishop of Oxford (1763–1811), 2319n., 3288n.
'Mother Hump', 1599n.
'Mountain', the: the Radical section of the Whig Party, 3344n.
Mount Charles, Henry Joseph Conyngham, Earl of (1795–1824), 3421
Mount Edgcumbe, 2nd Earl of (1764–1839), 631
Mountnorris, 1st Earl of (1744–1816), 2347
Muhammad Ali, Nawab of Arcot (1717–95), 72, 106, 134,
 letter from, 99
Mulgrave, 3rd Baron and 1st Earl of (1755–1831), 726, 837, 2076, 2362n., 2441, 2520, 2530n., 2654n., 2701n., 2715n.
 letter from, 2925
Muller, Captain, 1809
Mulso, Rev. Mr. (d. 1791), 618
Munro, Lieut.-Col. John, 2554
Munroe, Dr., see Monro
Münster, Prussian occupation of (1802), 1667
Münster, Count (1766–1839), 728n., 1624, 2402, 2684, 3098, 3114, 3131, 3221, 3234, 3256, 3256n., 3258n.
 letters from, 3177, 3202
Murat, Joachim, King of Naples (1771–1815), 3200
Murillo (1618–82), 2207
Murray, Lady Augusta (c. 1762–1830), 728, 802n., 947, 982, 1022, 1093, 1480, 1482, 1488, 1490, 1492, 1494, 1559, 1644, 1653, 1671, 1682, 1809, 2171n., 2299, 2322, 2322n.
 letters from, 1506n., 1509, 1600n., 1643, 1643n., 1671n., 2299n.
 letter to, 1506
 her daughter, see D'Este
 her son, see D'Este
Murray, Lieut.-Col. Alexander (1764–1842), 745, 799, 821, 1809

Vol. I: 1–444; Vol. II: 445–942; Vol. III: 943–1416; Vol. IV: 1417–1865; Vol. V: 1866–2287; Vol. VI: 2288–2693; Vol. VII: 2694–3056; Vol. VIII: 3057–3480.

551

Vol. I: 1–444; Vol. II: 445–942; Vol. III: 943–1416; Vol. IV: 1417–1865; Vol. V: 1866–2287; Vol. VI: 2288–2693; Vol. VII: 2694–3056; Vol. VIII: 3057–3480.

553

Vol. I: 1–444; Vol. II: 445–942; Vol. III: 943–1416; Vol. IV: 1417–1865; Vol. V: 1866–2287; Vol. VI: 2288–2693; Vol. VII: 2694–3056; Vol. VIII: 3057–3480.

557

Plomer, a singer, 1063
Plumer, Sir Thomas (1753–1824), 2304n., 2352n., 3108
Plunket, William Conyngham, 1st Baron (1764–1854), 3265
Plymouth Dock Police, memo respecting, 2681
Plymouth, 5th Earl of (1751–99), 639, 658
Plymouth elections, 631, 732, 2146, 2154, 2301, 3188, 3188n., 3210, 3215, 3219
    Governorship of, 2441, 2965, 2967, 3001
    Sound breakwater, 2980, 2980n.
Plymouth, Sarah, Countess of (1762–1838), 658
Pohl, Miss, 2117
Poix, Philippe, Prince de, 2nd Duc de Mouchy (1752–1819), 686
Pole, see Wellesley-Pole
Pole, Admiral Sir Charles Morice (1757–1830), 264, 266, 268, 281, 284, 343, 535, 2301n.
    M.P. for Plymouth, 3188, 3188n.
Pole, Christopher, 3228
Polignac, Comte de (1781–1855), 2497
Pollock, W., Chief Clerk in H.O., 1641n., 3133
Pollon, Chevalier de, Sardinian Minister in London, 22n.
Polyphemus, a 64-gun ship, 2443
Pomany, Captain, 809
Pomfret, Mary, Countess of (c. 1769–1839), 1861
Pomfret, Thomas, 1st Earl of (1698–1753), 2n.
Pond, John (1767–1836), 2884
Ponsonby, Sir Frederick Cavendish (1783–1837), 2961, 3249
Ponsonby, George (1755–1817), 410, 1735, 1820, 2156, 2161, 2232n., 2236n., 2239, 2289n., 2456, 2461, 2461n., 2483n., 2715n., 2761n., 2770, 2779, 2861, 2869, 2888, 2917, 2917n., 2934, 2996, 3055, 3057n., 3065n., 3320, 3341, 3344, 3344n., 3358, 3358n., 3363
Ponsonby, John, 2nd Baron (c. 1770–1855), 2801
Ponsonby, Richard (1772–1853), Bishop of Killaloe (1828), 3474
Ponsonby, Major-Gen. Sir William (1772–1815), killed at Waterloo, 3401
Ponsonby, William Brabazon, 1st Baron (1744–1806), 410, 1820
    letter from, 1239
Ponsonbys, the, 1735, 1976, 1987
Poole elections, 2145
Poole, Sir Ferdinando, 4th Bart. (d. 1804), 1528
Poole, Samuel, 2538n.
Pope, the, see Clement XIV and Pius VI
Pope, Alexander (1688–1714), 114
Pope, Dr., 2587, 2589, 2595, 2597, 2603, 2612, 2623, 2627, 2629–30, 2635–6, 2638–9, 2643, 2646, 2650–2, 2656, 2659, 2661–3, 2675, 2677, 2684–5, 2694, 2740, 2744
Popham, 888
Popham (d. 1788), 282
Popham, Alexander (c. 1729–1810), 334n.
Popham, Sir Home Riggs (1760–1820), 1515, 2350, 2419
    letter from, 2195
Porcher, Josias Dupré (c. 1761–1820), 2323

Porden (*sic*), 2682n.
Porrit, A., 1706
Portarlington, 1st Earl of (1744–98), 777
Porter, a servant, 2698
Porter(?), *letter to*, 2408
Porter, Walsh, *letters from*, 2078, 2207
Porteus, Beilby, Bishop of London (1731–1809), 1629, 3273
Portland, 3rd Duke of (1738–1809), 70, 79, 79n., 82–3, 90–1, 93, 215n., 218n., 219n., 221n., 311n., 323n., 331n., 354, 354n., 357, 357n., 375n., 393n., 404, 412n., 439n., 463, 463n., 489, 524, 553, 576, 708n., 843, 866, 877n., 907, 920, 975, 1013n., 1154, 1156, 1159, 1187, 1192, 1243, 1270, 1282, 1317, 1464, 1552n., 1592n., 1598n., 1651, 1696n., 1861, 1998, 2010, 2145, 2196n., 2282, 2288, 2352n., 2368n., 2387n., 2441, 2441n., 2477n., 2481, 2550n., 2576, 2578, 2578n., 2579n., 2582n., 2600, 2602, 2604, 2617, 2622–3, 2626, 2631n., 2632, 2637n., 2647, 2650, 2653, 2760, 2794, 2815–16, 2842, 2896, 3058, 3146n., 3157, 3180n., 3231n., 3373, 3472n.
    letters from, 73, 77, 80, 86, 88, 323n., 336, 353, 416, 496, 498, 503, 517, 531, 540, 549–50, 552, 671, 706, 708, 720, 720n., 845, 885n., 911, 915, 923, 923n., 930, 1013n., 1281, 1320
    letters to, 80, 88, 92, 323, 336, 706, 720, 845, 861, 907n., 910n., 924, 930n., 1029n., 1279
Portland family, the, 402
Portsmouth Dockyard, 26, 654
    elections, 840
Portugal, John, Prince of Brazil, later King of (1767–1826), 1600, 1639, 2445n., 2520, 2701, 2706, 2708, 3009, 3018, 3048, 3139, 3158n., 3181, 3189, 3221, 3294, 3351
Post Office, letters opened in the, 1215, 1323, 1326, 1334
Potato bread, the Queen's recipe for, 1012
Potsdam, description of, 78n.
Pott, Robert Percival,
    letter from, 752
    his brother, 752
Potter, William, 2474
Poulett, 4th Earl (1756–1819), 688, 2612, 2616, 2627, 2629
Poulett, Sophia, Countess (d. 1811), 688
Pouletts, the, 1379
Powell, 1809
Powell, a criminal, 2259
Powlet (*sic*), 1006
Powys, Thomas, 1st Baron Lilford (1743–1800), 215n., 361n., 3373
Poynings, Sir Edward (1459–1521), 153
Poyntz, Charlotte Louisa (1766–1840), 1094n., 1455, 1777
Poyntz, William (1734–1809), MS. Diary of, quoted, 546n., 560n., 644n., 656n.
Praed, William (1747–1833), 2083
Prescott, Robert (1725–1816), General, 954n., 1462n.

558

Vol. I: 1–444; Vol. II: 445–942; Vol. III: 943–1416; Vol. IV: 1417–1865; Vol. V: 1866–2287; Vol. VI: 2288–2693; Vol. VII: 2694–3056; Vol. VIII: 3057–3480.

Randel, 235

Randolph, Dr. Francis (1752–1831), 2508

Ranger, 1901

Ranjit Singh (1780–1839), 2554

Ransome, Morland and Hammersley, bankers, 531*n.*, 583, 1573, 1575*n.*, 1584

Raouska, Countess, 47

Raphael (1483–1520), 3307

Rashleigh, Charles (1747–1823), 572, 598, 734

Rashleigh, John (1742–1803), 1612

Rastatt, Congress of (1797), 1693

Rattler, sloop, 216, 239, 247

Rawdon, Lord, *see* Hastings

Rawdon, Charlotte (1769–1834), 1338, 1373

Rawdon, George (1761–1800), 1262, 1270, 1348, 1457

Rawdon, John Theophilus (1757–1808), 1013*n.*, 1270, 1373, 1577, 1577*n.*

Rawlinson, Sir Walter (1734–1805), 422

Raynsford, Nicolls (1755–1809), brother of Charles Justinian Raynsford (1757–1805), 1612, 2267, 2267*n.*

Raynsford, Mrs., 1612, 2267

Read, John, 1788

Reading, prevalence of lunacy in, 335

Reay, 5th Lord (1734?–68), 813

Recorder of London, *see* Silvester

Recorder's Reports, the, 2363*n.*, 2882, 3239, 3464, 3472

Red Ribbons, *see* Bath, Order of the

Red Rice, Errington's (Mrs. Fitzherbert's uncle's) house in Hampshire, 148

Red Sea, survey of the, 2350

Reder, M. de, 1341

Redvers, Barony of, 3365

Reeves, Mr. Justice, 1057*n.*

Reeves, John (*c.* 1752–1829), *letter from*, 1524

Regency Act (1811), 2787, 2827, 2833–4, 2836, 2878, 2897*n.*, 2976, 3124, 3204, 3283, 3297*n.*

Regent's Canal, the, 3346

Regleviez, Comte de, 806

Rehausen, Baron, Swedish Minister in London, 2325, 3232, 3248

Reichenbach, Convention of, 623

Reid, George, 372

Rembrandt (1606–69), 3307

Remiremont, Princess Christine-Chanoinese (*sic*), 3383

Rennie, John (1761–1821), civil engineer, 2154

Repton School, 2738–9

Resseli, musician, 892

Reventlow, Mme. de, *see* Hardenberg, Mme.

Reversion Bill, *see under* Offices

Révolutionnaire, frigate, 1843*n.*

Reynolds, Dr. Henry Revell (1745–1811), 293, 321*n.*, 335–6, 424, 1389, 1594, 1806*n.*, 1894, 1895*n.*, 2757*n.*, 2756, 2758, 2897*n.*, 3100, 3199

Rhine, the Confederation of the (1806), 2264

Rhymer, 39

Ribbands, the Regent's policy respecting conferment of, 2889

Richardson, Joseph (1755?–1803), 1690, 1697A, 1715

Richebourg, Jacques de Luxembourg, Seigneur de, 2046

Richmond, 3rd Duke of (1735–1806), 286, 302, 321, 332*n.*, 410*n.*, 793*n.*, 838, 1011*n.*, 1012, 1146, 1387, 2177, 2287, 2340*n.*, 2341, 2349, 2349*n.*

letters from, 768, 770, 785, 1892, 1905

letter to, 770

Richmond, 4th Duke of (1764–1819), 457, 457*n.*, 472, 2483*n.*, 2505*n.*, 2617, 2770*n.*, 2803*n.*, 2874, 2880, 2888, 2898, 2905, 2908, 2933, 2975, 3085, 3087*n.*, 3153, 3180*n.*, 3196, 3252, 3265, 3326

letters from, 3065*n.*, 3085*n.*, 3109*n.*, 3146*n.*, 3231*n.*

letters to, 2334*n.*, 2637*n.*, 2756*n.*, 2790*n.*, 2917*n.*, 3011*n.*, 3030*n.*, 3057*n.*, 3060*n.*, 3065*n.*, 3085*n.*, 3097*n.*, 3198*n.*, 3231*n.*, 3273*n.*, 3296*n.*, 3320*n.*, 3355*n.*, 3358*n.*

Richter, surgeon, 1051*n.*

Ricketts, Edward Jervis, 2313*n.*

Riddell, convict, 2939–40, 2944

Ridge, Army Agent, 1756, 1875, 2235

Ridges, 507

Rietz, Miss and Mrs., 792*n.*

Rigby, Mrs., 1225

Rigby, Richard (1722–88), 219*n.*

Rights of Man, Paine's, 740

Riley, 1542

Rimnik, Battle of the (1789), 1428

Rion, Comte de, 409

Rival Dukes, the, a pamphlet, 2736*n.*

Rival Princes, the, by Mary Anne Clarke, 2736, 2736*n.*

Rival Queens, the, a pamphlet, 2736*n.*

Rivers, 1st Baron (1721–1803), 788, 1385

Rivers, 2nd Baron (1751–1828), 3308

Rix, Thomas, 2259

Roberts, 2930, 3462

Roberts, William Hayward (*d.* 1791), 65

Robertson, 1775

Robertson, David, *letter from*, 1687*n.*

Robertson, Colonel William (*d.* 1821), 789

Robertson, William, Scottish Judge, 2095

Robespierre (1758–94), 856–7

Robinson, 1395

Robinson, Mrs., 2484*n.*

Robinson, Andrew, *letters from*, 737

letter to, 729

Robinson, Arthur (*d.* 1799), 229–30, 232, 235, 249*n.*, 1523

letter from, 232

letter to, 267

Robinson, Frederick John, Visct. Goderich and Earl of Ripon (1782–1859), 3459, 3466, 3472, 3474

letters to, 3431, 3440, 3442, 3448

Robinson, John (1727–1802), 108*n.*, 379*n.*, 426*n.*

letters from, 219*n.*, 379, 384

memo by, 383, (?)398

Robinson, Maria (or Mary Elizabeth), 'Perdita's' daughter (*d.* 1818), 1852

letter from, 1852

Robinson, Mary ('Perdita') (1758–1800), 42, 44n., 47, 235, 1852
Robson, Richard Bateman (d. 1827), 1256
Robust, a 74-gun ship, 26
Roch, Rev. Nicholas (c. 1772–1830), 2884
Rochambeau, Vicomte de (1750–1813), 2254
Rochambeau, Mme. de (1760–1837), 2254
Rochester, Prebend of, 574
Rochett, Mrs., 2117
Rockingham, 2nd Marquess of (1730–82), 399, 402, 490, 2246
Roden, 2nd Earl of (1756–1820), 1735
Rodney, Admiral Lord (1719–92), 30n., 3352
  letters from, 304, 580
Rodney, John (1765–1847), 1013, 2424
  letter to, 1013
Rogers, Sir Frederick Leman (1746–97), 732
Rohan, Duc de (d. 1816), 74
Rohan, Prince de, 857
Rolle, John, Lord (1756–1842), 242n., 384
  letter to, 268n.
Rolleston, a Foreign Office clerk, 3060n., 3314
Rollo, James, Lord (1773–1846), 1695n.
Romilly, Sir Samuel (1757–1818), 2113n., 2123, 2172, 2179, 2183n., 2305n., 2338n., 2564, 2679n., 2711, 2711n., 2901, 2966, 2989, 2989n., 3065n., 3106n., 3344n., 3363n.
Rooke, General James (c. 1740–1805), 2667
  his son, 2664
Roscoe, William (1753–1831), 3029n.
  letter from, 2231n.
  letters to, 1436n., 2231n.
Rose, 1549, 1571n.
Rose, of the Heralds College, 1403
Rose, George (1744–1818), 1013n., 1462n., 1572, 1590n., 1597n., 1783n., 1805n., 1806n., 1811n., 1812n., 1855, 1948, 2004n., 2145, 2171n., 2322n., 2597n., 2645n., 2749n., 2796n., 2825n., 2837n., 3344, 3364n.
  letters from, 1496, 1498, 2322n.
  letters to, 404n., 1552n., 1842n., 3087n.
Rosebery, 4th Earl of (1783–1868), his U.K. peerage, 3469
Rosen, Count, 3232
Rosenberg, 1886
Rosenhagen, 1216
Ross, Mr., 1213
Ross, Miss, 2745
Ross, General Alexander (1742–1827), 483
Ross, Col. Andrew (1773–1812), 1749, 1775
Ross, General Charles (c. 1729–97), 404
Rosslyn, Charlotte, Countess of (1751–1826), 3006
Rosslyn, Henrietta Elizabeth, Countess of (1771–1810), 2204n.
Rosslyn, Alexander Wedderburn, 1st Earl of, *see* Loughborough
Rosslyn, Sir James St. Clair Erskine, 2nd Earl of (1762–1837), 2204, 2204n., 2888n., 3474n.
  letters from, 2801n., 2861n.

Rowan, Archibald Hamilton (1751–1834), 2161
Rowcroft, 1736
Rowe, Rev. John, 1793, 2535
Rowland, Hugh, 3152
Rowles, Mr., 3214
'Royal', *see* Charlotte Augusta Matilda, Princess Royal
Royal Academy, the, 1711, 2533, 3067, 3335
Royal Dukes, Protests of the (1810), 2789, 2795, 2797, 2797n.
Royal Family's declaration (1804), 1810
Royal Hanoverian Guelphic Order, motto of, 3417
Royal Institution, the, 2327
Royal Lancasterian Institution, the, 3223n.
Royal Marriages Act (1772), 728n., 1480, 1995, 2019, 2322n., 2532, 2684n.
Royal Military College, the, 1634, 2126, 2347, 2370, 2682, 2938, 2947, 2965, 2967, 3011, 3136, 3155n.
Royal Society of Literature, the, 3415
Rubens, Peter Paul (1577–1640), 2207
Ruby, a 74-gun ship, 26
Ruffo de la Parc, the Marquis, 2985
Rumbold, Sir Thomas (1736–91), 72n., 99
Rundell, Bridge and Co., jewellers, 2959
Russell, a 74-gun ship, 748, 839
Russell, Francis, 2268, 2268n.
Russell, Lord John, later 6th Duke of Bedford (1766–1839), 69, 560n., 562n., 644n., 656n., 663n., 711n.
Russell, Lady John (d. 1801), 644n.
Russell, Lord William (1767–1840), 711n., 1194, 1908n.
Russia, Emperor of, *see* Alexander I
Russia, Sophia, Tsarina of (1759–1828), 1337
Rutland, Elizabeth, Duchess of (1780–1825), 1420n., 1422–3, 3392
Rutland, Mary Isabella, Duchess of (1756–1831), 447n., 877, 877n., 881, 1037n., 1420n., 1422n., 1436n., 1444, 1448, 1528n., 1546n., 1599n., 1607n., 1611n., 1937, 3373
  letters from, 1398, 1402, 3130
  letters to, 1402, 1422, 1425, 1427, 1436, 1556, 1579, 1596, 2165, 3390, 3393
Rutland, 4th Duke of (1754–87), 176n., 211n., 1037n., 1402, 1404, 2483n.
  his Garter, 3383
Rutland, 5th Duke of (1778–1857), 1402, 1420n., 1422, 1448, 1579, 1596, 3393
  letters from, 1404, 1423, 2936
  letters to, 1423, 1449, 2936, 3392
  his family, 3244
Ryan, J., *letter from*, 3219
Ryder, Richard (1766–1832), 1980n., 2751, 2757n., 2779, 2864, 2880n., 2888, 2919, 2924, 2933, 2989n., 3005, 3030–1, 3042n., 3060n., 3087n., 3133, 3179n., 3288, 3330, 3344, 3358, 3369
  letters from, 2362n., 2757n., 2857, 2867,

Vol. I: 1–444; Vol. II: 445–942; Vol. III: 943–1416; Vol. IV: 1417–1865; Vol. V: 1866–2287; Vol. VI: 2288–2693; Vol. VII: 2694–3056; Vol. VIII: 3057–3480.

561

Ryder, Richard—*cont.*
2874–5, 2880, 2882–3, 2898, 2905, 2908, 2917*n*., 2937, 2944, 2958, 2975, 3008, 3011*n*., 3030*n*., 3060*n*., 3065*n*., 3071, 3085*n*., 3108, 3154, 3160, 3196, 3198*n*., 3230, 3231*n*., 3259, 3273*n*., 3290*n*., 3313, 3319, 3320*n*., 3326, 3334, 3353
letters to, 2940, 3065*n*., 3085*n*., 3109*n*., 3146*n*., 3231*n*.
Ryder, Lady Susan (1772–1838), 1277, 1277*n*.
Rymer, 230
Rymer, Thomas (1641–1713), 2046

Saalfeld, battle of (1806), 2291
Sackville, 2nd Visct., later 5th Duke of Dorset (1767–1843), 562*n*.
Sadlers Wells, 3192
St. Albans, 5th Duke of (1740–1802), 518, 1412
St. Andrew, the Russian Order of, 3470
St. Asaph, Bishop of, *see* Shipley, Jonathan
St. Blankart (?), 471
St. David's College, Lampeter, building of, 3422
St. Étienne, Rabaud de, 650
St. Fai, Abbé de, 471
St. Fiorenzo, a 42-gun frigate, 1267*n*., 1277*n*.
St. George, the, a 98-gun ship, 535
St. George's Hospital, 235
St. Helens, Lord, *see* Fitzherbert, Alleyne
St. Ives, borough of, 2083, 2141
St. James's Palace, 31, 1855, 2729
St. John, General Frederick (1765–1844), 145, 1118
St. John, St. Andrew, 14th Baron St. John (1759–1817), 1654
St. John, Mrs., wife of Henry St. John, M.P., 3062
St. John-Mildmay, Sir Henry Paulet (1764–1808), *letter from*, 2407
St. Jules, Caroline, *see* Lamb, Mrs. George
St. Just (1767–94), 857
St. Laurent, Mlle. (or Mme.) de, 544, 561, 563, 800*n*., 954*n*., 1362, 1462*n*., 1487, 1487*n*., 1530, 1558, 1612, 1617, 1652, 1731, 1787, 1796, 1907, 1915, 1970, 2347, 2515
letter to, 543
St. Leger, Mrs. (*née* Blakeney), 2076
St. Leger, Anthony (1759?–1821), 484, 581, 609, 622–3, 636, 656*n*., 778–9, 945, 2448, 2484*n*.
letter from, 965
St. Leger, General John (1756–99), 44, 57, 579, 584, 591, 599, 616, 638, 679*n*., 733, 857, 877*n*., 1251, 3383
letters from, 581, 604, 636, 1216
letter to, 470
St. Leger, Lieut.-Gen. William (*c.* 1759–1818), 1691, 2076, 2554
St. Marsan, Comte, 3202
St. Michael, Order of, 2046
St. Patrick, Order of, 2162, 2167
St. Paul de Leon, Bishop of, 777
St. Vincent, *see* Jervis, Sir John

'Saints', the, 3057*n*., 3174*n*.
Salgas, M. de, 477*n*.
Salisbury, Mr., 2729
Salisbury, Marchioness of (1750–1835), 2678*n*.
Salisbury, 7th Earl and 1st Marquess of (1748–1823), 382, 894, 897, 1958, 2747*n*., 3218
Salisbury, Bishop of, *see* Douglas, John
Salle, Marquis de La, *see* La Salle
Sally, a royal housemaid of Windsor, 1937
Salm, Prince, *see* Solms-Braunfels
Saltoun, 16th Lord (1758–93), 517
Salvini, *see* Plomer
San Souci, Palace of, 597
Sandell, 2305
Sanderson, Sir James (1741–98), 970, 970*n*.
Sandford, *see* Sanford
Sandon, Visct., later Earl of Harrowby (1798–1882), 3432*n*.
Sandwich, a 90-gun ship, 26
Sandwich, 4th Earl of (1718–92), 26, 28, 307*n*., 354*n*., 357*n*., 646
letters from, 303, 307, 333, 348, 354, 357, 422, 648
letter to, 333
Sandwich, 5th Earl of (1744–1814), 357, 357*n*., 422*n*., 792*n*., 1853*n*.
Sanford, William Ayshford (*d.* 1833), 2627, 2629
Santague (Santhaque, Santhague), 52, 102, 1067
Sardinia, King of, *see* Victor Amadeus and Victor Emmanuel
Sastres, Francesco, 2983
Satchwell, R., 1493
Saumarez, Sir James, Baron de Saumarez (1757–1836), 863, 1657, 3111, 3111*n*., 3142*n*., 3167, 3212, 3232, 3256, 3256*n*.
Saunders, Sir Charles (*c.* 1713–75), 3352
Saunders, Dundas, *see* Dundas
Saunders, Dr. William (1743–1817), 2003*n*., 2257, 2292*n*., 2650, 2684–5
Saurin, William (*c.* 1757–1839), 2874, 2905
Savage, a 16-gun ship, 732
Savage, Francis (*c.* 1769–1823), 2003, 2289*n*.
Savile, Richard Lumley (1757–1832), *letter from*, 1047
Savile, Sir William Lumley (1769–1860), 1047
Savoye, M., 544
Sawbridge, Colonel Jacob, 869
Sawyer, Admiral Herbert (*c.* 1731–98), 250
Saxe-Coburg-Saalfeld, Prince Frederick Josias of (1737–1815), 730, 740, 745, 756*n*., 766, 787, 792, 816, 819, 825, 843, 850, 852, 856, 896
letter from, 756
Saxe-Teschen, Albert, Archduke of (1738–1822), 686
Saxony, King of, *see* Augustus I
Saxton, 1853
Saxton, Mrs., 1853
Saxton, Sir Charles (*c.* 1732–1808), 535
Saxton, Sir Charles, 2nd Bart. (1773–1838), 2790*n*.
Saye and Sele, 8th Lord (1769–1844), 1690

Seymour, Miss Frances, *see* Southampton, Frances Isabella, Lady

Seymour, Admiral Sir George Francis (1787–1870), 2218*n.*, 2248

Seymour, Georgiana, Lord Cholmondeley's ward, 1432, 1434–5

Seymour, Major Henry, *letter from*, 1943

Seymour, Lord Hugh, *see* Conway

Seymour, Mary Georgiana Emma (1798–1848), 1675, 1675*n.*, 1683, 1688, 1688*n.*, 1692, 1861, 1876, 1942, 1978*n.*, 2043, 2086, 2172*n.*, 2192*n.*, 2272, 2288*n.*, 2289*n.*, 2421, 2542*n.*, 2675*n.*, 2682*n.*, 2736, 3062
letters from, 2799, 2872
Mrs. Fitzherbert's 'beloved child', 3398

Seymour, Lord Robert, *see* Conway

Seymours, the, 2167

Shah Alam, the titular Mogul Emperor, 1757

Shakespear, 2377*n.*

Shakespear, John (1774–1858), 1687
letter from, 2155

Shakespeare, William (1564–1616), 1687, 3335

Shannon, 2nd Earl of (1728–1807), 262, 410

Shannon, 3rd Earl of (1771–1842), 3146*n.*

Shark, a 16-gun sloop, 30

Sharp, a surgeon, 1389

Sharp(e), George (1755–1830), huntsman to the Prince, 518

Sharpe, Mrs., on the Prince's pension list, 235

Shee, 45, 62

Shee, J. Annesley, *memo by*, 913

Shee, Sir George (*c.* 1754–1825), 1641*n.*, 2091*n.*
letter from, 1890

Sheerness, Governorship of, 2797

Sheffield, Anne, Lady (1764–1832), 1603, 1607, 1607*n.*, 1615*n.*, 2448, 2448*n.*, 2455
letter to, 2448

Sheffield, Earl of (1735–1821), 108, 582, 1620*n.*

Shelburne, Earl of, later 1st Marquess of Lansdowne (1737–1805), 79, 399, 465*n.*, 1338, 1601*n.*, 1937, 3383
letter from, 1737
letter to, 1636

'Shelburne gang', the, 324

Sheldon, Colonel, 157, 200

Sheldon, Ralph (*c.* 1741–1822), 2161, 3180*n.*

Shelley, 1422*n.*

Shelley, Sir John (1772–1852), 2431, 2679
letters from, 2415, 2431, 2457, 2478

Shelley, Elizabeth Jane Sidney, Lady, 2589

Shepley, Richard, 1908*n.*

Sherborne, James Dutton, 1st Baron (1744–1820), 2820
letter to, 2820*n.*

Sheridan, Charles Brinsley (1796–1843), 2284, 2467

Sheridan, Charles Francis (1750–1806), 2368

Sheridan, Charles Robert, *letter from*, 2368

Sheridan, Dr., 3259

Sheridan, Mrs. Elizabeth Ann (1754–92), 311*n.*, 435*n.*
letters from, 435, 2467
her father, *see* Linley

Sheridan, Mrs. Elizabeth Ann—*cont.*
her first Assembly, 435

Sheridan, Mrs. Esther Jane (*c.* 1776–1817), 1783, 2284*n.*
letters from, 2284, 2467

Sheridan, Richard Brinsley (1751–1816), 221, 291*n.*, 297, 354*n.*, 359*n.*, 361*n.*, 371*n.*, 375*n.*, 379*n.*, 380, 384*n.*, 435, 440, 463, 465, 553, 599*n.*, 706, 706*n.*, 708*n.*, 715, 877*n.*, 936, 1140, 1142, 1153, 1153*n.*, 1192, 1264, 1270, 1270*n.*, 1329*n.*, 1333, 1342, 1354, 1500, 1590*n.*, 1638, 1766–7, 1772, 1774*n.*, 1803, 1805*n.*, 1830*n.*, 1835, 1835*n.*, 1842*n.*, 1861, 1868*n.*, 1873, 1913*n.*, 1921, 1929*n.*, 1942, 2058, 2102, 2123, 2123*n.*, 2125, 2125*n.*, 2143*n.*, 2148*n.*, 2161, 2221–2, 2225, 2228, 2228*n.*, 2230, 2230*n.*, 2234, 2262, 2276, 2284, 2288, 2288*n.*, 2308, 2308*n.*, 2311*n.*, 2316, 2329, 2362*n.*, 2374*n.*, 2415, 2415*n.*, 2427, 2451, 2465, 2467, 2469, 2469*n.*, 2471, 2480*n.*, 2495, 2500, 2539, 2555, 2619*n.*, 2622*n.*, 2628*n.*, 2682, 2693, 2749, 2749*n.*, 2760, 2761*n.*, 2769, 2770*n.*, 2779, 2792, 2801, 2804*n.*, 2808, 2808*n.*, 2811, 2811*n.*, 2812*n.*, 2813*n.*, 2818, 2822*n.*, 2824*n.*, 2836*n.*, 2841, 2966, 3015, 3055*n.*, 3064*n.*, 3106*n.*, 3165*n.*, 3191–2, 3226, 3229, 3301, 3329, 3341, 3341*n.*, 3358, 3373
letters from, 286, 290, 292, 296, 302, 308–9, 311, 318, 323*n.*, 334, 346, 369, 466, 578, 844, 1138, 1815, 1815*n.*, 1860, 1922, 1999*n.*, 2125*n.*, 2221*n.*, 2236, 2244, 2261, 2311*n.*, 2451, 2469, 2495, 2622, 2679, 2750, 2774, 2812, 2816, 2816*n.*, 2840, 3046, 3203, 3306
letters to, 291, 319, 364, 366, 635, 1138, 1783, 1815*n.*, 1830, 2036*n.*, 2127*n.*, 2143, 2283, 2622, 3015
his theatrical property, 3203

Sheridan, Tom (1775–1817), 1715, 1783, 1783*n.*, 1830, 2082, 2261, 2261*n.*, 2308*n.*, 2469*n.*, 2679

Shiels, Lieut., 2739

Shipley, Jonathan (1714–88), *letter from*, 181

Shippon, Major-Gen., 1485

Shore, Sir John, Lord Teignmouth (1751–1834), 201*n.*, 520*n.*

Short, 244

Short, Rev. William (*c.* 1760–1826), 2717

Shrapnel, Henry (1761–1842), 2508

Shrapnell, the jeweller, 230

Shrewsbury House, Shooter's Hill, Princess Charlotte's residence, 1563, 2117

Shropshire election (1806), 2299*n.*

Shuckburgh, Sir George Augustus William (1751–1804), 1429

Shuldham, Lord (1717?–98), 572

Shuttleworth, Captain, 588

Sicard, John Jacob, the Princess of Wales's cook, 1615*n.*, 2572*n.*
letter from, 2157

Sicily, military situation in (1811), 3200

Siddons, Mrs. (1755–1831), 280*n.*, 1375, 3373

Sidmouth, Ursula Mary, Viscountess (1760–1811), death of, 3081

Sidmouth, Lord, *see* Addington, Henry

Sieyès, Emmanuel Joseph, Comte (1748–1836), 1507

Silva, Mme., 1593

Silvester, Sir John, Recorder of London, 1803–22 (1745–1822), 1906n., 2363n., 3353

Silviera, General, 3139

Simcoe, 2680

Simcoe, Lieut.-Gen. John Graves (1752–1806), 771, 1819, 2153, 2204, 2292, 2347, 2395

Simian (*sic*), Mme., 198

Simmons, Richard, 1901

Simmons, Dr. Samuel Foart (1750–1813), 1806n., 1814, 1878, 1878n., 1887–8, 1895n., 1896, 1915, 1925, 1925n., 1937, 2756n., 2757, 3129, 3185, 3201, 3205, 3217, 3224n., 3238, 3243
his son, 2756n.

Simolin, M., *letter to*, 75

Simpson, 1230, 1235, 1253, 1256

Sims, *see* Symes

Sinclair, Sir John (1754–1835), 366, 366n., 472, 669, 877n., 1243, 1270, 1842, 1862
letters from, 472, 478, 490, 573, 582, 669

Sinclair, Sir Robert (*d.* 1795), 472

Sindhia, Daulat Rao, 1757, 1762

Singleton, Mark (*c.* 1762–1840), 662

Sirius, a 36-gun frigate, 2782n.

Skinner, Alderman, 1218, 1253, 1256, 1908n.

Slade, General Sir John (1762–1859), 2530, 2530n.

Slater, 901

Slave Trade Abolition Bill (1807), the, 2682, 2682n., 3244

Sleath, W. Boultby, 2739

Sleigh, William, 531n., 583, 1541

Sligo, 1st Marquess of (1756–1809), 2246, 2407

Sligo, 2nd Marquess of (1788–1845), 3141

Sloper, Robert S., 2282

Sloper, General Sir Robert (*d.* 1802), 201, 562n.

Sloughter-Stanwix, General Thomas (*d.* 1815), 148n.

Smelt, Leonard (*c.* 1719–1800), sub-governor to the Princes, 23n.

Smith, 204

Smith, a mason, 1215

Smith, of Fowey, 593, 598, 637

Smith, Lieut., 2442

Smith, 2919

Smith, 3228

Smith, Adam (1723–90), 1764

Smith, Lady Anne Culling (*d.* 1844), 2923n.

Smith, Lady Charlotte Juliana (*d.* 1830), 1949

Smith, Culling Charles (*d.* 1853), Under-Sec. of State, 2959, 3114, 3135, 3142, 3142n., 3248, 3256, 3266n.
letters from, 2923, 3040
letter to, 3256n.

Smith, George (1765–1836), 2040

Smith, Major-Gen. Haviland (*d.* 1817), 2739

Smith, Sir James Edward (1759–1828), 3063
memo by, 3058

Smith, Col. John Carrington, 1949, 1956

Smith, John Spencer (1769–1845), Envoy to Wurtemberg, 1637, 1645

Smith, Joshua Jonathan, 3022

Smith, Letty, see Lade, Lady

Smith, Mrs., on the Prince's pension list, 235

Smith, Mrs., a wet-nurse, 1045

Smith, Sir Michael (1740–1808), 2156

Smith, Mrs., Lady Mayo's sister, 3299n.

Smith, General Richard (1734–1803), 659, 695

Smith, Robert, Baron Carrington (1752–1838), 937n.

Smith, Rev. Sydney (1771–1845), 2327, 2440n., 2896n.

Smith, William (1756–1835), 1908n., 3074

Smith, William, *letter from*, 748

Smith, Admiral Sir William Sidney (1764–1840), 1622, 1706, 2350, 2445n.
letter from, 529
wants a peerage, 3180n.

Smyth, Major-Gen. George Stracey, Duke of Kent's Groom, 1462n., 1787, 2080

Smyth, John Henry (1780–1822), 2941n.
letter from, 2297n.

Smyth, Sir William (1746–1823), *letters from*, 2215, 2265, 2270

Smythe, Mrs., Mrs. Fitzherbert's mother (*d.* 1808), 148, 1422, 1425

Smythe, John, Mrs. Fitzherbert's brother, 1375, 1454

Smythe, Walter, Mrs. Fitzherbert's brother (1757–1822), 2736

Sneyd, Colonel, 1996n.

Sneyd, Nathaniel (*c.* 1767–1833), 2003

Sneyd, Rev. Ralph (*c.* 1753–1808), *letter from*, 2227

Snow, George, 1328

Snow, R., banker, 1328

Society for the Improvement of British Wool, 573

Society of United Irishmen, 1265

Solms-Braunfels, Prince Frederick of (1770–1814), 1437n., 1515n.

Somerset, 7th Duke of (1684–1750), 2000

Somerset, Lord Arthur John Henry (1780–1816), 2555

Somerset, Lord Charles Henry (1767–1831), 562n., 663n., 857, 1378, 1385, 1389, 1391, 1398n., 1665, 1669, 1749, 2125, 2125n., 2170, 2194, 2194n., 2492n., 2667, 2861n., 2896
letters from, 2170, 2194, 2492

Somerset, Edward Adolphus, Duke of (1775–1855), 1468n.

Somerset, Lady Elizabeth (1766–1815), 1379, 1391, 1665, 1669

Somerset, Elizabeth (1790–1872), 2667

Somerset, Lord Robert Edward Henry (1776–1842), 2555, 2555n., 2760

Vol. I: 1–444; Vol. II: 445–942; Vol. III: 943–1416; Vol. IV: 1417–1865; Vol. V: 1866–2287; Vol. VI: 2288–2693; Vol. VII: 2694–3056; Vol. VIII: 3057–3480.

565

Vol. I: 1–444; Vol. II: 445–942; Vol. III: 943–1416; Vol. IV: 1417–1865; Vol. V: 1866–2287;
Vol. VI: 2288–2693; Vol. VII: 2694–3056; Vol. VIII: 3057–3480.

567

Sturt, Charles (1763–1812), 518, 1187n., 1253, 1448, 1524, 2944
  letters from, 551, 2939
Sublime Society of Beek Steaks, see Beef Steaks
Suchtelen, Van, 3377
Sudbury elections, 1658
Sudell, Henry, 2943n.
Sudermania, Prince of, see Charles XIII
Sudley, Arthur Saunders Gore, Visct. later Earl of Arran (1761–1837), 1379
Sudley, Mary, Viscountess (c. 1767–1832), later Countess of Arran, 1379
Sudleys, the, 1478
Suffolk, 15th Earl of (1739–1820), 2128n.
  memo by, 2487
Suffren (Suffrein), Mme. de, 1572
Sultan, the, 2708n., 2923
Sumner, Charles Richard (1790–1874), 3449
Sumpter, 1586
Sun, the (newspaper), 1916, 2083
Supervisor of Tin, office of, 460, 538
Surface, Joseph, a character in Sheridan's School for Scandal, 297
Surienne, Sir Francis, 2046
Surprise, cutter, 30
Surrey bowmen, the, 851
Surrey Theatre, the, 3192
Sussex, Duke of, see Augustus Frederick
  Lord Lieutenancy of, 2341
Sutton, 1445, 1785
Sutton, see Manners-Sutton
Sutton Pool Bill, the, 3054
Suvorov, Marshal Alexander (1729–1800), 1428, 1440, 1470
Swan, 14-gun sloop, 662
Swayne, Lieut.-Gen. Hugh (d. 1836), 3231
Sweden, King of, see Gustavus III and Gustavus IV
  Peace treaty signed with (1812), 3377
Swelly, see Schwellenberg
Sydenham, Benjamin (1777–1828), 2645
  letter from, 1517n.
Sydenham, Thomas (1780–1816), 2645n., 3190
Sydenham, Major-Gen. William (d. 1801), 2645n.
Sydney, 1st Visct. (1733–1800), 108n., 321, 332n., 457, 1548, 1548n.
Sydney, 2nd Visct. (1764–1831), 2775n.
Symes, Col. Richard, 146, 510, 588
  letters from, 548, 561, 563
Symmonds, see Simmons
Syracuse, Governor of, 2108

Tacitus, 581n.
Tackle, Jack, 1580
Talavera, battle of, 2587, 2591, 2701, 2747
Talbot, Captain, 477, 479, 676
Talbot, Earl (1777–1849), 2366, 3410
  recalled from Ireland, 3417
Talleyrand de Périgord, Charles Maurice, Comte de (1754–1838), 650, 794, 2264
Tankerville, 4th Earl of (1743–1822), 1375n., 2287

Tankerville, 5th Earl of (1776–1859), 1908n., 2287
Tankerville, Corisande Armandine Sophie Léonie Hélène, Countess of (1782–1865), 2287
Tant Mieux, see Villiers, George
Tara, Lord (1764–1821), 3146n.
Tarente, Prince, 644n., 663n.
Tarleton, Sir Banastre (1754–1833), 1586, 1850, 2861, 2909, 2934, 2966
Tarleton, John (1755–1820),
  letter from, 2006
  his nephew, 2006
Tarrant, Dr. (1724?–91), 574
Tatter, George, 581n.
Tattersall, Richard (1724–95), 653, 664, 743
Tauentzien, Count Friedrich (1756–1824), 1549
Taurade, C., the Prince's pastry cook, 465n.
Tavistock, Marquess of, later 7th Duke of Bedford (1788–1861), 3358
Tayler, John, letter from, 2271
Taylor, 1772
Taylor, actor, 1478
  his wife, 1478
Taylor, 2199, 2380
Taylor, Serjeant, 1370
Taylor, 2289
Taylor, Sir Charles William (1770–1857), 2313, 2313n.
Taylor, Mrs. Frances Anne, wife of Michael Angelo Taylor, 2145, 2289
Taylor, George Watson (c. 1770–1841), 2199, 3474
Taylor, Sir Herbert (1775–1839), 1630, 1772, 2330, 2384, 2462, 2500n., 2621, 2632n., 2811, 2897n., 2976, 3009n., 3032, 3194, 3308, 3310, 3310n., 3312, 3325, 3325n., 3333, 3349, 3425, 3463
  letters from, 2462, 2620, 2725
  letters to, 2620, 2726–8, 2733
Taylor, John, 2161
Taylor, Lady Lucy (d. 1814), 2189n.
Taylor, Michael Angelo (c. 1757–1834), 2289n., 2297n., 2804n., 3165n., 3320n.
  letters from, 2145, 3165
Taylor, Robert, 2642n.
Taylor, Thomas, shoemaker, 605, 609, 611, 894
Taylor, William (c. 1754–1825), 'Opera Taylor', 1375, 1426n., 2901, 3149
  letters from, 1426, 2305, 2414, 3240
Teckell, Lady Griselda (d. 1851), 2189n.
Tempest, Vane, see Vane-Tempest
Temple, Earl (1711–79), 19n., 2767
Temple, Earl, later 1st Marquess of Buckingham, see Buckingham
Temple, Earl, later, 2nd Marquess of Buckingham, later, Duke of Buckingham and Chandos (1776–1839), 728n., 1709n., 2385, 2519, 2626n., 2790n.
  letters from, 2153n., 2311n., 2380, 2461n.
  letter to 2468
  his absurd pretensions, 3447, 3449
Templer, 1870

Vol. I: 1–444; Vol. II: 445–942; Vol. III: 943–1416; Vol. IV: 1417–1865; Vol. V: 1866–2287; Vol. VI: 2288–2693; Vol. VII: 2694–3056; Vol. VIII: 3057–3480.

569

Vol. I: 1–444; Vol. II: 445–942; Vol. III: 943–1416; Vol. IV: 1417–1865; Vol. V: 1866–2287; Vol. VI: 2288–2693; Vol. VII: 2694–3056; Vol. VIII: 3057–3480.

571

Vernon, Edward Venables, Archbishop of York (1757–1847), 3128n., 3194
    letter from, 2324n.
Verschoyle, James (*d.* 1834), Bishop of Killala (1810–34), 3137
Verschoyle, John, Dublin banker, 1317
Vesey, John Agmond (*c.* 1772–1812), 946, 954n., 1377, 1388, 1462n., 2347, 2929, 2953
    letter from, 2030
Vestal, frigate, 520
Viale, Emanuel, 1775
Vickry, Rev. Christopher Cunningham (1754?–1792), 713
Victor, Claude Perrin, Duc de Belluno and Marshal of France (1764–1841), 2591n., 2954n.
Victor Amadeus III, King of Piedmont-Sardinia (1726–96), 20n., 639
Victor Emmanuel I, King of Sardinia (1759–1824), 3026
Victory, Nelson's flagship, 26, 738, 3111, 3232n., 3256n., 3290n.
Viereck, Mlle., 695
Vieuville, Marquis de La (*d.* 1653), 2046
Villettes, Major-Gen. William Anne (1754–1808), 3124
    Duke of Kent's Comptroller, 1680, 1749
Villiers, 2431
Villiers, Lady Caroline Elizabeth, *see under* Paget
Villiers, Lady Elizabeth (*d.* 1810), 1450
Villiers, George (1759–1827), 1996n., 2390, 2603, 2616, 2627, 2630, 2639n., 2671, 2684, 2718, 2740, 3375, 3425
    his sons, 3425
Villiers, John Charles, later Earl of Clarendon (1757–1838), 1674n., 2263, 2701
    letter to, 1722
Villiers, Lady Gertrude (1778–1809), 1187, 1187n.
Villiers, Maria Eleanor, later Countess of Clarendon (*c.* 1759–1844), 2263
Villiers, Visct., later (1805) 5th Earl of Jersey (1773–1859), 956n.
Villiers, Theresa (1775–1855), Lord Boringdon's sister, wife of George Villiers, 2390, 2616, 2627, 2630, 2650, 2684, 2684n., 2718, 2740, 2743, 2765, 3375
Vimiero, battle of (1808), 2509
Vincent, Sir Francis (*d.* 1809)
Vinter, *see* Vintner
Vintner, Lieut. George, 264, 268
Virago, a 12-gun brig, 2350
Virgil, 532
Vitoria, battle of (1813), 3390
Voice of Reason, the, 402
Voiture, Vincent (1598–1648), 1348
Voltaire, the French *philosophe* (1694–1778), 14
Vulliamy, 230, 2513
Vyse, General Richard (1746–1825), 847, 1252, 1785, 1841
Vyse, Major-Gen. Richard William Howard (1784–1853), 3320

Waddell, John, 2117
Waddington, Rev. Mr., 157, 502
Wakefield, Captain, 752
Walcheren, expedition to (1809), 2607, 2634, 2785
    inquiry into the, 2699, 2701, 2701n., 2711n.
    fever, 3137
Walcot, 2394
Waldegrave, Lady Caroline (1765–1831), 1187, 1293n., 1884
Waldegrave, Elizabeth, Countess (1760–1816), 656n.
Waldegrave, Mrs., later, Lady Radstock (*d.* 1839), 1455
Waldegrave, 4th Earl (1751–89), 396n., 656n.
Waldegrave, Admiral William, Baron Radstock (1753–1825), 894
Wales, the late Prince of, *see* Frederick Louis
Wales, the late Princess of, *see* Augusta
Walker, 883
Walker, the Prince's apothecary, 1799, 2243n., 2302n.
Walker, George, *letter from*, 3307
Walker, Lieut.-Gen. Sir George Townshend (1764–1842), 134
Walker, T., 1621n.
Wallace, 216
Waller, 473
Wallis, 247, 838
Wallmoden-Gimborn, Count Johann Ludwig von (1736–1811), 43, 818, 881, 885, 888, 901, 1031
Wallop, Coulson, 560n.
'Wally, old Mrs.,' 3401
Walmsley, Rev. T. T., *letter from*, 618
Walpole, Horace, 4th Earl of Orford (1717–97), 2n., 4n., 12n., 23n., 26n., 29n., 32n., 44n.
Walpoles, the, 219n.
Walsingham, 1005
Walsingham, 2nd Baron (1748–1818), 1609
Walter, solicitor, 2576
Walter, John (1739–1812), 467n., 501, 913, 3072, 3072n.
    letter from, 2543
Walter, John II (1776–1847), 2543, 3072
    letter from, 1781
Walter, William, eldest son of John Walter I, *letter from*, 3072
Wangenheim, Major-Gen. George von, 477n., 803, 1031
Warburton, Charles Mongan (1755?–1826), 1077, 2167, 2167n., 2203, 3252, 3261, 3262n.
    letters from, 3093, 3093n., 3137, 3273
    his son, Garnet, 1077
    his son, Augustus, 3137
Ward, Captain, 764
Ward (Warde), Rev. Edward, 1675, 1683
Ward, Elizabeth, 1615n.
Ward, John William, 1st Earl of Dudley (1781–1833), 2888, 3165n., 3344n.
Ward, Mary, housemaid, 2117
Ward (later Plumer Ward), Robert (1765–

William Henry, Duke of Clarence—*cont.*
2682*n.*, 2744*n.*, 2748, 2770*n.*, 2789, 2801,
2939–40, 3375
letters from, 30*n.*, 69*n.*, 89, 98, 101, 104*n.*,
105, 107, 110, 116, 118, 126, 140, 150, 152,
154, 157, 160, 166, 207, 212, 216, 239, 247,
250, 254, 258, 262, 264, 266, 268, 272, 281,
284, 343, 388, 507, 509, 511, 513, 516, 521,
523, 525, 527, 530, 606, 614, 624, 628, 851,
1013, 1026, 1042, 1046, 1056, 1123, 1248,
1414, 1751, 1768, 1770, 1776, 1942, 1949,
1956, 2279, 2370, 2483, 2500, 2503, 2530,
2646, 2660, 2682–3, 2700, 3136, 3140, 3155,
3231, 3299, 3377–8
letters to, 6, 29*n.*, 76*n.*, 89*n.*, 467*n.*, 855,
1949*n.*, 1954, 2370, 2700, 3155
and the Grand Duchess Catherine of Russia,
3378
wishes to marry Miss Tylney-Long, 3231,
3231*n.*, 3299*n.*
wishes to marry Mercer Elphinstone, 3231*n.*
wishes to marry Lady Berkeley, 3231*n.*,
3378*n.*
wishes to marry Lady Downshire, 3231*n.*
allegedly wishes to marry Lady Charlotte
Lindsay, 3231*n.*
appointed Admiral of the Fleet, 3299
separation from Mrs. Jordan, 3287, 3305
on the King's health, 3377
apparent wish to marry Grand Duchess Anne
of Russia, 3378
wishes to marry Grand Duchess Catherine of
Russia, 3378
accident to (1782), 3383
given £30,000 by the Prince, 3480
Williams, 1856, 2347
Williams, Mrs., 1856–7, 2347, 2710
letters to, 2710*n.*, 3123*n.*
Williams, Henry, *see* Wynn
Williams, John ('Anthony Pasquin'), journalist
(1761–1818), 1193
Willis, Dr. Francis (1718–1807), 309, 340*n.*,
344, 351, 378, 378*n.*, 384, 412*n.*, 1594, 1597,
1601, 2100
memo. respecting, 340
Willis, Henry Norton, 925, 2183
Willis, Dr. John (1751–1835), 340, 1594, 1597,
1806, 1806*n.*, 2756*n.*, 2757, 3127–9, 3185,
3205, 3217*n.*, 3224*n.*, 3227, 3238, 3243, 3246,
3349
Willis, Mrs., 340, 1017
Willis, Dr. Robert Darling (1760–1821), 1806,
2756*n.*, 2757, 2757*n.*, 2758, 2764, 2769*n.*,
2830, 2830*n.*, 2833, 3064, 3100, 3113, 3123,
3127–8, 3129, 3138, 3201, 3205, 3217, 3238,
3243
Willis, Dr. Thomas (1754–1827), 1594, 1597
letter from, 1598*n.*
Willises, the, 1802, 1806*n.*, 1808, 1814

Willoughby of Eresby, Lady (1761–1828), 274,
1094, 1167*n.*, 1170, 1170*n.*, 1193, 1200, 1202,
1204, 1208, 1208*n.*, 1211, 1396, 1434–5, 1572
Willoughby, Miss, 2224*n.*
Willsbourn, Jane, 1615*n.*
Willson, Lieut., 783
Willyams (*sic*), James, 539
Wilmot, John (*c.* 1749–1815), 108*n.*
Wilson, a groom, 1064
Wilson, at the Cape of Good Hope, 1216
Wilson, a soldier in the Prince's Regiment, 3171
his brother, 3171
Wilson, Captain, 1489, ?1741
Wilson, Harriette (1786–1846), 2645*n.*, 3451*n.*
Wilson, Mary, 1615*n.*
Wilson, Nathan, 3228
Wilson, Richard (1759–1834), the Duke of
Northumberland's Agent in Cornwall, 1628,
1690, 1690*n.*, 1697A, 1793, 1928, 2083, 2089,
2141, 2221*n.*, 2228, 2432, 2432*n.*, 2535, 2747,
2747*n.*, 2776, 3267
letters from, 1788, 1921, 1939, 2222, 2832
letters to, 2308*n.*, 2329*n.*, 2369*n.*
Wilson, General Sir Robert Thomas (1777–
1849), 2079, 2699*n.*
letters from, 1772, 1819
memo by, 1958
Wilson, Mrs. Selina,
letter from, 986*n.*
her husband, 986*n.*
Wilson, William, Gentleman Usher of the
Privy Chamber, *letter from*, 180
Wilton elections, 450
Wilton, Lord, *see* Grey de Wilton
Wimpen, M. de, 699
Wimpfen, Baron de, 1466
Winchelsea election (1806), 2299*n.*
Winchilsea and Nottingham, 9th Earl of (1752–
1826), 2*n.*, 42, 457*n.*, 2515, 3128, 3201, 3224,
3308, 3312, 3394
Windham, Mrs. Cecilia, 2338*n.*
Windham, William (1750–1810), 564*n.*, 777,
843, 978*n.*, 1259, 1556, 1690, 1709*n.*, 1735,
1780, 1811, 1812*n.*, 1861, 2091*n.*, 2123,
2123*n.*, 2128, 2149, 2170, 2229, 2232, 2232*n.*,
2236, 2239, 2267, 2288, 2347, 2701*n.*, 2971
letters from, 328, 837, 2267
his dissenting Cabinet Minutes (1806), 2338,
2338*n.*, 2385*n.*
Windham, an Indiaman captured by the
French, 2782*n.*
Windsor Castle, prints of (1784), 110
Prince of Wales's apartments in, 79, 299, 313,
316
building in progress at, 600*n.*, 1996*n.*, 3474
Constable of, 287*n.*, 3001
Windsor Great Park, 35
Winne, George, 264, 268, 268*n.*, 284, 343, 507,
516
Winne, Sally, 207*n.*, 264, 264*n.*, 266

Vol. I: 1–444; Vol. II: 445–942; Vol. III: 943–1416; Vol. IV: 1417–1865; Vol. V: 1866–2287;
Vol. VI: 2288–2693; Vol. VII: 2694–3056; Vol. VIII: 3057–3480.

575

Winston, 3186, 3192, 3197
Winter, an attorney, 2565
Wise, Ayshford (1786–1847), 2582n.
Withers, Rev. Mr. (d. 1790), 501
Wodford (sic), 1093
Woide, Rev. Charles Godfrey (1725–90), 514
Wolff, M. de, 531
Wombwell, Lady Anne (1768–1808), 1392, 1439, 1441, 2488
Wombwell, Sir George (1769–1846), 1439, 1441
Wood, Captain, 888
Wood, of Littleton, 2500
Wood, Miss (d. 1799), 1424
Woodfall, William (1746–1803), 36n.
Woodford, Lieut.-Col., 3401
Woodley, Captain John, R.N., 966
Woodthorpe, Henry, letter from, 2045
Worcester, Deanery of, 3472n.
Worontzov, Count Simon, Russian Minister in London (1744–1832), brother of Count Alexander Worontzov (1741–1805), 578, 578n., 1958
Worsley, Sir Richard (1751–1805), 2313, 2313n.
Wouwerman, Philip (1619–68), 3307
Wraxall, Sir Nathaniel William (1751–1831), 19n., 29n., 72n., 99n., 188n., 218n., 235n., 242n., 251n., 291n., 305n., 310n., 311n., 320n., 321n., 335n., 355n., 390n., 409n., 447n., 468n., 472n., 496n., 852n., 877n., 1025n., 1037n., 1172n., 1256n., 1390n., 1429n., 2150
letter from, 2150
Wrey, Sir Bourchier (1757–1826), 3035
Wright, Daniel, 2670n.
Wright, Francis, 2670n.
Wright, James, letter from, 710
Wright, Dr. Robert, the Duke of Sussex's physician, 266, 1653
Wright, Lieut.-Col. Robert, 2347
letters from, 1708–9
letters to, 1709n., 1749, 1775, 2347n., 2556n., 2670n., 2736n.
his brother, 1775
Wrottesley, Henry (1772–1825), 2299n.
Wurmb, 888
Wurtemberg, Duchy of, invaded by the French, 1437, 1453, 1551, 1623
Wurtemberg, Caroline Alexei, Princess of, later (1807), Baroness von Rottenburg, and (1825), Countess von Urach (1779–1853), 1542
Wurtemberg, Catherine, Princess of (1783–1835), 2524n.
Wurtemberg, Charles, Duke of (1728–93), 1309
Wurtemberg, Charlotte, Hereditary Princess of, later, Duchess of, see Charlotte Augusta Matilda
Wurtemberg, Dorothea, Duchess of (1736–98), 1309, 1337
Wurtemberg, Frederick, Duke of (1732–97), 1309, 1453
Wurtemberg, Frederick, Hereditary Prince of, later Duke of, later, King of (1754–1816), 562n., 1188, 1254, 1254n., 1259–60, 1267,

Wurtemberg, Frederick—cont.
1309, 1316, 1341, 1352, 1356, 1441, 1441n., 1453, 1466, 1470, 1542, 1542n., 1551, 1623, 1645, 1839, 2119, 2524, 2668, 2777
Wurtemberg, Prince Henry of (1772–1833), 1542, 1542n.
Wurtemberg, Queen of, see Charlotte Matilda
Wyatt, 1749, 1958, 2053
Wyatt, Benjamin Dean (1775–?1850), 3208, 3214
Wyatt, James, architect (1746–1813), 600n., 1014, 1958, 2053, 2602, 3148, 3214
Wyatt, Philip (d. 1836), 3208, 3214
Wyndham, see Windham
Wyndham, Charles William (1760–1828), 44, 959n.
Wynn, Charles Watkin Williams (1775–1850), 2351n., 3055, 3358, 3358n., 3449, 3472
letter to, 2461n.
resigns office (1828), 3472
Wynn, Glyn (c. 1739–93), 2305n.
Wynn, Sir Henry Watkin Williams (1783–1856), 2520, 2520n.
Wynn, Sir Watkin Williams (1748–89), 2520n.
Wynn, Sir Watkin Williams (1772–1840), 2912n.
letter from, 2912
Wynn-Belasyse, Thomas Edward, 2305
Wynne (sic), 2161
Wynne, Owen (c. 1756–1841), 2814n.
Wynne, Robert (1760–1838), 2814
Wynyard, Lady Matilda (b. 1774–?), 1434n., 2390n.
Wynyard, Captain W., Equerry to Duke of York, 249n.
Wynyard, General William (d. 1819), 1672
letter from, 2118

Yarborough, 1st Lord (1749–1823), 2313
Yarmouth, Francis, Earl of, later 3rd Marquess of Hertford (1777–1842), 1692, 2167A, 2213, 2254, 2297, 2328, 2377, 2423, 2469n., 2500, 2500n., 2590, 2593, 2637, 2790n., 3055n., 3065, 3167n., 3215, 3219, 3249, 3257, 3257n., 3263n., 3274, 3344n., 3349n.
letters from, 2709, 2712, 3178
letters to, 2255, 2372, 3395
Yarmouth, Maria Emily, Countess of, later Marchioness of Hertford (c. 1770–1856), 1958, 2213n., 2254, 3249
Yeates, Mr., 2658, 2902, 2915
Yonge, Sir George (1733–1812), 390n., 646
letters from, 723, 725, 725n.
York, Archbishop of, see Vernon
York, Duchess of, see Frederica, Duchess of York
York, Edward, Duke of (1739–67), George III's brother, 79n.
York, Frederick, Duke of, see Frederick, Duke of York
York, freedom of, for Prince of Wales, 468, 468n., 473

576

York, Henry Benedict Maria Clement, Cardinal (1725–1807), second son of titular James III, the 'Old Pretender', 564, 860, 1085, 2435, 3026

York, Lord Mayor of, 468

York Races, Prince of Wales visits, 468, 473

Yorke, Charles Philip (1764–1834), 1742, 1749, 1775, 1780, 1804n., 1806n., 1835n., 2545, 2701, 2701n., 2704n., 2713, 2813n., 2837n., 2888, 2893, 2928, 2933, 2952, 2981, 3011, 3074, 3094–5, 3111, 3116, 3174, 3212, 3285, 3290n.

letters from, 1868n., 2866, 2899, 2913, 2951, 2980, 3020, 3076, 3168, 3176

letter to, 1868n.

impending retirement of, 3347, 3352

Yorke, Sir Joseph Sydney (1768–1831), Rear-Admiral, 3212

Yorke, Captain, 2863

Yorks, the, 1044

Young, Admiral Sir George (1732–1810), memo signed by, 2681

Zastrow, 591, 594, 597, 601, 604–5, 611, 769, 775, 787, 792, 2296

Zéa, M., 3167

Zeppelin, Count Johann Karl von (1767–1801), Wurtemberg Minister, 1254n.

Zettwitz (sic), General, 78n.

Ziethen, General, 591

Zouch, Rev. Thomas (c. 1738–1815), 2339